Readings in
MANAGERIAL
ECONOMICS

Readings in MANAGERIAL ECONOMICS

Edited by

Thomas Joseph Coyne
John Carroll University

1985   FOURTH EDITION

BUSINESS PUBLICATIONS, INC.   Plano, Texas   75075

ISBN 0-256-02698-X

Library of Congress Catalog Card No. 84-71558

Printed in the United States of America

1 2 3 4 5 6 7 8 9 0 K 2 1 0 9 8 7 6 5

To Pat

Preface

Managerial economics is not merely another course in economic theory; it requires a different approach than found in a theory book of readings. An understanding of theory *is* mandatory; this book assumes at least elementary training in economic theory. But managerial economics is concerned with application of that theory, a special subject in itself. These articles allow you to see how theory is applied.

For the future manager few topics, if any, are as exciting as managerial economics. It is the study of why some businesses prosper and grow, why some simply survive, and why others fail at the marketplace and go under. As an academic subject it differs significantly from other economics courses.

Managerial economics goes straight to the heart of the U.S. mixed capitalistic system. Its topics include: demand and determinants of demand, supply and determinants of supply, cost conditions, production functions, capital budgeting procedures and techniques, risk and uncertainty in decision making, short-range and long-range forecasting, corporate profits, and the problems of pricing.

Managerial economics investigates the firm: the place it holds in an industry or field of business, its contributions to the economy as a whole, and even its impact on international affairs.

The study of managerial economics offers major benefits for students willing to pursue it seriously. It is here that you can learn practical applications for concepts already studied in the more traditional courses of micro- and macroeconomic theory. The tools you learn to apply by reading these articles will contribute significantly to your skills and reputation as a manager. How far you advance in management will depend, in large part, on your ability to use these techniques in matters useful to the daily operations of the firms that employ you.

For instance, you may be asked to determine how a price change will affect a company's principle product. You may someday have to determine the effects of raises or pay cuts on the productivity of hourly workers. Shifting demands for your company's products may require you to make high-priced decisions regarding plant capacity. Or you may be called upon by a puzzled chief executive officer to explain how changes in the price of oil from Saudi Arabia can alter the quantity of steel exported from Japan, and how these variables affect "our" business.

Managerial economics is woven through the great fabric of business and is found at the heart of any firm. It affects the sole proprietor who sells bicycles in a neighborhood shop as well as massive multinational corporations.

Solid grounding in managerial economics helps one decide many things important to a company's daily operations and short-run and long-run plans. This book of readings is designed to provide the necessary background. For instance: Which products and services should you produce? How much output can be achieved and at what prices? When should equipment be replaced? What are the best sizes and locations for new plants? How should available capital be allocated?

This book examines many aspects, topics, and examples of managerial economics. Some of the subjects to be covered include practical application of the concept of price elasticity, the alternative cost concept, transfer pricing, the profit contribution concept, how to apply the principles that describe the inverse relationship between the value of an asset and the interest rate, the notion that all factors of production relative to their price should be equal, and the incremental cost/price/profit concept.

Managerial economics is economics applied in decision making. It combines abstract theory with everyday practice, emphasizing the use of economic analysis in clarifying problems, in organizing and evaluating information, and in weighing alternative courses of action.

Although managerial economics is sometimes known as business economics, its tools, techniques, and perspective are useful in managing nonprofit organizations, public agencies, and government-owned businesses as well.

Economics is the study of how scarce and costly social resources are allocated throughout the world. *Managerial* economics, on the other hand, focuses directly on the firm and on individual units of management. As a subject, it is closely related to finance and financial management. Managerial economics is goal oriented—it aims for maximum achievement of objectives, and it is concerned with strategies and choices vital to a firm's survival and growth. In short, it deals with the total situation in which decisions are made.

This Fourth Edition retains those articles which reportedly appeal to economics scholars; however, it mostly contains research of interest to skills-oriented students who must learn when, how, and why certain tools and techniques of the economist are applicable.

A few articles in the first three versions of this publication were too complicated for some students; a few articles were too easy. An attempt is made here to alter this condition. Professors wanting to maximize application of economic theory may welcome this slight change of emphasis. Also, the first three editions did not contain a section dealing with risk, uncertainty, and factors to consider when making business decisions. Five articles dealing with these subjects now appear as Part Six in this edition.

The writings of the classical and socialistic economic theorists, which have contributed significantly to the literature, were not found in the first three versions and are not found in this fourth edition. Likewise, the unmistakable brilliance of the many economists who concerned themselves with the study and explanation of how an economy works and whether certain desirable goals such as full employment and price stability could be achieved are unnecessary in this kind of book. For the most part, those writers did not address themselves specifically to the price and output decisions that must be made daily by corporate executives, many of the tools for which *are* explained in this publication.

The purpose of this edition is to demonstrate that economic theory need not be confined to some ivory tower. Its objective is to supplement the reader's understanding of economic theory with enough knowledge of procedural technique(s) so that he or she will become a more effective decision maker, a more useful member of the management team.

Every economy, whether it be capitalistic, socialistic, or communistic, has little choice but to rely upon the subject matter of economics for meaningful decisions. Business executives as well as politicians will continue to lean heavily tomorrow on the "academic scribblers" of yesterday and today. In some small way, this publication should help them make significantly better decisions.

The price and output behavior of a firm operating in a mixed capitalistic system such as we have within the confines of the United States and Canada is, for the most part, the subject matter of this book. It has to do with economic organization and methodology; demand; costs; production and productivity; pricing; capital budgeting risk/uncertainty; and economic forecasting. It is an exciting undertaking and one that will prove beneficial to students who pursue it seriously.

The astute student will find that *Readings in Managerial Economics* investigates the place a firm holds within an industry, the contribution it makes to society, and the impact it has upon international affairs.

As a separate subject managerial economics is relatively new, its first serious treatment in textbook format being provided by Joel Dean in 1951. It applies concepts learned in the more traditional courses in microeconomic and/or macroeconomic theory—applies them in a manner useful in the daily operations of the firm. And why not? The last thing most organizations need is an economist steeped in economic theory but unable to communicate with other executives employed by the firm. This readings book helps to put economic theory and practice in proper perspective.

One hesitates to guess at the number of articles that were reviewed in the selection process for this edition. Suffice it to say that many were called but few were chosen. And the probability is high that some mistakes were made. Naturally, I assume full responsibility for these errors, judgmental or otherwise.

Suggestions received from several colleagues almost caused adoption of a more uniform level of abstraction throughout the volume. The temptation was overcome; consequently, the user has abstract articles that develop important principles mixed with elementary ones that illustrate those principles clearly.

Constraints common to the practice continue with this fourth edition; namely, space, coverage, and balance. A self-imposed limitation of not reprinting materials from books is retained.

Whenever possible, footnotes are removed, and, at times, textual material that does not contribute significantly to the overall aims of the book is omitted. To the greatest possible extent editorial changes are minimal.

A matrix of cross-references between several leading textbooks and specific articles in this publication is provided for the user. In addition, these chapters are cross-referenced with specific articles in the Table of Contents.

Very sincere thanks is expressed to the authors and publishers who provided permission to reprint these articles.

I have benefited from helpful comments received from a number of students and colleagues. In particular, I would like to acknowledge the help of Felix Livingston, Troy State University; John Peck, Indiana University at South Bend; and Norman Weed, University of Houston. John Carroll University student assistant Mary O'Toole made her fair share of trips to the Grasselli Library and to other libraries in the Greater Cleveland area. She has my sincere thanks. Clay Cerny contributed to preparation of the index.

I am particularly grateful to students for feedback and suggestions concerning many of the articles considered but not used. Because of them, this publication should contribute to a better understanding of applied price theory; however, if this Fourth Edition does not accomplish everything for the student that I hope it will, I will be comforted by this fact: he who achieves everything he sets out to achieve probably did not set out to achieve enough in the first place.

THOMAS JOSEPH COYNE

Contents and Text Cross-Reference*

PART ONE
Introduction to Managerial Economics

---

* Textbooks referenced include:

Coyne, Thomas J. *Managerial Economics: Analysis and Cases,* 5th ed. Plano, Texas: Business Publications, Inc., 1984.

Douglas, Evan J. *Managerial Economics: Theory, Practice, and Problems,* 2d ed. Englewood Cliffs, N.J.: Prentice-Hall, 1983.

Maurice, S. Charles, and Smithson, Charles W. *Managerial Economics,* Homewood, Ill.: Richard D. Irwin, 1981.

McGuigan, James R., and Moyer, R. Charles. *Managerial Economics,* 3d ed. St. Paul, Minn.: West Publishing Company, 1982.

Naylor, Thomas H., Vernon, John M., and Wertz, Kenneth L. *Managerial Economics: Corporate Economics and Strategy,* New York: McGraw-Hill, 1983.

Pappas, James L., Brigham, Eugene F., and Hirschey, Mark. *Managerial Economics,* 4th ed. Hinsdale, Ill.: Dryden Press, 1983.

Seo, K. K. *Managerial Economics: Text, Problems and Short Cases,* 6th ed. Homewood, Ill.: Richard D. Irwin, 1984.

Truett, Lila J., and Truett, Dale B. *Managerial Economics: Analysis, Problems and Cases,* Cincinnati, Ohio: South-Western Publishing, 1984.

PART THREE

Costs, Production and Productivity

PART FOUR

Pricing

PART FIVE

Financial Management

PART SIX

Risk, Uncertainty, and Factors to Consider when Making Business Decisions

PART SEVEN

Forecasting

TEXT CROSS-REFERENCES

	Part and Chapter Numbers						
Readings in this book	Part One Introduction to Managerial Economics	Part Two Demand	Part Three Costs, Production, and Productivity	Part Four Pricing	Part Five Financial Management	Part Six Risk and Uncertainty	Part Seven Forecasting
Coyne	1, 2, 3	4, 5	6, 7	8, 9, 10	11, 12	3, 5, 11, 12, 13, 14	4, 5, 13, 14
Douglas	1, 2, 3	3, 4, 5	6, 7, 8	1, 4, 9, 10, 11, 12, 14	12, 14	1, 2, 5	4, 5, 8
Maurice and Smithson	1	2, 4, 5	6, 7	2, 5, 10, 12, 13	3, 4, 13, 14	13, 14	3, 5, 14
McGuigan and Moyer	1	1, 5, 6, 8	10, 11, 12	6, 14, 15, 18	16, 17, 19 (App.)	2, 3, 5, 15, 16	7, 9
Naylor, Vernon, and Wertz	1	2, 3	3, 4	3, 4, 6, 7, 9, 10	9, 10, 11	3, 10, 12, 13	3, 12, 13
Pappas, Brigham and Hirschey	1	4, 5	6, 7, 8	4, 5, 10, 11, 12	13, 14 (App.)	3, 5, 11 (App. B), 13	5, App.B
Seo	1, 2	2, 3, 4, 5, 6, 7	9, 10, 11, 12	5, 6, 7, 13, 14, 15, 16	16, 18, 19	13, 14	2, 3, 4, 5, 6, 8, 17
Truett and Truett	1	4, 9, 10	1, 3, 4, 5, 6	5, 8, 9, 11, 11 (App.), 13	11, 13, 13 (App.), 14	1, 9 (App.), 14	5, 9, 10 (App.), 10, 17

PART ONE

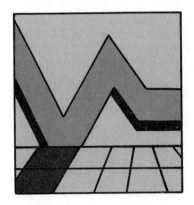

INTRODUCTION TO MANAGERIAL ECONOMICS

Managerial economics is not merely another course in economic theory; it requires a different approach than found in a theory text. Managerial economics is therefore manifestly different from microeconomic theory, but it is somehow related. Just what this relationship is, has been and continues to be a lively topic of debate. The extreme positions are, on the one hand, a naive belief that the most abstract of economic theories are applicable to the most complex of managerial problems; on the other, an equally repugnant belief that no part of economic theory is applicable to even the simplest of them.

The modern corporation is a complex economic institution. Evidence of its importance is expressed often in the tens of billions of dollars in corporate assets and sales and/or in the hundreds of thousands of employees who occupy their time and talent within the corporate structure on a daily basis. The functioning of the corporate system and its impact on the aggregate economy is explained in the opening article by Williamson. His view of the corporate organization can be studied for the contributions it makes to one's understanding of how the corporation, as explained in economic theory, may differ from the one that operates daily in the modern world.

Every economy, whether it be capitalist, socialist, or communist, is organized. The organization might appear somewhat haphazard (as in Iran in 1984) or highly structured and rigidly controlled (as in modern Russia). A person interested in managing resources effectively in any economic system needs to understand the organizational structure of his/her immediate environment. Even a prison camp has an economic environment, and the article by Radford explains the development and organization of an economy in such a restricted situation. He finds that a currency evolves (cigarettes) and price movements occur; paper markets develop; price fixing is a problem; and, of course, public opinion needs to be molded.

Regardless of the form of business organization (i.e., corporate, partnership, proprietorship) and regardless of whether it takes place in the real world or an isolated environment (P.O.W. camps), if the system is to function properly it must be managed by people who know what they are doing. More specifically, the level of economic literacy is of great importance to a society, and efforts must be made to improve upon it. The article by Heebner explains that the quality of economic knowledge is not uniformly high and existing institutions concerned with dissemination of that knowledge are not rapidly closing the knowledge gap. This piece by Heebner conveys a sense of urgency to the reader with respect to why business persons in general and business economists in particular need to combine their talents with the five general guidelines provided by him.

Edgar Fiedler calls attention to problems of stagflation in our modern economy. He fears we have too much inflation and too little productivity, and the situation has existed over an extended period of time. How can economic theory help resolve the problems about which Fiedler is concerned? William Baumol offers an approach.

How closely one chooses to weave other disciplines into economics depends primarily upon the range of questions being answered and the confidence placed by the economist in assumptions dealing with such things as static equilibrium. The piece by Baumol reveals the relevance of managerial economics to the price, output, and other problems found in a sophisticated, somewhat complex and highly structured, dynamic American economic system.

This well-known paper by William Baumol establishes a point of view for managerial economics; namely, that a managerial economist can make significant contributions as a member of the management group simply because he or she is an effective model builder. The economist's analytic tools and techniques help that person deal with problems facing an organization in a very rigorous and revealing manner. Managerial economists tend to probe deeper into complex problems than do persons without such training, and these problems, once solved, then may be presented to noneconomists in an easy-to-understand manner.

These five articles in Part One provide the reader with an opportunity to see that managerial economics, like all economics, is concerned with choice; but, among the various branches of economics, it is supremely pragmatic. It cuts through many of the refinements of theory. While it seems to avoid some of the most difficult issues of abstract economic theory, it inevitably faces complications that are ignored in pure theory, for managerial economics deals with the total situation in which all decisions are made.

1.

The Modern Corporation: Origins, Evolution, Attributes*

OLIVER E. WILLIAMSON

There is virtual unanimity with the proposition that the modern corporation is a complex and important economic institution. There is much less agreement on what its attributes are and on how and why it has successively evolved to take on its current configuration. While I recognize that there have been numerous contributing factors, I submit that the modern corporation is mainly to be understood as the product of a series of organizational innovations that have had the purpose and effect of economizing on transaction codes.

Note that I do not argue that the modern corporation is to be understood exclusively in these terms. Other important factors include the quest for monopoly gains and the imperatives of technology. These mainly have a bearing on market shares and on the absolute size of specific technological units; but decisions to make or buy, which determine the distribution of economic activity, as between firms and markets, and the internal organization (including both the shape and the aggregate size) of the firm are not explained, except perhaps in trivial ways, in these terms. Inasmuch as these are core issues, a theory of the modern corporation that does not address them is, at best, seriously incomplete.

---

* *Journal of Economic Literature* 19 (December 1981), pp. 1537–65.

Specifically, the study of the modern corporation should actively concern itself with, and provide consistent explanations for, the following features of the organization of economic activity: What are the factors that determine the degree to which firms integrate—in backward, forward, and lateral respects? What economic purposes are served by the widespread adoption of divisionalization? What ramifications, if any, does internal organization have for the long-standing dilemma posed by the separation of ownership from control? Can the "puzzle" of the conglomerate be unraveled? Do similar considerations apply in assessing multinational enterprise? Can an underlying rationale be provided for the reported association between innovation and direct foreign investment?

It is my contention that transaction-cost economizing figures prominently in explaining these (as well as related) major features of the business environment. Since transaction-cost economizing is socially valued, it follows that the modern corporation serves affirmative economic purposes. But complex institutions often serve a variety of purposes—and the corporation can and sometimes is used to pursue antisocial objectives. I submit, however, that (1) objectionable purposes can normally be recognized and dealt with separately and (2) failure to understand the main purposes of the corporation has been the source of much confusion and ill-conceived public policy. Specifically, antisocial purposes have often been attributed where none existed.

Inasmuch as a sensitivity to transactions and transaction-cost economizing can be traced to the 1930s, it is somewhat surprising that the importance of the modern corporation as a means of reducing transaction costs has been so long neglected. The main reason is that the origins of transaction costs must often be sought in influences and motives that lie outside the normal domain of economics. Accordingly, a large gap separated an identification of transaction costs, as the main factor to which the study of the organization of economic activity must repair, and efforts to give operational content to that insight.

This paper is organized in two parts. Sections 1 and 2 sketch the background and set forth the arguments that are subsequently employed to interpret a series of organizational innovations that have successively yielded the modern corporation. Sections 3 and 4 deal with these changes. My discussion of organizational innovation begins with the latter half of the 19th century. In this regard, I follow Alfred Chandler who traces the origins of complex hierarchical forms of business organization to this period. To be sure, others have identified interesting organizational developments in both Japanese and English business history that predate, if not prefigure, those in the United States. But these earlier developments were not widely adopted by other firms—and in any event represent very primitive forms of divisionalization. As a consequence, these earlier developments were of isolated economic importance and are properly distinguished from the general transformation of American industry that began in the 19th century and has continued since.

Key legal features of the corporation—limited liability and the transferability of ownership—are taken as given. Failure to discuss these does not reflect a judgment that these are either irrelevant or uninteresting. The main focus of this essay, however, is on the internal organization of the corporation. Since any of a number of internal structures is consistent with these legal features, an explanation for the specific organizational innovations that were actually adopted evidently resides elsewhere. Among the more significant of these innovations, and the ones addressed here, are: the development of line-and-staff organization by the railroads; selective forward integration by manufacturers into distribution; the development of the multidivisional corporate form; the evolution of the conglomerate; and the appearance of the multinational enterprise. The first three of these changes have been studied by business historians, the contributions of Chandler being the most ambitious and notable.

1. SOME BACKGROUND

1.1 General

Assessing the organization of economic activity in an advanced society requires that a bewildering variety of market, hierarchical, and mixed modes be evaluated. Economists, organization theorists, public policy specialists, and historians all have an interest and each have offered interpretations of successive organizational innovations. A coherent view, however, has not emerged.

Partly this is because the principal hierarchical structure to be assessed—the modern corporation—is formidably complex in its great size, diversity, and internal organization. The natural difficulties which thereby resulted would have been overcome sooner, however, had it not been for a number of conceptual barriers to an understanding of this institution. Chief among these are the following: (1) the neoclassical theory of the firm, which is the main referrent to which economists appeal, is devoid of interesting hierarchical features; (2) organization theorists, who are specialists in the study of internal organization and unencumbered by an intellectual commitment to neoclassical economic models, have been preoccupied with hierarchy to the neglect of market modes of organization and the healthy tension that exists between markets and hierarchies; (3) public policy analysts have maintained a deeply suspicious attitude toward nonstandard or unfamiliar forms of economic organization; and (4) organizational innovation has been relatively neglected by business and economic historians.

To be sure, this indictment sweeps too broadly. As discussed in 1.2 below, there have been important exceptions. The main features, however, are as I have described. Thus neoclassical theory treats the firm as a production function to which a profit maximization objective has been ascribed. Albeit useful for many purposes, such a construction is unhelpful in attempting to assess the purposes served by hierarchical modes of organization. The firm as production function needs to make way for the view of the *firm as governance structure* if the ramifications of internal organization are to be accurately assessed. Only recently has this latter orientation begun to make headway—and is still in a primitive state of development.

The preoccupation of organization theory specialists with internal organization is a potentially useful corrective. An understanding of the purposes served by internal organization has remained elusive, however, for at least two reasons. First, efficiency analysis plays a relatively minor role in the studies of most organization theory specialists—many of whom are more inclined to emphasize power. The economizing factors that are crucial to an understanding of the modern corporation are thus effectively suppressed. Second, and related, firms and markets are treated separately rather than in active juxtaposition with one another. The propositions that (1) firms and markets are properly regarded as alternative governance structures to which (2) transactions are to be assigned in discriminating (mainly transaction-cost economizing) ways are unfamiliar to most organization theory specialists and alien to some.

Public policy analysts with an interest in the modern corporation might also have been expected to entertain a broader view. In fact, however, many of these likewise adopted a production function orientation—whereby markets were regarded as the "natural, hence efficient" way by which to mediate transactions between technologically separable entities. This was joined by a pervasive sense that the purposes of competition are invariably served by maintaining many autonomous traders. Even sensitive observers were trapped by this combined technological/ atomistic logic. Thus Donald Turner, at a time when he headed the Antitrust Division, expressed skepticism over nonstandard business practices by observing that "I approach territorial and customer restrictions not hospitably in the common law tradition, but inhospitably in the tradition of antitrust law." The possibility that efficiency might be served by imposing restraints on autonomous market trading was evidently thought to be slight. This inhospitality tradition also explains ingrained public policy animosity towards vertical integration and conglomerate organization; more generally, industrial organization specialists were encouraged to discover what were often fanciful "distortions" at the expense of a more basic understanding of the modern corporation in economizing terms.

The neglect of organizational innovations by business and economic historians has been general but by no means complete and shows recent signs of being corrected. Mainly, however, interpretation has played a secondary role to description in most historial studies of organizational change—which, while understandable, contributes to the continuing confusion over the purposes served by the changing organizational features of the corporation.

This essay attempts to provide a coherent view of the modern corporation by (1) augmenting the model of the firm as production function to include the concept of the firm as governance structure, (2) studying firms and markets as alternative governance structures in a comparative institutional way, (3) supplanting the presumption that organizational innovations have anticompetitive purposes by the rebuttable presumption that organizational innovations are designed to economize on transaction costs, and (4) interpreting business history from a transaction cost perspective. Such an approach to the study of the modern corporation (and, more generally, to the study of organizational innovation) owes its origins to antecedent contributions of four kinds.

1.2 Antecedents

(a) Theory of Firms and Markets.   The unsatisfactory state of the theory of the firm was recognized by Ronald Coase in his classic 1937 article on "The Nature of the Firm." As he observed:

> Outside the firm, price movements direct production, which is coordinated through a series of exchange transactions on the market. Within a firm, these market transactions are eliminated and in place of the complicated market structure with exchange transactions is substituted the entrepreneur–coordinator, who directs production. It is clear that these are *alternative means of coordinating production.*

Coase went on to observe that firms arose because there were costs of using the price system. But internal organization was no cost panacea, since it experienced distinctive costs of its own. A balance is struck when the firm has expanded to the point where "the costs of organizing an extra transaction within the firm become equal to the costs of carrying out the same transaction by means of an exchange in the open market or the costs of organizing in another firm."

Related insight on the study of firms and markets was offered by Friedrich A. Hayek, who dismissed equilibrium economics with the observation that "the economic problem of society is mainly one of adaptation to changes in particular circumstances of time and place," and who held that the "marvel" of the price system was that it could accomplish this without "conscious direction." Setting aside the possibility that Hayek did not make adequate allowance for the limitations of the price system, three things are notable about these observations. First is his emphasis on change and the need to devise adaptive institutional forms. Second, his reference to particular circumstances, as distinguished from statistical aggregates, reflects a sense that economic institutions must be sensitive to dispersed knowledge of a microanalytic kind. And third was his insistence that attention to the details of social processes and economic institutions was made necessary by the "unavoidable imperfection of man's knowledge."

The organization of firms and markets has been a subject to which Kenneth Arrow has made repeated contributions. He has addressed himself not only to the economics of the internal organization but also to an assessment of the powers and limits of markets. Like Coase, he expressly recognizes that firms and markets are alternative modes of organizing economic activity. Moreover, whereas the limits of markets were glossed over by Hayek, Arrow specifically traces these to transaction-cost origins: "market failure is not absolute; it is better to consider a broader category, that of transaction costs, which in general impede and in particular cases block the formation of markets"—where by transaction costs Arrow has reference to the "costs of running the economic system."

(b) Organization Theory. Although organization theorists have not in general regarded efficiency as their central concern, there have been notable exceptions. The early works of Chester Barnard and Herbert Simon both qualify.

Barnard was a businessman rather than a social scientist and he addressed internal organizational issues that many would regard as outside the scope of economics. Economizing was nevertheless strongly featured in his approach to the study of organizations. Understanding the employment relation was among the issues that intrigued him. Matters that concerned him in this connection included: the need to align incentives, including noneconomic inducements, to achieve enterprise viability; the importance of assent to authority; a description of the authority relation within which hierarchical organizations operate; and the role of "informal organization" in supporting the working rules upon which formal organization relies. The rationality of internal organization, making due allowance for the attributes of human actors, was a matter of continuous concern to Barnard.

Simon expressly relies on Barnard and carries rationality analysis forward. A more precise vocabulary than Barnard's is developed in the process. Simon traces the problem of organization to the joining of rational purposes with the cognitive limits of human actors: "it is precisely in the realm where human behavior is *intendedly* rational, but only *limitedly* so, that there is room for a genuine theory of organization and administration." Intended rationality supplies purpose, but meaningful economic and organizational choices arise only in a limited (or bounded) rationality context.

Simon makes repeated reference to the criterion of efficiency, but he also cautions that organizational design should be informed by "a knowledge of those aspects of the social sciences which are relevant to the broader purposes of the organization." A sensitivity to subgoal pursuit, wherein individuals identify with and pursue local goals at the possible expense of global goals, and the "outguessing" or gaming aspects of human behavior are among these.

Although Simon examines the merits of centralized versus decentralized modes of organization, it is not until his later writing that he expressly addresses the matter of factoring problems according to rational hierarchical principles. The issues here are developed more fully in Section 2.

(c) **Nonstrategic Purposes.**   The "inhospitality tradition" referred to above maintained a presumption of illegality when nonstandard or unfamiliar business practices were brought under review. These same practices, when viewed "through the lens of price theory" by Aaron Director (and his students and colleagues at Chicago), were regarded rather differently. Whereas Turner and others held that anticompetitive purposes were being served, Director and his associates reported instead that tie-ins, resale price maintenance, and the like were promoting more efficient resource allocation.

In fact, nonstandard business practices (such as tie-ins) are anomalies when regarded in the full information terms associated with static price theory. Implicitly, however, Chicago was also relying on the existence of transaction costs—which, after all, were the reason why comprehensive price discrimination could not be effected through simple contracts unsupported by restrictive practices from the outset. Be that as it may, Chicago's insistence that economic behavior be assessed with respect to its economizing properties was a healthy antidote and encouraged further scrutiny of these same matters—with the eventual result that an economizing orientation is now much more widely held. Indirectly, these views have spilled over and influenced thinking about the modern corporation as an economizing, rather than mainly a monopolizing, entity.

(d) **Business History.**   The study of organizational innovation has been relatively neglected by business and economic historians. Aside from the Research Center in Entrepreneurial History at Harvard, which was established in 1948 and closed its doors a decade later, there has not been a concerted effort to work through and establish the importance of organizational innovation. Probably the most important reason for this neglect is that business history has not had "the support of an established system of theory."

Despite this general neglect, notable contributions have nevertheless been made. The works of Lance Davis and Douglass North, and of Alfred Chandler have been especially important. The first of these takes a sweeping view of institutional change and employs a market failure theory for assessing successive changes. It pays only limited attention, however, to the corporation as a unit whose attributes need to be assessed.

Chandler, by contrast, is expressly and deeply concerned with the organization form changes which, over the past 150 years, have brought us the modern corporation as we know it. The story is told in two parts, the first being the evolution of the large, multifunctional enterprise, the second being the subsequent divisionalization of these firms. Both of these transformations are described and interpreted in Sections 3 and 4 below. Suffice it to observe here that (1) Chandler's is the first treatment of business history that describes organizational changes in sufficient detail to permit a transaction-cost interpretation to be applied, (2) Chandler's 1962 book was significant not only for its business history contributions but because it clearly established that organization form had an important impact on business performance—which neither economics nor organization theory had done (nor, for the most part, even attempted) previously, and (3) although Chandler is more concerned with the description than with the interpretation of organizational change, his careful descriptions are nevertheless suggestive of the economic factors that are responsible for the changes observed.

2. TRANSACTION-COST ECONOMICS

Each of the antecedent literatures just described has a bearing on the transaction-cost approach to the study of economic institutions in general and the modern corporation in particular. Following Commons, the transaction is made the basic unit of analysis. Specifically, attention is focused on the transaction costs of running the economic system, with emphasis on adaptation to unforeseen, and often unforeseeable, circumstances. The issues of special interest are connected with the changing structure of the corporation over the past 150 years. Rather than regard these inhospitably, the new approach maintains the rebuttable presumption that the evolving corporate structure has the purpose and effect of economizing on transaction costs. These transaction-cost and business history literatures are linked by appeal to selective parts of the (mainly older) organization theory literature.

As Barnard emphasized, differences in internal organization often had significant performance consequences and could and should be assessed from a rationality viewpoint. Simon extended and refined the argument that internal organization mattered and that the study of internal organization needed to make appropriate allowance for the attributes of human actors—for what Frank Knight has felicitously referred to as "human nature as we know it." Then, and only then, does the comparative institutional assessment of alternative organizational forms take on its full economic significance.

2.1 Comparative Institutional Analysis

The costs of running the economic system to which Arrow refers can be usefully thought of in contractual terms. Each feasible mode of conducting relations between technologically separable entities can be examined with respect to the ex ante costs of negotiating and writing, as well as the ex post costs of executing, policing, and, when disputes arise, remedying the (explicit or implicit) contract that joins them.

A transaction may thus be said to occur when a good or service is transferred across a technologically separable interface. One stage of processing or assembly activity terminates and another begins. A mechanical analogy, while imperfect, may nevertheless be useful. A well-working interface, like a well-working machine, can be thought of as one where these transfers occur smoothly.

In neither case, however, is smoothness desired for its own sake: the benefits must be judged in relation to the cost. Both investment and operating features require attention. Thus extensive prior investment in finely tuned equipment and repeated lubrication and adjustment during operation are both ways of attenuating friction, slippage, or other loss of mechanical energy. Similarly, extensive precontract negotiation that covers all relevant contingencies may avoid the need for periodic intervention to realign the interface during execution so that a contract may be brought successfully to completion. Simultaneous attention to both investment (precontract costs) and operating expenses (harmonizing costs) is needed if mechanical (contractual) systems are to be designed effectively. The usual study of economizing in a production function framework is thus extended to include an examination of the *comparative costs of planning, adapting, and monitoring task completion under alternative governance structures*—where by governance structure I have reference to the explicit or implicit contractual framework within which a transaction is located (markets, firms, and mixed modes—e.g., franchising—included).

The study of transaction-cost economizing is thus a comparative institutional undertaking which recognizes that there are a variety of distinguishably different transactions on the one hand and a variety of alternative governance structures on the other. The object is to match governance structures to the attributes of transactions in a discriminating way. Microanalytic attention to differences among governance structures and microanalytic definition of transactions are both needed in order for this to be accomplished.

Although more descriptive detail than is associated with neoclassical analysis is needed for this purpose, a relatively crude assessment will often suffice. As Simon has observed, comparative institutional analysis commonly involves an examination of discrete structural alternatives for which marginal analysis is not required: "In general, much cruder and simpler arguments will suffice to demonstrate an inequality between two quantities than are required to show the conditions under which these quantities are equated at the margin."

2.2 Behavioral Assumptions

Human nature as we know it is marvelously rich and needs to be reduced to manageable proportions. The two behavioral assumptions on which transaction-cost analysis relies—and without which the study of economic organization is pointless—are bounded rationality and opportunism. As a consequence of these two assumptions, the human agents that populate the firms and markets with which I am concerned differ from economic man (or at least the common caricature thereof) in that they are less competent in calculation and less trustworthy and reliable in action. A condition of bounded rationality is responsible for the computational limits of organizational man. A proclivity for (at least some) economic agents to behave opportunistically is responsible for their unreliability.

The term *bounded rationality* was coined by Simon to reflect the fact that economic actors, who may be presumed to be "intendedly rational," are not hyperrational. Rather, they experience limits in formulating and solving complex problems and in processing (receiving, storing, retrieving, transmitting) information. Opportunism is related to but is a somewhat more general term than the condition of "moral hazard" to which Knight referred in his classic statement of economic organization. Opportunism effectively extends the usual assumption of self-interest seeking to make allowance for self-interest seeking with guile.

But for the *simultaneous* existence of both bounded rationality and opportunism, all economic contracting problems are trivial and the study of economic institutions is unimportant. Thus, but for bounded rationality, all economic exchange could be effectively organized by contract. Indeed, the economic theory of comprehensive contracting has been fully worked out. Given bounded rationality, however, it is impossible to deal with complexity in all contractually relevant respects. As a consequence, incomplete contracting is the best that can be achieved.

Ubiquitous, albeit incomplete, contracting would nevertheless be feasible if economic agents were completely trustworthy. Principals would simply extract promises from agents that they will behave in a stewardship fashion, while agents would reciprocally ask principals to behave in good faith. Such devices will not work, however, if some economic actors (either principals or agents) are dishonest (or, more generally, disguise attributes or preferences, distort data, obfuscate issues, and otherwise confuse transactions) and it is very costly to distinguish opportunistic from nonopportunistic types ex ante.

Although the dual assumptions of bounded rationality and opportunism complicate the study of economic behavior and may be inessential for some purposes, the study of alternative modes of organization does not qualify as an exception. To the contrary, failure to recognize and make allowance for both is virtually to invite mistaken assessments of alternative modes. Taking these two behavioral assumptions into account, the following compact statement of the problem of economic organization is suggested: Assess alternative governance structures in terms of their capacities to economize on bounded rationality while simultaneously safeguarding transactions against opportunism. This is not inconsistent with the imperative "maximize profits!," but it focuses attention somewhat differently.

2.3 Dimensionalizing

As Coase observed in 1972, his 1937 paper was "much cited but little used." The reasons for this are many, including a preoccupation by economists with other matters during the intervening 35 years. The main reason, however, is that transaction costs had not been operationalized and it was not obvious how this could be accomplished.

The postwar market failure literature, especially Arrow's insight that market failures had transaction-costs origins, served to focus attention on the troublesome issues. A recognition that market (and internal) failures of all kinds could be ultimately traced to the human factors described above was a second step. The remaining step was to identify the critical dimensions with respect to which transactions differ.

The attributes of transactions that are of special interest to the economics of organization are: (1) the frequency with which transactions recur, (2) the uncertainty to which transactions are subject, and (3) the degree to which transactions are supported by durable, transaction-specific investments. A considerable amount of explanatory power turns on the last.

Asset specificity can arise in any of three ways: site specificity, as when successive stations are located in cheek-by-jowl relation to each other so as to economize on inventory and transportation expenses; physical asset specificity, as where specialized dies are required to produce a component; and human asset specificity that arises in a learning-by-doing fashion. The reason why asset specificity is critical is that, once the investment has been made, buyer and seller are effectively operating in a bilateral (or at least quasi-bilateral) exchange relation for a considerable period thereafter. Inasmuch as the value of highly specific capital in other uses is, by definition, much smaller than the specialized use for which it has been intended, the supplier is effectively "locked into" the transaction to a significant degree. This is symmetrical, moreover, in that the buyer cannot turn to alternative sources of supply and obtain the item on favorable terms, since the cost of supply from unspecialized capital is presumably great. The buyer is thus committed to the transaction as well. Accordingly, where asset specificity is great, buyer and seller will make special efforts to design an exchange relation that has good continuity properties. Autonomous contracting gives way to more complex forms of market contracting and sometimes to internal organization for this reason.

2.4 Three Principles of Organizational Design

The criterion for organizing commercial transactions is assumed to be the strictly instrumental one of cost economizing. Essentially this takes two parts: economizing on production expense and economizing of transaction costs. In fact, these are not independent and need to be addressed simultaneously. The study of the latter, however, is much less well developed and is emphasized here.

The three principles of organizational design employed here are neither exhaustive nor refined. They nevertheless offer considerable explanatory power in dealing with the main changes in corporate organization reported by Chandler and addressed here. Transaction-cost reasoning supports all three, although only the first, the asset-specificity principle, is tightly linked to dimensionalizing. Bounded rationality and opportunism, however, operate with respect to all three.

The asset-specificity principle turns on the above described transformation of an exchange relation from a large-numbers to a small-numbers condition during the course of contract execution. The second, the externality principle, is often discussed under the heading of "free rider" effects. The more general phenomenon, however, is that of subgoal pursuit, that is, in the course of executing contracts, agents also pursue private goals which may be in some degree inconsistent with the contract's intended purpose. These two principles influence the choice of contracting form (mainly firm or market). In fact, however, the efficacy of internal organization depends on whether sound principles of internal organizational design are respected, which is to say that the details of internal organization matter. The hierarchical decomposition principle deals with this last.

It will be convenient to assume that transactions will be organized by markets unless market exchange gives rise to serious transaction costs. In the beginning, so to speak, there were markets. Both bureaucratic and production cost considerations favor this presumption. The bureaucratic argument is simply this: market exchange serves to attenuate the bureaucratic distortions to which internal exchange is subject. The production cost advantages of market procurement are three: static scale economies can be more fully exhausted by buying rather than making if the firm's needs are small in relation to the market; markets can aggregate uncorrelated demands, to thereby realize risk pooling benefits; and markets may enjoy economies of scope in supplying a related set of activities of which the firm's requirements are only one. Accordingly, transactions will be organized in markets *unless* transaction cost disabilities appear.

(a) **Asset-Specificity Principle (All Transactions).** Recall that transactions are described in terms of three attributes: frequency, uncertainty, and asset specificity. Although interesting organizational issues are posed when transactions are of only an occasional kind, this paper deals entirely with the governance of recurring transactions. Also, it will facilitate the analysis to hold uncertainty constant in intermediate degree—which is to say that we are dealing neither with steady state nor highly uncertain events. Accordingly, asset specificity is the transactional dimension of special interest. The first principle of efficient organizational design is this: *The normal presumption that recurring transactions for technologically separable goods and services will be efficiently mediated by autonomous market contracting is progressively weakened as asset specificity increases.*

The production cost advantages of markets decrease and the (comparative) governance costs of markets increase as assets become progressively more specific. Thus as assets become more fully specialized to a single use or user, hence are less transferable to other uses and users, economies of scale can be as fully realized when a firm operates the asset under its own internal direction as when its services are obtained externally by contract. And the market's advantage in pooling risks likewise shrinks. Simultaneously, the transactions in question take on a stronger bilateral character, and the governance costs of markets increase relatively.

The distinction between ex ante and ex post competition is essential to an understanding of this condition. What may have been (and commonly is) an effective large-numbers-bidding situation at the outset is sometimes *transformed* into a bilateral trading relation thereafter. This obtains if, despite the fact that large numbers of qualified bidders were prepared to enter competitive bids for the initial contract, the winning bidder realizes advantages over nonwinners at contract renewal intervals because nontrivial investments in durable specific assets are put in place (or otherwise accrue, say in a learning-by-doing fashion) during contract execution. As set out elsewhere, the efficient governance of recurring transactions will vary as follows: classical market contracting will be efficacious wherever assets are nonspecific to the trading parties; bilateral or obligational market contracting will appear as assets become semispecific; and internal organization will displace markets as assets take on a highly specific character.

Internal organization enjoys advantages over market contracting for transactions that are supported by highly specific assets at both contract-writing and contract-execution stages. Since highly specific assets cannot be redeployed without sacrificing productivity, both suppliers and purchasers will insist upon contractual safeguards before undertaking such projects. Writing and negotiating such contracts is costly. Additionally, implementation problems need to be faced. The internal direction of firms confers execution advantages over bilateral trading in three respects. First, common ownership reduces the incentives of the trading units to pursue local goals. Second, and related, internal organization is able to invoke flat to resolve differences whereas costly adjudication is needed when an impasse develops between autonomous traders. Third, internal organization has easier and more complete access to the relevant information when disputes must be settled. The incentive to shift bilateral transactions from markets to firms also increases as uncertainty increases, since the costs of harmonizing a relation among parties vary directly with the need to adjust to changing circumstances.

(b) Externality Principle (Forward Integration). Whereas the asset-specificity principle refers to transactions that are transformed from large- to small-numbers bidding situations—as buyers, who initially obtained assets or their services in a competitive market, subsequently face suppliers with some degree of monopoly power—the externality principle involves no such market transformation. Also, the asset-specificity principle applies to backward, forward, and lateral integration; by contrast, the externality principle mainly applies to distribution stages.

The externalities of concern are those that arise in conjunction with the unintended debasement of quality for a branded good or service. As discussed below, such debasement is explained by costly metering. The externality is thus a manifestation of the measurement problems to which North refers in his discussion of transaction costs. It appears mainly at the interface between production and distribution. The differential ease of inspecting, and thereby controlling, the quality of components and materials that are purchased from earlier-stage and lateral suppliers as compared with the cost of exercising quality controls over distributors is responsible for this condition.

End-games and fly-by-night distributors aside, the unintended debasement of quality by distributors poses a problem only where the activities of individual distributors affect one another, as when one retailer's poor service in installation or repair injures a product's reputation for performance and limits the sales of other retailers. More generally, if the quality enhancement (debasement) efforts of distributors give rise to positive (negative) externalities, the benefits (costs) of which can be incompletely appropriated by (assigned to) the originators, failure to extend quality controls over distribution will result in suboptimization. Autonomous contracting thus gives way to obligational market contracting (e.g., franchising) if not forward integration into distribution as demand interaction effects become more important. More generally, the second principle of efficient organizational design is this: *The normal presumption that exchange between producers of differentiated goods and distribution stages will be efficiently mediated by autonomous contracting is progressively weakened as demand externalities increase.*

Product differentiation is a necessary but not a sufficient condition for troublesome demand externalities to appear. Manufacturers can sometimes insulate a product against deterioration by special packaging (say by selling the item in hermetic containers with an inert atmosphere and providing replacement guarantees). If, however, such safeguards are very costly, and if follow-on checks and penalties to discourage distributors from debasing the quality image of a product are likewise expensive, autonomous trading will give way to forms of distribution that have superior quality control properties.

(c) Hierarchical-Decomposition Principle (Internal Organization). Merely to transfer a transaction out of the market into the firm does not, by itself, assure that the activity will be effectively organized thereafter. Not only are bounded rationality and opportunism ubiquitous, but the problems presented by both vary with changes in internal organization. Accordingly, a complete theory of value will recognize that firm structure as well as market structure matters.

Simon makes provision for bounded rationality effects in arguing that the organizational division of decision-making labor is quite as important as the neoclassical division of production labor, where, from "the information processing point of view, division of labor means factoring the total system of decisions that need to be made into relatively independent subsystems, each one of which can be designed with only minimal concern for its interactions with the others." This applies to both vertical and horizontal aspects of the organization. In both respects the object is to recognize and give effect to conditions of near decomposability. The vertical slice entails grouping the operating parts into separable entities, the interactions within which are strong and between which are weak. The horizontal slice has temporal ramifications of a strategic versus operating kind. Problems are thus factored in such a way that the higher frequency (or short run dynamics) are associated with the operating parts while the lower frequency (or long run dynamics) are associated with the strategic system. These operating and strategic distinctions correspond with the lower and higher levels in the organizational hierarchy, respectively. Internal incentives and information flows need, of course, to be aligned, lest distortions be deliberately or inadvertently introduced into the internal information summary and transmittal processes.

The hierarchical-decomposition principle can thus be stated as follows: *Internal organization should be designed in such a way as to effect quasi-independence between the parts, the high frequency dynamics (operating activities) and low frequency dynamics (strategic planning) should be clearly distinguished, and incentives should be aligned within and between components* so as to promote both local and global effectiveness.

Each of these three principles of organizational design is responsive to considerations of both bounded rationality and opportunism. Thus asset specificity would pose no problems if comprehensive contracting were feasible (which is tantamount to unbounded rationality) or if winning bidders could be relied upon to behave in an utterly reliable and trustworthy fashion (absence of opportunism). The externality principle is mainly a reflection of opportunism (autonomous distributors permit their suppliers' reputations to be degraded because they bear only part of the costs), but, of course, quality control checks would be unneeded if all relevant information could be costlessly displayed and assessed. The hierarchical-decomposition principle recognizes the need to divide problems into manageable units and at the same time prevent agents from engaging in dysfunctional pursuit of local goals, which reflect bounded rationality and opportunism concerns, respectively.

A more comprehensive analysis would embed these principles of organization within a larger optimizing framework where demand as well as cost consequences are recognized and where production versus transaction costs tradeoffs are made explicit. For the purposes at hand, however, which take product design as given and focus on distinguishably different rather than close cases, such refinements do not appear to be necessary.

3. THE 19TH CENTURY CORPORATION

The 1840s mark the beginning of a great wave of organizational change that has evolved into the modern corporation. According to Stuart Bruchey, the 15th-century merchant of Venice would have understood the form of organization and methods of managing men, records, and investment used by Baltimore merchants in 1790. These practices evidently remained quite serviceable until after the 1840s. The two most significant developments were the appearance of the railroads and, in response to this, forward integration by manufacturers into distribution.

3.1 The Railroads

Although a number of technological developments—including the telegraph, the development of continuous process machinery, the refinement of interchangeable parts manufacture, and related mass manufacturing techniques—contributed to organizational changes in the second half of the 19th century, none was more important than the railroads. Not only did the railroads pose distinctive organizational problems of their own, but the incentive to integrate forward from manufacturing into distribution would have been much less without the low-cost, reliable, all-weather transportation afforded by the railroads. Forward integration is discussed in 3.2 below; the railroads are treated here.

The appearance and purported importance of the railroads have been matters of great interest to economic historians. But with very few exceptions, the organizational—as opposed to the technological—significance of the railroads has been neglected. Thus Robert Fogel and Albert Fishlow "investigated the railroad as a construction activity and as a means of transport, but not as an organizational form. As with most economists, the internal workings of the railroad organizations were ignored. This appears to be the result of an implicit assumption that the organization form used to accomplish an objective does not matter."

The economic success of the railroads entailed more, however, than the substitution of one technology (rails) for another (canals). Rather, organizational aspects also required attention. As Chandler puts it:

> [the] safe, regular, reliable movement of goods and passengers, as well as the continuing maintenance and repair of locomotives, rolling stock, and track, roadbed, stations, roundhouses, and other equipment, required the creation of a sizeable administrative organization. It meant the employment of a set of managers to supervise these functional activities over an extensive geographical area; and the appointment of an administrative command of middle and top executives to monitor, evaluate, and coordinate the work of managers responsible for the day-to-day operations. It meant, too, the formulation of brand new types of internal administrative procedures and accounting and statistical controls. Hence, the operational requirements of the railroads demanded the creation of the first administrative hierarchies in American business.

The "natural" railroad units, as these first evolved, were lines of about 50 miles in length. These roads employed about 50 workers and were administered by a superintendent and several managers of functional activities. This was adequate as long as traffic flows were uncomplicated and short hauls prevailed. The full promise of the railroads could be realized, however, only if traffic densities were increased and longer hauls introduced. How was this to be effected?

In principle, successive end-to-end systems could be joined by contract. The resulting contracts would be tightly bilateral in negotiation, interpretation, and execution, however, since investments in site-specific assets by each party were considerable. Severe contractual difficulties would, therefore, predictably arise. Unless supporting governance structure were simultaneously created, the potential of the railroads for long-haul and high-density traffic would evidently go unrealized. One possibility was for heavily traveled end-to-end links to be joined under common ownership.

But while the consolidation of ownership reduced the restraints on long-haul operations, it did not guarantee that the end-to-end systems would work smoothly. Indeed, early operation of the Western and Albany road, which was just over 150 miles in length and was built in three sections each operated as a separate division with its own set of functional managers, quickly proved otherwise. As a consequence, a new organizational structure was fashioned whereby the first "formal administrative structure manned by full-time salaried managers" in the United States appeared.

This structure was progressively perfected, and the organizational innovation that the railroads eventually evolved is characterized by Chandler as the "decentralized line-and-staff concept of organization." This provided that "the managers on the line of authority were responsible for ordering men involved with the basic function of the enterprise, and other functional managers (the staff executives) were responsible for setting standards." Geographic divisions were defined and the superintendents in charge were held responsible for the "day-to-day movement of trains and traffic by an express delegation of authority." These division superintendents were on the "direct line of authority from the president through the general superintendent," and the functional managers within the geographic division—who dealt with transportation, motive power, maintenance of way, passenger, freight, and accounting—reported to them rather than to their functional superiors at the central office.

Confronted, as they were, by the contractual dilemmas that arise when highly specific assets are in place and by complexities that exceeded, perhaps by several orders of magnitude, those that had been faced by earlier business enterprise, the managements of the railroads supplanted markets by hierarchies of a carefully crafted kind. Although military organizations had earlier devised similar structures, the railroad innovators brought engineering rather than military backgrounds to the task. The hierarchical structure that they evolved was consistent, at least broadly, with the hierarchical principles stated by Simon. Thus support activities (lower frequency dynamics) were split off from operations (higher frequency dynamics), and the linkages within each of these classes of activity were stronger than the linkages between. This organizational innovation, in Chandler's judgment, paved the way for modern business enterprise. As with most significant organizational developments, it evolved in a piecemeal rather than a full-blown way. Failure to recognize the opportunities for decomposition of functions and to perfect the hierarchical governance structures by which these could be realized would have arrested the development of the modern corporation at a very primitive stage.

3.2 Forward Integration

Forward integration by manufacturers into distribution was one of the significant consequences of the appearance of the railroads. Low cost transportation combined with telegraph and telephone communication permitted manufacturers efficiently to service a larger market and, as a consequence, realize greater economies of scale in production. The points of connection between manufacturing, wholesaling, and retailing, however, also required attention. Forward integration was a common but by no means uniform response. To the contrary, it was highly selective rather than comprehensive, and it is this selectivity that is the matter of special interest to this paper.

At least four degrees of forward integration can be recognized. From least to most, these are:

A. None—in which event traditional wholesale and retail distribution was continued (many grocery, drug, hardware, jewelry, liquor, and dry goods items were of this kind).
B. Minor—efforts to presell product and to monitor wholesale inventories, but not to include the ownership and operation of wholesale plants, are examples. Certain branded nondurables (soups, soaps), especially those for which staling was a problem (cigarettes, cereals), are included.
C. Wholesale—this was undertaken for perishable, branded items that required special handling, often specialized investments in refrigeration were involved (meat and beer are examples).
D. Retail—integration into retail was rare and was reserved for "new, complex, high priced machines that required specialized marketing services—demonstration, installation, consumer credit, after-sales service and repair." Certain consumer durables (sewing machines, automobiles) and producer durables (some electrical machinery and office machines) were of this kind.

Actually, there is a variant of this fourth category that I will designate "mistaken" retail integration. Such integration involved none of the transaction specific investments in sales and service referred to above but had the purpose of foreclosing rivals. The ill-fated efforts of American Tobacco to integrate forward into the wholesaling and retailing of cigars and of American Sugar Refining to "drive its competitor John Arbuckle out of business by buying into wholesale and retail houses" are examples.

The question is how to interpret these developments. Although the data that would be needed for a quantitative analysis have yet to be

TABLE 1

Integration Class	Economies of Scope	Exter- nalities	Asset Specificity
A. None	++	0	0
B. Minor	+	+	0
C. Wholesale	~	+	+
D_1. Retail/viable	0	+	++
D_2. Retail/mistaken	+	0	0

worked up, a systematic qualitative interpretation along the lines of the discussion in Sections 2.2 and 2.3 above is nevertheless feasible. The attributes of the five integration classes are set out in Table 1, where ++ denotes considerable, + denotes some, ~ is uncertain, and 0 is negligible.

Markets remain the main mode for effecting distribution for classes A and B. Markets enjoy substantial economies of scope for these products while asset specificity is negligible and externalities are dealt with by monitoring inventory. Integration into wholesale occurs for products that involve some asset specificity (refrigeration) and the reputation of branded products needs protection. Integration into retail does not occur, however, until asset specificity at the retail level is great (and these are products for which separate sales and service entails negligible loss of scope economies). Finally, mistaken retail integration involves the sacrifice of scope economies without offsetting governance cost benefits (externalities and asset specificity are negligible). This pattern of integration is broadly consistent with transaction-cost reasoning and explains why forward integration occurred selectively rather than comprehensively in response to the transportation and communication infrastructure.

4. THE 20TH CENTURY CORPORATION

Three developments are particularly noteworthy in the evolution of the modern corporation in the 20th century. The first of these was the appearance of the multidivisional (or M–form) organization. Later developments are the conglomerate and the multinational corporation.

4.1 The Multidivisional Structure

The most significant organizational innovation of the 20th century was the development in the 1920s of the multidivisional structure. Surprisingly, this development was little noted or widely appreciated as late as 1960. Leading management texts extolled the virtues of "basic departmentation" and "line and staff authority relationships," but the special importance of multidivisionalization went unremarked.

Chandler's pathbreaking study of business history, *Strategy and Structure*, simply bypassed this management literature. He advanced the thesis that "changing developments in business organization presented a challenging area for comparative analysis" and observed that "the study of [organizational] innovation seemed to furnish the proper focus for such an investigation." Having identified the multidivisional structure as one of the more important of such innovations, he proceeded to trace its origins, identify the factors that gave rise to its appearance, and describe the subsequent diffusion of this organizational form. It was uninformed and untenable to argue that organization form was of no account after the appearance of Chandler's book.

The leading figures in the creation of the multidivisonal (or M–form) structure were Pierre S. du Pont and Alfred P. Sloan; the period was the early 1920s; the firms were Du Pont and General Motors; and the organizational strain of trying to cope with economic adversity under the old structure was the occasion to innovate in both. The structures of the two companies, however, were different.

Du Pont was operating under the centralized, functionally departmentalized or unitary (U–form) structure, General Motors, by contrast, had been operated more like a holding company by William Durant— whose genius in perceiving market opportunities in the automobile industry evidently did not extend to organization. Chandler summarizes the defects of the large U–form enterprise in the following way:

> The inherent weakness in the centralized, functionally departmentalized operating company . . . became critical only when the administrative load on the senior executives increased to such an extent that they were unable to handle their entrepreneurial responsibilities efficiently. This situation arose when the operations of the enterprise became too complex and the problems of coordination, appraisal, and policy formulation too intricate for a small number of top officers to handle both long-run, entrepreneurial, and short-run, operational administrative activities.

The ability of the management to handle the volume and complexity of the demands placed upon it became strained and even collapsed. Unable meaningfully to identify with, or contribute to, the realization of global goals, managers in each of the functional parts attended to what they perceived to be operational subgoals instead. In the language of transaction cost economics, bounds on rationality were reached as the U–form structure labored under a communication overload while the pursuit of subgoals by the functional parts (sales, engineering, production) was partly a manifestation of opportunism.

The M–form structure fashioned by du Pont and Sloan involved the creation of semi-autonomous operating divisions (mainly profit centers) organized along product, brand, or geographic lines. The operating affairs of each were managed separately. More than a change in decomposition rules were needed, however, for the M–form to be fully effective. Du Pont and Sloan also created a general office "consisting of a number of powerful general executives and large advisory and financial staffs" to monitor divisional performance, allocate resources among divisions, and engage in strategic planning. The reasons for the success of the M–form innovation are summarized by Chandler as follows:

> The basic reason for its success was simply that it clearly removed the executives responsible for the destiny of the entire enterprise from the more routine operational activities, and so gave them the time, information, and even psychological commitment for long-term planning and appraisal. . . .
>
> [The] new structure left the broad strategic decisions as to the allocation of existing resources and the acquisition of new ones in the hands of a top team of generalists. Relieved of operating duties and tactical decisions, a general executive was less likely to reflect the position of just one part of the whole.

In contrast with the holding company—which is also a divisionalized form but has little general office capability and hence is little more than a corporate shell—the M–form organization adds (1) a strategic planning and resource allocation capability and (2) monitoring and control apparatus. As a consequence, cash flows are reallocated among divisions to favor high yield uses, and internal incentive and control instruments are exercised in a discriminating way. In short, the M–form corporation takes on many of the properties of (and is usefully regarded as) a miniature capital market, which is a much more ambitious concept of the corporation than the term *holding company* contemplates.

Although the structure was imitated very slowly at first, adoption by U.S. firms proceeded rapidly during the period 1945 to 1960. Acceptance of this structure by European firms came later. Lawrence Franko reports that most large European companies administered their domestic operations through U–form or holding company structures until late in the 1960s, but that rapid reorganization along M–form lines has occurred since. The advent of zero tariffs within the European Economic Community and the postwar penetration of European markets by American multinationals were, in his judgment, important contributing factors.

As W. Ross Ashby has observed, it is not sufficient to determine the behavior of a whole machine to know the behavior of its parts: "only when the details of coupling are added does the whole's behavior become determinate." The M–form structure represented a different solution to the coupling problem than the earlier unitary form structure. It effected decomposability along product or brand lines to which profit center standing could be assigned and it more clearly separated operating from strategic decision making. It carried Simon's hierarchical-de-composition principles to a higher degree of refinement.

As compared with the U–form organization of the same activities, the M–form organization of the large, complex corporation served both to economize on bounded rationality and attenuate opportunism. Specifically:

> Operating decisions were no longer forced to the top but were resolved at the divisional level, which relieved the communication load. Strategic decisions were reserved for the general office, which reduced partisan political input into the resource allocation process. And the internal auditing and control techniques which the general office had access to served to overcome information impactedness conditions and permit fine timing controls to be exercised over the operating parts.

4.2 The Conglomerate

Chandler's studies of organizational innovation do not include the conglomerate and multinational form of corporate enterprise. These are more recent developments, the appearance of which would not have been feasible but for the prior development of the M–form structure. Inasmuch as transaction cost economizing is socially valued and has been relatively neglected by prior treatments, my discussion of both of these emphasizes affirmative aspects. But this is intended to redress an imbalance and should not be construed to suggest either that a transaction cost interpretation is fully adequate or that conglomerates and multinationals pose no troublesome public policy issues. Unrelieved hostility to these two forms of organization, however, is clearly inappropriate. Specifically, conglomerates that have the capacity to allocate resources to high valued uses and multinationals that use the M–form to facilitate technology transfer warrant more sympathetic assessments.

Although diversification as a corporate strategy certainly predates the 1960s, when general awareness of the conglomerate began to appear, the conglomerate is essentially a post-World War II phenomenon. To be sure, General Electric's profit centers number in the hundreds and GE has been referred to as the world's most diversified firm. Until recently, however, General Electric's emphasis has been the manufacture and distribution of electrical appliances and machinery. Similarly, although General Motors was more than an automobile company, it took care to limit its portfolio. Thus Sloan remarked that "tetraethyl lead was clearly a misfit for GM. It was a chemical product, rather than a mechanical one. And it had to go to market as part of the gasoline and thus required a gasoline distribution system." Accordingly, although GM retained an investment position, the Ethyl Corporation became a free-standing entity rather than an operating division. Similarly, although Durant had acquired Frigidaire, and Frigidaire's market share of refrigerators exceeded 50 percent in the 1920s, the position was allowed to deteriorate as rivals developed market positions in other major appliances (radios, ranges, washers, etc.) while Frigidaire concentrated on refrigerators. The suggestion that GM get into air conditioners "did not register on us, and the proposal was not . . . adopted." As Richard Burton and Arthur Kuhn conclude, GM's "deep and myopic involvement in the automobile sector of the economy, [prevented] product diversification opportunities in other market areas—even in product lines where GM had already achieved substantial penetration—[from being] recognized.

The conglomerate form of organization, whereby the corporation consciously took on a diversified character and nurtured its various parts, evidently required a conceptual break in the mind-set of Sloan and other prewar business leaders. This occurred gradually, more by evolution than by grand design; and it involved a new group of organizational innovators—of which Royal Little was one. The natural growth of conglomerates, which would occur as the techniques for managing diverse assets were refined, was accelerated as antitrust enforcement against horizontal and vertical mergers became progressively more severe. Conglomerate acquisitions—in terms of numbers, assets acquired, and as a proportion of total acquisitions—grew rapidly with the result that "pure" conglomerate mergers, which in the period 1948–53 constituted only 3 percent of the assets acquired by merger, had grown to 49 percent by 1973–77.

Morris Adelman's explanation for the conglomerate is that this form of organization has attractive portfolio diversification properties. But why should the conglomerate appear in the 1960s rather than much earlier? After all, holding companies, which long predated the conglomerate, can accomplish portfolio diversification. And individual stockholders, through mutual funds and otherwise, are able to diversify their own portfolios. At best the portfolio diversification thesis is a very incomplete explanation for the postwar wave of conglomerate mergers.

The Federal Trade Commission also ventured in early assessment of the conglomerate in which organization form features were ignored. The conglomerate was a natural target for the inhospitality tradition. Thus the FTC Staff held that the conglomerate had the following properties:

> With the economic power which it secures through its operations in many diverse fields, the giant conglomerate corporation may attain an almost impregnable economic position. Threatened with competition in any one of its various activities, it may sell below cost in that field, offsetting its losses through profits made in its other lines—a practice which is frequently explained as one of meeting competition. The conglomerate corporation is thus in a position to strike out with great force against smaller business in a variety of different industries.

I submit that some phenomena, of which changing internal organization is one, need to be addressed on their own terms. Adopting this view, the conglomerate is best understood as a logical outgrowth of the M–form mode for organizing complex economic affairs. Thus once the merits of the M–form structure for managing separable, albeit related, lines of business (e.g., a series of automobile or a series of chemical divisions) were recognized and digested, its extension to manage less closely related activities was natural. This is not to say that the management of product variety is without problems of its own. But the basic M–form logic, whereby strategic and operating decisions are distinguished and responsibilities are separated, carried over. The conglomerates in which M–form principles of organization are respected are usefully thought of as internal capital markets whereby cash flows from diverse sources are concentrated and directed to high yield uses.

The conglomerate is noteworthy, however, not merely because it permitted the M–form structure to take this diversification step. Equally interesting are the unanticipated systems consequences which developed as a byproduct. Thus once it was clear that the corporation could manage diverse assets in an effective way, the possibility of takeover by tender offer suggested itself. In principle, incumbent managements could always be displaced by waging a proxy contest. In fact, this is a very expensive and relatively ineffective way to achieve management change. Moreover, even if the dissident shareholders should succeed, there was still a problem of finding a successor management.

Viewed in contractual terms, the M–form conglomerate can be thought of as substituting an administrative interface between an operating division and the stockholders where a market interface had existed previously. Subject to the condition that the conglomerate does not diversify to excess, in the sense that it cannot competently evaluate and allocate funds among the diverse activities in which it is engaged, the substitution of internal organization can have beneficial effects in goal pursuit, monitoring, staffing, and resource allocation respects. The goal-pursuit advantage is that which accrues to M–form organizations in general: since the general management of an M–form conglomerate is disengaged from operating matters, a presumption that the general office favors profits over functional goals is warranted. Relatedly, the general office can be regarded as an agent of the stockholders whose purpose is to monitor the operations of the constituent parts. Monitoring benefits are realized in the degree to which internal monitors enjoy advantages over external monitors in access to information—which they arguably do. The differential ease with which the general office can change managers and reassign duties where performance failures or distortions are detected is responsible for the staffing advantage. Resource-allocation benefits are realized because cash flows no longer return automatically to their origins but instead revert to the center, thereafter to be allocated among competing uses in accordance with prospective yields.

This has a bearing on the problem of separation of ownership from control, noted by Adolph Berle and Gardiner C. Means in 1932. Thus they inquired, "have we any justification for assuming that those in control of a modern corporation will also choose to operate it in the interests of the stockholders." The answer, then as now, is almost certainly no. Indeed, the evident disparity of interest between managers and stockholders gave rise in the 1960s to what has become known as the managerial discretion literature.

There are important differences, however, between the U–form structure, which was the prevailing organization form at the time Berle and Means were writing, and the M–form structure, which in the United States was substantially in place by the 1960s. For one thing, as argued above, U–form managers identified more strongly with functional interests and hence were more given to subgoal pursuit. Secondly, and related, there was a confusion between strategic and operating goals in the U–form structure which the M–form served to rectify—with the result that the general office was more fully concerned with enterprise goals, of which profits is the leading element. Third, the market for corporate control, which remained ineffectual so long as the proxy contest was the only way to challenge incumbent managements, was activated as conglomerates recognized that tender offers could be used to effect corporate takeovers. As a consequence, managements that were otherwise secure and would have permitted managerial preferences to prevail were brought under scrutiny and induced to self-correct against egregious managerial distortions.

To be sure, managerial preferences (for salary and perquisites) and stockholder preferences for profits do not become perfectly consonant as a result of conglomerate organization and the associated activation of the capital market. The continuing tension between management and stockholder interests is evident in the numerous efforts that incumbent managements have taken to protect target firms against takeover. Changes in internal organization have nevertheless relieved these concerns. A study of capitalist enterprises which makes no allowance for organization form changes and their capital market ramifications will naturally overlook the possibility that the corporate control dilemma posed by Berle and Means has since been alleviated more by *internal* than it has by regulatory or external organizational reforms.

Not all conglomerates respected M–form principles when they were first organized. The above argument applies only to those where rational decomposition principles were observed and leads to the following testable proposition: conglomerates that were organized along holding company rather than M–form lines (as many were initially) would be less able to cope when adversity appeared, at which time they would be reorganized as M–form firms. Voluntary divestiture is also an interesting conglomerate phenomenon. Such a rationalization of assets is commonly accompanied by internal organizational reforms. Growth maximization theories are mainly at a loss to explain such behavior.

4.3 Multinational Enterprise

The discussion of the multinational enterprise (MNE) that follows deals mainly with recent developments and, among these, emphasizes organizational aspects—particularly those associated with technology transfer in manufacturing industries. As Mira Wilkins has reported, direct foreign investment by American firms has a long history: the book value of cumulative U.S. direct foreign investment, expressed as a percentage of GNP, was in the range of 7 to 8 percent in 1914, 1929, and 1970. Both the character of this investment and, relatedly, the organization structure within which this investment takes place have been changing, however. It is not accidental that the term MNE was coined neither in 1914 or 1929 but is of much more recent origin.

Thus whereas the ratio of the book value of U.S. foreign investments in manufacturing as compared with all other (petroleum; trade; mining; public utilities) was 0.47 in 1950, this had increased to 0.71 in 1970. Also, "what impressed Europeans about American plants in Europe and the United States [in 1929] was mass production, standardization, and scientific management; in the 1960s, Europeans were remarking that America's superiority was based on technological and managerial advantage . . . [and] that this expertise was being exported via direct investment."

The spread of the multinational corporation in the post-World War II period has given rise to considerable scrutiny, some puzzlement, and even some alarm. One of the reasons for this unsettled state of affairs is that transaction-cost economizing and organization form issues have been relatively neglected in efforts to assess MNE activity. An important exception is the work of Peter Buckley and Mark Casson.

Organization form is relevant in two related respects. First is the matter of U.S.-based as compared with foreign-based investment rates. Tsurumi reports in this connection that the rate of foreign direct investments by U.S. firms increased rapidly after 1953, peaked in the mid-1960s, and has leveled off and declined since. The pattern of foreign direct investments by foreign firms, by contrast, has lagged that of the United States by about a decade.

Recall that the conglomerate uses the M–form structure to extend asset management from specialized to diversified lines of commerce. The MNE counterpart is the use of the M–form structure to extend asset management from a domestic base to include foreign operations. Thus the domestic M–form strategy for decomposing complex business structures into semi-autonomous operating units was subsequently applied to the management of foreign subsidiaries. As noted in 4.1 above, the transformation of the corporation along M–form lines came earlier in the United States than in Europe and elsewhere. U.S. corporations were for this reason better qualified to engage in foreign direct investments at an earlier date than were foreign-based firms. Only as the latter took on the M–form structure did this multinational management capability appear. The pattern of foreign direct investments recorded by Tsurumi and reported above is consistent with the temporal differences of U.S. and foreign firms in adopting the M–form structure.

That U.S. corporations possessed an M–form capability earlier than their foreign counterparts does not, however, establish that they used it to organize foreign investment. John Stopford and Louis Wells have studied this issue. They report that while initial foreign investments were usually organized as autonomous subsidiaries, divisional status within an M–form structure invariably appeared as the size and complexity of foreign operations increased. This transformation usually followed the organization of domestic operations along M–form lines. The adoption of a "global" strategy or "worldwide perspective"—whereby "strategic planning and major policy decisions" are made in the central office of the enterprise—could only be accomplished within a multidivisional framework.

Even more interesting than these organization form issues is the fact that foreign direct investments by U.S. firms have been concentrated in a few industries. Manufacturing industries that have made substantial foreign direct investments include chemicals, drugs, automobiles, food processing, electronics, electrical and nonelectrical machinery, nonferous metals, and rubber. Tobacco, textiles and apparel, furniture, printing, glass, steel, and aircraft have, by comparison, done little foreign direct investment.

Stephen Hymer's "dual" explanation for the multinational enterprise is of interest in this connection. Thus Hymer observes that direct foreign investment "allows business firms to transfer capital, technology, and organizational skill from one country to another. It is also an instrument for restraining competition between firms of different nations."

Hymer is surely correct that the MNE can service both of these purposes and examples of both kinds can doubtlessly be found. It is nevertheless useful to ask whether the overall character of MNE investment, in terms of its distribution among industries, is more consistent with the efficiency purposes to which Hymer refers (transfer of capital, technology, and organizational skill) or with the oligopolistic restraint hypothesis. Adopting a transaction cost orientation discloses that the observed pattern of investment is more consistent with the efficiency part of Hymer's dual explanation.

For one thing, oligopolistic purposes can presumably be realized by portfolio investment coupled with a limited degree of management involvement to segregate markets. Put differently, direct foreign investment and the organization of foreign subsidiaries within an M–form structure are not needed to effect competitive restraints. Furthermore, if competitive restraints were mainly responsible for these investments, then presumably all concentrated industries—which would include tobacco, glass, and steel—rather than those associated with rapid technical progress would be active in MNE creation. Finally, although many of the leading U.S. firms that engaged in foreign direct investment enjoyed "market power," this was by no means true for all.

By contrast, the pattern of foreign direct investments reported by Tsurumi appears to be consistent with a transaction-cost economizing interpretation. Raymond Vernon's 1970 study of the *Fortune* 500 corporations disclosed that 187 of these firms had a substantial multinational presence. R&D expenditures as a percentage of sales were higher among these 187 than among the remaining firms in the *Fortune* 500 group. Furthermore, according to Vernon, firms that went multinational tended to be technological innovators at the time of making their initial foreign direct investments.

This raises the question of the attributes of firms and markets for accomplishing technology transfer. The difficulties with transferring technology across market interface are of three kinds: recognition, disclosure, and team organization. Of these three, recognition is probably the least severe. To be sure, foreign firms may sometimes fail to perceive the opportunities to apply technological developments originated elsewhere. But enterprising domestic firms that have made the advance can be expected to identify at least some of the potential applications abroad.

Suppose, therefore, that recognition problems are set aside and consider disclosure. Technology transfer by contract can break down if convincing disclosure to buyers effectively destroys the basis for exchange. A very severe information asymmetry problem exists, on which account the less informed party (in this instance the buyer) must be wary of opportunistic representations by the seller. Although sometimes this asymmetry can be overcome by sufficient ex ante disclosure (and veracity checks thereon), this may shift rather than solve the difficulty. The "fundamental paradox" of information is that "its value for the purchaser is not known until he has the information, but then he has in effect acquired it without costs."

Suppose, *arguendo*, that buyers concede value and are prepared to pay for information in the seller's possession. The incentive to trade is then clear and for some items this will suffice. The formula for a chemical compound or the blueprints for a special device may be all that is needed to effect the transfer. Frequently, however, and probably often, new knowledge is diffusely distributed and is poorly defined. Where the requisite information is distributed among a number of individuals all of whom understand their speciality in only a tacit, intuitive way, a simple contract to transfer the technology cannot be devised.

Transfer need not cease, however, because simple contracts are not feasible. If the benefits of technology transfer are sufficiently great, exchange may be accomplished either by devising a complex trade or through direct foreign investment. Which will be employed depends on the circumstances. If only a one-time (or very occasional) transfer of technology is contemplated, direct foreign investment is a somewhat extreme response. The complex contractual alternative is to negotiate a tie-in sale whereby the technology and associated know-how are transferred as a package. Since the know-how is concentrated in the human assets who are already familiar with the technology, this entails the creation of a "consulting team" by the seller to accompany the physical technology transfer—the object being to overcome start up difficulties and to familiarize the employees of the foreign firm, through teaching and demonstration, with the idiosyncracies of the operation.

Inasmuch as many of the contingencies that arise in the execution of such contracts will be unforeseen and as it will be too costly to work out appropriate ex ante responses for others, such consulting contracts are subject to considerable strain. Where a succession of transfers is contemplated, which is to say, when the frequency shifts from occasional to recurring, complex contracting is apt to give way to direct foreign investment. A more harmonious and efficient exchange relation—better disclosure, easier reconciliation of differences, more complete cross-cultural adaptation, more effective team organization and reconfiguration—all predictably result from the substitution of an internal governance relation for bilateral trading under these recurrent trading circumstances for assets, of which complex technology transfer is an example, that have a highly specific character.

The upshot is that while puzzlement with and concerns over MNEs will surely continue, a transaction cost interpretation of this phenomenon sheds insight on the following conspicuous features of multinational investment: (1) the reported concentration of foreign direct investment in manufacturing industries where technology transfer is of special importance; (2) the organization of these investments within M–form structures; and (3) the differential timing of foreign direct investment between U.S. and foreign manufacturing enterprises (which difference also has organization form origins). I furthermore conjecture that the application of transaction cost reasoning will lead to a deeper understanding of other specific features of MNE activity as these are discovered and/or become subject to public policy scrutiny.

5. CONCLUDING REMARKS

There is widespread agreement, among economists and noneconomists alike, with the proposition that the modern corporation is an important and complex economic institution. Such agreement is mainly explained by the obtrusive size of the largest firms—running to tens of billions of dollars of assets and sales, with employment numbering in the hundreds of thousands. The economic factors that lie behind the size, shape, and performance of the modern corporation, however, are poorly understood.

This puzzlement is not of recent origin. Edward Mason complained over 20 years ago that "the functioning of the corporate system has not to date been adequately explained. . . . The man of action may be content with a system that works. But one who reflects on the properties or characteristics of this system cannot help asking why it works and whether it will continue to work." The predicament to which Mason refers is, I submit, largely the product of two different (but not unrelated) intellectual traditions. The first of these holds that the structural features of the corporation are irrelevant. This is the neoclassical theory of the firm that populates intermediate theory textbooks. Structural differences are suppressed as the firm is described as a production function to which a profit maximization objective has been assigned. The second has public policy roots; this is the inhospitality tradition that I referred to earlier. In this tradition, distinctive structural features of the corporation are believed to be the result of unwanted (anticompetitive) intrusions into market processes.

The transaction-cost approach differs from both. Unlike neoclassical analysis, internal organization is specifically held to be important. Unlike the inhospitality tradition, structural differences are assumed to arise primarily in order to promote economy in transaction costs. The assignment of transactions between firms and markets and the economic ramifications of internal structure both come under scrutiny in these terms. The application of these ideas to the study of transactions in general and of the modern corporation in particular requires that (1) the transaction be made the principal unit of analysis, (2) an elementary appreciation for "human nature as we know it" supplant the fiction of economic man, (3) transactions be dimensionalized, (4) rudimentary principles of market and hierarchial organization be recognized, and (5) a guiding principle of comparative institutional study be the hypothesis that transactions are assigned to and organized within governance structures in a discriminating (transaction-cost economizing) way.

The view that the corporation is first and foremost an efficiency instrument does not deny that firms also seek to monopolize markets, sometimes by engaging in strategic behavior, or that managers sometimes pursue their own goals to the detriment of system goals. But specific structural preconditions need to be satisfied if strategic behavior is to be feasible—and most firms do not qualify, which is to say that strategic behavior is the exception rather than the rule. Furthermore, most firms will be penalized if efficiency norms are seriously violated for extended periods of time—which serves to curb managerial discretion. The strongest argument favoring transaction-cost economizing, however, is that this is the only hypothesis that is able to provide a discriminating rationale for the succession of organizational innovations that have occurred over the past 150 years and out of which the modern corporation has emerged.

To recapitulate, although railroad mergers between parallel roads can have monopolizing purposes, the joining of end-to-end systems under common management is explained by transaction-cost economics. The hierarchical structures evolved by the railroads were the outcome of internal efforts to effect coordination across interfaces to which common operating responsibilities had been assigned. Older and simpler structures were unable to manage such complex networks, while coordination by end-to-end contracts between successive stations was prohibitively costly.

Forward integration out of manufacturing into distribution was widespread at the turn of the century. More interesting, however, than this general movement is the fact that forward integration was selective—being extensive in some industries (e.g., sewing machines), negligible in others (e.g., dry goods), and mistaken in still others (e.g., sugar). This selective pattern is predicted by and consistent with transaction-cost reasoning—whereas no other hypothesis makes comparably detailed predictions.

The efficiency incentive to shift from the earlier U–form to the M–form structure is partly explained in managerial discretion terms: the older structure was more subject to distortions of a managerial discretion kind—which is to say that opportunism had become a serious problem in the large U–form firm. Equally and probably more important, however, is that the managerial hierarchy is the U–form enterprise was simply overburdened as the firm became large and complex. The M–form structure represented a more rational decomposition of the affairs of the firm and thereby served to economize on bounded rationality. The subsequent diffusion of this structure was hastened by a combination of product market (pressure on rivals) and capital market (takeover) competition.

The M–form structure, which was originally adopted by firms in relatively specialized lines of commerce was subsequently extended to manage diversified assets (the conglomerate) and foreign direct investments (MNE). A breadth-for-depth tradeoff is involved in the former case, as the firm selectively internalizes functions ordinarily associated with the capital market. MNE activity has also been selective—being concentrated in the more technologically progressive industries where higher rates of R&D are reported and technology transfer arguably poses greater difficulties than is true of technologically less progressive industries. This pattern of foreign direct investment cannot be explained as the pursuit of monopoly but is consistent with transaction-cost reasoning.

The upshot is that a transaction-cost approach to the study of the modern corporation permits a wide variety of significant organizational events to be interpreted in a coherent way. It links up comfortably with the type of business history studies that have been pioneered by Chandler. It has ramifications for the study of regulation and for antitrust enforcement. Applications to aspects of labor economics and comparative systems have been made, and others would appear to be fruitful. More generally, while there is room for and need for refinement, a comparative approach to the study of economic institutions in which the economy of transaction costs is the focus of analysis, appears to have considerable promise.

2.

The Economic Organisation
of a P.O.W. Camp*

R. A. RADFORD

INTRODUCTION

After allowance has been made for abnormal circumstances, the social institutions, ideas, and habits of groups in the outside world are to be found reflected in a Prisoner of War Camp. It is an unusual but a vital society. Camp organisation and politics are matters of real concern to the inmates, as affecting their present and perhaps their future existences. Nor does this indicate any loss of proportion. No one pretends that camp matters are of any but local importance or of more than transient interest, but their importance there is great. They bulk large in a world of narrow horizons and it is suggested that any distortion of values lies rather in the minimisation than in the exaggeration of their importance. Human affairs are essentially practical matters and the measure of immediate effect on the lives of those directly concerned in them is to a large extent the criterion of their importance at that time and place. A prisoner can hold strong views on such subjects as whether or not all tinned meats shall be issued to individuals cold or be centrally cooked, without losing sight of the significance of the Atlantic Charter.

One aspect of social organisation is to be found in economic activity, and this, along with other manifestations of a group existence, is to be found in any P.O.W. camp. True, a prisoner is not dependent on

* *Economica* 12 (November 1945), pp. 189–201.

his exertions for the provision of the necessaries, or even the luxuries of life, but through his economic activity, the exchange of goods and services, his standard of material comfort is considerably enhanced. And this is a serious matter to the prisoner: he is not "playing at shops" even though the small scale of the transactions and the simple expression of comfort and wants in terms of cigarettes and jam, razor blades and writing paper, make the urgency of those needs difficult to appreciate, even by an ex-prisoner of some three months' standing.

Nevertheless, it cannot be too strongly emphasized that economic activities do not bulk so large in prison society as they do in the larger world. There can be little production; as has been said the prisoner is independent of his exertions for the provision of the necessities and luxuries of life; the emphasis lies in exchange and the media of exchange. A prison camp is not to be compared with the seething crowd of higglers in a street market, any more than it is to be compared with the economic inertia of a family dinner table.

Naturally then, entertainment, academic and literally interests, games, and discussions of the "other world" bulk larger in everyday life than they do in the life of more normal societies. But it would be wrong to underestimate the importance of economic activity. Everyone receives a roughly equal share of essentials; it is by trade that individual preferences are given expression and comfort increased. All at some time, and most people regularly, make exchanges of one sort or another.

Although a P.O.W. camp provides a living example of a simple economy which might be used as an alternative to the Robinson Crusoe economy beloved by the textbooks, and its simplicity renders the demonstration of certain economic hypotheses both amusing and instructive, it is suggested that the principal significance is sociological. True, there is interest in observing the growth of economic institutions and customs in a brand-new society, small and simple enough to prevent detail from obscuring the basic pattern and disequilibrium from obscuring the working of the system. But the essential interest lies in the universality and the spontaneity of this economic life; it came into existence not by conscious imitation but as a response to the immediate needs and circumstances. Any similarity between prison organisation and outside organisation arises from similar stimuli evoking similar responses.

The following is as brief an account of the essential data as may render the narrative intelligible. The camps of which the writer had experience were Oflags and consequently the economy was not complicated by payments for work by the detaining power. They consisted normally of between 1,200 and 2,500 people, housed in a number of separate but intercommunicating bungalows, one company of 200 or so to a building. Each company formed a group within the main organisation and inside the company the room and the messing syndicate, a voluntary and spontaneous group who fed together, formed the constituent units.

Between individuals there was active trading in all consumer goods and in some services. Most trading was for food against cigarettes or other foodstuffs, but cigarettes rose from the status of a normal commodity to that of currency. RMks existed but had no circulation save for gambling debts, as few articles could be purchased with them from the canteen.

Our supplies consisted of rations provided by the detaining power and (principally) the contents of Red Cross food parcels—tinned milk, jam, butter, biscuits, bully, chocolate, sugar, etc., and cigarettes. So far the supplies to each person were equal and regular. Private parcels of clothing, toilet requisites and cigarettes were also received, and here equality ceased owing to the different numbers despatched and the vagaries of the post. All these articles were the subject of trade and exchange.

THE DEVELOPMENT AND ORGANISATION
OF THE MARKET

Very soon after capture people realised that it was both undesirable and unnecessary, in view of the limited size and the equality of supplies, to give away or to accept gifts of cigarettes or food. "Goodwill" developed into trading as a more equitable means of maximising individual satisfaction.

We reached a transit camp in Italy about a fortnight after capture and received one fourth of a Red Cross food parcel each a week later. At once exchanges, already established, multiplied in volume. Starting with simple direct barter, such as a nonsmoker giving a smoker friend his cigarette issue in exchange for a chocolate ration, more complex exchanges soon became an accepted custom. Stories circulated of a padre who started off round the camp with a tin of cheese and five cigarettes and returned to his bed with a complete parcel in addition to his original cheese and cigarettes; the market was not yet perfect. Within a week or two, as the volume of trade grew, rough scales of exchange values came into existence. Sikhs, who had at first exchanged tinned beef for practically any other foodstuff, began to insist on jam and margarine. It was realised that a tin of jam was worth one-half lb. of margarine plus something else; that a cigarette issue was worth several chocolate issues, and a tin of diced carrots was worth practically nothing.

In this camp we did not visit other bungalows very much and prices varied from place to place; hence the germ of truth in the story of the itinerant priest. By the end of a month, when we reached our permanent camp, there was a lively trade in all commodities and their relative values were well known, and expressed not in terms of one another—one didn't quote bully in terms of sugar—but in terms of cigarettes. The cigarette became the standard of value. In the permanent camp people started by wandering through the bungalows calling their offers—"cheese for seven" (cigarettes)—and the hours after parcel issue were Bedlam. The inconveniences of this system soon led to its replacement by an Exchange and Mart notice board in every bungalow, where under the headings "name," "room number," "wanted," and "offered" sales and wants were advertised. When a deal went through, it was crossed off the board. The public and semipermanent records of transactions led to cigarette prices being well known and thus tending to equality throughout the camp, although there were always opportunities for an astute trader to make a profit from arbitrage. With this development everyone, including nonsmokers, was willing to sell for cigarettes, using them to buy at another time and place. Cigarettes became the normal currency, though, of course, barter was never extinguished.

The unity of the market and the prevalence of a single price varied directly with the general level of organisation and comfort in the camp. A transit camp was always chaotic and uncomfortable: people were overcrowded, no one knew where anyone else was living, and few took the trouble to find out. Organisation was too slender to include an Exchange and Mart board, and private advertisements were the most that appeared. Consequently a transit camp was not one market but many. The price of a tin of salmon is known to have varied by two cigarettes in 20 between one end of a hut and the other. Despite a high level of organisation in Italy, the market was morcellated in this manner at the first transit camp we reached after our removal to Germany in the autumn of 1943. In this camp—Stalag VIIA at Moosburg in Bavaria—there were up to 50,000 prisoners of all nationalities. French, Russians, Italians, and Jugoslavs were free to move about within the camp: British and Americans were confined to their compounds, although a few cigarettes given to a sentry would always procure permission for one or two men to visit other compounds. The people who first visited the highly organised French trading centre, with its stalls and known prices, found coffee extract—relatively cheap among the tea-drinking English—commanding a fancy price in biscuits or cigarettes, and some enterprising people made small fortunes that way. (Incidentally we found out later that much of the coffee went "over the wire" and sold for phenomenal prices at black market cafés in Munich: some of the French prisoners were said to have made substantial sums in RMks. This was one of the few occasions on which our normally closed economy came into contact with other economic worlds.)

Eventually public opinion grew hostile to these monopoly profits—not everyone could make contact with the French—and trading with them was put on a regulated basis. Each group of beds was given a quota of articles to offer and the transaction was carried out by accredited representatives from the British compound, with monopoly rights. The same method was used for trading with sentries elsewhere, as in this trade secrecy and reasonable prices had a peculiar importance, but as is ever the case with regulated companies, the interloper proved too strong.

The permanent camps in Germany saw the highest level of commercial organisation. In addition to the Exchange and Mart notice boards, a shop was organised as a public utility, controlled by representatives of the Senior British Officer, on a no profit basis. People left their surplus clothing, toilet requisites and food there until they were sold at a fixed price in cigarettes. Only sales in cigarettes were accepted—there was no barter—and there was no higgling. For food at least there were standard prices: clothing is less homogeneous and the price was decided around a norm by the seller and the shop manager in agreement; shirts would average say 80, ranging from 60 to 120 according to quality and age. Of food, the shop carried small stocks for convenience; the capital was provided by a loan from the bulk store of Red Cross cigarettes and repaid by a small commission taken on the first transactions. Thus the cigarette attained its fullest currency status, and the market was almost completely unified.

Actually there was an embryo labour market. Even when cigarettes were not scarce, there was usually some unlucky person willing to perform services for them. Laundrymen advertised at two cigarettes a garment. Battle-dress was scrubbed and pressed and a pair of trousers lent for the interim period for 12. A good pastel portrait cost 30 or a tin of "Kam." Odd tailoring and other jobs similarly had their prices.

There were also entrepreneurial services. There was a coffee stall owner who sold tea, coffee, or cocoa at two cigarettes a cup, buying his raw materials at market prices and hiring labour to gather fuel and to stoke; he actually enjoyed the services of a chartered accountant at one stage. After a period of great prosperity he overreached himself and failed disastrously for several hundred cigarettes. Such large-scale private enterprise was rare but several middlemen or professional traders existed. The padre in Italy, or the men at Moosburg who opened trading relations with the French, are examples: the more subdivided the market, the less perfect the advertisement of prices, and the less stable the prices, the greater was the scope for these operators. One man capitalised his knowledge of Urdu by buying meat from the Sikhs and selling butter and jam in return: as his operations became better known more and more people entered this trade, prices in the Indian Wing approximated more nearly to those elsewhere, though to the end a "contact" among the Indians was valuable, as linguistic difficulties prevented the trade from being quite free. Some were specialists in the Indian trade, the food, clothing, or even the watch trade. Middlemen traded on their own account or on commission. Price rings and agreements were suspected and the traders certainly cooperated. Nor did they welcome new-comers. Unfortunately the writer knows little of the workings of these people: public opinion was hostile and the professionals were usually of a retiring disposition.

One trader in food and cigarettes, operating in a period of dearth, enjoyed a high reputation. His capital, carefully saved, was originally about 50 cigarettes, with which he bought rations on issue days and held them until the price rose just before the next issue. He also picked up a little by arbitrage; several times a day he visited every Exchange or Mart notice board and took advantage of every discrepancy between prices of goods offered and wanted. His knowledge of prices, markets, and names of those who had received cigarette parcels was phenomenal. By these means he kept himself smoking steadily—his profits—while his capital remained intact.

Sugar was issued on Saturday. About Tuesday two of us used to visit Sam and make a deal; as old customers he would advance as much of the price as he could spare then, and entered the transaction in a book. On Saturday morning he left cocoa tins on our beds for the ration, and picked them up on Saturday afternoon. We were hoping for a calendar at Christmas, but Sam failed too. He was left holding a big black treacle issue when the price fell, and in this weakened state was unable to withstand an enexpected arrival of parcels and the consequent price fluctuations. He paid in full, but from his capital. The next Tuesday, when I paid my usual visit he was out of business.

Credit entered into many, perhaps into most, transactions, in one form or another. Sam paid in advance as a rule for his purchases of future deliveries of sugar, but many buyers asked for credit, whether the commodity was sold spot or future. Naturally prices varied according to the terms of sale. A treacle ration might be advertised for four cigarettes now or five next week. And in the future market "bread now" was a vastly different thing from "bread Thursday." Bread was issued on Thursday and Monday, four and three days' rations respectively, and by Wednesday and Sunday night it had risen at least one cigarette per ration, from seven to eight, by supper time. One man always saved a ration to sell then at the peak price: his offer of "bread now" stood out on the board among a number of "bread Monday's" fetching one or two less, or not selling at all—and he always smoked on Sunday night.

THE CIGARETTE CURRENCY

Although cigarettes as currency exhibited certain pecularities, they performed all the functions of a metallic currency as a unit of account, as a measure of value and as a store of value, and shared most of its characteristics. They were homogeneous, reasonably durable, and of convenient size for the smallest or, in packets, for the largest transactions. Incidentally, they could be clipped or sweated by rolling them between the fingers so that tobacco fell out.

Cigarettes were also subject to the working of Gresham's Law. Certain brands were more popular than others as smokes, but for currency purposes a cigarette was a cigarette. Consequently buyers used the poorer qualities and the Shop rarely saw the more popular brands: Cigarettes such as Churchman's No. 1 were rarely used for trading. At one time cigarettes hand-rolled from pipe tobacco bagan to circulate. Pipe tobacco was issued in lieu of cigarettes by the Red Cross at a rate of 25 cigarettes to the ounce and this rate was standard in exchanges, but an ounce would produce 30 home-made cigarettes. Naturally, people with machine-made cigarettes broke them down and re-rolled the tobacco, and the real cigarette virtually disappeared from the market. Hand-rolled cigarettes were not homogeneous and prices could no longer be quoted in them with safety: each cigarette was examined before it was accepted and thin ones were rejected, or extra demanded as a make-weight. For a time we suffered all the inconveniences of a debased currency.

Machine-made cigarettes were always universally acceptable, both for what they would buy and for themselves. It was this intrinsic value which gave rise to their principal disadvantage as currency, a disadvantage which exists, but to a far smaller extent, in the case of metallic currency;—that is, a strong demand for nonmonetary purposes. Consequently our economy was repeatedly subject to deflation and to periods of monetary stringency. While the Red Cross issue of 50 or 25 cigarettes per man per week came in regularly, and while there were fair stocks held, the cigarette currency suited its purpose admirably. But when the issue was interrupted, stocks soon ran out, prices fell, trading declined in volume and became increasingly a matter of barter. This deflationary tendency was periodically offset by the sudden injection of new currency. Private cigarette parcels arrived in a trickle throughout the year, but the big numbers came in quarterly when the Red Cross received its allocation of transport. Several hundred thousand cigarettes might arrive in the space of a fortnight. Prices soared, and then began to fall, slowly at first but with increasing rapidity as stocks ran out, until the next big delivery. Most of our economic troubles could be attributed to this fundamental instability.

PRICE MOVEMENTS

Many factors affected prices, the strongest and most noticeable being the periodical currency inflation and deflation described in the last paragraphs. The periodicity of this price cycle depended on cigarette and, to a far lesser extent, on food deliveries. At one time in the early days, before any private parcels had arrived and when there were no individual stocks, the weekly issue of cigarettes and food parcels occurred on a Monday. The nonmonetary demand for cigarettes was great, and less elastic than the demand for food: consequently prices fluctuated weekly, falling towards Sunday night and rising sharply on Monday morning. Later, when many people held reserves, the weekly issue had no such effect, being too small a proportion of the total available. Credit allowed people with no reserves to meet their nonmonetary demand over the week-end.

The general price level was affected by other factors. An influx of new prisoners, proverbially hungry, raised it. Heavy air raids in the vicinity of the camp probably increased the nonmonetary demand for cigarettes and accentuated deflation. Good and bad war news certainly had its effect, and the general waves of optimism and pessimism which swept the camp were reflected in prices. Before breakfast one morning in March of this year, a rumour of the arrival of parcels and cigarettes was circulated. Within 10 minutes I sold a treacle ration, for four cigarettes (hitherto offered in vain for three), and many similar deals went through. By 10 o'clock the rumour was denied, and treacle that day found no more buyers even at two cigarettes.

More interesting than changes in the general price level were changes in the price structure. Changes in the supply of a commodity, in the German ration scale or in the make-up of Red Cross parcels, would raise the price of one commodity relative to others. Tins of oatmeal, once a rare and much sought after luxury in the parcels, became a commonplace in 1943, and the price fell. In hot weather the demand for cocoa fell, and that for soap rose. A new recipe would be reflected in the price level: The discovery that raisins and sugar could be turned into an alcoholic liquor of remarkable potency reacted permanently on the dried fruit market. The invention of electric immersion heaters run off the power points made tea, a drug on the market in Italy, a certain seller in Germany.

In August 1944, the supplies of parcels and cigarettes were both halved. Since both sides of the equation were changed in the same degree, changes in prices were not anticipated. But this was not the case: The nonmonetary demand for cigarettes was less elastic than the demand for food, and food prices fell a little. More important however were the changes in the price structure. German margarine and jam, hitherto valueless owing to adequate supplies of Canadian butter and marmalade, acquired a new value. Chocolate, popular and a certain seller, and sugar, fell. Bread rose; several standing contracts of bread for cigarettes were broken, especially when the bread ration was reduced a few weeks later.

In February 1945, the German soldier who drove the ration wagon was found to be willing to exchange loaves of bread at the rate of one loaf for a bar of chocolate. Those in the know began selling bread and buying chocolate, by then almost unsaleable in a period of serious deflation. Bread, at about 40, fell slightly; chocolate rose from 15; the supply of bread was not enough for the two commodities to reach parity, but the tendency was unmistakable.

The substitution of German margarine for Canadian butter when parcels were halved naturally affected their relative values, margarine appreciating at the expense of butter. Similarly, two brands of dried milk, hitherto differing in quality and therefore in price by five cigarettes a tin, came together in price as the wider substitution of the cheaper raised its relative value.

Enough has been cited to show that any change in conditions affected both the general price level and the price structure. It was this latter phenomenon which wrecked our planned economy.

PAPER CURRENCY—BULLY MARKS

Around D-Day, food and cigarettes were plentiful, business was brisk and the camp in an optimistic mood. Consequently the Entertainments Committee felt the moment opportune to launch a restaurant, where food and hot drinks were sold while a band and variety turns performed. Earlier experiments, both public and private, had pointed the way, and the scheme was a great success. Food was bought at market prices to provide the meals and the small profits were devoted to a reserve fund and used to bribe Germans to provide greasepaints and other necessities for the camp theatre. Originally meals were sold for cigarettes but this meant that the whole scheme was vulnerable to the periodic deflationary waves, and furthermore heavy smokers were unlikely to attend much. The whole success of the scheme depended on an adequate amount of food being offered for sale in the normal manner.

To increase and facilitate trade, and to stimulate supplies and customers therefore, and secondarily to avoid the worst effects of deflation when it should come, a paper currency was organised by the Restaurant and the Shop. The Shop bought food on behalf of the Restaurant with paper notes and the paper was accepted equally with the cigarettes in the Restaurant or Shop, and passed back to the Shop to purchase more food. The Shop acted as a bank of issue. The paper money was backed 100 percent by food; hence its name, the Bully Mark. The BMk was backed 100 percent by food: there could be no over-issues, as is permissible with a normal bank of issue, since the eventual dispersal of the camp and consequent redemption of all BMks was anticipated in the near future.

Originally one BMk was worth one cigarette and for a short time both circulated freely inside and outside the Restaurant. Prices were quoted in BMks and cigarettes with equal freedom—and for a short time the BMk showed signs of replacing the cigarette as currency. The

BMk was tied to food, but not to cigarettes: as it was issued against food, say 45 for a tin of milk and so on, any reduction in the BMk prices of food would have meant that there were unbacked BMks in circulation. But the price of both food and BMks could and did fluctuate with the supply of cigarettes.

While the Restaurant flourished, the scheme was a success: the Restaurant bought heavily, all foods were saleable, and prices were stable.

In August parcels and cigarettes were halved and the Camp was bombed. The Restaurant closed for a short while and sales of food became difficult. Even when the Restaurant reopened, the food and cigarette shortage became increasingly acute and people were unwilling to convert such valuable goods into paper and to hold them for luxuries like snacks and tea. Less of the right kinds of food for the Restaurant were sold, and the Shop became glutted with dried fruit, chocolate, sugar, etc., which the Restaurant could not buy. The price level and the price structure changed. The BMk fell to four fifths of a cigarette and eventually farther still, and it became unacceptable save in the Restaurant. There was a flight from the BMk no longer convertible into cigarettes or popular foods. The cigarette reestablished itself.

But the BMk was sound! The Restaurant closed in the New Year with a progressive food shortage and the long evenings without lights due to intensified Allied air raids, and BMks could only be spent in the Coffee Bar—relict of the Restaurant—or on the few unpopular foods in the Shop, the owners of which were prepared to accept them. In the end all holders of BMks were paid in full, in cups of coffee or in prunes. People who had bought BMks for cigarettes or valuable jam or biscuits in their heyday were aggrieved that they should have stood the loss involved by their restricted choice, but they suffered no actual loss of market value.

PRICE FIXING

Along with this scheme came a determined attempt at a planned economy, at price fixing. The Medical Officer had long been anxious to control food sales, for fear of some people selling too much, to the detriment of their health. The deflationary waves and their effects on prices were inconvenient to all and would be dangerous to the Restaurant which had to carry stocks. Furthermore, unless the BMk was convertible into cigarettes at about par it had little chance of gaining confidence and of succeeding as a currency. As has been explained, the BMk was tied to food but could not be tied to cigarettes, which fluctuated in value. Hence, while BMk prices of food were fixed for all time, cigarette prices of food and BMks varied.

The Shop, backed by the Senior British Officer, was now in a position to enforce price control both inside and outside its walls. Hitherto a standard price had been fixed for food left for sale in the shop, and prices outside were roughly in conformity with this scale, which was recommended as a "guide" to sellers, but fluctuated a good deal around it. Sales in the Shop at recommended prices were apt to be slow though a good price might be obtained: sales outside could be made more quickly at lower prices. (If sales outside were to be at higher prices, goods were withdrawn from the Shop until the recommended price rose: but the recommended price was sluggish and could not follow the market closely by reason of its very purpose, which was stability.) The Exchange and Mart notice boards came under the control of the Shop: advertisements which exceeded a 5 percent departure from the recommended scale were liable to be crossed out by authority: unauthorised sales were discouraged by authority and also by public opinion, strongly in favour of a just and stable price. (Recommended prices were fixed partly from market data, partly on the advice of the M.O.)

At first the recommended scale was a success: the Restaurant, a big buyer, kept prices stable around this level: opinion and the 5 percent tolerance helped. But when the price level fell with the August cuts and the price structure changed, the recommended scale was too rigid. Unchanged at first, as no deflation was expected, the scale was tardily lowered, but the prices of goods on the new scale remained in the same relation to one another, owing to the BMk, while on the market the price structure had changed. And the modifying influence of the Restaurant had gone. The scale was moved up and down several times, slowly following the inflationary and deflationary waves, but it was rarely adjusted to changes in the price structure. More and more advertisements were crossed off the board, and black market sales at unauthorised prices increased: eventually public opinion turned against the recommended scale and authority gave up the struggle. In the last few weeks, with unparalleled deflation, prices fell with alarming rapidity, no scales existed, and supply and demand, alone and unmellowed, determined prices.

PUBLIC OPINION

Public opinion on the subject of trading was vocal if confused and changeable, and generalisations as to its direction are difficult and dangerous. A tiny minority held that all trading was undesirable as it engendered as unsavoury atmosphere; occasional frauds and sharp practices were cited as proof. Certain forms of trading were more generally condemned; trade with the Germans was criticised by many. Red Cross toilet articles, which were in short supply and only issued in cases of actual need, were excluded from trade by law and opinion working in unshakable harmony. At one time, when there had been several cases of malnutrition reported among the more devoted smokers, no trade in German rations was permitted, as the victims became an additional burden on the depleted food reserves of the Hospital. But while certain activities were condemned as antisocial, trade itself was practised, and its utility appreciated, by almost everyone in the camp.

More interesting was opinion on middlemen and prices. Taken as a whole, opinion was hostile to the middleman. His function and his hard work in bringing buyer and seller together were ignored; profits were not regarded as a reward for labour, but as the result of sharp practices. Despite the fact that his very existence was proof to the contrary, the middleman was held to be redundant in view of the existence of an official Shop and the Exchange and Mart. Appreciation only came his way when he was willing to advance the price of a sugar ration, or to buy goods spot and carry them against a future sale. In these cases the element of risk was obvious to all, and the convenience of the service was felt to merit some reward. Particularly unpopular was the middleman with an element of monopoly, the man who contacted the ration wagon driver, or the man who utilised his knowledge of Urdu. And middlemen as a group were blamed for reducing prices. Opinion notwithstanding, most people dealt with a middleman, whether consciously or unconsciously, at some time or another.

There was a strong feeling that everything had its "just price" in cigarettes. While the assessment of the just price, which incidentally varied between camps, was impossible of explanation, this price was nevertheless pretty closely known. It can best be defined as the price usually fetched by an article in good times when cigarettes were plentiful. The "just price" changed slowly; it was unaffected by short-term variations in supply, and while opinion might be resigned to departures from the just price, a strong feeling of resentment persisted. A more satisfactory definition of the *"just price"* is impossible. Everyone knew what it was, though no one could explain why it should be so.

As soon as prices began to fall with a cigarette shortage, a clamour arose, particularly against those who held reserves and who bought at reduced prices. Sellers at cut prices were criticised and their activities referred to as the black market. In every period of dearth the explosive question of "should nonsmokers receive a cigarette ration?" was discussed to profitless length. Unfortunately, it was the nonsmoker, or the light smoker with his reserves, along with the hated middleman, who weathered the storm most easily.

The popularity of the price-fixing scheme, and such success as it enjoyed, were undoubtedly the result of this body of opinion. On several occasions the fall of prices was delayed by the general support given to the recommended scale. The onset of deflation was marked by a period of sluggish trade; prices stayed up but no one bought. Then prices fell on the black market, and the volume of trade revived in that quarter. Even when the recommended scale was revised, the volume of trade in the Shop would remain low. Opinion was always overruled by the hard facts of the market.

Curious arguments were advanced to justify price fixing. The recommended prices were in some way related to the calorific values of the foods offered: hence some were overvalued and never sold at these prices. One argument ran as follows—not everyone has private cigarette parcels: thus, when prices were high and trade good in the summer of 1944, only the lucky rich could buy. This was unfair to the man with few cigarettes. When prices fell in the following winter, prices should be pegged high so that the rich, who had enjoyed life in the summer, should put many cigarettes into circulation. The fact that those who sold to the rich in the summer had also enjoyed life then, and the fact that in the winter there was always someone willing to sell at low prices were ignored. Such arguments were hotly debated each night after the approach of Allied aircraft extinguished all lights at 8 P.M. But prices moved with the supply of cigarettes, and refused to stay fixed in accordance with a theory of ethics.

CONCLUSION

The economic organisation described was both elaborate and smooth-working in the summer of 1944. Then came the August cuts and deflation. Prices fell, rallied with deliveries of cigarette parcels in September and December, and fell again. In January 1945, supplies of Red Cross cigarettes ran out: and prices slumped still further: in February the supplies of food parcels were exhausted and the depression became a blizzard. Food, itself scarce, was almost given away in order to meet the nonmonetary demand for cigarettes. Laundries ceased to operate, or worked for £s or RMks: food and cigarettes sold for fancy prices in £s, hitherto unheard of. The Restaurant was a memory and the BMk a joke. The Shop was empty and the Exchange and Mart notices were full of unaccepted offers for cigarettes. Barter increased in volume, becoming a larger proportion of a smaller volume of trade. This, the first serious and prolonged food shortage in the writer's experience, caused the price structure to change again, partly because German rations were not easily divisible. A margarine ration gradually sank in value until it exchanged directly for a treacle ration. Sugar slumped sadly. Only bread retained its value. Several thousand cigarettes, the capital of the Shop, were distributed without any noticeable effect. A few fractional parcel and cigarette issues, such as one sixth of a parcel and 12 cigarettes each, led to momentary price recoveries and feverish trade, especially when they coincided with good news from the Western Front, but the general position remained unaltered.

By April 1945, chaos had replaced order in the economic sphere: sales were difficult, prices lacked stability. Economics has been defined as the science of distributing limited means among unlimited and competing ends. On 12th April, with the arrival of elements of the 30th U.S. Infantry Division, the ushering in of an age of plenty demonstrated the hypothesis that with infinite means economic organisation and activity would be redundant, as every want could be satisfied without effort.

3.

The Cause of Economic Literacy and the Business Economist*

A. GILBERT HEEBNER

It is hardly necessary to argue that the level of economic literacy—call it economic understanding or education if you prefer—is of great importance in a democratic society. Through the elective process and the pressure of public opinion the people will tend to get what they want in way of economic policies. And it takes no profound logic to conclude that the lower the level of understanding, the less satisfactory will be the country's economic policies and performance.

What could be a more conspicuous example of the importance of economic intelligence than the fact that the first of the Ford-Carter debates was primarily devoted to economic issues? Ostensibly the voters were going to formulate preferences for the candidates at least partly on the basis of their economic knowledge and policy viewpoints. But much of the reaction to the debate centered on the images created rather than the content of the answers given. While I don't dismiss the value of personal impressions, I think that a more economically informed public, including columnists, would have paid greater attention to what Mr. Ford and Mr. Carter actually said.

The level of economic literacy leaves much to be desired. That could, of course, also be said of economists and the body of economics. There

* *Business Economics*, January 1977, pp. 7–10.

is so much that we don't know. But the public's understanding of even the essentials of what we do know with reasonable confidence is seriously limited.

First, and most simply, there is lack of information, and even worse, misinformation, regarding important economic facts. You have all seen surveys of what people think is the average rate of corporate profits. Answers, even among college students, usually come out to be many times higher than, for instance, the actual average of about 5 percent of sales for all manufacturing corporations in nonrecession years. We cannot expect the layman to be saturated with economic statistics, and I think it would be a waste of money to provide each citizen with a gift subscription to the *Survey of Current Business*. Nevertheless, there is need to correct gross misunderstandings as to the magnitude and meaning of major economic measures.

BASIC FACTS

The low level of economic literacy is not, of course, only a matter of ignorance of essential facts. On the conceptual level, there is too little appreciation of the basic tenant that our means are limited while our wants are virtually unlimited. As Herbert Stein once put it, "we live in a world of scarcity," and "to live is to choose." So often this truth is ignored and the consequences are painful. Inflation has resulted when we have staked out claims on the national output that have exceeded potential output at existing prices. As the Vietnam War escalated, President Johnson told us that we could have both guns and butter when we could not.

To use more current examples, the benefits of improving environmental quality or reducing dependence on foreign oil cannot be obtained in a market economy without higher prices of energy and other goods and services. In the short run, adjustment to these price increases can even curtail employment and output. This summer I saw an automobile bumper sticker which read, "Out of work and hungry?—eat an environmentalist." Please be assured that I do not subscribe to this recommendation. But it cannot be sufficiently emphasized that trade-offs and choices are an integral part of economic life, and it is urgent that the public come to a better understanding of this economic truth. Indeed, "there is no such thing as a free lunch," even if an environmentalist were on the menu.

ECONOMIC POLICY

Economic policy is another subject that is poorly understood. The public often expects too much from policy and expects it too soon. Economists and policymakers are partly to blame. They sometimes give the impression that their policy prescriptions will produce attractive results, without placing emphasis on the uncertainties. I also believe, however, that overly ambitious policy objectives in part stem from the demands of an unenlightened public expressed through political processes. This often includes the demand that the government "do something" to get quicker results, even though the best option might be to continue on a given policy course.

It is well to recognize the limitations of economic policy, given the present state of the art. One of my concerns about the Humphrey-Hawkins bill, for example, is that it may promise more than can be delivered in setting an objective of 3 percent for the adult unemployment rate in four years. That is a fine objective in itself, but I am not at all confident that it can be achieved with available and yet-to-be developed policy tools. The result may well be both unfulfilled expectations and inflationary pressures as available demand management tools are used aggressively in a vain effort to reach the 3 percent goal.

You can easily add to the examples I have given of lack of economic understanding. I will not try to explain who or what is at fault. Politicians, professors, textbooks, the news media, special interest groups, and yes, business economists, probably should all share the blame. My purpose is not to find the villains, but to enter a plea for all competent parties to help in the cause of economic literacy. One of those parties, may I suggest, is the business economist.

A ROLE FOR BUSINESS ECONOMISTS

Your reaction may be an exasperated, "who me?" Yet I would submit that business economists have good qualifications for the challenge of educating the public in economics. Their formal education and professional experience are the foundation. Moreover, the skill that business economists have (or should have) to communicate clearly and simply particularly equips them to relate to the public. After all, in our jobs we have to convey information and conclusions to associates who are not professional economists. We are practiced in the art of explaining economics without resorting to esoteric theories and technical jargon.

The situation is different with our academic counterparts who are largely addressing themselves to other professors and students obliged to try to understand them. On the program of the recent meetings of the Allied Social Sciences Associations in Atlantic City there appeared such topics as, "The Identification of Casual Relationships for Bivariate Autoregressive Processes," and "On the Optimality of Rational Expectations Equilibria." Please don't misunderstand. I have awesome respect for the academic economists who conduct such research. I suspect, however, that business economists have a comparative advantage over them when it comes to explaining economics to the layman.

AIDING LEARNING

Assuming that as business economists you are at least partly persuaded of your unique qualifications for the cause I am espousing, may I humbly offer a few random suggestions for effective "teaching?"

1. Have patience. Economic concepts are not easily understood by many, and even clear and cogent explanations will probably require frequent repetition and elaboration. I am sure that you have been frustrated by people who ask skeptically, "how can you say that the rate of inflation is coming down when prices are still rising," or "how can the unemployment rate rise if employment increases?" If these apparent paradoxes are not easy for people to understand, it is no wonder that the more involved issues of economic policy and choice among conflicting goals are almost inexplicable.

2. Be sure that your purpose is economic education not propaganda. I always wince when I hear a businessman say that we need to do a better job of teaching economics so that people will appreciate the free enterprise system, much as there is to commend such a system. If you start with the objective of inculcating a preference for a particular system or policy, your effort can hardly serve a real educational purpose. An appropriate goal would have the broad and objective ring of the consensus developed in a survey study by the Conference Board a few years ago, namely, "to improve our understanding of the worlds in which we live." Interestingly, that reminds one of the words of Alfred Marshall, written more than a few years ago, that "economics is a study of mankind in the ordinary business of life. . . ."

3. Avoid subtly biased words and expressions (and, of course, grossly biased ones). It is tempting to sprinkle one's oral and written communication with such words as "prudent," "sober," "wise," and "sound." Frankly, I have never been able to determine what a "sound" policy is other than one that meets with my approval.

4. Distinguish between economic analysis and your value judgments. I would not attempt a learned discussion of where the line is drawn. Moreover, the torturous extremes to which some scholars in the past went to rule as off limits to an economist *qua* economist any sort of "what ought to be" judgments were, I think, a little silly. But we should honestly try to separate our own value preferences from the "if this, then that," reasoning of economic analysis.

5. Set forth your assumptions and qualifications. This is particularly necessary in the case of forecasting (and yes, forecasts can have educational value). Assumptions regarding such key questions as war, an oil embargo, the Russian wheat crop, who will occupy the White House, and even the proximity of anchovies to the coast of Peru, to name a few, are usually crucial to an analysis. Of course, people

don't want to hear the "ifs," but they must be included for the analysis to be scientific, and I might add, educational.

CHARTING THE COURSE

If you agree that business economists should help to increase economic understanding, how should we proceed? What can we do? At the organizational level, the National Association of Business Economists can make a contribution. One way is through its meetings, seminars, and publications, although admittedly we are largely speaking to each other in these. Within the limited budget of NABE, we might be able to afford some support of educational efforts.

Other possibilities might be recognized for our Association, but I mainly want to emphasize the role of the business economist in his or her individual career. Our first responsibility, of course, is to our employers. Nevertheless, they may be willing to allow time in our schedules for educational activities in keeping with the firm's social responsibility commitment. Even if a firm does not see it that way, there are always those extra hours in your 25-hour days.

The task of teaching economic truth is tough and frustrating. No dramatic results should be expected. Indeed you will probably not be able to measure the extent to which your effort has raised the level of public understanding. The cause of economic literacy is so important, however, that even a small contribution is a "pearl of great price."

4.

Stagflation: Our Pernicious Social Disease—That Our Antibiotics Can't Cure*

EDGAR R. FIEDLER

The economic news of 1983 has been surprisingly cheerful. In fact, by comparison with the dreary reports on the persistent inflation and sagging productivity growth of the past decade—the dismal combination known as "stagflation"—the news has been downright exhilarating. What was a very sick patient has now taken a pronounced turn for the better. Inflation has subsided dramatically. Production, employment, and all other measures of the business cycle have begun a strong recovery. The body economic suddenly shows a promising glow of health. Only a little more, and stagflation will be cured, right?

Wrong! Recent news *has* been good, and near-term prospects are also favorable. Over a longer horizon, however, the prognosis for exorcising stagflation from our economy is a gloomy one. Despite some marginal improvements, the underlying causes of our pernicious disease are still with us.

To understand such a melancholy judgment, it is necessary to probe a little deeper than usual into the internal mechanisms of our economic system. Sadly, most discussion of stagflation is based on relatively simple and short-term analysis. On inflation, for example, we regularly hear how the consumer price index went up this month because meat or

* *Business Economics,* January 1984, pp. 13–23.

gasoline or some other specific price increased—as though inflation were *caused* by rising prices. Tautologies are passed off as analysis, e.g., we often hear that rising wages force prices higher, or that rising prices force wages up. And of course we hear a lot about budget deficits, the money supply, and the burdens of government regulation. Well, fair enough, since each of these is an important part of the inflationary process.

But, as vital and as fascinating as these issues are, they do not get to the underlying source of our economic troubles. Stagflation is a complex social, political, and economic phenomenon, in the same way that heart disease and cancer are multidimensional medical conditions. Thus it is not enough to recognize that our poor economic performance is related to money and deficits and regulation and inadequate investment. These are only the *proximate* causes of high inflation and lagging productivity growth. Even if we understood those relationships thoroughly, it would not be enough. To get to the root causes, we must go beyond the immediate relationships and ask why these things take place: Why is the federal budget always in deficit? Why do we have such rapid monetary growth so often? Why are government policies so persistently biased toward inflation and against saving and investment? And why do regulatory decisions almost always add to costs and inhibit productive efficiency?

The answers to these questions are not so much economic in nature as they are social and political. There are occasional exceptions to this rule in the short run, but by and large the origins of stagflation are to be found in the way our social attitudes interact with our governing processes. The late Professor Fred Hirsch put it nicely:

> Inflation, a monetary phenomenon, is the end product of the existing monetary instrumentalities and the use made of them. The instrumentalities represent the technique: Their management or manipulation ultimately rests on political determination and on the social and economic forces that in turn underlie political decisions or confine them within a certain range. Economic factors, and they alone, can explain how inflation happens, but economic factors alone cannot explain why.

Over the past half-century, the American people have undergone two fundamental shifts in attitudes. First, they gradually adopted many new and extremely ambitious social objectives. Second, they decided these objectives should be pursued through collective, rather than individual means. That is, they have come to look more and more to government as having the basic responsibility for achieving these goals.

The American political system, however, was not up to the challenge. The demands placed on the economy by these new objectives far exceeded our ability to meet them. Within the political system, no systematic means existed to set priorities among the competing demands. No orderly political mechanism was in place to reconcile the economic conflict between too much demand and too few resources. The inevitable result was stagflation.

THE NEW SOCIAL OBJECTIVE

Economic Security. The most far-reaching of the new social goals adopted by the American people was the drive for economic security, especially job security. The desire for steady work is as old as the institution of employment, of course. What was new in recent decades was the change in public attitudes that made regular employment almost the inherent right of every individual, with that right guaranteed by government. In economic terms, we adopted a national commitment to full employment—in fact, to overfull employment.

The extent of this change in attitudes is fully appreciated only by those who remember the 1930s and 1940s. In those decades, if a worker lost his job and couldn't find another, it was considered to be his fault—a failing of ambition or diligence or some other virtue within his own personal control. He was looked upon as a malingerer.

Today, of course, those attitudes have shifted nearly 180 degrees. Employment is now almost an entitlement. Unemployment is society's fault, not the individual's. It is considered to be a failure of government policy, and any time the jobless rate rises above the accepted norm, government is expected to step in promptly both to alleviate the economic distress and to create more jobs. As a consequence, we have generous unemployment benefits, employment subsidies, aid to businesses in depressed areas, trade-adjustment assistance for workers whose jobs are "lost" to imports, a combined federal-state job-finding service, several public service employment programs (the largest of which, however, is mostly a way for the federal government to pay the salaries of state and city workers), educational grants for unemployed workers, and (until recently) an endless variety of training and retraining programs.

Our national commitment to full employment was only the first of a much broader series of commitments to protect individuals and their families against the everyday economic hazards of life. We created the social security system to provide almost everyone with income during retirement. We set up workers' compensation and other forms of disability insurance to guarantee income to injured workers. And government relief programs are mounted to alleviate the damage from hurricanes, drought, volcanic eruptions, and every other form of natural disaster.

In addition, government has put in place over the years an enormous number of statutory and administrative interventions designed to protect or enhance the established positions of various economic groups. The minimum wage, for example. The Davis-Bacon Act, which maintains high wage rates on government construction and thereby also on competitive projects in the private sector. Constraints on the harvest of federal timber. Agricultural marketing orders that limit the amount of produce brought to market. Import restrictions. Subsidies to various industries. Restrictive licensing practices and building codes, mostly at the local level. The list goes on and on. A tabulation put together within the federal government a few years back ran on for 55 pages! And every intervention not only protects some group's vested interest but also has the unintended but inevitable effect of raising costs or retarding efficiency or both.

Income Redistribution. The second ambitious social goal adopted by the American people in recent decades was to provide more economic security for persons outside the labor market. This venture went by a number of names: the "war on poverty," "egalitarianism," "social justice," or simply "welfare." But whatever the label, the common denominator is a greater redistribution of income from the "haves" to the "have-nots."

Here, too (as with job security) the objective is not a new one. The class struggle over income shares has been going on for millennia. What is new in the past couple of decades versus a half-century ago and earlier is how much redistribution is called for and the dominant role of government in achieving it.

This redistribution has been pursued primarily through two channels: the tax system and transfer payments. From the mid-1960s through the 1970s, the tax system was repeatedly restructured toward a greater degree of progressivity. During the same period, welfare programs designed to aid the poor and disadvantaged proliferated—although in many instances, because of both faulty design and bad administration, assistance flowed far up into the middle range of incomes. In 1980, the federal government was reported to have 182 separate income-support programs lodged in 16 different departments. Some of these, of which Aid to Families with Dependent Children and Supplementary Security Income are the largest, disburse direct cash assistance. Many others provide income in kind: food stamps, school breakfasts and lunches, public housing, medicare and medicaid, legal services for the poor, half-price bus fares for senior citizens, and so on. In addition, the widespread public sympathy for redistribution motivated some government agencies with no direct welfare function—e.g., utility rate commissions—to alter their practices in ways that served the egalitarian goal.

Although government has played the dominant role in redistributing income, the change in attitudes that brought this social goal to the forefront has had pervasive effects throughout society. One important example is the startling shift of occupational choices by our young people. As Albert Wojnilower of First Boston Corporation has observed, "Ten or 12 years ago we graduated four times as many engineers as lawyers.

Currently the numbers are close to equal. We used to graduate twice as many physicists as psychologists—now it is the other way around." On the relative number of lawyers and engineers, the figures on practitioners are even more dramatic than the data on graduates cited by Wojnilower, as the accompanying chart demonstrates. In the same vein, personnel counseling is reported to be the nation's fastest growing job title. This mounting emphasis on occupations in the legal profession, psychology, and personnel work reflects the growing importance to Americans of fairness, justice, peace of mind, and self-indulgence (the "me generation"). Alternatively, the declining prestige and popularity of occupations in engineering and science reflect the subordination of goals such as production and efficiency.

Where our primary concern used to be how to bake a bigger pie, we now focus more on how to divide up the present pie. To quote Wojnilower again, "As you can see we have shifted our economic effort very considerably in the direction of perfecting the allocation and consumption as contrasted with the production of material wealth."

Social Regulation.   The third major social goal of recent decades was to reduce a variety of risks that are not always strictly economic in nature. Massive legislative and regulatory initiatives were undertaken to lessen the dangers to health from a polluted atmosphere and impure water supplies, to enhance safety both within and outside the work place (e.g., restrictions on waste disposal, nuclear energy development, plant siting, and transportation of hazardous materials), and to provide equal opportunity, both economic and noneconomic, for women and various minority groups.

These regulatory efforts imposed heavy burdens on the economy. In a few places the impact can be seen quite clearly. In mining, for example, where the regulations were probably the most onerous, the industry had a particularly dismal productivity record, declining from 4.3 percent annual growth during 1950–65 to 1.9 percent during 1965–73 and then to a *minus* 6.1 percent during 1973–77. Similarly, environmental and safety requirements are estimated to have added over $1,000 to the price of an automobile. In most cases, however, the cost imposed by each individual regulation is small and well-hidden. But the costs are rarely considered at all. Although some progress toward our health and safety goals has been achieved, there is little doubt it came at a high price to the economy.

In summary, the American people have adopted the monumental aspiration of achieving a nearly risk-free society. Job security is to be the rule in the labor market, income security is to be provided for everyone else, and no one is to be exposed to serious health and safety risks. The American people have been demanding something approach-

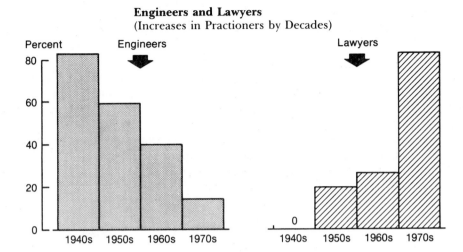

Engineers and Lawyers
(Increases in Practioners by Decades)

ing "cradle to grave" security. The predominant attitude comes close to a belief that no one should be uncomfortable—ever.

To these ends government is called on at every turn. And in its response to these demands, government has taken over functions that were formerly the responsibility of others in our society. The Federal Reserve's role as "lender of last resort" is well known. Today, government has also become the employer of last resort, the charity of last resort, the religion of last resort, and even to some degree the family of last resort.

THE POLITICAL DEFICIENCIES

To point out that these grandiose social objectives are part of the process that creates inflation and retards productivity growth is not to suggest they are somehow wrong. Quite the contrary: What could be more virtuous and more altruistic than efforts to prevent illness and assist unfortunate victims of recession and natural disasters? Furthermore, such undertakings do not create stagflation *in and of themselves.* Their effects can be offset by appropriate government policies. However, they do stultify investment and innovation and they do add heavily to total economic demand, and thus *they are both inflationary and growth-inhibiting in a society that lacks sufficient political discipline to set priorities among its goals and to reconcile systematically the gap between too much demand and too few resources.* Government in the United States, in common with other democracies and indeed with political systems of various kinds, is seriously inadequate in this way.

Political Irresponsibility.   One of the inadequacies of our system is the venality of both political leaders and the voters. Clearly, many politicians regularly take positions on legislation or other policy issues, not from their own convictions or principles but simply as a way of buying votes. They pander to the general public by supporting broad-gauged tax cuts. They promote specifically targeted spending programs to win the favor of special interest groups.

A classic example was the emphatic guarantee President Carter made to construction union officials in October 1979 that he would not fight inflation with the jobs of construction workers, a statement he made only a few months after pledging an uncompromising fight against inflation and endorsing the restrictive monetary policies of the Federal Reserve. In light of the sensitivity of construction to high interest rates, the two commitments were almost patently inconsistent. It was a guarantee he could not make with any confidence. And as it turned out, construction activity declined in the months following his statement to the union leaders. In 1980, after the Carter Administration and the Federal Reserve collaborated on another major tightening of credit policy, the economy dipped into a short but sharp recession and the unemployment of construction workers increased substantially, along with almost all other groups in the labor force.

This is not to suggest that Mr. Carter was the only president to speak out of both sides of his mouth. It is, unfortunately, a common occurrence among political leaders. In a *Newsweek* column Meg Greenfield reproached:

> . . . all those well-known budget balancers and austerity types jostling and shoving to be first and most lavish and least serious in promising the voters a juicy tax cut. But there were also the who-got-what stories just prior to the Congressional recess. Something for this pressure group, something for that, an incautious benefits increase here, a wholly ill-founded subsidy there—the legislation reads like somebody's will.

> . . . Congress is . . . paying shut-up money to the voters. You could call it something nicer, like "tribute," or something less nice, like "extortion," but this is essentially the relationship that has developed between the public and its elected representatives in both the legislature and the higher reaches of the executive branch.

Special-interest politics, or as it is sometimes called, single-issue politics, is a particularly important form of political irresponsibility. The way to get elected, politicians have learned, is to appeal to many different minority groups simultaneously. Sometimes these are very substantial minorities, such as employees in a certain industry who want import restrictions or farmers who want acreage curtailments or elderly persons who want more generous social security benefits. In other cases, the group might be small but, if the issue that is their special concern is fairly narrow, it will nevertheless pay the candidate to take a strong stand in their favor. Putting together a coalition of just a handful of these single-issue minorities is often enough to guarantee victory in the election.

Special-interest politics leads to inflation in two ways. First, the commitments made to all the separate groups add up to far more than the economy can produce. The expectations of the people are raised to unrealistic levels and efforts to deliver what's been promised bring only inflation. Second, inflationary consequences arise out of special-interest politics because of the way our governments are organized. The cabinet system in the executive branch and the committee systems of both the Congress and the state legislatures almost guarantee that the concerns of every individual group are dealt with separately, whereas almost no one in government feels much responsibility to look after the interests of society as a whole.

What was described earlier as the "class struggle over income shares" is not limited to the haves versus the have-nots. It goes on incessantly on hundreds of battlegrounds, with each special-interest group trying to win an advantage over the rest of society. Industry demands subsidies and import limitations. Unions demand the Davis-Bacon Act and friendly appointments to the National Labor Relations Board. Optometrists and lawyers demand restrictions on advertising. Doctors and taxi drivers demand restraints on entry into the occupation. Farmers demand price supports and a grain reserve. Professors demand tenure. And so on. Everyone demands a bigger slice of the pie and less risk of losing what they've gained.

This is not, of course, the announced purpose of the demands! The stated intent is to assure the quality of the product, to protect the health and safety of the customer, or some other unselfish goal. Partly because of this propaganda but mostly because nobody else is paying enough attention, the special-interest groups and the politicians who collaborate in arranging the subsidy or the anticompetitive regulations can ignore the cost of their actions to society. They can pretend that granting a benefit to one group does not involve taking something away from everyone else. Of course, nothing is taken away *overtly;* rather it is done through the stealth of higher inflation and lower productivity. Mancur Olson, in his book, *The Rise and Decline of Nations,* built a persuasive theory of differential growth rates around the social rigidities created by "distributional coalitions," which is his term for special-interest groups.

There are a variety of other forms of political irresponsibility that exacerbate our economic difficulties. On occasion politicians will delay action for long periods simply to avoid making tough choices. They will do this even in the face of mandated deadlines as, for example, Congress has done several times in its budget process. Sometimes they pass legislation without ever considering the consequences or the costs, as appears to have been the case with various environmental bills and also with the Age Discrimination Act of 1975. A particularly outrageous example was the legislative requirement that public transportation be altered to provide easy access for the handicapped, which the Government Accounting Office later costed out at $38 per trip.

On other occasions legislatures enact enormously costly benefits completely unintentionally, simply because they didn't know precisely what they were voting—e.g., when Congress "double indexed" social security benefits in the early 1970s. Sometimes the legislation will prove to be impossibly vague, or will mandate conflicting goals, both of which strategies allow the politicians to appear as benefactors to all competing factions, while hiding the costs and sloughing off the dirty work of making the implementational decisions to the regulators who have to make the legislation work or to the courts.

Although all these forms of political irresponsibility are essentially immoral, it would be wrong to judge them too critically, because they are easily understandable. Although some political leaders take such actions quite consciously, others do so unintentionally. What could be more natural than for a politician to stress what he wants government to "give" to the people and to ignore, or at least deemphasize, what is to be taken away? Surely it is as human for politicians to pursue their self-interest, reelection, this way as it is for workers to seek higher pay and business executives higher profits. And if politicians frequently promise their constituents more than can be delivered, is this any different from the excessive claims businesses often make in advertising to their customers, or union leaders make to their members about the wages and benefits to be won from employers? There is probably little difference in style or degree. There is one important difference, however, which is that workers and businesses are subject to the discipline of either competition or regulation or both, whereas in politics the only competition seems to be who can make the most grandiose promises. Nevertheless the behavior patterns of the politicians are quite understandable and quite human.

Furthermore, vote-buying politicians can get by with this practice only because there is a vote-selling public ready to believe it can gain from the exchange. It takes two to tango. A political transaction of this sort is just like any free-market transaction: Both parties have to believe they will gain from it. Many voters support activist, free-spending politicians out of a belief they will benefit from the government programs but will not have to ante up their full share of the cost. The free lunch syndrome still lives, and sometimes it works.

Myopia. A second serious flaw in our political process is its short-sightedness and impatience. The American people have a limited attention span. They habitually focus on the near term and demand simple, instant, costless solutions to every problem, no matter how deep-seated and complex it may be.

We are a nation in a hurry. The success of instant coffee, instant cake mixes, and TV dinners attests to this universal wish to save time—and in some cases it also attests to our willingness to sacrifice a considerable measure of quality in exchange. And why shouldn't we demand the "quick fix" from our politicians? After all, if James Bond can unravel even the most complex international conspiracy in a two-hour movie, why should anyone argue with the Humphrey-Hawkins bill and its lofty prescription to simultaneously achieve highly ambitious targets for unemployment and inflation in a few years.

Just as there is an impatient public demanding instant solutions, so is there a corresponding shortsightedness on the part of the politicians who are always ready to respond with expediencies that provide short-run gratification at the expense of long-run discipline. To reduce unemployment, for example, cut taxes; to curb inflation, impose mandatory price and wage controls. In both cases, the quick-fix solutions will work temporarily. The initial response to the tax cut is a rise in spendable income, increased consumption, a step-up in production, and lower unemployment. Similarly, at the beginning controls will suppress inflation. As with the first effects of alcohol, for a while it all feels so good!

However, although the economic goodies come first, the baddies will inevitably follow. Before long, the feeling of well-being turns sour and the hangover sets in. An overstimulated economy will develop excesses and maladjustments that lead inevitably into recession and high unemployment. Similarly, direct price and wage restraints invariably crumble under their own weight and produce a "catch-up" burst of increases that leaves inflation at least as bad as before and probably worse. In both cases, the effort at short-run gratification does more harm than good in the long run.

Yet as long as the American people are impatient and vote into office politicians who promise instant solutions, those are inevitably the kinds of economic policies that will be adopted. With Congress up for reelection every two years and presidents every four years, government officials do not have the luxury of undertaking the long-run discipline that might produce lasting solutions to complex problems like inflation, productivity growth, and energy. As Lester Thurow has pointed out about the problems of achieving energy independence:

> For a long time, sacrifices must be made to construct the necessary mines and plants. Benefits emerge only near the end of the process. The politician who must incur the costs (raise the necessary revenues and incur the anger

of those who are hurt as the projects are constructed) is unlikely to be around to collect the credits when energy independence has been achieved.

Arnold Weber, president of the University of Colorado, once summed this up with a quip: "An economist's lag is a politician's nightmare." A more cynical version is: "To a politician, the long term is the time between now and the next election."

The problem, it should be noted, is not limited to politicians. A recent *New York Times* article was headlined, "Stock Choices For Long Haul." It turned out that the reporter was referring to a time horizon of a year and a day, which is enough to qualify for long-term capital gains tax treatment, but hardly appropriate for "long haul." Similarly, the penchant of the American consumer for instant gratification is well known, best exemplified by our buy-now, pay-later mentality and by our highly developed consumer credit markets, which are by far the most advanced in the world. Many business leaders, too, are biased toward the short run. This bias may stem from their own impatience, or from compensation arrangements that tie their bonuses to annual earnings, or from the demands of investors for improved earnings every quarter without interruption. Whatever the reasons, the effect is to divert attention toward the quick fix and other expediencies and away from longer term solutions, including long-lived investment projects.

Democracy's Internal Conflict.   Another interplay between politics and economics in our system that nurtures stagflation—as pointed out by my Conference Board colleague Albert T. Sommers and the late Arthur M. Okun of Brookings Institution, among others—is the inherent and fundamental conflict that exists between equally distributed voting rights and unequally distributed economic power. On the one side we distribute political power throughout the population on the basis of one vote for each adult—per capita equality. On the other side, the qualities that determine an individual's economic power—intelligence, energy, industriousness, self-discipline, imagination, entrepreneurship, and ambition, plus various conferred advantages such as education and inherited wealth—are distributed unequally. In a society where economic activity is organized on the basis of private property and freedom of choice (a "meritocracy"), the wide differences that exist in the personal characteristics of individuals are sure to produce a distribution of income and wealth that is highly uneven. (It is probably less skewed in democracies than in societies organized on other principles, but it is nevertheless substantially unequal.)

These two conditions—equally distributed voting rights and unequally distributed economic power—get in each other's way. They are fundamentally incompatible. Concentrations of economic power can subvert the equal distribution of political power—e.g., through their ability to finance election campaigns. Similarly, the principle of equality before the law is frustrated to some degree by the greater ability of the rich to hire superior defense counsel.

At the same time, the economic have-nots unite in a political effort to contravene the tendency toward economic disparity. As an old slogan of the British Labour Party puts it, "The rich man has his money, the poor man has his politics." Accordingly, every voter with less economic power than political power has an incentive to use the latter to enhance the former. The coalition that forms often lacks cohesion and a sharp focus (because this issue is only one of many that command the attention of voters) but sooner or later the have-nots will come together to bring their majority political power to bear in the struggle with the haves.

Albert Sommers identified this conflict in 1974 as follows: "Where private property and universal suffrage coexist, it would seem almost inevitable that a powerful tide of social change will develop, to mediate between them. All modern democracies are experiencing that tide in the 1970s." He later described it in more detail:

> For the democratic ethic turns out to be basically distributive, egalitarian, oriented to consumption, unimpressed with incentive, and concerned with the "average man" and eager to believe in his perfectibility. The free market, on the other hand, is basically cumulative, organized on dominance and leadership, a machine driven by incentive and reward, antiegalitarian, and darkly suspicious of altruism. Capitalism fuses risk and reward in a rigid gel of market logic; democracy treats them as partly independent variables. Democracy seeks a more equal distribution of income; capitalism depends on an unequal distribution for saving, investment, and growth. Democracy legislates values, arrays priorities, praises, and condemns. The free market offers no priorities, no values, no end, no purpose; it makes do with man as it found him. In refusing to bend to purpose, the free market protects us from the purposes of others, and it liberates the enormous energies contained within self-interest. Democracy struggles to direct the energies toward its won purposes; in so doing, if often treads on the incentives that are responsible for the energy in the first place.
>
> . . . The description suggests, properly, an unequal struggle. All over the West, the free market has been on the defensive and in retreat. Democracy has invaded the marketplace, altering its institutions, breaking down its natural defenses against inflation, and forcing outcomes that are all but unrecognizable by conventional economic reasoning.
> . . . In modern societies, fiscal and monetary policies may be enabling conditions of inflation, but they do not "cause" inflation. . . . All three phenomena—inflation, budget deficits, and rapid money growth—are coordinate reflections of the ethical invasion of free markets.

As an outgrowth of this inherent conflict, there has been a persistent steepening of the progressivity of the tax structure and a proliferation of welfare programs in recent decades. How much income redistribution has been achieved is debatable. Analysts are divided on this question but the guess here is that some narrowing of overall differentials in income and wealth have taken place, although much less than is widely assumed. What we can be certain of is that the changes have had many harmful economic side effects in the form of disincentives, inefficiencies and increased production costs.

Policy Paralysis. A fourth shortcoming of our political system that nurtures inflation and stultifies productivity growth is the tendency for governmental processes to freeze into immobility whenever difficult and controversial policy issues arise. The way our political system operates, agreement among many groups usually has to be achieved before significant action can be taken on a major issue. The key players are the White House, the many committees of Congress and the independent regulatory agencies. Other units are also powerful, such as labor unions, coalitions of trade associations, and various lobbying groups, all of which work through their supporters in Congress and the regulatory agencies. Usually, each of these groups has the power to block any action not to its liking. None can unilaterally force its own will on the rest of the system, but each has an effective veto. The result is sometimes referred to as the institutional constipation of government. Just last week a *Wall Street Journal* editorial labelled it "terminal proceduritis." Once when President Ford asked for Congressional action to be completed in nine days, political satirist Mark Russell said, "The only thing Congress could do in nine days is make Minute Rice!"

When it comes to making tough economic policy decisions, Washington is like the overindulgent parent who can't bear to refuse a child's demand for more candy, no matter now apparent it is that the brat has already had far too much. When inflation threatens, no way can be found to cut spending or raise taxes. The classic example is the policy response to the inflationary outburst of the mid-1960s. At first the politicians left the anti-inflation effort to the Federal Reserve. Once it was proven that the Fed couldn't do the job by itself, the president and the Congress went into political gridlock over what was to be done next. The impasse lasted a year and a half before a compromise was reached, and in the meantime the inflation accelerated and became more deeply entrenched.

Two other illustrations of Congressional inaction arising from an unwillingness to face up to difficult but unavoidable policy decisions are worth mentioning. The egregious error of "double-indexing" social security benefits mentioned earlier was discovered soon after it was made, but remedial legislation was not enacted for some six years. The second illustration is the five-year stalemate that developed over energy policy following the oil embargo and quadrupling of crude-oil prices in 1973–74. Everyone agreed there was a crisis. But no mechanism existed to compel action and thus no way could be found to force a decision, one way or another.

The impasse over energy policy provides an excellent example of how special-interest groups exercise their power beyond the legislative halls. Coal is often cited as a major part of the answer to our dangerous dependence on imported oil. Yet few of the environmental constraints on the use of coal, a number of which were of doubtful value in the first place, have yet been overcome. Environmental groups (among others) have learned that it is relatively easy to use our legal system to delay a new project almost indefinitely, often until the costs and uncertainties generated by the delays kill the project altogether. The delays are such a major part of the strategy that one group has a name for it—analysis paralysis. On the other side of the issue, the difficulty of increasing the use of coal has spawned a different derisive comment: "Yes, coal is a great source of energy—it's just that you can't mine it, you can't move it, and you can't burn it."

The entropy that often grips the Congress can be explained in part by "Dale's Paradox." Edwin L. Dale, Jr., observed that, "The inefficiency and unpredictability of Congress rise in direct proportion to the ability and energy of its members." Thus, the better the quality of the individuals elected to Congress, the less it is able to accomplish as an organization. Some observers are inclined to attribute this to a lack of leadership, but Dale looked on it more as a lack of followership. As has been quipped elsewhere, the problem is that Congress is made up of 535 prima donnas running off in all directions simultaneously.

Economic Ignorance. A fifth major shortcoming of our political process is the severe lack of understanding by the American people of how their economic system works. In some cases they are simply unaware of basic economic facts, such as the typical corporate profit margin, which they badly overestimate, or how much oil the United States has to import to meet its energy needs, which they badly underestimate.

The public is also ignorant, to a large extent, of some of the most fundamental economic relationships. Probably the two most important misconceptions are related to time and resources. The first is the general failure to recognize how pervasive and deep-seated such problems as inflation and slow productivity growth are, and thus how long it takes to correct them. This misconception is implicit in the myopia and impatience discussed earlier.

The second fundamental concept of economics the American people consistently fail to grasp—one especially relevant to inflation—is the resource and production limitations of the economy. Americans often behave as though there are no limits. They do not recognize that in the long run, if more output of one type is wanted, something else has to be cut back. If more income is to be transferred to the poor or if more funds are to be devoted to the military, then the necessary resources must be extracted from elsewhere in the system—this is a concept they consistently ignore. In particular they are reluctant to recognize that more investment means less consumption.

In part this misconception may go back to the depression, when the existence of massive unused capacity meant that more spending for one thing did not have to come out of some other type of spending. Alternatively, the misperception may have been an outgrowth of World War II from which the United States emerged as unquestionably the preeminent nation worldwide, economically as well as militarily. A feeling of supreme self-confidence, even omnipotence, may have helped feed the myth that no limits apply to the U.S. economy. Whatever its source, the misperception has no doubt led to persistently high rates of resource utilization and the inflationary pressures that accompany them.

Professor Simon Rottenberg of the University of Massachusetts, Amherst, has identified several other economic misperceptions that have been held by many Americans in recent decades to the detriment of our economic performance:

> A failure to appreciate that the market is an instrument of discipline, that market transactions are consensual, that the power of buyers and sellers in competitive markets is not unequal, and that the market resolves conflict in ways that are reciprocally advantageous to the contenders.
>
> A disdain for profit-seeking ventures, as though profit were not a payment for service to the consumer.
>
> A belief that collective choice through the political process is usually superior to collective choice through the aggregation of individual decisions.
>
> A confusion of equity with equality.
>
> A belief that the market pays too much for entrepreneurial risk but too little for occupational and consumer risk.

Investment Climate.   Another political condition that was economically enfeebling in recent decades especially to productivity, was the unfriendly environment for savings and investment. At its roots productivity growth is a cultural phenomenon, dependent on the attitudes of the populace. What value do the people place on current consumption as opposed to the increased future consumption that comes from saving and investment? Do they encourage innovation and welcome change, or are they more comfortable with the status quo? Are they intellectually curious or mostly uninterested in learning? Do they respect and admire successful entrepreneurs who earn large profits, or are they only envious and suspicious of them? How high is freedom on their list of priorities, and how high is security? These are the intangible but fundamental issues that are at the heart of productivity growth.

Historically, America was a country that revered freedom, tolerated unconventional thought, welcomed change, encouraged risk taking, esteemed saving, acclaimed moneymakers, and was always pushing on to the next frontier. Some of that spirit is still present, but a good bit of it has been lost in recent decades. In part, the change is a legacy of the Great Depression, which created a lasting policy bias toward demand stimulation and consumption, but the shift in attitudes seems to be much broader than that. High profits, once admired, are now more often disparaged as a "rip-off" of "obscene." Innovations are now more often rebuffed than welcomed, out of anxiety that they will disturb the status quo. The quest for security has in part replaced the quest for growth. The use of debt to increase current consumption has supplanted savings as the prevailing orthodoxy. Conformity has displaced creativity.

A prerequisite of vibrant productivity growth is a social and political climate that fosters creativity, saving, and investment. This would consist of public attitudes that say, in effect, "Go ahead Mr. Innovator, try out your new idea, take the risks, and if successful you will be welcome to the rewards of the investment. (Of course, if your idea fails, you will have to accept the loss.) Furthermore, we won't change the rules on you in midstream." Such a climate has been absent in the United States for many years, and our productivity performance has suffered for it.

FIXING THE RESPONSIBILITY

By themselves, neither our ambitious social goals nor the shortcomings of our political processes necessarily lead to stagflation. But together they form a kind of double whammy that inevitably fosters the immediate causes of burgeoning inflation and deteriorating productivity performance:

Massive and almost continuous deficits in the federal budget.

Excessive growth of money and credit.

Persistently high rates of resource utilization.

A bias that consistently favors consumption and discriminates against saving and investment.

An altering of incentives in ways that penalize hard work, innovation, and risk-taking, while rewarding nonperformance.

A regulatory burden that adds heavily to production costs.

The argument is thus clear. The root causes of stagflation reach down to our social ambitions and our political institutions. Our appetites are voracious. Our discipline is flimsy. Our government processes are inadequate. Feverish inflation and lethargic productivity are the inevitable consequence.

Who, then, should be found guilty of the crime of stagflation? Certainly there is no shortage of suspects, starting with greedy unions, profiteering businesses and rapacious OPECs, and going on through the

Washington crowd including the irresponsible budget-busters, the monetary libertines at the Federal Reserve and the inefficient, overregulating bureaucrats. And then there are the activist groups: the environmental freaks, safety mongers, poverty pimps, antinuclear knaves, health charlatans, and consumer quacks. These nefarious groups are often blamed for our economic failings and, as my facetious labels are meant to imply, I do not regard them as entirely pure and innocent. But if the theory described in this paper is at all valid, we cannot find these groups accountable for the crime, at least not to any substantial degree.

Well, if not these rascals, who *is* to blame? The answer, I believe, is to be found in the marvelous insight of that great American philosopher, Pogo, who said "We have met the enemy and they is us." The American people, in their individual and collective behavior, are responsible—at least they are responsible for much of the largest part of the high inflation and slow productivity growth of the past two decades. At any given moment, with the investigative lens set at short focus, circumstances can be found that make it appropriate to hold the actions of OPEC or some other specific event responsible for a large part of the poor statistical record *of that brief span.* But over the long haul, no. Over the long haul the net of responsibility has to be cast much wider, to take in the great majority of the American people.

Not everyone will agree with that conclusion, of course. In particular, some analysts will want to assign most of the blame to one or both of two groups not mentioned thus far. The first is made up of the very senior officials of government, including the president and the most senior members of his cabinet, the leaders of Congress, the Federal Reserve and the regulatory agencies. These executives have their hands on the control levers of economic policy and, the argument goes, if they do not behave responsibly the economic results can be attributed directly to them. The second group is the so-called new class, comprised of academics, bureaucrats, journalist, various public-interest activists, and other "elitists." Some believe that these generally "liberal" groups, through their roles in the schools and the news media, have shaped public opinion and thus have wielded a disproportionate influence in determining our social priorities and undermining the political processes. They are, therefore, held responsible for leading us down the garden path of deteriorating economic performance.

No doubt both groups deserve some of the blame; perhaps each group deserves slightly more than its proportionate share. But where is there a reason to absolve the American people as a whole? If they have been led down the wrong path, certainly they went willingly. In this democratic system of ours there is always competition among ideas, and the voters made their choice freely.

There is a further point to consider about the responsibility of senior government officials: Their independence is highly limited. Those who would exercise too much of it are voted out of office very quickly. How, therefore, can we really expect political leaders to choose a policy very different from the wishes of their constituents, even if the leader's inner voice tells him that the alternative is the truly responsible choice? To expect that is to expect too much i.e., it is asking a politician not to behave like a politician. All of the elected official's training and experience condition him the other way. The judgment here, therefore, is that in the end the predominant responsibility for our deplorable economic performance has to be traced back to the voting public.

LOOKING AHEAD

This theory of the root causes of our economic troubles is frustrating and disheartening. Ideally, my essay should conclude with a set of concrete prescriptions to restore the economy to full health—such therapeutic dicta as: slow monetary growth, balance the budget, reform sclerotic regulations, strengthen saving incentives, and introduce discipline into the political process. But easier said than done. Gluttonous public appetites are not curbed simply by admonition. Every regulatory intervention has vigorous and politically powerful defenders, which is why farm price supports, import quotas, and maritime subsidies are often referred to as "sacred cows," i.e., not easily slain.

Finding effective medicines to cure the disease of stagflation is difficult, because neither our public attitudes nor our political institutions are easily reformed. Absent crisis, both are stubbornly resistant to change. There is an obvious need for public education on these issues, but education is a painfully slow route to reform. Thus the chances of turning our social attitudes around, curbing our appetites and rectifying our political deficiencies anytime soon are slim. Correspondingly, as much as I would prefer to, I think it's only realistic to conclude that we are unlikely to restore price stability and a vibrant growth of productivity for some years ahead.

On the political side, the one reform that holds some promise is the proposal to lengthen presidential and congressional terms but to limit incumbents to a single term in office. Presidents might be restricted to a single 6-year term, senators to a single 6- or 8-year term, and representatives to one or two 4-year terms. Such a change would, hopefully, lengthen the time horizon over which economic policy is shaped, and reduce the pressure for politicians to pander to the immediate appetites of their constituents. But clearly this one simple-but-unlikely reform, although helpful, could not be expected to fully rectify the political weaknesses that have contributed so much to our economic policy errors.

Beyond that one reform it is difficult to imagine beneficial changes that would not alter our democratic system in unacceptable ways. Some things are more important than optimal economic performance, and freedom is at the top of my list. As Churchill noted, democracy is the worst possible type of government except for every other type ever devised.

On the attitudes of the American people, there are many who will say the picture is not nearly as bleak as I imply. Over the past couple of years, they point out, the public has shown more self-discipline and a greater willingness to tolerate austerity than could reasonably have been expected from the political climate of the past couple of decades. As a result, inflation has been cut to less than half its former rate, and meaningful changes have been made in our tax structure to strengthen savings and investment incentives. Give us more time, they say, and we'll cure this stagflation altogether.

Parts of that argument are valid. There has been a significant change of attitudes and several important antistagflation steps have been taken. The slowdown of inflation is for real. Part of the slowdown was fortuitous—the declines in food, fuel, and imported goods prices helped speed up the deflationary process a lot, but they are one-shot phenomena and are reversible—as this summer's drought has reminded us. But the most important reason inflation slowed was indeed the change in public attitudes, which accepted the high unemployment costs of a stringent monetary policy long enough to convince both managers and workers that if they continued to push up prices and wages in the "normal" way all they would do would be to price themselves out of the market and into the bankruptcy courts and unemployment lines.

As we look to the future, the major question on inflation is whether the shift in attitudes will prove to be deep and sustained enough to administer the *coup de grace*. Monetary policy was relaxed last October, and for this and other reasons a vigorous cyclical recovery has developed. Already the leading indicators of new inflationary pressures—rising prices for raw industrial commodities and rapid increases in credit— are poking up their heads. Inflation is down but not out. Whether the policymakers will be able to exert enough fiscal and monetary discipline to prevent the recovery from reigniting a full-fledged inflationary conflagration is open to serious question. The high probability of long-term megadeficits in the federal budget says that the monetary authorities are not going to be able to sustain a steadfast anti-inflationary policy. Sooner or later, they will be forced to monetize the deficits and subsequently, inflation will burgeon anew.

On productivity, unlike inflation, no signs of progress are visible. The improvement in the latest quarterly numbers is only the usual revival for this stage of the business cycle, and not an encouraging revival at that. But in view of the long-term nature of the productivity process, we should not expect to see progress this soon, only a couple of years after the policy changes were implemented.

What of the productivity trend over the longer term? Is there reasonable hope for a step-up in growth from the three fourths of 1 percent annual rate of the past 10 years to the 2½–3 percent historical norm? Although productivity is clearly not a one-dimension problem, the central issue seems to me to boil down to whether or not our society will generate enough saving and investment. Despite the policy changes made thus far, we have no reason to believe the historically thin slice of the total economic pie devoted to new capital formation is going to increase. Resources we use for one purpose are not available for something else. Thus, unless we are willing to cut back on consumption or government spending, we won't make room in the economy for more productivity-stimulating investment.

Here, too, the deficits are the signal that the old priorities are still very much intact. We want more consumption, which the 1981 tax cuts make possible. We want more military spending, where a powerful uptrend is firmly established. And we're not willing to pare back federal social spending; indeed, the latest soundings from Washington suggest a new lease on life for some of the previously curbed programs.

It's this spending by consumers and governments that crowds out investment, but the process works through the capital markets. And in the absence of major budget surgery, which is unlikely, the deficit is going to preempt more than half the available supply of savings. Thus the net result seems sure to be a further shaving down of that already thin investment slice and, correspondingly, lengthy odds against rejuvenation of the productivity trend.

Consequently, it is difficult to avoid an unhappy conclusion for the long term. The social appetites of the American people, while less voracious than before, remain excessive. Correspondingly, we have not found a way to impose discipline on our political processes. As Arnold Weber put it long ago, "With the inevitability of a mudslide in California, the Old Profligacy will ooze back and submerge the New Austerity."

I am not suggesting catastrophe—no bout with hyperinflation is likely, nor an enduring fall in living standards. Disaster conclusions of that sort make for good drama, but little else. Furthermore, one of these years we might experience something of a crisis that will shake our society out of its comfortable rigidities and release a new surge of noninflationary growth energies. But in the meantime, I worry that we are in for a grinding, nagging, persistent deficiency in our economic performance—too much inflation and too little productivity growth over an extended period.

Stagflation is here to stay.

5.

What Can Economic Theory Contribute to Managerial Economics?*

WILLIAM J. BAUMOL

What to me is one of the most significant aspects of economic theory for management science was brought out very clearly in a talk I had some time ago with a biologist friend of mine. This biologist is an eminent authority on clock mechanisms in animals. There is a remarkable and well-known periodicity in the behavior of a large variety of animal species—in fact, probably among all of them. To illustrate the point, the emergence of adult fruit flies from their pupae usually occurs shortly after dawn. Even if the flies are placed in a darkened room whose temperature, humidity, and other evidences of passage of time are carefully controlled, they will continue to emerge from the pupae at just about the same time day after day. However, if after being kept under these controlled laboratory conditions they are suddenly shown some light in order to produce the effect of a false dawn, there is a permanent shift of phase and, after some transient behavior, they will change the time at which they emerge from the pupae to that corresponding to the dawn which they were last shown. This suggests that there is a very definite way in which these animals can tell the time; that is to say, in which they can recognize when 24 hours are over, even though there is nothing conscious about it.

* *American Economic Review* 51, no. 2 (May 1961), pp. 142–46.

Of course a clock mechanism suggests periodicity, and periodicity, to any good cycle theorist, suggests difference or differential equations. And in fact, after this biologist had been working on the subject for some time, he became aware of this possibility and set out to find a mathematician who could help him to determine an appropriate equation. This was done, a relationship was fitted by statistical methods, and it turned out that it was appropriate to use a nonlinear differential equation. It was found that one such equation could fit a great variety of the data which this man had available. Not only could it do that, but with the aid of the equation he was able to make a number of interesting predictions which were subsequently very closely confirmed by data which he was able to collect.

Here is where we come to the point of the story—the contrast between the situation of the biologist and that of the economic theorist—for the biologist who had obtained a very nice relationship on the basis of empirical data was totally unable to give any sort of analytical explanation of what he had. He had absolutely no model on which he could base a derivation of his mathematical relationship. We may, perhaps, generalize by remarking that biologists, with some notable exceptions, have data without models, whereas we in economic theory have models which usually are created without data. And in this way we have summarized one of the economic theorist's greatest weaknesses and one of his greatest strengths.

I would now like to emphasize the latter, the more pleasant, side: the fact that the economist is an expert model builder. Indeed, there are very few disciplines which produce model builders with such practice and such skill. This, I think, is one of the most important things which the economic theorist can contribute to the work of management science. In management science it is important—in fact, absolutely essential—to be able to recognize the structure of a managerial problem. In order to be able to analyze it at all and to be able to do so systematically, it is necessary to do several things: first of all, to undertake a judicious simplification—an elimination of minor details which are peripheral to the problem and which, if included in the model, would prevent any successful and systematic analysis. Second, it is important to capture in a formal statement the essence of all the interrelationships which characterize the situation, because it is only after stating these interrelationships so explicitly that we can hope to use the powerful techniques of rigorous analysis in the investigation of a managerial problem. It is the model which incorporates both these features; it is the central focus of the entire analysis which must capture the essence of the situation which is being investigated.

Thus, in any of the complex situations which are encountered in the systematic analysis of management problems, model building is a critical part of the investigation. Problems as diverse as the optimal size and composition of a department store product line or the location of a company's warehouses have one thing in common: their complexity—which arises to a large extent out of the network of interrelationships among their elements. An increase in the number of items carried in a store reduces the capacity for carrying stocks of other items: on the one hand it makes it more likely that the customer will find what she wants when she enters the store; on the other she may find more often that although the store usually carries what she desires, it happens to be out of it temporarily. The length of time a customer must search for an item is affected by a change in product line; the likelihood of "impulse" purchases is also affected, etc. The drawing together of such a diversity of strands is the major function of the model, without which most of our tools will not function. Moreover, in my experience it is not atypical that nearly half of the time spent in the investigation of such a problem is devoted to model building—to capturing the essence of the situation in a set of explicit relationships. For there are no cut and dried rules in model building. It is essentially a matter of discovery, involving all of the intangibles of discovery—hunch, insight, and intuition, and no holds are barred. Only after the model has been built can the problem sometimes be reduced to a routine by use of standard rules of calculation.

To my knowledge there are few classroom courses in this critical skill of model building, and, because it has no rules, it cannot be taught like trigonometry or chemistry. But apparently it can be learned by experience. And, as I have said, the economic theorist has had a great deal of experience in the construction and use of such models. When he employs some differential equations, you can almost be certain that he has derived them from a model which he built, not, like the biologist, from some data which he has collected.

This, then, is one of the major contributions which the economic theorist can, in my opinion, make to managerial analysis. It is, however, a skill and a predisposition that he brings with him, not a series of specific results.

This takes me to the second major point that I wish to make: the other way in which I think economic theory can be helpful to management science. I believe the most important thing a managerial economics student can get out of a course in economic analysis is not a series of theorems but rather a set of analytical methods. And for that reason I think it is far more important for him to learn the basis of these theorems, their assumption and their methods of derivation, than to end up with a group of conclusions. I can say quite categorically that I have never encountered a business problem in which my investigation was helped by any specific economic theorem, nor, may I add, have I ever met a practical problem in which I failed to be helped by the method of reasoning involved in the derivation of some economic theorem.

One of the major reasons that the proposition of economic theory are not directly applicable to management poblems is that the theory does not deal with the major concerns of the businessman. Product line, advertising, budgeting, sales force allocation, inventory levels, new product introduction are all relative strangers to the idealized firm of value theory whose major concern is price-output policy. Certainly there is little in the theoretical literature which refers directly to the warehouse location or the department store product line problems which were mentioned previously.

Even where more familiar theoretical matters, such as pricing problems, arise in practice, the results of the theory provide only limited help. This is because theorems in economic analysis deal with rather general abstract entities, with firms which have the peculiar and most interesting characteristics of actual companies eliminated from them in order to enable the analyst to draw conclusions which apply to the entire economy and not just to one or several particular firms. As a result, when attempting to apply these theorems, one finds that they have abstracted some of the features it is most essential to retain in order to analyze the specific situation with which one is faced in the market. The theory offers us fairly general admonitions, like the one which tells us that marginal cost must equal marginal revenue if we are to maximize profits—surely a statement which is not very much of a guide in application. I repeat that in my applied work I have never found any occasion to use either this theorem or any other such specific proposition of economic analysis.

But I have often found it absolutely essential to use the techniques of marginal analysis as it occurs in the theory of the firm, the theory of production, and in welfare economics. Several times I have even found it helpful to use the techniques and derivations of some of the elasticity theorems. This last illustration perhaps merits a little expansion. It may appear extraordinary that the elasticity theorems were of any use in application at all for they would seem to provide the ultimate illustration of tools whose use requires the availability of extensive data. However, the point I am making is that it was not the theorems but the methods of analysis and derivation which were employed. For example, an analogue of the elementary proposition that unit elasticity is the borderline between increasing and decreasing total revenue in response to a decrease in price can be applied in other situations. In fact, it is precisely because of the lack of data that it often becomes necessary to decide just where such break-even points occur, and in a number of cases I have found that the ability to prove that this critical point is sufficiently beyond what may reasonably be expected is an adequate substitute for the availability of data. Thus knowledge of the method of derivation of the theorems—and, indeed, of the spirit of the theorems themselves—often enables one to do things without data which otherwise would be pretty much out of the question.

But this is not the major point. If it is true—and it certainly has been true in my experience—that every firm and every managerial situation requires a model which is more or less unique, none of the standard theorems is going to fit in with it. It will be necessary, in effect, to derive special theorems which enable one to deal with that specific situation. Here one is helped, then, not by the generalized propositions which have been developed by the theorist, but by the methods which have enabled him to achieve his results which show us how analogous conclusions or analogous analyses can be conducted for the problems at hand. It is for this reason that I make my plea about the teaching of economics and economic theory to the managerial economist. The plea is not only that economic theory should be taught to the business student but that it should be presented to him pretty much as it is taught to the liberal arts student, with the emphasis not on a series of canned conclusions but on the methods of investigation on the derivations behind the results—on the analytic tools and methods.

There is a third way in which economic theory can help in managerial analysis—and, perhaps strangely, here the more elementary concepts of economics are primarily involved or, rather, concepts which though relatively sophisticated are used in a very elementary way. These elementary concepts can imbue the economist with habits of thought which enable him to avoid some significant pitfalls. For example, consider the case of external economies and diseconomies. How much can familiarity with this concept tell us about the dangers involved in directing one branch of an enterprise to maximize its profits in disregard of the effects of its actions on other parts of the firm! Similarly, we economists are made very sensitive by marginal analysis to the perils of resource allocation by average cost and profit—resource allocation rules of thumb which are so frequently encountered in business practice. Such bits of reasoning once led one of my colleagues, who was reviewing some of the cases cited in the literature of managerial analysis, to remark that he was amazed at how often this reading had forced him to recall his sophomore economics!

To summarize, then, I have suggested very little by way of concrete contribution from economic theory to managerial economics. With some exceptions, I have not said that this particular result or that particular body of discussion is essential or even particularly helpful for the managerial economist. I have been able to offer no illustrations of managerial problems in which I was able to use very specific pieces of the body of economic analysis. But this is right in line with the very nature of my major point: the assertion that a managerial economist can become a far more helpful member of a management group by virtue of his studies of economic analysis, primarily because there he learns to become an effective model builder and because there he acquires a very rich body of tools and techniques which can help him to deal with the problems of the firm in a far more rigorous, a far more probing, and a far deeper manner.

PART TWO

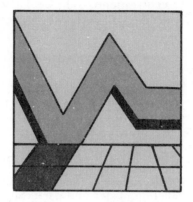

DEMAND

INTRODUCTION

The theoretical foundations of demand analysis are useful to the managerial economist. Useful also are empirical studies of demand. In empirical studies a demand curve, once established, holds true for the period of time and under the market conditions cited. Such being the case, empirical studies do not always correspond to the demand curves of economic theory. An understanding of this difference is necessary for the practicing business economist.

An understanding of demand for a firm's product requires identification of those factors which determine or influence existing sales volume. After a firm or industry defines as precisely as possible why its product is selling at current levels, it may be in a better position to consider certain changes; consequently, this Part Two dealing with demand is a necessary prelude to the one on forecasting, Part Seven.

Demand analysis is important to decision making in two ways: (1) it provides the basis for analyzing market influences on the firm's products and thus helps the firm adapt to the influences and (2) it provides guidance to the manipulation of demand itself. Some decisions require a passive adaptation to market forces, while others require the active shifting of those forces.

Unfortunately, the results of very few empirical demand analyses have stood up. The classic article by E. J. Working tells us why.

Demand for certain goods and services is created often by somewhat subjective notions held by the ultimate consumer. The desire of some consumers to be "in style" exists. Other consumers attempt to attain exclusiveness and, in fact, are somewhat snobbish in their behavior. The persistent existence of Veblen's "conspicuous consumption" are incorporated into the theory of consumer's demand by H. Leibenstein. This is a very unique and interesting approach to determination of a demand curve.

Most market studies of demand are either cross-sectional or time series. The article by Rodger D. Carlson derives the potential dollar demand for toothpaste in San Bernardino, California. The technique used in this article is illustrative of what could be done in any market, for any product for which data are available.

The research piece by Clements and Johnson illustrates how the system-wide approach to consumer demand can be extended so that it can be applied to narrowly defined commodity groups. This paper uses the consumption of beer, wine, and spirits to show how the approach can be applied to estimate income and price elasticities of demand for each. Assuming the ultimate consumer's utility function for alcoholic beverages can be separated, the paper establishes a demand model for a number of simulations designed to analyze the rapid growth of wine consumption. The methodology employed here is applicable to a large and growing number of situations in which the manager of scarce and costly resources finds him or herself.

Generally speaking, a demand curve may be elastic, inelastic, or unitary. In addition, demand functions are subject to systematic risk. But what about the demand for money? The paper by John B. Carlson examines the theoretical relationship of money to economic activity. It describes the fundamental ways in which new cash-management practices affect the demand (level) of cash balances.

6.

What Do Statistical "Demand Curves" Show?*

E. J. WORKING

Many questions of practical importance hinge upon the elasticity of demand, or of demand and supply. The economist can answer them only in a vague and indefinite manner, because he does not know the nature of the demand curve. What will be the effect of a five-million-bushel increase in the corn crop upon the price of corn and of hogs? What will be the effect of a tariff on imports and prices; on the protected industry; on the balance of international payments? How large an indemnity can Germany pay? The answers all depend in greater or less measure upon the elasticity of demand of the various commodities in question.

Such are the needs of the theorist, and in recent years a great deal of attention has been turned to the construction of statistical demand curves. Beef, corn, cotton, hay, hogs, pig iron, oats, potatoes, sweet potatoes, sugar, and wheat are on the list of commodities for which we have statements of the "law of demand." Many economists have been skeptical, while others have been enthusiastic, on the significance of such demand curves. In consequence of this divergence of opinion, it may be well to consider some of the theoretical aspects of what the demand curves constructed by our statistical experts may be expected to show. Do they correspond to the demand curves of economic theory? If so, it would seem that they represent something tangible by which our theories may be tested and turned to better account.

* *Quarterly Journal of Economics* 41, no. 2 (February 1927), pp. 212–35.

Among the statistical studies of demand that have been made, there are cases in which the same commodity has been studied by more than one investigator, and their results indicate varying degrees of elasticity of demand. But despite this, in all but one of the cases the demand curves have been negatively inclined—they have been in accord with Marshall's "one general *law of demand.*"

In the case of pig iron, however, Professor H. L. Moore finds a "law of demand" which is not in accord with Marshall's universal rule. He finds that the greater the quantity of pig iron sold, the higher will be the prices. If this is the nature of the statistical demand curve for pig iron, surely statistical demand curves must be of a very different sort from the demand curves of traditional economic theory!

Professor Moore holds that the statistical "law of demand" at which he arrives is a *dynamic* law, while that of theory is a *static* law. He says in part: "The doctrine of the uniformity of the demand function is an idol of the static state—the method of *cœteris paribus*—which has stood in the way of the successful treatment of dynamic problems." If it be true that statistical demand curves and the demand curves of theory differ so utterly from each other, of what value is statistical analysis to the theorist—of what value is economic theory to the statistical analyst? It would seem that so far as the study of demand is concerned, the statistical analyst and the economic theorist are on paths so divergent as to be wholly out of touch with each other. Before we accede to such a discouraging thought, let us examine a little more closely the nature of statistical demand curves as they may be viewed in the light of economic theory.

Let us first consider in what way statistical demand curves are constructed. While both the nature of the data used and the technique of analysis vary, the basic data consist of corresponding prices and quantities. That is, if a given quantity refers to the amount of a commodity sold, produced, or consumed in the year 1910, the corresponding price is the price which is taken to be typical of the year 1910. These corresponding quantities and prices may be for a period of a month, a year, or any other length of time which is feasible; and, as has already been indicated, the quantities may refer to amounts produced, sold, or consumed. The technique of analysis consists of such operations as fitting the demand curve, and adjusting the original data to remove, insofar as is possible, the effect of disturbing influences. For a preliminary understanding of the way in which curves are constructed, we need not be concerned with the differences in technique; but whether the quantities used are the amounts produced, sold, or consumed is a matter of greater significance, which must be kept in mind.

For the present, let us confine our attention to the type of study which uses for its data the quantities which have been sold in the market. In general, the method of constructing demand curves of this sort is to take corresponding prices and quantities, plot them, and draw a curve which will fit as nearly as possible all the plotted points. Suppose, for example, we wish to determine the demand curve for beef. First, we find out how many pounds of beef were sold in a given month and what was the average price. We do the same for all the other months of the period over which our study is to extend, and plot our data with quantities as abscissas and corresponding prices as ordinates. Next we draw a curve to fit the points. This is our demand curve.

In the actual construction of demand curves, certain refinements necessary in order to get satisfactory results are introduced. The purpose of these is to correct the data so as to remove the effect of various extraneous and complicating factors. For example, adjustments are usually made for changes in the purchasing power of money, and for changes in population and in consumption habits. Corrections may be made directly by such means as dividing all original price data by "an index of the general level of prices." They may be made indirectly by correction for trends of the two time series of prices and of quantities. Whatever the corrections and refinements, however, the essence of the method is that certain prices are taken as representing the prices at which certain quantities of the product in question were sold.

With this in mind, we may now turn to the theory of the demand-and-supply curve analysis of market prices. The conventional theory runs in terms substantially as follows. At any given time, all individuals within the scope of the market may be considered as being within two groups—potential buyers and potential sellers. The higher the price, the more the sellers will be ready to sell and the less the buyers will be willing to take. We may assume a demand schedule of the potential buyers and a supply schedule of the potential sellers which express the amounts that these groups are ready to buy and sell at different prices. From these schedules supply and demand curves may be made. Thus we have our supply and demand curves showing the market situation at any given time, and the price which results from this situation will be represented by the height of the point where the curves intersect.

This, however, represents the situation as it obtains at any given moment only. It may change; indeed, it is almost certain to change. The supply and demand curves which accurately represent the market situation of today will not represent that of a week hence. The curves which represent the average or aggregate of conditions this month will not hold true for the corresponding month of next year. In the case of the wheat market, for example, the effect of news that wheat which is growing in Kansas has been damaged by rust will cause a shift in both demand and supply schedules of the traders in the grain markets. The same (or a greater) amount of wheat will command a higher price than would have been the case if the news had failed to reach the traders. Since much of the buying and selling is speculative, changes in the market price itself may result in shifts of the demand and supply schedules.

If, then, our market demand-and-supply curves are to indicate conditions which extend over a period of time, we must represent them as shifting. A diagram such as the following, Figure 1, may be used to indicate them. The demand and supply curves may meet at any point within the area a, b, c, d, and over a period of time points of equilibrium will occur at many different places within it.

But what of statistical demand curves in the light of this analysis? If we construct a statistical demand curve from data of quantities sold and corresponding prices, our original data consist, in effect, of observations of points at which the demand and supply curves have met. Although we may wish to reduce our data to static conditions, we must remember that they originate in the market itself. The market is dynamic and our data extend over a period of time; consequently our data are of changing conditions and must be considered as the result of shifting demand and supply schedules.

Let us assume that conditions are such as those illustrated in Figure 2, the demand curve shifting from D_1 to D_2 and the supply curve shifting in similar manner from S_1 to S_2. It is to be noted that the chart shows approximately equal shifting of the demand and supply curves.

Under such conditions there will result a series of prices which may be graphically represented in Figure 3. It is from data such as those represented by the dots that we are to construct a demand curve, but evidently no satisfactory fit can be obtained. A line of one slope will give substantially as good a fit as will a line of any other slope.

FIGURE 1
Utility and Demands

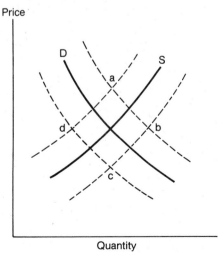

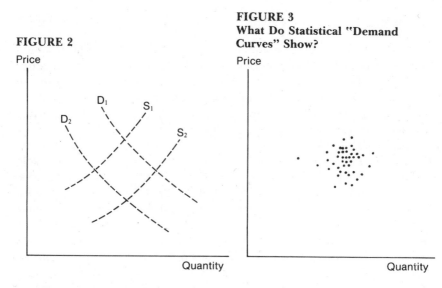

FIGURE 2

Price

FIGURE 3
What Do Statistical "Demand Curves" Show?

Price

Quantity

Quantity

But what happens if we alter our assumptions as to the relative shifting of the demand and supply curves? Suppose the supply curve shifts in some such manner as is indicated by Figure 4, that is, so that the shifting of the supply curve is greater than the shifting of the demand curve. We shall then obtain a very different set of observations—a set which may be represented by the dots of Figure 5. To these points we may fit a curve which will have the elasticity of the demand curve that we originally assumed, and whose position will approximate the central position about which the demand curve shifted. We may consider this to be a sort of typical demand curve, and from it we may determine the elasticity of demand.

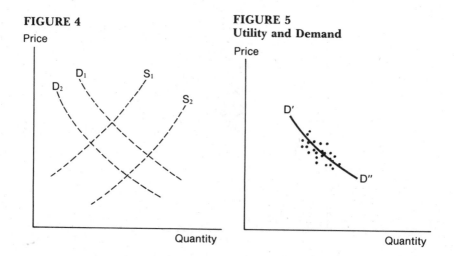

FIGURE 4

Price

FIGURE 5
Utility and Demand

Price

Quantity

Quantity

If, on the other hand, the demand schedules of buyers fluctuate more than do the supply schedules of sellers, we shall obtain a different result. This situation is illustrated by Figure 6. The resulting array of prices and quantities is of a very different sort from the previous case, and its nature is indicated by Figure 7. A line drawn so as most nearly to fit these points will approximate a supply curve instead of a demand curve.

If this analysis is in accord with the facts, is it not evident that Professor Moore's "law of demand" for pig iron is in reality a "law of supply" instead? The original observations of prices and corresponding quantities are the resultant of both supply and demand. Consequently, they do not necessarily reflect the influence of demand any more than that of supply. The methods used in constructing demand curves (particularly if the quantity data are of quantities sold) may, under some conditions, yield a demand curve, under others, a supply curve, and, under still different conditions, no satisfactory result may be obtained.

In the case of agricultural commodities, where production for any given year is largely influenced by weather conditions, and where farmers sell practically their entire crop regardless of price, there is likely to be a much greater shifting of the supply schedules of sellers than of the demand schedules of buyers. This is particularly true of perishable commodities, which cannot be withheld from the market without spoilage, and in any case the farmers themselves can under no conditions use more than a very small proportion of their entire production. Such a condition results in the supply curve shifting within very wide limits. The demand curve, on the other hand, may shift but little. The quantities which are consumed may be dependent almost entirely upon price, so that the only way to have a much larger amount taken off the market

FIGURE 6

Price

FIGURE 7

Price

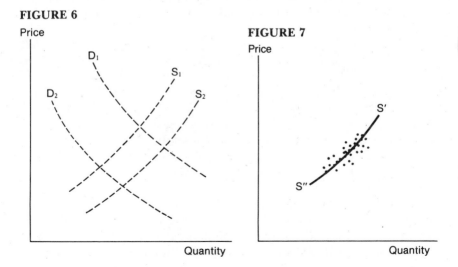

Quantity   Quantity

is to reduce the price, and any considerable curtailment of supply is sure to result in a higher price.

With other commodities, the situation may be entirely different. Where a manufacturer has complete control over the supply of the article which he produces, the price at which he sells may be quite definitely fixed, and the amount of his production will vary, depending upon how large an amount of the article is bought at the fixed price. The extent to which there is a similar tendency to adjust sales to the shifts of demand varies with different commodities, depending upon how large overhead costs are and upon the extent to which trade agreements or other means are used to limit competition between different manufacturers. In general, however, there is a marked tendency for the prices of manufactured articles to conform to their expenses of production, the amount of articles sold varying with the intensity of demand at that price which equals the expenses of production. Under such conditions, the supply curve does not shift greatly, but rather approximates an expenses-of-production curve, which does not vary much from month to month or from year to year. If this condition is combined with a fluctuating demand for the product, we shall have a situation such as that shown in Figures 6 and 7, where the demand curves shift widely and the supply curves only a little.

From this, it would seem that, whether we obtain a demand curve or a supply curve, by fitting a curve to a series of points which represent the quantities of an article sold at various prices, depends upon the fundamental nature of the supply and demand conditions. It implies the need of some term in addition to that of elasticity in order to describe the nature of supply and demand. The term *variability* may be used for this purpose. For example, the demand for an article may be said to be "elastic" if, at a given time a small reduction in price would result in a much greater quantity being sold, while it may be said to be "variable" if the demand curve shows a tendency to shift markedly. To be called variable, the demand curve should have the tendency to shift back and forth, and not merely to shift gradually and consistently to the right or left because of changes of population or consuming habits.

Whether a demand or a supply curve is obtained may also be affected by the nature of the corrections applied to the original data. The corrections may be such as to reduce the effect of shifting of the demand schedules without reducing the effect of the shifting of the supply schedules. In such a case the curve obtained will approximate a demand curve, even though the original demand schedules fluctuated fully as much as did the supply schedules.

By intelligently applying proper refinements, and making corrections to eliminate separately those factors which cause demand curves to shift and those factors which cause supply curves to shift, it may be possible even to obtain both a demand curve and a supply curve for the same product and from the same original data. Certainly it may be possible, in many cases where satisfactory demand curves have not been obtained, to find instead the supply curves of the articles in question. The supply curve obtained by such methods, it is to be noted, would be a market supply curve rather than a normal supply curve.

Thus far it has been assumed that the supply and demand curves shift quite independently and at random; but such need not be the case. It is altogether possible that a shift of the demand curve to the right may, as a rule, be accompanied by a shift of the supply curve to the left, and vice versa. Let us see what result is to be expected under such conditions. If successive positions of the demand curve are represented by the curves D_1, D_2, D_3, D_4, and D_5 of Figure 8, while the curves S_1, S_2, S_3, S_4, and S_5 represent corresponding positions of the supply curves, then a series of prices will result from the intersection of D_1 with S_1, D_2 with S_2, and so on. If a curve be fitted to these points, it will not conform to the theoretical demand curve. It will have a smaller elasticity, as is shown by $D'D''$ of Figure 8. If, on the other hand, a shift of the demand curve to the right is accompanied by a shift of the supply curve to the right, we shall obtain a result such as that indicated by $D'D''$ in Figure 9. The fitted curve again fails to conform to the theoretical one, but in this case it is more elastic.

If there is a change in the range through which the supply curve shifts, as might occur through the imposition of a tariff on an imported good, a new fitted curve will result, which will not be a continuation of the former one—this because the fitted curve does not correspond to the true demand curve. In case, then, of correlated shifts of the demand and supply curves, a fitted curve cannot be considered to be the

FIGURE 8
Utility and Demand

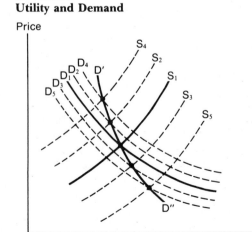

Price

Quantity

FIGURE 9

Price

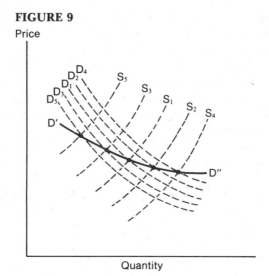

Quantity

demand curve for the article. It cannot be used, for example, to estimate what change in price would result from the levying of a tariff upon the commodity.

Perhaps a word of caution is needed here. It does not follow from the foregoing analysis that, when conditions are such that shifts of the supply and demand curves are correlated, an attempt to construct a demand curve will give a result which will be useless. Even though shifts of the supply and demand curves are correlated, a curve which is fitted to the points of intersection will be useful for purposes of price forecasting, provided no new factors are introduced which did not affect the price during the period of the study. Thus, so long as the shifts of the supply and demand curves remain correlated in the same way, and so long as they shift through approximately the same range, the curve of regression of price upon quantity can be used as a means of estimating price from quantity.

In cases where it is impossible to show that the shifts of the demand and supply curves are not correlated, much confusion would probably be avoided if the fitted curves were not called demand curves (or supply curves), but if, instead, they were called merely lines of regression. Such curves may be useful, but we must be extremely careful in our interpretation of them. We must also make every effort to discover whether the shifts of the supply and demand curves are correlated before interpreting the results of any fitted curve.

*   *   *   *   *

In assuming that we are dealing with quantities actually sold in the market, and in disregarding the fact that for many commodities there is a whole series of markets at various points in the marketing chain, we have simplified our problem. But it has been more than mere simplification, for the interpretation which is to be placed on statistical demand curve is a "particular" or a "general" demand curve, depends upon whether or not we use quantities sold. Whether it represents consumer or dealer demand, depends upon the point in the marketing chain to which the quantities sold refer.

Most theorists are acquainted with the concept of the general demand curve as it is presented by Wicksteed and Davenport. Briefly, the idea is that demand should be considered as including not merely the quantities that are bought, but rather all those in existence. The general demand curve, then, includes the possessors of a commodity as having a demand for it at any price below their reservation price, even if they are prospective sellers. Instead of showing the amounts that will be bought at various prices, it shows the marginal money valuation which will be placed upon varying quantities of an existing supply.

Wicksteed even indicates that the supply curve ought not to be considered at all. The following gives an intimation of his viewpoint:

> But what about the "supply curve" that usually figures as a determinant of price, coördinate with the demand curve? I say it boldly and badly: There is no such thing. When we are speaking of a marketable commodity, what is usually called a supply curve is in reality a demand curve of those who possess the commodity; for it shows the exact place which every successive unit of the commodity holds in their relative scale of estimates. The so-called supply curve, therefore, is simply a part of the total demand curve.[1]

Thus the general demand curve is an expression of the relation between the supply of a commodity and its valuation.

* * * * *

The amount of a commodity sold at one point in the marketing chain may differ from that sold at another in much the same way that the amount produced may differ from the amount sold. This is particularly true if monthly data are used. A case in point would be the demand for eggs. The amount of eggs sold by farmers in the spring of the year is greatly in excess of the amount sold by retail dealers, while in the winter months it is much less. Since differentials between the prices received by farmers and those received by retail dealers remain fairly constant, very different demand curves would be obtained. The consumers' demand curve would be very much less elastic than that of the dealers who buy from farmers.

Differences between dealer demand and consumer demand are

---

[1] P. H. Wicksteed, "The Scope and Method of Political Economy in the Light of the 'Marginal Theory of Value,'" *Economic Journal*, March 1914, p. 1.

largely dependent upon whether we are considering short or long periods. Over long periods of time, dealer demand tends to conform to consumer demand. This difference, however, is not a thing which depends upon the length of period over which the data extend, but of the length of period to which the individual observations of prices and quantities refer. In the case of eggs, if yearly data were used, the principal difference which would be found between the elasticity of consumer and dealer demands would be due to price differentials alone.

The questions whether statistical demand curves are static or dynamic is a perplexing one and rather difficult to deal with. This is largely due to uncertainty as to just what is meant by the terms *static* and *dynamic*. Moore holds that his "laws of demand" are dynamic, and that this is an eminently desirable feature. Schultz, while considering it most desirable to obtain both a static and a dynamic law by means of multiple correlation, holds that the statistical devices of relative changes and of trend ratios give a static "law of demand."

Conditions are often defined as being static or dynamic on two different grounds. They may be called static if they refer to a point of time; or else they may be said to be static if all other things are held equal. Statements such as these, however, lack much in clarity and accuracy. How can a statement be made as to prices at which different quantities of a commodity will sell at a *point* of time? Is it really supposed that *all* other things must be held equal in order to study the demand of the commodity? Rather, the real supposition, though it may not be accurately expressed, is that the relationships between the various economic factors should be the same as those which exist at a given point of time, or that the relationships between these factors should remain constant.

The data used in a statistical study of demand must, of course, extend over a period of time, but they may in effect conform to conditions at a point of time if trend is removed and if there is no other change in the relationship between quantity and price. Of course, the shifting of the demand and supply curves constitutes a change in the relationship between the quantity and price, but the process of curve fitting corresponds to that of averaging. Consequently, the fitted curve may be considered to depict the average relationship between quantity and price. This amounts to the same thing as representing the relationship at a point of time which is typical for the period studied. In this sense, then, of relating to a point of time, Moore's "laws of demand" are static instead of dynamic.

Holding "all other things equal," however, is a different matter. Schultz states the difficulty in the following manner:

> In *theory* the law of demand for any one commodity is given only on the assumption that the prices of all other commodities remain constant (the

old *ceteris paribus* assumption). This postulate fails in the case of commodities for which substitutes are available. Thus when the price of beef is changed markedly, the prices of such rival commodities as mutton, veal, and pork cannot be supposed to remain constant. Likewise, the price of sugar cannot be increased beyond a certain point without affecting the prices of glucose, corn sugar, and honey.[2]

Marshall makes similar restrictions as to the need for other things to be held equal, and suggests that in some cases it may be best to "group together commodities as distinct as beef and mutton," in order to obtain a demand curve which will not be too restricted because of other things being equal.

The question arises, however, whether it is desirable to hold all other things equal in any case. Is it not better to have a demand curve for beef which expresses the relation between the price and quantity of beef while the prices of pork, mutton, and veal, vary as they normally do, with different prices of beef? Furthermore, may not this be called a static condition? The point can perhaps be made clearer if we take an extreme example. If we are studying the demand for wheat, it would be almost meaningless to get the demand curve for No. 2 Winter wheat while holding the price of all other grades of wheat constant. Other grades of wheat can be so readily substituted that the demand would be almost completely elastic. The difference between this and holding the prices of pork, mutton, and veal constant, while the price of beef varies, is only one of degree—a difference which depends upon the ease with which substitutes can be used in place of the article whose demand is being studied.

All other things being held equal is not a condition represented by a statistical law of demand or, strictly interpreted, of any useful demand curve theory. Some of the things that are correlated with the price of the commodity in question may be held equal, but it is impossible for all things to be held equal. However, a statistical law of demand represents a condition under which the relationships between factors may be considered to have remained the same, or, to put it more accurately, a condition which is an average of the relationships during the period studied.

In conclusion, then, it is evident that the mere statement that the demand for a commodity has a given elasticity is meaningless. As with the results of all other statistical analysis, statistical demand curves must be interpreted in the light of the nature of the original data and of the methods of analysis used. There are four questions, the answers to which are particularly important to know. They concern (1) whether the supply or demand curve is more variable, (2) the market to which

---

[2] Henry Schultz, "The Statistical Law of Demand," *The Journal of Political Economy* (October and December 1925). See pp. 498–502 of October issue.

the price and quantity data refer, (3) the extent to which "other things are held equal," and (4) whether the shifting of the supply and demand curves is correlated or random.

For precision, it is preferable that the data of price and quantity should refer to the same market. Yet this may be out of the question. In a study of the demand for wheat, for example, if we want to obtain a demand curve of the quantity demanded by the entire country, we cannot use prices for all different points and for all different grades. Instead, the price at one market and for one grade may be used as representative, and the demand of the entire country determined for various prices at the one marketplace. If the price at any other market or for any other grade were used, the elasticity of demand might be different.

Furthermore, the point in the market chain must be specified and the results interpreted accordingly. As is the case with geographical points, it is preferable that the quantities and prices should refer to the same stage in the marketing process. If this is not the case, the interpretation should be made with the situation in view.

It is to be expected that the methods used in constructing statistical demand curves should be such as to give a demand curve which presents a point of time, that is, that trends in both quantities and prices are removed, or else multiple correlation is used to effect the same result. If, in addition to this, other things are held constant, the fact should be noted and the elasticity of demand should be stated as referring to a condition where these other things are held constant.

The matter of correlation between shifts of the demand and supply curves is a more difficult problem to deal with. Every effort should be made to discover whether there is a tendency for the shifting of these to be interdependent. In case it is impossible to determine this, it should be carefully noted that the demand curve which is obtained is quite likely not to hold true for periods other than the one studied, and cannot be treated as corresponding to the demand curve of economic theory.

7.

Bandwagon, Snob, and Veblen Effects in the Theory of Consumers' Demand*

H. LEIBENSTEIN

I. THE NATURE OF THE PROBLEM

The desire of some consumers to be "in style," the attempts by others to attain exclusiveness, and the phenomena of "conspicuous consumption," have as yet not been incorporated into the current theory of consumers' demand. My purpose, in this paper, is to take a step or two in that direction.

1. "Nonadditivity" in Consumers' Demand Theory

This enquiry was suggested by some provocative observations made by Professor Oskar Morgenstern in his article, "Demand Theory Reconsidered." After examining various aspects of the relationship between individual demand curves and collective market demand curves Professor Morgenstern points out that in some cases the market demand curve is not the lateral summation of the individual demand curves. The following brief quotation may indicate the nature of what he calls "nonadditiv-

* *Quarterly Journal of Economics* 64 (February 1950), pp. 183–207.

ity" and gives some indication of the problem involved. "Nonadditivity in this simple sense is given, for example, in the case of fashions, where one person buys because another is buying the same thing, or vice versa. But the phenomenon of nonadditivity is in fact much deeper; since virtually all collective supply curves are nonadditive it follows that the demand of the firms for their labor, raw materials, etc. is also nonadditive. This expands the field of nonadditivity enormously."

Since the purpose of Professor Morgenstern's article is immanent criticism he does not present solutions to the problems he raises. He does clearly imply, however, that since coalitions are bound to be important in this area only the "Theory of Games" . . . is likely to give an adequate solution to this problem. The present writer is not competent to judge whether this is or is not the case, but he does believe that there are many markets where coalitions among consumers are not widespread or of significance, and hence abstracting from the possibility of such coalitions may not be unreasonable. Should this be the case we may be able to make some headway through the use of conventional analytical methods.

What we shall therefore be concerned with substantially is a reformulation of some aspects of the static theory of consumers' demand while permitting the relaxation of one of the basic implicit assumptions of the current theory—namely, that the consumption behavior of any individual is independent of the consumption of others. This will permit us to take account of consumers' motivations not heretofore incorporated into the theory. To be more specific, the proposed analysis is designed to take account of the desire of people to wear, buy, do, consume, and behave like their fellows; the desire to join the crowd, be "one of the boys," etc.—phenomena of mob motivations and mass psychology either in their grosser or more delicate aspects. This is the type of behavior involved in what we shall call the "bandwagon effect." On the other hand, we shall also attempt to take account of the search for exclusiveness by individuals through the purchase of distinctive clothing, foods, automobiles, houses, or anything else that individuals may believe will in some way set them off from the mass of mankind—or add to their prestige, dignity, and social status. In other words, we shall be concerned with the impact on the theory created by the potential nonfunctional utilities inherent in many commodities.

2. The Past Literature

The past literature on the interpersonal aspects of utility and demand can be divided into three categories: sociology, welfare economics, and pure theory. The sociological writings deal with the phenomena of fashions and conspicuous consumption and their relationship to social status and human behavior. This treatment of the subject was made famous by Veblen—although Veblen, contrary to the notions of many, was neither the discoverer nor the first to elaborate upon the theory of conspicuous consumption. John Rae, writing before 1834, has quite an extensive treatment of conspicuous consumption, fashions, and related matters pretty much along Veblenian lines. Rae attributes many of these ideas to earlier writers, going so far as to find the notion of conspicuous consumption in the Roman poet Horace; and a clear statement of the "keeping up with the Joneses" idea in the verse of Alexander Pope. An excellent account of how 18th and 19th century philosophers and economists handled the problem of fashion is given in Norine Foley's article "Fashion." For the most part, these treatments are of a "sociological" nature.

The economist concerned with public policy will probably find the "economic welfare" treatment of the problem most interesting. Here, if we examine the more recent contributions first and then go backward, we find examples of current writers believing they have stumbled upon something new, although they had only rediscovered what had been said many years before. Thus, Professor Melvin Reder in his treatment of the theory of welfare economics claims that ". . . there is another type of external repercussion which is rarely, *if ever*, recognized in discussions of welfare economics. It occurs where the utility function of one individual contains, as variables, the quantities of goods consumed by other persons." It can only be lack of awareness of the past literature that causes Reder to imply that this consideration has not been taken up before. Among those who considered the problem earlier are J. E. Meade, A. C. Pigou, Henry Cunynghame, and John Rae.

The similarity in the treatment of this matter by Reder and Rae is at times striking. For example, Reder suggests that legislation forbidding "invidious expenditure" may result in an increase in welfare by freeing resources from "competitive consumption" to other uses. In a similar vein Rae argued that restrictions on the trade of "pure luxuries" can only be a gain to some and a loss to none, in view of the labor saved in avoiding the production of "pure luxuries." It is quite clear from the context that what Rae calls "pure luxuries" is exactly the same as Reder's commodities that enter into "competitive consumption."

One reason why the interpersonal effects on demand have been ignored in current texts may be the fact that Marshall did not consider the matter in his *Principles.* We know, however, from Marshall's correspondence, that he was aware of the problem. Both Cunynghame and Pigou pointed out that Marshall's treatment of consumers' surplus did not take into account interpersonal effects on utility. Marshall seemed to feel that this would make the diagrammatical treatment too complex. Recently, Reder and Samuelson noticed that external economies and diseconomies of consumption may vitiate (or, at best, greatly complicate) their "new" welfare analysis, and hence, in true academic fashion, they assume the problem away. This, however, is not the place to examine the question in detail.

The only attack on the problem from the point of view of pure theory that the writer could find is a short article by Professor Pigou. In this article Pigou sets out to inquire under what circumstances the assumption of the additivity of the individual demand curves "adequately conforms to the facts, and, when it does not so conform, what alternative assumption ought to be substituted for it." It is obvious that the particular choice of alternative assumptions will determine (a) whether a solution can, given the existing analytical tools, be obtained and (b) whether such a solution is relevant to the real world. Pigou's treatment of the problem is, unfortunately, exceedingly brief. He attempts to deal with nonadditivity in both supply and demand curves within the confines of six pages. In examining the additivity assumption he points out that it is warranted when (1) the demand for the commodity is wholly for the direct satisfaction yielded by it or (2) where disturbances to equilibrium are so small that aggregate output is not greatly changed. After briefly suggesting some of the complexities of nonadditivity he concludes that the ". . . problems, for the investigation of which it is necessary to go behind the demand schedule of the market as a whole, are still, theoretically, soluble; there are a sufficient number of equations to determine the unknowns." This last point, which is not demonstrated in Pigou's article, is hardly satisfying since it has been shown that the equality of equations and unknowns is not a sufficient condition for a determinate solution, or indeed for any solution, to exist.

3. The Approach and Limits of the Ensuing Analysis

It should, perhaps, be pointed out at the outset that the ensuing exposition is limited to statics. In all probability, the most interesting parts of the problem, and also those most relevant to real problems, are its dynamic aspects. However, a static analysis is probably necessary, and may be of significance, in order to lay a foundation for a dynamic analysis. In view of the limitations to be set on the following analysis, it becomes necessary to demarcate clearly the conceptual borderline between statics and dynamics.

There are, unfortunately, numerous definitions of statics and there seems to be some confusion on the matter. In view of this it will not be possible to give *the* definition of statics. All that we can hope to do is to choose *a* definition that will be consistent with, and useful for, our purposes—and also one that at the same time does not stray too far from some of the generally accepted notions about statics. Because of the fact that we live in a dynamic world most definitions of statics will imply a state of affairs that contradicts our general experience. But this is of necessity the case. What we must insist on is internal consistency but we need not, at this stage, require "realism."

Our task, then, is to define a static situation—a situation in which static economics is applicable. Ordinarily, it is thought that statics is in some way "timeless." This need not be the case. For our purposes, a static situation is not a "timeless" situation, nor is static economics timeless economics. It is, however, "temporally orderless" economics. That is, we shall define a static situation as one in which the order of events is of no significance. We, therefore, abstract from the consequences of the temporal order of events. The above definition is similar to, but perhaps on a slightly higher level of generality than, Hicks's notion that static deals with "those parts of economic theory where we do not have to trouble about dating."

In order to preserve internal consistency, it is necessary to assume that the period of reference is one in which the consumer's income and expenditure pattern is synchronized. And, we have to assume also that this holds true for all consumers. In other words, we assume that both the income patterns and the expenditure patterns repeat themselves *every* period. There is thus no overlapping of expenditures from one period into the next. This implies, of course, that the demand curve reconstitutes itself every period. The above implies also that only one price can exist during any unit period and that price can change only from period to period. A disequilibrium can, therefore, be corrected only over two or more periods.

II. FUNCTIONAL AND NONFUNCTIONAL DEMAND

At the outset it is probably best to define clearly some of the basic terms we are going to use and to indicate those aspects of demand that we are going to treat. The demand for consumers' goods and services may be classified according to motivation. The following classification, which we shall find useful, is on a level of abstraction which, it is hoped, includes most of the motivations behind consumers' demand.

A. Functional
B. Nonfunctional
   1. External effects on utility
      a. Bandwagon effect
      b. Snob effect
      c. Veblen effect
   2. Speculative
   3. Irrational

By functional demand is meant that part of the demand for a commodity which is due to the qualities inherent in the commodity itself.

By nonfunctional demand is meant that portion of the demand for a consumers' good which is due to factors other than the qualities inherent in the commodity. Probably the most important kind of nonfunctional demand is due to external effects on utility. That is, the utility derived from the commodity is enhanced or decreased owing to the fact that others are purchasing and consuming the same commodity, or owing to the fact that the commodity bears a higher rather than a lower price tag. We differentiate this type of demand into what we shall call the "bandwagon" effect, the "snob" effect, and the "Veblen" effect. By the bandwagon effect, we refer to the extent to which the demand for a commodity is *increased* due to the fact that others are also consuming the same commodity. It represents the desire of people to purchase a commodity in order to get into "the swim of things"; in order to conform with the people they wish to be associated with; in order to be fashionable or stylish; or, in order to appear to be "one of the boys." By the snob effect we refer to the extent to which the demand for a consumers' good is *decreased* owing to the fact that others are also consuming the same commodity (or that others are increasing their consumption of that commodity). This represents the desire of people to be exclusive; to be different; to dissociate themselves from the "common herd." By the Veblen effect we refer to the phenomenon of conspicuous consumption; to the extent to which the demand for a consumers' good is increased because it bears a higher rather than a lower price. We should perhaps emphasize the distinction between the snob and the Veblen effect—the former is a function of the consumption of others, the latter is a function of price. This paper will deal almost exclusively with these three types of nonfunctional demand.

For the sake of completeness there should perhaps be some explanation as to what is meant by speculative and irrational demand. Speculative demand refers to the fact that people will often "lay in" a supply of a commodity because they expect its price to rise. Irrational demand is, in a sense, a catchall category. It refers to purchases that are neither planned nor calculated but are due to sudden urges, whims, and so forth, and that serve no rational purpose but that of satisfying sudden whims and desires.

In the above it was assumed throughout that income is a parameter. If income is not given but allowed to vary, then the income effect on demand may in most cases be the most important effect of all. Also, it may be well to point out that the above is only one of a large number of possible classifications of the types of consumers' demand—classifications that for some purposes may be superior to the one here employed. We therefore suggest the above classification only for the purposes at hand and make no claims about its desirableness, or effectiveness, in any other use.

III. THE BANDWAGON EFFECT

1. A Conceptual Experiment

Our immediate task is to obtain aggregate demand curves of various kinds in those cases where the individual demand curves are nonadditive. First we shall examine the case where the bandwagon effect is important. In its pure form this is the case where an individual will demand more (less) of a commodity at a given price because some or all other individuals in the market also demand more (less) of the commodity.

One of the difficulties in analyzing this type of demand involves the choice of assumptions about the knowledge that each individual possesses. This implies that everyone knows the quantity that will be demanded by every individual separately, or the quantity demanded by all individuals collectively at any given price—after all the reactions and adjustments that individuals make to each other's demand has taken place. On the other hand, if we assume ignorance on the part of consumers about the demand of others, we have to make assumptions as to the nature and extent of the ignorance—ignorance is a relative concept. A third possibililty, and the one that will be employed at first, is to devise some mechanism whereby the consumers obtain accurate information.

Another problem involves the choice of assumptions to be made about the demand behavior of individual consumers. Three possibilities suggest themselves: (1) The demand of consumer A (at given prices) may be a function of the total demand of all others in the market collectively. Or, (2) the demand of consumer A may be a function of the demand of all other consumers both separately and collectively. In other words, A's demand may be more influenced by the demand of some than by the demand of others. (3) A third possibility is that A's demand is a function of the number of people that demand the commodity rather than the number of units demanded. More complex demand behavior patterns that combine some of the elements of the above are conceivable. For present purposes it is best that we assume the simplest one as a first approximation. Initially, therefore, we assume that A's demand is a function of the units demanded by all others collectively. This is the same as saying that A's demand is a function of total market demand at given prices, since A always knows his own demand, and he could always subtract his own demand from the total market demand to get the quantity demanded by all others.

In order to bring out the central principle involved in the ensuing analysis, consider the following *gedankenexperiment*. A known product is to be introduced into a well-defined market at a certain date. The nature of the product is such that its demand depends partially on the functional qualities of the commodity, and partially on whether many or few units are demanded. Our technical problem is to compound the nonadditive individual demand curves into a total market demand curve, given sufficient information about the individual demand functions. Now, suppose that it is possible to obtain an accurate knowledge of the demand function of an individual through a series of questionnaires. Since an individual's demand is, in part, a function of the total market demand, it is necessary to take care of this difficulty in our questionnaires. We can have a potential consumer fill out the first questionnaire by having him assume that the total market demand, at all prices, is a given very small amount—say 400 units. On the basis of this assumption the consumer would tell us the quantities he demands over a reasonable range of prices. Subjecting every consumer to the same questionnaire, we add the results across and obtain a market demand curve that would reflect the demand situation if every consumer believed the total demand were only 400 units. This, however, is not the real market demand function under the assumption of the possession of accurate market information by consumers, since the total demand (at each price) upon which consumers based their replies was not the actual market demand (at each price) as revealed by the results of the survey. Let us call the results of the first survey "schedule No. 1."

We can now carry out a second survey, that is, subject each consumer to a second questionnaire in which each one is told that schedule No. 1 reflects the total quantities demanded, at each price. Aggregating the replies we obtain schedule No. 2 Schedule No. 1 then becomes a parameter upon which schedule No. 2 is based. In a similar manner we can obtain schedules No. 3, No. 4, . . . , No. *n* in which each schedule is the result of adding the quantities demanded by each consumer (at each price), *if each consumer believes that the total quantities demanded (at each price) are shown by the previous schedule.* Now, the quantities demanded in schedule No. 2 will be greater than, or equal to, the quantities demanded in schedule No. 1 for the same prices. Some consumers may increase the quantity they demand when they note that the total quantity demanded, at given prices, is greater than they thought it would be. As long as some consumers or potential consumers continue to react positively to increases in the total quantity demanded the results of successive survey will be different. That is, some or all of the quantities demanded in schedule No. 1 will be less than the quantities demanded at the same prices, in schedule No. 2, which in turn will be equal to or less than the quantities demanded, at the same prices, in schedule No. 3, and so on.

At this point it is appropriate to introduce a new principle with the intention of showing that this process cannot go on indefinitely. Sooner or later two successive schedules will be identical. If two successive surveys yield the same market demand schedules, then an equilibrium situation exists since the total quantities demanded, at each price, upon which individual consumers based their demand, turns out to be correct. Thus, if schedule No. n is identical with schedule No. n-1, then schedule No. n is the actual market demand function for the product on the assumption that consumers have accurate information of market conditions.

The question that arises is whether there is any reason to suppose that sooner or later two successive surveys will yield exactly the same result. This would indeed be the case if we could find good reason to posit a principle to the effect that for every individual there is some point at which he will cease to increase the quantities demanded for a commodity, at given prices, in response to incremental increases in total market demand. Such a principle would imply that beyond a point incremental increases in the demand for the commodity by others have a decreasing influence on a consumer's own demand; and, further, that a point is reached at which these increases in demand by others have no influence whatsoever on his own demand. It would, of course, also be necessary to establish that such a principle holds true for every consumer. It would not be inappropriate to call this the principle of diminishing marginal consumption effect. Does such a principle really exist? There are some good reasons for believing that it does. First, the reader may note that the principle is analogous to the principle of diminishing marginal utility. As the total market demand grows larger, incremental increases in total demand become smaller and smaller proportions of the demand. It sounds reasonable and probably appeals to us intuitively that an individual would be less influenced, and indeed take less notice of, a 1 percent increase in total demand, than of a 10 percent increase in total demand, though these percentage increases be the same in absolute amount. Second, we can probably appeal effectively to general experience. There are no cases in which an individual's demand for a consumers' good increases endlessly with increases in total demand. If there were two or more such individuals in a market then the demand for the commodity would increase in an endless spiral. Last but not least, the income constraint is sufficient to establish that there must be a point at which increases in a consumer's demand must fail to respond to increases in demand by others. Since every consumer is subject to the income constraint, it must follow that the principle holds for all consumers.

Now, to get back to our conceptual experiment, we would find that after administering a sufficient number of surveys, we would sooner or later get two surveys that yield identical demand schedules. The result of the last survey would then represent the true demand situation that would manifest itself on the market when the commodity was offered for sale. We may perhaps justly call such a demand function the equilibrium demand function—or demand curve. The equilibrium demand curve is the curve that exists when the marginal external consumption effect for every consumer, but one, at all alternate prices is equal to zero. All other demand curves may be conceived as disequilibrium curves that can exist only because of temporarily imperfect knowledge by consumers of other people's demand. Once the errors in market information were discovered such a curve would move to a new position.

2. The Bandwagon Effect— Diagrammatical Method

The major purpose of going through the conceptual experiment with its successive surveys was to illustrate the diminishing marginal external consumption effect and to indicate its role in obtaining a determinate demand curve. There is, however, a relatively simple method for obtaining the market demand function in those cases where external consumption effects are significant. This method will allow us to compare some of the properties of the "bandwagon demand curve" with the usual "functional" demand curve; and, it will also allow us to separate the extent to which a change in demand is due to a change in price, and the extent to which it is due to the bandwagon effect.

Given a certain total demand for a commodity as a parameter, every individual will have a demand function based on this total market demand. Let the alternative total market demands that will serve as parameters for alternate individual demand functions be indicated as superscripts $a, b, \ldots n$ (where $a < b < \ldots < n$). Let the individual demand functions be $d_1, d_2, \ldots d_n$; where every subscript indicates a different consumer. Thus d_3^a is the individual demand curve for consumer 3 if the consumer believes that the total market demand is a units. Similarly d_{500}^m is the individual demand curve for the 500th consumer if he believes that the total market demand will be m units. We could now add across $d_1^a, d_2^a, d_3^a, \ldots, d_n^a$ which will give us the market demand curve D^a, which indicates the quantities demanded at alternate prices if all consumers believed that the total demand was a units. In the same manner we can obtain $D^b, D^c, \ldots, D^n$. These hypothetical market demand curves $D^a, D^b, D^c, \ldots, D^n$ are shown in Figure 1. Now, if we assume that buyers have accurate knowledge of market conditions (i.e., of the total quantities demanded at every price) then only one point on any of the curves $D^a, D^b, \ldots, D^n$ could be on the real or equilibrium demand curve. These are the points on each curve $D^a, D^b, \ldots, D^n$ that represent the amounts on which the consumers based their individual demand curves; that is, the amounts that consumers expected to be the total market demand. These points are labeled in Figure 1 as $E^a, E^b, \ldots, E^n$. They are a series of virtual equilibrium points. Given that consumers possess accurate market information, $E^a, E^b, \ldots, E^n$, are the only points that can become actual quantities demanded. The locus of all

FIGURE 1

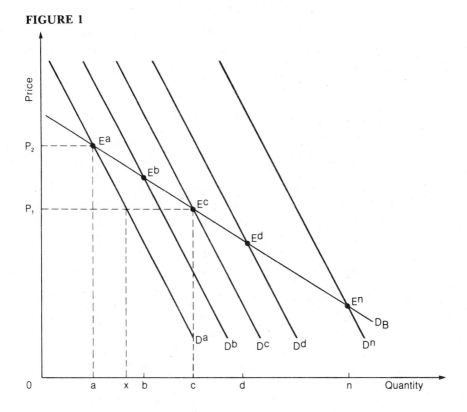

these points D_B is therefore the actual demand curve for the commodity.

It may be of interest, at this point, to break up changes in the quantity demanded due to changes in price into a price effect and a bandwagon effect; that is, the extent of the change that is due to the change in price, and the extent of the change in demand that is due to consumers adjusting to each other's changed consumption. With an eye on Figure 1 consider the effects of a reduction in price from P_2 to P_1. The increase in demand after the change in price is ac. Only part of that increase, however, is due to the reduction in price. To measure the amount due to the reduction in price we go along the demand curve D^a to P_1 which tells us the quantity that would be demanded at P_1 if consumers did not adjust to each other's demands. This would result in an increase in demand of ax. Due to the bandwagon effect, however, an additional number of consumers are induced to enter the market or to increase their demands. There is now an additional increase in demand of xc after consumers have adjusted to each other's increases in consumption. Exactly the same type of analysis can, of course, be carried out for increases as well as for decreases in price.

We may note another thing from Figure 1. The demand curve D_B

is more elastic than any of the other demand curves shown in the diagram. This would suggest that other things being equal, the demand curve will be more elastic if there is a bandwagon effect than if the demand is based only on the functional attributes of the commodity.

3. Social Taboos and the Bandwagon Effect

Social taboos, to the extent that they affect consumption, are, in a sense, bandwagon effects in reverse gear. That is to say, some people will not buy and consume certain things because other people are not buying and consuming these things. Thus, there may not be any demand for a commodity even though it has a functional utility, although, apart from the taboo, it would be purchased. Individual A will not buy the commodity because individuals B, C, and D do not, while individuals B, C, and D may refrain from consumption for the same reasons. It is not within the competence of the economist to investigate the psychology of this kind of behavior. For our purposes we need only note that such behavior exists and attempt to analyze how such behavior affects the demand function.

We can proceed as follows. Let d_1^x be the demand curve of the least inhibited individual in the market, where the superscript x is the total quantity demanded in the market upon which he bases his individual demand. Suppose that at market demand x consumer 1 will demand at some range of prices one unit of the commodity, but at no price will he demand more. If he believes, however, that the total market demand is less than x units he will refrain from making any purchases. Since, *ex hypothesi*, consumer 1 is the least inhibited consumer, he will, at best, be the only one who will demand one unit of the commodity if consumers expect the total market demand to be x units. It must be clear, then, that x units cannot be a virtual equilibrium point, since only points where the total expected quantity demanded is equal to the actual quantity demanded can be points on the real demand curve, and the quantity x cannot at any price be a point where expected total demand is equal to actual total demand. Now, if the total expected demand were $x + 1$ the actual demand might increase, say, to 2 units. At expected total demands $x + 2$ and $x + 3$, more would enter the market and the actual demand would be still greater since the fear of being different is considerably reduced as the expected demand is increased. With given increases in the expected total demand there must, at some point, be more than equal increases in the actual demand, because, if a real demand curve exists at all, there must be some point where the expected demand is equal to the actual demand. That point may exist, say, at $x + 10$. That is, at an expected total demand of $x + $

10 units a sufficient number of people have overcome their inhibitions
to being different so that, at some prices, they will actually demand
$x + 10$ units of the commodity. Let us call this point "T"—it is really
the "taboo breaking point." The maximum bid (the point T^1 in Figure
2) of the marginal unit demanded if the total demand were T units
now give us the first point on the real demand curve (the curve D_B).

How social taboos may affect the demand curve is shown in Figure
2. It will be noted that the price axis shows both positive and negative
"prices." A negative price may be thought of as the price it would be
necessary to *pay* individuals in order to induce them to consume in
public a given amount of the commodity; that is, the price that it would
be necessary to pay the consumers in order to induce them to disregard
their aversion to be looked upon as odd or peculiar.

As we have already indicated, the point T in Figure 2 is the "taboo
breaking point." T represents the number of units at which an *expected*
total quantity demanded of T units would result in an *actual* quantity
demanded of T units at some *real* price. Now, what has to be explained

FIGURE 2

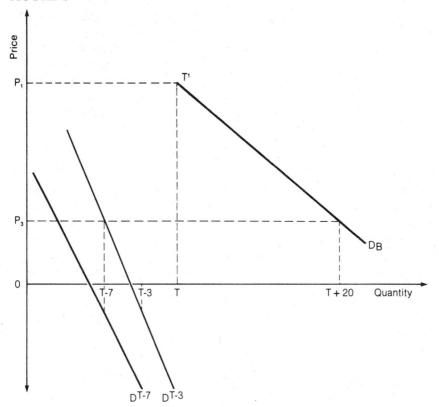

is why an expected demand of less than T units, say $T - 3$ units, would not yield an actual demand of $T - 3$ units at a positive price but only at a "negative price." Let the curve D^{T-3} be the demand curve that would exist if consumers thought the total demand was $T - 3$. Now, at any positive price, say P_3, the amount demanded would be less than $T - 3$, say $T - 7$. The price P_3 can therefore exist only if there is inaccurate information of the total quantity demanded. Once consumers discovered that a P_3 only $T - 7$ was purchased, and believed that this was the demand that would be sustained, their demand would shift to the D^{T-7} curve. At P_3 the amount purchased would now be less than $T - 7$ and demand would now shift to a curve to the left of the D^{T-7} curve. This procedure would go on until the demand was zero at P_3. We thus introduce a gap into our demand function and focus attention on an interesting psychological phenomenon that may affect demand. What we are suggesting, essentially, is that given "accurate expectations" of the total quantity demanded at any real price. In other words, this is a case in which a commodity will either "go over big" or not "go over" at all. It will be noted that at P_3 zero units or $T + 20$ units (Figure 2) may be taken off the market given "accurate expectations" of the total quantity demanded. It would seem, therefore, that "accurate expectations" of the total quantity demanded at P_3 can have two values depending upon whether people are generally pessimistic or optimistic about other consumers' demands for the commodity in question. If everybody expects that everybody else would not care much for the commodity, then zero units would be the accurate expectation of the total quantity demanded; if everybody, on the other hand, expects others to take up the commodity with some degree of enthusiasm, then $T + 20$ units would be the accurate expectation of the total quantity demanded. The factors that would determine one set of expectations rather than the other are matters of empirical investigation in the field of social psychology. The factors involved may be the history of the community, the people's conservatism or lack of conservatism, the type and quantity of advertising about the commodity under consideration, etc.

The really significant point in Figure 2 is T^1, the first point on the real demand curve D_B. As already indicated, it is the point at which the maximum bid of the marginal unit demanded is P_t and the total market demand is T units. If the price were higher than P_t, the Tth unit would not be demanded and all buyers would leave the market because of the effect of the taboo at less than a consumption of T units. By way of summary we might say that the whole point of this section is an attempt to show that in cases where social taboos affect demand the real demand curve may not start at the price-axis but that the smallest possible quantity demanded may be some distance to the right of the price-axis.

IV. THE SNOB EFFECT

Thus far, in our conceptual experiment and diagrammatic analysis, we have considered only the bandwagon effect. We now consider the reverse effect—the demand behavior for those commodities with regard to which the individual consumer acts like a snob. Here, too, we assume at first that the quantity demanded by a consumer is a function of price and of the total market demand, but that the individual consumer's demand is negatively correlated with the total market demand. In the snob case it is rather obvious that the external consumption effect must reach a limit although the limit may be where one snob constitutes the only buyer. For most commodities and most buyers, however, the motivation for exclusiveness is not that great; hence the marginal external consumption effect reaches zero before that point. If the commodity is to be purchased at all, the external consumption effect must reach a limit, at some price, where the quantity demanded has a positive value. From this it follows that after a point the principle of the diminishing marginal external consumption effect must manifest itself. We thus have in the snob effect an opposite but completely symmetrical relationship to the bandwagon effect.

The analysis of markets in which all consumers behave as snobs follows along the same lines as our analysis of the bandwagon effect. Because of the similarity we will be able to get through our analysis of the snob effect in short order. We begin, as before, by letting the alternate total market demands that serve as parameters for alternate individual demand curves be indicated by the superscripts $a, b, \ldots ,$ n (where $a < b < n$). Let the individual demand functions be $d_1, d_2,$ $\ldots d_n$, where there are n consumers in the market. Again, d_3^a signifies the individual demand curve for consumer 3 on the assumption that he expects the total market demand to be "a" units. By adding

$$d_1^a + d_2^a + \cdots + d_n^a = D^a$$
$$d_1^b + d_2^b + \cdots + d_n^b = D^b$$
$$\vdots \qquad \vdots \qquad \qquad \vdots$$
$$d_1^n + d_2^n + \cdots + d_n^n = D^n$$

we obtain the market demand functions on the alternate assumptions of consumers expecting the total market demands to be $a, b, \ldots , n$. Due to snob behavior the curves $D^a, D^b, \ldots , D^n$ move to the left as the expected total market demand increases. This is shown in Figure 3. Using the same procedure as before we obtain the virtual equilibrium points $E^a, E^b, \ldots , E^n$. They represent the only points on the curves $D^a, D^b, \ldots , D^n$ that are consistent with consumers' expectations (and hence with the assumption of accurate information). The locus of these virtual equilibrium points is the demand curve D_S.

FIGURE 3

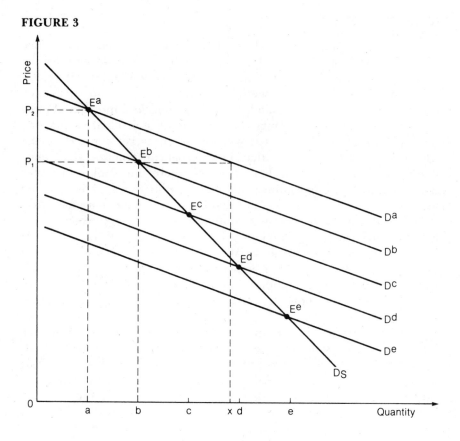

Now, given a price change from P_2 to P_1 we can separate the effect of the price change into a price effect and a snob effect. In Figure 3 we see that the net increase in the quantity demanded due to the reduction in price is ab. The price effect, however, is ax. That is, if every consumer expected no increase in the total quantity demanded then the total quantity demanded at P_1 would be Ox. The more extreme snobs will react to this increase in the total quantity demanded and will leave the market. The total quantity demanded will hence be reduced by bx. The net result is therefore an increase in demand of only ab.

It may be of interest to examine some of the characteristics of the curves in Figure 3. First we may note that all the points on the curves other than D_S (except E^a, E^b, . . . , E^n) are theoretical points that have significance only under conditions of imperfect knowledge. Second, we may note from the diagram that the demand curve for snobs is less elastic than the demand curves where there are no snob effects. The reason for this, of course, is that the increase in demand due to a reduction in price is counterbalanced, in part, by some snobs leaving the market because of the increase in total consumption (i.e., the decrease in the snob value of the commodity). It should be clear, however, that the snob effect, as defined, can never be in excess of the price effect since this would lead to a basic contradiction. If the snob effect were greater than the price effect, then the quantity demanded at a lower price would be less than the quantity demanded at a higher price. This implies that some of the snobs in the market at the higher price leave the market when there is a reduction in the total quantity demanded; which, of course, is patently inconsistent with our definition of snob behavior. It therefore follows that the snob effect is never greater than the price effect. It follows, also, that D_S is monotonically decreasing if D^a, D^b, . . . , D^n are monotonically decreasing.

Finally, it may be interesting to note another difference between the usual functional demand curve and the D_S curve. In the usual demand curve the buyers at higher prices always remain in the market at lower prices. That is, from the price point of view, the bids to buy are cumulative downward. This is clearly not the case in the D_S curve. Such terms as intramarginal buyers may be meaningless in snob markets.

V. THE VEBLEN EFFECT

Although the theory of conspicuous consumption as developed by Veblen and others is quite a complex and subtle sociological construct we can, for our purposes, quite legitimately abstract from the psychological and sociological elements and address our attention exclusively to the effects that conspicuous consumption has on the demand function. The essential economic characteristic with which we are concerned is the fact that the utility derived from a unit of a commodity employed for purposes of conspicuous consumption depends not only on the inherent qualities of that unit, but also on the price paid for it. It may, therefore, be helpful to divide the price of a commodity into two categories; the real price and the conspicuous price. By the real price we refer to the price the consumer paid for the commodity in terms of money. The conspicuous price is the price other people think the consumer paid for the commodity and which therefore determines its conspicuous consumption utility. These two prices would probably be identical in highly organized markets where price information is common knowledge. In other markets, where some can get "bargains" or special discounts the real price or conspicuous price need not be identical. In any case, the quantity demanded by a consumer will be a function of both the real price and the conspicuous price.

The market demand curve for commodities subject to conspicuous consumption can be derived through a similar diagrammatical method (summarized in Figure 4). This time we let the superscripts 1, 2, . . . , n stand for the expected conspicuous prices. The real prices are P_1,

FIGURE 4

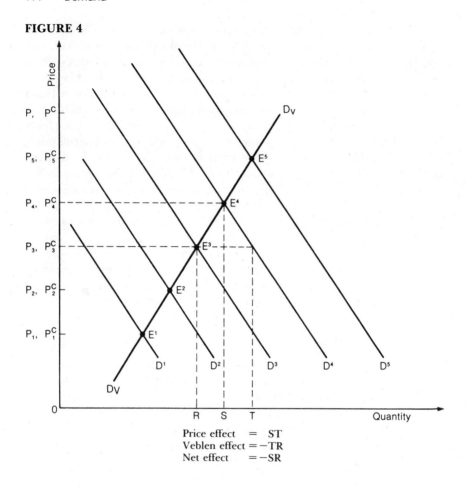

Price effect   = ST
Veblen effect = −TR
Net effect   = −SR

$P_2, \ldots, P_n$. The individual demand functions are $d_1, d_2, \ldots, d_n$. In this way d_6^3 stands for the demand curve of consumer number 6 if he expects a conspicuous price of P_3^c. We can now add across $d_1^1, d_2^1, \ldots, d_n^1$ and get the market demand curve D^1 which indicates the quantities demanded at alternate prices if all consumers expected a conspicuous price of P_1^c. In a similar manner we obtain $D^2, D^3, \ldots, D^n$. The market demand curves will, of course, up to a point, shift to the right as the expected conspicuous price increases. Now on every curve $D^1, D^2, \ldots, D^n$ in Figure 4 only one point can be a virtual equilibrium point if we assume that consumers possess accurate market information—the point where the real price is equal to the conspicuous price (that is, where $P_1 = P_1^c, P_2 = P_2^c, \ldots, P_n = P_n^c$). The locus of these virtual equilibrium points $E^1, E^2, \ldots, E^n$ gives us the demand curve D_V.

As before, we can separate the effects of a change in price into two effects—the price effect, and, what we shall call for want of a better term, the Veblen effect. In Figure 4 it will be seen that a change in price from P_4 to P_3 will reduce the quantity demanded by RS. The price effect is to increase the quantity demanded by ST; that is, the amount that would be demanded if there were no change in the expected conspicuous price would be OT. However, at the lower price a number of buyers would leave the market because of the reduced utility derived from the commodity at that lower conspicuous price. The Veblen effect is therefore RT.

It should be noted that unlike the D_S curve, the D_V curve can be positively inclined, negatively inclined or a mixture of both. It all depends on whether at alternate price changes the Veblen effect is greater or less than the price effect. It is possible that in one portion of the curve one effect may predominate while in another portion another may predominate. It is to be expected, however, that in most cases, if the curve is not monotonically decreasing it will be shaped like a backward S, as illustrated in Figure 5A. The reasons for this are as follows: First, there must be a price so high that no units of the commodity will be purchased at that price owing to the income constraint (among other reasons). This is the price P_n in Figure 5A, and it implies that there must be some point at which the curve shifts from being positively inclined to being negatively inclined as price increases. Second, there must be some point of satiety for the good. This is the point T in Figure 5A. It therefore follows that some portion of the curve must be monotonically decreasing to reach T if there exists some minimum price at which the Veblen effect is zero. It is of course reasonable to assume that there is some low price at which the commodity would cease to have any value for purposes of conspicuous consumption. If this last assumption does not

FIGURE 5

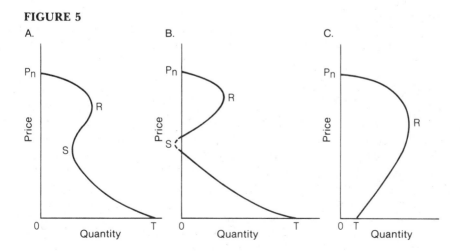

hold, which is unlikely, then the curve could have the shape indicated in Figure 5C. Otherwise, it would have the general shape indicated in Figure 5A, or it might be in two segments as illustrated in Figure 5B.

VI. MIXED EFFECTS

Any real market for semidurable or durable goods will most likely contain consumers that are subject to one or a combination of the effects discussed heretofore. Combining these effects presents no new formal difficulties with respect to the determination of the market demand curve, although it complicates the diagrammatic analysis considerably. The major principle, however, still holds. For any price there is a quantity demanded such that the marginal external consumption effect (or the marginal Veblen effect) for all buyers but one, is zero. This implies that for every price change there is a point at which people cease reacting to each other's quantity changes, regardless of the direction of these reactions. If this is so, then for every price there is a determinate quantity demanded, and hence the demand curve is determinate.

Now, for every price change we have distinguished between the price effect and some other, such as the snob, the Veblen, or the bandwagon effect. In markets where all four effects are present we should be able to separate out and indicate the direction of each of them that will result from a price change. That is, every price change will result in two positive and two negative effects—two which, other things being equal, will increase the quantity demanded, and two which, other things being equal, will decrease it. Which effects will be positive and which will be negative will depend on the relative strength of the Veblen effect as against the price effect. The Veblen and the price effects will depend directly on the direction of the price change. An increase in price will therefore result in price and bandwagon effects that are negative, and Veblen and snob effects that are positive, provided that the price effect is greater than the Veblen effect; that is, if the net result is a decrease in the quantity demanded at the higher price. If, on the other hand, the Veblen effect is more powerful than the price effect, given a price increase, then the bandwagon effect would be positive and the snob effect negative. The reverse would of course be true for price declines.

The market demand curve for a commodity where different consumers are subject to different types of effects can be obtained diagrammatically through employing the methods developed above—although the diagrams would be quite complicated. There is no point in adding still more diagrams to illustrate this. Briefly, the method would be somewhat as follows: (1) Given the demand curves for every individual, in which the expected total quantity demanded is a parameter for each curve, we can add these curves laterally and obtain a map of aggregate demand curves, in which each aggregate curve is based on a given total quantity demanded. (2) The locus of the equilibrium points on each aggregate demand curve (as derived in Figure 1) gives us a market demand curve that accounts for both bandwagon and snob effects. This last curve assumes that only one conspicuous price exists. For every conspicuous price there exists a separate map of aggregate demand curves from which different market demand curves are obtained. (3) This procedure yields a map of market demand curves in which each curve is based on a different conspicuous price. Employing the method used in Figure 4 we obtain our final market demand curve which accounts for bandwagon, snob, and Veblen effects simultaneously.

VII. CONCLUSION

It is not unusual for a writer in pure theory to end his treatise by pointing out that the science is really very young; that there is a great deal more to be done; that the formulations presented are really of a very tentative nature; and that the best that can be hoped for is that his treatise may in some small way pave the road for future formulations that are more directly applicable to problems in the real world. This is another way of saying that work in pure theory is an investment in the future state of the science where the returns in terms of applications to real problems are really very uncertain. This is probably especially true of value theory where the investment in time and effort is more akin to the purchase of highly speculative stocks rather than the purchase of government bonds. Since this was only a brief essay on one aspect of value theory, the reader will hardly be surprised if the conclusions reached are somewhat less than revolutionary.

Essentially, we have attempted to do two things. First, we have tried to demonstrate that nonadditivity is not necessarily an insurmountable obstacle in effecting a transition from individual to collective demand curves. Second, we attempted to take a step or two in the direction of incorporating various kinds of external consumption effects into the theory of consumers' demand. In order to solve our problem, we have introduced what we have called the principle of the diminishing marginal external consumption effect. We indicated some reasons for believing that for every individual, there is some point at which the marginal external consumption effect is zero. We have attempted to show that if this principle is admitted, then there are various ways of effecting a transition from individual to collective demand curves. The major conclusion reached is that under conditions of perfect knowledge (or accurate expectations) any point on the demand curve, for any given price, will be at that total quantity demanded where the marginal external consumption effect for all consumers but one, is equal to zero.

In comparing the demand curve in those situations where external consumption effects are present with the demand curve as it would be where these external consumption effects are absent, we made three basic points. (1) If the bandwagon effect is the most significant effect, the demand curve is more elastic than it would be if this external consumption effect were absent. (2) If the snob effect is the predominant effect, the demand curve is less elastic than otherwise. (3) If the Veblen effect is the predominant one, the demand curve is less elastic than otherwise, and some portions of it may even be positively inclined; whereas, if the Veblen effect is absent, the curve will be negatively inclined regardless of the importance of the snob effect in the market.

8.

Demand Analysis for Toothpaste*

RODGER D. CARLSON

In such fields as marketing research and econometrics an attempt is often made to estimate the total size of a market for a product or service. The estimate enables a person to segment different types of markets and to relate the estimate to corresponding industry data which brings out a comparison of market shares and other competitive factors. In estimating market size, the type of market should first be classified in order to reduce ambiguity because of the many possible interpretations. In this study the classification is by nature of the product. The product is toothpaste which is a single consumer good produced primarily for direct sale to families or individuals. In order to clear up any misunderstanding, toothpaste encompasses dentrifices whether in the form of powder, paste, or liquid. Consequently, when the word *toothpaste* is used in this study, it implies any preparation which aids in cleaning teeth such as Crest, Colgate or Gleem toothpaste, Pearl Drops paste, or Pepsodent powder, but it would not include such items as baking soda or any other household substance not specifically made for cleaning teeth.

NATURE OF THE INVESTIGATION

The nature of this investigation (demand analysis) is to arrive at the total dollar demand for toothpaste for the city of San Bernardino,

---

* *Business Economics* 12 (September 1977), pp. 61–66.

California, for the year of 1970. The year 1970 was chosen due to the availability of Census Data for that year.

Most market studies are either cross-sectional or time-series approaches. This study extends the work of Palda and Blair who put cross-sectional and time-series techniques together in a pioneering work. The work of Palda and Blair is extended by applying their coefficients and analytical techniques to determine the total potential dollar value of sales in a specific market. The technique used is illustrative of what could be done in any market for which comparable data are available.

ASSUMPTIONS

It is assumed there should be a correlation between toothbrushing frequently and the amount spent on toothpaste. However, my model is not an aggregate model using a macro-approach to estimate demand, because rather than starting with aggregate data and working downward, the data will be aggregated forward to arrive at the demand. Therefore, the model may be classified as a building block model or a micro-approach to estimating demand. This approach to estimating demand is explained by Uhl and Schoner who state that: "the census method involves querying or estimating the number of units that will be purchased by each (and every) user (and prospective user) on the buyer's side of the market." First the analyst must determine who the users and prospective users are and then he must be able to discern the quantity of the product or service each of them anticipates buying from the sellers.

METHODOLOGY

This investigation uses the causal-comparative method of research. In other words, the effect, or dependent variable, is demand for toothpaste while the causes, or independent variables, whose effect upon the dependent variable is being studied are: (1) household size, (2) ages of children in the household, (3) education of the head of the household, (4) occupation of the head of household, (5) race of the head of household. These independent variables have been selected based on a previous demand analysis for toothpaste conducted by Palda and Blair. Consequently, this study follows a pattern developed by them with some modifications so that it can be applied for this San Bernardino study. For example, the family's cross-sectional effect variable along with the area dummy variables have been dropped for purposes of this study since they are inapplicable. Consequently, the demand equation for this study is:

$$D = a + f(Yit, Yi, Hd1, Hd2, Hd3, Cd1, Cd2, Ed1, Ed2, Od1, Rd1, Rd2)$$

with symbols defined as follows:

a = intercept (.25)
Yit = income in thousands of dollars (.06)
Yi = average income over 5 years (.14)
$Hd1$ = 3, 4, or 5 persons (household) (.79)
$Hd2$ = 6 or 7 persons (household) (.46)
$Hd3$ = 8 or more persons (household) (1.17)
$Cd1$ = children under 6 years of age in household (.13)
$Cd2$ = children 6–17 in household (1.41)
$Ed1$ = completed high school (household head) (.79)
$Ed2$ = any college (household head) (.44)
$Od1$ = professional or executive (occupations of household head)
      (.36)
$Rd1$ = Black (race of household head) (−.34)
$Rd2$ = other than Black or White (race of household) (.63)

composite values of coefficient as calculated by Palda and Blair in parentheses

Palda and Blair measured and established systematic relationships among the variables. Consequently, their demand function specified variables that affect the demand for toothpaste. Consumer panel data enabled them to detect variables through regression analysis so that they could be included in the demand function, along with the use of dummy variables. In using dummy variables, the procedure is to assign numbers to each variable. As will be shown later in this paper, one variable which influences the expenditure for toothpaste is the occupational classification of the household head. For professional household heads a value of one would be assigned (next to its coefficient of $Od1$ which is .36). For nonprofessional heads of households a value of zero would be assigned. In this study, the independent variable of household size has been broken down into three categories: 3, 4, or 5 persons for ($Hd1$), 6 or 7 persons for ($Hd2$), and 8 or more persons for ($Hd3$).

The total population of the city of San Bernardino was used for this study. Demand will be calculated by predicting the amount a household is willing to spend on toothpaste for the year 1970 taking into account variations of certain independent variables in relation to Census Data for the city. This annual figure per type of household will be aggregated forward so that total demand for all households in the city can be estimated in terms of total annual expenditure in dollars.

The method used to gather data concerning toothpaste expenditures was provided through the Market Research Corporation of America (MRCA) panel data. If it were not for my preliminary research into this topic in which panel data were obtained, such a study would not have been attempted.

With reference to the Census Data for San Bernardino, the figures are subject to sampling variability because they are based on 5 and 15 percent sample questionnaires. In order to apply the method used by Palda and Blair, certain assumptions had to be made and applied to the available data with the following revisions. Palda and Blair used income in increments of a thousand dollars but the income data from the sources listed was in groupings in this study. Consequently, the median income has been used to best represent the variability in income levels for the city. Therefore, very large incomes have no influence on the value of the median, whereas the arithmetic mean of income would distort the true picture of income for San Bernardino. The annual median income for whites is $8,656; blacks, $6,164; browns, $7,484. In order to compute the five year average, I used a 7 percent figure (cost of living) to adjust the income levels which then became respectively by race—$8,050, $5,733, and $6,960.

In addition to the change above, Palda and Blair used the actual household size in each individual case in their analysis, and my study uses the average household size. The average household size for blacks was 4.50 persons; 3.39 persons for whites; and browns 4.28.

Although some households do not have children, it will be assumed that they do because of lack of data. Of all the households, the ratio is approximately two households with children aged 6–17 to one household with children under 6. Therefore, of the 34,581 households in San Bernardino, 23,054 of them have children in ages 6–17 and 11,527 have children under 6 years of age. Since education by head of household is not available, the median school years completed of those 25 years old and over (12.1) in the city shall be used. For the number of professional persons by race, the national average will be used since no other data were available. Palda and Blair do not define professionals or executives, so it will be assumed that professionals, technicians, managers, and administrators fall under this category. The number of such black households is 4,292, browns number 6,772, and whites total 23,517. In terms of the race variable, those classified "other than black or white" will only be those classified as people with Spanish surname or Spanish language since other races are combined in the census classifications.

COMPUTATIONS

In order to show how the outlay in dollars on toothpaste was calculated I will provide the following illustration:

> How can we predict what a household is going to spend on toothpaste in the year 1970, if the head of household is white, had completed high school, is a nonprofessional; the household income is $8,656 annually (median income for whites) and over the last five years averaged $8,050; it lives in San Bernardino and has five family members including children under 6 years old?

Based on the covariance regression results by Palda and Blair the estimate is $3.62. This is calculated as the intercept (0.25) plus the coefficient of the income in thousands of dollars from the regression (.06) times the income (8.7 rounded off from $8,656), using the demand equation and associated coefficients.

In order to compute the outlay in dollars on toothpaste for households, the various types of households were defined taking into consideration a combination of all independent variables. To reduce the original number of combinations down from 48, it was necessary to do some grouping. For example, groups were formed of the annual median income for whites, blacks, and browns. This saved much time and confusion since listing six or seven income levels for each race would have caused the types of different households to increase sharply. Also, as can be seen from the outlay for households listed below, the average number of persons per household including all three races was below five; therefore, the coefficient .79 was used in all cases. But, if average size per household for blacks had turned out to be 6.2, then the combinations would have increased as the coefficient .46 would be used instead of .79. However, such was not the case. In terms of the variable for the presence of children in the household, there were two choices, children under 6 and children from 6–17. The median level of education for the head of households, 12.1 years, was used in order to get away from two choices in the education variable. Consequently, the coefficient .79 was used throughout since it was intended for persons who had completed high school. For the occupation variable, either the head of household was, or was not, a professional person. The race variable did not cause an increase in the number of combinations since it was used to match up with the median income variable by race. In other words, if black median income was used, then the coefficient .34 was subtracted from the computations. The other races followed along the same lines. By combining such factors, there were 12 household types with different characteristics.

Average expenditure per household was calculated along the lines indicated above. These calculations should be obvious, but if they are not, the author will be pleased to supply details to interested readers. Total toothpaste expenditures for San Bernardino were then constructed by multiplying the number of each type of household in the city by the calculated average expenditure for that type of household.

Of the total number of households, there are 4,292 blacks, 6,772 browns, and 23,517 whites. However, a problem arises concerning the composition of the 4,292 black households, the 6,772 brown households, and the 23,517 white households among four types. In order to do so, an attempt was made to find out how many of the household heads for each race in San Bernardino were professional and nonprofessional. But, such data were not available. Therefore, from the *Occupational Char-*

acteristics 1970 Census Population for the United States, it was ascertained that 8.03 percent of all blacks employed were professionals, 7.44 percent of all browns were professionals, and 15.24 percent of all whites were professionals. Although those percentages are U.S. averages, it was assumed that in San Bernardino they were distributed in approximately the same way. The Census Data for San Bernardino contained an error in that age groups were listed for all races, whites, and blacks. It would have been easy to subtract children under 6 and from 6–17 for blacks and whites from the total figure for all races to arrive at a figure for browns. However, the age distribution for whites must have included figures for browns because the figures for whites and blacks was equal to the total for all races. Therefore, the figures for the following distribution of household types are the same for the children variable (2:1 or .334:.166). This 2:1 ratio should be representative for each race since the ratio for blacks alone was also approximately 2:1. As one will recall from the previous calculations for the 12 types of households, the children variable and the occupation variable were the only ones which had two solutions. The other variables either had a median value (i.e., education 12.1) so only one dummy variable was used, or another average was used.

The characteristics of households are listed in Table 1 followed by variable weightings for the children and occupation variables. Looking at black households (Table 1), weightings of .166 for children under 6 years of age and .334 for ages 6–17 can be found (this is because the ratio is 2:1). The weightings under the occupational variable are .460 and .040 for nonprofessionals and professionals respectively. It can be

TABLE 1

Characteristics of Household	Children Weight	Occupation Weight
Black, children under 6, nonprofessional	.166	.460
Black, children under 6, professional	.166	.040
Black, children 6–17, nonprofessional	.334	.460
Black, children 6–17, professional	.334	.040
	1.000	1.000
Brown, children under 6, nonprofessional	.166	.463
Brown, children under 6, professional	.166	.037
Brown, children 6–17, nonprofessional	.334	.463
Brown, children 6–17, professional	.334	.037
	1.000	1.000
White, children under 6, nonprofessional	.166	.424
White, children under 6, professional	.166	.076
White, children 6–17, nonprofessional	.334	.424
White, children 6–17, professional	.334	.076
	1.000	1.000

noted that approximately 8 percent of blacks are professionals; for blacks there are two household types which include professionals so the 8 percent is split or a value weighting of .040. If 8 percent of blacks are professionals, then 92 percent are nonprofessionals or for the purposes here are classified as others. Since there were two black households which were nonprofessionals, the 92 percent was split or .460. The same method was used for brown and white households except that value weightings for the occupational variable was different since brown professionals comprise 7.44 percent and white professionals 15.24 percent of their respective total employed.

By adding the weightings of the children variable and the occupational variable for each household type and dividing by two, the percentage of households in the total was found. (In other words, looking at the black household with children under 6 and the household head being a nonprofessional, the figures would be .166 + .460 = .626/2 or 31 percent, shown in Table 2.) Consequently, 31 percent of the total number of black households (4,292) is equal to 1331; 1331 times the expenditure per family ($2.79) is equal to $3,713.49. The same procedure is followed for all 12 household types. If the total expenditure

TABLE 2

Combination of Children Weight and Occupation Weight		Percent of Households		Total Expenditure		
.626/2 = 31.3 or	31%	31% of 4,292 =	1,331	1,331 @ $2.79 = $		3,713.49
.206/2 = 10.3 or	10	10% of 4,292 =	429	429 @	3.15 =	1,351.35
.794/2 = 39.7 or	40	40% of 4,292 =	1,717	1,717 @	4.07 =	6,988.19
.374/2 = 18.7 or	19	19% of 4,292 =	815	815 @	4.43 =	3,610.45
	100%		4,292			$ 15,663.48
.629/2 = 31.4 or	31	31% of 6,772 =	2,099	2,099 @ $4.02 = $		8,437.98
.203/2 = 10.2 or	10	10% of 6,772 =	677	677 @	4.38 =	2,965.26
.797/2 = 39.8 or	40	40% of 6,772 =	2,709	2,709 @	5.30 =	14,357.70
.371/2 = 18.6 or	19	19% of 6,772 =	1,287	1,287 @	5.66 =	7,284.42
	100%		6,772			$ 33,045.36
.590/2 = 29.5 or	30%	30% of 23,517 =	7,055	7,055 @ $3.62 = $		25,539.10
.242/2 = 12.1 or	12	12% of 23,517 =	2,822	2,822 @	3.98 =	11,231.56
.758/2 = 37.9 or	38	38% of 23,517 =	8,937	8,937 @	4.90 =	43,791.30
.410/2 = 20.4 or	20	20% of 23,517 =	4,703	4,703 @	5.26 =	24,737.78
	100%		23,517			$105,299.74

Total demand expenditures for toothpaste in San Bernardino for 1970

Total black households = $ 15,663.48
Total brown households =   33,045.36
Total white households =   105,299.74
All Households   = $154,008.58

for every household type is added, the total (demand) expenditures for toothpaste in San Bernardino in 1970 should have been $154,008.58.

CONCLUSIONS

In conclusion, in order to estimate demand for toothpaste for the city of San Bernardino, a microapproach was used as a building block model. The model used was based on a previous demand analysis conducted by Palda and Blair in which consumer panel data from MRCA served as a basis for developing their regression analysis. By acquiring data from the 1970 Census and other sources, use was made of the model developed by Palda and Blair. The number of factors that affect the demand for toothpaste are many, but the ones used in this study are most important for it is necessary to limit the number of factors to make the demand function operational.

The implications of the findings in this demand analysis can serve as a basis for sales forecasting and therefore, dentrifice manufacturers would be quite interested in such a study because actual sales in 1970 for San Bernardino might have been low relative to demand. However, the total demand for toothpaste for San Bernardino is not the only important finding of this study. The demand by type of household has some very important implications. For example, a toothpaste manufacturer could aim his advertising to those households which show the most promise and increase advertising effectiveness.

Obviously, the analytical techniques and the use of those techniques demonstrated here could be applied to consumer behavior in any area, and the work undertaken here might also usefully serve as a "stepping stone" for further research in consumer behavior.

9.

The Demand for Beer, Wine, and Spirits: A Systemwide Analysis*

KENNETH W. CLEMENTS
LESTER W. JOHNSON

I. INTRODUCTION

The systemwide approach to the analysis of consumer demand considers the multivariate structure of the problem in which the consumer allocates his income to all goods simultaneously. This approach combines the theory of the consumer with empirical analysis and has enjoyed much popularity over the past decade.

Most previous applications of the systemwide approach have used national accounts commodity groups (food, clothing, housing, and so on). For many business and government policy purposes, however, these groups are much too broad. For example, to analyze the effects on consumption of all but the simplest changes in indirect taxes, we would need considerably more disaggregation. Similarly, market researchers need to analyze demand at the individual product level for purposes of forecasting and formulating pricing and other policies. The objective of this paper is to use the consumption of beer, wine, and spirits to illustrate how the approach can be applied to give insights into the structure of demand for more narrowly defined commodity groups.

* *Journal of Business* 56, no. 3 (July 1983), pp. 273–304.

When the consumer's utility function is appropriately separable in alcoholic beverages and all other goods, it is possible to confine our attention to the three beverages and ignore all other goods. In Section II of the paper we set out the so-called differential version of the systemwide approach. In Section III we use the alcohol data to estimate demand equations for beer, wine, and spirits. We then use the demand model in Sections IV and V to (1) explain the rapid growth of wine consumption and (2) measure the welfare cost of alcohol taxes. Section VI contains concluding comments.

II. DIFFERENTIAL DEMAND EQUATIONS

In this section we first formulate the consumer's demand equations for all n goods in terms of differentials. These are unconditional demand equations as they depend on all prices and total expenditure. The coefficients of these equations are not necessarily taken to be constant, so the model is general. We then block the n goods such that they form groups that are separable in the consumer's utility function. This leads to a composite demand equation for each group, as well as conditional demand equations within each group. The variables of the conditional equation are exclusively concerned with the group to which the good belongs, allowing us to focus attention on demand within the group. Finally, for estimation we set out a Rotterdam paramenterization.

Unconditional Demand

We write p_i, q_i for the price and quantity demanded for good i ($i = 1, \ldots, n$), $M = \Sigma_{i=1}^n p_i q_i$ for total expenditure ("income" for short) and $w_i = p_i q_i / M$ for the ith budget share. Under general conditions, the demand for good i can be written as

$$w_i d(\log q_i) = \theta_i d(\log Q) + \sum_{j=1}^n v_{ij} d\left(\log \frac{p_j}{P'}\right), \qquad (1)$$

where $\theta_i = \partial(p_i q_i)/\partial M$ is the ith marginal share; $d(\log Q) = \Sigma_{i=1}^n w_i d(\log q_i)$ is the Divisia volume index of the change in the consumer's real income; $d(\log p_j/P')$ is to be interpreted as the change in the deflated price of $j d(\log p_j) - d(\log P')$, where $d(\log P') = \Sigma_{i=1}^n \theta_i d(\log p_i)$ is the Frisch price index; and

$$v_{ij} = \lambda p_i u^{ij} p_i / M \qquad (2)$$

is the (i,j)th price coefficient, where λ is the marginal utility of income and u^{ij} is the (i,j)th element of the inverse of the Hessian of the utility function $[\partial^2 u/\partial q_i \partial q_j]^{-1}$. In view of (2), the symmetry of this Hessian means that the matrix of price coefficients $[v_{ij}]$ is also symmetric. A

sufficient second-order condition for a budget-constrained maximum
is that the Hessian be negative definite; (2) thus implies that $[\nu_{ij}]$ is
negative definite. The price coefficients are subject to the constraint
that the row sums of $[\nu_{ij}]$ are proportional to the corresponding marginal
shares,

$$\sum_{j=1}^{n} \nu_{ij} = \phi\theta_i \qquad i = 1, \ldots, n, \tag{3}$$

where $\phi = (\partial \log \lambda/\partial \log M)^{-1}$ is the reciprocal of the income elasticity
of the marginal utility of income. We shall refer to ϕ as the income
flexibility.

Block-Independent Preferences

Let the n goods now be divided into G groups, $S_1, \ldots, S_G$, such
that each good belongs to only one group. Further, let the consumer's
preferences be such that the utility function is the sum of G subutility
functions, each involving the quantities of only one group,

$$u(\mathbf{q}) = \sum_{g=1}^{G} u_g(\mathbf{q_g}), \tag{4}$$

where $\mathbf{q} = [q_1, \ldots, q_n]'$ and $\mathbf{q_g}$ is the vector of the q_i's that fall under
S_g. Then, when the goods are numbered appropriately, the Hessian
$[\partial^2 u/\partial q_i \partial q_j]$ and its inverse become block-diagonal. Accordingly, specification (4) is known as block-independent preferences.

Under block independence, $\nu_{ij} = 0$ for i and j in different groups
(see [2]) and (3) for $i \in S_g$ becomes

$$\sum_{j\in S_g} \nu_{ij} = \phi\theta_i \qquad g = 1, \ldots, G. \tag{5}$$

The demand equation (1) for $i \in S_g$ becomes

$$w_i d(\log q_i) = \theta_i d(\log Q) + \sum_{j\in S_g} \nu_{ij} d\left(\log \frac{p_j}{P'}\right), \tag{6}$$

so that the only deflated prices which appear are those of goods belonging to the same group as i.

Composite Demand Equations

We write $W_g = \Sigma_{i\in S_g} w_i$ and $\Theta_g = \Sigma_{i\in S_g}\theta_i$ for the average and
marginal shares of group g, and define the group volume and Frisch
price indexes as $d(\log Q_g) = \Sigma_{i\in S_g} (w_i/W_g)d(\log q_i)$, $d(\log P'_g) = \Sigma_{i\in S_g}$
$(\theta_i/\Theta_g)d(\log p_i)$. If we then add (6) over $i \in S_g$ and use (5) and the
symmetry of $[\nu_{ij}]$, we obtain the composite demand equation for S_g as
a group,

$$W_g d(\log Q_g) = \Theta d(\log Q) + \theta\Theta_g d\left(\log\frac{P'_g}{P'}\right). \tag{7}$$

Thus only the deflated price of the group $d(\log P'_g/P') = d(\log P'_g) - d(\log P')$ and income affects the demand for the group as a whole. The income and own-price elasticities for the group are Θ_g/W_g and $\phi\Theta_g/W_g$, respectively.

Conditional Demand Equations

Combining (6) and (7) we obtain

$$w_i d(\log q_i) = \frac{\theta_i}{\Theta_g} W_g d(\log Q_g) + \sum_{j\in S_g} v_{ij} d\left(\log\frac{p_j}{P'_g}\right). \tag{8}$$

This is the demand equation for $i \in S_g$, given the demand for the group as a whole $W_g d(\log Q_g)$. As the variables on the right of this equation are exclusively concerned with the group S_g to which the ith commodity belongs, it is known as a conditional demand equation. The term θ_i/Θ_g is the conditional marginal share of i within the group S_g, with $\sum_{i\in S_g}\theta_i/\Theta_g = 1$.

Equation (8) can be formulated in terms of absolute (undeflated) prices by using the definition of $d(\log P'_g)$ (see above [7]) to write the price term as

$$\sum_{j\in S_g} v_{ij}\left[d(\log p_j) - \sum_{k\in S_g}\frac{\theta_k}{\Theta_g}d(\log p_k)\right]$$

$$= \sum_{j\in S_g} v_{ij}d(\log p_j) - \phi\theta_i\sum_{k\in S_g}\frac{\theta_k}{\Theta_g}d(\log p_k) \tag{9}$$

$$= \sum_{j\in S_g}(v_{ij} - \phi\Theta_g\theta'_i\theta'_j)d(\log p_j)$$

$$= \sum_{j\in S_g}\pi^g_{ij}d(\log p_j),$$

where the first step is based on (5), $\theta'_i = \theta_i/\Theta_g$ is the conditional marginal share of i, and

$$\pi^g_{ij} = v_{ij} - \phi\Theta_g\theta'_i\theta'_j \qquad i,j\in S_g \tag{10}$$

is the (i,j)th conditional Slutsky coefficient. Substitution of the fourth member of (9) in (8) gives the absolute price version of the conditional demand equation for $i \in S_g$,

$$w_i d(\log q_i) = \theta'_i W_g d(\log Q_g) + \sum_{j\in S_g}\pi^g_{ij}d(\log p_j). \tag{11}$$

By dividing both sides of this equation by w_i, we find that $(\theta_i/\Theta_g)(W_g/w_i) = (\theta_i/w_i)/(\Theta_g/W_g)$ is the ratio of the income elasticity of the good to that of the group to which it belongs. We shall refer to this ratio as the conditional income elasticity of i. We also find that π_{ij}^{g}/w_i is the conditional price elasticity, that is, the elasticity of q_i with respect to the absolute price p_j $(i,j \in S_g)$.

It follows from (5) and (10) and the fact that $\Sigma_{j \in S_g} \theta'_j = 1$ that

$$\sum_{j \in S_g} \pi_{ij}^{g} = 0 \qquad i \in S_g. \tag{12}$$

This reflects the homogeneity proposition that a proportionate change in all prices in the group, total consumption of the group remaining unchanged, does not affect the demand for any good in the group. We shall refer to (12) as demand homogeneity.

If S_g consists of n_g commodities, the $n_g \times n_g$ matrix of price coefficients referring to S_g is a principal submatrix of the $n \times n$ price coefficient matrix $[\nu_{ij}]$. As the latter matrix is symmetric, so is the former. It then follows from (10) that the conditional Slutsky matrix $[\pi_{ij}^{g}]$ is symmetric,

$$\pi_{ij}^{g} = \pi_{ji}^{g} \qquad i,j = 1, \ldots , n_g. \tag{13}$$

We shall refer to this as Slutsky symmetry. The negative definiteness of $[\nu_{ij}]$ together with (10) and (12) imply that $[\pi_{ij}^{g}]$ is negative semidefinite with rank $n_g - 1$.

A Parameterization of the Conditional Demand Equations

To apply (11) to finite-change data, we replace w_i with its arithmetic average over the periods $t - 1$ and t, $\overline{w}_{it} = (w_{it} + w_{i,t-1})/2$, and $d(\log x)$ with $Dx_t = \log x_t - \log x_{t-1}$, the log change in x. We also use the Rotterdam parameterization of treating the coefficients of (11) as constants, so that the estimating equations are

$$\overline{w}_{it}Dq_{it} = \theta'_i \overline{W}_{gt}DQ_{gt} + \sum_{j=1}^{n_g} \pi_{ij}^{g}Dp_{jt} + \epsilon_{it}, \qquad i = 1, \ldots , n_g, \tag{14}$$

where $\overline{W}_{gt} = \Sigma_{i=1}^{n_g} \overline{w}_{it}$; $DQ_{gt} = \Sigma_{i=1}^{n_g} (\overline{w}_{it}/\overline{W}_{gt})Dq_{it}$; and the ϵ_{it}'s are serially independent, normally distributed disturbances with zero means and a constant contemporaneous covariance matrix.

III. DEMAND EQUATIONS FOR ALCOHOLIC BEVERAGES

In this section we first present price-quantity data for the consumption of beer, wine, and spirits. We then use these data to estimate (14) under two conditions, that total consumption of alcohol is a predetermined variable and that it is endogenously determined. Finally, we give the unconditional demand responses.

The Data

Our data refer to the consumption of beer, wine, and spirits in Australia over the period 1955–56/1976–77. Table 1 gives the price-quantity data and Table 2 the budget shares. As can be seen, on average, beer consumption per capita increased by about 1.2 percent per annum, wine by 4.5 percent, and spirits by 2.2 percent. The budget share for total alcohol has remained more or less constant over this period at about 6 percent (Table 2). Expenditure on beer, expressed as a percentage of total alcohol expenditure, has fallen by about 10 percentage points to 66 percent in 1976–77 (see the third to last col. of Table 2). This relative decline in beer expenditure mirrors the dramatic growth of the share of wine in total alcohol, which increased from 8.6 percent in 1956–57 to 18.6 percent in 1976–77. One of our objectives is to explain this rapid growth in the wine share. The spirits share in total alcohol has been relatively stable at about 16 percent. Further details of the data and sources are given in a separate appendix, available on request.

TABLE 1
Alcohol Quantity and Price Log-Changes, Australia, 1955–1956/1976–1977

	Beer		Wine		Spirits	
	Quantity	Price	Quantity	Price	Quantity	Price
Year	(Dq_1)	(Dp_1)	(Dq_2)	(Dp_2)	(Dq_3)	(Dp_3)
1956–57	−5.359	14.205	−2.447	5.982	−10.427	0
1957–58	.209	1.230	−.730	4.879	1.220	0
1958–59	.476	.366	.684	6.108	4.853	0
1959–60	1.735	.849	.901	7.514	8.429	0
1960–61	−.292	1.795	−2.960	7.363	−.390	8.406
1961–62	−.410	.709	.479	1.361	.289	1.315
1962–63	1.235	.587	3.039	1.584	−2.588	5.656
1963–64	3.355	1.971	4.608	1.082	7.639	.894
1964–65	3.083	1.368	.708	5.809	7.271	1.982
1965–66	.045	8.152	8.737	7.395	−11.977	13.734
1966–67	2.452	4.291	11.501	4.709	−.712	−5.069
1967–68	3.304	4.114	10.430	6.953	11.586	0
1968–69	3.032	3.025	8.657	12.275	−1.068	6.766
1969–70	2.612	3.477	8.094	6.004	10.476	2.856
1970–71	1.699	6.274	−3.016	9.198	.939	3.041
1971–72	−.135	5.104	1.904	5.850	5.653	.264
1972–73	3.010	5.238	10.084	−.873	12.249	.875
1973–74	7.028	7.623	11.430	2.924	.643	20.202
1974–75	1.060	13.327	11.200	14.993	−4.268	25.660
1975–76	−2.130	22.672	6.158	18.523	−3.534	12.946
1976–77	−.965	8.943	4.463	7.748	9.773	.386
Mean	1.193	5.491	4.473	6.542	2.193	4.758

Note: The quantities are per capita. The year 1956–57, e.g., refers to the transition from 1955–56 to 1956–57. All entries are to be divided by 100.

TABLE 2
Arithmetic Averages of Unconditional and Conditional Budget Shares for Alcohol: Australia, 1955–1956/1976–1977

	Unconditional				Conditional		
Year	Beer $(\overline{w}_1)$	Wine $(\overline{w}_2)$	Spirits $(\overline{w}_3)$	Total Alcohol $(\overline{W}_g)$	Beer $(\overline{w}_1/\overline{W}_g)$	Wine $(\overline{w}_2/\overline{W}_g)$	Spirits $(\overline{w}_3/\overline{W}_g)$
1956–57	4.6325	.5256	.9587	6.1168	75.734	8.593	15.673
1957–58	4.7115	.5274	.8823	6.1211	76.970	8.616	14.414
1958–59	4.6336	.5415	.8847	6.0597	76.465	8.936	14.599
1959–60	4.4809	.5552	.8991	5.9351	75.497	9.354	15.149
1960–61	4.3314	.5609	.9247	5.8170	74.462	9.643	15.896
1961–62	4.2709	.5661	.9477	5.7846	73.831	9.785	16.383
1962–63	4.1877	.5673	.9408	5.6957	73.524	9.959	16.517
1963–64	4.1115	.5656	.9446	5.6217	73.137	10.061	16.802
1964–65	4.0759	.5676	.9747	5.6181	72.549	10.102	17.349
1965–66	4.1326	.6059	.9802	5.7185	72.266	10.594	17.140
1966–67	4.2397	.6778	.9164	5.8339	72.674	11.618	15.707
1967–68	4.2709	.7525	.8839	5.9073	72.299	12.738	14.963
1968–69	4.2805	.8550	.9028	6.0383	70.889	14.160	14.951
1969–70	4.2479	.9492	.9278	6.1248	69.355	15.497	15.148
1970–71	4.2308	.9749	.9387	6.1444	68.857	15.866	15.277
1971–72	4.1829	.9686	.9139	6.0654	68.964	15.969	15.067
1972–73	4.0888	.9646	.9200	5.9734	68.451	16.148	15.401
1973–74	4.0500	.9588	.9632	5.9720	67.817	16.054	16.129
1974–75	3.9724	.9969	1.0088	5.9781	66.449	16.676	16.875
1975–76	3.9885	1.0839	.9927	6.0651	65.761	17.872	16.367
1976–77	3.9918	1.1303	.9496	6.0716	65.745	18.616	15.639
Mean	4.2434	.7569	.9359	5.9363	71.509	12.708	15.783

Note: The year 1956–57, e.g., refers to arithmetic averages of budget shares in 1955–56 and 1956–57. All entries are to be divided by 100.

Estimates with Total Alcohol Consumption Predetermined

We assume that the total consumption of alcohol $(\overline{W}_{gt}DQ_{gt})$ and prices (Dp_{jt}) are predetermined variables and use maximum likelihood to estimate (14) for $i = 1, 2, 3$, subject to the homogeneity and symmetry restrictions (12) and (13). The estimates are given in Table 3. Constant terms have been added to each equation to take account of trendlike changes in tastes and other factors. A preliminary analysis indicated that two constants are needed in each equation, one for the first 9 observations (α_i) and one for the remaining 12 (β_i). As can be seen, there is a significant trend into wine and out of spirits in the second part of the period. The estimate of β_i for wine implies that per capita consumption is growing autonomously at an exponential rate of $.53/(\overline{w}_{it} \times 1000) = .53 \times 100/1.13 \times 1000 = 4.7$ percent per annum in 1976–

TABLE 3
Conditional Demand Equations for Alcoholic Beverages, Australia, 1955–1956/1976–1977

$$\overline{w}_{it}Dq_{it} = \alpha_i D_t + \beta_i(1 - D_t) + \theta'_i \overline{W}_{gt}DQ_{gt} + \sum_{j=1}^{3} \pi^g_{ij} Dp_{jt} + \epsilon_{it}$$

	Constants		Conditional Marginal Share (θ'_i)	Conditional Slutsky Coefficients				
Beverage	$\alpha_i \times 1,000$	$\beta_i \times 1,000$		$\pi^g_{i1} \times 100$	$\pi^g_{i2} \times 100$	$\pi^g_{i3} \times 100$	R^2	DW
Beer	−.039	−.107	.539	−.464	.135	.329	.92	2.20
	(.103)	(.115)	(.046)	(.153)	(.117)	(.101)		
Wine	.066	.525	.095	—	−.300	.165	.74	1.49
	(.078)	(.084)	(.033)		(.122)	(.074)		
Spirits	−.027	−.419	.366	—	—	−.494	.78	1.66
	(.100)	(.112)	(.044)			(.105)		

Note: $D_t = 1$ for 1956-57/1964-65, 0 otherwise. R^2 is the squared correlation coefficient between actual and predicted values of dependent variable and thus lies in the range [0, 1]. DW (with the usual single-equation definition) tests for autocorrelation of residuals from restricted model. Asymptotic SEs in parentheses.

77. The conditional marginal shares are estimated quite precisely and they indicate that when alcohol expenditure increases by $1, expenditure on beer rises by 54 cents, wine by 10 cents, with the remaining 37 cents being spent on spirits. All the diagonal elements of the conditional Slutsky matrix are negative, as they should be, and significant. The off-diagonal π_{ij}^{g}'s are positive, indicating that the three beverages are pair-wise substitutes, and only one is insignificantly different from zero. The fit of the equations is satisfactory given that they are in first-difference form.

The compatibility of the homogeneity and symmetry restrictions with the data can be verified by means of a likelihood ratio test. The unrestricted version of the model is (14), including constant terms, without the constraints (12) and (13). Asymptotically, minus twice the difference between the log-likelihood values for the restricted and unrestricted models is distributed as $X^2(3)$. The observed value of the test statistic is 4.05, less than the critical value at the 5 percent level of 7.81. Thus we are unable to reject homogeneity and symmetry.

Table 4 gives the conditional demand elasticities evaluated at the beginning and end of the sample period, as well as at sample means. At sample means, the conditional income elasticities are .8, .8, and 2.3, for beer, wine, and spirits, respectively. This indicates that, within alcohol, beer and wine are necessities and spirits is a strong luxury. Note, however, that at the beginning of the period wine has a conditional income elasticity greater than one. All the conditional price elasticities are less than one in absolute value, with the own-price elasticities being

TABLE 4
Conditional Demand Elasticities for Alcoholic Beverages, Australia, 1955–1956/1976–1977

Beverage	Conditional Income Elasticity $(\theta_i' \bar{W}_{gt}/\bar{w}_{it})$	Conditional Price Elasticities		
		$\pi_{i_1}^{g}/\bar{w}_{it}$	$\pi_{i_2}^{g}/\bar{w}_{it}$	$\pi_{i_3}^{g}/\bar{w}_{it}$
1956–57:				
Beer	.71	−.10	.03	.07
Wine	1.11	.26	−.57	.31
Spirits	2.34	.34	.17	−.52
1976–77:				
Beer	.82	−.12	.03	.08
Wine	.51	.12	−.27	.15
Spirits	2.34	.35	.17	−.52
Sample means:				
Beer	.75	−.11	.03	.08
Wine	.75	.18	−.40	.22
Spirits	2.32	.35	.18	−.53

Source: Based on Table 3 estimates and Table 2 data.

$-.1$, $-.4$, and $-.5$ (at sample means). As expected, there is only a moderate amount of substitutability between the three beverages.

Estimates with Total Alcohol Consumption Endogenous

We now let total alcohol consumption $\overline{W}_{gt}DQ_{gt}$ become endogenously determined by adding the composite demand equation to the three conditional equations. The composite equation in terms of infinitesimal changes is (7). As before, we replace budget shares with their arithmetic averages and infinitesimal logarithmic changes by finite log changes; and treat the coefficients as constants. Numbering goods such that the alcoholic beverages are the first three, the estimating equation is thus

$$\overline{W}_{gt}DQ_{gt} = \Theta_g DQ_t + \phi\Theta_g \left(\sum_{i=1}^{3} \theta'_i Dp_{it} - \sum_{j=1}^{n} \theta_j Dp_{jt} \right) + E_{gt}, \qquad (15)$$

where $DQ_t = \sum_{i=1}^{n} \overline{w}_{it} Dq_{it}$ and E_{gt} is a serially independent, normally distributed disturbance with a zero mean and a constant variance.

Equations (14) and (15) form a system of four simultaneous equations with endogenous variables $\overline{w}_{it}Dq_{it}$ ($i = 1, 2, 3$) and $\overline{W}_{gt}DQ_{gt}$. The variables taken to be predetermined are the prices and DQ_t. Note that (15) implies that the only random component of $\overline{W}_{gt}DQ_{gt}$ is the disturbance E_{gt}. Hence, we can treat $\overline{W}_{gt}DQ_{gt}$ as predetermined in (14) if E_g is independent of the disturbance in (14) ϵ_{it}. Remarkably, Theil's theory of rational random behavior implies that these disturbances are independent. Thus, our previous estimates of (14) by itself are consistent under the theory of rational random behavior.

In this subsection we do not rely on this theory and estimate (14) and (15) simultaneously, allowing the disturbances E_{gt} and ϵ_{it} to be correlated. A comparison of the two sets of estimates can be interpreted as an informal test of the theory. In addition, the estimation of (15) allows us to obtain the unconditional demand responses.

The overall Frisch price index in (15) can be written as

$$\sum_{j=1}^{n} \theta_j Dp_{jt} = \Theta_g \sum_{j=1}^{3} \theta'_j Dp_{jt} + (1 - \Theta_g) \sum_{k=4}^{n} \frac{\theta_k}{\sum_{l=4}^{n} \theta_l} Dp_{kt}, \qquad (16)$$

as $\theta'_j = \theta_j/\Theta_g$ and $\Theta_g = \sum_{i=1}^{3}\theta_i = 1 - \sum_{l=4}^{n}\theta_l$. In words, the overall Frisch price index is a weighted average of the Frisch indexes for alcohol and all other, the weights being the group marginal shares. The estimation procedure can be simplified by eliminating the marginal shares not involving alcohol. We do this by approximating the Frisch index of all other in (16), $\sum_{k=4}^{n}(\theta_k/\sum_{l=4}^{n}\theta_l)Dp_{kt}$, by the change in the consumer price index excluding alcohol DP_{0t}, so that

$$\sum_{j=1}^{n} \theta_j Dp_{jt} \approx \Theta_g \sum_{j=1}^{3} \theta_j' Dp_{jt} + (1 - \Theta_g) DP_{0t}. \tag{17}$$

For estimation we substitute in (15) the right side of (17) for $\sum_{j=1}^{n} \theta_j Dp_{jt}$. We also approximate the change in real income DQ_t by the difference between the log change in per capita total consumption expenditure and that of the consumer price index.

The maximum likelihood estimates are given in Table 5. All the estimates for the conditional demand equations are highly consistent with those of Table 3. This result gives support to the theory of rational random behavior, which allows $\overline{W}_{gt} DQ_{gt}$ to be treated as predetermined. Looking at the estimates for the composite equation, there is a significant autonomous trend out of alcohol in the first part of the period. The marginal share for the group is highly significant and indicates that a $1 rise in income leads to a 6 cent increase in alcohol expenditure. Finally, the value of the income flexibility is quite close to previous estimates. Testing the homogeneity and symmetry restrictions, as before, gives an observed X^2 value of 5.66, again less than the critical value of $X^2(3)$ at the 5 percent level.

Table 6 gives the conditional demand elasticities and the income and own-price elasticities for the group. As is to be expected, the conditional elasticities are similar to those of Table 4. The income elasticity of demand for alcoholic beverages as a whole is 1.0, while the own-price elasticity is $-.6$.

The Unconditional Demand Responses

The conditional demand equation (14) depends on total alcohol consumption and the prices of the three beverages. Accordingly, the conditional Slutsky coefficient π_{ij}^{g} measures the effect of a change in the price of alcoholic beverage j on the consumption of beverage i with total alcohol consumption held constant. From equation (15), this total also depends on the price of j. Thus a change in p_j has a direct effect on i, via the conditional demand equation, and an indirect effect via the composite demand equation. These two effects can be combined to give the total effect by substituting the right side of (15) for $\overline{W}_{gt} DQ_{gt}$ in (14). This yields

$$\overline{w}_{it} DQ_{jt} = \theta_i DQ_t + \sum_{j=1}^{3} \pi_{ij} Dp_{jt} + \pi_{i0} DP_{0t} + \eta_{it}, \tag{18}$$

where

$$\theta_i = \Theta_g \theta_i' \tag{19}$$

is the unconditional marginal share of i;

TABLE 5
Conditional and Composite Demand Equations for Alcoholic Beverages, Australia, 1955–1956/1976–1977

$$\bar{w}_{it}Dq_{it} = \alpha_i D_t + \beta_i(1-D_t) + \theta_i'\bar{W}_{gt}DQ_{gt} + \sum_{j=1}^{3}\pi_{ij}^{g}DP_{jt} + \epsilon_{it}$$

$$\bar{W}_{gt}DQ_{gt} = \gamma D_t + \lambda(1-D_t) + \Theta_g EQ_t + \phi\Theta_g\left(\sum_{i=1}^{3}\theta_i'Dp_{it} - \sum_{j=1}^{n}\theta DP_{jt}\right) + E_{gt}$$

Beverage	Constants		Conditional Marginal Share	Conditional Slusky Coefficients				
	$\alpha_i \times 1{,}000$	$\beta_i \times 1{,}000$	(θ_i')	$\pi_{i1}^{g} \times 100$	$\pi_{i2}^{g} \times 100$	$\pi_{i3}^{g} \times 100$	R^2	DW
Beer	−.065	−.196	.590	−.390	.150	.240	.67	1.72
	(.106)	(.115)	(.045)	(1.45)	(.114)	(.097)		
Wine	.062	.517	.099	—	−.293	.144	.68	1.24
	(.078)	(.084)	(.035)		(.124)	(.072)		
Spirits	.003	−.321	.311	—	—	−.384	.69	2.34
	(.104)	(.111)	(.042)			(.102)		
	$\gamma \times 1{,}000$	$\lambda \times 1{,}000$	Θ_g			ϕ		
Total alcohol	−.686	.209	.0576	—	—	−.595	.76	1.73
	(.332)	(.342)	(.0095)			(.130)		

Note: R^2 refers to reduced form. See nn. to Table 3.

TABLE 6
Conditional and Composite Demand Elasticities for Alcoholic Beverages,
Australia, 1955–1956/1976–1977

Beverage	Conditional Income Elasticity $(\theta_i'\overline{W}_{gt}/\overline{w}_{it})$	Conditional Price Elasticities			Composite Income Elasticity $(\Theta_g/\overline{W}_{gt})$	Composite Own-Price Elasticity $(\phi\Theta_g/\overline{W}_{gt})$
		$\pi_{i1}^g/\overline{w}_{it}$	$\pi_{i2}^g/\overline{w}_{it}$	$\pi_{i3}^g/\overline{w}_{it}$		
1956–57:						
Beer	.78	−.08	.03	.05	—	—
Wine	1.15	.29	−.56	.27	—	—
Spirits	1.98	.25	.15	−.40	—	—
Total alcohol	—	—	—	—	.94	−.56
1976–77:						
Beer	.90	−.10	.04	.06	—	—
Wine	.53	.13	−.26	.13	—	—
Spirits	1.99	.25	.15	−.40	—	—
Total alcohol	—	—	—	—	.95	−.56
Sample means:						
Beer	.83	−.09	.04	.06	—	—
Wine	.78	.20	−.39	.19	—	—
Spirits	1.97	.26	.15	−.41	—	—
Total alcohol	—	—	—	—	.97	−.58

Source: Based on Table 5 estimates and Table 2 data.

$$\pi_{ij} = \pi_{ij}^g + \phi\Theta_g(1-\Theta_g)\theta_i'\theta_j' \qquad \pi_{i0} = -\phi\Theta_g(1-\Theta_g)\theta_i' \qquad (20)$$

are unconditional Slutsky coefficients; and $\eta_{it} = \epsilon_{it} + \theta_i'E_{gt}$. In deriving
(18) we have used the right side of (17) to substitute for $\Sigma_{j=1}^n\theta_jDp_{jt}$ in
(15). From (18) it can be seen that the unconditional income and price
elasticities are $\theta_i/\overline{w}_{it}$, $\pi_{ij}/\overline{w}_{it}$, and $\pi_{i0}/\overline{w}_{it}$.

We use the Table 5 estimates to evaluate (19) and (20) for $i, j =$
1, 2, 3. The results are given in Table 7. Thus the direct and indirect
effects of a \$1 rise in income is to increase expenditure on beer by
3.4 cents, wine by .6 cents and spirits by 1.8 cents. All the own-Slutsky
coefficients are estimated quite precisely and each is more negative than
the corresponding conditional coefficient of Table 5. The reason is that
an increase in the price of beverage i lowers total alcohol consumption,
which also lowers the consumption of i as the estimate of θ_i' is positive
for each i. This negative indirect effect is then added to the conditional
Slutsky coefficient π_{ii}^g (<0) to give an unconditional coefficient π_{ii} larger
in absolute value than π_{ii}^g. For a similar reason the estimates of π_{12}
and π_{13} are negative, indicating that beer is an unconditional complement
for wine and spirits, whereas these beverages are conditional substitutes
(π_{12}^g, $\pi_{13}^g > 0$; see Table 5). Finally, each of the three beverages is a
substitute for all other goods.

Table 8 gives the unconditional elasticities. As the income elasticity
for the group is about unity (see Table 6), the unconditional income

TABLE 7
Unconditional Demand Equations for Alcoholic Beverages, Australia,
1955–1956/1976–1977

$$\overline{w}_{it}Dq_{it} = \delta_i D_t + \psi_i(1 - D_t) + \theta_i DQ_t + \sum_{j=1}^{3} \pi_{ij}Dp_{jt} + \pi_{i0}DP_{0t} + \eta_{it}$$

	Constants			Slutsky Coefficients			
Beverage	δ_i $\times$ 1,000	ψ_i $\times$ 1,000	Marginal Share (θ_i)	π_{i1} $\times$ 100	π_{i2} $\times$ 100	π_{i3} $\times$ 100	π_{i0} $\times$ 100
Beer	−.469	−.073	.0340	−1.514	−.039	−.353	1.906
	(.236)	(.235)	(.0062)	(.299)	(.125)	(.146)	(.377)
Wine	−.006	.537	.0057	—	−.325	.044	.319
	(.092)	(.089)	(.0023)		(.132)	(.080)	(.132)
Spirits	−.210	−.256	.0179	—	—	−.697	1.006
	(.139)	(.139)	(.0037)			(.130)	(.202)

Note: The estimates from Table 5 are used in eq. (19) and (20) to obtain the (unconditional) marginal shares and Slutsky coefficients. The constant term δ_i is defined as $\alpha_i + \theta_i'\gamma$, with estimates taken from Table 5; and similarly for ψ_i. See nn. to Table 3.

elasticities given in Table 8 are quite close to the corresponding conditional elasticities. The high income elasticity for spirits agrees well with the notion that in Australia the more affluent tend to be spirits drinkers. For the reason given above, the own-price elasticities are substantially larger (in absolute value) than those of Table 6. At sample means, the unconditional own-price elasticities are −.4, −.4, and −.7 for beer, wine, and spirits, respectively.

TABLE 8
Unconditional Demand Elasticities for Alcoholic Beverages, Australia, 1955–1956/1976–1977

Beverage	Income Elasticity $(\theta_i/\overline{w}_{it})$	Price Elasticities			
		$\pi_{i1}/\overline{w}_{it}$	$\pi_{i2}/\overline{w}_{it}$	$\pi_{i3}/\overline{w}_{it}$	$\pi_{i0}/\overline{w}_{it}$
1956–57:					
Beer	.73	−.33	−.01	−.08	.41
Wine	1.08	−.07	−.62	.08	.61
Spirits	1.87	−.37	.05	−.73	1.05
1976–77:					
Beer	.85	−.37	−.01	−.09	.48
Wine	.50	−.03	−.29	.04	.28
Spirits	1.89	−.37	.05	−.73	1.06
Sample means:					
Beer	.80	−.36	−.01	−.08	.45
Wine	.75	−.05	−.43	.06	.42
Spirits	1.91	−.38	.05	−.74	1.07

Source: Based on Table 7 estimates and Table 2 data.

IV. WHY HAS WINE CONSUMPTION GROWN SO RAPIDLY?

As indicated in the previous section, wine consumption per capita grew by 4.5 percent per annum over our sample period; and the share of wine in total alcohol expenditure increased by 10 percentage points. In this section we analyze the reasons for this rapid growth by using the demand equations to (1) decompose the growth into a number of components and (2) simulate alcohol consumption under several different scenarios.

A Decomposition of the Change in the Budget Share

Recalling that the ith budget share is defined as $w_i = p_i q_i / M$, its change is $dw_i = w_i d(\log p_i) + w_i d(\log q_i) - w_i d(\log M)$. This can be expressed in terms of the relative price of i and real income by adding and subtracting from the right side the Divisia cost of living index $d(\log P) = \sum_{i=1}^{n} w_i d(\log p_i)$. This gives

$$dw_i = w_i d\left(\log \frac{p_i}{P}\right) + w_i d(\log q_i) - w_i d(\log Q), \qquad (21)$$

where $d(\log p_i/P) = d(\log p_i) - d(\log P)$ is the change in the relative price of i and $d(\log Q) = d(\log M) - d(\log P) = \sum_{i=1}^{n} w_i d(\log q_i)$ is the change in real income.

Equation (21) states that dw_i is made up of relative price, quantity, and real income components. From the consumer's viewpoint prices and income are given, while the quantity demanded is to be determined. Thus we use the demand equation (1) to express the quantity component in terms of income and relative prices,

$$dw_i = (\theta_i - w_i)d(\log Q) + \sum_{j=1}^{n} \nu_{ij} d\left(\log \frac{p_j}{P'}\right) + w_i d\left(\log \frac{p_i}{P}\right). \qquad (22)$$

Thus a rise in income causes the budget share of i to increase if the marginal share (θ_i) exceeds the average share (w_i); that is, if this good is a luxury. The second component on the right of (22) is the price substitution term, which gives the effect of changes in relative prices on w_i via q_i. The final term is the direct effect of the relative price of i on the budget share.

To apply (22) to the finite-change data for alcoholic beverages, we use the right side of equation (18) to substitute for the quantity component in (21). This gives

$$\Delta w_{it} = (\theta_i - \overline{w}_{it})DQ_t + \sum_{j=1}^{3} \pi_{ij} Dp_{jt} + \pi_{i0} DP_{0t}$$
$$+ \overline{w}_{it}(Dp_{it} - DP_t) + \eta_{it} + 0_3, \qquad (23)$$

where $\Delta w_{it} = w_{it} - w_{i,t-1}$ and 0_3 is a remainder term of third degree (Theil 1975-76, pp. 37-40, 215). Note that (12) and (20) imply $\Sigma_{j=1}^3 \pi_{ij} + \pi_{i0} = 0$, which is a reflection of demand homogeneity. We use this to deflate the absolute prices in (23) Dp_{jt} and DP_0t by DP_t to give

$$\Delta w_{it} = (\theta_i = \overline{w}_{it})DQ_t + \sum_{j=1}^3 \pi_{ij}(Dp_{jt} - DP_t) \tag{24}$$
$$+ \pi_{i0}(DP_{0t} - DP_t) + \overline{w}_{it}(Dp_{it} - DP_t) + \eta_{it} + 0_3.$$

To evaluate (24) we use the estimates given in Table 7 and the log change in the consumer price index for DP_t. The constant term in the demand equation $\delta_i D_t + \psi_i(1 - D_t)$ means that this is an additional component of Δw_i. The results are given in Tables 9–11. Looking at Table 9, on average the budget share of beer fell by .029 percentage points per annum. The shift in preferences away from beer accounts for .024 of this. The growth in real income, together with the fact that beer is a necessity, accounts for .019 of the fall. The rise in the relative price of beer accounts for .008, while the other relative prices have a negligible effect. Finally, offsetting the fall in the beer share is the direct relative price component of .022. The conclusion that emerges is that the shift in preferences away from beer and the growth in real income are the two most important reasons for the decline in the budget share of beer.

As can be seen from Table 10, the most important component of growth in the wine share on average is the shift in preferences toward wine. This is then followed by the direct relative price component, caused by the price of wine rising more rapidly than the CPI. Offsetting these two terms are the effects due to growth in real income and own-price substitution. For spirits (Table 11) on average the growth in income has the effect of almost offsetting the negative shift in preferences; and the other components are quite small.

The importance of the shift in preferences raises the question of what lies behind this shift. Possible explanations include (1) Southern Europeans migrating to Australia and bringing with them their alcohol consumption patterns; (2) changes in demographic structure, such as members of the postwar baby boom reaching drinking age over this period; and (3) advertising and innovation in packaging and marketing, such as the introduction of wine casks.

Simulation of Alcohol Consumption

In this subsection we attempt to isolate the key factors responsible for the rapid growth of wine consumption by using the demand model for counterfactual simulations. We simulate alcohol consumption with (1) alcohol tax rates held constant; (2) a wine tax rate equal to the

TABLE 9. Decomposition of Change in Budget Share of Beer, Australia, 1955–1956/1976–1977

| Year | Change in Budget Share of Beer Δw_1 (1) | Constant $\delta_1 D + \psi_1 \times (1-D)$ (2) | Income $(\theta_1 - \bar{u}_1)DQ$ (3) | Components of Δw_1 — Price Substitution |||| | Direct Relative Price $\bar{u}_1(Dp_1 - DP)$ (9) | Demand Equation Residual η_1 (10) |
				Beer $\pi_{11} \times (Dp_1 - DP)$ (4)	Wine $\pi_{12} \times (Dp_2 - DP)$ (5)	Spirits $\pi_{13} \times (Dp_3 - DP)$ (6)	Total Alcohol $\sum_{j=1}^{3} \pi_{1j} \times (Dp_j - DP)$ (7)	All Other $\pi_{10} \times (DP_0 - DP)$ (8)		
1956–57	21.31	−4.69	1.77	−12.91	−.01	2.01	−10.91	−.69	39.50	−3.63
1957–58	−5.52	−4.69	−2.15	−.38	−.15	.34	−.19	−.05	1.19	.34
1958–59	−10.06	−4.69	−1.76	1.82	−.18	.55	2.19	.09	−5.57	−.23
1959–60	−20.50	−4.69	−5.07	2.47	−.20	.88	3.15	.14	−7.31	−6.78
1960–61	−9.39	−4.69	.31	3.34	−.13	−1.55	1.66	.07	−9.56	2.82
1961–62	−2.72	−4.69	−.43	−.40	−.04	−.31	−.74	−.05	1.12	2.05
1962–63	−13.91	−4.69	−3.88	−.55	−.05	−1.92	−2.52	−.15	1.53	−4.20
1963–64	−1.33	−4.69	−3.39	−1.64	−.01	−.00	−1.65	−.09	4.46	4.04
1964–65	−5.81	−4.69	−1.48	3.51	−.08	.60	4.02	.20	−9.44	5.58
1965–66	17.15	−.73	−.35	−6.96	−.15	−3.59	−10.71	−.63	19.01	10.62
1966–67	4.28	−.73	−2.60	−2.51	−.08	2.72	.13	−.03	7.02	.50
1967–68	1.97	−.73	−3.24	−1.31	−.14	1.15	−.31	−.07	3.70	2.56
1968–69	−.06	−.73	−3.06	−.67	−.38	−1.48	−2.53	−.28	1.90	4.70
1969–70	−6.47	−.73	−3.78	−.48	−.11	.11	−.49	−.08	1.36	−2.78
1970–71	3.06	−.73	−2.16	−2.47	−.18	.57	−2.08	−.20	6.90	1.34
1971–72	−12.64	−.73	−1.10	2.24	.03	2.23	4.50	.26	−6.19	−9.38
1972–73	−6.16	−.73	−2.68	.96	.26	1.76	2.98	.28	−2.59	−3.46
1973–74	−1.59	−.73	−1.86	6.89	.36	−2.83	4.41	.40	−18.42	14.65
1974–75	−13.95	−.73	−1.40	3.22	.02	−3.60	−.36	−.03	−8.45	−2.99
1975–76	17.17	−.73	2.37	−15.86	−.25	−.26	−16.37	−1.00	41.77	−4.12
1976–77	−16.53	−.73	.48	6.05	.20	4.43	10.68	.68	−15.95	−11.70
Mean	−2.94	−2.43	−1.91	−.75	−.06	.09	−.72	−.06	2.19	−.00

Note: Column (1) = (2) + (3) + (4) + (5) + (6) + (7) + (8) + (9) + (10) + a remainder term of third degree. The year 1956–57, e.g., refers to the transition from 1955–56 to 1956–57. All entries are to be divided by 10,000.

TABLE 10. Decomposition of Change in Budget Share of Wine, Australia, 1955–1956/1976–1977

| | | | | Components of Δw_2 | | | | | | |
| | | | | | Price Substitution | | | | | |
Year	Change in Budget Share of Wine Δw_2 (1)	Constant $\delta_2 D + \psi_2 \times (1-D)$ (2)	Income $(\theta_2 - \bar{w}_2)DQ$ (3)	Beer $\pi_{21} \times (Dp_1 - DP)$ (4)	Wine $\pi_{22} \times (Dp_2 - DP)$ (5)	Spirits $\pi_{23} \times (Dp_3 - DP)$ (6)	Total Alcohol $\sum_{j=1}^{3} \pi_{2j} \times (Dp_j - DP)$ (7)	All Other $\pi_{20} \times (DP_0 - DP)$ (8)	Direct Relative Price $\bar{w}_2(Dp_2 - DP)$ (9)	Demand Equation Residual η_2 (10)
1956–57	−.40	−.06	−.06	−.33	−.10	−.25	−.68	−.12	.16	.40
1957–58	.76	−.06	.07	−.01	−1.27	−.04	−1.32	−.01	2.06	.07
1958–59	2.06	−.06	.04	.05	−1.48	−.07	−1.50	.02	2.46	1.10
1959–60	.67	−.06	.07	.06	−1.64	−.11	−1.68	.02	2.79	−.45
1960–61	.48	−.06	−.00	.09	−1.09	.19	−.81	.01	1.88	−.61
1961–62	.55	−.06	.00	−.01	−.30	.04	−.27	−.01	.52	.33
1962–63	−.30	−.06	.01	−.01	−.44	.24	−.22	−.03	.77	−.78
1963–64	−.02	−.06	.02	−.04	−.06	.00	−.11	−.02	.11	.07
1964–65	.41	−.06	.01	.09	−.69	−.07	−.68	.03	1.21	−.14
1965–66	7.26	5.37	−.02	−.18	−1.25	.45	−.98	−.11	2.33	.74
1966–67	7.14	5.37	−.33	−.06	−.67	−.34	−1.08	−.00	1.41	1.75
1967–68	7.80	5.37	−.68	−.03	−1.20	−.14	−1.38	−.01	2.79	1.75
1968–69	12.71	5.37	−.99	−.02	−3.15	.18	−2.98	−.05	8.29	3.08
1969–70	6.13	5.37	−1.69	−.01	−.93	−.01	−.95	−.01	2.70	.74
1970–71	−.99	5.37	−1.05	−.06	−1.48	−.07	−1.61	−.03	4.44	−8.14
1971–72	−.26	5.37	−.56	.06	.24	−.28	.02	.04	−.71	−4.38
1972–73	−.54	5.37	−1.54	.02	2.19	−.22	2.00	.05	−6.50	.10
1973–74	−.63	5.37	−1.11	.18	3.01	.35	3.54	.07	−8.87	.37
1974–75	8.25	5.37	−1.04	.08	.15	.45	.68	−.00	−.46	3.74
1975–76	9.15	5.37	−2.07	−.41	−2.06	.03	−2.43	−.17	6.85	1.62
1976–77	.11	5.37	.46	.16	1.69	−.55	1.29	.11	−5.87	−1.25
Mean	2.87	3.04	−.50	−.02	−.50	−.01	−.53	−.01	.87	.00

Note: Column (1) = (2) + (3) + (4) + (5) + (6) + (8) + (9) + (10) + a remainder term of third degree. The year 1956–57, e.g., refers to the transition from 1955–56 to 1956–57. All entries are to be divided by 10,000.

TABLE 11. Decomposition of Change in Budget Share of Spirits, Australia, 1955–1956/1976–1977

| Year | Change in Budget Share of Spirits Δw_3 (1) | Constant $\delta_3 D + \psi_3 \times (1-D)$ (2) | Income $(\theta_3 - \bar{w}_3)DQ$ (3) | Components of Δw_3 — Price Substitution | | | | | Direct Relative Price $\bar{w}_3(Dp_3 - DP)$ (9) | Demand Equation Residual η_3 (10) |
				Beer $\pi_{31} \times (Dp_1 - DP)$ (4)	Wine $\pi_{32} \times (Dp_2 - DP)$ (5)	Spirits $\pi_{33} \times (Dp_3 - DP)$ (6)	Total Alcohol $\sum_{j=1}^{3} \pi_{3j} \times (Dp_j - DP)$ (7)	All Other $\pi_{30} \times (DP_0 - DP)$ (8)		
1956–57	−13.98	−2.10	−1.20	−3.01	.01	3.96	.96	−.37	−5.45	−5.92
1957–58	−1.30	−2.10	1.49	−.09	.17	.68	.76	−.03	−.86	−.49
1958–59	1.77	−2.10	1.29	.42	.20	1.09	1.72	.05	−1.39	2.08
1959–60	1.12	−2.10	4.18	.58	.22	1.73	2.53	.07	−2.23	−1.32
1960–61	4.00	−2.10	−.29	.78	.15	−3.07	−2.14	.04	4.07	4.44
1961–62	.62	−2.10	.41	−.09	.04	−.60	−.66	−.03	.82	2.18
1962–63	−2.02	−2.10	4.18	−.13	.06	−3.79	−3.86	−.08	5.11	−5.21
1963–64	2.79	−2.10	4.03	−.38	.01	−.00	−.38	−.05	.01	1.22
1964–65	3.25	−2.10	1.79	.82	.09	1.19	2.10	.11	−1.66	3.06
1965–66	−2.18	−2.56	.39	−1.62	.17	−7.10	−8.55	−.33	9.98	−1.16
1966–67	−10.59	−2.56	2.70	−.58	.09	5.37	4.88	−.01	−7.06	−8.49
1967–68	4.10	−2.56	3.37	−.31	.16	2.26	2.12	−.04	−2.87	4.05
1968–69	−.32	−2.56	3.08	−.16	.43	−2.92	−2.65	−.15	3.78	−1.83
1969–70	5.32	−2.56	3.85	−.11	.13	.21	.22	−.04	−.28	4.11
1970–71	−3.12	−2.56	2.22	−.58	.20	1.12	.74	−.11	−1.50	−1.86
1971–72	−1.85	−2.56	1.23	.52	−.03	4.41	4.90	.14	−5.78	.18
1972–73	3.07	−2.56	3.39	.22	−.30	3.48	3.41	.15	−4.60	3.31
1973–74	5.58	−2.56	2.37	1.61	−.41	−5.60	−4.40	.21	7.73	2.24
1974–75	3.54	−2.56	1.91	.75	−.02	−7.11	−6.38	−.01	10.30	.27
1975–76	−6.76	−2.56	3.22	−3.70	.28	−.52	−3.94	−.53	.74	−3.70
1976–77	−1.87	−2.56	−.69	1.41	−.23	8.75	9.93	.36	−11.92	3.01
Mean	−.42	−2.36	2.04	−.17	.07	.17	.06	−.03	−.15	.01

Note: Column (1) = (2) + (3) + (4) + (5) + (6) + (8) + (9) + (10) + a remainder term of third degree. The year 1956–57, e.g., refers to the transition from 1955–56 to 1956–57. All entries are to be divided by 10,000.

beer tax rate; and (3) no constant terms in the demand equations. These simulations answer the question to what extent the growth in wine is due to (1) changes in all alcohol taxes; (2) the fact that beer is subject to a substantial tax, while wine is not; and (3) trend-like changes in tastes toward wine.

Table 12 gives the data on alcohol taxes, in terms of both revenue and tax rates. As can be seen, although beer represents the most important source of revenue, its tax *rate* has almost halved over this period (from 117% to 63%). Aside from the early 1970s, the tax on wine is negligible, while the tax rate for spirits has increased.

We simulate consumption with the tax rates held constant at their 1955–56 values of 117 percent, 0, and 38 percent for beer, wine, and spirits, respectively. With p_i the posttax price of i, p_i^0 the pretax price and t_i the tax rate, we have $p_{it} = (1 + t_{it})p_{it}^0$, so that $Dp_{it} = D(1 + t_i) + Dp_{it}^0$, where D is the log-change operator (as before). Accordingly, we can simulate the constant tax rates by replacing in the demand equations the observed price log change Dp_{it} with $Dp_{it} - D(1 + t_{it})$, which is the price change purged of its tax change component. Using equation (18), the simulated quantity log change is

$$Dq_{it}^s = (\theta_i/\overline{w}_{it})DQ_t + \sum_{j=1}^{3} (\pi_{ij}/\overline{w}_{it})[Dp_{jt} - D(1 + t_{jt})]$$
$$+ (\pi_{i0}/\overline{w}_{it})DP_{0t} + \eta_{it}/\overline{w}_{it}.$$

Subtracting from this the observed quantity log change Dq_{it} and using (18) gives

$$Dq_{it}^s - Dq_{it} = -\sum_{j=1}^{3} (\pi_{ij}/\overline{w}_{it})D(1 + t_{jt}). \tag{25}$$

Converting from changes to levels, the simulated quantity is $q_{it}^s = \exp(Dq_{it}^s + \log q_{i,t-1}^s)$. Finally, to evaluate (25) we use the estimates given in Table 7.

The results of this simulation are given in the first three columns of Table 13 (for changes) and in columns 4–6 of Table 14 (levels). As the observed tax rate for beer fell over this period and that for spirits rose, the constant tax rate policy causes beer consumption to be lower than otherwise and spirits to be higher. By 1976–77, simulated per capita consumption is 125 liters, 13.4 liters, and 3.23 liters for beer, wine, and spirits (see Table 14). Accordingly, this tax package causes beer consumption to be $(124.57 - 136.14)/136.14 = 8.5$ percent lower than otherwise, wine to be $(13.3616 - 13.6533)/13.6533 = 2.1$ percent lower, and spirits to be $(3.2300 - 3.1663)/3.1663 = 2.0$ percent higher. The reasons for the lower consumption of wine are (1) that it is an unconditional complement for beer (see Table 7) and in the simulation we increase the price of beer; and (2) wine and spirits are unconditional substitutes and the price of spirits increases less rapidly in the simulation.

TABLE 12
Alcohol Taxes, Australia, 1955–1956/1976–1977

	Tax Revenues ($per capita)				Tax Rates × 100 (percent pretax prices)		
Year	Beer $\left(\dfrac{t_1}{1+t_1}\,p_1q_1\right)$	Wine $\left(\dfrac{t_2}{1+t_2}\,p_2q_2\right)$	Spirits $\left(\dfrac{t_3}{1+t_3}\,p_3q_3\right)$	Total Alcohol $\left(\sum_{i=1}^{3}\dfrac{t_i}{1+t_i}\,p_iq_i\right)$	Beer (t_1)	Wine (t_2)	Spirits (t_3)
1955–56	18.33	0	2.14	20.47	117.198	0	38.351
1956–57	21.72	0	2.27	23.99	141.132	0	48.401
1957–58	21.77	0	2.27	24.04	137.090	0	47.588
1958–59	21.17	0	2.39	23.56	126.086	0	47.704
1959–60	21.59	.01	2.63	24.23	124.296	.201	48.524
1960–61	21.51	.01	2.64	24.16	119.236	.192	43.421
1961–62	21.41	.01	2.67	24.09	117.250	.189	43.133
1962–63	21.72	.01	2.59	24.32	116.272	.180	39.602
1963–64	22.45	.01	2.78	25.24	111.358	.170	38.773
1964–65	23.17	.02	3.00	26.19	108.372	.320	37.927
1965–66	26.34	.02	3.31	29.67	119.674	.273	42.436
1966–67	27.43	.02	3.67	31.12	112.929	.232	53.891
1967–68	28.45	.03	4.09	32.57	104.365	.292	53.254
1968–69	29.26	.04	3.96	33.26	97.793	.316	46.589
1969–70	29.88	.05	4.41	34.34	90.491	.343	44.862
1970–71	30.08	.75	4.38	35.21	79.073	5.064	41.995
1971–72	30.53	.96	4.63	36.12	74.356	6.057	41.749
1972–73	31.65	.32	5.23	37.20	68.654	1.767	41.213
1973–74	34.31	.09	7.70	42.10	61.598	.425	53.584
1974–75	34.81	.11	10.73	45.65	50.353	.400	64.601
1975–76	50.17	.15	11.83	62.15	64.761	.426	64.965
1976–77	53.23	.18	13.40	66.81	62.615	.452	67.507
Mean	28.23	.13	4.67	33.02	100.225	.786	47.730

TABLE 13
Simulation of Consumption of Alcoholic Beverages, Australia, 1955–1956/1976–1977

Year	Alcohol Tax Rates Held Constant			Wine Tax Rate Equal to Beer Tax Rate			No Constant Terms in Demand Equations		
	Beer	Wine	Spirits	Beer	Wine	Spirits	Beer	Wine	Spirits
1956–57	3.95	.19	8.95	−.74	−54.43	4.04	1.01	.11	2.19
1957–58	−.58	−.08	−1.11	.01	1.04	−.08	1.00	.11	2.38
1958–59	−1.55	−.35	−1.83	.04	2.85	−.24	1.01	.11	2.37
1959–60	−.22	.02	.11	.01	.58	−.05	1.05	.11	2.34
1960–61	−1.08	.11	−3.51	.02	1.32	−.11	1.08	.11	2.27
1961–62	−.34	−.05	−.49	.01	−.52	−.04	1.10	.11	2.22
1962–63	−.37	.16	−2.02	.00	.25	−.02	1.12	.11	2.23
1963–64	−.90	−.12	−1.30	.02	1.31	−.11	1.14	.11	2.22
1964–65	−.58	.04	−.96	.02	.90	−.07	1.15	.11	2.15
1965–66	2.21	.08	4.19	−.05	−2.86	.24	.18	−8.86	2.61
1966–67	−.47	−.70	4.68	.03	1.48	−.15	.17	−7.92	2.79
1967–68	−1.49	−.16	−1.97	.04	1.80	−.21	.17	−7.14	2.90
1968–69	−1.52	.09	−4.71	.03	1.25	−.16	.17	−6.28	2.84
1969–70	−1.44	−.09	−2.32	.03	1.30	−.18	.17	−5.66	2.76
1970–71	−2.34	1.38	−4.02	.10	3.59	−.51	.17	−5.51	2.73
1971–72	−.97	.22	−1.21	.03	1.21	−.17	.17	−5.54	2.80
1972–73	−1.30	−1.51	−1.37	−.01	−.27	.04	.18	−5.57	2.78
1973–74	−.88	−1.01	4.57	.03	1.00	−.13	.18	−5.60	2.66
1974–75	−2.13	−.60	2.26	.07	2.34	−.31	.18	−5.39	2.54
1975–76	3.49	.33	3.41	−.09	−2.74	.40	.18	−4.95	2.58
1976–77	−.36	−.10	.63	.01	.38	−.06	.18	−4.75	2.70
Mean	−.42	−.10	.09	−.02	−1.77	.10	.56	−3.44	2.53

Note: The entries are $Dq_{it}^t - Dq_{it}$, where Dq_{it}^t is the simulated log change in the quantity consumed per capita of i and Dq_{it} is the actual log change. The year 1956–57, e.g., refers to the transition from 1955–56 to 1956–57. All entries are to be divided by 100.

TABLE 14
Actual and Simulated Consumption of Alcoholic Beverages, Australia, 1955–1956/1976–1977
(Liters per Capita)

Year	Actual Consumption			Simulated Consumption with Alcohol Tax Rates Constant			Simulated Consumption with Wine Tax Rate Equal to Beer Tax Rate			Simulated Consumption with No Constant Terms in Demand Equations		
	Beer	Wine	Spirits	Beer	Wine	Spirits	Beer	Wine	Spirits	Beer	Wine	Spirits
1955–56	105.98	5.3374	1.9977	105.98	5.3374	1.9977	105.98	5.3374	1.9977	105.98	5.3374	1.9977
1956–57	100.45	5.2084	1.7999	104.50	5.2182	1.9684	99.71	3.0223	1.9741	101.47	5.2144	1.8398
1957–58	100.66	5.1705	1.8220	104.11	5.1762	1.9705	99.93	3.0317	1.8955	102.70	5.1823	1.9072
1958–59	101.14	5.2060	1.9126	103.00	5.1936	2.0309	100.45	3.1409	1.9851	104.24	5.2237	2.0501
1959–60	102.91	5.2531	2.0808	104.57	5.2415	2.2119	102.21	3.1878	2.1586	107.18	5.2766	2.2832
1960–61	102.61	5.0999	2.0727	103.14	5.0943	2.1274	101.94	3.1359	2.1479	108.03	5.1282	2.3265
1961–62	102.19	5.1244	2.0787	102.37	5.1162	2.1232	101.53	3.1674	2.1532	108.78	5.1583	2.3855
1962–63	103.46	5.2825	2.0256	103.25	5.2824	2.0276	102.79	3.2734	2.0977	111.37	5.3231	2.3771
1963–64	106.99	5.5316	2.1864	105.82	5.5250	2.1603	106.32	3.4731	2.2619	116.49	5.5800	2.6234
1964–65	110.34	5.5709	2.3513	108.51	5.5662	2.3011	109.67	3.5294	2.4307	121.53	5.6256	2.8827
1965–66	110.39	6.0795	2.0859	110.98	6.0793	2.1288	109.66	3.7431	2.1615	121.80	5.6185	2.6250
1966–67	113.13	6.8205	2.0711	113.20	6.7726	2.2150	112.42	4.2618	2.1430	125.04	5.8231	2.6802
1967–68	116.93	7.5703	2.3255	115.27	7.5049	2.4386	116.24	4.8161	2.4013	129.46	6.0181	3.0979
1968–69	120.53	8.2549	2.3008	117.03	8.1909	2.3016	119.85	5.3178	2.3720	133.67	6.1629	3.1531
1969–70	123.72	8.9508	2.5549	118.41	8.8734	2.4971	123.07	5.8414	2.6292	137.45	6.3148	3.5993
1970–71	125.84	8.6849	2.5790	117.66	8.7291	2.4213	125.30	5.8753	2.6406	140.04	5.7988	3.7337
1971–72	125.67	8.8518	2.7290	116.36	8.9161	2.5313	125.17	6.0612	2.7893	140.10	5.5915	4.0631
1972–73	129.51	9.7910	3.0846	118.36	9.7144	2.8224	128.99	6.6861	3.1540	144.64	5.8499	4.7222
1973–74	138.94	10.9766	3.1045	125.87	10.7814	2.9734	138.42	7.5710	3.1701	155.45	6.2011	4.8807
1974–75	140.42	12.2775	2.9748	124.53	11.9875	2.9145	139.99	8.6691	3.0281	157.39	6.5722	4.7969
1975–76	137.46	13.0573	2.8715	126.24	12.7908	2.9108	136.92	8.9709	2.9348	154.36	6.6518	4.7513
1976–77	136.14	13.6533	3.1663	124.57	13.3616	3.2300	135.62	9.4165	3.2341	153.15	6.6327	5.3823
Mean	116.16	7.6251	2.3716	112.75	7.6722	2.3955	116.01	5.0568	2.4601	127.35	5.7594	3.2458

The conclusion from this simulation is that although changes in all alcohol taxes have contributed to the rapid growth of wine, this contribution is a small component of the overall growth.

To simulate the effects of taxing wine at the same rate as beer, we impose a wine tax equal to the beer tax in 1956–57 and then adjust it in all subsequent years to keep it equal to the beer tax. To do this, we write t_2^s for the simulated value of the tax rate for wine and define it as follows. In 1955–56 it takes the value zero (which is also the observed value of t_2 in that year: see Table 12) and in all subsequent years it is equal to the observed beer tax rate t_1. Applying the same argument that led to equation (25), simulated minus actual consumption can then be expressed as

$$Dq_{it}^s - Dq_{it} = (\pi_{i2}/\overline{w}_{it})[D(1 + t_{2t}^s) - D(1 + t_{2t})].$$

The results of this simulation are given in columns 4–6 of Table 13 and columns 7–9 of Table 14. On average, the tax causes the annual growth in wine consumption to be about 1.8 percentage points lower than actual. Simulated consumption of wine in 1976–77 is 9.4 liters per capita, which is $(9.4165 - 13.6533)/13.6533 = 31.0$ percent lower than actual. The effect of the wine tax is to lower beer consumption by a small amount to 135.6 liters in 1976–77 and to increase spirits consumption to 3.23 liters. Hence, the fact that wine escaped a substantial tax does account for a large part of the observed growth in consumption over this period.

In the final simulation we take out the trendlike changes in tastes by setting to zero the constant terms in the demand equations of Table 7. Simulated minus actual consumption can be expressed for this case as

$$Dq_{it}^s - Dq_{it} = -[(\delta_i/\overline{w}_{it})D_t + (\psi_i/\overline{w}_{it})(1 - D_t)],$$

and the results are given in the last three columns of Tables 13 and 14. From Table 13, taking out this trend has the effect on average of beer consumption growing by .6 percentage points per annum more than actual, wine growing by 3.4 percentage points less, and spirits 2.5 points more.

To summarize, the simulations indicate that there are two reasons for the rapid growth of wine consumption. First, wine has not attracted a substantial tax, whereas beer has done so. Second, there has been a significant trendlike shift in preferences toward wine, away from beer and spirits. We also found that the observed changes in all alcohol taxes contributed very little to the growth of wine.

V. THE WELFARE COST OF ALCOHOL TAXES

In this section we measure the welfare cost of alcohol taxes by the reduction in consumer surplus not offset by government revenue from the taxes. This welfare cost can be expressed as

$$W = -\tfrac{1}{2} \sum_{i=1}^{3} \sum_{j=1}^{3} T_i \, S_{ij} \, T_j, \qquad (26)$$

where $T_i = t_i p_i^0$ is the tax per unit of i measured in terms of dollars and $S_{ij} = \partial q_i / \partial p_j$ with real income constant. Dividing (26) by income M, the cost can be formulated as a fraction of M as

$$\frac{W}{M} = -\tfrac{1}{2} \sum_{i=1}^{3} \sum_{j=1}^{3} \frac{t_i}{1 + t_i} \, \pi_{ij} \frac{t_j}{1 + t_j} \,, \qquad (27)$$

where π_{ij} is the (i,j)th unconditional Slutsky coefficient and $t_i = T_i / p_i^0$ is the tax rate on i. Using (20), (27) can be decomposed into the cost *within* the alcoholic beverages group and *between* alcoholic beverages and all other goods,

$$-\tfrac{1}{2} \sum_{i=1}^{3} \sum_{j=1}^{3} \frac{t_i}{1 + t_i} \, \pi_{ij} \frac{t_j}{1 + t_j} \qquad \text{(total cost)}$$

$$= -\tfrac{1}{2} \sum_{i=1}^{3} \sum_{j=1}^{3} \frac{t_i}{1 + t_i} \, \pi_{ij}^{g} \frac{t_j}{1 + t_j} \qquad \begin{array}{l}\text{(cost within al-}\\\text{coholic bever-}\\\text{ages group)}\end{array}$$

$$-\tfrac{1}{2} \phi \Theta_g (1 - \Theta_g) \sum_{i=1}^{3} \sum_{j=1}^{3} \frac{t_i}{1 + t_i} \, \theta_i' \theta_j' \frac{t_j}{1 + t_j} \qquad \begin{array}{l}\text{(cost between al-}\\\text{coholic bever-}\\\text{ages and all}\\\text{other goods).}\end{array}$$

$$(28)$$

We evaluate (28) with the tax data given in Table 12 and the estimates given in Tables 5 and 7. The results are given in Table 15. In 1976–77 the welfare cost is .2 percent of income (total consumption expenditure) or \$7.91 per capita (in current dollars). This represents 3.7 percent of expenditure on alcoholic beverages and 11.8 percent of government revenue from alcohol taxes. The within group component represents about 10 percent of the total cost.

In the previous section we simulated the effects of the imposition of a tax on wine at the same rate as that on beer. The simulated taxes are given in Table 16. We now apply the above analysis to measure the welfare cost of this tax package; the results are given in Table 17. As the imposition of the wine tax goes in the direction of having uniform tax rates, the within group cost falls. However, the between group and

TABLE 15
Welfare Cost of Actual Alcohol Taxes, Australia, 1955–1956/1976–1977

Welfare Cost as Fraction of Total Consumption Expenditure × 100

Year	Within Alcoholic Beverages Group $-\frac{1}{2}\sum_{i=1}^{3}\sum_{j=1}^{3}\pi_{ij}^{g}\frac{t_i}{1+t_i}\frac{t_j}{1+t_j}$	Between Alcoholic Beverages and All Other Goods $-\frac{1}{2}\phi\Theta_g(1-\Theta_g)\sum_{i=1}^{3}\sum_{j=1}^{3}\frac{t_i}{1+t_i}\theta_i'\theta_j'\frac{t_j}{1+t_j}$	Total = Within + Between $-\frac{1}{2}\sum_{i=1}^{3}\sum_{j=1}^{3}\pi_{ij}\frac{t_i}{1+t_i}\frac{t_j}{1+t_j}$	Total Welfare Cost		
				Dollars per Capita $\frac{(3)}{100}\times M$	Percentage of Alcohol Expenditure $100\times(4)/M_g$	Percentage of Revenue from Alcohol Taxes $100\times(4)/R$
	(1)	(2)	(3)	(4)	(5)	(6)
1955–56	.036	.264	.300	2.25	4.93	10.99
1956–57	.041	.322	.364	2.85	5.91	11.88
1957–58	.040	.315	.355	2.85	5.83	11.86
1958–59	.037	.298	.335	2.78	5.56	11.80
1959–60	.037	.297	.334	2.97	5.71	12.26
1960–61	.036	.278	.314	2.90	5.42	12.00
1961–62	.035	.275	.310	2.88	5.36	11.96
1962–63	.035	.266	.301	2.95	5.36	12.13
1963–64	.034	.256	.289	3.00	5.14	11.89
1964–65	.033	.249	.282	3.10	5.02	11.84
1965–66	.036	.277	.313	3.59	5.37	12.10
1966–67	.034	.288	.321	3.90	5.50	12.53
1967–68	.031	.271	.302	3.93	5.06	12.07
1968–69	.029	.247	.276	3.81	4.52	11.46
1969–70	.027	.229	.256	3.82	4.17	11.12
1970–71	.019	.206	.225	3.61	3.66	10.25
1971–72	.016	.197	.213	3.70	3.56	10.24
1972–73	.018	.179	.197	3.78	3.31	10.16
1973–74	.019	.180	.199	4.44	3.33	10.55
1974–75	.019	.165	.185	4.93	3.10	10.80
1975–76	.022	.203	.226	7.07	3.66	11.38
1976–77	.022	.201	.224	7.91	3.74	11.84
Mean	.030	.248	.278	3.77	4.69	11.51

TABLE 16
Simulated Alcohol Taxes, Australia, 1955–1956/1976–1977

Year	Tax Revenues ($ per capita)				Tax Rates × 100 (% pretax prices)		
	Beer $\left(\dfrac{t_1^s}{1+t_1^s}p_1^s q_1^s\right)$	Wine $\left(\dfrac{t_2^s}{1+t_2^s}p_2^s q_2^s\right)$	Spirits $\left(\dfrac{t_3^s}{1+t_3^s}p_3^s q_3^s\right)$	Total Alcohol $\left(\sum_{i=1}^{3}\dfrac{t_i^s}{1+t_i^s}p_i^s q_i^s\right)$	Beer (t_1^s)	Wine (t_2^s)	Spirits (t_3^s)
1955–56	18.33	0	2.14	20.47	117.198	0	38.351
1956–57	21.56	3.36	2.36	27.28	141.132	141.132	48.401
1957–58	21.61	3.43	2.36	27.41	137.090	137.090	47.588
1958–59	21.02	3.48	2.48	26.98	126.086	126.086	47.704
1959–60	21.44	3.74	2.73	27.91	124.296	124.296	48.524
1960–61	21.37	3.81	2.74	27.91	119.236	119.236	43.421
1961–62	21.27	3.83	2.77	27.87	117.250	117.250	43.133
1962–63	21.58	3.99	2.68	28.25	116.272	116.272	39.602
1963–64	22.31	4.10	2.88	29.28	111.358	111.358	38.773
1964–65	23.03	4.29	3.10	30.42	108.372	108.372	37.927
1965–66	26.17	5.41	3.43	35.01	119.674	119.674	42.436
1966–67	27.26	6.10	3.80	37.15	112.929	112.929	53.891
1967–68	28.28	6.82	4.22	39.32	104.365	104.365	53.254
1968–69	29.10	7.98	4.08	41.15	97.793	97.793	46.589
1969–70	29.72	8.60	4.54	42.87	90.491	90.491	44.862
1970–71	29.95	7.92	4.48	42.36	79.073	79.073	41.995
1971–72	30.41	8.07	4.73	43.21	74.356	74.356	41.749
1972–73	31.52	8.49	5.35	45.36	68.654	68.654	41.213
1973–74	34.18	9.00	7.86	51.05	61.598	61.598	53.584
1974–75	34.70	9.79	10.92	55.42	50.353	50.353	64.601
1975–76	49.97	15.68	12.09	77.74	64.761	64.761	64.965
1976–77	53.03	17.19	13.69	83.91	62.615	62.615	67.507
Mean	28.08	6.59	4.79	39.47	100.225	94.898	47.730

Note: t_i^s is the simulated tax rate on i; $p_i^s = p_i(1 + t_i^s)/(1 + t_i)$ is the simulated posttax price of i, where p_i is the actual (posttax) price and t_i the actual tax rate; and q_i^s is the simulated per capita consumption given in cols. 7–9 of Table 14.

TABLE 17
Welfare Cost of Simulated Alcohol Taxes, Australia, 1955–1956/1976–1977

	Welfare Cost as Fraction of Total Consumption Expenditure × 100			Total Welfare Cost		
Year	Within Alcoholic Beverages Group $-\frac{1}{2}\sum_{i=1}^{3}\sum_{j=1}^{3}\frac{t_i^s}{1+t_i^s}\pi_{ij}^g\frac{t_j^s}{1+t_j^s}$	Between Alcoholic Beverages and All Other Goods $-\frac{1}{2}\phi\Theta_g(1-\Theta_g)\sum_{i=1}^{3}\sum_{j=1}^{3}\frac{t_i^s}{1+t_i^s}\theta_i'\theta_j'\frac{t_j^s}{1+t_j^s}$	Total = Within + Between $-\frac{1}{2}\sum_{i=1}^{3}\sum_{j=1}^{3}\frac{t_i^s}{1+t_i^s}\pi_{ij}\frac{t_j^s}{1+t_j^s}$	Dollars per Capita $\frac{(3)}{100}\times M$	Percentage of Alcohol Expenditure $100\times(4)/M_g^s$	Percentage of Revenue from Alcohol Taxes $100\times(4)/R^s$
	(1)	(2)	(3)	(4)	(5)	(6)
1955–56	.036	.264	.300	2.25	4.93	10.99
1956–57	.013	.411	.424	3.32	6.66	12.17
1957–58	.012	.402	.414	3.33	6.58	12.15
1958–59	.010	.379	.390	3.23	6.26	11.97
1959–60	.010	.377	.387	3.45	6.41	12.36
1960–61	.011	.355	.366	3.38	6.11	12.11
1961–62	.011	.350	.361	3.36	6.03	12.06
1962–63	.012	.340	.352	3.46	6.07	12.25
1963–64	.012	.327	.339	3.52	5.83	12.02
1964–65	.011	.318	.330	3.63	5.69	11.93
1965–66	.012	.354	.366	4.19	6.03	11.97
1966–67	.006	.363	.370	4.49	6.09	12.09
1967–68	.005	.342	.347	4.51	5.58	11.47
1968–69	.006	.312	.318	4.40	5.01	10.69
1969–70	.005	.290	.295	4.40	4.62	10.26
1970–71	.004	.254	.258	4.13	4.09	9.75
1971–72	.003	.240	.243	4.23	3.98	9.79
1972–73	.002	.223	.225	4.32	3.70	9.52
1973–74	.000	.222	.223	4.96	3.65	9.72
1974–75	.001	.201	.202	5.37	3.34	9.69
1975–76	.000	.250	.250	7.83	3.96	10.07
1976–77	.000	.246	.247	8.72	4.03	10.39
Mean	.008	.310	.319	4.30	5.21	11.16

all other goods cost rises sufficiently to increase the total cost to $8.72 per capita in 1976–77.

VI. CONCLUDING COMMENTS

In this paper we have indicated how the systemwide approach to consumer demand can be extended so that it can be applied to quite narrowly defined commodity groups. Such applications have a number of attractions from the viewpoint of policy analysis for business and government. We analyzed the consumption of beer, wine, and spirits to illustrate the general principles and used the demand model for (1) a number of simulations designed to analyze the rapid growth of wine consumption and (2) to measure the welfare cost of alcohol taxes.

The approach of this paper focused on income, prices, and a time trend as the systematic determinants of demand. It is clear, however, that the methodology could be extended to allow for other factors such as product quality, demographic characteristics, advertising, and so on; as indicated in Section IV, these factors may well lie behind the time trend in our demand equations. As the effects of advertising are likely to be distributed over time, the incorporation of this factor would require a dynamic formulation of the approach. As a possible area of future research, the methodology could be applied to individual product data, including the analysis of the demand for different brands of the same commodity.

10.

Money Demand:
Cash Management
and Deregulation*

JOHN B. CARLSON

I. INTRODUCTION

The relationship of money to economic activity is one of the most closely studied relationships in economics. Prior to 1974, these seemed to be consensus about the stability of an empirical form of this relationship, known as the *money-demand function*. The basic theoretical underpinnings of this function are the models of Baumol and Tobin who treat money as an asset that is held primarily for transactions purposes. As estimated, the money-demand function includes a positive relationship to income and a negative relationship to interest rates with partial adjustment of money balances (measured as M-1) to desired levels in the short run. While many variations on the basic model were estimated, almost every specification was reported as functionally stable before the mid-1970s. That is, the estimated parameters linking money to income and interest rates did not change significantly over time.

The stability of the relationship of money to income and interest rates had important implications for monetary policy. Functional stability suggested that the level of money balances provided reliable information concerning the current level of economic activity, which is not observable

---

* *Economic Review*, Spring 1983, pp 2–15.

until several months after the fact. More importantly, functional stability suggested that monetary aggregates might serve as readily observable targets. Monetary policymakers could aim at these targets to promote price stability, economic growth, and high employment. In fact, during the 1970s monetary aggregates evolved as the primary targets of monetary policy. Ironically, as the role of the narrow money measures grew in importance, their relationship to income became less stable. Specifically, between the mid-1970s and late 1981, M-1 grew on average at a much slower rate than any of the money-demand functions would have predicted for the existing levels of interest rates and income. The literature suggests that the shortfall in money demand occurred in two episodes: one in the period 1974–76, and another around 1980–81. The second episode may be obscured in part by deregulation, particularly the introduction of interest-bearing checking accounts for households.

The breakdown in the money-demand function has been viewed in two (but not mutually exclusive) ways. One view holds that the instability of money demand results from a measurement problem. Financial innovations, such as overnight repurchase agreements (RPs) and money market mutual funds (MMMFs), are not included in M-1 but are close substitutes for assets in M-1. Because these assets are not included, their growth has depressed the growth of M-1 relative to its historical relationship to income and interest rates. Initially, the solution seemed simple: just add the new substitutes to M-1. Their tremendous growth since 1979, however, suggested that these assets had qualities making them suitable to serve both as transactions balances and investment media. The measurement view has led to research on methods obtaining an index of transactions services from a broad class of assets.

The other view of money-demand instability emphasizes the consequences of developments in cash-management technology and deregulation. Rather than focusing on new assets arising from financial innovation, this second approach analyzes from a microeconomic perspective the effects of developments on the opportunity cost of cash balances. The demand for money has been reduced, in principle, because it has become cheaper to economize systematically on money balances. Explicit behavioral models suggest alternative specifications of money demand. These specifications are used to estimate the impact of indirect measures of cost and support the role of cash management in explaining the shortfalls in M-1.

This article describes the fundamental ways in which new cash-management practices affect the level of cash balances. Part III of this article reviews some empirical studies of these effects. Part IV presents an empirical finding that raises questions about money demand not addressed in previous studies of cash mangement. In the context of the conventional money-demand regression, this study finds a sharp increase in the speed of adjusting cash balances to desired levels. While this change may be consistent with the cash-management process, it may also be explained by alternative hypotheses. To the extent that this result reflects a money-demand effect, it has important implications for monetary control. Specifically, the result suggests that, in the short run, the responsiveness of M-1 to changes in opportunity cost is much stronger than was previously thought.

II. THE CASH-MANAGEMENT PROCESS

Cash management—the control of payments, receipts, and any resulting transactions balances—has become increasingly sophisticated over the past decade. High interest rates have made it feasible for many firms to invest in information and forecasting systems that accelerate the collection of receivables and reduce uncertainty about the timing of receipts and clearing of disbursements. Recent developments in computer and communications technology have sharply reduced the costs of these systems, thereby increasing their rates of return. Declining costs of funds transfers have reduced the costs of concentrating receipts in one account. Investing collected balances in larger denominations enables balance holders to reduce average investment costs by spreading fixed costs over a larger volume.

The development of markets for immediately available funds (IAFs), such as overnight RPs, and other very liquid assets, such as MMMFs, has facilitated the growth of more intensive cash management. There are now investment opportunities for periods as short as one day, making profitable cash-management techniques that free funds only temporarily. Because of new, high-yielding, short-term assets, particularly MMMFs, it is worthwhile for households and small-to-medium size firms to manage their own demand-deposit balances more carefully.

Effects of Cash Management

Porter, Simpson, and Mauskopf studied the role of more intensive cash management in explaining the first episode of money-demand shortfall. Essentially, they identified three fundamental elements of this process: declining information costs, reduced uncertainty regarding cash flow, and reduced costs of funds transfers. They stressed the incentives that high market rates of interest create for managers to implement available cash-management techniques. The cash-management process has reduced the cost of shifting in and out of assets yielding market rates of interest, increasing the opportunity cost of holding transactions deposits not yielding market rates. Thus, a proximate impact of more intensive cash management has been to reduce the demand for transactions balances.

Other effects of cash management are specific to the basic types of cash-management techniques being adopted. Observing these effects may give clues to the intensity of cash-management practices and hence the impact on money demand. One important effect is shown by *controlled disbursement,* a payment technique adopted by many large corporations. Controlled disbursement allows a firm to control the funding of its disbursement account so that, for a given day, the firm need not deposit funds in excess of the clearings against such an account for that day. Because it is not *known* what the clearings will be on the *next* day, excess funds are freed for only one day; hence, investment opportunities are limited to the market for overnight instruments, e.g., the RP and Eurodollar markets. Although funds may be released for only one day, average balances may be reduced permanently, in some cases to zero. Fixed transactions costs make this arrangement feasible only for firms with large disbursements (e.g., $1 million or more). The RP market accelerated sharply during the first wave of cash management when disbursement techniques were being adopted by many of the largest firms.

Techniques that tend to accelerate receipts, on the other hand, tend to release funds for broader investment opportunities. An example of this technique is the use of lock boxes. The *lock-box system* enables businesses to decentralize the processing and collection of their receipts, locating this function near the source of payment. The firm receives payment earlier by eliminating mailing time (*mail float*) and may obtain earlier availability of funds by reducing the collection time once the payment enters the banking system (*bank float*).[1]

The key implication of these practices is that released balances become "permanently" available. That is, users of these techniques are not confined to invest these funds in IAFs, but may use them for any purpose. The lock-box system is often a profitable arrangement for intermediate-size firms not large enough to take advantage of disbursement techniques. It is largely this class of firms that became eligible for cash-management services when short-term rates peaked in 1981. Unfortunately, there is no close correspondence between the balances made available for investment and growth in any one set of short-term instruments to corroborate empirical significance of this technique.

Cash management by small businesses and households, on the other hand, is typically limited to the use of financial assets as a buffer for the variability of cash flow created by the lack of synchronization between

---

[1] The reduction in the aggregate money supply results from the elimination of mail float, which has never been subtracted from demand deposits. The impact of the reduction of mail float on the money supply depends on the behavior of the drawers of the checks. If the drawers were formerly successful in exploiting mail float, then money balances are not affected because the drawers actually had been using the balances and need to hold additional balances to offset the decline in mail float. On the other hand, if the drawers considered the funds extinguished at the time the checks were written, then the impact on demand-deposit balances equals the amount of mail float eliminated.

receipts and expenditures. Historically, direct investment of cash balances has been inhibited by the round lot (or size) requirements of the investment and by transactions costs. Treasury bills, for example, are sold only in lots of $10,000 or more and are not redeemable before they mature; hence, if the funds are needed, the sale of the bill would involve a cost. Innovations such as MMMFs pool funds of many investors and thereby reduce denomination requirements and transactions costs for any one investor. Their development has facilitated more efficient cash management by small-balance holders. Increased cash management by small businesses and households also has contributed to the explosive growth of MMMFs since 1979. Thus, the MMMF growth can be viewed as both a cause and an effect of the cash-management process.

Because MMMFs are also attractive as a store of value, they have lured funds from nontransactions sources. The MMMF explosion also reflects factors other than cash-management usage, e.g., cyclical buildup of precautionary balances. Thus, it is not likely that the impact of the cash-management process is mirrored in any simple sum of assets not included in M-1. This raises doubts about using alternative, broader measures (simple-sum) of transactions balances to remedy the shortfall problem. Nevertheless, monitoring growth in assets linked to cash management may be useful in anticipating effects on transactions balances. The growth of money market instruments, such as MMMFs, indicates a broadening of the scope of cash management over time. The second wave of cash management involved more participants as techniques became attractive to smaller businesses and households.

Deregulation and Cash Management

Since the early 1970s the financial industry has faced a large number of regulatory changes, most of which have led to a less restrictive financial environment. Deregulation has important implications for cash management, particularly for households and small businesses. Because these deposit holders typically maintain relatively small average balances, their investment opportunities have been limited. Deregulation has expanded such opportunities and reduced the investment costs for the small-balance holder.

Assets created under deregulation can serve both as complements and as substitutes for cash-management techniques. By reducing investment costs, new *nontransactions* accounts—such as money market certificates (MMCs), small-savers certificates (SSCs), and money market deposit accounts (MMDAs)—have increased incentives to economize on transactions balances not bearing interest or subject to interest-rate ceilings. Thus, deregulation has served to complement more efficient cash management, especially during periods of high interest rates and effective interest-rate ceilings.

The new interest-bearing transactions assets, on the other hand, have reduced incentives for adopting new cash-management practices. Many households do not have sufficient funds to maintain the minimum requirements of the most convenient investment opportunities (e.g., $1,000 for most MMMFs and $2,500 for MMDAs). Prior to interest-bearing checking accounts, cash management for many small-balance holders could be characterized chiefly by going to the bank to transfer excess transactions balances into a passbook savings account. These over-the-counter transfers involved obvious fixed costs and seemed worthwhile only when the amount of funds transferred was relatively large. The advent of negotiable order of withdrawal (NOW) and automatic transfer service (ATS) accounts and credit union share drafts (CUSDs) meant that transactions balances could earn interest without the "shoe leather" costs. The new accounts reduced incentives for such transfers, especially since the explicit yield on these accounts has been only about 25 basis points less than on passbook savings. Parke and Taubman estimate that in the first five months of 1981 approximately 7 percent of the funds flowing into NOWs came from savings deposits held by the same institution where a NOW account was opened. This suggest that some NOWs were opened for savings and hence served to substitute for a common cash-management practice of households.

In providing for assets that *complement* cash management, deregulation *raises* the opportunity cost of holding transactions balances and hastens the cash-management process. To the extent that these assets are priced attractively, they enhance cash-management practices and thereby could reduce the demand for transactions balances. Conversely, by authorizing instruments that *substitute* for cash management, deregulation *lowers* the opportunity cost of these balances and could limit or even reverse the impact of the cash management process. The net impact on money demand also depends on the relative prices (or perhaps the perception of these prices) of the new instruments.

III. EMPIRICAL FORMS OF THE CASH-MANAGEMENT HYPOTHESIS

The cash-management hypothesis essentially views the money-demand shortfall as a consequence of incomplete specification of the money-demand function. A "complete" form, in principle, would include the return on investment (or profitability) of cash-management techniques to determine the level of money balances, particularly noninterest-bearing transactions deposits. Because profitability of cash management is so closely linked to transactions costs, a measure of these costs alone might capture the effects of cash management.

Several studies have attempted to estimate the effects of cash management indirectly. Enzler, Johnson, and Paulus and Quick and Paulus use past peaks of interest rates as a proxy for the incentive to adopt new cash-economizing methods. Building on this approach, Simpson and Porter propose a more flexible proxy variable, also with a ratchet property, to represent the perceived profitability of investment in cash management:

> One justification for using the previous peak in interest rates is that there might be an awareness threshold that is related to interest rate peaks and once the previous peak has been surpassed more attention is drawn to the opportunity cost of holding money balances and to the profitability of investing in new techniques. Or, alternatively, if interest rate peaks imply a higher level of rates in the future than prevailed in the past—as would be the case, for example, if rates followed a random walk—then firms might be willing to undertake investments in new money management techniques that were previously judged unprofitable. In essence, this approach suggests that once a past peak has been surpassed, investments are made in new money management techniques that lead to a more permanent effect on money demand, even after market rates have dropped below the previous peak. That is, once the fixed costs of an investment are borne, it remains in place and is not discarded even though rates have declined.
>
> The relationship between peaks in interest rates and the subsequent impact on cash management, and thereby money demand, may be lengthy and somewhat variable for a number of reasons. If the threshold effects are large, the new investments to be undertaken may be more sizable than otherwise and take a longer time to implement. Such episodes may also spur the development of new technologies, new research and development efforts and the promotion of new practices by the suppliers of cash management services. Bringing the new technology in line—learning by doing—takes time as does recruiting the skilled labor force to operate it. Finally, it takes time before the new technology is diffused throughout the industry.

The particular ratchet variable used by Simpson and Porter is given by:

$$S_t = \sum_{j=1}^{t} (r_j - \frac{1}{12} \sum_{i=j-13}^{i=j} r_i)^+, \tag{1}$$

where

r_i = the five-year Treasury bond rate (chosen to be the relevant opportunity cost of evaluating a cash-management investment),

$(\ )^+$ = the nonnegative values, and

S_t = the cumulative sum of the nonnegative deviations of r_t from its 12-period moving average.

This approach differs from that of Quick and Paulus by using a moving average of the opportunity cost rather than a past peak. Hence, the Simpson-Porter approach is somewhat more flexible, ratcheting up more continuously both before and after new peaks in the opportunity cost.

Simpson and Porter include the ratchet variable in several different money-demand regressions, each a special case of the following equation:

$$\ln (M/P) = \beta_0 + \sum_{j=0}^{3} \beta_{1j} \ln r_{it-j}$$

$$+ \beta_2 \ln r_{2t} + \sum_{j=0}^{2} \beta_{3j} \ln Y_{t-j} + \sum_{j=0}^{5} \beta_{4j} g(S_{t-j)}, \tag{2}$$

where

M/P = real M-1 balances,
r_1 = three-month T-bill rate,
r_2 = commercial bank passbook rate,
y = real GNP, and
g = one of three functions of S:
$\quad S_t, S_t \times \ln (S_t), \text{ or } S_t^\lambda$.

The regressions are estimated over the periods 1955:IQ through 1974:IIQ and 1955:IQ through 1980:IIQ, using a Schiller-lag technique. The results are then compared with the standard specifications of money demand, which do not account for the effects of cash management. Simpson and Porter find equations that include the ratchet variable overall are superior to those that do not, particularly on the basis of post-sample forecasting performance since 1974. For example, the mean forecast errors of all the alternative cash management specifications are at least as small as the lowest mean forecast error of the standard specifications estimated. The mean error of the best cash-management equation is less than one half the mean error of the best of the standard forms. Thus, their approach offers at least some measure of improvement on the standard form.

More recently Porter and Offenbacher have pursued the idea that what is truly relevant about the effect of cash management (on money demand) is captured sufficiently in transactions costs of the "brokerage fee." Based on the analytical results of the Miller and Orr transactions model, Porter and Offenbacher derive indirect estimates of the brokerage fee. Essentially, the Miller-Orr model explains the levels of both average money balances and "financial debits" in terms of brokerage fees, the variability of cash flows, and the opportunity cost of money. These relationships are used to solve for two measures of brokerage fees, one in terms of financial turnover (the ratio of average money balances to debits) and the other in terms of debits. When these proxies for transactions costs are added to the standard money-demand function, evidence of money-demand shortfall diminishes significantly. While the approach must overcome some obstacles in estimation (too lengthy to discuss here), it builds on the well-defined theories of Baumol, Tobin, and Miller and Orr.

Kimball proposes another approach for estimating the impact of cash management. He posits that, because most cash-management techniques involve the use of wire transfers, the number of wire transfers can be used as a proxy variable to estimate the impact of cash-management techniques on money balances. Kimball finds that respecification of the relationship between money and transactions to include the number of wire transfers greatly reduces money-demand forecast errors in the post-1974 period using annual data.

Dotsey also uses wire-transfer data as a proxy for cash-management effects, finding that this measure performs well relative to other proxies in an annual model. He analyzes the influence of six different proxies on the demand for demand deposits, since it is largely this component of M-1 that seems to be most affected by cash management. The proxies are divided into two classes: measures representing the equilibrium level of demand deposit economization and measures for technological innovation. The first class includes the number and real value of electronic funds transfers (EFTs) and the ratio of demand-deposit debits to consumption. Like Kimball, Dotsey argues that EFT usage is directly related to most of the major cash-economizing techniques adopted in the mid-1970s—lockboxes, cash concentration, and zero balancing. The ratio of debits to consumption reflects the increase in financial transactions relative to spending.

The proxies for technological innovation include the real price of office computing and accounting equipment, a Simpson-Porter ratchet, and a time trend. Because the price index was adjusted for quality (hedonic), it dropped sharply in the 1970s. It was assumed that the decline in the cost of this technology represents the inducement to adopt the more sophisticated techniques, causing demand deposits to decline. Lieberman initially proposed the rationale for a time trend, i.e., the adoption of new technology will be fairly uniform and proceed at a smooth rate.

Dotsey analyzes the influence of the various proxies on the basis of three criteria: how they affect other coefficients of money demand, the out-of-sample predictive power, and the stability of money demand over the whole sample period (1920–79). The money-demand model used takes an inventory approach originally proposed by Barro and Santomero.[2] Without controlling for cash management, Dotsey finds that the model is not stable when the sample period is divided at 1965. Most notably, after 1965 the coefficient of transactions income (proxied by consumption) diminishes sharply, and the coefficient of the value of time (real wage rate) increases sharply. When each of the cash-manage-

---

[2] This specification differs from the conventional approach in several distinct ways. First, the model uses consumption rather than income as the scale variable. It also includes two variables not found in the conventional specification: an implicit interest rate on demand deposits and the real wage rate. The latter variable is included as a measure of the value of time of cash managers. Finally, the model assumes complete adjustment on average.

ment proxies is included separately and the model is re-estimated, each has the desired effect of restoring parameter estimates to levels comparable to estimates of the pre-1965 sample. Of the alternatives, the specification using the number of EFTs had the smallest standard error of estimate (SEE). In a comparison of one-step-ahead forecasts beginning in 1966, the specification including the number of EFTs produces the smallest forecast root mean square error, although the predictive power of the basic model is improved greatly when any of the proxies is included. Finally, in tests of functional stability, only with the model including EFTs could the data reject the hypothesis of instability.

Although these results suggest that the number of EFTs is the best proxy for the effects of cash management, it is not possible to extend this conclusion to apply to quarterly models without explicit comparisons using quarterly data. The standard errors of the Dotsey regression models are much higher than those of typical quarterly money-demand regressions that employ similar proxies for cash management. Nevertheless, the message that seems to emerge from empirical investigations is that the effects of cash management are large and important regardless of the way in which one proxies the cash-management process.

IV. THE ADJUSTMENT OF CASH BALANCES

Although some theoretical models of the cash-management process account for interaction among the determinants of money, empirical forms thus far have not been as general. Simply adding cash-management proxies to log-linear forms of money demand implies that cash management has no effect on the parameters linking money to its other determinants. However, as cash management has become more broadly based over the last several years, M-1 has appeared to become more responsive to changes in interest rates and income. That is, the short-run elasticities of the determinants of money seem to have increased, suggesting that cash holders are adjusting their M-1 balances to desired levels more quickly. The hypothesis of higher short-run elasticities can be examined in the context of the conventional model.

The Conventional Specification

The conventional money-demand specification has followed a basic approach proposed by Chow and also associated with Goldfeld. The basic feature of this approach is to allow temporary differences between the observed stock of money and the public's desired balances, a long-run equilibrium level. The mechanism guiding adjustment of actual money to its desired level is most frequently defined as follows:

$$\frac{m_t}{m_{t-1}} = \left(\frac{m_t^*}{m_{t-1}} \right)^{\gamma}, \tag{3}$$

or equivalently in log form

$$\ln m_t - \ln m_{t-1} = \gamma(\ln m_t^* - \ln m_{t-1}), \qquad (4)$$

where

$m = $ money deflated by the price level (P),
$\gamma = $ the adjustment rate, and
$* = $ desired.

Because it is assumed that $0 < \gamma < 1$, real money balances adjust only partially to the gap between the desired balances—the quantity of money demanded in the long run—and the holdings of the previous period. In the absence of a firm theoretical basis, the partial adjustment framework is often defended on the grounds that transactions costs inhibit complete adjustment to equilibrium.[3] That is, adjustment speed depends on transactions costs.

The determinants of desired money (i.e., the long-run equilibrium level) are based on the theoretical underpinnings of Baumol and Tobin, who relate the demand for real money balances to the level of real income and "the" interest rate:

$$m^* = \alpha_0 y^{\alpha_1} r^{\alpha_2}, \qquad (5)$$

where

$m_t = $ money deflated by the price level,
$y_t = $ real income, and
$r_t = $ opportunity cost of holding money.

According to the theory, the parameter α_0 is related to transactions costs. Thus, transactions costs can also affect equilibrium levels of money. In addition, the basic theoretical result of the Baumol model implies that the elasticities of y_t and r_t (α_1 and α_2) should equal ½ and $-½$, respectively.

Most estimated forms include two interest-rate variables, a money market rate—often the three-month Treasury bill (rtb_t)—and the commercial bank passbook rate (rcb_t). In log form, desired money is specified as

$$\ln m^* = \ln \alpha_0 + \alpha_1 \ln y_t + \alpha_2 \ln rtb_t + \alpha_3 rcb_t. \qquad (6)$$

Because desired balances are not observable, m^* is eliminated by substituting Equation 6 into Equation 4, yielding the familiar empirical form in terms of observed money:

---

[3] This rationale has been criticized, especially since the estimated adjustment rate is commonly too low to be defended on adjustment costs alone. It is not the intent here to defend the partial adjustment approach but to identify further evidence of change in the conventional specification that could be related to the cash-management process.

$$\ln m_t = a_0 + a_1 \ln y_t + a_2 \ln rtb_t + a_3 \ln rcb_t + a_4 m_{t-1}, \qquad (7)$$

where

$a_0 = \gamma \ln \alpha_0,$
$a_i = \gamma \alpha_i$ for $i = 1, 3,$ and
$a_4 = (1 - \gamma).$

Thus, all parameters of Equation 4 and Equation 6 can be identified exactly from this log-linear form.

To test for a shift in the adjustment rate, the adjustment scheme was modified to include the factor $(1 + \delta DG_t)$, where DG_t is a dummy variable that equals 0 prior to 1979:IVQ and 1 thereafter and δ is an additional parameter to be estimated:

$$\ln m_t - \ln m_t = \gamma(1 + \delta DG_t)(\ln m_t^* - \ln m_{t-1}). \qquad (8)$$

The desired money-demand specifications examined include a cash-management proxy. Two variables were used, both based on the Simpson-Porter ratchet formula. The first (SP-1) was a simple linear version proposed in Simpson and Porter, i.e., Equation 1. The second ratchet (SP-2) was also in linear form but was initiated in 1970 and assumed a shorter lag length (four quarters), making it more flexible than the former.[4] All equations included a dummy variable ($D1$) to test for an intercept shift in mid-year 1974.[5]

$$\ln m^* = \ln \alpha_0 + \alpha_1 \ln y_t + \alpha_2 \ln rtb_t + \alpha_3 \ln rcb_t + \alpha_4 SP_t + \alpha_5 Dl_t. \qquad (9)$$

Modifying the conventional framework to test for a change in the adjustment rate poses some problems for estimation. Specifically, substitution of Equation 9 into Equation 8 does not yield a linear form that allows identification of the parameters of the model; hence, nonlinear methods were employed to estimate the parameters of both equations directly.

Estimation results for two measures of money, M-1 and M-1 adjusted for NOWs (M-1a), are shown in Table 1. The results indicate a large change in the rate of adjustment that is statistically significant for all

---

[4] Money demand appeared stable prior to 1970. There is little evidence to suggest intensive adoption of techniques that were permitted by developments in information and communications systems during the 1970s. Thus, if the ratchet is in fact a relevant proxy variable for the waves of cash management in the 1970s, it should not be effective before then.

[5] This variable was included to examine whether the cash-management proxy accounted for all the unexplained shifts in the conventional equation. Hafer and Hein found that before 1979 the stability of the conventional equation could be restored if the regression accounted for an intercept shift between 1974:IQ and 1974:IIQ. Although the dummy variable reported in Table 1 assumes that the shift occurred between 1974:IIQ and 1974:IIIQ, the Hafer-Hein shift variable was also examined. The results were not significantly affected. The choice of which dummy variable to report was based on which equation fit the data better.

TABLE 1
Nonlinear Model
(Estimation Period: 1960:IQ to 1981:IVQ*)

Estimated Parameters†

Money Measure ‡	Ratchet Variable	γ	$1+\delta$	Long-Run Elasticities				
				α_1	α_2	α_3	α_4	α_5
M-1a	SP-2	0.353 (5.18)	2.34 (2.88)	0.463 (11.75)	−0.041 (−2.68)	−0.046 (−1.48)	−0.010 (−11.43)	0.054 (5.58)
	SP-1	0.200 (5.88)	2.80 (2.82)	0.671 (10.75)	−0.104 (−4.66)	−0.039 (−0.75)	−0.308 (−6.19)	0.093 (7.02)
M-1	SP-2	0.349 (5.10)	2.54 (2.85)	0.453 (11.06)	−0.041 (−2.78)	−0.045 (−1.38)	−0.006 (6.69)	0.067 (6.83)
	SP-1	0.251 (6.03)	2.76 (2.74)	0.573 (11.24)	−0.076 (−4.61)	−0.042 (−0.95)	−0.186 (−4.58)	0.090 (8.53)

Implied Short-Run Elasticities

Money Measure‡	Ratchet Variable	Period	Adjustment Rate	Income	T-Bill Rate	Passbook Rate	Ratchet
M-1a	SP-2	Through 1979:IIIQ	0.353	0.163	−0.014	−0.016	−0.004
		After 1979:IIIQ	0.826	0.382	−0.034	−0.038	−0.008
	SP-1	Through 1979:IIIQ	0.200	0.134	−0.021	−0.008	−0.062
		After 1979:IIIQ	0.561	0.377	−0.058	−0.022	−0.173
M-1	SP-2	Through 1979:IIIQ	0.349	0.158	−0.014	−0.016	−0.002
		After 1979:IIIQ	0.888	0.403	−0.037	−0.040	−0.005
	SP-1	Through 1979:IIIQ	0.251	0.144	−0.019	−0.010	−0.047
		After 1979:IIIQ	0.692	0.396	−0.052	−0.029	−0.129

* The model was estimated using "Program for Computation," IBM version 9.
† t-Statistics are in parentheses.
‡ This variable was measured on an end-of-period basis as an average of the two two months surrounding the end of the quarter.

TABLE 2
Test of Complete Adjustment*
(After 1979:IIIQ H_0: $\gamma(1 + \delta) = 1$)

Money Measure	Ratchet Variable	t-Statistic	Reject Null Hypothesis†
M-1a	SP-2	0.91	No
	SP-1	2.88	Yes
M-1	SP-2	0.53	No
	SP-1	1.74	Yes

* This test was based on results of large sample theory presented by Rao (1973, pp. 386–89). The estimated variance of $\gamma(1 + \delta)$ is given by

$$\hat{\sigma}_{11}(1 + \delta)^2 + 2\,\hat{\sigma}_{12}\,\hat{\gamma}(1 + \delta) + \hat{\sigma}_{22}\,\hat{\gamma}^2.$$

† One-tailed test with 0.05 acceptance level.

specifications. Adjustment rates jump about two and one-half times after 1979:IIIQ. For the M-1a measure, this implies an adjustment rate as high as 0.89 in the latter period. The data do not reject the hypothesis that, after 1979, the adjustment rate is statistically equal to 1 in two equations examined (see Table 2). In these equations lagged money is no longer a relevant explanatory variable. This clearly creates a new puzzle for the partial adjustment approach to money demand.

Table 3 shows the same basic specifications estimated for a sample ending in 1979 before the apparent shift. Because all parameters of this model could be identified from the parameters of a linear form, they were estimated in the linear form, using a maximum likelihood iterative routine that corrected for serial correlation. The short-run elasticity estimates are comparable with those in Table 1. An interesting result is that the marginal significance of the cash-management proxies increased over the longer sample periods, indicating that the ratchet proxy was no less useful during the second wave of cash management.

The evidence of quicker adjustment would seem easy to rationalize from the cash-management view. It could simply reflect lower transactions costs. But if this hypothesis were true, one would expect to find other systematic changes in the adjustment rate as transactions costs have declined relative to the opportunity cost of money in recent years. Several additional specifications were estimated to test whether the speed of adjustment had changed around 1974 or whether it was systematically related to the Simpson-Porter proxies of cash management. No evidence of such effects was found.

The absence of such effects in the earlier period could reflect the limited scope of the cash-management process then. As indicated above, the dominant effects of cash management seemed to be reflected largely by the significant development of the market for IAFs. This suggested

TABLE 3
Linear Model
(Estimation period: 1960:IQ to 1979:IVQ*)

Money Measure†	Ratchet Variable	Adjustment Rate	Income	Short-Run Elasticities			
				T-Bill Rate	Passbook Rate	Ratchet Variable	Intercept Shift
M-1a	SP-2	0.316 (10.78)	0.156 (6.09)	−0.016 (−4.18)	−0.017 (−1.47)	−0.004 (−3.53)	0.015 (3.29)
	SP-1	0.169 (17.86)	0.124 (5.49)	−0.023 (−6.51)	−0.007 (−0.636)	−0.059 (−2.42)	0.017 (3.85)
M-1	SP-2	0.334 (9.76)	0.162 (5.97)	−0.016 (−3.91)	−0.019 (1.59)	−0.003 (−3.06)	0.017 (3.58)
	SP-1	0.206 (15.58)	0.138 (5.84)	−0.021 (−6.20)	−0.010 (−0.93)	−0.060 (−2.48)	0.019 (4.07)

* t-Statistics are in parentheses.
† This variable was measured on an end-of-period basis as an average of the two months surrounding the end of the quarter.

that the cash-management process could be characterized adequately by large firms learning to conduct transactions with fewer (in some cases zero) demand deposits, with the result mirrored in the growth of IAFs. The adjustment rates of large firms were probably close to one (within three months) before the advent of the new technology. Thus, these techniques probably did little to change average speed of adjustment in the aggregate. The cash-management process then would affect only the long-run, or "desired," level of M-1 balances during the first wave.

Although many innovations suitable to a broader scope of cash holders were available during the first wave, the extent of their adoption was limited—perhaps by information costs. The availability of MMMFs, for example, which were introduced in 1973, sharply reduced investment costs for small-balance holders. However, MMMFs grew to only $3.5 billion by the mid-1970s. As interest rates began to rise in the late 1970s, the advantages of MMMFs as an investment vehicle became widely known. MMMF growth exploded, reaching a level over $230 billion by the end of 1982.

Because MMMFs were clearly being used by a broader scope of cash holders—particularly those with fewer investment opportunities— it is likely that widespread usage facilitated faster adjustment to desired M-1 levels in addition to affecting the desired level. A consumer who needed $10,000 to invest in a Treasury bill in 1974 (most consumers were unaware of MMMFs at that time) learned by the late 1970s that a share of this investment could be bought for as little as $500. Household balances now need not accumulate for as long before average adjustment costs are low enough to make a financial transaction. Since the previously high transactions costs for small-balance holders probably accounted for the slow adjustment speed of total balances, the widespread participation of households in the second wave of cash management suggests their transactions costs had been reduced sharply.

Other Qualifications

Evidence of a change in the short-run relationships among the variables included in the money-demand function appears substantial. However, the structural interpretations must be qualified. Recent critiques of the conventional money-demand function suggest alternative explanations that are especially relevant in light of the October 6, 1979, change in operating procedure—the procedure the Federal Reserve uses to control the money supply.

Goodfriend illustrates one way a change in operating procedure could affect the estimates of the parameters of the conventional money-demand function. Specifically, Goodfriend offers an interpretation of the conventional function that does not rely on a partial adjustment rationalization. Instead, he posits that money demand adjusts completely each period to appropriate current interest-rate and transactions variables that in turn are generated by independent first-order autoregressive processes. He shows that if the regressors are not measured correctly, the coefficient on lagged money is positive, even though lagged money plays no role in the true money-demand function. Lagged money enters significantly because, under the hypothesis, it helps to predict money. Goodfriend also shows that each of the coefficients in the conventional money-demand regression is a function of all the parameters in true money-demand models and all the regressor-generating process parameters. Thus, to the extent the change in operating procedure implies a change in the process-generating interest rates, it could produce a change in the estimated coefficient of the lagged dependent variable, which under the hypothesis does not imply a change in the adjustment rate.

The coincidence of a change in operating procedure and a stronger short-run association between changes in money income and interest rates also raises questions about the exogeneity of interest rates. A common criticism of the conventional approach is that it assumes interest rates are independent of money. Under the new operating procedure, if interest rates systematically respond to changes in money, the relationship between interest rates and income is simultaneous, and the methods typically used to estimate the model are not appropriate.

A popular defense for assuming the exogeneity of interest rates was based on the contention that the Federal Reserve pegged interest rates in the short run. Thus, the Fed had to supply the quantity of money demanded. The perfectly elastic supply curve implied that money was endogenous—not interest rates. Under the operating procedure implemented between October 1979 and mid-1982, changes in money were not fully accommodated at a pegged interest rate. Deviations of money from target led to an automatic impact on the federal funds rate in the same direction. As money moved above (below) its target path, interest rates tended to increase (decrease).

The parameter estimates in Table 1 indicate that the short-run elasticity of the Treasury bill rate was significantly higher after the change in the operating procedure, i.e., more like that of a demand curve than a supply curve. This elasticity is more negative than for any short-run interest-rate elasticities reported in a recent survey of the literature. To the extent simultaneity was a problem before 1979, it would seem to be less so afterward. Nevertheless, little solace should be taken in these results, as the simultaneity problem is still an open issue.

Finally, other shortcomings of the conventional model also could account for an "apparent" change in the adjustment rate. Brayton, Farr, and Porter present evidence that the response of transactions balances to their opportunity cost increases with the level of interest rates. This implies that the conventional approach, which restricts this elasticity to be constant, would have underpredicted the M-1 impact of interest-rate changes since 1979—a period when interest rates have been historically high. Because the partial adjustment framework restricts the adjustment pattern of money holdings to be the same with respect to all determinants of money, it is conceivable that the estimated shift in adjustment rate inappropriately reflects the nonlinearity in the interest-rate elasticity.

V. SOME CONCLUDING REMARKS

Although it is difficult to assess the precise impact of cash management on M-1, the results of a variety of studies indicate that the impact is large and cannot be ignored. Furthermore, it is evident in the conventional money-demand framework that the parameter estimates linking money with income and interest rates (contemporaneously) have changed significantly since 1979. Interpreted in this context, the evidence implies that cash managers are adjusting their balances to desired levels more quickly than before. To the extent M-1 is more responsive to changes in its opportunity cost, closer monetary control need not imply greater interest-rate volatility. But, this article also questions the basis of the conventional model. Qualified interpretations are presented to highlight important empirical issues in need of closer examination.

Attempts to study this issue more closely are likely to be obscured by continued deregulation. It has been argued that new interest-bearing assets have reduced the opportunity cost of holding transactions balances. If the yields of the new instruments are market-determined and parallel the yields of other short-term assets, then small-balance holders may find little incentive to manage these balances so closely. This implies that adjustment rates of this class of cash holder could decline. Furthermore, the stronger the covariability between yields on transactions and nontransactions assets, the more difficult it would be for the Federal Reserve to affect the opportunity cost of transactions balances, especially after 1986 when NOW rates will be decontrolled. Thus, although M-1 may respond more quickly to changes in opportunity cost, the Federal Reserve may not be able to take advantage of this in a demand-oriented procedure for monetary control.

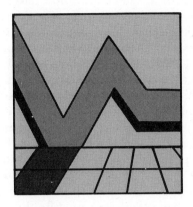

COSTS, PRODUCTION, AND PRODUCTIVITY

INTRODUCTION

The central focus of Part Three is cost theory, a theory developed from an underlying theory of production. Economically feasible production is any economic activity that transforms resource inputs into outputs having greater value. Management know-how plus land, labor, and capital carry a price that the firm must incur if it is to have use of certain resources. These prices are the explicit and implicit costs of producing a firm's goods or services. The fact is, therefore, that in a price-oriented economy, nothing of substance gets produced without incurring costs. Moreover, even with the payment of fixed, variable, financial, real, opportunity, short-run, long-run, sunk, and/or other costs, production levels may not be high enough to allow a firm to break even.

The word *cost* means different things to different people, and business people are prone to overwork this word at times. The words *production* and *productivity* appear to be no less susceptible to the same problem. Yet mastery of cost concepts places the formally trained economist in a position to make a larger contribution to the overall goals and objectives of his/her firm than otherwise would be the case.

The literature on empirical cost studies has become increasingly technical over the years as data and econometric problems continue to exist. The research piece by Caves, Christensen, and Tretheway is relatively brief and provides insight into the research difficulties associated with establishment of cost elasticities.

Standard cost systems, and the variances resulting from comparisons between standard and actual costs, have been recognized for a long time according to James A. Largay III, Philip D. York, and Willis R. Greer, Jr. Their article reveals that separate cost variances have been developed for control purposes in the decision-making process. They describe the opportunity cost variance; review some major theoretical contributions made by other authors; and suggest to the reader some areas where their theories can be applied.

Classical methods of statistical estimation are not used by all cost analysts. George J. Stigler applies the "survivor" principle to the investigation of economies of scale; fundamental to problems associated with this approach is acquisition of reliable raw data with which to work.

John F. Stewart's paper models an electricity producing firm's choice of technology for a generating plant in a way that recognizes that planned output is described best by a load increment composed of an instantaneous rate and a time duration, and that the cost of capital equipment is dependent on the size and fuel efficiency of the plant. The major finding of his paper is that plant size has relatively little effect on average cost; plant utilization is *the* major element leading to reductions in average costs as cumulative output expands. The methodology employed here is, and should be, of tremendous interest to public utilities in general and, of course, electric power generating plants in particular.

Statistical cost functions are useful devices (1) for describing the relationships which exist currently between various measurable variables and (2) for forecasting the effects of changes in one or more of these variables. Using the Federal Reserve System's functional cost analysis data, William A. Longbrake applies this technique to the commercial banking industry.

11.

Flexible Cost Functions for Multiproduct Firms*

DOUGLAS W. CAVES
LAURITS R. CHRISTENSEN
MICHAEL W. TRETHEWAY

The application of duality theory to economic analysis has fostered rapid development of econometric techniques for modeling the structure of cost. Diewert's path-breaking contribution showed that the researcher could make very general functional representations of the structure of cost while maintaining classical restrictions on the underlying structure of production. A specific cost function can be chosen for econometric convenience, provided only that it satisfies certain regularity conditions. Diewert proposed the generalized Leontief functional form for the cost function. This form has the attractive features of being linear in the parameters yet imposing no a priori restrictions on the elasticities of substitution among the factor inputs. Other cost functions having these attractive features of linearity and flexibility have also been proposed. The most widely-used in empirical work has been the translog form proposed by Christensen, Jorgenson, and Lau.

Since the early work of Cobb and Douglas, empirical studies of production and cost have generally assumed that production processes involve a single output produced from aggregate capital and aggregate labor input. Recently, empirical studies have recognized the importance

* *Review of Economics and Statistics* 62, no. 3 (August 1980), pp. 477–81.

of materials and energy inputs, as well as the importance of treating separately dissimilar types of capital and labor. The logical parallel step is the recognition that most production processes result in two or more outputs. Indeed the recent literature—both theoretical and empirical—contains an increasing emphasis on multiproduct production processes.

The duality relationships between transformation functions and multiproduct cost functions are straightforward extensions of the single output case. In a formal sense it is also straightforward to generalize functional forms from the single to the multiple output case. However, all of the cost functions that have been proposed contain flaws which limit their attractiveness for empirical work in the multiproduct setting. These flaws include: (1) violation of regularity conditions on the structure of production, (2) an excessive number of parameters to be estimated, and (3) an inability to accommodate observations which contain zero levels for some of the outputs. The purposes of this paper are to review the flaws of existing multiproduct cost functions, and to propose a new multiproduct cost function which exhibits none of these flaws.

I. FUNCTIONAL FORMS FOR THE MULTIPRODUCT COST FUNCTION

The total cost of production for a firm can be expressed as $C(Y, W)$, where Y is an m dimensional vector of output levels, and W is an n dimensional vector of input prices. Provided that C satisfies certain regularity conditions, it is said to be dual to the transformation function $T(Y, X)$, where X is an n dimensional vector of input levels. The duality between C and T ensures that they contain the same information about production possibilities. The regularity conditions on C are that it be nonnegative, real valued, nondecreasing, strictly positive for nonzero Y, and linearly homogeneous and concave in W for each Y.

Empirical implementation of the cost function approach requires specification of a functional form for C. It is desirable to specify a form which is flexible, in the sense that no a priori restrictions are imposed on its first and second order derivatives. We discuss three flexible forms which are possible candidates to represent the multiproduct cost function (MCF).

Diewert proposed the generalized Leontief functional form for the cost function and the generalized linear form for the production function. Hall suggested that these could be combined to form the "hybrid Diewert" multiproduct cost function (HDMCF):

$$C = \sum_i^m \sum_j^m \sum_k^n \sum_l^n \alpha_{ijkl} (Y_i Y_j W_k W_l)^{1/2}. \tag{1}$$

Although the HDMCF contains no a priori restrictions on elasticities of substitution among factor inputs, it imposes constant returns to scale on the relationship between total cost and the output levels. Generalizing the HDMCF to permit flexibility in scale economies necessitates a large increase in the number of parameters. Burgess used the translog functional form to represent the multiproduct cost function (TMCF):

$$\ln C = \alpha_0 + \sum_{i}^{m} \alpha_i \ln Y_i + \sum_{i}^{n} \beta_i \ln W_i$$

$$+ \frac{1}{2} \sum_{i}^{m} \sum_{j}^{m} \delta_{ij} \ln Y_i \ln Y_j$$

$$+ \frac{1}{2} \sum_{i}^{n} \sum_{j}^{n} \gamma_{ij} \ln W_i \ln W_j$$

$$+ \sum_{i}^{m} \sum_{j}^{n} \rho_{ij} \ln Y_i \ln w_j. \tag{2}$$

A third flexible form which might be used to represent the MCF is the quadratic (QMCF), suggested by Lau:

$$C = \alpha_0 + \sum_{i}^{m} \alpha_i Y_i + \sum_{i}^{n} \beta_i W_i + \frac{1}{2} \sum_{i}^{m} \sum_{j}^{m} \delta_{ij} Y_i Y_j$$

$$+ \frac{1}{2} \sum_{i}^{n} \sum_{j}^{n} \gamma_{ij} W_i W_j + \sum_{i}^{m} \sum_{j}^{n} \rho_{ij} Y_i W_j. \tag{3}$$

To be attractive for empirical applications a flexible form for the MCF should be linearly homogeneous in input prices for all possible price and output levels; be parsimonious in parameters; and contain the value zero in the permissible domain of output quantities.

Linear homogeneity in input prices is a precondition for the existence of a duality relationship between the cost and transformation functions. The HDMCF satisfies this requirement, and the TMCF satisfies it upon imposition of appropriate linear restrictions. The QMCF does not satisfy the homogeneity condition; nor can homogeneity be imposed by parametric restrictions without sacrificing the flexibility of the form. Thus it is not an attractive form of the MCF.

Given that a functional form is flexible, it is desirable that the number of parameters to be estimated is small. The TMCF dominates both the QMCF and HDMCF in terms of number of parameters. When restricted to be linearly homogeneous in prices, the TMCF has $(m(m+1)/2) + (n(n+1)/2) + mn$ parameters. The QMCF has $m + n + 1$ more parameters than the TMCF. The HDMCF restricted to constant returns to scale has $m(m+1)n(n+1)/4$ parameters. This exceeds the number for the TMCF except when there are only two inputs and two outputs. When the HDMCF is generalized to allow for scale economies, it may have several times as many parameters as the TMCF. Thus the HDMCF is generally unsuitable for estimation.

A third desirable characteristic of a multiproduct cost function is that it permit the value zero for one or more outputs. For many multiproduct industries, firms exist which produce only a subset of the feasible outputs. To obtain global information on the production function it is necessary that such firms be included in the analysis. The QMCF and the HDMCF permit zero output values. However, in the TMCF all of the outputs enter in logarithmic form; thus the TMCF has no finite representation if any output has a zero value.

We conclude that each MCF we have discussed contains a flaw. The QMCF does not satisfy the regularity condition of linear homogeneity in factor prices. The HDMCF contains too many parameters to be attractive for estimation. The TMCF is not suitable when there are zero output observations in the sample.

II. THE GENERALIZED TRANSLOG MULTIPRODUCT COST FUNCTION

The purpose of this section is to propose a functional form for the MCF which does not have any of the three flaws discussed in the previous section. The flaws possessed by the QMCF and the HDMCF are not readily conducive to remedy. However, the TMCF can be generalized to permit zero output levels without introducing either of the other two flaws.

The translog is a member of a class of functions known as general quadratic flexible forms. Following Blackorby, Primont, and Russell, this class of functions can be expressed as

$$F(q) = \alpha_0 + \sum_i^r \alpha_i f_i(q_i) + \sum_i^r \sum_j^r \beta_{ij} f_i(q_i) f_j(q_j). \qquad (4)$$

The translog form is obtained by choosing the natural logarithm as the metric for F and for each argument f_i. It is the use of the log metric on input prices and total cost that allows homogeneity of degree one for the TMCF via simple parametric restrictions. However, the use of the log metric for the outputs is unnecessary for this homogeneity property, and it prevents the use of any observations with zero output values. In searching for an unflawed form for the MCF it seems natural to maintain the log metric for input prices and total cost but to choose for outputs a metric that is well defined for zero values. A metric is available that not only permits zero values, but also contains the natural logarithm metric as a limiting case. We refer to the metric proposed by Box and Cox: $f_i(Y_i) = (Y_i^\lambda - 1)/\lambda$, $(\lambda \neq 0)$; $f_i(Y_i) = \ln Y_i$, $(\lambda = 0)$. Provided that λ is strictly positive, the Box-Cox metric is well defined for zero output levels: $f_i(0) = -1/\lambda$. We further note that the natural log metric is a limiting case of the Box-Cox metric:

$$\lim_{\lambda \to 0} (Y_i^\lambda - 1)/\lambda = \ln Y_i.$$

If we form a general quadratic flexible form using the natural log as the metric for cost and input prices and the Box-Cox metric for output quantities, the resulting MCF contains none of the flaws discussed above. We refer to the form as the generalized translog multiproduct cost function (GTMCF). This function is well defined for zero output values. The requirement of linear homogeneity in input prices is met by imposing the same restrictions as for the TMCF. Finally, although the GTMCF has one more parameter than the TMCF, it is still far more parsimonious in parameters than the HDMCF.[1]

III. APPLICATION OF THE GENERALIZED TRANSLOG MULTIPRODUCT COST FUNCTION

We illustrate the use of the GTMCF with cross-sectional data from the U.S. Railroad industry in 1963. The sample consists of 41 firms that produced significant amounts of both passenger and freight service and 15 firms that provided freight service but little or no passenger service. Hereafter we refer to the total of 56 firms as the full sample and the 41 firms that provided both freight and passenger service as the truncated sample. We distinguish two categories of output, revenue ton-miles of freight and revenue passenger-miles, and three categories of factor inputs, fuel, labor, and capital.

Following the methodology of Christensen and Greene, we obtain efficient estimates of the parameters of the MCF by treating the MCF and its associated input cost share equations as a multivariate regression. The cost share equations can be derived for the GTMCF using Shephard's Lemma:

$$\frac{W_i X_i}{C} = \frac{\partial C}{\partial W_i} \cdot \frac{W_i}{C} = \frac{\partial \ln C}{\partial \ln W_i}$$

$$= \beta_i + \sum_j^n \gamma_{ij} \ln W_j + \sum_j^m \rho_{ji}(Y_j^\lambda - 1)/\lambda. \qquad (5)$$

Since the share equations (5) sum to unity for each observation, the covariance matrix of disturbances appended to (5) is singular. The estimation of the GTMCF with equations (5) requires a modification of Zellner's method for seemingly unrelated regressions: At the first stage we include all $n + 1$ equations, but prior to the second stage one of the n share equations is deleted. These estimates are invariant to the equation deleted and are asymptotically equivalent to maximum likelihood estimation, but avoid the expense of iterating to obtain maximum likelihood estimates. We estimated the parameters of the GTMCF for

---

[1] One could further generalize the GTMCF by specifying a distinct λ for each output, or by replacing Y_i^λ with $(Y_i + \psi_i)^\lambda$. However, these generalizations needlessly complicate estimation.

both the truncated and full samples and the TMCF ($\lambda = 0$) for the truncated sample. The results are presented in Table 1.[2] The three sets of estimates satisfy the regularity conditions at every data point.

The effect of allowing λ to be non-zero can be assessed by comparing the properties of the estimated GTMCF and TMCF functions. Because the most significant differences between columns 1 and 2 involve the δ_{ij}, the parameters of the second order output terms, we expect the estimated GTMCF and TMCF to differ primarily in their implications for the relationship between cost and output levels. These differences can be assessed by comparing the estimated cost elasticities from the two functions. The formula for the elasticity of cost with respect to freight output is

$$\frac{\partial \ln C}{\partial \ln F} = [\alpha_F + \delta_{FF}(F^\lambda - 1)/\lambda + \delta_{FP}(P^\lambda - 1)/\lambda$$
$$+ \Sigma_i \rho_{Fi} \ln W_i]F^\lambda, \tag{6}$$

where F is freight output and P is passenger output. The corresponding formula for the elasticity of cost with respect to passenger output can be obtained by interchanging P and F subscripts.

When all variables are equal to their means from the full sample, the freight and passenger cost elasticities are given simply by α_F and α_P, which have similar estimates for the GTMCF and the TMCF. In Table 2 we present estimated cost elasticities at output levels other than the sample mean, holding prices fixed at their sample means. The freight elasticities for the two forms are practically identical for firms with very large freight output and moderate passenger output. But for other output configurations there are some large differences in the elasticities.

The standard errors of the parameters and of the cost elasticities near the sample mean are generally smaller for the GTMCF than for the TMCF. Away from the mean the GTMCF elasticities generally have larger standard errors than those of the TMCF. The higher variance of the GTMCF elasticities is not unexpected since the GTMCF does not incorporate the constraint $\lambda = 0$ in estimation. However, it is interesting that this constraint does not result in more favorable standard errors for the TMCF over the full range of outputs.

Both the TMCF and the GTMCF yield negative passenger cost elasticities for low levels of freight output in the truncated sample. This must be taken as an indication that both forms have difficulty representing the structure of cost over the full range of outputs. Of the 41 firms in the truncated sample 11 have negative estimated passenger cost elas-

---

[2] The data were standardized by dividing each output and price variable by its mean in the full sample.

TABLE 1
Parameter Estimates for the TMCF and the GTMCF (standard errors in parentheses)
Parameter Subscripts: F(freight), P(passenger), K(capital), L(labor), E(fuel)

Parameter	Truncated Sample		Full Sample	Parameter	Truncated Sample		Full Sample
	GTMCF (1)	TMCF (2)	GTMCF (3)		GTMCF (1)	TMCF (2)	GTMCF (3)
λ	−.182 (.058)	0	.115 (.051)	γ_{LL}	.028 (.080)	.015 (.082)	.018 (.077)
α_0	19.124 (.030)	19.089 (.027)	19.138 (.036)	γ_{EE}	.000 (.011)	−.002 (.011)	.005 (.008)
α_F	.756 (.048)	.774 (.053)	.776 (.050)	γ_{KL}	−.039 (.077)	−.026 (.079)	−.027 (.075)
α_P	.239 (.037)	.201 (.042)	.165 (.037)	γ_{KE}	−.012 (.014)	−.009 (.014)	−.013 (.010)
δ_{FF}	.111 (.059)	−.082 (.068)	−.113 (.084)	γ_{LE}	.011 (.018)	.011 (.017)	.008 (.012)
δ_{PP}	.107 (.029)	.108 (.044)	.024 (.013)	ρ_{FK}	−.023 (.010)	−.020 (.011)	−.021 (.008)
δ_{FP}	−.024 (.030)	.013 (.048)	.001 (.017)	ρ_{FL}	.023 (.010)	.019 (.011)	.018 (.008)
β_K	.583 (.008)	.583 (.008)	.586 (.007)	ρ_{FE}	.000 (.002)	.001 (.002)	.002 (.001)
β_L	.387 (.008)	.388 (.008)	.385 (.007)	ρ_{PK}	.006 (.007)	.002 (.009)	.006 (.004)
β_E	.030 (.002)	.029 (.001)	.029 (.007)	ρ_{PL}	−.007 (.007)	−.003 (.008)	−.006 (.004)
γ_{KK}	.051 (.078)	.036 (.080)	.040 (.075)	ρ_{PE}	.001 (.001)	.001 (.001)	−.000 (.001)

TABLE 2
Cost Elasticities with Respect to Outputs (standard errors in parentheses), Truncated Sample

	Generalized Translog Multiproduct Cost Function						Translog Multiproduct Cost Function					
	Freight Cost Elasticity			Passenger Cost Elasticity			Freight Cost Elasticity			Passenger Cost Elasticity		
Ton Miles (billion)	.002*	.02*	.04*	.002*	.02*	.04*	.002*	.02*	.04*	.002*	.02*	.04*
0.5	.935 (.248)	.718 (.223)	.668 (.263)	−1.946 (.615)	−.264 (.100)	−.029 (.125)	.952 (.046)	.982 (.047)	.992 (.047)	−.442 (.025)	−.194 (.031)	−.119 (.034)
1	.951 (.172)	.782 (.122)	.744 (.157)	−1.310 (.383)	−.073 (.075)	.094 (.097)	.904 (.047)	.935 (.048)	.944 (.048)	−.358 (.027)	−.110 (.034)	−.035 (.036)
10	.838 (.080)	.765 (.044)	.748 (.057)	−.184 (.095)	.220 (.034)	.263 (.046)	.745 (.052)	.775 (.053)	.784 (.053)	−.079 (.033)	.169 (.041)	.244 (.044)
15	.805 (.074)	.742 (.045)	.728 (.055)	−.084 (.082)	.239 (.033)	.269 (.048)	.717 (.053)	.747 (.054)	.756 (.054)	−.030 (.034)	.218 (.043)	.293 (.045)
30	.747 (.068)	.698 (.049)	.687 (.055)	.043 (.066)	.257 (.040)	.272 (.057)	.669 (.055)	.699 (.056)	.708 (.057)	.054 (.036)	.302 (.045)	.377 (.048)
50	.702 (.068)	.662 (.055)	.653 (.058)	.110 (.057)	.262 (.049)	.269 (.066)	.633 (.057)	.664 (.058)	.673 (.059)	.116 (.038)	.364 (.047)	.439 (.050)

* Ratio of passenger miles to ton miles.

ticities for the TMCF, while 8 have negative estimated passenger cost elasticities for the GTMCF.

A comparison of columns 1 and 3 in Table 1 indicates the impact on the parameter estimates of using the full range of output values. The parameters associated with the input prices and interactions between output levels and the input prices, the β_i, γ_{ij}, and ρ_{ij}, have very similar estimates in columns 1 and 3. The standard errors of these estimates are uniformly smaller for the full sample. The chief differences between columns 1 and 3 are for α_P, which is 50 percent larger for the truncated sample than for the full sample, and for the δ_{ij}. Characterization of the cost structure at the sample mean is considerably altered by use of the full sample. Consider an increase of 1 percent in both outputs at the mean of the full sample. The associated percentage increase in costs is given by $\alpha_F + \alpha_P$, which is 1.00 from the truncated sample and 0.93 from the full sample. Thus the full sample indicates that there are positive scale economies.

For output levels away from the sample means, Tables 2 and 3 can be used to compare the cost elasticities of the GTMCF from the truncated and full samples. The most interesting difference is that the full sample yields more stable estimates for both the freight and passenger cost elasticities over wide ranges of output variation. One beneficial result of this change is that the estimated cost elasticities are now positive for all firms.

TABLE 3
Cost Elasticities with Respect to Outputs (standard errors in parentheses), Full Sample

	Generalized Translog Multiproduct Cost Function						
Ton Miles (billion)	Freight Cost Elasticity				Passenger Cost Elasticity		
	0*	.002*	.02*	.04*	.002*	.02*	.04*
0.5	.737	.740	.741	.742	.033	.066	.080
	(.044)	(.071)	(.085)	(.090)	(.016)	(.029)	(.033)
1	.754	.758	.760	.760	.041	.081	.098
	(.045)	(.056)	(.072)	(.079)	(.016)	(.028)	(.034)
10	.759	.765	.768	.768	.082	.153	.183
	(.139)	(.050)	(.048)	(.053)	(.019)	(.033)	(.046)
15	.747	.754	.756	.757	.092	.171	.204
	(.167)	(.068)	(.059)	(.061)	(.021)	(.038)	(.054)
30	.713	.722	.725	.725	.112	.205	.245
	(.228)	(.117)	(.101)	(.099)	(.026)	(.051)	(.072)
50	.676	.686	.689	.690	.129	.235	.280
	(.285)	(.169)	(.149)	(.146)	(.032)	(.065)	(.091)

* Ratio of passenger miles to ton miles.

IV. CONCLUDING REMARKS

The generalized translog multiproduct cost function maintains the desirable features of the translog form while extending the domain of admissible output values to the entire nonnegative orthant. Our application to U.S. railroad data demonstrates the importance of including firms that do not produce any passenger output. Estimates of the structure of cost which include these firms are clearly preferable to the estimates which exclude them.

12.

Opportunity Cost Variances*

JAMES A. LARGAY III
PHILIP D. YORK
WILLIS R. GREER, JR.

Standard cost systems, and the variances resulting from comparisons between standard and actual costs, have long been recognized as useful tools for controlling operations. These tools have been used both for identifying problems (signaled by deviations from standard) and evaluating performance. During the past few years, however, a new thrust has begun to appear in the accounting literature. This new line of inquiry has suggested using variances to control the decision-making process *itself*.

In this latter context, separate variances have been developed for control of the decision process. These variances recognize that, once plans are formulated, changes in cost factors can cause different plans to be preferred to the ones adopted. The difference between actual performance and the performance suggested by an optimal decision is the opportunity cost. *Opportunity cost variances* attempt to measure this cost. In this paper, we (1) describe the opportunity cost variance, (2) briefly review the major theoretical contributions in the area, and (3) suggest some aspects of practical implementation.

---

* *Cost and Management*, November/December 1982, pp 34–40.

The Opportunity Cost Variance

We begin by developing the concept of an opportunity cost variance with a numerical illustration. While one would seldom encounter a situation as simple as the one used, the basic concepts shown can be generalized to a more realistic level.

Assume a firm participates in a market such that the only determinant of the periodic quantity sold is the price established by the firm. To quantify, let

$$Q = 50 - \frac{1}{2} P$$

so that if the firm established a price of, say, $70 the periodic quantity sold would be 15 units. Further, assume that the price must be established at the beginning of the period, *before* the cost structure is known with certainty. However, the decision maker *expects* the costs to be

$$C = 100 + 60\ Q.$$

That is, the periodic fixed cost is expected to be $100 and variable costs of $60 per unit are anticipated.

Suppose in making the pricing decision the decision maker employs the following profit maximization model:

$$Q = 50 - \frac{1}{2} P \qquad \text{(demand equation)}$$

or

$$P = 100 - 2\ Q. \qquad \text{(pricing equation)}$$

Therefore, total revenue is

$$R = P \times Q,$$

or

$$R = 100\ Q - 2\ Q^2. \qquad \text{(revenue equation)}$$

The periodic cost function is expected to be

$$C = 100 + 60\ Q \qquad \text{(cost equation)}$$

Since profit is given by

$$\Pi = R - C,$$

then

$$\Pi = -100 + 40\ Q - 2\ Q^2. \qquad \text{(profit equation)}$$

Taking the first derivative of the profit equation,

$$\frac{d\Pi}{dQ} = 40 - 4\,Q,$$

and setting it equal to zero, we find the optimal demand level,

$$Q^* = 10.$$

We return to the pricing equation to determine the optimal price,

$$P^* = 80.$$

Having established the price, \$80, the decision maker expects the following results for the period:

Revenue (10 × \$80)	\$800
Costs [\$100 + (10 × \$60)]	700
Profit	\$100

Now let us suppose there is an unanticipated 20 percent increase in the price of the variable cost elements in the firm's cost structure—that variable costs actually turn out to be \$72 per unit rather than \$60—but that everything else progresses according to expectations. The actual results would be:

Revenue (10 × \$80)	\$800
Costs [\$100 + (10 × \$72)]	820
Loss	(\$ 20)

Conventional variance analysis would attribute the \$120 disappointment in earnings to the \$120 unfavorable impact of the higher-than-expected price for the cost elements; an unfavorable price variance of \$120. But this tells only part of the story.

Had the decision maker known beforehand that the variable cost per unit would be \$72 rather than \$60, the pricing decision would have been different. In fact, the profit equation (using the new variable cost) turned out to be,

$$\Pi = -100 + 28\,Q - 2Q^2.$$

With this profit equation, the maximization model would have called for a different optimal demand level:

$$\frac{d\Pi}{dQ} = 28 - 4\,Q, \; Q^* = 7.$$

This would have led to a selling price of \$86 rather than \$80 which, in turn, would have produced the following actual results:

Revenue (7 × $86)	$602
Costs [$100 + (7 × $72)]	604
Loss	($ 2)

A $2 loss is obviously better than a $20 loss. While neither is as desirable as a $100 profit, the loss could have been reduced had the decision maker known *ex ante* that the variable cost was going to be $72 rather than $60.

The total variance indeed is $120, unfavorable. But of that $120 only $102 [$100 − ($2)] is directly attributable to the cost increase. The other $18 [($2) − ($20)] is an opportunity loss due to imperfect decision making. This says nothing of course about why incorrect information entered the decision model (any more than a price variance says why prices were high or low); it simply quantifies the effect.

A report which would summarize the above information might look something like this:

Periodic Variance Report

Price variance	$102 U
Opportunity cost variance	$ 18 U
Total profit variance	$120 U

The effect of ignoring the quantification of the opportunity cost variance would have been to overstate the unfavorable price variance. Had the price variance been favorable, the reverse would have been true. To illustrate, suppose that the unanticipated 20 percent change in the price of the variance cost elements had been a decrease rather than an increase. The actual results would then have been:

Revenue (10 × $80)	$800
Costs [$100 + (10 × $48)]	580
Profit	$220

This profit figure is $120 higher than anticipated, so the price variance would conventionally be measured as $120 favorable.

Again, however, the pricing decision was suboptimal. The profit equation in fact was,

$$\Pi = -100 + 52\,Q - 2\,Q^2.$$

Optimizing, we have,

$$\frac{d\Pi}{dQ} = 52 - 4\ Q,\ Q^* = 13,\ P^* = \$74.$$

This combination would yield:

Revenue (13 × $74)	$962
Costs [$100 + (13 × $48)]	724
Profit	$238

The appropriate analysis would disclose the following:

Periodic Variance Report

Price variance	$138 F
Opportunity cost variance	$ 18 U
Total variance	$120 F

Several additional insights can be gained at this point. For example, let the expected value of a range of possible future unit variable costs be $60, and the range be extended symmetrically from $48 to $72. The decision maker could project an expected total variance of $0 by establishing the $80 selling price. Nevertheless, the *expected opportunity cost variance* is unfavorable (note that an unfavorable opportunity cost variance resulted when the actual cost was either $48 or $72, if the decision was based on an expected cost of $60). This is true because any departure from optimal plans will generate an unfavorable opportunity cost variance.

A similar analysis can be undertaken if the actual quantity sold differed from the expected $Q^* = 10$. Parameter changes might have occurred in the demand equation, the pricing equation, or both. Had the decision maker been able to anticipate these changes ex ante, a different pricing decision and profit expectation would have resulted. Alternatively, an unanticipated change in the quantity sold might be due to a temporary change in demand (i.e., the structural forms of the demand and pricing equations remain valid). In this situation, one component of the total profit variance would be a sales quantity variance.

The expected opportunity cost variance will be zero only in a world of perfect certainty, if the firm consistently has access to perfect forecasts, or if the decision could not have been changed to incorporate new information. In these cases optimal decisions, once made, would not be rendered suboptimal by future developments. While we do not live in a world of perfect certainty, there are steps which can be taken to *reduce* cost structure uncertainty and to improve decisions under uncertainty. These would include careful monitoring of potentially volatile cost elements, development of better forecasting techniques, and more frequent revision of standards.

The monitoring, forecasting, and cost analysis activities which might reduce cost structure uncertainty are themselves costly. The incurrence of these costs must be weighed against the benefits—the opportunity losses which would be avoided by the improved decision making. Thus the opportunity cost variance must be calculated under various potential scenarios to determine the firm's exposure to opportunity losses. Once the potential losses attributable to imperfect decision making are quantified, the desirability of uncertainty-reducing activities can be evaluated.

In our numerical example, suppose that the probability of each variable cost value—$48, $60 and $72—was one third. Then the expected opportunity cost variance is $12 U [(1/3 × $18 U) + (1/3 × $0) + (1/3 × $18 U)]. Therefore, a maximum of $12 could be spent to determine which cost value will actually prevail.

This has been only one of many possible illustrations of the ways in which opportunity cost variances could be used to extend the control benefits of standard costing to the level of the decision-making process itself. By examining some of the important prior work in the area, we can see several others.

The Major Theoretical Contributions

Although accountants have long recognized that persistent cost variances in a given direction may signal the need for revised standards, Zannetos was among the first to observe that such signals, by revising the marginality conditions, can lead to changes in plans. In other words, a change in the standard cost of labor can affect not only the desirability of using labor rather than capital in the production process, but the relative profitability of labor-intensive products as well. Although Zannetos did not label it as such, failure to make the required changes in the production process suggested by the revised marginality conditions represents an opportunity cost equal to the difference between actual costs and the new minimum cost.

Opportunity costs were linked to responsibility accounting by Samuels within the context of a linear programming model used to develop the optimal production plan for three departments where each department's production was limited by a resource constraint. Samuels proposed a responsibility accounting system in which the "standard costs" charged to each department were the shadow prices or marginal values of the limiting resource constraints. In a subsequent paper, Bernhard showed that Samuels' reporting system could have undesirable behavioral effects and recommended certain changes.

Samuels' basic approach has been extended by Greer to sequential production process situations. Greer shows that where there are constraints controlling the total amount of time available for a sequence of processes, and where the consumption of additional resources is required to accelerate production rates, conventional standard cost systems tend to motivate process managers toward suboptimal behavior patterns. He develops a system whereby each process manager is charged for the incremental costs a "downstream" process is required to incur due to his own departure from the authorized optimal plan. The motivational characteristics of this revised system are such that each process manager, in turn, has incentives to comply with the optimal plan.

Dopuch, Birnberg, and Demski joined the ideas of Samuels and Zannetos into one conceptual framework wherein variance analysis is used to effect both process control and decision model control. To control the decision model effectively, two prerequisites must be met. First, the control system must be designed around the formal decision model used by the firm, and the decision variables for which variances need to be calculated must be identified. Second, the control system must be able to distinguish between controllable and noncontrollable deviations or variances.

Demski refined and extended these ideas in subsequent work. He introduced the concept of *ex post analysis* and linked it to the opportunity cost variance. At the end of the accounting period, the original decision model is re-solved using the actual parameters (variables) reported. The resulting solution is the ex post optimum. The following notation is employed to evaluate systematically the ex post results:

Π° = original budgeted profit resulting from the optimal solution of the decision model using the original parameters (variables).

Π^a = actual profit reported by the accounting system.

Π^p = ex post budgeted profit resulting from the optimal solution of the decision model using the actual parameters (variables).

Since the ex post optimum represents the best the firm *could have done* with the actual reported parameters (variables), the amount $\Pi^p - \Pi^a$ is the opportunity cost of not revising plans as suggested by the ex post solution. The example used in the first section of this paper illustrates these concepts. Decision model control is therefore linked to process control via the ex post optimum program.

To this point, our discussion of opportunity cost variances has focused on the control of short-run decision models and has assumed fixed productive capacity. Ronen has applied ex post analysis to longer-run decisions dealing with the acquisition of plant capacity and has developed a set of capacity variances to measure the cost of incorrect capacity decisions. These opportunity cost variances address issues of decision implementation as well as parameter (variable) misspecification. They provide an intriguing theoretical framework for evaluation of capital expenditure decisions.

In another interesting application of the opportunity cost variance concept, Ijiri and Itami employed an ex post analysis to evaluate formally the cost associated with timing of the receipt of information. Although accountants have long believed that timeliness is an important characteristic of information, it has rarely been studied systematically. Ijiri and Itami show that, in some situations, a cost/benefit analysis of the timing of information is feasible. Their "forecast delay variance" relates to the delay before a firm order for the period's production is received and focuses on the opportunity cost of untimely information. The avoidance of this opportunity cost is one benefit of *timely* information; against this benefit the cost of obtaining timely information can be compared. For example, what would it cost the producing department, in terms of price concessions or other considerations, to obtain a firm order at the *beginning* of the periodic production process, rather than at some time *during* the production process?

Aspects of Practical Implementation

The currently available literature has firmly established several important concepts. First, the actual level and structure of costs incurred (and benefits received) are sometimes different from what was anticipated when a decision was made. Prices of input factors do change unexpectedly. Expected demand levels sometimes do not materialize.

Second, these unanticipated differences frequently cause suboptimal results. That is, had the decision maker been able to foresee the actual cost of input factors or the actual level of demand, the decision itself would have been different and the different decision would have produced higher profits. This means the unanticipated differences caused the incurrence of opportunity costs.

Third, the frequency of unanticipated differences, and therefore the amount of opportunity cost incurred, can be reduced by incurring other kinds of costs. Firms can monitor factor price markets more closely. Standard costs can be updated more frequently. Selling price policies could be changed and final product market forecasts may be improved. All of these activities can reduce the frequency and magnitude of unanticipated differences, but they all require making economic sacrifices.

The main problem lies in actually measuring the relationships. In practice, simple mathematical decision models which can just be solved again with new data seldom exist. Rather, decision processes are often complex, undefinable and intuitive. We will suggest, however, that an approximation can provide useful information. Our question, then, is how the opportunity cost variance can actually be *estimated.*

As a first step for practical estimation, the decisions to be evaluated must be identified. This may sound trivial but it is an important step. Every day in every organization thousands of decisions are made. It would be impossible to estimate the opportunity cost associated with all of them. Decisions which are fairly important and easily separable from routine operations might be likely candidates for initial efforts. We are thinking of pricing decisions for new product lines, make-or-buy decisions, purchase quantity decisions on major inventory items or even large capital expenditure decisions.

Once the decisions are selected, the values of the variables which were important to the decision maker should be recorded. These would include elements such as variable cost per unit, storage costs, ordering cost, estimated price/demand relationships, projected tax rates and so on. Ideally this step would take place at the time of the decision.

After sufficient time has passed, the economic results of the decision will be known. The actual values of the variables considered as important at the time the decision was made should be determined and organized for presentation to the decision maker.

The next step is probably the most crucial to the success of an effort to estimate an opportunity cost variance. The decision maker must be asked to specify what his decision would have been with the *benefit of hindsight*. In other words, with knowledge about the actual values of the critical variables, what would his decision have been? Together, then, the decision maker and the analyst can estimate what the economic consequences of the revised decision would have been. Using Demski's terminology, the output of this step is the ex post budgeted profit resulting from the optimal decision, Π^p. This figure is compared with the actual profit, Π^a, to determine the opportunity cost variance.

In some cases the decision maker's response will be that the original decision could not have been altered. If this is so, the opportunity cost variance will be zero even if the expected profit did not materialize. The total difference would be directly attributable to price or efficiency discrepancies.

A more troublesome response to the actual values of the variables would be that nothing would have been done. That is, the capital expenditures would not have been made (with hindsight) or the new product line would not have been introduced. The problem is that "doing nothing" does *not* imply that Π^p = zero. Rather, the available capital or the production time would probably have been put to some other use. Conceivably an estimate of the economic value of the alternative use could be made, but such an estimate is likely to be highly speculative and unreliable. An alternative approach would be to use the firm's estimated cost of capital to approximate the foregone returns on the investments in idle production capacity.

As a final step, the degree to which hindsight *could* have been obtained before the decision was made must be analyzed—and the costs of doing so must be determined. Would it have been possible to forecast future demand levels more accurately at the time of the decision? How much would it have cost to do so? Could the cost of materials have been more accurately estimated? What amount of analysis would have been required? These kinds of questions would lead to an understanding of the profit potential for systematically reducing the opportunity cost variance.

As long as decisions are susceptible to modification, it is clearly impossible to eliminate the opportunity cost variance completely. It would also be economically unwise to attempt to do so. It may well be, however, that a given firm is now attempting to do more or less than it should, and that profits could be enhanced by addressing the issue.

13.

The Economies of Scale*

GEORGE J. STIGLER

The theory of the economies of scale is the theory of the relationship between the scale of use of a properly chosen combination of all productive services and the rate of output of the enterprise. In its broadest formulation this theory is a crucial element of the economic theory of social organization, for it underlies every question of market organization and the role (and locus) of governmental control over economic life. Let one ask himself how an economy would be organized if every economic activity were prohibitively inefficient upon alternately a small scale and a large scale, and the answer will convince him that here lies a basic element of the theory of economic organization.

The theory has limped along for a century, collecting large pieces of good reasoning and small chunks of empirical evidence but never achieving scientific prosperity. A large cause of its poverty is that the central concept of the theory—the firm of optimum size—has eluded confident measurement. We have been dangerously close to denying Lincoln, for all economists have been ignorant of the optimum size of firm in almost every industry all of the time, and this ignorance has been an insurmountable barrier between us and the understanding of the forces which govern optimum size. It is almost as if one were trying to measure the nutritive values of goods without knowing whether the consumers who ate them continued to live.

The central thesis of this paper is that the determination of the optimum size is not difficult if one formalizes the logic that sensible

---

* *The Journal of Law and Economics* 1 (October 1958), pp. 54–71.

men have always employed to judge efficient size. This technique, which I am old-fashioned enough to call the survivor technique, reveals the optimum size in terms of private costs—that is, in terms of the environment in which the enterprise finds itself. After discussing the technique, we turn to the question of how the forces governing optimum size may be isolated.

I. THE SURVIVOR PRINCIPLE

The optimum size (or range of sizes) of enterprises in an industry is now ascertained empirically by one of three methods. The first is that of direct comparison of actual costs of firms of different sizes; the second is the comparison of rates of return on investment; and the third is the calculation of probable costs of enterprises of different sizes in the light of technological information. All three methods are practically objectionable in demanding data which are usually unobtainable and seldom up to date. But this cannot be the root of their difficulties, for there is up-to-date information on many economic concepts which are complex and even basically incapable of precise measurement (such as income). The plain fact is that we have not demanded the data because we have been unable to specify what we wanted.

The comparisons of both actual costs and rates of return are strongly influenced by the valuations which are put on productive services, so that an enterprise which over- or undervalues important productive services, will under- or overstate its efficiency. Historical cost valuations of resources, which are most commonly available, are in principle irrelevant under changed conditions. Valuations based upon expected earnings yield no information on the efficiency of an enterprise—in the limiting case where all resources are so valued, all firms would be of equal efficiency judged by either average costs or rates of return. The ascertainment on any scale of the maximum value of each resource in alternative uses is a task which only the unsophisticated would assume and only the omniscient would discharge. The host of valuation problems are accentuated by the variable role of the capital markets in effecting revaluations and the variable attitudes of the accountants toward the revaluations.

The technological studies of costs of different sizes of plant encounter equally formidable obstacles. These studies are compounded on some fairly precise (although not necessarily very relevant) technical information and some crude guesses on nontechnological aspects such as marketing costs, transportation rate changes, labor relations, etc.—that is, much of the problem is solved only in the unhappy sense of being delegated to a technologist. Even ideal results, moreover, do not tell us the optimum size of firm in industry A in 1958, but rather the optimum size of new plants in the industry, on the assumption that the industry starts *de novo* or that only a small increment of investment is being made.

The survivor technique avoids both the problems of valuation of resources and the hypothetical nature of the technological studies. Its fundamental postulate is that the competition of different sizes of firms sifts out the more efficient enterprises. In the words of Mill, who long ago proposed the technique:

> Whether or not the advantages obtained by operating on a large scale preponderate in any particular case over the more watchful attention, and greater regard to minor gains and losses usually found in small establishments, can be ascertained, in a state of free competition, by an unfailing test. . . . Wherever there are large and small establishments in the same business, that one of the two which in existing circumstances carries on the production at the greater advantage will be able to undersell the others.[1]

Mill was wrong only in suggesting that the technique was inapplicable under oligopoly, for even under oligopoly the drive of maximum profits will lead to the disappearance of relatively inefficient sizes of firms.

The survivor technique proceeds to solve the problem of determining the optimum firm size as follows: Classify the firms in an industry by size, and calculate the share of industry output coming from each class over time. If the share of a given class falls, it is relatively inefficient, and in general is more inefficient the more rapidly the share falls.

An efficient size of firm, on this argument, is one that meets any and all problems the entrepreneur actually faces: strained labor relations, rapid innovation, government regulation, unstable foreign markets, and what not. This is, of course, the decisive meaning of efficiency from the viewpoint of the enterprise. Of course, social efficiency may be a very different thing: the most efficient firm size may arise from possession of monopoly power, undesirable labor practices, discriminatory legislation, etc. The survivor technique is not directly applicable to the determination of the socially optimum size of enterprise, and we do not enter into this question. The socially optimum firm is fundamentally an ethical concept, and we question neither its importance nor its elusiveness.

Not only is the survivor technique more direct and simpler than the alternative techniques for the determination of the optimum size of firm, it is also more authoritative. Suppose that the cost, rate of return, and technological studies all find that in a given industry the optimum size of firm is one which produces 500 to 600 units per day, and that costs per unit are much higher if one goes far outside this range. Suppose also that most of the firms in the industry are three times as large,

---

[1] *Principles of Political Economy* (Ashley ed.), p. 134. Marshall states the same argument in Darwinian language: "For as a general rule the law of substitution—which is nothing more than a special and limited application of the law of survival of the fittest—tends to make one method of industrial organization supplant another when it offers a direct and immediate service at a lower price." *Principles of Economics*, p. 597 (8th ed., 1920).

and that those firms which are in the 500 to 600 unit class are rapidly failing or growing to a larger size. Would we believe that the optimum size was 500 to 600 units? Clearly not: An optimum size that cannot survive in rivalry with other sizes is a contradiction, and some error, we would all say, has been made in the traditional studies. Implicitly all judgments on economies of scale have always been based directly upon, or at least verified by recourse to, the experience of survivorship.

This is not to say that the findings of the survivor technique are unequivocal. Entrepreneurs may make mistakes in their choice of firm size, and we must seek to eliminate the effects of such errors either by invoking large numbers of firms so errors tend to cancel or by utilizing time periods such that errors are revealed and corrected. Or the optimum size may be changing because of changes in factor prices or technology, so that perhaps the optimum size rises in one period and falls in another. This problem too calls for a close examination of the time periods which should be employed. We face these problems in our statistical work below.

We must also recognize that a single optimum size of firm will exist in an industry only if all firms have (access to) identical resources. Since various firms employ different kinds or qualities of resources, there will tend to develop a frequency distribution of optimum firm sizes. The survivor technique may allow us to estimate this distribution; in the application below we restrict ourselves to the range of optimum sizes.

The measure of the optimum size is only a first step toward the construction of a theory of economies of scale with substantive content, but it is the indispensable first step. We turn in later sections of this paper to the examination of the methods by which hypotheses concerning the determinants of optimum size may be tested.

II. ILLUSTRATIVE SURVIVORSHIP MEASURES

The survivor principle is very general in scope and very flexible in application, and these advantages can best be brought out by making concrete applications of the principle to individual industries. These applications will also serve to display a number of problems of data and interpretation which are encountered in the use of the survivor technique. We begin with the American steel industry.

In order that survivorship of firms of a given size be evidence of comparative efficiency, these firms must compete with firms of other sizes—all of the firms must sell in a common market. We have therefore restricted the analysis to firms making steel ingots by open-hearth or Bessemer processes. Size has perforce been measured by capacity, for production is not reported by individual companies, and capacity is expressed as a percentage of the industry total to eliminate the influence of the secular growth of industry and company size. The geographical

TABLE 1
Distribution of Output of Steel Ingot Capacity by Relative Size of Company

Company Size (percent of industry total)	1930	1938	1951
	1. *Percent of Industry Capacity*		
Under 0.5	7.16	6.11	4.65
0.5 to 1	5.94	5.08	5.37
1 to 2.5	13.17	8.30	9.07
2.5 to 5	10.64	16.59	22.21
5 to 10	11.18	14.03	8.12
10 to 25	13.24	13.99	16.10
25 and over	38.67	35.91	34.50
	2. *Number of Companies*		
Under 0.5	39	29	22
0.5 to 1	9	7	7
1 to 2.5	9	6	6
2.5 to 5	3	4	5
5 to 10	2	2	1
10 to 25	1	1	1
25 and over	1	1	1

Sources: *Directory of Iron and Steel Works of the United States and Canada,* 1930, 1938; *Iron Age,* January 3, 1952.

extent of the market is especially difficult to determine in steel, for the shifting geographical pattern of consumption has created a linkage between the various regional markets. We treat the market as national, which exaggerates its extent, but probably does less violence to the facts than a sharp regional classification of firms. The basic data are given in Table 1.

Over two decades covered by Table 1 (and, for that matter, over the last half century) there has been a persistent and fairly rapid decline in the share of the industry's capacity in firms with less than half a percent of the total, so that we may infer that this size of firm is subject to substantial diseconomies of scale.[2] The firms with 0.5 to 2.5 percent of industry capacity showed a moderate decline, and hence were subject to smaller diseconomies of scale. The one firm with more than one fourth of industry capacity declined moderately, so it too had diseconomies of scale. The intervening sizes, from 2.5 to 25 percent of industry capacity, grew or held their share so they constituted the range of optimum size.

---

[2] In 1930 the firm with 0.5 percent of the industry capacity had a capacity of 364,000 net tons; in 1951, 485,000 net tons. Of course, we could have employed absolute firm size classes, but they are less appropriate to many uses.

The more rapid the rate at which a firm loses its share of the industry's output (or, here, capacity), the higher is its private cost of production relative to the cost of production of firms of the most efficient size. This interpretation should not be reversed, however, to infer that the size class whose share is growing more rapidly is more efficient than other classes whose shares are growing more slowly; the difference can merely represent differences in the quantities of various qualities of resources. In the light of these considerations we translate the data of Table 1 into a long-run average cost curve for the production of steel ingots and display this curve in Figure 1. Over a wide range of outputs there is no evidence of net economies or diseconomies of scale.

FIGURE 1

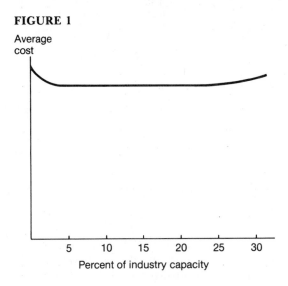

Although the survivor test yields an estimate of the shape of the long-run cost curve, it does not allow an estimate of how much higher than the minimum are the costs of the firm sizes whose shares of industry output are declining. Costs are higher the more rapid the rate at which the firm size loses its share of industry output, but the rate at which a firm size loses a share of industry output will also vary with numerous other factors. This rate of loss of output will be larger, the less durable and specialized the productive resources of the firm, for then exit from the industry is easier. The rate of loss will also be larger, the more nearly perfect the capital and labor markets, so that resources can be obtained to grow quickly to more efficient size. The rate of loss will be smaller, given the degree of inefficiency, the more profitable the industry is, for then the rate of return of all sizes of firms is larger relative to other industries.

By a simple extension of this argument, we may also estimate the

TABLE 2
Distribution of Output of Steel Ingot Capacity

Plant Size (percent of industry total)	1930	1938	1951
1. Percent of Industry Capacity			
Under 0.25	3.74	3.81	3.25
0.25 to 0.5	6.39	5.81	7.20
0.5 to 0.75	6.39	4.18	3.82
0.75 to 1	9.42	12.29	10.93
1 to 1.75	21.78	15.56	20.67
1.75 to 2.5	13.13	16.73	17.01
2.5 to 3.75	23.49	17.18	8.10
3.75 to 5	8.82	12.07	12.46
5 to 10	6.82	12.37	16.56
2. Number of Plants			
Under 0.25	40	29	23
0.25 to 0.5	20	16	18
0.5 to 0.75	11	7	6
0.75 to 1	11	14	12
1 to 1.75	18	13	15
1.75 to 2.5	6	8	8
2.5 to 3.75	8	6	3
3.75 to 5	2	3	3
5 to 10	1	2	3

Sources: *Directory of Iron and Steel Works of the United States and Canada,* 1930, 1938; *Iron Age,* January 3, 1952.

most efficient size of *plant* in the steel ingot industry during the same period (Table 2). We again find that the smallest plants have a tendency to decline relative to the industry, and indeed this is implied by the company data. There is no systematic tendency toward decline in shares held by plants between 0.75 percent and 10 percent of the industry size. We may therefore infer that the tendency of very small plants and companies to decline relative to the industry is due to the diseconomy of a small plant, and the tendency of the largest company (U.S. Steel) to decline has been due to diseconomies of multiplant operation beyond a certain scale.

An equally important and interesting industry, passenger automobiles, uncovers different problems. Here we can use production data instead of capacity, and have no compunctions in treating the market as national in scope. The basic data for the individual firms are given in Table 3.

A striking feature of the automobile industry is the small number of firms, and this poses a statistical problem we have glossed over in our discussion of steel: What confidence can be attached to changes in the share of industry output coming from a firm size when that size

TABLE 3
Percentages of Passenger Automobiles Produced in United States by Various Companies, 1936–1941 and 1946–1955

Year	General Motors	Chrysler	Ford	Hudson	Nash	Kaiser	Willys Over-land	Packard	Stude-baker	Other
1936	42.9	23.6	22.6	3.3	1.5	—	0.7	2.2	2.4	0.8
1937	40.9	24.2	22.6	2.7	2.2	—	2.0	2.8	2.1	0.5
1938	43.9	23.8	22.3	2.5	1.6	—	0.8	2.5	2.3	0.3
1939	43.0	22.7	21.8	2.8	2.3	—	0.9	2.6	3.7	0.3
1940	45.9	25.1	19.0	2.3	1.7	—	0.7	2.1	3.1	0.1
1941	48.3	23.3	18.3	2.1	2.1	—	0.8	1.8	3.2	0.1
1946	38.4	25.0	21.2	4.2	4.6	0.6	0.3	1.9	3.6	0.2
1947	40.4	21.7	21.3	2.8	3.2	4.1	0.9	1.6	3.5	0.5
1948	40.1	21.2	19.1	3.6	3.1	4.6	0.8	2.5	4.2	0.7
1949	43.0	21.9	21.0	2.8	2.8	1.2	0.6	2.0	4.5	0.2
1950	45.7	18.0	23.3	2.1	2.8	2.2	0.6	1.1	4.0	0.1
1951	42.2	23.1	21.8	1.8	3.0	1.9	0.5	1.4	4.2	0.1
1952	41.5	22.0	23.2	1.8	3.5	1.7	1.1	1.4	3.7	—
1953	45.7	20.3	25.2	1.2	2.2	1.0		1.3	3.0	—
1954	52.2	13.1	30.6	1.7		0.3		0.5	1.6	—
1955	50.2	17.2	28.2	2.0		0.1			2.3	—

Source: Ward's Automotive Yearbook 1951, 1955, 1956.

contains very few firms? For the automobile industry (unlike steel) we possess annual data, and can therefore take into account the steadiness of direction or magnitude of changes in shares of various firm sizes, and to this extent increase our confidence in the estimates. We may also extend the period which is surveyed, although at the risk of combining periods with different sizes of optimum firms. Aside from recourse to related data (the survivorship pattern of the industry in other countries, for example), there is no other method of reducing the uncertainty of findings for small number industries.

The survivorship record in automobiles (summarized in Table 4) is more complicated than that for steel. In the immediate prewar years there was already a tendency for the largest company to produce a rising share and for the 2.5 to 5 percent class to produce a sharply declining share; the smallest and next to largest sizes showed no clear tendency. In a longer span of time, however, the smallest companies reveal a fairly consistently declining share. In the immediate postwar period, the 2.5 to 5 percent size class was strongly favored by the larger companies' need to practice price control in a sensitive political atmosphere, and the same phenomenon reappeared less strongly in the first two

TABLE 4
Percentage of Passenger Automobiles Produced by Companies of Various Sizes

	Company Size (as percent of industry)				Number of Companies	
Year	Over 35 (percent)	10–35 (percent)	2.5–5 (percent)	Under 2.5 (percent)	2.5–5 (percent)	Under 2.5 (percent)
1936	42.9	46.2	3.3	7.6	1	5*
1937	40.9	46.8	5.5	6.8	2	4*
1938	43.9	46.1	5.0	5.0	2	4*
1939	43.0	44.4	9.1	3.5	3	4*
1940	45.9	44.1	3.1	6.9	1	6*
1941	48.4	41.6	3.2	6.8	1	5
1946	38.4	46.2	12.4	3.0	3	4
1947	40.4	43.0	13.6	3.0	4	3
1948	40.1	40.3	18.0	1.5	5	2
1949	43.0	42.9	10.0	4.0	3	4
1950	45.7	41.3	6.8	6.1	2	5
1951	42.2	44.9	7.2	2	5	
			5.7			
1952	41.5	45.2	7.2	6.1	2	5
1953	45.6	45.5	3.0	5.8	1	4
1954	52.2	43.7	0	4.1	0	4
1955	50.2	45.4	0	4.4	0	3

Source: Table 3.
* Or more.

years after the outbreak of Korean hostilities. From this record we would infer that there have been diseconomies of large size, at least for the largest size of firm, in inflationary periods with private or public price control, but substantial economies of large scale at other times. The long-run average cost curve is saucer shaped in inflationary times, but shows no tendency to rise at the largest outputs in other times.

The automobile example suggests the method by which we determine whether changing technology, factor prices, or consumer demands lead to a change in the optimum firm size. We infer an underlying stability in the optimum size in those periods in which the survivorship trends are stable. Indeed it is hard to conceive of an alternative test; one can judge the economic importance, in contrast to technological originality, of an innovation only by the impact it has upon the size distribution of firms.

Before we leave these applications of the survivorship technique we should indicate its flexibility in dealing with other problems which seem inappropriate to our particular examples. For example, a Marshallian may object that firms must begin small and grow to optimum size through time, so that the size structure of the industry in a given period will reflect this historical life pattern as well as the optimum size influences. In an industry such as retail trade this interpretation would be quite plausible. It can be met by studying the survivor experience of firm sizes in the light of the age or rate of growth of the firms. Again, one may argue that firms of different sizes have different comparative advantages at different stages of the business cycle. Such a hypothesis could be dealt with by comparing average survivorship patterns in given cycle stages with those calculated for full cycles.

Let us now turn to the methods by which one may test hypotheses on the determinants of optimum size.

III. INTERINDUSTRY ANALYSES OF THE DETERMINANTS OF OPTIMUM SIZE

Once the optimum firm size has been ascertained for a variety of industries, the relationship between size and other variables can be explored. This is, in fact, the customary procedure for economists to employ, and the present investigation differs, aside from the method of determining optimum size, only in being more systematic than most such investigations. For example, numerous economists have asserted that advertising is a force making for large firms, and they usually illustrate this relationship by the cigarette industry. Will the relationship still hold when it is tested against a list of industries which has not been chosen to illustrate it? This is essentially the type of inquiry we make here.

Although the survivor method makes lesser demands of data than other methods to determine optimum firm size, it has equally exacting requirements of information on any other variable whose influence is to be studied. In the subsequent investigation of some 48 ("three-digit) manufacturing industries, whose optimum firm size is calculated from data in *Statistics of Income,* we have therefore been compelled to exclude some variables for lack of data and to measure others in a most imperfect manner. The industries we study, and the measures we contrive, are given in Table 5; we describe their derivation below.

1. Size of Firm. The optimum size of firm in each industry is determined by comparing the percentage of the industry's assets possessed by firms in each asset class in 1948 and 1951.[3] Those classes in which the share of the industry's assets was stable or rising were identified, and the average assets of the firms within these sizes were calculated. The range of optimum sizes is also given in Table 5. An industry was excluded if it had a very large noncorporate sector (for which we could not measure firm size) or gave strong evidence of heterogeneity by having two widely separated optimum sizes (as, for example, in "aircraft and parts").

2. Advertising Expenditures. We have already remarked that extensive advertising is often mentioned as an explanation for the growth of large firms, especially in consumer goods industries such as cigarettes, liquor, and cosmetics. The argument supporting this view can take one of three directions. First, national advertising may be viewed as more efficient than local advertising, in terms of sales per dollar of advertising at a given price. Second, long-continued advertising may have a cumulative impact. Finally, and closely related to the preceding point, the joint advertising of a series of related products may be more efficient than advertising them individually. We measure the variable by the ratio of advertising expenditures to sales, both taken from *Statistics of Income.*

3. Technology and Research. A host of explanations of firm size are related to technological characteristics and research. Complicated production processes may require large companies, or at least large plants. The economies of research are held to be substantial; the outcome of individual projects is uncertain, so small programs are more risky; a balanced research team may be fairly large; and much capital may be required to bring a new process to a commercial stage and to wait for a return upon the outlay.

At present there is no direct measure available for either the impor-

---

[3] These particular dates were dictated by the data; there were large changes in industry classification in 1948, and no minor industry data were tabulated for 1952. A better, but more laborious, determination of optimum size could have been made if the data for intervening years were utilized.

TABLE 5. **Basic Data on 48 Manufacturing Industries**

Industry	Optimum Company Size (in thousand dollars of total assets) (1948–51)	Optimum Range Class Limits (in thousand dollars)		Average Establishment Size (in thousand dollars of value added) (1947)	Number of Chemists and Engineers per 100 Employed (1950)	Advertising Expenditure as Percent of Gross Sales (1950)
		From	To			
Motor vehicles, incl. bodies and truck trailers	$827,828	$100,000	$open	$ 3,715	1.5879	0.4395
Petroleum refining	765,716	100,000	open	3,420	6.9171	0.4562
Blast furnaces, steel works, and rolling mills	525,485	100,000	open	8,310	2.0956	0.1321
Dairy products	446,483	100,000	open	110	0.7865	1.5221
Distilled, rectified, and blended liquors	248,424	100,000	open	2,090	0.9041	1.3674
Pulp, paper, and paperboard	203,794	100,000	open	1,645	1.4927	0.3357
Paints, varnishes, lacquers, etc.	175,404	100,000	open	394	6.0431	1.3539
Railroad equipment, incl. locomotives and streetcars	150,217	100,000	open	3,407	2.7171	0.3611
Tires and tubes	141,600	10,000	open	11,405	2.0974*	0.9453
Grain mill products ex. cereals preparations	128,363	100,000	open	210	1.0344	1.2492
Drugs and medicines	123,662	100,000	open	552	6.2599	8.3858
Smelting, refining, rolling, drawing, and alloying of nonferrous metals	100,398	10,000	open	1,658	2.9845†	0.4088
Office and store machines	65,914	10,000	open	1,411	2.5860	1.5812
Bakery products	58,960	50,000	100,000	192	0.2359	2.1335
Yarn and thread	44,375	10,000	open	687	0.4461	0.3238
Carpets and other floor coverings	37,337	10,000	100,000	1,119	1.2391	1.7295
Broadwoven fabrics (wool)	31,265	10,000	open	1,211	0.4461	0.3400
Watches, clocks, and clock work operated devices	31,025	10,000	50,000	705	1.2027	5.3238
Cement	29,554	10,000	100,000	1,600	2.1277‡	0.2726
Malt liquors and malt	28,922	10,000	open	1,750	0.9041	4.7962
Agricultural machinery and tractors	28,291	1,000	open	684	2.1816	0.8956
Structural clay products	24,001	10,000	100,000	253	1.6292	0.4552
Newspapers	23,428	10,000	100,000	168	0.1348§	0.1948
Knit goods	17,918	10,000	100,000	273	0.1244	0.8522
Confectionery	13,524	5,000	50,000	335	0.5950	2.6481
Commercial printing including lithographing	11,939	5,000	50,000	97	0.1348§	0.6474
Furniture—household, office, public building and professional	11,378	5,000	50,000	209	0.3990‖	0.9152

TABLE 5 (*concluded*)

Industry	Optimum Company Size (in thousand dollars of total assets) (1948–51)	From	To	Average Establishment Size (in thousand dollars of value added) (1947)	Number Chemists and Engineers per 100 Employed (1950)	Advertising Expenditure as percent of Gross Sales (1950)
Men's clothing	$ 10,077	$ 5,000	$ 50,000	$ 247	0.0456#	0.8795
Dyeing and finishing textiles, excl. knit goods	9,625	5,000	50,000	545	0.1223	0.3472
Canning fruit, vegetables, and seafood	6,536	1,000	open	240	0.9144	1.8462
Broadwoven fabrics (cotton)	5,847	50	open	2,595	0.4461**	0.2822
Footwear, exc. rubber	4,359	1,000	100,000	524	0.1474	1.1619
Paperbags, and paperboard containers and boxes	4,127	1,000	100,000	428	0.6939	0.1854
Cigars	3,753	250	50,000	174	0.2274††	2.3188
Meat products	2,665	500	100,000	322	0.5983	0.4264
Nonferrous foundries	2,365	500	50,000	172	2.9845†	0.2793
Fur goods	1,966	1,000	5,000	55	0.0456#	0.4119
Partitions, shelving, lockers, etc.	1,545	500	50,000	121	0.3990‖	0.8678
Narrow fabrics and other small wares	1,382	500	5,000	226	0.4461**	0.3212
Wines	1,304	500	5,000	227	0.9041‡‡	3.5854
Women's clothing	1,304	500	50,000	150	0.0456#	0.9150
Books	1,137	50	50,000	399	0.1348§	2.8796
Periodicals	1,117	250	10,000	307	0.1348§	0.5245
Leather—tanning, curing, and finishing	764	0	10,000	720	0.8140	0.1813
Concrete, gypsum, and plaster products	762	250	10,000	53	2.1277‡	0.6855
Window and door screens, shades, and venetian blinds	667	100	10,000	110	0.3990‖	1.0581
Nonalcoholic beverages	546	100	50,000	75	0.9041‡‡	4.0740
Millinery	468	250	5,000	108	0.0456#	0.4438

* Rubber products.
† Primary nonferrous.
‡ Cement, and concrete, gypsum, and plaster products.
§ Printing, publishing, and allied industries.
‖ Furniture and fixtures.
Apparel and accessories.
** Yarn, thread, and fabric mills.
†† Tobacco manufactures.
‡‡ Beverage industries.

tance of research or the intricacy of technology. We use an index, chemists and engineers as a ratio to all employees, that may reflect both influences, but probably very imperfectly. When it becomes possible to make a division of these personnel between research and routine operation, a division which would be very valuable for other purposes also, the interpretation of an index of technical personnel will be less ambiguous.

4. Plant Size. Plant size normally sets a minimum to company size, and therefore exerts an obvious influence on the differences among industries in company size. We are compelled to resort to a measure of plant size—value added per establishment in 1947—which is not directly comparable to company size because the 1947 Census of Manufacturers did not report corporate establishments at the requisite level of detail.

Preliminary analysis revealed that there is no significant relationship between firm size and advertising expenditures, so this variable was omitted from the statistical calculations. The average ratio of advertising expenditures to sales was 1.97 percent in consumer goods industries and 0.57 percent in producer goods industries, but in neither group was there a significant relationship between the ratio and firm size.[4]

A regression analysis confirms the impression one gets from Table 5 that the other variables we examine are positively related to optimum firm size.

$$X_1 = -5.092 + 34.6 \ X_2 + 42.7 \ X_3,$$
$$(10.8) \qquad (12.2)$$

where

X_1 is firm size, in millions of dollars of assets,
X_2 is plant size, in millions of dollars of value added,
X_3 is engineers and chemists per 100 employees.

The standard errors of the regression coefficients are given below the coefficients.

An examination of Table 5 suggests that the correlation would be higher if the data were somewhat more precise. The size of plant is unduly low in motor vehicles, because of the inclusion of suppliers of parts. Moreover the plant sizes have not been estimated by the survivor technique. Technological personnel are exaggerated in nonferrous foundries because we are compelled to use the ratio for a broader class, and the same is true of concrete products. The relatively small size of company in footwear, as compared to plant size, is at least partially due to the fact that the machinery was usually leased, and hence not

---

[4] The respective rank correlation coefficients were $-.187$ and $-.059$.

included in assets. Industries which are "out of line" have not been omitted, however, for similar considerations may have caused other industries to be "in line." Yet the general impression is that the correlation would rise substantially with improved measurements of the variables.

The range of optimum sizes is generally wide, although the width is exaggerated, and our measurements impaired, because the largest asset class (over $100 million) embraces numerous firms of very different sizes—growth and inflation are outmoding the size classes used in *Statistics of Income*. In 10 industries only this largest size has had a rising share of industry assets, and in another nine industries it is included in the range of sizes with rising shares. When the upper limit of optimum sizes is known, the range of optimum sizes is typically three or four times the average size of the firms in these sizes.

The results of this exploratory inter-industry study are at least suggestive—not only in their specific content but also in pointing out a line of attack on the economies of scale that escapes that confession of failure, the case method. The chief qualifications that attach to the findings are due to the imperfections of the data: the industry categories are rather wide; and the measure of technical personnel is seriously ambiguous. At least one finding—a wide range of optimum firm sizes in each industry—is so general as to deserve to be taken as the standard model in the theory of production.

IV. INTRAINDUSTRY ANALYSIS OF THE DETERMINANTS OF OPTIMUM SIZE

One may also examine the varying fates of individual firms within an industry in the search for explanations of optimum size. If, for example, firms moving to optimum size were vertically integrated and those moving to or remaining in nonoptimum size were not so integrated, we could infer that vertical integration was a requisite of the optimum firm in the industry. This approach has the advantage over the inter-industry approach of not requiring the assumption that a determinant such as advertising or integration works similarly in all industries.

The intraindustry analysis, however, has a heavy disadvantage, it can be applied only to those variables for which we can obtain information on each firm and in industries with numerous firms hardly any interesting variables survive this requirement. Because we could examine so few influences, and because the results were so consistently negative, we shall be very brief in describing our results in the industry—petroleum refining—in which this approach was tried.

The basic survivor experience for companies and plants in petroleum refining is given in Tables 6 and 7, for the postwar period 1947–1954. In each case only operating plants are included, and asphalt plants and companies are excluded. Capacities are measured in terms of crude

TABLE 6
Distribution of Petroleum Refining Capacity
by Relative Size of Company

Company (percent of industry capacity)	1947	1950	1954
1. Percent of Industry Capacity			
Under 0.1	5.30	4.57	3.89
0.1 to 0.2	4.86	3.57	3.00
0.2 to 0.3	2.67	2.16	2.74
0.3 to 0.4	2.95	2.92	1.65
0.4 to 0.5	2.20	0	.89
0.5 to 0.75	3.04	4.66	5.05
0.75 to 1.00	.94	0	1.58
1.0 to 2.5	11.70	12.17	10.53
2.5 to 5	9.57	16.70	14.26
5 to 10	45.11	42.15	45.69
10 to 15	11.65	11.06	10.72
2. Number of Companies			
Under 0.1	130	108	92
0.1 to 0.2	34	24	22
0.2 to 0.3	11	9	11
0.3 to 0.4	8	8	5
0.4 to 0.5	5	0	2
0.5 to 0.75	5	8	8
0.75 to 1.00	1	0	2
1.0 to 2.5	6	7	6
2.5 to 5.0	3	5	5
5.0 to 10.0	7	6	7
10.0 to 15.0	1	1	1
Total	211	176	161

Source: Bureau of Mines, Petroleum Refineries, including Cracking Plants in the United States, January 1, 1947, January 1, 1950, January 1, 1954, Information Circulars 7455 (March 1948), 7578 (August 1950), and 7693 (July 1954).

oil; as in the case of steel plants, actual outputs cannot be obtained for all companies.

There is a family resemblance between the data for petroleum and steel companies: in each case there has been a substantial reduction in the share of the largest company. In the petroleum refining industry, the size range from 0.5 percent to 10 percent has contained all the size classes which have stable or rising shares of industry capacity.

The plant survivor data suggest that the disappearance of the smaller companies has been due to the relative inefficiency of the smaller plants, for all plant size classes with less than 0.5 percent of the industry's capacity have also declined substantially. The sizes between 0.5 percent and 2.5 percent of industry capacity have all grown relatively, and the top plant size has declined moderately, so that the growth of company

TABLE 7
Distribution of Petroleum Refining Capacity
by Relative Size of Plant

Plant Size	1947	1950	1954
	1. *Percent of Industry Capacity*		
Under 0.1	8.22	7.39	6.06
0.1 to 0.2	9.06	7.60	7.13
0.2 to 0.3	6.86	4.95	3.95
0.3 to 0.4	5.45	4.99	7.28
0.4 to 0.5	4.53	6.56	4.06
0.5 to 0.75	9.95	10.47	11.82
0.75 to 1.0	5.35	7.07	8.33
1.0 to 1.5	12.11	10.36	13.38
1.5 to 2.5	17.39	23.64	22.45
2.5 to 4.0	21.08	16.96	15.54
	2. *Number of Plants*		
Under 0.1	184	158	138
0.1 to 0.2	64	53	51
0.2 to 0.3	27	19	16
0.3 to 0.4	15	14	21
0.4 to 0.5	10	15	9
0.5 to 0.75	17	16	19
0.75 to 1.0	6	8	10
1.0 to 1.5	10	8	11
1.5 to 2.5	9	12	12
2.5 to 4.0	7	5	5
Total	349	308	292

Source: Bureau of Mines, Petroleum Refineries, including Cracking Plants
in the United States, January 1, 1947, January 1, 1950, January 1, 1954, Information Circulars 7455 (March 1948), 7578 (August 1950) and 7693 (July 1954).

sizes beyond 2.5 percent of industry capacity has presumably been due
to the economies of multiple plant operation.

It has been claimed that backward integration into crude oil pipelines
was necessary to successful operation of a petroleum refinery. We tabu-
late some of the material bearing on this hypothesis in Table 8. There
does not appear to be any large difference between the changes in market
shares of firms with and without pipelines. Since all firms with more
than 0.75 percent of industry refining capacity have some pipelines, a
comparison (not reproduced here) was made between changes in their
market shares and crude pipeline mileage per 1,000 barrels of daily
refining capacity. There was no relationship between the two variables.

The intraindustry analysis has its chief role, one may conjecture,
in providing a systematic framework for the analysis of the data commonly employed in industry studies. A complete analysis of the plausible
determinants of firm size requires such extensive information on the
individual firms in the industry as to make this an unattractive method
of attack on the general theory.

TABLE 8
Industry Shares of Petroleum Refining Companies
with and without Crude Pipelines in 1950

Company Size (average of 1947, 1950, and 1954 percentage of industry capacity)	Companies with Pipelines			Companies without Pipelines		
	Number 1950	Share 1947	Share 1954	Number 1950	Share 1947	Share 1954
Under 0.1	25	1.40	1.12	60	2.87	2.18
0.1 to 0.2	17	2.19	2.50	5	0.77	0.77
0.2 to 0.3	6	1.48	1.63	2	0.34	0.50
0.3 to 0.4	5	1.90	1.63	0	—	—
0.4 to 0.5	1	0.40	0.55	2	0.54	1.22
0.5 to 0.75	7	3.59	4.72	1	0.38	0.61
0.75 to 1.0	0	—	—	0	—	—
1.0 to 2.5	7	11.54	13.10	0	—	—
2.5 to 5.0	4	11.11	11.69	0	—	—
5.0 to 10.0	7	45.11	45.69	0	—	—
10.0 to 15.0	1	11.65	10.72	0	—	—
Not in existence all years	16	2.30	0.05	79	2.43	1.33
Total	96	92.67	93.40	149	7.33	6.60

Source: *International Petroleum Register.*

V. CONCLUSION

The survivor technique for determining the range of optimum sizes of a firm seems well adapted to lift the theory of economies of scale to a higher level of substantive content. Although it is prey to the usual frustrations of inadequate information, the determination of optimum sizes avoids the enormously difficult problem of valuing resources properly that is encountered by alternative methods.

Perhaps the most striking finding in our exploratory studies is that there is customarily a fairly wide range of optimum sizes—the long-run marginal and average cost curves of the firm are customarily horizontal over a long range of sizes. This finding could be corroborated, I suspect, by a related investigation: if there were a unique optimum size in an industry, increases in demand would normally be met primarily by near proportional increases in the number of firms, but it appears that much of the increase is usually met by expansion of the existing firms.

The survivor method can be used to test the numerous hypotheses on the factors determining the size of firm which abound in the literature. Our exploratory study suggests that advertising expenditures have no general tendency to lead to large firms, and another experiment (which is not reported above) indicates that fixed capital-sales ratio are also unrelated to the size of firms. The size of plant proves to be an important variable, as is to be expected, and the survivor method should be employed to determine the factors governing plant size. A rather ambiguous variable, the relative share of engineers and chemists in the labor force, also proves to be fairly important, and further data and work is necessary to disentangle research and routine technical operations. The determination of optimum size permits the investigator to examine any possible determinants which his imagination nominates and his data illuminate.

14.

Plant Size, Plant Factor, and the Shape of the Average Cost Function in Electric Power Generation: A Nonhomogeneous Capital Approach*

JOHN F. STEWART

1. INTRODUCTION

The technology of electric power generation has been the subject of intense empirical study. Perhaps the most consistently obtained result of this body of literature is the conclusion that significant scale economies exist in electric power generation at the plant level.[1] The majority of the empirical studies reaching this conclusion have relied on the neoclassical production model as a framework. Thus the existence of scale economies can be interpreted as a production function with a degree of

---

* *Bell Journal of Economics,* Autumn 1979, pp. 549–65.

[1] The terms plant and unit are used interchangeably throughout the rest of the paper. A unit is a collection of capital equipment performing the function of converting the energy contained in fossil fuel into electricity. A plant at a given physical location may house more than one generating unit, but our concern will be limited to single-unit plants or to plants where multiple identical units are employed.

homogeneity greater than unity or a total cost function that increases less than proportionately with cumulative output.

This paper will argue that the empirical models derived from the neoclassical production framework fail to capture two of the important characteristics of the process of electric power generation, and therefore may produce misleading or incomplete conclusions. The characteristics of electric power generation not captured are the multidimensional nature of output and the nonhomogeneity of capital.[2] The question of interest is the rate at which ex ante average cost declines with the planned capacity of a plant. In the remainder of the paper we argue that cumulative output is an imperfect index of a two-dimensional output vector composed of instantaneous rate and duration. When we use a model capable of distinguishing the two components of output, we find that the decline in average cost resulting from increased plant size is of much smaller magnitude than suggested in the main body of empirical research. We shall also show that by specifying a model with a nonhomogeneous capital input, it is possible to identify the technological sources of scale economies in electric power generation.

2. ELECTRIC POWER GENERATION

Electric power is produced by creating heat energy from fuel and converting that heat energy mechanically into electricity.[3] Initially, the neoclassical production function would seem ideally suited to model such a production process. Fuel and capital are combined according to a technological relationship to produce output. The difficulty one encounters is developing the appropriate empirical definitions of the theoretical concepts of output and capital. It is at this point that the typical neoclassical assumptions of scalar output and homogeneous inputs clash with the realities of multidimensional output and nonhomogeneous capital in the production of electricity.

Defining Output

The output of an electric generation plant can usefully be thought of as being two dimensional. The first dimension, which can be called *power*, is usually measured in kilowatts (KWs) and can be thought of as the instantaneous rate of output. The second dimension, which can

---

[2] These characteristics of electric power generation are well understood by engineers and power system planners and have been incorporated by a number of economists in analyzing the electric power industry. It is in the area of econometric estimation of cost and production functions that these characteristics have been neglected.

[3] Other inputs, including production labor, maintenance labor, and materials, go into the process as well. In the interest of simplification these are omitted from the present analysis.

be called *energy,* is usually measured in kilowatt hours (KWHs) and can be thought of as the cumulative output. Though rate and volume are related,[4] failure to recognize their potentially differential effect on costs can create problems.[5] In the case of electric power generation, empirical studies have typically relied on KWHs as the scalar measure of output. There are two factors in electric power generation, however, that make the inclusion of multidimensional output in the model crucial. First, technology is such that electricity usually cannot be economically stored, and thus the instantaneous rate of output must conform to the instantaneous rate of demand at all times if demand is to be satisfied. Second, the instantaneous demand for electric power varies considerably over a daily as well as a seasonal cycle. The institutional regime under which electric utilities operate requires that the demands for electricity be met as they occur, thus determining one characteristic of a utility's operation; the utility must have sufficient capacity to meet the maximum instantaneous demand that will occur over the cycle. Most electric utilities are multiplant operations. The requirement to meet instantaneous demand means that the sum of the capacities of the plants must meet or exceed the instantaneous demand for power. Given that the instantaneous rate of demand varies over a shorter cycle than it is possible to vary capacity, some of the utility's capacity will not be fully utilized at all times. It is possible to observe plants with the same maximum instantaneous rate of output producing different cumulative levels of output or to observe plants with the same cumulative level of output producing different maximum instantaneous rates of output. Therefore, it is reasonable to expect that a firm building a new plant would consider *both* dimensions of output in making ex ante factor choice and technology decisions. As a result, it may be inappropriate to rely on an empirical specification that relates inputs or costs to only one dimension of output, or to an imperfect index of the two dimensions.

Defining Capital

The capital equipment used in electric power generation has two major engineering characteristics. The first is the size of the generating unit. We shall describe the size of a generating unit as the maximum instantaneous rate of output the unit is capable of producing. The second characteristic of a generating unit is its efficiency. We shall describe the fuel efficiency of a unit by the quantity of fuel the unit requires to produce a given amount of electric energy. These characteristics are

---

[4] If the instantaneous rate at time t is $KW(t)$, then the cumulative output over the time period T can be defined by KWH $= \int_0^T KW(t)dt$.

[5] Alchian noted the relationship between rate, volume, and production timing and cost structure, but this approach to describing production technologies has failed to enter the mainstream of economic analysis.

embedded in the piece of capital equipment, and once set, cannot be altered. Note that there is a direct relationship between the first dimension of output and the first characteristic of generating capital. If the planned maximum instantaneous demand that will be placed on a new plant is known, the size characteristic of the new plant's capital is known.

In the neoclassical production model the input capital is usually interpreted as the flow of services from a piece of capital equipment, where one unit of capital services is equivalent to any other unit of capital services (i.e., the service of capital is a homogeneous input). In the preceding representation of generating capital, capital services become distinctly nonhomogeneous.[6]

Direct observation confirms that plants of various fuel efficiencies are operated, and, more importantly, that the cost of a KW of capital service varies not only with the money cost of capital (i.e., the interest rate), but also with the number of KWs of service that are combined in a particular unit and the fuel efficiency of the unit.

All theory is, of course, a slight mutation of reality, and one cannot expect the assumption of the theory to be mirrored exactly by the data used in empirical research. Virtually no measure of an input truly measures physical units of a strictly homogeneous input and no real pattern of output can be exactly measured by a scalar. Our purpose here is only to narrow the gap between theory and reality in a few specifics and to examine the differences in the results.

3. SIMPLE PRODUCTION AND COST MODEL WITH MULTIDIMENSIONAL OUTPUT AND NONHOMOGENEOUS CAPITAL

This section considers a model of the firm's ex ante technology for a plant intended to produce a given pattern of output. The model employs the engineering production function approach used by Cowing, McKay, and Stewart. We assume the following about the environment in which the firm makes its planning decisions:

1. The utility faces a load duration curve that describes the time pattern of instantaneous demands for power that will be made over the period of a year. The utility takes the load duration curve as given and is required to meet the load as it occurs.
2. In planning a new plant, the utility decides what increment of the load the new plant will serve. The load increment is defined by an

---

[6] In a weak sense, capital services are a homogeneous input if they are measured in terms of KWs, since any KW of capital can be replaced with any other KW of capital with no effect on either dimension of output. However, the fuel required to produce that pattern of output may change if the KW of capital removed and the one substituted in its place are not of identical fuel efficiencies.

instantaneous rate (the KW capacity of the new plant) and the duration (the number of yearly hours the plant will produce that rate).[7] Turvey used a two-dimensioned increment to load as the appropriate ex ante measure of output. It is the incorporation of the load increment concept into the engineering production function that differentiates this paper from Cowing.

Our concern here is with the factor choice of the firm, *given* a particular load increment to be served by the new plant. The investment decision of the firm will encompass determining both the segment of total demand the new plant will serve and the configuration of the new plant. The complete investment decision of the firm will be considerably more complicated than the portion of the investment decision being modeled here, because the firm's decision will have to include such factors as the technical configuration of existing plant, construction lags of various types of equipment, regulatory constraints, and reliability constraints.

Given the load increment, the following identity defines the cumulative demand on the plant:

$$Q = 8760bk, \tag{1}$$

where

Q = yearly KWH demand;
8,760 = hours per year;
b = percent of yearly hours the load is incurred; and
k = KW increment of the load.

Ex Post Production Process

We assume that electric power is produced by combining fuel and equipment and that the range of available equipment can be fully defined by the equipment's size (KW capacity) and the equipment's fuel requirements.[8] We also assume that the fuel requirement of a given piece of equipment is constant and fixed.[9] Thus, once the unit is in place, neither the size of the unit nor its fuel requirements can be altered. The ex post production function for a plant of given characteristics can be defined by a fixed coefficient production function:

---

[7] This is a simplification in that at any instant a plant may produce at less than its maximum rate. The analysis is somewhat more complicated if plant's load duration curves are allowed to be nonrectangular and the data do not exist to specify the load duration curves of individual plants.

[8] Again, this is a simplification. Plants are also available with various production labor requirements and maintenance requirements.

[9] This is the final simplification. In fact, the heat rate varies nonlinearly with the percent of plant capacity used at any instant. Unfortunately data are limited to the plant's average heat rate.

$$Q = \min\left[\frac{F}{\alpha_0}, \quad 8760 \cdot K_0\right],$$ (2)

where

F = BTUs of fuel per year;
α_0 = the plant's heat rate (BTUs/KWH); and
K_0 = the plant's capacity (KWs).

Ex Post Cost Function

Once a particular plant is in place, it is possible to write total cost as a function of cumulative output, given the price per BTU of fuel (P_F), the cost per KW of constructing the particular plant (P_{K_0}), and the yearly cost of money capital including depreciation (r):

$$TC(Q, P_F, P_{K_0}, r, \alpha_0, K_0) = \alpha_0 8760 b_0 K_0 P_F + r P_{K_0} K_0 \text{ for } Q \le 8760 K_0. \quad (3)$$

Note that under this specification, short-run average cost must decline with cumulative output.

Ex Ante Factor Choice

Ex ante the firm has the choice of technology it will use to produce the planned load increment (defined by b and k). The cost per KW of constructing plants is assumed to vary with the fuel requirements of the plant and its size. The cost of plant function is written:

$$P_K = P_K(\alpha, K).$$ (4)

This function represents both the market conditions in the equipment industry and the technological aspects of plant design. It is reasonable to expect that the cost of plants will increase with the fuel efficiency of the plant $(\partial P_K/\partial\alpha < 0)$. It is also reasonable to assume that as one approaches the technological limit of fuel efficiency, plant cost will increase at an increasing rate, $(\partial^2 P_K/\partial\alpha^2 > 0)$. One may also expect that the cost per KW of capacity will decline, at least over some range, with the size of plants being constructed, $\partial P_K/\partial K < 0$. Finally, it may be possible that the additional cost of increased fuel efficiency may be lower in large plants $(\partial^2 P_K/\partial\alpha\partial K < 0)$.

The ex ante accounting cost for a plant intended to meet a given load increment (K_0, b_0) and facing factor prices P_F and r is a function of heat rate alone:

$$TC(\alpha, K_0, b_0, P_F, r) = \alpha 8760 b_0 K_0 P_F + r P_K(\alpha, K_0) K_0.$$ (5)

Minimizing the total cost of producing the planned output pattern would require selecting a fuel intensity (heat rate) α^* such that $\partial TC/\partial\alpha = 0$:

$$8760 b_0 P_F = - r \left. \frac{\partial P_K(\alpha_i K_0)}{\partial \alpha} \right|_{\alpha^*}. \tag{6}$$

The verbal interpretation of this condition is exactly analogous to the cost-minimizing condition of the neoclassical model. A plant can produce the same pattern of output at a lower total cost by increasing fuel efficiency only so long as the marginal savings from increased fuel efficiency are greater than the marginal cost of achieving additional fuel efficiency.

Several additional implications can be deduced from the cost-minimizing condition. The higher the planned utilization rate, everything else held constant, the lower the optimal heat rate will be. The higher the money cost of capital (r), the higher the optimal heat rate will be. Finally, the higher the cost of fuel, the lower the optimal heat rate will be. Each of these observations is consistent with intuition and casual empiricism.

We can derive the ex ante economic cost function, the minimum cost of producing any particular pattern of output (K,b), given technology and factor prices, by implicitly solving Equation (6) for α^*

$$\alpha^* = g(K, b, P_F, r) \tag{7}$$

and substituting into Equation (5)

$$TC^*(K, b, P_F, r) = g(K, b, P_F, r) 8760 b K P_F + r P_K(g(K, b, P_F, r), K) K. \tag{8}$$

Total costs are still represented as a function of output and factor prices, but the measure of output is two dimensional, thereby allowing for different effects on total cost if cumulative output is increased by increasing capacity or by increasing plant factors. Note that the cost function is not necessarily homogeneous of degree one in factor prices, but will depend on the relative magnitudes of $\partial g / \partial P_F, \partial g / \partial r$, and $\partial P_K / \partial \alpha$.[10] Finally, in this model the concept of scale economies must be interpreted as the shape of the long-run economic cost function, rather than the degree of homogeneity of the production function, and that "scale economies" can occur in two dimensions. Total cost can increase by an equal, greater, or lesser proportion as capacity is proportionally expanded (economies of unit size). Total costs can increase by an equal, greater, or lesser proportion as plant factor is proportionately expanded (economies of plant factor).

---

[10] In a strict sense, the cost function *is* homogeneous of degree one in r and P_F. Increasing both by the same proportion will not alter the solution of equation (6) (i.e., α^* does not change). Thus total cost will increase by the same proportion. However, a general proportional increase in all prices would also shift the cost of plant function upward, which would alter the solution of equation (6). The expectation is that a proportional increase of all prices would result in a greater than proportional increase in total cost.

4. THE COST OF PLANT FUNCTION

This section will examine in more detail the cost of plant function $(P_K(\alpha,k) = $ dollars per KW of plant with heat rate α and plant size K) and will present estimates of the cost of equipment function.

The working hypothesis from Section 3 is that the factor decision of the firm can be reduced to a decision by the firm as to what characteristics a new plant will have. For simplicity, we consider only two characteristics: the KW capacity of the plant and the fuel efficiency of the plant. We assume that the utilities are price takers in the equipment market and face an array of all technical feasible plant sizes and fuel efficiencies, each with known price. Again, the cost of plant function embodies two phenomena, one technological and one related to the equipment market. Technologically, it should cost different amounts to build equipment with different characteristics; however, unless the sellers' side of the equipment market behaves in a competitive fashion, the differences in prices between plants with different characteristics may not reflect technological considerations alone.

It is desirable to specify the cost of plant functions in a sufficiently general form so that all major phenomena that may exist can potentially appear in the estimation. These phenomena include the following:

1. *Changes in the cost of plant function related to the size of plant:* One engineering fact that is commonly related to the economic concept of scale economies is the "two-thirds rule." This rule merely notes the mathematical fact that for most geometric shapes, surface area grows less rapidly than volume. If output is closely related to the volume of a piece of equipment (e.g., a boiler, a pipe, or a turbogenerator) and fabrication cost is related to surface area (e.g., the amount of material required to construct the equipment), then the cost of equipment should increase less than proportionately with its volume. The "continuous process" nature of electric power generation leads us to believe that this phenomenon might be present in the cost of generating plants. There is no reason, however, to believe the phenomenon would continue indefinitely. At some point, larger volumes may necessitate the use of extra structural reinforcement, special materials, or construction techniques. Thus, it is desirable to specify the cost of plant functions so that $\partial P_K / \partial K$ can take on positive, negative, or zero value, depending on the size of the plant. Our expectations are that $\partial P_K / \partial K$ will take on negative values at low capacities and possibly become positive for large capacity plants.

2. *Changes in the cost of plant functions related to fuel efficiency:* It is reasonable to expect that a more fuel-efficient piece of equipment should be more expensive to build than a less fuel-efficient piece of equipment (i.e., $\partial P_K / \partial \alpha < 0$). The thermal efficiency of generating equipment depends on the temperature, pressure, and friction generated in the

unit. It is reasonable to assume that increasing operating temperatures and pressures and reducing friction would all require more sophisticated engineering, materials, and fabrication techniques, all of which should add to plant cost.

It is also necessary to introduce a constraint on the cost of plant functions. The process of generating electricity is the process of converting one form of energy (fossil fuel) into another (electric energy). This process must conform to the physical laws of thermodynamics. Given the law of conservation of energy, it is theoretically (and physically) impossible to produce a KWH of electricity with less than 3,412 BTUs of fuel. Given the state of engineering and metallurgy, it is impossible to produce a KWH of electricity with less than approximately 6,000 BTUs of fuel. We would like to incorporate this fact into the cost of plant functions by requiring the cost per KW of plants to go to infinity as the heat rate approaches 6,000 BTUs from above.

Cross Effects of Size and Efficiency

There are two counteracting forces that will determine the sign of the cross partial $\partial^2 P_K / \partial\alpha\partial K$. On the one hand, since heat losses will be more closely related to surface area than to volume, it may be relatively cheaper to achieve additional fuel efficiency in larger units. On the other hand, the engineering and fabrication requirement from the temperature and pressure increases needed to increase fuel efficiency may be more extensive on larger plants than on smaller plants.

Functional Form and Estimation

To allow sufficient flexibility to incorporate the desired possibilities, we used a translog specification to estimate the cost of plant functions:

$$\ln P_K = A + \gamma_\alpha \ln(\alpha - \bar{\alpha}) + \gamma_{\alpha\alpha}(\ln(\alpha - \bar{\alpha}))^2 + \gamma_K \ln(K)$$
$$+ \gamma_{KK}(\ln(K))^2 + \gamma_{\alpha K}\ln(K)\ln(\alpha - \bar{\alpha}) + \sum_i \gamma_i X_i + u, \quad (9)$$

where

P_K = the dollar cost per KW of the generating unit (building excluded);

α = the average heat rate of the unit (BTUs/KWH);

$\bar{\alpha}$ = the asymptotic heat rate (6,000 BTU/KWH);

K = the capacity of the unit (KW);

X_i = shift variables which will be discussed later; and

u = a random error term.

We estimated equation (9) on a cross section of 58 newly constructed fossil-fuel plants that went into service between 1970 and 1971. We obtained the data from *Steam Electric Construction Cost and Operating Expense* and *Gas Turbine Construction Cost and Operating Expense.* The sample contains only single unit plants or plants with multiple identical units. All of the plants in the sample are of the same vintage, so problems of technological progress are avoided.

We also used four shift variables in the regression. Since the reported cost includes both equipment cost and some installation costs, we included regional dummy variables to capture possible differences in labor or transportation costs.[11] The regions were: the West (FPC regions VI, VII, VIII), the Northeast (FPC region I), the Gulf (FPC region V), and the Central and Southeast (FPC regions II, III, IV). The cost of plant function is based on the generating unit. Since some of the plants observed had multiple units, we entered a shift variable for the number of units in a given plant in logarithmic form. We expect that installing two identical units on the same site will be less than twice as expensive as installing one. The heat rates used in the regressions were the average heat rates of the plants reported in 1972. We used data for 1972 because abnormal conditions may persist in the break-in period of the plant.

The sample contains both conventional fossil-fuel steam units and gas turbine units. Nineteen of the sample plants were steam electric and 39 were gas turbine. The steam electric plants varied in unit size from 800 MW to 200 MW, the gas turbines from 187 MW to approximately 20 MW. The cost of plants ran from about $160 per KW to about $60 per KW, heat rates running from a low of 9,100 BTU/KWH to a high of 19,000 BTU/KWH. From an engineering standpoint steam technology and gas turbine technology differ significantly. Gas turbines directly convert combustion energy into mechanical energy to drive the generator, while steam plants first convert combustion energy into steam and the steam then produces the mechanical energy to drive the generator. It is conceivable that the shape and position of the cost of plant function may differ, depending on which technology is being considered. It must also be remembered that the cost of plant function describes both a technological relationship between the characteristics of the equipment and its cost and the pricing behavior of equipment manufacturers. Few people would argue that the electric equipment industry is competitively structured, and it is conceivable that there may be some smoothing of the cost of plant function at the interface between the two technologically distinct equipment types.

For these reasons we estimated two forms of Equation (9). First we estimated Equation (9) over the entire sample, with the coefficients on the size and heat rate variables restricted to be equal for both steam

---

[11] Another potential shift variable would be building type, since the cost of equipment used might vary depending on whether it was intended for indoor or outdoor installation. We did not use this variable because of the strong correlation between region and type of construction.

TABLE 1
Regression Results (Restricted Specification) Dependent Variable:
ln (Unit Cost per KW)

Independent Variable	Coefficient	Standard Error
Constant	152.323	65.2664†
Dummy steam (DS)	.5019	.2759
ln (heat rate—6,000)	−28.6544	13.2009†
(ln (heat rate—6,000))²	1.3969	.6700†
ln (unit capacity)	−9.4629	3.5078†
(ln (unit capacity))²	.1802	.0571*
ln (heat rate—6,000) ln (unit capacity)	.8794	.3458†
ln (number of units in plant)	−.0645	.0390
Dummy North Central	−.0574	.1222
Dummy Gulf	−.2036	.1361
Dummy Central–South	.1710	.1169

$R^2 = .6460$
$F(10,47) = 8.5766$ * Significant at 99 percent.
S.E. $= .1926$ † Significant at 95 percent.

and gas turbine plants and with only a dummy variable for steam plants to allow for fundamental differences in the fuel-handling equipment required by the two technologies. In the second estimation we used interactive dummy variables to allow the slope coefficients on the heat rate variable, the unit size variable, and their interaction to assume different values for gas turbine and steam units.[12]

The results of the ordinary least squares regressions for the two specifications appear in Tables 1 and 2. In general, the coefficients of the heat rate and unit size variables are of plausible signs and are statistically significant for both specifications. Though the number of units variable has the expected sign, it is not significant. The regional dummy variables also are not significant. A comparison of the two specifications indicates that there is reason to believe that the cost of equipment function differs significantly by plant type, so the remainder of the discussion will concentrate on the unrestricted model.

Several interesting implications of the regression results should be noted. First, plant cost does decline at a decreasing rate as heat rate increases for both types of plants for a reasonable range of heat rates and unit sizes; thus the conditions necessary for the existence of a unique cost-minimizing heat rate are satisfied.[13] For gas turbine plants, the cost

---

[12] The inclusion of dummy variable interaction terms on all independent variables was precluded by problems of multicollinearity.

[13] It is also interesting to note that the implied elasticities of the price of plant with respect to the difference between heat rate and asymptotic heat rate are relatively large (on the order of −1.5 at 9,000 BTU/KW for a 600 MW unit). In McKay's study the Cobb-Douglas functional form restricted the elasticity to be constant. His estimate of −.37 yields implied optimal heat rates that are very close to the 6,000 BTU/KWH asymptotic heat rate he used, and the optimal heat rates obtained from his data and estimation are considerably lower than the observed heat rates of the plants in his sample.

TABLE 2
Regression Results (Unrestricted Specification) Dependent Variable:
ln (Unit Cost per KW)

Independent Variable	Coefficient	Standard Error
Constant	241.729	101.749†
Dummy steam (DS)	−153.062	55.6617†
ln (heat rate—6,000)	−46.8038	21.4353†
ln (heat rate—6,000) DS	18.4932	6.5546*
(ln (heat rate—6,000))²	2.3191	1.1330†
ln (unit capacity)	−13.6287	5.5313†
ln (unit capacity) DS	−24.2139	9.1254†
(ln (unit capacity))²	.2333	.0697*
ln (heat rate—6,000) ln (unit capacity)	1.2975	.6016†
ln (heat rate—6,000) ln (unit capacity) DS	−2.9176	1.0625†
ln (number of units in plant)	−.0553	.0369
Dummy North Central	−.1017	.1160
Dummy Gulf	−.2459	.1360
Dummy Central–South	.1500	.1106

R² = .7139
F(13,44) = 8.4457   * Significant at 99 percent.
S.E. = .1789   † Significant at 99 percent.

of plant function assumes a reasonable shape over the entire observed range of heat rates and unit sizes. For steam plants, the function only assumes a reasonable shape for plants with heat rates in the 8,500– 10,000 BTU/KWH range, and unrealistically low plant costs are predicted for units less than 250 MW in size. This is not of great concern, since only one steam unit in the sample is smaller than 240 MW and only one unit falls outside the reasonable range of heat rates.[14] The second interesting result is that unit size has a relatively small impact on the cost of equipment. For gas turbine units, plant cost declines with unit size over only part of the range of unit sizes. At the mean heat rate of the gas turbines in the sample (about 14,000 BTU/KWH), plant cost declines with unit size only for units smaller than 70 MW. For steam plants, per KW plant cost declines with unit size only for very small units of relatively low fuel efficiency, and plant cost increases with unit size over most of the reasonable range of unit sizes and fuel efficiencies, though at a relatively modest rate.[15] See Table 3. Finally,

---

[14] One steam plant in the sample has an observed heat rate of 11,178, and there is one 200 MW unit in the sample of steam plants.

[15] It should be noted that relatively little faith can be put on the sign of the elasticity of steam plant cost with respect to unit size. The hypothesis that the coefficient on the unit size variable plus the coefficient on the unit size variable interacted with the steam dummy differs from zero must be rejected at any normal confidence level. In the restricted specification the cost of equipment per KW declines with size over the entire range of unit sizes. However, the elasticities are quite close to zero (−.18 for a 500 MW plant at 9,000 BTU/KWH).

the sign of the interaction term between heat rate and unit size is positive for gas turbine plants and negative for steam plants, which suggests that it becomes more expensive, at the margin, to achieve additional fuel efficiency in gas turbine plants as unit size is increased and less expensive in steam plants.

TABLE 3
Elasticity of Plant Cost with Respect to Unit Capacity

Gas Turbine Plants				Steam Plants				
	Heat Rate (BTU/KWH)				Heat Rate (BTU/KWH)			
Unit Size (MW)				Unit Size (MW)				
	12,000	14,000	16,000		8,500	9,000	9,500	10,000
40	−.62	−.25	.04	300	.57	.28	.03	−.19
60	−.43	−.06	.23	500	.81	.51	.26	.05
80	−.30	.08	.37	700	.97	.67	.42	.20
100	−.19	.18	.47					
150	−.003	.37	.65					
200	.13	.50	.79					

In the next section of the paper we shall offer evidence that the model being employed produces reasonable estimates of cost. Then we shall use simulations to explore the implications of the regression results on the question of scale economies.

5. THE COST FUNCTION

In the previous section the cost of plant function was estimated for a cross section of generating plants. With this estimate, given the plant's size load factor and factor prices, it is then possible to compute estimates of average cost (cost per KWH) for each plant in the sample by assuming cost minimization and using equation (8). Since the functional form for the cost of plant function does not permit explicitly solving for $g(K,b,P_F,r)$, given the factor prices faced by each plant (P_F,r) and the estimated parameters of the cost of plant function, we used numerical techniques to find the minimum average cost of producing each two-dimensional output vector in the sample (K,b). The price of fuel we used is the actual price paid for fuel used in the plant in 1972; the cost of money capital is the interest rate on new long-term debt paid by the firm at the time the plant was constructed plus the depreciation rate. The parameters of the cost of plant function come from the unrestricted specification.

To test the reasonableness of the model, we compared the observed heat rates of the plants with the cost-minimizing heat rates predicted by the model and the observed average costs with the minimum average costs predicted by the model. Least squares regression of actual heat rates on predicted heat rates yielded a coefficient of .968, with a standard error of .0115 and an R^2 of .77. Least squares regression of actual average cost on predicted average cost yielded a coefficient of .927, with a standard error of .0139 and an R^2 of .95. Perfect prediction by the model would require that these coefficients equal unity. A t-test would lead us to reject this hypothesis. There are unfortunately several plausible explanations for the downward bias of predicted heat rate and average cost. One is the lag time between the time the plant is planned and when it comes into operation. If at the time the plant's characteristics were finalized, fuel prices were expected to be different from what they actually were when the plant came on line, then, given a knowledge of the fuel price that actually occurred, the designed heat rate would differ from the cost-minimizing heat rate. It is also plausible that decisions are made in a dynamic rather than static context. Since the heat rate of a plant is virtually fixed once the plant is installed, expectations of increasing fuel prices would lead to selecting a design with lower heat rates if the object was to minimize the present value of cost over the life of the plant rather than static cost minimization. The systematic downward bias of the predicted average cost could also be explained by nonminimizing behavior.[16] Finally, it should be noted that the model has simplified the problem by omitting labor and maintenance costs and that there are certainly tradeoffs between fuel efficiency, plant reliability, and maintenance expense.

Despite these deficiencies in the model's predictions, it still predicts average cost quite well, especially when one considers that the entire model is based only on the estimated relationship between the equipment characteristics and the equipment cost, an accounting relationship between the equipment's characteristics and the cost of output, and the assumption of cost minimization.

Simulated Cost Function

To analyze the relationship between cost per unit of output and the two quantities defining a load increment, KW capacity and plant factor, we calculated the minimum average cost of meeting a grid of

---

[16] The usual form of nonminimizing behavior attributed to electric utilities is the Averch-Johnson bias due to the rate of return constraint of the regulatory mechanism. In terms of the present model, the A-J bias would manifest itself as a systematic selection of capital equipment that was more fuel efficient (thus more expensive) than necessary to minimize cost. If an A-J bias were present, one would expect to find predicted cost consistently lower than actual costs and predicted heat rates consistently higher than actual heat rates. Our results show that the bias between actual and predicted heat rates runs in an opposite direction. Other researchers have found cost inefficiencies as high as 17 percent.

load increments. The grid encompassed units from 10 MW to 900 MW size which operated at load factors from 10 to 90 percent. We calculated minimum average costs for each point in the grid on the basis of an assumed fuel price of $.50 per million BTU and a 10 percent rate of return (interest plus depreciation). The prices used are representative of those appearing in the sample, as are the ranges of unit size and utilization rates. We assumed gas turbine technology for units of 200 MW or less and for plant factors between 10 and 60 percent; we assumed steam technology for units larger than 200 MW and for plant factors between 40 and 90 percent.[17] The simulated minimum average costs and corresponding optimal heat rates appear in Tables 4 and 5.

The simulations can illustrate several interesting results. First, given a plant utilization rate, costs decline with unit size only for gas turbine units. Costs actually increase with unit size for steam plants over the entire range. However, the effect that unit size has on average cost is quite small. The calculated arc elasticity of average cost with respect to unit size falls in the range of −.05 to −.12 for gas turbine plants and in the range of .09 to .12 for steam plants. Doubling the size of a gas turbine plant from 40 to 80 MW results in a cost advantage of about 10 percent. Doubling the size of a steam plant from 400 to 800 MW results in a cost disadvantage of about 8 percent.[18]

On the other hand, average costs decline for all unit sizes as the

---

[17] These ranges were selected to conform roughly with the characteristics of the plants in the sample. The gas turbine plants in the sample fall into the size range of 14 to about 200 MW, with plant utilization factor of roughly 2 to 35 percent. The steam plants in the sample ran from about 200 MW to a little over 800 MW, with plant utilization factors of 35 to 75 percent. These ranges tend to delineate reasonable "bounds" on the simulations. For gas turbine plants on the high end of both the size and utilization rate ranges, the simulated optimal heat rates get unrealistically low, and for steam plants with below 30-percent utilization rates, the simulated average costs do not converge to a minimum.

[18] Several cautions should be made concerning the interpretation of these results. As will be shown later, the increase in average cost in steam units and the decrease in average cost in gas turbines as unit size increases are primarily a result of the effect of unit size on equipment cost. While our results strongly suggest that the cost per KW falls as gas turbine unit size increases, the result that cost per KW increases as steam plant unit size increases is not sufficiently strong to argue that substantial diseconomies of scale exist in the steam technology. If we use the coefficients from the restricted specification, average cost declines with unit size over the entire range, but at a very modest rate. (The calculated are elasticities of average cost with respect to unit size are never smaller than −.28 and for typical unit size and utilization rates they run about −.05.) The omission of labor may also contribute to the finding of decreasing returns to scale. It is reasonable to assume that some of the production labor is invariant with unit size. Thus, labor cost per KWH would fall with unit size. Labor is a relatively small proportion of total cost, so the effect would not be large. It is also worth noting that in general the fuel used by gas turbine equipment is more expensive than the fuel used by steam equipment, particularly if coal-fired steam equipment is used. Finally, the simulations assume the same fuel price for both technologies. If different fuel prices are used, the average cost of generation is considerably higher for gas turbine plants than is indicated by the simulation results.

TABLE 4
Minimum Average Cost; Mills/KWH
Fuel Price = 0.5000, Rate of Return = 0.1000

MW Capacity*	Plant Factor								
	.1	.2	.3	.4	.5	.6	.7	.8	.9
20.	17.6294	12.5756	10.7920	9.8457	9.2436	8.8192			
40.	15.5777	11.1650	9.6139	8.7937	8.2738	7.9085			
60.	14.7039	10.5380	9.0794	8.3108	7.8251	7.4845			
80.	14.2083	10.1685	8.7587	8.0184	7.5509	7.2240			
100.	13.8883	9.9206	8.5407	7.8170	7.3616	7.0472			
150.	13.4421	9.5518	8.2062	7.5234	7.1137	6.8406			
200.	13.2247	9.3587	8.0641	7.4168	7.0285	6.7696			
250.				7.2896	6.7063	6.3127	6.0279	5.8115	5.6408
300.				7.4548	6.8557	6.4513	6.1582	5.9352	5.7590
350.				7.5931	6.9814	6.5680	6.2682	6.0401	5.8598
400.				7.7114	7.0896	6.6688	6.3640	6.1317	5.9481
450.				7.8145	7.1843	6.7581	6.4485	6.2127	6.0262
500.				7.9056	7.2685	6.8377	6.5244	6.2855	6.0966
550.				7.9869	7.3443	5.9093	6.5929	6.3516	6.1606
600.				8.0605	7.4131	6.9747	6.6556	6.4122	6.2194
650.				8.1277	7.4763	7.0346	6.7134	6.4680	6.2734
700.				8.1893	7.5345	7.0900	6.7669	6.5197	6.3239
750.				8.2461	7.5882	7.1419	6.8166	6.5681	6.3708
800.				8.2987	7.6384	7.1899	6.8633	6.6133	6.4152
850.				8.3482	7.6854	7.2352	6.9071	6.6559	6.4566
900.				8.3838	7.7294	7.2777	6.9483	6.6964	6.4959

* Gas turbine plant to 200 MW steam plants 250–900 MW.

TABLE 5
Optimal Heat Rates; BTU/KWH
Fuel Price = 0.5000, Rate of Return = 0.1000

MW Capacity*	Plant Factor								
	.1	.2	.3	.4	.5	.6	.7	.8	.9
20.	15,400.	14,700.	14,200.	13,850.	13,550.	13,300.			
40.	13,800.	13,250.	12,800.	12,500.	12,250.	12,050.			
60.	13,000.	12,500.	12,150.	11,900.	11,650.	11,500.			
80.	12,500.	12,050.	11,700.	11,450.	11,250.	11,100.			
100.	12,100.	11,700.	11,400.	11,150.	10,950.	10,950.			
150.	11,500.	11,150.	10,950.	10,950.	10,950.	10,950.			
200.	11,100.	10,950.	10,950.	10,950.	10,950.	10,950.			
250.				8,800.	8,700.	8,650.	8,600.	8,550.	8,550
300.				8,950.	8,900.	8,850.	8,750.	8,700.	8,700
350.				9,100.	9,050.	8,950.	8,900.	8,850.	8,800
400.				9,250.	9,150.	9,100.	9,050.	9,000.	8,950
450.				9,350.	9,300.	9,200.	9,150.	9,100.	9,050
500.				9,500.	9,400.	9,350.	9,250.	9,200.	9,150
550.				9,600.	9,500.	9,450.	9,350.	9,300.	9,250
600.				9,700.	9,600.	9,500.	9,450.	9,400.	9,300
650.				9,800.	9,700.	9,600.	9,550.	9,450.	9,400
700.				9,900.	9,800.	9,700.	9,600.	9,550.	9,500
750.				9,950.	9,850.	9,750.	9,700.	9,600.	9,550
800.				10,050.	9,950.	9,850.	9,750.	9,700.	9,600
850.				10,100.	10,000.	9,900.	9,850.	9,750.	9,700
900.				10,200.	10,100.	10,000.	9,900.	9,800.	9,750

* Gas turbine plants to 200 MW, steam plants 250–900 MW.

utilization rate is increased over the entire range. Here the cost reductions are considerably larger. Doubling the utilization rate of a 200 MW plant from 10 to 20 percent decreases the average cost by 40 percent, while doubling the utilization rate of a 600 MW plant from 40 to 80 percent decreases average costs by 25 percent.

These numbers demonstrate forcefully the potential dangers in formulating a discussion of the shape of the average cost curve of electric power generation in terms of cumulative output. One plant can exhibit double the KWH output of another if its capacity is twice as large and its utilization rate the same, its utilization factor twice as large and capacity the same, or an appropriate combination of the two. The simulations indicate that an ex ante doubling of cumulative output could reduce average cost by as much as 40 percent or increase average cost by as much as 10 percent, depending on whether a change in the planned plant utilization factor or a change in plant size increased cumulative output.

We can also demonstrate these results in a more conventional way. We fitted a very simple cost function to the sample of plants, and regressed the log of average cost on the logs of fuel price, the log of the cost of money capital, and the log of plant size. We also estimated the same regression with plant utilization rates included as an independent variable (see Table 6). When utilization rate is not included, the regressions show a highly significant coefficient on the plant size variable. One would conclude that average cost declines with plant size. When utilization rates are included, the coefficient on plant size becomes smaller by a factor of almost 10 and loses significance, and the regression shows that average cost declines with utilization rate. These results hold up, though not quite so dramatically, if the sample is divided by plant type or if KWHs are used instead of KWs as the index of size.

The data generated by the simulation permit some speculation as to the technical source of scale economies. As the size of plant is increased and the utilization rate is held constant, changes in the average cost can come from two sources: (1) changes in the per KW cost of

TABLE 6
Independent Variable Log Cost per KWH

Independent Variable	$R^2 = .78$		$R^2 = .92$	
	Coefficient	Standard Error	Coefficient	Standard Error
Constant	4.282*	.184	3.829*	.125
Log fuel price	.898*	.118	.364*	.094
Log cost of capital	.545	.409	.953*	.260
Log plant size	−.188†	.043	−.023	.032
Utilization rate			−2.239†	.244

* Significant at 99 percent.
† Significant at 95 percent.

capital when the heat rate is held constant and (2) net changes in cost from changes in the optimal heat rate (a declining heat rate implies decreasing fuel expenditure but an increasing equipment cost). For example, at a 20 percent utilization rate, an 80 MW gas turbine has an average cost 8.8 percent lower than a 40 MW unit. Sixty-two percent of the total difference in cost is a result of increasing unit size when the heat rate is held constant. The other 38 percent is a result of the differences in the optimal heat rate of the two plants. At a 60 percent utilization rate, a 700 MW steam unit has a 3.2 percent cost disadvantage over a 500 MW unit. This is a 3.4 percent cost disadvantage due to unit size when the heat rate is held constant, which is partially offset by net changes in average cost due to differences in heat rates. Qualitatively this result holds across all utilization rates. The simulation results seem to point to the conclusion that the dominant factor in producing plant-size-related average cost changes is the cost of equipment. This result cannot be obtained from a strictly neoclassical framework.

As the plant factor is increased with plant size held constant, decreases in average cost again can come from two sources: (1) decreases in average cost which are the result of spreading the cost of a given number of KWs of plants over a larger number of KWHs of output with the heat rate held constant and (2) the net changes in cost resulting from changes in the optimal heat rate as the plant factor is varied. Here the results are most startling. At low utilization rates, over 90 percent of the reduction in average cost is a result of spreading capital over a large output. Even at utilization rates as high as 70 percent, less than 10 percent of the cost reduction is a result of the net impact of changes in the optimal heat rate. The major source of average cost reduction as cumulative output expands is a result of increased plant factor, and the major component of cost reduction from plant factor economies is merely the spreading of capital expenses.

6. CONCLUSIONS

This paper has developed a model to describe factor choice and cost in electric power generation at the unit level and has done so in a way that is appreciative of the facts that electric power is a multidimensional output and that the capital equipment used to produce electric power is heterogeneous. The estimation of the cost of plant function confirms that the price per KW of equipment varies as expected with the fuel efficiency of the capital and with the "amount" of capital—KWs—contained in a single unit. The predicted average costs computed by the model conform reasonably well with the observed average costs in the sample. The most interesting results come from a simulation of the economic average cost function over a grid of the two dimensions defining output, KW capacity and plant utilization factor. The simulations show that scale economies, typically defined in economics as the reduction in average cost as plant size is increased, are of relatively minor significance in electric power generation at the unit level. The major source of cost reduction at the unit level comes from increases in the plant utilization factor, not from increases in the size of the unit, and the cause of declining average cost is primarily a result of the ability of plants with higher utilization rates to spread capital expenses over a greater volume of output. That econometric studies have consistently found average cost declining with cumulative plant output is not surprising, given that larger plants are generally operated at higher plant factors.

These results should be viewed with considerable care. Our finding that costs do not decline significantly with unit size cannot and should not be directly extended to statements concerning the average cost curve of the firm. The findings of the paper only suggest that when one looks for the sources of scale economies in electric power generation at the firm level, one might expect to find that the ability of a larger firm to employ larger units, *every thing else held equal,* will be of minor significance. The findings also suggest that an examination of the relation between firm size and the configuration of the firm's load duration curve would be a fruitful direction in which to pursue scale economies at the firm level.

15.

Statistical Cost Analysis*

WILLIAM A. LONGBRAKE

Statistical techniques provide information useful in making many types of business decisions. For several reasons, however, statistical analysis is seldom used in analyzing production and other costs. Standard costing procedures, such as time and motion studies and direct costing procedures based on past experience and modified by anticipated changes, are sufficient in many decision-making situations.

Data limitations frequently hinder the employment of statistical analysis. To use it, data concerning costs, output, and product characteristics must exist for a sufficient number of time periods in one business firm or, alternatively, these data must be available for one time period for several firms producing essentially the same product. Another impediment is the general lack of knowledge about statistical cost analysis.

This article will demonstrate the use of statistical analysis for product costing, incremental costing, and cost forecasting. While the illustrations are developed specifically for use by commercial banks in making decisions about demand deposit operations, the basic techniques could be modified for cost analysis of products in other industries or products of a single firm.

Detailed cost accounting and production data exist for a sample of nearly 1,000 banks that have voluntarily participated in the Federal Reserve Banks' Functional Cost Analysis (FCA) program. Development of uniform accounting classifications and methods of allocating costs by the FCA has enabled participating banks to compare their perfor-

* *Financial Management* 2, no. 1 (Spring 1973), pp. 49–55.

mance with the average performance of similarly-sized banks. As a result, the accuracy and consistency of FCA data is excellent. Hence, the data afford a good basis for demonstrating the use of statistical analysis.

METHODOLOGY

Before statistical analysis can take place, it is necessary to construct a cost function that describes accurately all relevant factors. First, cost categories must be defined. For example, three types of costs are incurred in providing services to demand deposit customers—fixed maintenance costs, variable maintenance costs, and transactions costs. Fixed maintenance costs arise from routine operations performed on a regular basis for every account, e.g., carrying a master record of an account on a ledger card and preparing and sending monthly statements. Variable maintenance costs, such as FDIC insurance and "free" service, vary with the size of an account. Transactions costs vary directly with the volume of transactions.

Second, measurable variables must be found that explain variations in each general cost category.

Third, other factors that may indirectly influence the costs of providing demand deposit services should be identified, and variables should be defined that explain their effects. For example, to the extent that common production costs exist and cannot be allocated precisely, the level of time deposit operations may have an influence on demand deposit costs. Other factors arise when the cost behavior of several firms is being analyzed. For instance, legal organizational form—unit, branch, or holding company affiliate—may influence the organization of demand deposit operations and, therefore, influence operating costs as well. In addition, wage rates prevailing in local labor markets will have an important effect on demand deposit costs because of the large amount of labor required.

It may be impossible to determine the separate effects of each of these factors because of their complex interrelationships. Moreover, if the volume of output affects the unit cost related to any one of these factors, the accountant's use of standard costs may overlook important variations that occur with changes in the level of output. Thus, a cost function may be a useful alternative to ordinary accounting practices.

Bell and Murphy and Longbrake have demonstrated that a log-linear cost function of the type defined in the following equation is appropriate for commercial banks and explains most of the variation in demand-deposit operating costs among banks:

$$\log C = \log H + \delta_1 \log N + \delta_2 \log S + \psi_1 \log T_1 + \psi_2 \log T_2$$
$$+ \psi_3 \log T_3 + \psi_4 \log T_4 + \psi_5 \log T_5 + \psi_6 \log T_6$$
$$+ \alpha_1 \log B + \alpha_2 \log M + \alpha_3 \log w + \alpha_4 \log I,$$

where C is total *direct* operating costs allocated by a bank to the demand deposit function. A glossary of the symbols in the equation appears in the inset. The reader is asked to peruse them before proceeding, and refer to them as necessary in company with the following exposition.

Glossary of Symbols

C = total *direct* operating costs allocated by a bank to the demand deposit function.

$\log H$ = cost function constant.

N = average number of accounts per banking office.

S = average dollar size of a demand deposit account.

T_1 = average number of home debits (items posted to the debit column in the ledger for each account) per account.

T_2 = average number of deposits per account.

T_3 = average number of transit checks (checks written on banks other than the home bank) deposited per account.

T_4 = average number of official checks issued per account.

T_5 = average number of checks cashed per account.

T_6 = average number of transit checks cashed per account.

B = number of offices operated by a bank.

M = ratio of the number of regular checking accounts to the sum of both regular and special accounts.

w = average annual wage rate per demand deposit employee.

I = ratio of the dollar volume of demand deposits to the dollar volume of demand and time deposits, measures the effects of time deposit production activities on demand deposit costs.

$\delta_i, \psi_i, \alpha_i$ indicate that percentage change in total cost that occurs when a particular variable changes by 1 percent, given that all other variables remain unchanged.

Coefficients of the variables in the cost equation shown above—δ_i, ψ_i, and α_i—indicate that percentage change in total cost occurring when a particular variable changes by 1 percent, with all other variables unchanged. The effect on costs of the addition of a new account with characteristics *identical* to the existing "average" account is measured by the coefficient of $\log N$. The indicated percentage change in costs will include additional fixed maintenance, variable maintenance, and transactions costs. The percentage change in costs caused by an increase in the average size of account S will indicate primarily increases in variable maintenance costs associated with account size. The percentage change in costs caused by an increase in T_1 will show the change in transactions costs due to a large number of home debits per account. Changes in the other transactions variables can be interpreted in a similar fashion.

If a regular account is substituted for a special account, the coefficient of log M will indicate whether costs increase or decrease. The change in costs may result from differences in either fixed maintenance, variable maintenance, or transactions costs for two accounts which are identical in all respects except that one is a special account and the other is a regular account. The coefficient of log w indicates the percentage change in costs which occurs when the wage rate changes. Differences in local wage rates or differences in the mix of personnel engaged in demand deposit operations could cause differences in total costs. Therefore, the effects of maintenance, transactions, and other factors on demand deposit costs are contained within the cost function. Although the cost of a specific demand deposit production operation may not be identifiable, the statistical cost function can be used to determine the costs which occur for a given set of production relationships.

Data for estimating the coefficients of the cost equation shown above were obtained from 964 banks that participated in the 1971 FCA program. These banks ranged in size from $5 million to $6 billion in total deposits. Regression analysis was used to estimate the coefficients; the results are presented in Exhibit 1. These results will serve as a base for developing illustrations of product costing, incremental costing, and cost forecasting below.

EXHIBIT 1
Regression Results for the 1971 Demand Deposit Cost Function*

$$\log C = -1.7345 + .9503 \log N + .3936 \log S + .0467 \log T_1$$
$$ (.1792)\ \ (.0127) (.0248) (.0268)$$
$$ + .1427 \log T_2 + .0742 \log T_3 + .0583 \log T_4 +$$
$$ (.0348) (.0126) (.0111)$$
$$ + .0183 \log T_5 - .0046 \log T_6 + 1.0150 \log B +$$
$$ (.0105) (.0124) (.0092)$$
$$ - .0626 \log M + .4312 \log w + .0113 \log I$$
$$ (.0251) (.0470) (.0311)$$

$\bar{R} = .9630$
Standard Error of Estimate $= .0998$
F-Ratio $= 2087.5$

* Numbers in parentheses are standard errors of the regression coefficients.

PRODUCT COSTING

Accountants generally recognize two methods of product costing—job order costing and process costing. In job order costing, each job is an accounting unit to which material, labor, and other costs are assigned. However, in process costing, attention centers on total costs incurred by a department for a given time period in relation to the units processed. Dividing total costs by the quantity of units produced gives the average unit cost. Process costing is usually more appropriate for mass production.

Statistical analysis of costs is more applicable in process than in job order costing. Costs are accumulated over a period of time for a specific department, and data concerning production activities in the department are collected for the same time period. However, rather than employing traditional accounting methods to ascertain average unit costs, average unit costs are estimated through a statistical analysis of the cost-output relationship as defined in a cost function. Traditional accounting methods must assume a rather uncomplicated relationship between output and costs (or various categories of costs); however, if complex interrelationships prevail among the various factors influencing total costs, statistical methods may be more appropriate. It must be remembered that data are required for several time periods or for several firms producing essentially the same product before statistical analysis is feasible. Traditional accounting methods do not have such a requirement.

In many respects, servicing demand deposits in a bank is similar to a continuous production process in manufacturing and thus will serve as a good general illustration. Tellers perform several operations including counting cash, verifying deposit amounts, and issuing receipts. The proof department sorts checks by type and identifies questionable checks. The bookkeeping department posts deposits and checks to appropriate accounts. Furthermore, many other activities, in addition to those mentioned above, occur on a regular and continuing basis.

Two kinds of demand deposit accounts—regular and special—customarily exist in most banks. Special accounts have no minimum balance requirement whereas regular accounts do. As a result of the no minimum balance feature, special accounts tend to be held by individuals rather than businesses and they tend to be less active and have smaller average balances than regular accounts. Thus, regular and special accounts are distinct products; however, production operations for both always occur simultaneously. Consequently, the cost of servicing each type of account is not easily separable.

In Exhibit 2, it is shown how the total and average cost per $100 of an average regular and an average special account can be determined from the results of the statistical analysis shown in Exhibit 1. For convenience, values of the various account characteristics and bank characteristics have been selected that are approximately equal to the sample geometric means of these characteristics. In the cost computations for regular accounts, it is assumed that no special accounts exist. However, in the cost computations for special accounts, it is assumed that 1 percent of the accounts are regular. This assumption is required because the log of the mix variable (M) is undefined when there are no regular accounts.

EXHIBIT 2
Computation of Average Unit Costs for Regular and Special Checking Accounts

	(1)	(2) Regular Account	(3)	(4)	(5)	(6) Special Account	(7)
	Value	Log of Value	Cost Function Coefficient	Product of Columns 2 and 3	Value	Log of Value	Product of Columns 3 and 6
Characteristics of average account							
S Account size	$2,100	3.32222	.3936	1.30763	$ 300	2.47712	.97499
T_1 Home debits/accounts	230	2.36173	.0467	.11029	100	2.00000	.09340
T_2 Deposits/accounts	40	1.60206	.1427	.22861	25	1.39794	.19949
T_3 Transit checks deposited/accounts	180	2.25527	.0742	.16734	20	1.30103	.09654
T_4 Official checks/accounts	3	.47712	.0583	.02782	2	.30103	.01755
T_5 Checks cashed/accounts	30	1.47712	.0183	.02703	30	1.47712	.02703
T_6 Transit checks cashed/accounts	14	1.14613	−.0046	−.00527	16	1.20412	−.00554
Bank characteristics							
N Number of accounts	3,250	3.51188	.9503	3.33734	3,250	3.51188	3.33734
B Number of offices	3	.47712	1.0150	.48428	3	.47712	.48428
M Regular accounts/all accounts	100%	.00000	−.0626	.00000	1%	−2.00000	.12520
w Annual wage rate	$5,700	3.75587	.4312	1.61953	$5,700	3.75587	1.61953
I Demand deposits/total deposits	40%	−.39794	.0113	−.00450	40%	−.39794	−.00450
H Cost function constant				−1.73447			−1.73447
Total cost (log)				5.53860			5.23084
(antilog)				$345,623.00			$170,054.00
Average cost per account				35.45			17.44
Average cost per $100				1.69			5.81

The average regular account in Exhibit 2 is more than twice as costly to service as the average special account. However, the average regular account is only 29 percent as costly per *dollar* of deposits as the average special account. Product costs developed in this way can be used to develop pricing policy. In the case of banks, this kind of information is useful in establishing service schedules. It should be noted that the average unit cost of an account need not be the same for each set of account characteristic and bank characteristic variables. Any bank which knows its values for the variables in Exhibit 2 may determine its average unit costs by following the demonstrated computational procedure.

This method of product costing would be useful in any business enterprise that produces more than one product on a regular and continuing basis using essentially the same types of resources. For example, different types of telephone service—private, party, or commercial—could be costed using the methods described above. Other possible applications might include the manufacture of canned and processed foods, book publishing, manufacture of apparel, manufacture of consumer durable goods such as automobiles, refrigerators, television sets, appliances, and lawn mowers.

INCREMENTAL COSTING

Incremental or differential costs are the increases or decreases in total costs, or the changes in specific elements of cost, that result from some variation in operations. An incremental costing approach to decision making is important when certain costs are fixed and, as such, are not influenced by changes in operations. Ordinarily such a situation occurs in the short run when scale of operations cannot be changed. When the decision is whether or not to accept another order or expand output from a given level, and certain costs are fixed or are relatively inflexible, use of standard costs or average unit costs may lead to the wrong decision. This could happen because the incremental cost of the additional output may differ from the change in total costs indicated by multiplying the additional output by the average unit cost.

Situations in which an incremental cost approach to decision making may be appropriate include: taking on new orders; increasing, decreasing, or eliminating production of certain products; replacing old equipment with new; and so forth. In commercial banks, it may be useful to know the incremental costs of a new demand deposit account, especially if it is tied to a loan arrangement, so that an appropriate pricing strategy can be developed. Incremental costs can also be developed for specific types of demand deposit accounts that differ in various respects from the average account.

The usual accounting approach to differential costing is to identify variable and fixed costs. Then, in a particular situation the affected variable costs can be used to determine the differential cost. However, if variable costs cannot be determined easily, or if variable costs do not remain constant per unit of output at various levels of output, the usual accounting techniques may prove to be insufficient.

Statistical cost analysis may improve the accuracy of incremental cost determination in such circumstances because estimates of incremental (marginal) costs can be derived directly from the cost function for every variation in the basic product that might exist. For example, incremental costs can be determined for each type of transaction that is identified in the demand deposit cost function. Thus, the incremental cost of one additional home debit per account is the change in total cost, C, which results from an increase in home debits per account, T_1, while all other variables in the cost equation shown above remain unchanged. This incremental cost is computed by taking the partial derivative of total cost, C, with respect to home debits per account, T_1. In the present instance, the incremental cost of one additional home debit per account is equal to the cost function coefficient of T_1 (ψ_1) times total cost (C) divided by T_1. Thus, the incremental cost of an additional home debit per regular demand account is computed in column 3 of Exhibit 3 by multiplying the appropriate cost function coefficient in column 1 (.0467) by total cost ($345,623) and then dividing by the number of home debits per regular account (230). Incremental cost per unit, shown in column 4, is obtained by dividing the incremental cost figure in column 3 by the number of regular accounts (9,750). Incremental costs for other variations in the product are calculated in a similar fashion and the results are shown in Exhibit 3.

The incremental cost of an additional regular demand deposit account that is *identical* to the average regular account is $33.69. This is less than the average unit cost of $35.45 for an existing regular account as indicated in Exhibit 2. However, the incremental cost of an additional special account is slightly larger than the average unit cost of a special account. Thus, increases in the number of regular accounts would reduce average unit cost, but increase in the number of special checking accounts would increase average unit cost. To the extent that unutilized capacity exists, management may wish to promote regular rather than special accounts.

An additional dollar in a special account is more than three times as costly to service as an additional dollar in a regular account. This indicates that the cost of providing extra services to small special checking accounts is greater per dollar than the cost of providing additional services to large regular checking accounts. This also implies that the incremental cost associated with an additional dollar of deposits most likely depends on the size of the deposit, i.e., fixed account maintenance costs can be spread over more dollars in large accounts. Home debits

EXHIBIT 3
Incremental Costs for Various Characteristics of Regular and Special Accounts

		(1)	(2) Regular Accounts	(3) Regular Accounts	(4) Regular Accounts	(5)	(6) Special Accounts	(7) Special Accounts
	Characteristics	Cost Function Coefficient	Value	Incremental Cost	Incremental Cost per Unit*	Value	Incremental Cost	Incremental Cost per Unit*
N†	Account	$\delta_1 = .9503$	9,750	$ 33.69	$33.6867	9,750	$ 17.67	$17.6664
S	Account size	$\delta_2 = .3936$	$ 2,100	64.78	.0066	300	223.11	.0229
T_1	Home debits/accounts	$\psi_1 = .0467$	230	70.18	.0072	100	79.42	.0081
T_2	Deposits/accounts	$\psi_2 = .1427$	40	1,233.01	.1265	25	970.67	.0996
T_3	Transit checks deposited/accounts	$\psi_3 = .0742$	180	142.47	.0146	20	630.90	.0647
T_4	Official checks/accounts	$\psi_4 = .0583$	3	6,716.61	.6889	2	4,957.07	.5084
$(T_5 - T_6)$‡	Nontransit checks cashed/accounts	$\psi_5 = .0183$	16	210.83	.0216	14	103.73	.0106
T_6	Transit checks cashed/accounts	$\psi_6 = -.0046$ $\alpha_2 = -.0626$	14	97.27	.0100	16	54.84	.0056
C	Total costs		$345,623			$170,054		

* Incremental cost per unit is determined by dividing incremental cost by 9,750 accounts.

† The number of accounts variable (N) includes both regular and special accounts. However, the mix variable also contains both regular and special accounts. Let $N = (N_R + N_S)/B$ and $M = N_R/(N_R + N_S)$. Then, the incremental cost of another regular account $= (\delta_1 - \alpha_2)[C/N_R + N_S)] + \alpha_2(C/N_R)$. The incremental cost of another special account $= (\delta_1 - \alpha_2)[C/N_R + N_S)]$.

‡ Nontransit checks cashed per account equals $(T_5 - T_6)$ while transit checks cashed equals T_6. The sum of these two categories is total checks cashed (T_5). The incremental cost of nontransit checks cashed $= \psi_5(C/A_5)$. The incremental cost of transit checks cashed $a = \psi_5(C/A_5) + \psi_6(C/T_6)$.

are associated with highly routinized operations which may explain why there is little difference in the incremental costs of home debits in regular and special checking accounts. With the exception of transit checks deposited, incremental costs of changes in other account characteristics are greater for regular accounts than they are for special accounts. There are only one ninth as many transit checks deposited annually in special accounts as in regular accounts. The difference in incremental costs for transit checks deposited in regular and special accounts may occur if the cost of handling the first few transit checks is high while the cost of handling each additional transit check declines.

Suppose management wishes to know the cost of a specific regular checking account that differs in identifiable ways from the average regular account. Incremental cost analysis can be used to help determine the cost of this *example* regular account. Characteristics of the example regular account to be costed are shown in column 1 of Exhibit 4 and characteristics of the average account are contained in column 2. Column 3 is the difference of the first two columns. The incremental cost in column 5 is the product of the figure in column 3 and the incremental cost per item in column 4, which was computed in Exhibit 3.

Although the cost of the example regular account in Exhibit 4 is considerably greater than the cost of the average regular account, the cost per $100 is lower because of the larger balance. This result suggests that service charge rates should be based on account size and the number of various types of transactions. Knowledge of incremental costs can be used to establish variable-rate service charge schedules which reflect the actual cost incurred in servicing a particular account more accurately than using average unit costs or some kind of standard costing procedure.

Such an approach to pricing may be useful in nonfinancial firms that produce a product or service capable of being differentiated or varied in several ways. For example, the incremental costing method may be useful in establishing the cost of selling particular types of merchandise in retailing firms or in determining the cost of handling particular types of customer credit accounts.

COST FORECASTING

When management contemplates or expects some change in operations at a future date, it is important to forecast the effects of this change on costs. The use of statistical analysis in forecasting, especially for forecasting sales, is well established. However, cost forecasts ordinarily are based on a nonstatistical evaluation of the production facilities, equipment, labor, and materials required to produce enough to meet the sales forecast. When statistical methods are used to forecast costs, it usually involves either a simple regression analysis of volume and cost or, in rare cases, a multiple regression analysis.

EXHIBIT 4
Computation of the Cost of a Regular Checking Account Which Differs from the Average Regular Checking Account

Characteristics	(1) Value Example Account	(2) Value Average Account	(3) Difference (1) – (2)	(4) Incremental Cost per Item	(5) Change in Average Cost per Account
S Account size	$5,000	$2,100	$2,900	$.0066	$19.14
T_1 Home debits/account	400	230	170	.0072	1.22
T_2 Deposits/account	50	40	10	.1265	1.26
T_3 Transit checks deposited/account	300	180	120	.0146	1.75
T_4 Official checks/account	5	3	2	.6889	1.38
$(T_5 - T_6)$ Nontransit checks cashed/account	20	16	4	.0216	.09
T_6 Transit checks cashed/account	20	14	6	.0100	.04
Total					$24.88
Cost of average regular account					+35.45
Cost of example regular account					$60.33
Cost per $100 of the example regular account					1.21

The principal danger inherent in statistical cost forecasting is that future behavior may differ substantially from past cost behavior, thus making forecasts unreliable. Changes in plant and equipment, materials, products, production techniques, personnel, internal organization, prices paid for materials and labor, and many other factors will tend to impair the reliability of statistical cost forecasts. Nevertheless, in some circumstances statistical cost forecasting may provide helpful information. For example, if prices of materials and labor have varied in the past, this information can be included in the statistical cost function. Then, the effect of expected future changes in these prices on costs can be determined. In a firm that operates several plants or branches, all producing and selling the same product, statistical cost analysis may prove useful in forecasting the costs of *operating* a new plant or branch. Statistical analysis is not as likely to be useful in determining the cost of constructing a new plant. Several illustrations of cost forecasting are given below.

Turning to the banking example, suppose a branch bank is operating three offices with an average of 3,250 demand deposit accounts per office. It is considering opening a new office that it expects to be able to attract 3,250 new demand deposit accounts having characteristics essentially similar to those of existing demand deposits. Management is concerned about the effect of this expansion on its costs of operation for demand deposits. The change in costs can be forecast by making appropriate changes in the statistical cost function shown in the cost equation below:

$$\begin{aligned}
\log C_1 &= \log C_0 + \alpha_1 (\log B_1 - \log B_0) \\
&= 5.53860 + 1.0150 (.60206 - .47712) \\
&= 5.53860 + .12681 \\
&= 5.66541
\end{aligned}$$

Total costs are \$345,623 before the addition of the new branch and will be \$462,820 afterwards, an increase of \$117,197. Average unit cost before expansion is \$35.45, but after expansion it will be \$35.60. The \$.15 increase in average unit cost reflects added costs of coordination associated with the operation of the new branch.

Suppose that this branch bank is not considering opening a new branch but expects the number of demand deposits handled by each branch to increase from 3,250 to 4,333. The change in costs that occurs when 1,083 new demand accounts are added to each of the three existing branches can be computed in the same manner as described above: $5.53860 + .9503(3.63682 - 3.51188) = 5.65733$. Total costs will be \$454,289 and average cost per account will be \$34.95, a decline of \$.50 per account. In both of the cost forecasting examples given here, there will be 13,000 accounts and \$27.3 million in deposits (assuming that average account size is \$2,100). In one example, though, there are four offices while in the other there are only three. Having one more branch for the same number of accounts and the same amount of deposits causes a difference of $7,531 or nearly 2 percent in total operating costs.

Management can also forecast the effect of an increase in the average annual wage paid per employee. Suppose management expects wages to rise by 10 percent from $5,700 to $6,270. Total costs will be: 5.53860 + .4312 (3.79727 − 3.75587) = 5.55645 or $360,125. Average unit costs will be $36.94, an increase of $1.49 per account.

The effects of other anticipated changes, in addition to those illustrated above, can be determined in the same way. In fact, the effects of all expected changes on total costs can be forecast simultaneously.

Any business firm able to construct its own cost function can use it to forecast the effects of changes in any or all of its variables. This procedure is legitimate so long as there is no significant change in the production-cost relationship.

CONCLUDING REMARKS

These uses of statistical cost analysis were demonstrated for commercial banks. However, any business enterprise which produces its products on a relatively regular and continuing basis and which maintains detailed records about output, resource prices, product characteristics, and costs can construct its own statistical cost function and use it for product costing, incremental costing, or cost forecasting. Thus, a host of business enterprises have the potential to use some kind of management-oriented statistical cost analysis.

If the production-cost relationship is more complex than that presumed in break-even analysis or variable budgeting, statistical cost analysis may provide useful supplemental information that these more conventional cost accounting techniques are incapable of providing. It is not suggested that information derived from employing statistical techniques should supplant other types of information; rather, it is urged that statistical cost information be used in conjunction with other cost accounting information to help *improve* decision making.

PART FOUR

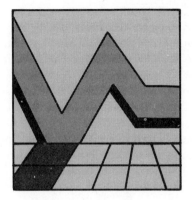

PRICING

INTRODUCTION

Business firms are attempting to maximize something when they establish a price(s). It may be profits, total revenue, position in the community; nonetheless, all firms must sell their product at some price. How should that price be established?

The article by Coyne studies the price and subsequent profits realized by investor-owned electric utilities during the decade of the 1970s. The article finds that electric utility industry profits, when correctly measured, are about the same as profits recorded by other firms and industries.

Domestic and imported steel products do not sell at the same price. James M. Jondrow, David E. Chase, and Christopher L. Gamble explain why. The price differential as well as the characteristics that cause domestic and imported steel to differ are documented. In addition, the reader is shown how to estimate a price differential that compensates the users of imported steel for the price difference(s).

Joel Dean's classic article treats the separate issue of transfer pricing and the impact it has on profits. It is the standard introduction to this subject and directs attention to the main principles of rational pricing policy in any context. This subject is as disturbing as it is important, for Dean states that to be economically effective autonomous divisions of most large companies must establish transfer prices. Most existing transfer price systems are inadequate, and huge quantities of time and patience are required to install competitive transfer prices. Yet once a "good" system is obtained, executives should be prepared to meet certain objections that critics always raise.

The reader is reminded by Dean's article that firms not only buy and sell from one another; in addition, they buy from themselves. Wholly owned subsidiary A quite often enters into a number of transactions with another wholly owned subsidiary of the same company. At what prices should such internal transactions take place? Robert G. Eccles agrees the transfer price should be a fair one, but quite often neither the buyer nor the seller may agree as to what is "fair."

Eccles concludes that a workable transfer pricing policy is one wherein top management persons monitor the interaction between units of their company and alter the transfer price if such adjustment is necessary to reflect changes in overall corporate strategy.

Price elasticity measures the responsiveness of changes in price to changes in quantity demanded. It is a relative measure of the sensitivity of sales to price changes. For manufacturers who sell their products through independent dealer or distributor networks, the price elasticity of consumer demand for the product may be misleading since dealer inventory may cause the elasticity of demand at the manufacturer or wholesale level to differ. A methodology is developed by H. Frederick Gallasch, Jr., relating price elasticities of demand at retail and wholesale levels via an elasticity of price transmission. Empirical studies of new car demand provide elasticity estimates with which this methodology is demonstrated.

16.

Financial Returns to Equity: The Profitability of the Electric Utility*

THOMAS J. COYNE

The allegation that American public utilities in general and electric companies in particular made huge profits during the decade of the 1970s and continue to do so into the 1980s may be gaining widespread support throughout the United States; meanwhile, electric utility companies are filing routinely with public utility commissions across the nation asking for, and often receiving, increasingly larger rate hikes. The Edison Electric Institute reported, for example, that 86 utilities asked for almost $6 billion in rate relief with the filing of 108 rate requests during the first six months of 1980; in addition, it is common for an electric utility to file a rate request almost immediately upon receipt of a rate increase. Such increases were unheard of prior to the 1970s; in fact, rates often went down, not up. Electric companies at that time were realizing economies of large-scale production and they passed these lower production costs to the consumer.

Higher construction, fuel, and interest expenses are cited often by electric utility executives as reasons for requested rate relief; the pangs of inflation, however defined, unemployment, recession, and similar factors are cited by opponents as reasons why electric utility rates are high enough or too high. In addition and of importance to this study, oppo-

---

* *Public Utility Fortnightly,* February 1982, pp. 19–26.

nents charge, the electric utilities are making more than a "fair return."

Apparently, a large percentage of the total population considers the word "price" or "rate" to be synonymous with profit. Electric utility industry critics have proposed various methods of reducing profits ranging from more stringent public utility commission control of prices to nationalization of the industry. Some critics are demanding a voice in the selection process of key executive positions; others want routine management audits to determine how and why top management cannot or will not perform better.

If high electric utility rates and high profits are almost perfectly correlated, this relationship should be revealed in higher financial returns obtained by electric companies on equity invested. This article analyzes financial returns to equity and comments upon the need for and the likelihood of greater rate increases being permitted or greater control being exercised over electric utility industry activities, or both. Following generally accepted accounting principles, the article assumes all profits after taxes are available to holders of equity.

Prices and profits are related to a principal pricing goal of major electric companies, a goal based on a philosophy of "fair return." This goal is achieved by pricing in a manner that allows the firm to charge a somewhat uniform rate per kilowatt-hour used, with recognition in recent years being given by some firms to peak-load demand pricing. Electric companies appear to seek with this pricing policy a fair return (profit) on their investment but, generally speaking, they do not define this return with uniformly specific figures. Electric industry critics also fail to define what they consider a "fair" profit to be and public utility commissions do not appear to know either. In the absence of a defined fair return profit level, it may be ludicrous to claim the profit level has been achieved or exceeded.

Over the years, the rate structure of most large electric companies has appeared similar in another way: Each firm has wanted to maintain its market share while simultaneously pursuing a position of price stabilization. This approach allowed electric companies to enjoy satisfactory, if not fair, profits over a prolonged period of time. Only one notable exception to past practice has changed at this writing: These firms no longer pursue policies of price stabilization. To even the most casual of observers, prices have not been very stable in the electric industry in recent years; instead, they are fluctuating rapidly in an upward direction. Moreover, higher prices paid recently for electricity have received the somewhat predictable response from consumer and government regulatory groups; namely, charges of inefficiency, price gouging, and profiteering.

This article studies profits received by each of the seven largest firms in the electric industry in the state of Ohio and compares the results with returns obtained by the six largest firms in the oil industry, by leading commercial banks (16), savings and loan associations (3), and trucking companies (4). Each firm and each industry of which that firm is a member is analyzed via application of a return to equity model to determine if average returns over time for the electric industry in Ohio have been equal to, less than, or greater than returns on equity for all or any segment of selected financial or nonfinancial industries.

RETURN ON EQUITY (ROE)

Net income, total revenue minus total expense, is a simplified and somewhat traditional way of viewing corporate profitability. It may not be an adequate measure. Even if one could agree with respect to the precise entries to include in the revenue and expense categories (construction work in progress?), the resultant "profit" figure would represent only a before-tax entry. Such an entry may or may not result in any reported profitability for a company in the short run because investment tax credits, depletion allowances, depreciation schedules, and "write-downs" for unprofitable and discontinued facilities are used to shield (reduce) a firm's nominal profit from tax; therefore, a firm's reported short-term profitability figure can be manipulated if net income is assumed to present a valid picture of a firm's profit.

Based on the assumption that profitability is a primary justification for the existence of a privately owned corporation, a different and better measurement of profit could, and perhaps should, be used. This measure of profitability compares net equity with total dollar profits generated after tax and is the one used here.

Equity represents the difference between what a firm owns and what it owes. It is a balance sheet entry revealing the stockholders' ownership and financial position in the company. Generally speaking, the larger the equity for a given number of shares of stock outstanding, the better the financial condition of the stockholder group. Financial returns to stockholders' equity are calculated by dividing the firm's profit after tax but before dividends by the equity figure. Once calculated, this return allows comparison of stockholder profits to stockholder investment.

Return on equity is a figure that allows comparison of (1) the stockholders' financial well-being over time, (2) the financial returns between companies in the same industry, and (3) financial returns to companies in different industries. The return on equity figure is an adequate measure of overall corporate profitability; therefore, throughout this article, profitability by definition is synonymous with return on equity.

TURNOVER, MARGIN, RETURN ON INVESTMENT (ROI), AND EQUITY MULTIPLIER

In considering the price and output behavior of a firm and its resultant profitability, if any, it is important to remember that no single variable provides an adequate indication of what is required to influence profitability. Public utility commissions may have lost sight of this truism. As all principles of economics students throughout the country should know by now, an increase in price (rate) is not associated automatically with an increase or decrease in profitability; in addition, an increase in one or more of a firm's operating expenses need not decrease profitability. To the extent that an increase in petroleum products or coal costs (or both) would represent an overall increase in expenses to an electric company in the short run, one would be naive to believe the firm's profitability would have to decrease because of such an increase.

If a higher petroleum product cost is imposed at a time when all other costs are relatively constant or, perhaps, increasing slightly, a firm's profit margin could increase, decrease, or remain unchanged. For electric companies in Ohio these profit margins declined over the 11 years studied. Declines of this nature, alone, do not cause profits to suffer.

A declining profit margin could cause return on investment to decline, unless asset turnover increases by an amount great enough to offset the decrease in profit margin. According to Table 1, turnover for electric companies in Ohio remained relatively constant while net operating margins declined in the last 11 years; return on investment declined also.

TURNOVER

The asset turnover to which one refers here is the ratio of revenue to total assets (revenue ÷ total assets). This ratio reveals the relative efficiency with which resources are used within and by the firm. For electric companies, the higher this ratio the more efficiently the firm is using previously acquired power-generating plants and other equipment. Increasing asset turnover associated with *decreasing* profit margins caused, perhaps, by too low a price per kilowatt-hour or too high a cost—i.e., oil, coal, labor—could result in return on investment *rising*. Undoubtedly, diminishing returns to increased asset turnover exist for electric companies; however, at this writing no sufficient published research appears to define, explain, or describe this point of diminishing returns. Most certainly, electric companies do not appear to be anywhere close to such a point.

The question that needs to be answered is: If Ohio electric industry turnover did not change much in the last 10 years, could it be made to do so during the next decade? If so, profitability could rise, even if net profit margin and ROI continued to fall. If not, another round of rate increases might improve neither profitability nor image for the average electric utility. In fact, and as indicated by the table, each of the seven firms in Ohio has been characterized in recent years by the existence of *declining* ROIs and *declining* profit margins and almost no change in efficiency of resource utilization. However, Cincinnati Gas and Electric

TABLE 1
Electric Utility Profitability: Seven Firms, Ohio

(1)	(2)	(3)	(4) Return on Investment‡ (ROI) (Col. 2 × Col. 3)	(5) Equity Multiplier§	(6) Return on Equity (Profitability) (ROE)‖ (Col. 4 × Col. 5)
Year	Turnover*	Margin†			
Cincinnati Gas and Electric Company					
1979	.4293	10.38%	4.46%	2.54	11.33%
1978	.4644	10.06	4.67	2.28	10.65
1977	.4627	11.03	5.10	2.27	11.58
1976	.3963	9.94	3.94	2.40	9.46
1975	.3838	10.36	3.98	2.37	9.43
1974	.3643	10.94	3.99	2.33	9.30
1973	.3440	14.37	4.94	2.08	11.26
1972	.3566	14.46	5.16	2.44	12.59
1971	.3576	12.82	4.58	2.54	11.63
1970	.3689	14.12	5.21	2.51	13.08
1969	.3974	14.13	5.62	2.60	14.61
Cleveland Electric Illuminating Company					
1979	.3028	14.50%	4.39%	2.33	10.23%
1978	.3032	14.00	4.24	2.25	9.54
1977	.3064	17.23	5.28	2.32	12.25
1976	.2888	15.35	4.43	2.49	11.03
1975	.3385	12.64	4.28	2.56	10.96
1974	.3371	13.31	4.49	2.68	12.03
1973	.2802	15.30	4.29	2.58	11.07
1972	.2724	17.02	4.64	2.58	11.97
1971	.2978	15.61	4.65	2.57	11.95
1970	.2964	16.83	4.99	2.85	14.22
1969	.2901	18.20	5.28	2.71	14.31
Columbus and Southern Ohio Electric Company					
1979	.2858	14.52%	4.14%	2.45	10.14%
1978	.2674	11.99	3.21	2.36	7.58
1977	.2545	17.11	4.35	2.31	10.05
1976	.2502	19.52	4.88	2.34	11.42
1975	.2698	16.52	4.46	2.64	11.77
1974	.2297	11.28	2.59	3.05	7.90
1973	.2338	16.43	3.84	2.74	10.52
1972	.2345	15.81	3.71	2.75	10.20
1971	.2290	12.92	2.96	2.99	8.85
1970	.2410	14.83	3.57	2.88	10.28
1969	.2526	14.49	3.66	2.95	10.80
Dayton Power and Light Company					
1979	.3852	10.79%	4.16%	2.34	9.73%
1978	.4164	8.99	3.74	2.21	8.27
1977	.3939	9.13	3.60	2.29	8.24
1976	.3954	11.07	4.38	2.30	10.07
1975	.3934	11.69	4.60	2.31	10.63
1974	.3546	10.17	3.61	2.34	8.45
1973	.3116	11.97	3.73	2.36	8.80
1972	.3231	12.62	4.08	2.38	9.71
1971	.3235	12.52	4.05	2.53	10.25
1970	.3134	12.66	3.99	2.59	10.33
1969	.3173	14.50	4.60	2.68	12.33

TABLE 1 *(concluded)*

(1)	(2)	(3)	(4) Return on Investment‡ (ROI) (Col. 2 × Col. 3)	(5) Equity Multiplier§	(6) Return on Equity (Profitability) (ROE)‖ (Col. 4 × Col. 5)
Year	Turnover*	Margin†			
Ohio Edison Company					
1979	.2717	16.06%	4.36%	2.26	9.85%
1978	.2717	11.73	3.19	2.26	7.21
1977	.2730	16.73	4.57	2.10	9.60
1976	.2579	19.22	4.96	2.23	11.06
1975	.2737	16.60	4.54	2.28	10.35
1974	.2548	14.77	3.76	2.48	9.32
1973	.2405	20.29	4.88	2.36	11.52
1972	.2566	19.10	4.90	2.51	12.30
1971	.2615	18.26	4.77	2.52	12.02
1970	.2641	20.38	5.38	2.33	12.54
1969	.2683	22.26	5.97	2.01	13.19
Ohio Power Company					
1979	.3722	13.77%	5.13%	2.73	14.00%
1978	.3313	11.86	3.93	2.68	10.53
1977	.2910	16.06	4.67	2.70	12.61
1976	.2935	21.01	6.17	2.59	15.98
1975	.2900	17.48	5.07	2.69	13.64
1974	.2486	17.35	4.31	2.85	12.28
1973	.1878	22.99	4.32	2.79	12.05
1972	.1934	21.84	4.22	2.70	11.39
1971	.2051	20.04	4.11	3.01	12.37
1970	.2162	18.60	4.02	3.35	13.47
1969	.2291	18.51	4.24	3.28	13.91
Toledo Edison Company					
1979	.2149	16.33%	3.51%	2.71	9.51%
1978	.2311	16.45	3.80	2.64	10.03
1977	.2141	18.10	3.88	2.57	9.97
1976	.2078	18.22	3.79	2.66	10.08
1975	.2092	19.11	4.00	2.80	11.20
1974	.1845	17.32	3.20	2.99	9.57
1973	.1924	18.87	3.63	3.00	10.89
1972	.2190	16.67	3.65	3.01	10.99
1971	.2230	15.18	3.39	3.32	11.25
1970	.2235	16.38	3.66	3.32	12.15
1969	.2303	17.00	3.92	3.14	12.31

* Turnover = revenue ÷ total assets
† Net operating margin = net income ÷ operating revenue
‡ ROI = net income ÷ total assets
§ Equity multiplier = total assets ÷ stockholders' equity
‖ ROE = net income ÷ total assets, or ROI × equity multiplier.
 Sources: *"Moody's Public Utility Manual"*; *"Annual Reports"*; Standard & Poor's *"Standard Stock Reports"*; and other data, yearly, 1969 through 1979.

Company, Dayton Power and Light Company, and Ohio Power Company may be exceptions to this statement![1] The turnover statistic increased over the time frame studied for each of these three firms. The other firms, except Toledo Edison Company, had virtually no change in turnover. TE *decreased* its turnover statistic from .2303 in 1969 to .2149 in 1979. No other firm and no industry with which those electric companies are compared had a decrease in this important variable during the time period studied.

Asset turnover had doubled in the oil industry on average during the past 10 years, whereas turnover had remained relatively constant for the other industries included in this study. Data analyzed reveal that certain electric and other firms utilize their resources less efficiently, on average, but enjoyed greater net operating profit margins than oil firms; yet, electric firms continue to seek rate relief. In fact, electric companies in Ohio as revealed in the table have had, and continue to have, net profit margins two and three times *greater* on average than oil and most other firms with which they are compared.

The oil companies on average, doubled the efficiency of plant and equipment utilization during the decade of the 1970s. Standard Oil Company of California, for example, saw its turnover jump 160 percent, from .62 in 1969 to 1.65 in 1979. Had the Columbus and Southern Ohio Electric Company been efficient enough to double its turnover statistic during the same 10-year period, to say, .5052 in 1979, retaining a 14.52 net profit margin, its return on investment would have been 7.33; CS's ROE would have been 17.97. The fact is CS did not increase its operating efficiency; it was acquired by a larger and presumably more efficiently managed corporation.

TURNOVER INCENTIVES

Revenue generated by an electric company is a function of its so-called rate base. The formula for calculating the amount of total revenue allowed by a public utility commission to an electric company is:

$$RR = OM + D + T + (G - AD)R$$

where:

RR = revenue requirement
OM = operation and maintenance expenses
D = annual depreciation
T = taxes
G = gross value of the property
AD = accrued (or observed) depreciation on the property

---

[1] Some of the difference in turnover results may be attributable to the natural gas operations at Cincinnati Gas and Electric and Dayton Power and Light.

R = rate of return; this figure is often the firm's average cost of capital.

Included in the rate base is the dollar value of the firm's plant and equipment, its assets. The higher the rate base, the higher the total revenue allowed by the regulatory commission. Conspicuous by its absence in this formula is mention, recognition, or incentive for the firm to use its plant and equipment more efficiently. As a result, electric company executives may believe relatively constant turnover statistics measure up to the minimum standards of excellence expected of them. These executives may think constant turnover ratios are okay. The more power-generating plants a firm can justify the higher its rate base and, of course, the higher its total revenue, according to the formula. The larger the number of plants, the larger in size and cost of precipitation and other pollution control device equipment per plant, the higher the total revenue to the firm. This is the opposite situation one would seek if he or she were interested in maximizing utilization and financial returns to scarce and costly resources.

Electric utilities complain often that governmental authorities insist upon pollution control devices, that the dollars invested in such equipment are wasted, that this additional investment is somehow detrimental to the stockholder. Not true insofar as potential income to the stockholder is concerned! To the extent that dollars invested in equipment designed to control pollution are approved by the utility commission and the courts, these costs appear eventually in the rate base. When multiplied by the firm's cost of capital (R), pollution control and other devices generate increased profitability to the stockholder. The more expensive the equipment, the higher the rate base and the ultimate profits to the firm.

The installation of pollution control equipment can serve to increase a company's net profit margin but decrease its asset turnover. On net balance, return on investment increases, decreases, or remains unaffected in the short run, dependent upon how quickly higher costs can be converted to higher rates. The degree of profitability (ROE) also depends heavily upon how it is financed (equity multiplier).

RETURN ON EQUITY AND THE EQUITY MULTIPLIER

Return on equity may be the most important measure of profitability for electric companies. It may be calculated by application of a firm's (1) asset turnover, (2) profit margin, (3) return on investment, and (4) equity multiplier figures.[2] ROE is ROI multiplied by the equity multiplier.

---

[2] A much less revealing but equally valid calculation could be made by dividing net income by net equity.

Assuming constant or increasing profit margins, the higher the asset turnover figure, the greater the firm's ROI. If the equity multiplier remains unchanged, this ROI is directly related to a firm's return on equity. It is possible for an electric company to increase or hold its profitability constant from, say 1969 through 1979, despite *decreasing* profit margins and *decreasing* ROIs by adjusting its equity multiplier.

A decrease in the asset turnover statistic associated with a constant or decreasing profit margin will result in decreasing ROIs and may result in decreasing returns to equity *unless* the equity multiplier is increased; also, decreasing profit margins and constant or increasing asset turnover figures may be associated with decreasing ROIs and decreasing returns to equity unless the equity multiplier is increased. Obviously, increases or decreases in ROI are based upon interrelationships between changes in asset turnover or profit margins (or both). Changes in returns to equity (profitability) are affected also by these factors but more importantly, perhaps, by the equity multiplier.

"Fair returns" can be achieved by an electric company and defended successfully at a public utility commission hearing by paying closer attention to factors other than the rate base; more specifically, one should watch turnover of this base, net operating margin, ROI, and the equity multiplier. Of these variables, turnover and the equity multiplier may be the most crucial for it is these variables that may be overlooked most easily.

If profitability is "too high" as alleged by some electric industry critics, and if profit may be defined for the moment in the traditional sense as being equal to net income, it is probable that denial or partial approval of a rate increase would be associated with: (a) a decrease in electric company net operating margins, (b) an increase, decrease, or no change in their turnover statistic, and (c) an increase, decrease, or no movement in its ROI; however, assuming inelasticity of demand for the final product in the short run, (d) the equity multiplier might be increased. Such an increase could cause electric company returns to equity to rise, not fall. And at the very time the critics said profits were too high.

The point is this: If profitability for financial or nonfinancial firms, including electric companies, is "high" or "low," it is that way because of a number of factors only one of which might be price, rate, or rate base of the company. To the extent that greater control over the affairs of electric companies is being considered because these companies have successfully imposed a succession of price rises on the public, the probability may be quite low that these more stringent controls over prices or imposition (or both) of expensive management audits and other controls will result in reduced electric company profitability (ROE). Let us take a closer look at profit margins.

PROFIT MARGIN

Profit or net operating margin is calculated by taking the firm's profit after tax and dividing that figure by total sales. Profit after tax is total operating income minus total costs. Included in total costs is the cost of goods produced or sold plus operating expenses, interest expense, and taxes. Public hearings, expert witnesses, attorneys, economists, and other personnel that must be hired as a self-protection measure by the firm serve to increase the firm's total costs. This increase in total costs is passed to the ultimate consumer via price increases if the demand function is price inelastic. Under such a set of circumstances, the net operating margin for the firm need not fall. On the other hand, should the demand function turn out to be relatively price elastic, an improbable assumption in the short run as viewed by this observer, net operating margin could but would not have to decline, if price rises.

To the extent that unnecessary costs are imposed, and represent a new cost to the firm, these higher costs are passed to the ultimate consumer via price increases if the demand for the product is relatively price inelastic in the short run. Profit margin(s) need not suffer. If the degree of inelasticity is significantly greater than 1.0 in the local market, demand for electricity elsewhere in the United States might be high enough to allow nonlocal consumers to absorb the higher cost. In either event, the probability may be high that electric company profitability (ROE) will not decline, even with the imposition of higher necessary or unnecessary costs. Why? (1) Profit margins might not decline because of the cost; (2) costs other than the one(s) that rose might decline; and (3) if profit margins are adversely affected by higher cost, increases in the firm's (a) turnover or (b) equity multiplier (or both) could serve to more than offset the impact of decreasing net operating margins on ROE. This offset could result in higher than ever profitability to an electric company.

Ohio Power Company, for example, had about the same profitability in 1979 as it had in 1969, despite decreases in its net operating margin. Modest improvement of its plant and equipment utilization, from .2291 to .3722, caused its ROI to jump from 4.24 to 5.13 percent. During this time period, OP allowed its equity multiplier to slip from 3.28 to 2.73. Had this shift in method of financing not occurred, OP would have had an ROE of 16.83 (3.28 × 5.13 percent) in 1979.

EQUITY MULTIPLIER

Turnover is an excellent measure of how efficiently the firm is utilizing the assets it owns; profit margin expresses nicely the relationship between profit after tax and operating revenues. The multiplication of these two variables produces a statistic referred to often as return on investment. Quite clearly, this ROI can continue to increase if one of the two variables decreases by an amount less than the increase in the other variable. For example, decreases in profit margin which are more than offset by increases in asset turnover could result in *increased* ROI. However, as indicated earlier, even if ROI decreases, profitability of the firm need not decrease provided the equity multiplier is rising.

As we have seen, profitability to the firm is the product of its return on investment and its equity multiplier. By definition, this equity multiplier is the ratio of the firm's assets to its equity. The higher this ratio, the larger the firm's short- or long-term liabilities (or both). These liabilities are debts owed by the firm and in the jargon of financial managers may be expressed as "financial leverage."

Firms using financial leverage obviously believe the name of the game is to make money with the use of someone else's money and have all parties to the transaction happy with the arrangement. Positive or favorable financial leverage for the firm exists when it earns more with borrowed money than it pays for it. Generally speaking, a long-term corporate bond costing 18 percent or so in interest expense should yield something greater than 18 percent, on average, for use of the bonded indebtedness to be beneficial to the firm.[3] Most major American corporations use leverage to the greatest extent feasible. Electric companies are no exception to this rule.

TAX AND RATE INCREASES

Leverage can be used to enhance a company's profits; however, at times, some highly visible firms run the risk of having special attention called to their profits when leverage is used successfully. As with the electric industry, such is the case with the oil industry.

In June 1979, the House of Representatives passed a windfall profits tax. Passage of this House version of the bill assumed that "excess" or "windfall" profits had been, were being, or would be, made by oil companies; moreover, these profits were to be subjected to a special 50 percent tax rate. Comparison of oil industry profits to the seven electric companies in Ohio and to selected financial and nonfinancial corporations elsewhere allows one to test HR 3919's basic assumption and to measure the degree by which oil company profits exceed the profits of other firms and industries with which oil is compared.

Return on equity figures for firms located in the oil, Commercial

---

[3] Technically, of course, the firm expects its internal rate of return to be equal to, or greater than, its marginal cost of capital. The long-term bond used here for illustrative purposes only would be one component of the firm's cost of capital; however, it is neither necessary nor expected that the firm's marginal cost of capital be equal to the cost of this or any other single component.

Bank (in New York city and outside of New York city), savings and loans, and trucking industries for the period 1969–79 have been analyzed. In each year tested, the electric companies whose data are presented in the table compare favorably with profitability generated by all firms studied. Overall, the table reveals that profitability of electric companies in Ohio often exceeds, and always compares very favorably with, oil and other industry profits.[4] This latter statement is particularly pronounced for the period 1969 through 1978. The year 1979 saw oil company profits at levels greater than returns generated by the electric companies.

If electric company profits compare favorably with oil and other firms with which electric returns are compared, can additional requests for rate relief be justified? On what grounds? If electric industry profits are not generating a "fair return," what is the magnitude of the shortage? How do we know?

Regardless of fair returns or lack thereof, the electric firms mentioned herein have shared more or less equally in these profits. Profitability for each electric firm in the table has approximated more than 10 percent on average over the 11 years tested; in addition, double-digit profitability has existed for most firms in every year tested.

SUMMARY AND CONCLUSIONS

Financial returns to equity are presented for each of the seven major firms in the electric industry in the state of Ohio, yearly 1969 through 1979. These returns have been compared with returns generated within selected financial and nonfinancial industries.

Profitability is defined as being synonymous with return on equity. In calculating return on equity, careful consideration is given to asset turnover, net operating margin, return on investment, and the equity multiplier. Attention is directed to the following points:

1. Neither the electric companies nor their critics define "fair" profit levels. Consequently, "fair return" levels of profit, per se, may not have been exceeded.

2. The public utilities commission in Ohio and elsewhere might profit by giving stronger consideration to real and potential changes in a firm's equity multiplier and other measures of financial and operating

---

[4] Comparison of industries in this manner assumes similarity of risk. This assumption may not be justifiable; in fact, many if not most observers would argue that risk is less for electric firms than for any other firm or industry represented here. These lower risks are attributable to the greater differences in economic, political, environmental, and social problems faced by modern electric firms. Generally speaking, the less the risk, the less the expected reward; consequently, if adjusted for differences in risk, electric industry returns as presented in the table might have to be *significantly* lower than they are to be considered normal, much less economic profits. In other words, once adjusted for risk, these electric industry returns might be something *greater* than normal profits.

leverage as it considers the merits of requested rate relief. A good equity multiplier can make a lot of difference.

3. Turnover of assets is an important measure of a firm's earning power. Increases in turnover reveal improved utilization of a firm's assets and contribute positively to its profitability. For electric companies, turnover figures remained almost constant during the 11 years studied. If electric companies could generate greater operating efficiency (turnover), they could improve profitability and would not need recurrent increases in rates charged per kilowatt-hour.

4. Electric firms have experienced *declining* net profit margins over the time frame studied; yet these margins are significantly higher than margins for any firm or industry tested. If electric prices (rates) had been rising at a rate more rapid than cost, these margins might have increased; however, declining profit margins alone do not and did not cause electric company profitability to suffer. Had these net operating margins increased, profitability would not necessarily have risen.

5. Ohio Power notwithstanding, return on investment *declined* or remained about the same, on average, for firms in the electric industry in Ohio for the years studied. With the exception of commercial banks nationally, ROI increased slightly or remained relatively constant for selected industries with which electric companies are compared over the same period of time; however, ROI alone is an incomplete measure of profitability, particularly for purposes of establishing electric rates. Decreases in ROI alone do not and did not cause profitability to suffer.

6. The equity multiplier is the ratio of the firm's assets to its net equity. The higher this ratio, the larger the share of the firm's assets financed with debt; also, the higher this ratio, the greater the firm's potential profitability once a break-even point is reached. When this ratio is multiplied by ROI, the firm's profitability is determined. Electric firms everywhere might benefit by paying greater attention to this equity multiplier. For too many years, perhaps, electric company executives have demanded excellence in engineering skills while simultaneously ignoring finance functions. This may be a luxury they can no longer afford. For example, if Ohio Power had had in 1979 the same equity multiplier it had in 1969, its profitability would have been 16.83 in 1979 as opposed to 14, all other variables remaining unchanged. With improved financing, subsequent rate relief requests might have been considered unnecessary.

7. Profitability for the electric industry (ROE), even when not adjusted to reflect the higher risks implicit in traditional investments of selected firms, may be *higher* than profitability for some and lower than other industries for each year tested; however, on average, electric company profits in Ohio were about the same as profits reported by all other firms and industries tested. This favorable profitability position for electric companies is maintained even when compared with profitabil-

ity achieved by some of the largest oil firms in the nation, firms that were said to be making too much money and ones against which an excess profit tax was levied. In some years tested, oil firms had *lower* profitability than electric companies in Ohio (see Texaco, 1975–78); yet, governmental regulatory authorities imposed an excess profits tax on the oil industry and granted higher rates (prices) in the electric industry. Neither position taken by the respective regulatory authority appears justifiable based on profits of the industry in question.

8. The probability appears low that *(a)* increased control or *(b)* management audits (or both) will reduce electric company profitability; instead, such factors serve to increase costs which, in turn, cause prices of electricity to rise and revenue of electric companies to rise even further.

9. If electric industry profits are too high or too low, they are that way because of a number of factors only one of which is price, rate, or the so-called rate base. Increases or decreases in any *one* of the following variables will not cause electric company (industry) profitability to rise or fall: *(a)* price, *(b)* cost (tax), *(c)* asset turnover, *(d)* net operating margin, *(e)* return on investment, or *(f)* equity multiplier. Additional government control(s) of any one or more of these variables could serve primarily to interfere with an industry that could be allowed to develop efficient market mechanisms.

10. It might be premature to call electric industry profits too high or too low for, as indicated herein, these profits compare favorably with profits generated by selected industries. However, if one were to quantify the relative political, economic, and other risks associated with electric industry activity vis-a-vis other industries with which electric firms have been compared, electric profits may be marginally higher than profits earned by other firms and industries.

11. If electric company profits (ROE) are high and have been providing a fair return to the investor, on what grounds do additional rounds of rate relief rest?

17.

The Price Differential between Domestic and Imported Steel*

JAMES M. JONDROW
DAVID E. CHASE
CHRISTOPHER L. GAMBLE

INTRODUCTION

Since the late 1950s, the quoted price of imported steel has generally been below the domestic price. This fact has been a recurrent source of worry for steelworkers and producers who fear that imports will force many domestic mills out of business. Congress seems to share this concern, as indicated by its acquiescence to a series of barriers to steel imports, such as the "voluntary" quotas of 1969–72 and the recent trigger prices. Little help is expected from buyer loyalty to American steel: Steel is steel, and the buyer need only find the cheapest source.

The concerns of the steel producers and workers seem, at first, well founded in economic theory: Identical products cannot sell at different prices; either the higher price will fall to meet the competition, or production of the higher priced one will stop.

But the production of domestic steel has not stopped, even though domestic producers have lost some ground to imports. Since the late 1950s, when imports first became low priced, the demand for imports

* *Journal of Business* 55, no. 3 (1982), pp. 383–97.

has grown steadily—and sometimes suddenly, as in 1968. Still, the amazing story is not that imports have increased but that they have increased slowly. In 1962, imports accounted for 6 percent of the U.S. market. Fourteen years later, they accounted for 14 percent. Each year, on average, imports have increased their share of the market by less than 1 percentage point.

Why have imports grown so gradually? That is the central question of this paper. We explore two answers, one briefly, the other in more detail. The first possible answer is that imports only seem to be lower in price but actually are not. This is not a trivial possibility. Quoted prices of domestic products are often said to differ from actual transaction prices. Import-price quotes are at least as suspect. The second possible answer is that buyers do not consider imported steel to be a perfect substitute for domestic steel—to them, steel is not steel.

It turns out that one major difference between imported and domestic steel is in lead time. To find out why the longer lead time for imported steel is an important detriment, we apply a standard model of optimal inventory levels.

The inventory problem and its relation to price differentials have been the subjects of several recent studies. A theoretical study by DeVany argues that a monopolist can raise his price by expanding capacity and shortening waiting times for his customers. Gould considers the case of a competitive equilibrium in which some suppliers offer high prices and short waiting times and others offer low prices and long waiting times. This offers an explanation of the observed multiplicity of prices, an alternative to the usual explanation that buyers have imperfect information about prices. A number of other empirical implications are also noted. A study by Carlton examines the social welfare implications of a competitive equilibrium in which both consumers and producers trade off waiting time against price (for consumers) or cost (for producers). Our work can be viewed as an empirical counterpart of these studies.

The possibility that buyers distinguish between imported and domestic products, even when their physical characteristics seem to be the same, has implications for both policy and research.

The implication for policy is that imports will not dominate the market suddenly; the gains derived from removing trade barriers need not come at the cost of sudden, massive layoffs in domestic industries. The adjustment of employment comes only after substantial warning.

The implication for research is that the demand for imports should be specified as a function of (at least) two distinct prices—the import price and the domestic price. For examples of empirical work using this assumption, see Kreinin; Houthakker and Magee; Magee; Price and Thornblade; Burgess; Richardson; Murray and Ginman; Jondrow, Chase, and Gamble; and Crandall. (Some of the theory of functional form under imperfect substitution has been worked out by Armington.) These demand curves, by incorporating imperfect substitution, make possible a model of the import market that includes the assumption of extremely elastic supply curves for both domestic and imported steel. Indeed, estimated supply curves for manufactured products do tend to be quite elastic. Empirical supply curves regarding imports are almost entirely absent from the economic literature, but the limited share of U.S. imports in world consumption of most manufactured goods suggests that the "small country" assumption of elastic supply is applicable.

The distinction between imported and domestic products also has implications for the theoretical analysis of international trade. It argues that imports and domestic products are often imperfect substitutes, a thought that runs counter to the perfect-substitution assumption of much theoretical work.

IS THE PRICE DIFFERENTIAL ILLUSORY?

Economic data are widely regarded as imperfect. This is especially true of price data and even more of import price data. Import prices are typically estimated by prices quoted in trade journals (such as prices of steel in *Metal Bulletin*) or by unit values (the ratio of value to tonnage). Accordingly, it would not be at all surprising to find that the price differential between imported and domestic steel is a statistical artifact.

Instead, we found evidence of a genuine price differential. Documentation comes from a number of sources, including formal studies, informal accounts in the press, congressional hearings, a survey conducted for the U.S. International Trade Commission, and our interviews with steel purchasers and producers.

In one study, for instance, Rosenberg compares price lists on "U.S. base price and extras" with cost plus insurance and freight (CIF) prices of four popular types of Japanese and European steel. Some of the quoted differentials are small: For example, the 1970 U.S. price of hot-rolled sheet was 4 percent above the import price. Other differentials were large: 16.2 percent in March 1971 for hot-rolled sheet and 13.3 percent in mid-1972.

In another study, Kravis and Lipsey use interviews with purchasers to compare export prices for various countries in selected years between 1953 and 1964. If the U.S. export price was the same as the internal price, domestic steel sold for about 30 percent more than Japanese steel in 1964.

Reports in the press also indicate that at times there has been a substantial difference between the prices of domestic and imported steel. *The Wall Street Journal,* for example, reported in 1975 that "the era of cheap foreign steel has gone the way of cheap foreign oil." An earlier article in *The Wall Street Journal* described the beginning of a price war among major steel companies, precipitated by price shading meant to bring domestic prices closer to foreign prices.

In 1968, the staff of the Senate Committee on Finance reported the results of a survey of domestic steel producers; the survey included detailed information on delivered prices for domestic and imported steel. For hot- and cold-rolled carbon sheets, about which the most replies were received, the reported differential ranged from 4 percent to 35 percent. As an example, one price comparison in Michigan showed domestic hot-rolled sheets delivered at $149 per ton and imported at $107, a 28 percent differential.

The price comparisons further indicate that the differential was not purely a function of inland transportation costs. In some cases, differentials were clearly inland and substantial. For example, hot-rolled carbon sheets sold at an 18 percent differential in Kentucky, a 12 percent differential in Tennessee, and a 16 percent differential in Missouri.

During congressional hearings in 1968, a major importer reported delivered prices for imported and domestic steel covering the period 1965–68. The quoted differentials were usually smaller than those quoted by U.S. producers, but there were still differentials. For example, in the period 1965–68, imported hot-rolled coils sold at 7.0–22.3 percent less than equivalent domestic steel. More recently, a mail survey by the U.S. International Trade Commission found differentials in stainless-steel plate ranging from 0 percent to 30 percent at various times between 1971 and 1975.

IS THE PRICE DIFFERENTIAL BETWEEN IMPORTED AND DOMESTIC STEEL ACCOUNTED FOR BY DIFFERENCES IN CHARACTERISTICS?

We tested in several ways the hypothesis that imports differed from domestic steel. First, we checked to find out whether imported steel was described as different from domestic steel in the technical literature. Second, we asked buyers and sellers of steel. Third, for two characteristics, security of supply and lead time between order and delivery, we made illustrative calculations of the added costs to users of imported steel. Fourth, we estimated a hedonic price regression to see how well the prices of steel from alternative sources of supply, including sources other than imports and domestic mills, could be explained by these same two characteristics.

Before reviewing this evidence, it is useful to list the characteristics that may distinguish imported and domestic steel: (1) quality of products, (2) delivery lead time, (3) certainty of delivery lead time, (4) credit conditions, (5) required size of purchase, (6) availability and cost of nonbase extras, (7) familiarity with domestic product, (8) transactions cost, and (9) security of supply.[1]

---

[1] "Security of supply," as used here, means that the consumer is assured of a specified price in the future and that he can obtain his normal supply.

Evidence of Differing Characteristics in the Literature

The literature cites several respects in which domestic and imported steel differ. Hogan, in his history of the steel industry, cites as disadvantages of imported steel (in the mid-1960s): long lead time, the need to buy in large quantities, the cost of unloading and unwrapping, and, in some cases, unknown quality. Miller says that purchasers regard the availability of foreign steel as "at best a cyclical phenomenon" and that imports cannot match the day-to-day continuity of supply provided by domestic sources, continuity that purchasers consider crucial. An importer testified at 1968 congressional hearings that imports must sell below domestic products because of slower delivery, problems of communication, transport hazards, and the necessity for users to carry large inventories to compensate for inflexible delivery schedules. Kravis and Lipsey, though they do not cite evidence about steel, do note that, with aluminum, one large consumer switched to domestic suppliers despite a 5–10 percent differential, because relying on imports meant that he had to maintain costly stocks to provide a margin of safety.

Finally, Crandall, in his recent book on the steel industry, explains his finding of less than perfect substitution between domestic and imported steel as an indication "that the U.S. steel market consists of two types of buyers: those desiring long-term arrangements with secure domestic suppliers and those more interested in minimizing their short-term cost of steel."

Evidence from Interviews

For additional information about the relative importance of various characteristics, we spoke with a number of buyers, sellers, and others close to the steel market—not to generate data for statistical analysis but to elicit comments from people close to the steel market.

The reasons most often given for buying or not buying imports are listed in Table 1. These reasons reinforced the impression that, except for the shortage period, imports have usually been priced well below domestic steel. One respondent noted that "in most instances, foreign steel has to be sold at lower than domestic prices, or there is no reason for purchase." Most respondents felt that import quality was higher (i.e., less was unusable because of such defects as cracks and blemishes) and speculated that this higher quality was a result of the higher cost of reshipping imports, if defects caused them to be returned. A number of interviewees said that foreign steel shipments has longer lead times—3 months rather than 1 month or less—and were less reliable. Security of supply, the requirement to make large purchases, "buy American" clauses, and the need for large inventories also worked against imports. (We interpret the larger inventories as a consequence of longer lead time; details are discussed later.) Credit conditions, information, and transaction costs were not considered important differences between imported and domestic steel.

TABLE 1
Interview Responses to Questions about Factors Influencing Choice between Imports and Domestic Steel

Characteristic of Imports	Most Important Positive	Positive for Imports	Negative for Imports	Most Important Negative	Not Important
Security of supply		2	4	8	2
Delivery lead time			15	1	1
Certainty of lead time			15		1
Required size of purchase			10		4
Inventory requirements			10		3
"Buy American" clause			8		3
Availability and cost of nonbase extras			7		4
Familiarity with domestic products			3		7
Relative transaction cost			3		11
Credit conditions		2	3		9
Quality		8	3	1	7
Price	15	1			1

Note: The columns do not sum to the number of interviews (28) because different interviews concentrated on different questions. A single interview typically covered about half the questions.

THE COST OF SOME CHARACTERISTICS OF IMPORTS

In the following sections, we analyze two of the competitive disadvantages of imports: supply insecurity and long lead time. Our purpose is to provide rough estimates of the cost that purchasers might plausibly impute to these disadvantages. The estimates require strong assumptions and will therefore be of interest primarily for their orders of magnitude.

The Cost of Insecurity of Import Supply

Our interviews indicated that insecurity of import supply is a major selling point for domestic steel. In this section, we limit the analysis to one aspect of "supply insecurity": the situation in which import prices rise sharply and domestic producers do not accept new customers. The assumption is that the relative prices of domestic and foreign steel do not vary enough over the cycle to eliminate excess demands or supplies. Instead, domestic suppliers provide implicit insurance against shortages by charging higher prices than foreign producers when demand is slack and allowing steady customers to buy at the (then) lower prices when demand is temporarily heavy. Indeed, during the steel shortages of 1973–74, domestic mills allocated supplies on the basis of 1972 purchases. The premium paid for this "insurance" may explain part of the price discount on imports during periods of slack demand.

To estimate the appropriate discount for imported steel when demand is slack and import prices are low, we make use of a strong assumption: When import prices are high, users cannot switch to domestic steel.[2] Given this assumption, a first approximation to the appropriate discount in slack periods is one that equates the average price of imports over the cycle to the average price of domestic steel.

But this first approximation omits several facts about the steel market. First, when steel prices are particularly high (during boom periods), some users can substitute other factors of production. Hence, their loss of profits is not so great as would first appear.[3] Second, import prices tend to be high during boom times, when, presumably, output prices are higher. Some allowance must, therefore, be made for the fact that imports become expensive at exactly the time when output demand is heaviest. Therefore, instead of calculating the price differential that equalizes the import and domestic *price* averages over the business cycle, we calculate the differential that equalizes *profits*.

Our method for estimating the equal-profit differential is shown in Figure 1. Line *D1* represents the demand for imports under boom conditions, and line *D2* represents slack demand. Both curves are drawn holding the domestic price constant at *p*. The demand curves reflect our assumption that steel users do not switch back and forth between domestic and imported steel, that they act instead as though bound to one source of supply by an implicit contract, and that they rarely negotiate new contracts. The demand curves, accordingly, do not represent substitutions between imported and domestic steel.

Suppose that during a shortage, the import price is *pm*. If the user has specialized in domestic steel, he can purchase domestic steel at price *p*. A consumer-surplus-type measure of the lost profits of import users relative to domestic users is equal to area *A + B*. To make up for this loss, the import purchaser requires some discount during nonshortage times *(pm')*. This discount yields the purchaser a gain in profits measured by the area to the left of the nonshortage demand curve *(D2)* between

---

[2] We also assume that imports are not bought when cheap and then stored. As will be seen later, the cost of storing steel for several years would be prohibitive. Hence, storing is limited to short periods.

[3] This would suggest that, *ceteris paribus*, buyers with close substitutes for steel would be more willing to buy imported steel than those with no good alternatives. Crandall found that imports of hot- and cold-rolled sheet steel—for which aluminum and other materials may be substituted—are more price sensitive than are imports of structural steel, steel plate, and steel bars.

FIGURE 1
The Difference in Profit from Using Imported and Domestic Steel

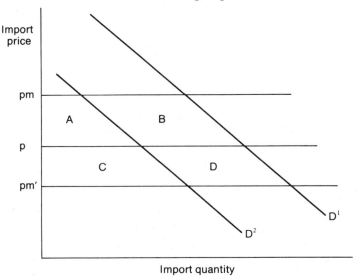

Import quantity

prices p and pm'. Ignoring present value considerations, the appropriate nonshortage import price is the one that equates area $A + B$ with area C, where each area is weighted by the frequency with which it is expected to occur.

Though this graphical analysis describes two periods, the actual calculations of the discount are made for each quarter of a typical cycle. We calculated the discount by simulating a simplified quarterly model of the market for imported and domestic steel. By successive simulations of the model, we find the discount that foreign producers must offer during slack periods to provide purchasers with the same present value of profits they would enjoy if they bought domestic steel.

The Model. The model includes six equations: one expressing the demand for imported steel, two describing domestic and foreign steel production, one for world steelmaking capacity, and two describing the prices of domestic and foreign steel.

The units of measurement for the variables can be chosen for convenience, provided only that the prices of imported and domestic steel are based on the same quantity units. Hence, the equations are so written that several of the variables are indices with value 1 in the first period of simulation: world capacity (k), the domestic steel price (p), and the U.S. price of steel-using commodities (py). The time trend (t) begins at 0 and increases by 1 each quarter. For the other variables, units are determined by the equations:

import demand:

$$m = \left(\frac{pm}{py}\right)^{-.345} y;$$ (1)

output of steel-using commodities in the United States:

$$Y = e^{.006\,t}\{1 + .054 \text{ sine } [.449(t + 7)]\};$$ (2)

world steel output:

$$s = e^{.006\,t}\{1 + .050 \text{ sine } [.449(t + 7)]\};$$ (3)

world steelmaking capacity:

$$k = e^{.006\,t};$$ (4)

domestic prices:

$$p = ae^{.026\,t};$$ (5)

import prices:

$$pm = Ae^{.026\,t}\left(\frac{s}{k}\right)^{1.84}$$ (6)

Equation (1) says that import demand (m) depends on the price of imports relative to the price of output (pm/py) and on the level of output (y) in the steel-using industries. The form of the equation can be derived from the assumption of a constant elasticity of substitution (CES) production function for output (y). That demand is proportional to output results from an assumption of constant returns to scale. The elasticity of substitution (.345) was estimated empirically by Jondrow.

Equations (2) and (3) describe trends and cycles in the output of steel-using commodities in the United States (y) and in world steel output(s). Both are assumed to grow exponentially at 0.602 percent per quarter, the rate of growth of nonresidential investment in the United States, used here as a proxy for the rate of growth of steel-using activity, domestic and foreign. The growth rate is calculated as a least-squares trend in the log of investment, 1966:III–1973:III, peak to peak over two cycles. Cycles about the trend are introduced by a sine wave. The length of the wave is 14 quarters, since the two investment cycles cover 28 quarters.

The cycle in world steel output was assumed to coincide with the cycle in U.S. output of steel-using commodities but with differing amplitudes. The amplitude of the U.S. cycle was estimated from the two cycles discussed earlier; the amplitude of the world cycle was estimated from the amplitude of cycles in world utilization over the period from 1956 to 1976. Accordingly, the parameters determining amplitude of the foreign and domestic cycles are different, 0.050 and 0.054, respectively. Each cycle is shifted 7 quarters by use of $t + 7$ as an argument in the sine functions of Equations (2) and (3). This simply begins the cycle at the beginning of the trough, when the import price drops below its trend. World steelmaking capacity is assumed to be a simple exponential trend (eq. [4]), with the rate of growth equal to that for world steel output. It is measured as an index, set equal to 1 in the first period of the simulation.

U.S. prices of steel (p) and steelmaking output (y) are both assumed to grow by 2.6 percent per quarter. This was calculated as the least-squares trend in the logarithm of wholesale price index from the first quarter of 1972—when recent inflation began to exceed 5 percent—to the second quarter of 1977. Historically, any price response of domestic steel to demand fluctuations has been mild; therefore, no influence of demand on price is built into the basic model. We do consider a variation with mild price response.

The price of imported steel (Equation [6] in the model) has the same rate of growth as the price of domestic steel. In addition, the import price shows a strong response to world market conditions, as measured by the ratio of world steel production to world capacity. The coefficient in this ratio, 1.84, is taken from Jondrow.

The remaining parameter (α) is so adjusted that the lower prices of imports during troughs offset the premium during booms, in the sense that the present value of profits is the same whether imported or domestic steel is used. To discount, we first deflate by the price of steel-using output, then use a real rate of return of 7 percent, a rate consistent with long-term, real returns on securities listed on the New York Stock Exchange.

For individual quarters, the added profit from using imports is the area to the left of the demand for imports and between the import price and the domestic price, illustrated earlier as area $A + B$ in Figure 1. To make numerical estimates of this area, we integrate the demand for imports (Equation [1]) between the import and domestic price. This integral is

$$\frac{y \, py^{.345}}{(1 - .345)py} \, (p^{1-.345} - pm^{1-.345}).$$

Parameter α is adjusted until the present value of this integral sums to 0 over the cycle. Once this has been done, there are a number of outputs of the simulation over the cycle. We report only the one of major interest, the price differential in the trough of the cycle, 9 percent. Suppliers of imports must offer a 9 percent discount during the trough of the cycle to compensate purchasers for the insecurity of import supply. This result assumes that the U.S. price does not respond to demand.

An alternative assumption of mild responsiveness in price[4] lowers the discount from 9 percent to 8 percent.

The Costs of Long Lead Times to Importers

That larger inventories will be needed is suggested by several characteristics of imports, including longer waiting times, less certainty about waiting time, and larger order requirements. In this section, we focus on longer lead time, and we use a standard inventory model to estimate the higher inventory cost. (We do not make corresponding estimates for larger order requirements or uncertainty about waiting time.)

One basic question is this: Why do longer lead times increase costs at all? If the lead time is longer, why not just plan earlier? The answer is that planning far in advance is costly. One important cost is the risk that predictions will be inaccurate and that too much or too little will be ordered. This risk can plausibly be expected to be higher for predictions that reach farther into the future.

Application of Inventory Model. The inventory model used is a standard one, based on trade-offs among three costs: the costs of ordering, the costs of storing inventories (including carrying charges), and the costs of running out of the material (outage costs). If inventories are large, the storage costs are high and the outage costs low; if inventories are small, storage costs are low, but outages are more frequent and costly. The inventory model tells how to minimize the expected sum of these costs by selecting an appropriate average level of inventory, size of order, and rule for when to reorder.

The model used is described in detail in Hadley and Whitin. These inputs are required: (1) *Expected lead-time demand:* This is the expected demand for the product between placement of the order and receipt of the material. (2) *The standard deviation of lead-time demand:* The variation in lead-time demand comes from two sources—variation in demand per period and variation in the lead time around its mean. (3) *The form of lead-time demand:* We use a normal distribution. When substantial probability is associated with negative demand, the distribution is truncated at 0. (4) *Unit inventory cost:* This is the cost of holding one unit of inventory for 1 year, expressed as a percentage of purchase price. (5) *The cost of ordering:* This is the transaction cost. (6) *The cost of outage:* This is the cost of not having material when it is needed.

In applying the model, we had data on only some of the parameters. To derive values for the unknown parameters, we used the observed levels of inventory held by steel purchasers, 1.82 months. (This is the

---

[4] The specific responsiveness was that a change in capacity utilization from .9 to .95 leads to a 1 percent change in price.

ratio of end-of-quarter inventories to consumption, each averaged over the period from 1970 to 1975.) This observed level allowed us to solve the model backward to determine permissible values of the unknown parameters. Though any number of sets of parameters can be derived in this way, the overall results of this section are not greatly affected by the specific combinations of parameters we chose. The parameters we used to estimate inventory costs are shown in Table 2.

Using these inputs, the model projects an average inventory level of 1.82 months (the parameters were so chosen as to ensure this), an order size of 103 tons, and, most important, an annual inventory cost of 3.2 percent of the purchase price. It is this last cost that must be compared with the corresponding cost of imports.

To estimate the corresponding costs for users of imported steel, we assume that the expected lead time increases from one to three months while the variance of lead time remains unchanged. Because lead time is longer, predictions must be made farther into the future, and errors in prediction increase. Hence, the variance of lead-time demand grows, even though the variance of lead time itself does not.

The question now becomes, By how much will this variance increase? To derive the increase in variance, we assumed that the errors of prediction increase proportionately with the length of projections. Clearly, this assumption cannot hold for predictions far into the future without implying massive errors. Yet the assumption is reasonable for a period of one–three months, the range of interest in this paper. The assumption about the dependence of errors on the length of projection is important. We checked it by examining recent projections of total steel production in the United States made by a large econometric model and found that the assumption predicted well relative to the assumption that the size of the error is uncorrelated with the length of time to be projected.

TABLE 2
Parameters for Inventory Model: Manufacturers Using Domestic Steel

Parameter	Value
Expected lead-time demand (tons)*	100
Standard deviation of lead-time demand (tons)†	50
Unit inventory cost (%)‡	16.5
Observed level of inventories (months)§	1.82
Cost of outage ($)†	550
Cost of ordering ($)†	200

* Arbitrary. The absolute figure is unimportant. What matters is the relation to the standard deviation of lead-time demand.

† These parameters were chosen as a set to generate the observed level of inventories (see text).

‡ The sum of interest cost (7%), housing cost (6.8%), obsolescence (1.5%), and inventory taxes and insurance (1.2%). All except the interest cost are drawn from "How the Steel Center Institute Figures Carrying Charges," *Purchasing World* 16 (July 1972), p. 82.

§ The ratio of end-of-quarter inventories to monthly consumption, both averaged from 1970 to 1975. Raw data are from *Survey of Current Business.*

(The proportional increase in error can also be generated by the assumption that future demand is a random walk.

These assumptions allowed us to adjust the parameters of the inventory model so they describe importers. The expected lead time was lengthened from one month to three months, expected lead-time demand was increased from 100 tons to 300, and the standard deviation of lead-time demand was increased from 50 tons to 248 tons.

With the new parameters for import users, the inventory model predicts an optimal inventory level of 7.47 months, an optimal order size of 228 tons, and, most important, an inventory cost of 11.9 percent of price. Because inventory costs are 11.9 percent of purchase price for import users and 3.2 percent for domestic users, inventory costs associated with lead-time differences can explain a price differential of about 8.7 percent.

An Interpretation of the Estimates

We have suggested that for imports the combined costs of supply insecurity and long lead times are about 18 percent of price, each type of cost accounting for about 9 percent. But imports are not necessarily priced 18 percent below domestic steel. Different prospective purchasers have different costs of using imports. For example, a purchaser whose output experiences large cyclical fluctuations in demand will, everything being equal, find it costlier to use imports because the cost of supply insecurity is higher. Similarly, a manufacturer who produces steel-using articles to order rather than for stock may be able to predict his demand several months ahead and hence will experience a lower inventory cost from using imports. Because the costs of imports vary among users, the differential is not fixed; it takes different values for different purchasers. At a small differential, there are few purchasers; at a larger differential, there are more.

Our estimates refer to a "typical" user of imported steel. Suppose, for illustration, that this user is the median in terms of the differential he requires before switching to imports, then the 18 percent differential we have calculated gains imports a 50 percent market share. Because the current share is much smaller, generating it requires a smaller price differential.

Evidence from Hedonic Regressions

If imported steel must cost less than domestic steel because of lead time and supply insecurity, other forms of steel with these same disadvantages would also sell at discounts, and sources of supply with favorable characteristics would sell at a premium above domestic steel. We considered five sources of supply: major mills, small mills, importers, warehouses, and brokers.

To see how well these prices can be explained by lead time and insecurity of supply, we made use of a regression with pooled data covering all five sources of supply and every quarter of the period 1973:I–1975:IV but omitting the shortage quarters, 1973:III–1974:IV. (Not reported are the coefficients on a set of dummy variables, one for each time period except the first.) The estimated equation is as follows:

$$P = 11.9 - .206S - .49T, \; R^2 = .54,$$
$$(17.0) \; (-1.7) \; (3.1)$$

where P is the price per hundred pounds. An attempt was made to incorporate discounts and premiums from list price. The source of the adjustment for discounts was the same as for lead time, and the two measures, therefore, refer to the same "typical" transaction. Security of supply, S, is stated as the difference (in 1967 dollars) between the highest price and the lowest price in the period 1973:I–1975:IV. The lead time in months is T. Lead time was assumed to be 0 for brokers and warehouses. Times for domestic mills were obtained from articles in *American Metal Market*. It was assumed that times for small mills were the same as for large mills. The articles in *American Metal Market* were quite descriptive, and we think we have good information on major mills and imports. Though information about small mills was much less firm, the assumption of equality with major mills seems reasonable.

The serious problems of identification with hedonic regressions are well known. Still, to the extent that the regression represents the preferences of purchasers, the hypothesized effect of lead time receives strong support, and the hypothesized effect for supply insecurity receives some support. Here, is a rough idea of the orders of magnitude involved: For 1973:I, the regression predicts that imports had to be priced 8.3 percent below the domestic mill price because of insecurity of supply, and that an additional 10.6 percent discount was needed because of longer lead time; both figures are close to our earlier estimates.

SUMMARY

In this paper, we have considered two attempts to explain why domestic steel retains most of the market, even though imports usually cost less. One hypothesis is that the price differential is entirely a consequence of difficulties in measurement. The evidence, drawn from the literature and interviews, does not support this hypothesis; there usually is a real difference in price. A second hypothesis is that imports must be priced below domestic steel because of unfavorable service characteristics, such as long lead times and insecurity of supply. This hypothesis is supported by evidence from a variety of sources: discussions in the literature, interviews with buyers and sellers of steel, illustrative calculations of the cost (to import users) of two characteristics, and a hedonic regression involving alternative sources of steel supply.

18.

Decentralization and Intracompany Pricing*

JOEL DEAN

A fist fight determined the intracompany transfer price policy that is in effect today in a major oil company. The issue was the price at which gasoline would be transferred from the company's refinery to its marketing division.

The present heads of the marketing and refining divisions had witnessed, as loyal but appalled lieutenants, the contentious negotiations that culminated in the fight. When these two men came to power, they vowed that their interdivisional bliss would not be marred by any arguments over intracompany pricing as had their predecessors'.

They finally found a way to abolish all disagreements about transfer prices. They simply abolished transfer prices, thereby neatly tossing out the baby with the bath.

This story—now a legend in the company—is probably exaggerated, and other events certainly contributed to the outcome. It does show, however, that the subject of this article is as disturbing as it is important: how and where to set prices for products that are transferred between divisions (or between different stages of processing and distribution) inside the company.

Our industrial system today is made up of many large, multiple-product, multiple-process companies. As these companies have expanded, it has become generally recognized that the best pattern for

*Reprinted by permission of the Harvard Business Review. "Decentralization and Intracompany Pricing" by Joel Dean (July/August 1955). Copyright © 1955 by the President and Fellows of Harvard College; all rights reserved.

their managerial organization is one of decentralization, i.e., the setting up of more or less autonomous operating divisions within a company. But as more and more large companies have adopted divisional management, they are finding that splitting up the enterprise and exhorting the divisional managers to go out and set new records for sales or production does not always accomplish the hoped-for profit results.

For an autonomous division to be an economically effective operation it has to follow the same basic rules of behavior as any independent firm competing with other independent firms, and this implies the same standards of economic performance—profits. But how can it be held to such competitive standards if there is no sound way to price the products transferred to it or from it in dealings with other divisions of the same company? In that question lies the reason for this article.

In the course of the discussion I shall set forth these propositions:

1. Transfer prices are necessary for almost all large companies. Trying to do without them sacrifices so much that it is no solution at all.

2. Intracompany price discrimination is not good business, either for the individual firm or for private enterprise in general.

3. There is need of a new system of transfer prices featuring: (a) profit centers with operational independence, access to sources and markets, separable costs and revenues, and profit intent and (b) competitive pricing among these centers.

4. Such a system has many advantages. It brings the division manager's interests closer to those of top management, provides a more accurate basis for evaluating his performance, bulwarks his independence, and gives him sound guides in purchasing and marketing decisions.

5. Most present systems for setting transfer prices, by contrast, are inadequate. They employ economically indefensible methods, keep many losses hidden, and have a negative value in the making of management decisions.

6. It takes time and patience to install competitive transfer prices. Top management will find it easier to make the change-over if it follows eight rules drawn from experience. Executives should also be prepared to meet certain objections which critics are likely to raise.

Here are the key terms which will be used in this article:

1. *Transfers* mean movement of product between operating units within the largest policy-making unit, regardless of corporate entities; for example, transfers within the family of companies represented by the Cities Service Oil Company or among the divisions of E. I. du Pont de Nemours & Company.

2. *Product* should be broadly interpreted to include raw materials, components, and intermediate products and services as well as finished products in the ordinary sense of the word.

3. *Transfer price* refers to the net value per unit that records the transaction for the purposes of operating statements.

NEED FOR SOUND PRICING

Why not do the same as the oil company referred to at the start of this article and dispose of the problem altogether by doing without transfer prices?

For most large firms this solution sacrifices too much. Our peace-loving oil company, for example, now has no knowledge of the cost and value of gasoline, heating oil, and other petroleum products at various stages of refining and distribution. Abolition of transfer prices prevents meaningful measurement of the profits of individual operating units, such as refineries, bulk stations, and service stations. It also prevents accurate estimates of the earnings on proposed capital projects. Basic decisions about market penetration, pricing, and capital expenditures are cut adrift from cost or profit moorings. And there is no way to assure that the product will be directed where it will produce the highest dollar return, either as among alternative processes or as among alternative channels and levels of distribution. The river of crude oil suddenly goes underground, disappearing from cost and profit sight, and comes up again at the consumers' doors, millions of processing dollars away.

So abolition is not the right answer. In fact, it is no solution at all. For most large companies the problem remains one of learning how to live with and use some system of internal transfer pricing. Sound transfer prices give division managers both the economic basis and the incentives for correct decisions. They also provide top management with profit and loss information indispensable for evaluation of the results of complex combinations of managerial skills and diverse facilities. Thus correct transfer prices are the basis for attaining the managerial decentralization sought by virtually every large American enterprise today.

One reason this has been such a problem for executives is that no systematic analysis of transfer pricing principles and policies has, so far as I can learn, heretofore been available.

Transfer prices have significance for public policy as well as for private policy. Criticism of vertical integration has focused on pricing of intracompany transfers. It is alleged that discrimination within the company hurts competition. For example, oil refineries are supposed to gain an advantage by charging their marketing affiliates lower prices than their independent customers, and aluminum and copper producers are supposed to benefit similarly in favoring their fabricating affiliates. Actually, shoving the profits around inside the company and into safe corners serves no useful purpose and succeeds only in confusing both operating managers and top management. But the fact that intracompany price discrimination is not the good business that many companies think it is hardly makes public criticism less damaging.

Fortunately, the correct economic solution for the company's managerial problem—transfer prices determined competitively—also solves this public policy problem.

NEW CONCEPT

How can the hodgepodge of intracompany pricing methods that is found in many large companies today be avoided? What is an economically realistic basis for intracompany pricing applied uniformly throughout the whole company? The answer lies in a new system of executive control which has the two intermeshed features of profit centers and competitive transfer prices.

Profit Centers

Before responsibility for profits or losses can be assigned, it is necessary that the management of the particular operation be in fact made primarily responsible for its economic performance. Four characteristics distinguish this type of autonomous unit from service functions.

1. Operational Independence. Each profit center must be an independent operating unit, and its manager must have a large measure of control over most if not all operational decisions that affect his profits. This means that he must have considerable discretion in determining the volume of production, methods of operation, product mix, and so forth, subject only to broad policy discretion from top management. The areas of the company where this independence of action cannot exist should properly be considered as service centers. For them, the volume and character of services rendered are to a large extent determined by decisions originating outside their division; an example is the public relations department.

2. Access to Sources and Markets. The profit-center manager must have control over all decisions relating to sources and markets. He must be genuinely free to buy and sell in alternative markets both outside the company and inside. For example, the manager of the canned meat division of an integrated meat packer must know that it is just as respectable to buy uncured hams outside the company as to buy from the company's own pork division.

Freedom to trade is essential to the new concept because it dissolves alibis. Brother buyer and seller have ample incentive to reach agreement on prices if neither is restricted to a particular source or market. They have almost no incentive, and everybody feels cheated, if these channels are predetermined.

The required access to sources and markets cannot be created by edict; outside sources or markets must either be there or be capable of creation. To illustrate, crank shaft and other major components of an automobile engine require highly specialized machine tools already in the possession of the supplying division. It is impracticable to get a sound figure on what it would cost to supplant the intracompany manufacturing source, since an outside supplier will not make a realistic bid unless the company signifies its willingness to make a long-run commitment sufficient to cover his installation of major facilities. Without this commitment, freedom to trade in such cases is meaningless.

3. Separable Costs and Revenues. A profit center must be able to split off its costs and find an economically realistic price of the end products; otherwise measurement of its profit performance is impossible. This requirement eliminates service-type staff activities from consideration.

4. Management Intent. A distinction between a profit center and a service center can also be drawn in terms of management's intention. Only if the basic goal is profits should the operation be treated as a profit center.

A service activity may contribute as much or more *in fact* to the company's profitability as an operating division, but still not qualify because top management does not and should not judge its performance solely on the basis of profitability. For example, the legal department could be run as a captive law firm and be judged by its performance in producing profits by chasing ambulances inside the company. But despite its ability to meet the requirements of operational independence, access to outside customers and talent, and separable costs and revenues, the legal department should not be made a profit center because individual decisions cannot be controlled by the profit motive.

In surveying operations within the company to determine which should be profit centers, management may want to restudy the fundamental objectives of each operation. The proclivity to view many activities as service center lean-tos for major divisions or the company as a whole should not lead top executives to ignore the advantages of conducting every possible operation as a profit center. Particular care should be taken in marginal cases like this one—

A captive steel mill that produces a substantial part of the requirements of a large manufacturer of equipment turns in a poor profit performance. This is due in part to the fact that it is not judged by profits alone; management's intent is to meet the requirements and specifications of the fabricating divisions at the expense of efficient scheduling and profitable product mix. Under these circumstances, the mill is viewed as a service function. It could, however, be operated as a profit center. While the difficulties of negotiating price premiums for special steels and special scheduling would be great, a price on the mill's unique services to the fabricating divisions would lead to correct allocation and remove the wasteful illusion that these special services are free.

To summarize, the modern integrated, multiple-product firm functions best if it is made into a sort of miniature of the competitive, free-enterprise economic system. The firm should be comprised of independent operating units that act like economic entities, free to trade outside the company as well as inside. Each such entity or profit center will, in seeking to maximize its own profits, do what will also maximize the profits of the entire company, just as individual firms in a private-enterprise society, by seeking their selfish advancement, generate the high productivity and well-being of a competitive economy.

Competitive Pricing

The underlying requisite for profit-center controls is competitive prices negotiated in arm's length bargaining by division managers who are free to go outside the company if unhappy with prices paid by or to brother division managers.

Small differences in the unit price of transferred products can make big differences in the division's profits and executive bonuses. Intracompany pricing must preserve the profit-making autonomy of the division manager so that his selfish interests will be identical with the interests of the company as a whole. This can be accomplished by following three simple principles:

1. Prices of all transfers in and out of a profit center should be determined by negotiation between buyers and sellers.
2. Negotiators should have access to full data on alternative sources and markets and to public and private information about market prices.
3. Buyers and sellers should be completely free to deal outside the company.

The practical benefits of sound transfer pricing for profit-center control are not always obvious. Many companies—especially if they are decentralized—seem to get along fine without it, never knowing what they are missing. This is because decentralization "digs gold with a pickax." In the flush of gratification for this great improvement over old authoritarian ways management may neglect the tools to get the most out of it.

In a big company there is danger that interest in making profits will be diluted as a result of managerial specialization and the separation of operation from ownership. The parochial ambitions of operating managers need to be held in check; performance should be judged in terms of alibi-proof, objectively measured profits. When transfer prices are economically correct and profit centers are properly established, top management can delegate and still have peace of mind, because the division manager's targets and incentives will be so set up that his interests are identical to those of top management.

How to protect the independence of operating divisions against the insidious encroachment of staff advice, the restrictions of policy rules, and the fettering effect of top-level supervision is an ever present problem. The fact that top management finds it necessary to protest so much about the independence of its division managers often shows how limited this independence is in reality. Competitively negotiated transfer prices bulwark the independence of operating divisions by making possible meaningful measurement of economic performance.

The harm that can be done by arbitrary and authoritative pricing of intracompany transfers is hidden. Such prices lead to sins of omission as well as sins of commission. They fail to give definitive indication of the profitability of added volume. They rob management of an economically correct basis for evaluating various profit figures. They provide a distorted and incorrect measure of the economic desirability of different channels of distribution. Bad transfer prices can also misdirect capital investment and cause friction and dissension among executives.

But negotiated competitive transfer prices can prevent these losses. They can make the division's procurement, processing, pricing, and distribution sensitive to market requirements and responsive to competitive alternatives. They provide sound guidance in making purchasing decisions, indicate the extent to which additional processing will be profitable, and direct the flow of products so as to make the greatest net profit for the company. Furthermore, the very process of negotiation avoids arbitrariness and tends to create agreement. This eliminates the cause of much friction and ill feeling.

OTHER PRICING SYSTEMS

What about existing systems of setting transfer prices? How adequate or inadequate are they? Various bases are now in use, such as:

1. *Published market prices.*   Example: uncured hams priced to the canning division at prices reported in the *National Provisioner*.
2. *Marginal cost.*   Example: electric motors transferred to the refrigerator division at cost of materials plus direct labor.
3. *Full cost plus.*   Example: gasoline transferred to the transportation division at the refineries' full costs plus a "fair" profit markup.
4. *Sales minus.*   Example: transfers of gasoline from the refinery at the retail price minus an allowance for the marketing department's services in getting it from the refinery to the customer.
5. *Traditional prices.*   Example: the transfer price of financing service, a customary 6 percent.

The choice among the different transfer pricing systems depends both on the kinds of information that are available and on the objectives that the management hopes to accomplish through the system.

If no measurement of the competitive market price exists for the intermediate product, some type of cost basis may have to be used, unless a negotiated price can be based on indirect alternatives of buying and selling units. But choice among cost bases may be narrowed by the kind of cost records used.

In the event that available information does permit a free choice, then what management wishes to accomplish by intracompany pricing should determine the system to be followed. For example, if a company wishes to use intracompany pricing as the primary means for controlling costs and profits, for measuring operational results, and for directing the product flow in the most profitable ways, some sort of market price system is clearly indicated.

Now let us examine the relative advantages and disadvantages of the different systems used today for setting transfer prices, so that we can see how they compare with the competitive pricing method advocated here.

Published Market Prices

Basing intracompany transfers on published statistical reports of market price has much merit. It often approximates the ideal of a competitive transfer pricing system. But practical difficulties arise from three sources:

1. *Conditions may make published statistics an inaccurate statement of the market price for the size, quality, timing, and location of the intracompany transaction.* Market price statistics often have systematic time lages which make them an inaccurate picture of the true market at near turning points. Also, they may represent a different quantity, grade, type of package, or duration from the intracompany transaction.

For example, published prices of intermediate products and services usually pertain to the spot price, whereas the intracompany transfer calls for a long-term contract price, which is usually lower and more stable. Thus, rates for chartered oil tankers, which fluctuate wildly, are not an adequate basis for pricing stable intracompany water transport.

Some of these deficiencies in the published market price can be partly remedied by market-determined price spreads for term contracts as opposed to spot prices, carload lots as opposed to small lots, and bulk as opposed to packaged products. But if these spreads are large, it is likely that they cannot be established objectively in a manner that will be satisfactory to buyer and seller without negotiation.

2. *The market place may not offer a real alternative for the intracompany buyer or seller.* The volume traded on the market may be so small com-

pared with intracompany transactions that an attempt to get supplies there would drive up the price. Or the quality standards of its market plan may be lower than those of the company or fail to meet the peculiarities of design and appeal of the company's own brand, so that price comparisons are futile.

3. *It may be difficult to distinguish between nominal price quotations and real ones.* No matter how honestly and carefully prices are reported, there are times when a very few strategically placed transactions can make a big difference in the published price. When these published prices affect the divisional manager's promotion and pay, he cannot be expected to be blind to opportunities to "make" the market. Cunning maneuvers of this sort are hardly in the company's interest.

Marginal Cost

Next to negotiated transfer pricing, marginal-cost pricing is most defensible economically. Under this plan transfer prices are based on the additional cost caused by the production of an additional unit of the product. Moderately close approximation to marginal cost can be made by confining costs to those that vary with volume and are traceable—i.e., direct costs. This is the best of the authoritarian pricing schemes for these reasons: (1) it determines cost of underlying processes in terms that are relevant for short-run operating decisions on pricing, promotion, and product policy; (2) the buying division has a guide as to when it is in the company's interest to acquire a product or material from outside sources so long as it knows the short-run marginal cost of producing the product inside the company; and (3) troublesome and contentious problems of assigning overhead costs to joint product operations and changing overhead loadings as a result of variations in operating rates are avoided.

Marginal-cost pricing has, however, several distinct disadvantages:

1. Divisional profit and loss statements are made meaningless as a measure of economic performance. All contributions to profits are passed along to the final operation, and therefore no profits appear for earlier divisions. This gives the last division, frequently the sales division, a big cushion for maneuvering. No wonder sales divisions like marginal-cost transfer pricing!

2. Where many divisions handle products in succession, operating management may overlook profitable changes in methods or product flows because the inefficiencies of one division are covered up by the low costs of more efficient divisions that worked on the product in earlier stages.

3. Commercial abilities that are so desirable in a well-rounded division manager are stunted under marginal-cost transfer pricing. He is isolated from the pitfalls and opportunities of the market and is confined to the role of a service division manager.

Full Cost Plus

Cost-plus pricing sets intracompany prices on the basis of the complete costs of the producing unit plus some allowance for profit. Many variations of the system, both as to the cost base and the add-on, are possible.

The commonest cost base is orthodox accounting costs for the latest period. Normal cost and standard cost are sometimes used. The add-on or profit ranges from a niggardly coverage of overheads to a markup on sales which produces a handsome return on investment. The standard for the amount of profit takes two principal forms: (a) a margin on sales and (b) a rate of return on investment. In practice, partly because of the difficulty of determining profit margins on reasonably similar operations, the margin is usually set arbitrarily.

Bare costs with no add-on were more common in the past than now. They are frequently justified on moral grounds: that it is wrong to take profit out of the hide of a brother division. Today, full cost plus a "reasonable" rate of return on the investment of the selling division appears to be gaining wider acceptance.

Supporters of full cost-plus pricing of transfers claim these conflicting virtues of the system:

1. That the company is assured of an adequate profit on the entire process if transfer prices at each stage force the addition of a profit.
2. That no company can make money by selling things to itself and allowing divisions to exploit each other; therefore prices limited to costs plus a fair margin should be used to prevent conflict and promote cooperation.
3. That cost-plus pricing assures that the economic benefits of integration will be achieved and will be passed on to the company's customers.
4. That cost-plus pricing makes the producing and supplying units attend to the business of producing cheaply without being diverted by concern about commercial problems of pricing sharply.

None of these virtues, however, minimize the fact that cost-plus pricing is arbitrary and authoritarian. As such, it provides a poor basis for evaluating division performance, it beclouds profits, and it inevitably diverts production into uneconomic channels.

Sales Minus

Basing intracompany transfer prices on what the customers pay has considerable vogue, particularly in organizations which are strongly market oriented. Transfer prices are geared to final selling prices by subtracting allowances that more or less completely provide for the costs and profits of intervening operations. For example, retail price lines of sheets and pillow cases once governed transfer prices for the textile mill subsidiary of a merchandising organization. Similarly, in the case of an integrated wholesale distribution unit, $4 was subtracted from the price paid by the retailer on a certain kind of canned food to get the transfer price from the canning factory to the distribution department. The factory allowed $2 a case for direct costs (transportation, promotion, etc.) and another $2 a case for overhead and profits.

This system has the virtue of being oriented toward the market value of the final product. However, it shifts the full impact of fluctuations in final price to the basic production units of an integrated firm, with the intermediate processing and marketing operations sheltered by an assured margin. In a buyer's market like that recently experienced in textiles, sales-minus pricing for gray goods would come close to what outside textile mills, hungry for business, could be forced to sell at. Under these supply and demand conditions, transfer prices that would approximate competitive market prices and realistically negotiated prices would result from sales-minus pricing. In a seller's market, by contrast, sales-minus pricing will undershoot the market; a division will not be able to get from intracompany transfers what it could get from outsiders or what it could negotiate at arm's length with brother divisions.

Traditional Prices

A weird throwback to medieval times when the concept of "just" price prevailed is occasionally encountered in modern business. The use of traditional prices in transfer pricing belongs in this category. An example is the costing of financial services at 6 percent in intracompany charges; such a rate has borne no relationship to the market place within the memory of today's executives.

It is hard to see any advantages in this method, beyond the fact that it is as convenient and consistent as most of the concepts of feudalism. But the other methods now in vogue are not much more useful. All have serious shortcomings; none can be relied on to produce profit-oriented decisions by division managers.

INSTALLATION AND OPERATION

We turn now to the more mundane problems of what needs to be done to install and operate competitive transfer pricing.

Comprehensive Study

A practical starting point is a systematic, impartial study of the intracompany pricing methods the company is now using, and the facts that can be marshaled concerning market prices and market price relation-

ships. The next thing to do is to lay the foundation of understanding
of the economic and management philosophy, the benefits, and the problems of this new concept of competitively negotiated intracompany dealings.

Managers of profit centers and of service centers need a new orientation—one that is pointed toward the economics of their operation rather
than exclusively toward the technology of the operation. When they
become managers of profit centers rather than merely managers of facto-
ries, they need a new set of ideas, values, and facts, with dimensions
broad enough to embrace marketplace choices and competitive return
on capital expenditures. All this takes time as well as education. Overnight installation by a presidential decree of the new transfer-price and
profit-center policy is not likely to succeed or last.

Gradual Progress

After the research and educational foundation has been laid, a program of gradual installation can be tailored to the company's needs.
The following rules should prove helpful:

1. *Widen the coverage gradually.* start with areas where competitively
negotiated pricing is easiest and take on the tougher ones as know-
how improves.

2. *Apply first to basic volume.* Start with negotiated prices on the minimum basic quantities needed for planned future production. Negotiate
term contracts for the distant future, so that both buyer and seller will
have maximum fluidity and alternatives. Then gradually move toward
arrangements for the fluctuating sector of volume for which real alternative outside sources get quite restricted. For these negotiations the trading experience and regard for long-term interests gained in previous
dealings will help to steady the bargaining by curbing temptations toward
exploitation in the short run.

3. *Establish pricing guides through research.* For products and components where the producing division has had no occasion to study market
prices and outside trading opportunities, a foundation of knowledge
must be laid so that neither brother division will be handicapped by
ignorance in negotiating a competitive price. It takes time to dig this
information up and to familiarize operating executives with its use.

4. *Set pricing limits temporarily.* These initial limits on the range of
prices over which bargaining can take place will become as vestigial as
the hip bone of a whale when the system gets into operation. But they
provide assurance and prevent undue exploitation of ignorance at the
outset. For example, a lower limit on price might be set by an estimate
of the marginal cost, and the upper limit might be the commercial price
charged outsiders plus 5 percent.

5. *Limit the volume of outside trading initially.* The freedom to trade

outside can be temporarily restricted by setting volume limits as, for instance, 75 percent inside the company, 25 percent outside the company. Those who fear that the advantages of integration will be dissipated are reassured by this expedient.

Price Mediator

One executive is needed to (a) pull together the transfer-price and profit-center investigations, (b) organize the conferences and training sessions, and (c) supervise the gradual installation of the new system of economic controls. To ease the transition, both emotionally and economically, this executive also can temporarily undertake to mediate the negotiation of some transfer prices.

Note that the price mediator should not attempt to arbitrate. The experience with price arbitration is almost universally bad. It is expensive and time consuming, and the results do not satisfy either party. Everyone feels cheated, and everyone has an alibi for his profit and volume results. Instead the mediator should aim at securing agreement by keeping the negotiations going, by supplying information, and by exercising business judgment on issues of fact as well as on commercial alternatives. For example, one transfer-price mediator in a meat packing firm reviewed and substantially deflated cost information which was burdened with fictitious charges for packaging and shipping sausage material at successive stages of processing. Up to this time the selling division had been using these costs in good faith for internal decisions as well as in transfer-price bargaining with other divisions. The delusion that these were rock-bottom incremental costs led the selling division to set its refusal price at a level which was above the market. Such a price would have led to idle facilities and would have sacrificed incremental profits if the buying division had been forced to go outside to get the supplies.

One of the functions of the mediator, particularly in the early stages of installation, is to distill the truth from conflicting, misguided, exaggerated, and prejudiced pricing facts which the negotiating parties often bring to a mediation conference. To illustrate again—in negotiating transfer prices for a pharmaceutical firm, the participants faced two major common problems: (a) the outside market was very thin, with a wide spread resulting between highest and lowest prices at which sales were made and (b) the transactions covered by this range differed from the intracompany transactions in volume, packaging, location, and so on. Quite naturally, each party came to the negotiations with a highly biased sample of market transactions to support its point of view. The triumph of the transfer-price mediator was to demonstrate to both parties that extreme prices, ranging from $.50 a pound to $1.50 a pound, were inapplicable; he managed to narrow the range within which both parties agreed that the real market lay for the transactions in question.

As profit-center managers gain experience in using the competitive pricing system and grow to appreciate its value, the effective mediator will work himself out of a job.

Term Contracts

The period over which the transfer prices are to be negotiated should be at least as long as the planning period required to design and schedule production, or to dig up satisfactory alternative outside sources, whichever time period is longer. For example, the planning and design period for automobiles is so long that in the short run, say over the next quarter, the divisions which make basic engine components have no real alternative market for their product. Similarly, the vehicle divisions could not on short notice dig up alternative outside sources for properly designed engine parts. Many operations are characterized by short-run inflexibility of alternatives especially where design, quality, and packaging must conform to rigid and publicized specifications. A product made to such specifications has passed the point of no return.

In such cases, *short*-run negotiations (less than three or four months for the automobile manufacturer) concerning transfer prices have the hallmark of bilateral monopoly; they are similar to wage-rate negotiations. They generate heat, bad temper, and rarely produce economic transfer prices that are gauged and policed by outside alternatives and freedom to use them.

But over a long period even a branded product like an automobile can properly be subject to transfer prices that have the virtues and characteristics of a free-enterprise system. If long-term specifications contracts are negotiated, the buying unit will generally be able to get outsiders to bid on products made to its requirements, and a producing unit will have a real choice—either to adapt its output to other uses or to again assume the commitments on design, volume, and productive facilities which are tied to the branded product.

Good Businessmen

Successful operation of a profit center under a miniature free-enterprise system within the corporate fold calls for talents and experience often summed up by the tag, "He is a good businessman."

These abilities need to be systematically cultivated because they are not likely to have survived in a big corporate bureaucracy where transfer prices have been authoritarian. Executives of highly centralized companies are likely to have been reared as if they were in one big happy family, in which each child has an assigned set of chores and emphasis is on cooperation and the subordination of individual desires to group interests. Some executives may have forgotten how to make independent decisions. They will need help in taking responsibility for decisions in a profit-center controlled company where anything that affects their profit is their business, where performance is judged by how much profit they can make, and where right, independent opinions quickly improve the executives' profit and loss statements.

ANSWERING OBJECTIONS

Any new system of transfer prices will be criticized, and this one particularly because it removes needed alibis and may blemish careers by exposing executives' inadequacies. In addition, it may appear to be fundamentally opposed to the reason for existence of a large multi-product corporation. Therefore anyone who is considering this new system of intracompany pricing and profit control needs to give some thought to the objections that are likely to be viewed as most telling by those who doubt. The following questions are ones which I have encountered constantly in work in the field.

"Why can't our company get along without transfer prices?" Some companies can. There is no need for management coordination through an apparatus of economic transfer prices and profit achievement measures if all complicated managerial functions can be competently exercised by one small, closely knit group of men. This was found to be true of a regional grocery chain. But very few large companies have such an administrative setup.

In some situations it may be possible to devise mathematical models which can solve empirically all the problems of allocating facilities, materials, and intermediate and finished products without continued exercise of managerial judgment and know-how. In these cases transfer prices are not essential, either. In using the new computers that are here and on the horizon management is handicapped, however, by the shortage of analytical ability and judgment needed to set up models which will adequately reflect fluid and changing alternatives at every stage.

"Why worry, since we already have that kind of transfer price?" Many companies think they have competitive transfer prices, but most of them do not. The consequences of noncompetitive transfer prices are present, but they seem to spring from such other causes as selfishness and lack of team spirit. There are two clear symptoms of noncompetitive pricing which cannot be explained away: *(a)* a continuous awareness of a conflict between the interest of the operating unit and what appears to its managers to be the interest of the company as a whole, reflected in self-congratulation for putting the company's interest before that of the division and *(b)* the prevalence of exhortations not to let transfer prices prevent the company from making money.

"Will the benefits of integration be lost?" Integration which is actually economically justified has such great and clear benefits to both buying

and selling divisions that competitive transfer pricing is not a threat. Only integration which does not produce economies—which does not profit both the buying and the selling division—will be eliminated by virtue of division buyers and sellers going outside the company. This assumes that the division managers are alert to the possible conflict between their short-run and long-run interests, both in maintaining customer relations and in having a stable and sure source of supply.

"Will cooperation be undermined?" Measuring profit-center performance on a competitive economic basis motivates each unit to do what is in its own best profit interest. These interests, if the transfer prices are determined economically and the profit centers properly defined, are identical with the interests of the company. Rivalry to make the best profit showing will certainly encourage shrewd, hard-headed negotiations, but the promotion of mutual economic interests will, as always, stimulate cooperation.

"Does perishability of a product rule out negotiable transfer pricing?" Physical perishability does not create a new kind of problem. Physical perishability causes price sacrifices, and it is this economic perishability alone that matters. Negotiated prices have proved practical for perishable products; indeed, they have been used for them in the market place for thousands of years.

"Will the system work if there is no true market price?" This does not matter. Sometimes the negotiated price will be above the general market average, sometimes below. So long as buyers and sellers are free to know and to choose competitive alternatives, the price will be mutually agreeable and will be determined by supply and demand forces for that particular kind of transaction.

Published data on market prices are likely to be too fragmentary and too unreliable to determine transfer prices; they should be used as a guide only. Sometimes negotiation leads to agreement to use the particular published price as a bench mark. However, this is not because the figure is published but because the negotiating parties agree to its economic validity.

"Will profit centers be shortsighted in their quest for gain?" No system of transfer prices and performance measurement makes judgment unnecessary in appraising the value of hanging on to a customer, and in balancing long-run and short-run interests. Shortsightedness is no more likely with good transfer prices than with bad. Profit-center managers have a big stake in their long-run future, and good supervision can clarify this stake and induce a long view when short-run profits conflict.

"Will the sales organization sell too cheaply?" The rather general mistrust of the business acumen of the marketing organization is a peculiarity of the big bureaucracy. From it stem the practices of kidding the sales organization about costs, pushing products down its throat, and rigging transfer prices to make marketing operations look like losers. The result

is the atrophy of commercial instincts sometimes associated with sales specialization.

Under the proposed system the sales organization will control factors that determine its profits; will be held responsible for the profits; and will have its profit performance measured. Given this encouragement, there is no reason to expect that salesmen should be any less capable of acting like businessmen than are engineers or accountants.

The company's interests require, not simply top price or top volume, but top profit. Sometimes a larger profit contribution comes from a bigger volume at lower price; sometimes it is the other way around. With this method, sales units will have the knowledge, the authority, and the incentive to sell the product at prices that will produce the greatest profits for themselves and therefore for the company. These advantages in turn will put the units in a better position to develop and attract men who are competent merchandisers.

CONCLUSION

Difficulties of installation and operation *can* be overcome; questions of criticism and skepticism *can* be met. Management will do well to make the necessary effort in view of the deficiencies of existing transfer pricing systems:

1. Economically indefensible methods of intracompany pricing are widely used in American industry.

2. Losses sustained from bad transfer prices do not show up on any set of books, because what would have happened under economically correct transfer prices will never be known. Anyone who has tried to restate in terms of correct transfer prices what has been reported in terms of wrong ones will testify to the practical impossibility of measuring the foregone profits. In other words, whatever losses result from noneconomic transfer prices are well and forever hidden.

3. Bad transfer prices do not necessarily lead to losses; but if they do not, it is because no attention is paid to them in making decisions. In some companies the critical decisions concerning flow of product, degree of processing, and channels and geography of distribution can be made without reference to any internal costs or prices. In such companies bad transfer prices may do no harm—they also do no good. And if the operations of these companies do not require an economically correct system of transfer prices, they probably require no intracompany pricing at all.

As a practical matter the chances are strong that an unsound system of transfer pricing *will* cause harm. For a large integrated organization with a diversified product line which is sold to a variety of industrial, commercial, and consumer market levels, the only system which will accomplish the needs of management is one based on negotiated competitive prices.

19.

Control with Fairness
in Transfer Pricing*

ROBERT G. ECCLES

Imagine the following conversation in a company president's office. He is talking with the general manager of a division selling products internally (seller), the general manager of a division buying these products (buyer), and a professor who has read everything that has ever been written about transfer pricing.

President: I wish somebody could tell me once and for all how we should do our transfer pricing. All the methods we've tried have problems, and often both the buyer and the seller claim they're being treated unfairly.

Professor: The answer is really very simple. When the product of the selling division is sold in a perfectly competitive market, the buying division should pay market price, with perhaps a discount to recognize that selling costs and other such expenses are saved on internal transactions. The buyer should be free to obtain this product either internally or from external suppliers.

Seller: That's a pretty fair arrangement. Of course, selling internally is usually more trouble than selling externally, so I don't think a discount is appropriate. After all, the buyer treats me in ways he wouldn't dare treat an outside supplier. He delays and cancels orders and demands product with short lead times. What's more, why should the company lose out on profits by buying outside when I have spare capacity?

Buyer: In the real world, Professor, there are very few perfectly competitive markets. I don't think market price is necessarily the best idea, although I agree that I should be free to buy from whoever I want. After all, my performance is measured by how well my business does. It isn't fair to hold me responsible for profits and then interfere with those kinds of decisions. I can usually get better prices, sales support, service, and technical cooperation from outside suppliers.

Professor: Well, you're right that market price isn't the best approach in imperfectly competitive markets. In that case the best method, when there is spare capacity, is to use marginal cost and require that you buy inside. That'll maximize company profits.

President: That sounds good to me.

Buyer: Our accounting system doesn't measure marginal costs, but if they're something like variable costs, I think it's fair. The price will be so much lower that I'll live with the inferior product and service I'm used to getting.

Seller: You've got to be kidding! I have fixed costs to pay for, and I should get a fair profit on internal sales, just like I do on external sales. I'm evaluated and rewarded on the performance of my business. My reported earnings would be unrealistically low, which would lower my people's morale. Do you mean to tell me that the products I make especially for you, that use up my capacity, should be transferred at marginal cost?

Professor: Well, now you're talking about a different situation. If the amount is fairly small, you should get a markup on full cost to approximate what the market price would be, so that you get a fair return.

Seller: That's more like it. I always knew you professors could reach intelligent decisions if given enough information.

Buyer: Wait a second. How are you going to determine a fair market price on something that isn't sold in the market? You professors have no idea how much time we spend arguing about what a fair market price is, even on products that *are* sold on the outside. But you've changed the subject. Let's get back to products sold inside.

Professor: My theory answers that problem as well.

Seller: It had better answer for situations where I don't have spare capacity. There are times when demand for my product is very high, and he's lucky to have an assured source of supply. Are you telling me I should get only marginal cost when I have customers knocking down my door, willing to pay premium prices so they can keep up with their own demand? Some of these customers are his competitors. If I sell to them, *he'll* lose sales. I think my product is worth a whole lot more than your stupid marginal cost.

Professor: Oh dear, you're making things more complicated, but that's no reason to get upset. My theory addresses this problem, known in academic circles as "demand dependence." Here it is necessary to use sophisticated mathematical programming techniques. While the procedure is too complicated to explain, shadow prices can be used to derive the transfer price that maximizes profits. It's somewhere between marginal cost and market price.

Buyer: Look, Professor, we're talking about *real* products and *real* costs—not this shadow world of yours. What you're ignoring is the fact that I'm one of his largest customers, and without my volume his costs would be much higher, which would make his profits much lower. Somehow your theory had better take account of the profits I'm making for him.

Professor: Well, I'm afraid you're now talking about what we call "technological dependence," a much more complicated situation. To be honest with you, I'm not sure it's always possible to find a mathematical solution when this condition holds. However, I'm sure that given enough time and a sufficiently large computer, I could develop the necessary equations and work out their solutions. Of course, we would have to specify the constraint equations for the algorithm used to solve the objective function, and a global optimum exists only—

President: Hold it! I haven't the faintest idea what you're talking about. It seems to me that if your solution is too complicated to explain, it's too complicated to use. And all this talk about time and computers—we have to make decisions *today*. Until you professors come up with something useful in practice, we'll just have to muddle along as best we can.

ATTACK ON THE ISSUE . . .

Since the invention of profit centers more than 60 years ago, corporate managers and academics alike have been looking for a solution to the nagging transfer pricing problem. It has two parts: the sourcing decision and the pricing decision. How should a business unit choose between internal and external suppliers, and what price should be placed on the good if the internal supplier is used? (*Business unit* refers of course to any part of an organization acting as a buyer or seller in internal transactions and includes divisions, manufacturing and sales functions, and product-business-program dimensions in a matrix structure.) The transfer price may be determined first and become an input to the sourcing decision, or the decision to buy inside may be made before the transfer price is decided on.

Most of the research academics have done on this problem has been of little use to executives. Studies usually recommend marginal cost and mathematical programming solutions, but the few surveys that have been conducted show that these approaches virtually do not exist in practice. For one thing, they are simply too cumbersome. And, ironically, in spite of their complexity, they require simplifying assumptions that ignore the many factors managers must take into account.

I decided that the best way to study transfer pricing and to develop a theory that would have clear implications for practice would be to focus on managers' experience. In pursuit of this objective, I interviewed nearly 150 executives (CEOs, CFOs, group and business general managers, financial managers, and others) in 13 companies. Their industries are chemicals, electronics, machinery, and machinery components.

These interviews left no doubt that the key to the transfer pricing problem is strategy. Transfer pricing schemes are a means of generating information and control for implementing corporate, business unit, and product strategy. The managers involved consider these schemes to be more or less fair. It is not always possible to satisfy both the control and the fairness objectives through the transfer pricing scheme alone.

There is no simple solution to the problem. It requires continuous attention through management processes. A company's transfer pricing policy and the processes for administering it depend on the particular situation and the direction the organization is going in.

Analysis in Two Dimensions

To help managers think analytically about the problem, I have developed a simple framework that recognizes transfer pricing's complexity in the real world. Two broad dimensions of strategy, applicable at the corporate, business unit, and product levels, are the basis for the framework I call the manager's analytical plane (MAP).

The first dimension of the MAP is vertical integration, that is, the extent to which the company carries on production and distribution activities that other companies could perform. Vertical integration results in interdependence between profit centers when each stage of the production and distribution processes is evaluated on the basis of profitability.

The second dimension is diversification, that is, the extent to which the company is engaged in different businesses. Diversification is determined by the extent of product-market segmentation. It results in an emphasis on the independent contributions of each business when they are separated as profit centers.

Although the dimensions can operate simultaneously, they are distinct. A company may integrate backward without diversifying by manufacturing a component that is not sold to external customers. Conversely, a company may add a product that requires no change in manufacturing and distribution capabilities. Often a company will use several transfer pricing policies depending on the strategy of the groups, business units, and products involved.

An executive can use the plane defined by these two dimensions to analyze his or her company (or business unit), since each location determined by the two strategic dimensions is associated with particular organizational characteristics. Five especially important characteristics are the nature of corporate strategy and the strategic planning process; the primary means of control by top management; the criteria for performance measurement, evaluation, and reward; the definition of fairness in the company; and the nature of the managerial processes. The framework appears as a plane to emphasize the difficulty of categorizing organizations as discrete types and to acknowledge the complexity of the real world.

For analytical purposes, however, I present four "pure" types to

EXHIBIT 1

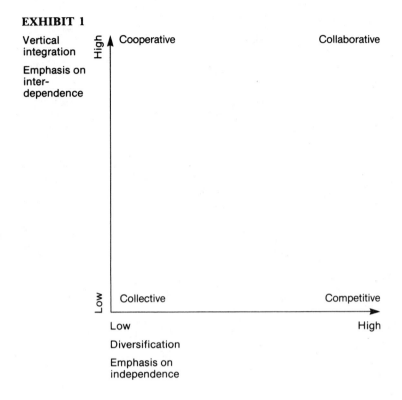

help a manager think about the situation. These four types correspond to the corners of the MAP as shown in Exhibit 1. Three of these, the *competitive, cooperative,* and *collaborative* types, are important for understanding the transfer pricing problem. (There is no transfer pricing in the *collective* organization.)

Exhibit 2 summarizes the characteristics of the three types. A company's transfer pricing policy (I use this term to include internal or external sourcing policy as well) depends on the organization's location on the plane and the direction in which it wishes to move. I'll take up each of these types in turn.

. . . IN COMPETITIVE ORGANIZATIONS

Highly diversified organizations that have little vertical integration between business units represent the *competitive* type. The most dramatic examples are the conglomerate and the holding company. But more common are companies with several relatively autonomous divisions having all the necessary functions of a complete business and having little interdivisional dependence. Corporate strategy is the sum of the

EXHIBIT 2
Characteristics of Competitive, Cooperative, and Collaborative Organizations

Characteristic	Competitive	Cooperative	Collaborative
Strategy	Aggregate of division's strategies	Total company strategy	Mutually defined total company business perspectives
Structure	Multidivisional	Functional	Matrix
Systems	Profits, ROI compared with budget, internally and externally	Costs compared with budgets and history	Combination of costs, profit, and ROI compared with budget
Processes	Bottom-up; distributive bargaining	Top-down; integrative bargaining	Iterative; mixed-mode bargaining
Method of managers' fairness evaluation	Impartial spectator	Shared fate	Rational trust
Top management control	Through systems on outcomes	Through structure on actions	Through processes balancing structure and systems

business unit strategies, and the strategic planning process is bottom-up.

The main control mechanism is management systems that measure the results of business unit actions, although organizational structure is also important. In these organizations, strategy implementation is most clearly reflected in these measurement systems. Since the business unit general manager has great authority over resources, upper management's control is exercised by measuring performance and comparing it with objectives. The entrepreneurial responsibility of business unit managers receives emphasis through measurement of the units as profit or investment centers.

The criteria for performance measurement, evaluation, and reward stress comparison of business unit performance with a budget or plan, similar competitors, and even sibling units. Use of similar performance measures for all units generates enormous internal competition. Since the measurement and evaluation of the use of resources and their allocation in a competitive organization resembles resource allocation in a market, the definition of fairness is similar to judgment meted out by an impartial spectator, namely the market.

Competitive organizations usually decentralize decision-making responsibility to the business unit level. This results in a bottom-up process for handling corporate-business unit relationships and a distributive bargaining process in business unit-business unit relationships. The latter is characterized by "win-lose" bargaining, which results from the attempt of each business unit to maximize its objectives, even at the expense of the other.

When the business units do not depend on each other very much, the costs of local decisions that are not best from a corporate perspective are small compared with the problems created by a transfer pricing policy that interferes with the stance of the impartial spectator and with the bottom-up and distributive bargaining processes. In its purest form, a competitive organization would have no transfer pricing policy, leaving the business units free to establish trading relationships as companies in the open market. A "no policy" default on top management's part, however, frustrates vertical integration because it creates disincentives to internal trading.

The general manager of the semiconductor group in one of the electronics companies I studied explained the problem: "In my experience, sister divisions are more antagonistic to each other than to outsiders. Basically this is due to competition as to who is the best performer. There is the suspicion that other divisions are doing something to get more than their share, especially when a product is forced on a division. Sister divisions are under more pressure because word about the first missed step could be picked up by the board."

Market-Based Pricing

A response to this problem is a policy of market-based transfer prices with constrained sourcing, such as giving inside suppliers a "last look" chance to meet outside quotes. In competitive organizations, transfer prices are used to select suppliers and customers and to value internal exchanges in a way consistent with the measurement of business unit performance.

One kind of market-based transfer price is cost-plus-profit markup. A buying unit may source a unique or proprietary good from a selling unit for which there is no market price since it is not sold externally. The seller establishes a cost intended to approximate the price if the product were on the market. Methods for determining the markup include comparable products, average gross profits, and average return on assets of the selling unit. Several of the electronics companies in my study used the cost-plus-profit method for proprietary products.

In competitive organizations, headquarters normally leave the determination of market prices up to the business units involved. The result is distributive bargaining processes as each unit tries to negotiate the most favorable price. When top management does set policies that influence the transfer price, such as "list price less 25 percent," the ability of the units to establish "true" market price obviously is hampered.

A reason often given for using market-based transfer prices less some discount is the presumed absence of selling costs, receivables carrying costs, and credit risk. But as internal transactions come to resemble external ones, through the use of salespeople assigned to internal accounts, for example, the less justified this discount becomes in the eyes of the selling business unit.

One of the companies I studied that had the characteristics of the competitive type gave its divisions autonomy on sourcing decisions—they were free to buy inside or outside—and they were under no obligation to sell internally if the terms were unfavorable. Regardless of the size of their purchase, internal customers received goods at the most favorable price obtained by outsiders with the largest quantity discount. Nevertheless, in a number of instances, external vendors were chosen over internal ones. To top management and the division heads, these outcomes were in the best interests of the divisions and the company as a whole. As one manager put it, "We don't want to do anything that would give a division general manager an excuse for not meeting his plan."

There are real advantages to leaving the decision to the business units. A manager of the semiconductor division of a second electronics company had recommended against a division's replacing its outside semiconductor supplier with the internal supplier even though the internal source stood to gain an additional $4 million to $6 million in sales. He explained why: "As long as Intel's product line is more comfortable and they'll jump through hoops to give us good quality, it's in the corporation's interest to stay with them."

When top management establishes constraints favoring internal transactions, as did a third electronics company by requiring that a "substantial percent" of semiconductor purchases be made internally during recessionary periods, both business units may find it unfair. A year after this policy took effect a division manager who bought semiconductors noted with a wry smile: "I think we're still in a recessionary period. They raised prices a lot and were willing to lose a share of their business with us. The president deemed that the prices should hold and that we had to buy inside. They aren't happy, and we aren't either. They'd rather make investments in other areas that are more profitable for them and growing faster, some of them at 100 percent a year. But they had to continue to invest in areas that support our products."

Unit heads think that the no-policy default is the fairest situation because top management does not interfere with their autonomy—which is consistent with exercising control through results. As the head office gets more involved with interunit relationships, complaints of unfairness may rise. Nevertheless, top management may want to increase internal transfers because of excess capacity in the selling unit or to take advantage of proprietary technologies. One way of accomplishing this while attempting to preserve fairness is through a dual pricing policy.

Dual Pricing

This policy combines the advantages of market-based pricing (the profit incentive for the selling unit) and of mandatory internal sourcing (e.g., the buildup of volume of the transferred good to reduce unit manufacturing costs). The buying unit receives the transferred good at cost, and the selling unit is credited with the market price. (The double-counting of profits is eliminated at a higher level in the organization.) As compensation for the interference with its flexibility, the buyer receives the product at less than market price, which enables it to show greater profits.

Just as a transfer pricing policy can be used to maintain a company's location on the MAP, it can be used to move a company in the direction of a desired future position. A competitive organization can use a dual pricing policy to increase its vertical integration, moving the company "north" on the MAP. Three of the electronics companies I studied that were located in the competitive region of the MAP used this policy from time to time.

A dual pricing policy has its problems too. (Two of the three companies that had adopted it reverted to market-based transfer prices with sourcing freedom.) If the double-counting elimination is not forecast properly, the net income of the whole company will be disturbingly less than the sum of the net profits of the units. This is especially likely if the financial and control systems are inadequate, or if business is poor and the selling unit can't meet its external quota and so generates excessive internal sales.

Moreover, since the buying unit gets the product at cost, it has little incentive to negotiate the most favorable market price on the transaction. Actually, neither division has the same incentive to monitor the performance of the other, which is a central characteristic of the competitive organization.

Sometimes the cost can be even greater than the market price, as it is at the beginning of the product life cycle for products with significant learning curve effects. This occurred at an electronics company, which had to make an exception for semiconductors.

Because of the problems, companies probably cannot use dual pricing for a long period of time for all products, although they may employ it for a few strategically important items. One electronics company, for example, set a dual pricing policy to enable a division selling batteries as a replacement part to price more competitively and regain lost market share.

Dual pricing is also used occasionally to bolster internal sales. An executive of an electronics company that used this policy for a few years described the experience this way: "The bookkeeping system didn't have the ability to handle it. It didn't work out well since it was difficult to administer. But it did get more transfers going, so it was the right move at the right time."

. . . IN COOPERATIVE ORGANIZATIONS

In competitive organizations, the business units must compete with each other; in *cooperative* organizations they must cooperate with each other. An example of the latter is a highly vertically integrated chemical company, organized on a functional basis, where all the units are cost centers except for a single sales force that acts as a revenue center.

More generally, business units turning out intermediate products have two roles, as a profit center for external sales and as a cost center for internal transfers. Corporate strategy is established for the company as a whole, and business unit strategies are derived from it.

The primary mechanism of control in cooperative organizations is the organizational structure. Since responsibility for many decisions rests at the top of the organization, especially for those involving exceptions to corporate policy or trade-offs between functions, the authority vested in hierarchical position or generated through expertise is especially important for specifying the actions of business units.

Business unit managers in cooperative companies do not have nearly as much autonomy and as wide a range of responsibility as their counterparts in competitive organizations. Top management is more directly involved in day-to-day operations and exercises control directly through interactions with subordinates. It relies less on management information systems. In these organizations, executives pay a great deal of attention to learning the unique aspects of the company.

The criteria for performance measurement, evaluation, and reward are also very different in cooperative organizations. Although managers use objective quantitative criteria—budgeted costs and revenue—these are largely based on comparisons with historical performances or budgets. Because of the interdependence between the units, top management uses more subjective criteria to determine whether a unit manager made her "numbers look good" at the expense of other units or whether, for example, the manufacturing unit stayed on a long production run rather than interrupt it and give priority to an important customer.

In cooperative organizations, because measurement and evaluation criteria are different for each unit, units compete with each other much less than they do in competitive organizations. Also, bonuses, salary increases, and promotions for individual managers and budgets for the business units are based primarily on total corporate performance. Thus, the definition of fairness in cooperative organizations is that of shared fate.

The philosophy in cooperative organizations is to centralize those decisions involving the interdependencies between business units that affect total corporate performance. Consequently, corporate-business unit relationships are managed through top-down processes, while integrative bargaining occurs between business units. In its win-win bargaining, each business unit tries to maximize corporate objectives, even at the expense of its own performance measures. Because a unit's contribution is not determined solely through quantitative means, the units have an incentive to perform well.

Because transfer prices strictly refer to exchanges between profit centers, in its purest form a cooperative organization would have *no* transfer prices. Many organizations, however, while closely approximating the pure cooperative type, have units that sell substantial quantities both inside and outside, forming quasi or partial profit centers. The transfer pricing policy for these organizations follows from the structure and systems. Internal transfers are mandated for both buying and selling units and the transfer price is full cost. Unlike in competitive organizations where the transfer price is a market price that determines whether sourcing will be internal or external, the transfer price in cooperative organizations is determined after the decision to source inside has already been made.

The mandating of transfers is a direct consequence of the vertical integration strategy whereby the large capital investments involved make any other approach impractical. Cooperative organizations measure performance of the total product flow across units, not of units as stand-alone profit centers. The purpose of transfer prices is to accumulate total costs as if the end products were manufactured completely within a single business unit.

Actual Full Cost

When a company transfers actual costs and its units share each other's fortunes, it approaches a pure cooperative type. Actual full costs are calculated by dividing all fixed and variable expenses for a period into the number of units produced. Because product costing involves valuing inventory, allocating joint product costs, and costing by-products, none of which is a precise science, costs are defined and calculated through management judgment and consensus.

The major difficulty with actual full-cost transfers is that the price of the intermediate good fluctuates. If either internal or external demand falls and the volume of the selling unit decreases, the transfer price to internal buyers increases. Also, buying units do not know the price until the period is finished and the selling unit can calculate the actual costs.

A multibillion-dollar chemical company with a sophisticated management control system used actual full-cost transfer prices. (Actual full cost is not the chosen method of only the unsophisticated.) In this company, buying divisions were told which plant to purchase from. Top management made these complex sourcing decisions to minimize transportation costs and to balance plant loadings for greatest manufacturing efficiency.

Because product costs varied according to the producing plant, some managers were unhappy with this approach. Overall, however, managers showed little desire to change to standard-cost or market-based transfer prices. The company's controller explained: "The alternatives, such as using market-based pricing or keeping track of who gets favorable and unfavorable variances, are worse than what we have. Financial information is important but it doesn't give managers yes or no decisions. We will pay them to run the business."

Performance measurement, evaluation, and reward at this company were consistent wit the actual-cost transfer pricing policy in that they emphasized the business unit's contribution to the company rather than its own financial results. Subjective judgment played a large role in evaluating a business unit manager. Company performance, business unit performance, and especially personal performance determined bonuses.

Standard Full Cost

If a company uses standard full-cost transfers, it can substantially reduce the variation in price the buying unit receives. This approach makes it possible to measure more precisely each unit's contribution, especially when variances are charged to the unit responsible for them. It also makes it possible to more clearly separate the profit-center (external sales) and cost-center (internal transfer) roles of the selling unit. Although nothing can eliminate it, standard full-cost transfers reduce the effect interdependence has on performance measures.

Given the assumptions about volume, raw materials, and other expenses, standard costs are the expected unit costs of producing a product for some period. Standard costs are usually based on what it would cost to produce the good if the plant were running at nearly full capacity. A good standard-cost system attempts to identify the changes in volume or raw material costs that make the actual costs either higher or lower than the standard cost.

A standard-cost system can also isolate the effects the buying unit has on the selling unit, such as when the former buys less than anticipated. Some systems include a "take or pay" provision in internal transfers. When buying units are responsible for negative volume variances if other customers don't turn up, a portion of the selling unit's capacity has to be identified as dedicated to a particular buyer. Disputes can arise about whether a buying unit's capacity was used to meet the demand of another customer.

Determining whether variances are the responsibility of the buying or the selling unit is not easy. When selling unit managers have to interrupt long production runs for special orders, they may complain that the buying units are responsible for the resulting inefficiencies. Buying divisions may argue that because cost decreases such as those for raw materials or utilities are not due to the purchasing acumen of the selling unit but to changes in market prices, the positive variances should be credited to the buying unit.

The integrity of the standard-cost system depends on how the system is designed and operated. At issue is whether managers believe that the standard costs are what the costs really would be for an efficiently run operation. Buying unit managers have to believe that selling unit managers are doing their best to forecast raw material costs accurately. A common complaint is that these estimates are purposefully conservative so that the selling unit can show positive variances.

No ultimate accounting method can solve the problems inherent in standard full-cost transfers. These problems must be managed through processes that recognize the limitations of quantitative measures of performance.

A chemical company in my study illustrates how a standard full-cost transfer pricing policy can be effective even when it does not include take-or-pay provisions. The company's transfer pricing approach had evolved out of a standard-cost system that had been implemented in the early 1960s. In the mid-1960s, as part of a reorganization to a matrix structure, a task force recommended a market-based system to allocate variances. Top management preferred the standard-cost approach and rejected the team's proposal.

At the time, the CEO explained his reasons this way: "I can tell how well the entire company is doing based on the performance of a few of our key chemicals. But in order to do this, I need to see all of the variances in one place, not scattered across 50 to 60 downstream products."

Twenty years after the implementation of standard-cost transfer prices the sentiment is pretty much the same. One manager acknowledges that market-based transfer prices would have some advantages: "There is a lot of merit to a market-price system. It shows on one accounting document the relative contributions to profits of the individual products. If we were to evaluate on this basis we would have to have a better way of showing the products' contributions."

In this company, however, relative profitability doesn't count for much. Managers are evaluated on the basis of their contribution to the company in ways other than the profitability of their business units.

The company is located in a small town; nearly all of its managers are chemists and chemical engineers who were recruited right out of college and promoted within the company. They know each other well and have an intimate understanding of the company's businesses and strategy, which have been constant for years. One senior executive explained how managers are assessed: "They are measured on profit before taxes, but we evaluate them more based on the quality of their effort. It is a largely subjective judgment and includes a poll of their colleagues."

Bonuses are based on total corporate performance and on an individual's performance appraisal—not unit results. One manager explained this shared-fate concept of fairness: "Our objective is total corporate profits. I can make a decision that costs my division money, but if it makes the company money, I'll be okay. It's an inherent philosophical and intellectual thing. We react to overall optimization."

Cost plus Investment

Even when managers mostly agree about what fair standard costs and variance allocations are, the standard full-cost method still causes problems. The selling unit does not receive a profit on internal transfers, resulting in lower profit margins and return on investment percentages. Even though top management does not attach much meaning to unit comparisons of net profit and ROI, some selling unit managers may feel that some of "their" profits are showing up in the performance measures of buying units.

One solution to this and other problems is to use a cost-plus-investment method for establishing the transfer price while retaining mandated internal sourcing. Several chemical companies, an electronics company, and a heavy machinery company in my study used this approach at some point. This method transfers the intermediate good on a full-cost basis, but it also "transfers" the portion of the selling unit's assets used for internal needs to the books of the buying unit. This approach essentially splits up the selling unit into an investment center based on external sales only and a cost center for internal transfers, and makes the buying unit responsible for profits and ROI on all internal resources used to manufacture its products.

Cost plus investment plays a function in cooperative companies similar to the one that dual pricing plays in competitive organizations. In both cases the objective is to obtain some of the advantages of the other organizational type. But whereas dual pricing accomplishes this by using both of the two basic approaches, cost-plus-investment pricing is a financial technique that "eliminates" the structural arrangement that requires a transfer in the first place.

Cost-plus-investment transfer pricing also has its problems, many of which are related to allocating costs and investments. As conditions change, allocations, which are inevitably somewhat arbitrary, may not fairly reflect the balance between internal and external sales.

One company took nearly three years to make a cost-plus-investment approach work, and even then some key managers remained vehemently opposed to it. The problems included a selling unit manager who wanted his unit to remain a profit center and so purposely set standard costs that would result in a positive variance; a take-or-pay provision combined with spot market-price transfer prices on products desired in excess of budget; disagreements about which unit should benefit from purchasing and energy variances; and some buying unit managers who felt that some of the selling units' plant investments were excessive.

. . . IN COLLABORATIVE ORGANIZATIONS

Companies that are *collaborative* emphasize both the interdependence of vertical integration and the independent contributions of the business units as diversified businesses. They combine characteristics of both competitive and cooperative organizations. As individual profit centers, the units compete; but as a result of high interdependence, they must cooperate. The inherent tension in this situation makes it possible for companies to obtain the benefits of the cooperative and competitive types but also makes them vulnerable to their problems. For collaborative organizations, the transfer pricing problem is most complex.

It is not clear on the MAP where an organization passes from competitive to collaborative or from cooperative to collaborative. As an organization moves toward the collaborative area—either through changes in transfer pricing policies or through increased strategic emphasis on interdependence through vertical integration or on independence through diversification—the transfer pricing problem becomes more difficult to manage. As this occurs, management processes become increasingly important in designing the transfer pricing policy.

In collaborative organizations the interplay of top-down and bottom-up planning approaches establishes strategy. As the balance between the objectives of the units working together and their individual objectives changes with conditions, the corporate strategy shifts.

Collaborative organizations are usually organized as matrix structures or as multidivisional structures that are substantially interdependent. Business units might share such resources as corporate manufacturing or sales units. The structures of collaborative organizations are more complicated and messier than the clean multidivisional form of the competitive organization or the clean functional form of the cooperative organization. Supporting the diversification dimension of strategy are the results-oriented systems of the competitive type for top management control, while the hierarchical structure of the cooperative organization gives top management control in support of the interdependent vertical integration dimension of strategy.

Because of the tension between structure and systems in collaborative organizations, the primary mechanism of control is through management processes. This is a higher order form of control than in either of the other types. Top management must constantly guard against an excessive use of the functional structure or of the business unit systems; either can lead to the deterioration of the dimension of strategy associated with the other control mechanism.

The management processes shaping corporate-business unit relationships are iterative in nature. They combine both the bottom-up processes of the competitive type and the top-down processes of the cooperative type. Similarly, the processes shaping interbusiness-unit relationships are those of mixed-mode bargaining. These processes combine distributive bargaining of the competitive type with integrative bargaining of the cooperative type. Iterative and mixed-mode bargaining processes are complex and require that the managers involved have sophisticated conflict resolution skills. They also increase stress, which, if excessive, can hurt performance.

Iterative processes are used in strategic planning: guidelines are issued from the top down; the units then communicate up in such a way that alters the top level's definition of strategy. Iterative processes make possible shifts of influence and control between levels and units as circumstances dictate.

Mixed-mode bargaining processes between business units are a consequence of their simultaneously competitive and cooperative relationships. Due to the emphasis on systems for measuring quantitative results, business units have an incentive to win at the expense of others. Structural interdependence, however, acts as an incentive for each business unit to be concerned with the performance of the other as it affects total corporate results.

The dual focus that exists in measuring, evaluating, and rewarding performance reflects the mixed-mode bargaining. One the one hand, collaborative organizations use largely quantitative, objective criteria to assess individual business unit performance and to reward this performance. Executives take great efforts to establish objectives that contain measures of profitability and return on investment and to compare performance along these dimensions with similar external competitors.

On the other hand, given the very real dangers of managers attempting to improve unit performance at the expense of total corporate performance and the difficulty of finding comparable outside competitors, management tempers the quantitative approach with internal criteria such as cost-efficiency, total product performance, and other, more subjective, assessments. Bonuses for managers and capital budgets for units take into account both independent and interdependent contributions in a necessarily difficult-to-define combination of cooperative and competitive criteria.

The sense of fairness in collaborative organizations is based on a rational trust the unit managers have in top management. The rational component signifies the impartial spectator standards of fairness appropriate for competitive organizations. The trust component signifies the shared-fate standards of fairness appropriate for cooperative organizations.

Management Processes and Conflict

In collaborative organizations the required internal sourcing part of the transfer pricing policy of cooperative organizations is combined with the market-based transfer prices (including cost-plus-profit-markup) part of the transfer pricing policy of competitive organizations.

Some companies move from the cooperative to the collaborative area because of increased diversification and a desire to put greater emphasis on individual unit performance. Others want to increase entrepreneurial spirit to prepare for and facilitate increased diversification. In companies that place a large emphasis on decentralized profit responsibility, selling unit managers are not likely to accept the argument that because cost transfers are built into the budget and objectives, they do not distort performance measures. As one manager in this situation put it, "I want to be able to compare my performance with competitors' and internal divisions' so everyone will know what this business is contributing to company profits."

When companies move from the competitive to the collaborative area it may be because they want to increase vertical integration and emphasize internal cooperation and the total product flow.

In collaborative organizations, market-based transfer prices play a different role than do prices in external markets and competitive organizations. In economic theory, price is a single-number transmitter of a great deal of information. Companies allocate resources and make decisions on trading relationships according to this number. Market-based transfer prices play a similar role in competitive organizations. Although they have less impact on capital allocation decisions, they do determine whether a buying unit sources internally or externally.

When top management requires internal sourcing, market-based transfer prices become a source of conflict through which management can gather information and obtain control. The conflict occurs because there is no completely satisfactory way to determine a fair market price. Very large volumes of internal transactions do not have external counterparts, and the specifications of the product sold internally may vary from those of the product sold externally. Both units can argue that the transfer price is not a true market price because changes in transfer prices can significantly affect the performance measures of business units as profit centers and thus perceptions of their relative contributions to company profits.

In making these arguments, the unit managers are likely to present information on roughly comparable external transactions or bids, differences in the cost of product sold internally compared with product sold externally, lack of cooperation in the relationship (poor R&D and service support or short lead times and canceled orders), inadequate or inflated gross margins, and so forth.

This information gives top management the control it needs to manage the business from a total product flow perspective. It is the kind of information that top managements in cooperative organizations have ready access to because their direct involvement is more accepted. When internal sourcing is required, both units actively seek the involvement of top management to solve the transfer price conflict. Control comes from top management's using each unit to keep the other on its toes.

Conflict is an inevitable element in the iterative and mixed-mode bargaining processes top management uses to exercise control in collaborative organizations. Because it can arise when changes in external conditions put pressures on existing objectives, conflict can warn top management to reexamine strategy. Just as time spent on budgeting and allocating capital is productive to the company, so may be time spent on resolving the conflict related to transfer pricing. Suppressing or alleviating this conflict beyond a certain point actually becomes undesirable. Top management may even want to take steps to increase conflict in order to overcome any reluctance managers may have about bringing disputes—and the attendant information—to the top.

In collaborative organizations, it is impossible to find a transfer pricing policy that will satisfy top management's needs for control and be perceived as fair by the units involved. Indeed, achieving fairness between units would reduce the utility of transfer prices as a mechanism for generating information and control. Nevertheless, to keep business unit managers motivated, management must still try to achieve fairness in *its* relationships with business units. When unit managers perceive that their individual rewards and units' resource allocations are independent of the numbers generated by transfer prices, they'll see the system as fair. It is a mistake to tie individual rewards to individual unit performance, as is done in competitive organizations. As in cooperative organizations, top management must allocate rewards—bonuses, praise, symbols of status, and so forth—subjectively to a certain extent.

A Collaborative Company's Approach

One of the chemical companies in my study provides a perfect illustration of a collaborative organization. One of its major businesses is the largest producer in its industry. Its two largest customers are internal users. All three businesses are critical to the success of the company.

These businesses are capital intensive and their managers accept internal sourcing without question. Transfer prices are market based, less a small discount to reflect the fact that sales effort and other expenses are not required.

The selling unit's product comes in several grades and in several degrees of finish. The largest internal user buys the product in a degree of finish less than for that sold on the outside, which makes finding comparable market prices impossible. The oligopolistic nature of the market for the intermediate good and the extent of vertical integration in the industry also make it difficult to determine a fair market price and an appropriate volume discount, if any.

Disputes about the transfer price of this product have raged off and on for nearly 20 years. Recently, the argument heated up again. The price of the intermediate good rose on the external market and the selling unit general manager set a new transfer price on the good internally. The result was a conflict that generated a series of memos and internal studies providing a great deal of information. In presentations to the president, the buying unit managers reported their performance using both cost- and market-based transfer prices.

The CEO has managed all three of these businesses at different points in his career and understands them very well. When managing these businesses he had shifted to a cost-plus-investment approach because he said he wanted to improve the profits and motivation of the buying units. Others speculated that doing so helped him gain information he needed for capital allocation negotiations. On becoming CEO, he shifted back to a market-based approach for these businesses.

All three managers of these businesses are key members of his management team. They report to group general managers (the selling unit manager to one and the buying unit managers to another) and so are one layer removed from the president. These group general managers are due to retire soon.

The conflict the market-based approach has generated gives the CEO the necessary information and control he needs to be sure that the right balance between vertical integration and diversification is maintained. This is especially important as the company increasingly emphasizes the selling unit's role as an internal supplier over its role as an external supplier. Another strategic concern is the poor performance of one buying unit due to industry conditions. At the time I did the study, the company was about to make a major capital investment to lower this unit's costs and make it more competitive.

None of the managers feels he is being treated unfairly by the chief executive officer. All of them think that he fairly evaluates their performances and that they get the recognition and financial compensation they deserve. They also think that the appropriate capital investments are being made in their businesses.

The CEO has made special efforts to let managers know that he recognizes their individual contributions to the company. What's more, his word carries weight because he receives much information and also has a deep understanding of all three businesses. Because the company is placing more emphasis on measuring unit profitability and return on investment, the CEO's knowledge and judgment are especially reassuring to the unit managers.

Managers feared that others in the company who lack the president's depth of understanding would underestimate the contributions their businesses make; such feelings of unfairness were directed toward each other. Perceptions of unfairness go far beyond mere financial compensation to include pride, concern with others in the unit, and personal values about what is just. In this company these feelings were exacerbated by the distrust that existed between the managers of the buying and selling units due to differences in personal style.

USING THE MAP

Managers can use the MAP, which associates organizational characteristics (including transfer pricing policies) appropriate for various combinations of the two strategic dimensions, to analyze their existing transfer pricing policies. This analysis takes five steps, each of which requires substantial managerial judgment to complete. Because the strategic relationships between business units vis-à-vis vertical integration and diversification depend on the business units involved, this analysis is best performed on a product (or group of similar products) basis.

Step 1: Locate interbusiness-unit relationships on the MAP. Define measures of diversification and vertical integration appropriate to the company. Place interbusiness-unit relationships on the MAP according to strategies of business units and strategy for their relationship.

Step 2: Compare location to existing transfer pricing policy. Determine what transfer pricing policy is most appropriate according to *Exhibit 3*. The exhibit summarizes the transfer pricing policies appropriate for varying degrees of emphasis on interdependence through vertical integration and independence through diversification. Compare to existing transfer pricing policy, and consider a change in either the strategy or the pricing policy if there isn't a fit.

Step 3: Analyze organizational characteristics. Determine which organizational characteristics from competitive, cooperative, or collaborative types (*Exhibit 2*) are most appropriate given the corporate strategy. Compare to existing organizational characteristics; consider making some changes in organizational characteristics if there isn't a fit.

EXHIBIT 3

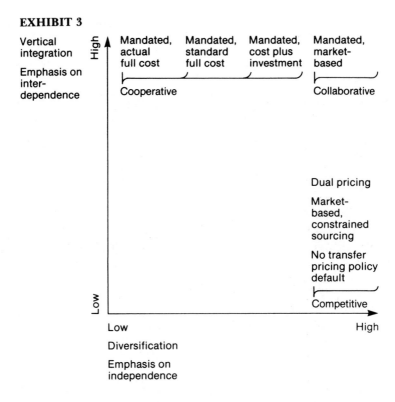

Step 4: Look for special problems.   If strategy, transfer pricing policy, and organizational characteristics are consistent but managers still complain, they may do so because of one of the five special problems noted in the next section. Resolution of the conflict will depend on its underlying source and will have little to do with transfer pricing.

Step 5: Consider future strategy.   Anticipate that changes in strategy may require changes in transfer pricing policy. Make a decision about the timing of this change. A change in transfer pricing policy prior to a change in strategy may signal and facilitate this new strategy, but expect and accept problems during the transition. Or a change in policy may occur after the new strategy is in place; the inevitable problems that will result as the old policy becomes increasingly inappropriate for the new strategy can help spur the change.

While providing a useful framework for thinking about transfer pricing, the MAP must be supplemented by management judgment. For example, the MAP enables a manager to determine if conflict is useful, as it is in collaborative organizations, or not, as is more likely in competitive or cooperative organizations. But by itself the MAP does not enable a manager to determine if the conflict is a result of other factors having little to do with transfer pricing.

COMMON TRANSFER PRICING PROBLEMS

Even if the company has a transfer pricing policy appropriate for its strategy, five common problems can lead to conflict. Here, too, management processes are far more important than any attempt to find technical solutions.

1. Performance Problems.   When either unit is having trouble meeting its profit objectives, changing the transfer price is one of the easiest fixes for the bottom line. If both businesses are doing poorly, as in times of recession, conflict will be especially severe, but at these times no change in the transfer price approach will alleviate the difficulties since the underlying problems are due to external factors that are independent of the transfer price.

2. Interpersonal Disputes.   Disputes over transfer prices may simply be the mechanism by which managers act on an interpersonal conflict unrelated to transfer prices. Arguing over transfer prices seems a more legitimate way of conducting this dispute than name-calling. The interpersonal and the substantive issues can get confused.

3. Power Imbalance.   A unit manager who feels there is a power imbalance due to his greater dependency on the other unit (such as when a buying unit sources a product internally that is a significant part of his cost of goods sold but in amounts insignificant to the selling unit) may initiate conflict to try to correct this imbalance.

4. Demand Fluctuation.   When demand for the intermediate good is high, the buying unit is glad to have assured supplies on a full-cost basis that will be much below market price. This is precisely the time, however, when external customers are especially attractive to the selling unit. The reverse situation occurs when demand for the intermediate good is low and outside suppliers are willing to sell at market prices below full cost.

5. Product Pricing.   A complaint about market-based transfer prices is that the final good's price becomes uncompetitive. The response to this is that because external suppliers of the intermediate good would receive a profit, profit should be earned at each stage of the production process. A complaint about cost-based transfer prices is that the final good will not be priced aggressively enough, resulting in lost profits or pursuit of market share at the expense of profitability. The response to this is either that vertically integrated competitors supply the intermediate good on a cost basis or that external suppliers have lower cost structures due to specialization and lower overhead and can make a profit at a lower price than would be required for internal transfers. In both of these cases, the problem requires recognition that product pricing involves issues other than cost. It is a complex problem in and of itself, and its analysis includes estimates of customer value and competitors' prices in addition to costs set up by transfer prices.

Conclusion

Although no simple solution to the transfer pricing problem exists, it can be effectively managed. The ability to do so rests on recognizing that the nature of the transfer pricing problem varies according to a company's (group's, unit's, or product's) location on the MAP and the direction in which management wishes to move. Effective management of transfer pricing requires policies and organizational characteristics that are consistent with strategy. Appropriate processes are essential for achieving the desired objectives of fairness and control.

20.

Price Elasticities of Demand at Retail and Wholesale Levels: An Automotive Example*

H. FREDERICK GALLASCH, JR.

Often the business economist is confronted with econometric models which describe consumer demand behavior when it is important to determine how dealer or distributor orders will respond to price changes. The new car market is an especially good example since consumer new car demand becomes dealer demand for the manufacturers' products only when dealers translate consumer demand into factory orders.

Most econometric models of new car sales provide little information about manufacturer level demand. However, using simplifying assumptions, a methodology is demonstrated, and estimates of dealer and manufacturer demand elasticities are obtained.

RETAIL-WHOLESALE PRICE RELATION

Since new car prices are determined by the interaction of consumer demand and dealer supply, the relevant price relation is between dealer or wholesale price, *DP*, and retail price, *p* (i.e., prices which dealers pay manufacturers and which consumers pay dealers). Assuming dealer

---

* *Business Economics*, January 1984, pp. 61–62.

margins, M, consist of absolute, M_0, and percentage, M_1, margins, one can describe the margin relation as follows:

$$M = M_0 + M_1 \tag{1}$$

where

$$M_1 = k\,DP \tag{2}$$

with k being the percentage of dealer price. Given the assumed margin description (1), the retail-wholesale price relation becomes:

$$p = M_0 + (1 + k)DP \tag{3}$$

ELASTICITIES OF DEMAND AND PRICE TRANSMISSION

Given retail and wholesale levels of demand for new cars, there are two corresponding demand elasticities, $E_{q \cdot p}$ and $E_{q \cdot DP}$, respectively. Dealers face consumer demand with price elasticity of:

$$E_{q \cdot p} = \frac{\partial q}{\partial p} \cdot \frac{P}{q} \tag{4}$$

and automobile manufacturers experience demand price elasticities of:

$$E_{q \cdot DP} = \frac{\partial q}{\partial DP} \cdot \frac{DP}{q} \tag{5}$$

Applying these demand elasticities and the assumed price relation (3), one describes consumer price elasticity as:

$$E_{q \cdot p} = \frac{\partial q}{\partial [M_0 + (1 + k)DP]} \cdot \frac{P}{q} \tag{6}$$

With the assumption of constant percentage margins at all prices, the price elasticity of consumer demand becomes:

$$E_{q \cdot p} = \frac{\partial q}{(1 + k)\,\partial DP} \cdot \frac{P}{q} \tag{7}$$

From the retail-wholesale price relation (3), the price transmission differential is:

$$\frac{\partial p}{\partial DP} = (1 + k) \tag{8}$$

and the elasticity of price transmission is:

$$\eta = \frac{\partial p}{\partial DP} \cdot \frac{DP}{p} \tag{9}$$

Substitution of the price transmission differential (8) into (7) provides

$$E_{q \cdot p} = \frac{\partial q}{\partial DP} \cdot \frac{\partial DP}{\partial p} \frac{P}{q} \tag{10}$$

which in elasticity terms becomes:

$$E_{q \cdot DP} = E_{q,p} \cdot \eta \tag{11}$$

Several observations arise. First, the relative responsiveness of the two levels of demand to price changes depends upon the elasticity of price transmission, η. Second, the assumed margin relation (1) implies that the two price elasticities of demand are the same if dealers use no absolute margin (i.e., $M_0 = 0$). Third, consumer demand is more price responsive than dealer demand as long as the price transmission elasticity is less than one (i.e., $M_0 > 0$).

EMPIRICAL EVIDENCE FOR NEW CAR DEMAND PRICE ELASTICITIES

The ideal method for estimating price elasticities of demand for new cars at retail and wholesale levels is with a simultaneous equation model relating consumer demand and dealer supply at one level and relating dealer demand and manufacturer supply at the other. Such a complex model is unavailable but two studies provide evidence of these elasticities. First, Luckey provides an estimate of the elasticity of price transmission of 1.1. Unfortunately, his model's construction does not provide price elasticities of demand.

Second, Gallasch provides a unique simultaneous equation model of the retail new car market which describes consumer demand, dealer supply, and dealer inventories. This model has retail new car prices endogenously determined with wholesale prices being exogenous. The final form provides an estimate of the price transmission elasticity, namely, 1.1. Further Gallasch provides a price elasticity of consumer demand of -1.0. Using relation (11), one obtains an implied price elasticity of demand at the manufacturer level of -1.1.

CONCLUSIONS

The above discussion and automotive example provide a procedure for estimating the price elasticity of demand faced by manufacturers who market their products through independent dealer or distributor networks. Given independent dealers' expectations and inventory behavior, this elasticity is often more useful than the more readily available consumer price elasticity of demand.

PART FIVE

FINANCIAL MANAGEMENT

INTRODUCTION

Capital budgeting is a major topic in many managerial economics texts. Capital budgeting procedures and techniques are utilized by companies planning long-term investment projects. It is a process which requires an understanding of the time value of money and, simultaneously, the cost of capital; also, its use assumes one's ability to predict net cash inflows and outflows from a specific investment.

Known also as investment decision making, equipment replacement analysis, and the analysis of capital expenditures, it is concerned with choices among the investment alternatives available to the firm, with the goal of accepting the most profitable alternatives and rejecting the others.

Main parts of capital budgeting include (1) the cost of capital, (2) replacement policy and the estimation of useful life, (3) ranking criteria, and (4) uncertainty.

In economics, it is not uncommon for wide disparities to exist between theory and practice. Capital budgeting does not differ in this regard. The theory of capital budgeting assumes the existence and application of sophisticated analytical techniques; in practice, executives may ignore results of such analysis. James C. T. Mao surveys this condition and suggests ways in which current theory may be modified to make it more operationally useful.

Permeating all of modern financial theory is the notion that business managers need to know more about the behavior of financial and capital markets and the impact such markets have on a company's cost of equity capital. A central tool in application of modern financial theory is the capital asset pricing model (CAPM). Does the CAPM work? How important is it? David W. Mullins, Jr., describes a method for arriving at the CAPM and explains its principle advantages. Mullins reveals also those situations in which the model should be avoided.

The role played by the cost of capital in financial decisions is still under debate. J. Walter Elliott explains how the cost of capital concept can be misleading when applied to decisions on capital structure and when used as a hurdle rate in making investment decisions. Technical problems associated with using the cost of capital as a hurdle rate appear to be somewhat refined, but the cost of *equity* continues to account for much difficulty in cost of capital calculation and application. The Elliott study was prompted by the fact that "virtually no empirical results exist at present to support either the choice of one cost of capital measure over another or to support the decision that we remain indifferent among the alternatives that have been presented."

The return on an investment should be equal to, or greater than, the investor's cost of capital, if the net asset value of the investor is to increase. But not all investments are created equal.

The conventional wisdom of the late 1960s and early 1970s was that common stocks represented the best possible hedge against price inflation; yet the period from 1965 to 1975 represented one of excess returns to real estate vis-a-vis returns to alternative investment opportunities. The study by Coyne, Goulet, and Picconi examines the validity of these "excess returns to real estate" when financial leverage is considered. They find that rewards to real estate investments are not always better, but risk makes a difference.

Concluding Part Five on financial management is the article by Charles Lieberman. His study notes the absence of empirical evidence in support of a cost of capital effect on inventory investment. Approximately three quarters of the variance in gross national product is accounted for by changes in inventory investment. Lieberman finds it truly remarkable that so little econometric evidence exists to indicate a cost of capital effect on inventory, the most variable component of GNP. Consequently, Lieberman reexamines the size and significance of the theoretically important cost of capital effect on inventory investment. He utilizes specific cost of capital measures, as suggested by finance theory literature, and does so in a pooled cross-section econometric analysis of inventory behavior. Lieberman finds that finished goods inventories are quite sensitive to the cost of capital for firms that produce to stock, while work in process inventories are most sensitive to the cost of capital for firms that produce to order.

21.

Survey of Capital Budgeting: Theory and Practice*

JAMES C. T. MAO

I. INTRODUCTION

There exists a wide disparity between the theory and practice of capital budgeting. During the past 15 years, the theory of capital budgeting has been characterized by the increased application of such analytical techniques as utility analysis, mathematical programming, probability and statistical theory. The practice of capital budgeting has no doubt changed at the same time, but business executives do not appear to have adopted many of the new techniques. The purpose of this paper is to compare current theory with practice: (1) to discuss the nature of the gap and the reason for its existence, and (2) to try to lessen this disparity by suggesting ways of modifying theory to make it more operationally meaningful. To aid discussion, this paper is divided into four sections: objective of financial management, risk analysis in investment decisions, profitability criteria for investment selection, and conclusions.

It is difficult, if not impossible, to characterize the current theory of capital budgeting in a few words. By current theory, I shall mean the type of work on capital budgeting that appears in journals such as *Management Science, Journal of Finance, Journal of Financial and Quantitative*

* *Journal of Finance.* 25, no. 2 (May 1970) pp. 349–60.

Analysis, and *Engineering Economist.* These theories generally make use of modern quantitative tools. By current practice, I shall present the findings of case studies I conducted during the summer of 1969. In all, I interviewed eight medium and large companies in the following industries: electronics, aerospace, petroleum, household equipment, and office equipment. I held full-day discussions in each company interviewed. Because of the small sample I do not wish to put forward any statistical generalizations about current practice. However, since the companies studied were chosen for the efficiency of their management, they do give a preliminary view of current capital budgeting practices in firms with progressive management.

II. OBJECTIVE OF FINANCIAL MANAGEMENT

Theory

Any theory of optimal investment decisions is premised on the existence of an objective function which the firm maximizes. Current financial theory generally assumes that the firm should maximize the market value of its common shares. There is a growing body of literature that explains how share values are determined under conditions of uncertainty. For example, according to John Lintner, a perfect capital market with homogeneous investor expectations, the risk of a security in a portfolio is measured by the weighted average of the variance of its return and the covariances between its return and other returns. The price of a share, then, is a function of its expected earnings, the pure rate of interest, the price of risk, and risk measured in this way.

Before discussing what financial executives regard as their objective, let us examine the objective of maximizing share value from an operational viewpoint. In order to implement this objective, the financial executive needs criteria for choosing between alternative time patterns of share prices within his planning horizon. Current theory does not provide this. Of course, this issue will not arise under conditions of certainty and perfect capital market, since the action which maximizes share value at the end of the firm's horizon also maximizes share prices throughout the horizon. (See figure 1A.) Since curve I dominates curve II, it is clearly preferable. However, under conditions of uncertainty and imperfect capital market, the relative share prices at the end of the horizon do not necessarily determine the relationship between the prices during the time span. Two possible courses of action could thus easily result in time patterns of share prices with multiple crossings. (See Figure 1B). In the latter case, the objective of maximizing share value has no operational meaning until there are criteria for choosing between crisscrossing price patterns. To make this choice, we may wish to consider the duration for which one pattern exceeds the other, as well as the

FIGURE 1

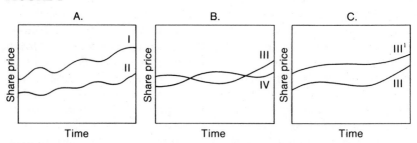

timing and size of the difference. One formula which incorporates these considerations is the following:

$$\phi = \int_0^T (P_t - P'_t)e^{-rt}\, dt \tag{1}$$

where P_t and P'_t stand for share prices as depicted by curves III and IV respectively, r stands for the rate of discount, and T stands for the time horizon. A simple rule would be to choose time pattern III if $\phi \geq 0$, and to select time pattern IV otherwise. It should be noted that this problem is quite similar to choosing between criss-crossing loss functions in decision theory, and perhaps some of its criteria could be used to choose alternatives here.

Let us suppose that time pattern III is preferred. How is it possible to improve curve III further so that the share price will be raised at every point along the time pattern? (See Figure 1C.) To put it differently, if there is an earnings per share (eps) series that corresponds to price pattern III, how should the eps series be modified to raise share prices from curve III to curve III'? B. G. Malkiel has shown that under conditions of certainty the price-earnings ratio of any stock is equal to the price-earnings of a standard reference stock, adjusted for the difference in growth rates and the duration of this difference. Although he applied his model to conditions of uncertainty, the complexities involved prevented him from constructing a full uncertainty model. Here, we shall make a simple extension of Malkiel's certainty model by introducing the risk factor. Risk is to be measured by the standard deviation to the eps series, calculated with regard to its trend. An eps series with a higher trend and less risk would result in a uniformly higher price.

To illustrate how this risk measure can be implemented, let us say that eps at any time t, denoted as $x(t)$, is the sum of three components:

$$x(t) = a + bt + c \sum_{h \in H} \sin \frac{t}{h} + u \tag{2}$$

where a, b, c are constants, h is an element of a set of incommensurate real numbers and t stands for time. Component $a + bt$ is the trend, component $\sum_{h \in H} \sin \frac{t}{h}$ is the sum of a set of sine functions with incommensurate periods, which results in nonperiodic oscillations; and component u is the source of random fluctuations. If we denote $x*(t)$ as the trend value of $x(t)$, then our risk measure, the standard deviation about the trend, is given by the formula:

$$\sigma = \left\{ \frac{1}{N} \sum [x(t) - x*(t)]^2 \right\}^{1/2} \tag{3}$$

where N stands for the number of observations. It should be noted that the concept of risk presented here is the risk of a security considered by itself. This risk concept needs to be modified if investors have sufficient resources to diversify their portfolios. In that case, the distinction made by some financial writers between diversifiable and nondiversifiable risks is relevant. It is the nondiversifiable component that determines the risk of a security in a portfolio context.

Practice

The executives interviewed were asked what they regarded as the objective of financial management. More specifically, they were asked whether they chose between alternative courses of action so as to maximize the value of the firm. Here is a sample of the answers given:

> Our objective is to finance the high growth rate of this company. Since we do not use debt, we have to make sure that we earn enough profit to finance the growth. It may be that share value is maximized as well, but we don't think about that.

> We have a goal of earnings per share which we manage astutely every quarter. Because this is a young, growing company, it is important in terms of future financing that we do not disappoint the investing public.

> The thing that means the most to the stockholder is the value of their stock. In determining the value of stock, the most critical factor is probably the earnings per share, but it also involves the fact that you are not static but moving forward and increasing your earnings per share. To increase earnings, you have to have sales growth which is the life blood of any business.

> The goal of the financial manager is to have his company produce a record that will enable it to raise capital at the lowest possible cost. To accomplish this goal, he needs a proper concept of stability and a proper concept of growth. In this company, we try to achieve a growth rate of 15 to 18 percent, compounded annually, in both sales and earnings.

Although most of the comments are self-explanatory, three points should be noted. First, while some executives did not explicitly state that the maximization of the value of the firm was their goal, this reason was implicit in all their answers. Since the management is operationally oriented, the goal of maximizing share value is translated into operating targets of growth and stability in the earnings stream. Second, the executives tend to view the value of their company independently of the effect of diversification by the investing public. From a practical standpoint, this approach has the advantage of being simple. Theoretically, this approach to valuation is adequate if the nondiversifiable risk represents a substantially large proportion of the total risk. Third, if the maximization of share value depends upon consistent growth, then it becomes vital for executives to have a constant flow of new ideas. Although the executives may search continually for new ideas, financial theorists have not contributed much to understanding how new ideas can be generated.

III. RISK ANALYSIS IN INVESTMENT DECISIONS

Concept of Risk

Theory.   A central aspect of any theory of capital budgeting is the concept of risk. Most financial writers argue that firms should choose portfolios rather than projects, and they measure the risk of a portfolio by the variance of its return.[1] This approach to the analysis of risk is a straightforward adaptation of Markowitz's quadratic programming model of portfolio selection. Although the variance is easy to manipulate mathematically, financial writers have not been completely satisfied with the concept of risk. In fact, Markowitz himself had reservations about choosing variance as a measure of risk. Besides variance, he considered five other alternative measures of risk: the expected value of loss; the probability of loss; the expected absolute deviation; the maximum expected loss; and the semi-variance. The first four measures were rejected for one reason or another as unsuitable. For the remaining two measures, variance and semi-variance, Markowitz preferred the latter for theoretical reasons, but chose the former because of its familiarity and ease of computation.

Why is semi-variance a better measure of risk than ordinary variance? Consider investment return, R, as a random variable with known probability distribution. If h stands for a critical value against which the actual values of R are compared, and $(R - h)^-$ if $(R - h) \leq 0$ and for zero if $(R - h) > 0$, then S_h (semi-variance with h as the reference point) is given by the formula:

$$S_h = E[(R - h)^-]^2 \tag{4}$$

---

[1] Return could refer to either internal rate of return, net present value, payback period, or some other measure. We are purposefully leaving the term *return* undefined, so that we can proceed with the discussion of risk.

where E is the expectation operator. In words, semi-variance is the expected value of the squared negative deviations of the possible outcomes from an arbitrarily chosen point of reference. In contrast, variance is the expected value of the squared deviations (whether positive or negative) of the possible outcomes from the mean of the random variable. This means that semi-variance evaluates the risks associated with different distributions by reference to a fixed point which is designated by the investor. The variance measure introduces no such refinement, but uses the means of the distributions, which may vary widely, to make the judgments. Also, in computing semi-variance, positive and negative deviations contribute differently to risk, whereas in computing variance, a positive and a negative deviation of the same magnitude contribute equally to risk. In essence, then, since capital has an opportunity cost, the risk of an investment decision is measured primarily by the prospect of failure to earn the return foregone. Semi-variance is more consistent with this concept of investment risk than ordinary variance.

Practice. The business executives interviewed were asked what they understood by the term *investment risk:*

> Risk is the prospect of not meeting the target rate of return. That is the risk, isn't it? If you are 100 percent sure of making the target return, then it is a zero risk proposition.

> Risk is financial in nature. It is primarily concerned with downside deviations from the target rate of return. However, if there is a good chance of coming out better than you forecast, that is negative risk (a sweetener) which is taken into account in determining the security of an investment.

> There are three things that concern me in evaluating the risk of an investment: the chances of losses exceeding a certain percent of my total equity, the chances of earning the required rate of return, and the chances of breaking even on a cash flow basis. Cash break-even is kind of a survival point. [The investment decisions in this company are few, but large in size.]

> There are some projects in the company which I don't think are going to pay off, and I disagree with the fellows who are running the show. These projects are the risky investments. Also, I never worry about the project return going above the target return. Risk is what might happen when the return is going to be less.

These statements give rise to two observations. First, when the investment decision involves only a small portion of the resources of the company, risk is primarily considered to be the prospect of not meeting some target rate of return. However, when the investment concerns a large proportion of the company's resources, risk also involves the danger of insolvency. Second, the executives' emphasis on downside risk indicates that their concept of risk is better described by semi-variance than by ordinary variance.

FIGURE 2

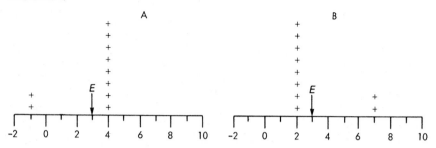

To verify further the empirical relevance of semi-variance as a risk measure, a test was designed in which the business executives were asked to choose between two hypothetical distributions of investment returns. Each investment is assumed to cost x dollars now, and after one year to return the cost of x dollars plus the profit (or loss) as given by the probability distributions in Figure 2. In this figure, each asterisk represents one possible investment outcome, and hence distribution A has a mean of 3, variance of 4 and a semi-variance of 1, whereas distribution B has a mean of 3, variance of 4, and a semi-variance of zero.[2] For this test, it is necessary to use a cost figure that the executive is familiar with, and which produces a rate of return that is reasonably close to his target rate of return as to call for considerable deliberation before arriving at a decision. Although both the target rate of return and the assumed cost of investment varied from company to company, for the sake of discussion we shall assume this cost to be $100,000 and the target rate of return 20 percent. The executives were asked to assume a position of capital rationing in which they had to choose either A or B. About one third of the executives chose A, another third chose B, and the remaining third indicated that their choice would depend on circumstances.

The reasons given for the decisions vary from company to company, but the following quotes summarize the major viewpoints:

> Why do I pick A? Well, I am going to earn a profit of 4 in 8 out of 10 times and suffer a loss of 1 in the other times. Sure, the investment is risky, but that is part of the game. I would be very much surprised that anyone in our industry wouldn't pick A because we face this kind of risk all the time.

> Because of the current tight money situation, I am worried about capital replacement in the event of loss. If we were in a period when capital could be easily replaced at a reasonable cost, then I would have an enhanced willingness to take on risky investments. In any case, I would never pick

---

[2] For this example, the critical value h in the definition of semi-variance is taken to be zero.

A unless I could get a reasonable repetition of the projects to enable the averages to come home.

Our present portfolio has a sufficient number of high risk–high return projects in it, so I would probably select B. But at another point in time I might look at those projects in terms of the portfolio aspect and pick A.

Project B has an 80 percent chance of returning 20 percent on my investment. Since my target return is 20 percent, I would probably play safe and accept B. Also, I prefer B because I have seen more heads roll as a result of negative returns.

Executives seemed more likely to choose A if their businesses accustomed them to that degree of risk, if they personally preferred risky ventures, and if they could control the loss possibility in A through diversification. When these conditions are absent, the executive is more likely to pick B because the absence of loss possibility makes it a more secure investment.

The previous analysis was concerned with a choice between two individual investments. It is equally important to examine the risk concept from the portfolio viewpoint. The executives were asked to imagine the same alternatives on a larger scale, where x represented the total company investment, and questioned as to which portfolio they would select. The answer was unanimously B, and their reasons were most succinctly voiced by the statement of one executive:

The key is survival. We will take a chance on evaluating individual projects rather optimistically, but we will not take a chance on the main company. One of our obligations is to sustain this company in life and every time we put it in a minus position, it dies a little bit if not in total.

This evidence is consistent with semi-variance as a concept of risk. If semi-variance is used by the business executives, there is a possibility that it may also be the risk concept used by security investors. If so, the definition of the risk of individual securities within a portfolio needs to be adjusted, with corresponding alterations to the existing theory of share valuation under uncertainty.

Method of Incorporating Risk

Theory.   For the present, let us accept variance as a measure of risk. How does current theory incorporate risk into investment analysis such that, given two investments with different returns and different risks, the factors can be adjusted to reach a single figure with which to compare the investments? Two methods can be distinguished: the certainty equivalent approach and the risk-adjusted discount rate approach. When the method of certainty equivalent is used, the value of an investment is calculated by discounting the random cash flows at the pure rate of interest. The resulting expected value and variance are converted into their certainty equivalent with the risk eliminated. This certainty equivalent figure determines the profitability of the investment. Under the method of risk-adjusted discount rate, the value of an investment is calculated by discounting the expected cash flow at a rate that allows for the time value of money and also for the risk present in the cash flow. The investment is profitable if the resulting value is positive.

Whichever approach is used, the investor must also decide between the single project or the portfolio framework of investment selection. This distinction can be illustrated most easily by using the certainty equivalent approach to risk analysis. In current theory, the single project approach is justified if the firm contemplates only one investment during its planning horizon. A good example of this analysis is the work of Frederick S. Hillier who derived formulas for calculating the expected value and variance of NPV from the cash flow distributions associated with an investment. However, when more than one investment may be taken, the firm's optimal selection of investments must be based on an examination of all possible combinations of investments, rather than the examination of single investments. When the portfolio approach is used, the model is generally an adaptation of the Markowitz portfolio selection model with 0–1 conditions imposed on the decision variables to reflect project indivisibility. A different model which also employs the portfolio approach is the chance-constrained model of R. Byrne, A. Charnes, W. W. Cooper, and K. Kortanek in which they imposed a probabilistic payback constraint over all investments simultaneously. The objective is to pick those projects which satisfy the constraints while maximizing expected net present value.

Practice. The executives' method of incorporating risk is primarily the risk-adjusted discount rate approach. In all companies interviewed, although the executives talked about the concept of probability, none used an explicit probabilistic framework for investment analysis. The operating division proposing a project has the responsibility of forecasting the incremental cash flows associated with the investment. In some companies, three sets of figures are forecast: optimistic, pessimistic, and most likely. The optimistic and pessimistic figures denote the range of possibilities. The "most likely" figure does not mean the mode: it is a conservative estimate which the executives consider as having a probability of about .75 of being attained or exceeded. In fact, one executive requires a minimum probability of .80 from his staff.

In most instances, the chief financial executive will receive the analysis of an investment based upon the most likely figure, and containing all the underlying assumptions. The executives were questioned as to what particular aspects of a report were most instrumental in their decisions:

> The project justification may run into volumes, but I am still going to ask my project manager one question: Why do you believe we can get a 5, or 10, or 15 percent share of the market against our competition. If he sells me on this and on the accuracy of his cost estimate, then it is a worthwhile risk venture.

> Before committing myself, I ask what else can we use the investments for, if things should go wrong. A project may have a fast payout, but it is not a good investment if we can't hedge our risk of failure.

> Sometimes I make a decision truly on the basis that I have enthusiastic support from the people that are going to implement it. I also look at their track record.

In essence, the executive is trying to check the accuracy of the most likely figure. He is modifying the projected outcome by considering the human factor and by introducing a contingency plan. His dilemma is the uncertain nature of his forecasts. The real difficulty is the search for a reliable probability distribution of cash flows to base the decision upon. Thus, if a theorist begins his analysis with an assumed probability distribution, he has assumed away one critical aspect of the problem involved.

Next, although the firms do use the portfolio approach to investment, the method of implementation and the reasons for its use differ from current theory. Current theory visualizes the investor in a portfolio framework as follows. He obtains the cash flows for the set of investments, and derives from them the means, variances, and covariances of the returns. He then chooses that portfolio of investments which gives the best combination of risk and return. But in reality, since these project analyses are submitted independently by separate divisions, no allowance is made in the risk assessment for the covariances between projects. In other words, the proposals top management receive do not contain the figures necessary for evaluating project risks on a portfolio basis in the manner presented by current theory.

The executives were asked how they introduced the portfolio approach in their investment decisions, and more specifically what was the objective and method of diversification. Diversification is thought of in terms of major activities, not with regard to every piece of capital expenditure. In practice, this involves a long-range plan (usually five years) which sets out broad guidelines for the operating divisions. The plan may call for changing, or adhering to the emphasis placed on existing activities, or for incorporating brand new ideas or products. This is where critical decisions regarding diversification are made. In formulating this plan, the executives group the many activities of the company into larger, global areas of concern, not into particular, isolated investments. Details of variances and covariances are generally left in the background. Theoretically, diversification is concerned with stabilizing the earnings stream; but, in practice, the executive is often more concerned with growth.

IV. CRITERIA FOR INVESTMENT SELECTION

Theory. In the above discussion of return and risk, we purposefully used the term *return* in its generic sense, without defining it as internal rate of return (IRR), net present value (NPV), payback period, or accounting profit, so that we could focus on the concept of risk. Current theory generally regards IRR, or its equivalent NPV, as a better measure of return than either the payback period or the accounting profit. The reason for this preference is that under conditions of certainty, of two investments of equal size, the one which has a higher IRR results in higher value for the firm. This preference has been carried over to conditions of uncertainty without sufficient critical analysis. Both the payback period and accounting profit have been regarded as inferior, because at best they can only be used to approximate the IRR. However, since the payback period is usually justified as a method of incorporating risk, a much more pertinent criticism is the limited applicability of the payback period as a method of risk analysis. Also, since reported earnings do affect share prices, investment decisions must consider the effect on accounting profit, if the goal is to maximize share values.

Although theorists have advocated IRR and NPV for measuring return, they are aware that the majority of business still use the payback period and/or the accounting profit criterion. Two reasons have been advanced to explain the relatively slow acceptance of the IRR and NPV criteria. One explanation focuses on the failure of IRR and NPV criteria to consider the effect of an investment on reported earnings. Thus, in choosing between two investments, the application of the IRR (or NPV) criterion may result in the acceptance of those investments which have a higher level of earnings, but which also produce an erratic eps pattern. Since the price-earnings ratio tends to vary inversely with the stability of earnings, the strict application of IRR criterion does not guarantee the maximum value for the firm. The other approach shows how the payback period can incorporate factors which the IRR does not pay full attention to. In their paper, Byrne, Charnes, Cooper, and Kortanek attempted to explain the common use of the payback period as a way of minimizing the risk of lost opportunities. More recently, H. Martin Weingartner tries to explain the payback method as a measure of the "liquidity" of an asset and as a simple device for "the resolution of uncertainty." In the next subsection, we shall look at the practice to determine which measure is actually used and why.

Practice. Of the eight companies questioned about investment criterion, two make primary use of the IRR, four use IRR together with accounting profit and payback, and two use accounting profit, payback, and an "exposure index," which measures the probability that the maximum investment loss will exceed a specified percentage of the firm's total equity. The two companies using primarily IRR are growth companies with closely held stock which finance growth through internal generation of funds, and whose typical investments are small in relation to the total resources of the firm. The four companies which use IRR together with accounting profit and payback are publicly held companies which rely heavily on external sources to finance growth, and whose businesses are fairly risky and competitive. The remaining two companies are similar to the above four in terms of stock ownership and in their reliance on outside capital. However, they differ in one major aspect. Their investments are more risky because of strong industry competition and because of their few, but large, investments.

These findings suggest that the payback period is primarily a risk measure. Accounting profit, since this is what the financial community focuses on, is especially important if the company is widely held and relies on external sources of financing. IRR is most likely to be the major criterion in closely held firms which are less worried by erratic patterns in their per share earnings, which finance themselves, and which make many small investments so that the risk in any one investment is not critical.

V. CONCLUSIONS

In making these case studies, I have focused on the essential points of disparity between the theory and practice of capital budgeting. The evidence suggests that there are at least six ways in which current theory can be modified to make it more operationally meaningful:

1. If we accept the objective of investment decisions to be maximizing the value of the firm, then we must provide the financial executive with a criterion for choosing between criss-crossing time patterns of share prices. The choice criteria in decision theory may be relevant to this analysis.

2. Current theory generally explains the equilibrium value of a firm in a static model. However, the financial executives need a dynamic model which explains how investors appraise eps series which exhibit different patterns over time.

3. Variance is the generally accepted measure of investment risk in current capital budgeting theory. There are theoretical reasons for preferring semi-variance and the evidence is more consistent with semi-variance than variance.

4. Accurate estimates of cash flows are crucial to the investment

decision process. To date, theorists have emphasized the analysis of investments with assumed cash flow distributions. Theorists can contribute even more by developing concepts and techniques which will enable the executives to make more reliable cash flow forecasts.

5. Current theory views diversification as a means to stabilize earnings. In fact, the executive may be more concerned with the objective of stable growth. More emphasis by theorists on ways to search for new and profitable growth opportunities seem appropriate.

6. While theorists recommended the IRR (or NPV) criterion of investment appraisal, this study confirms the prevalence of the payback period and the accounting profit criteria in practice. The theorists must identify the reason why financial executives prefer these alternative criteria and modify the IRR (or NPV) method to make it more generally applicable.

22.

Does the Capital Asset Pricing Model Work?*

DAVID W. MULLINS, JR.

Although its application continues to spark vigorous debate, modern financial theory is now applied as a matter of course to investment management. And increasingly, problems in corporate finance are also benefiting from the same techniques. The response promises to be no less heated. CAPM, the capital asset pricing model, embodies the theory. For financial executives, the proliferation of CAPM applications raises these questions: What is CAPM? How can they use the model? Most important, does it work?

CAPM, a theoretical representation of the behavior of financial markets, can be employed in estimating a company's cost of equity capital. Despite limitations, the model can be a useful addition to the financial manager's analytical tool kit.

The burgeoning work on the theory and application of CAPM has produced many sophisticated, often highly complex extensions of the simple model. But in addressing the above questions I shall focus exclusively on its simple version. Even so, finding answers to the questions requires an investment of time to understand the theory underlying CAPM.

* Reprinted by permission of the Harvard Business Review. "Does the Capital Asset Pricing Model Work?" by David W. Mullins (January/February 1982), pp. 105–14. Copyright © 1982 by the President and Fellows of Harvard College; all rights reserved.

WHAT IS CAPM?

Modern financial theory rests on two assumptions: (1) securities markets are very competitive and efficient (that is, relevant information about the companies is quickly and universally distributed and absorbed); (2) these markets are dominated by rational, risk-averse investors, who seek to maximize satisfaction from returns on their investments.

The first assumption presumes a financial market populated by highly sophisticated, well-informed buyers and sellers. The second assumption describes investors who care about wealth and prefer more to less. In addition, the hypothetical investors of modern financial theory demand a premium in the form of higher expected returns for the risks they assume.

Although these two assumptions constitute the cornerstones of modern financial theory, the formal development of CAPM involves other, more specialized limiting assumptions. These include frictionless markets without imperfections like transaction costs, taxes, and restrictions on borrowing and short selling. The model also requires limiting assumptions concerning the statistical nature of securities returns and investors' preferences. Finally, investors are assumed to agree on the likely performance and risk of securities, based on a common time horizon.

The experienced financial executive may have difficulty recognizing the world postulated by this theory. Much research has focused on relaxing these restrictive assumptions. The result has been more complex versions of the model that, however, are quite consistent with the simple version of CAPM examined in this article.

Although CAPM's assumptions are obviously unrealistic, such simplification of reality is often necessary to develop useful models. The true test of a model lies not just in the reasonableness of its underlying assumptions but also in the validity and usefulness of the model's prescription. Tolerance of CAPM's assumptions, however fanciful, allows the derivation of a concrete, though idealized, model of the manner in which financial markets measure risk and transform it into expected return.

Portfolio Diversification

CAPM deals with the risks and returns on financial securities and defines them precisely, if arbitrarily. The rate of return an investor receives from buying a common stock and holding it for a given period of time is equal to the cash dividends received plus the capital gain (or minus the capital loss) during the holding period divided by the purchase price of the security.

Although investors may expect a particular return when they buy a particular stock, they may be disappointed or pleasantly surprised, because fluctuations in stock prices result in fluctuating returns. Therefore common stocks are considered risky securities. (In contrast, because the returns on some securities, such as Treasury bills, do not differ from their expected returns, they are considered riskless securities.) Financial theory defines risk as the possibility that actual returns will deviate from expected returns, and the degree of potential fluctuation determines the degree of risk.

An underpinning of CAPM is the observation that risky stocks can be combined so that the combination (the portfolio) is less risky than any of its components. Although such diversification is a familiar notion, it may be worthwhile to review the manner in which diversification reduces risk.

Suppose there are two companies located on an isolated island whose chief industry is tourism. One company manufactures suntan lotion. Its stock predictably performs well in sunny years and poorly in rainy ones. The other company produces disposable umbrellas. Its stock performs equally poorly in sunny years and well in rainy ones. Each company earns a 12 percent average return.

In purchasing either stock, investors incur a great amount of risk because of variability in the stock price driven by fluctuations in weather conditions. Investing half the funds in the suntan lotion stock and half in the stock of the umbrella manufacturer, however, results in a return of 12 percent regardless of which weather condition prevails. Portfolio diversification thus transforms two risky stocks, each with an average return of 12 percent, into a riskless portfolio certain of earning the expected 12 percent.

Unfortunately, the perfect negative relationship between the returns on these two stocks is very rare in the real world. To some extent, corporate securities move together, so complete elimination of risk through simple portfolio diversification is impossible. However, as long as some lack of parallelism in the returns of securities exists, diversification will always reduce risk.

Two Types of Risk

Some of the risk investors assume is peculiar to the individual stocks in their portfolios—for example, a company's earnings may plummet because of a wildcat strike. On the other hand, because stock prices and returns move to some extent in tandem, even investors holding widely diversified portfolios are exposed to the risk inherent in the overall performance of the stock market.

So we can divide a security's total risk into *unsystematic risk,* the portion peculiar to the company that can be diversified away, and *systematic risk,* the nondiversifiable portion that is related to the movement of the stock market and is therefore unavoidable. Examples of systematic and unsystematic risk factors appear in Exhibit 1.

EXHIBIT 1
Some Unsystematic and Systematic Risk Factors

Unsystematic risk factors

A company's technical wizard is killed in an auto accident.

Revolution in a foreign country halts shipments of an important product ingredient.

A lower-cost foreign competitor unexpectedly enters a company's product market.

Oil is discovered on a company's property.

Systematic risk factors

Oil-producing countries institute a boycott.

Congress votes a massive tax cut.

The Federal Reserve steps up its restrictive monetary policy.

Long-term interest rates rise precipitously.

Exhibit 2 graphically illustrates the reduction of risk as securities are added to a portfolio. Empirical studies have demonstrated that unsystematic risk can be virtually eliminated in portfolios of 30 to 40 randomly selected stocks. Of course, if investments are made in closely related industries, more securities are required to eradicate unsystematic risk.

The investors inhabiting this hypothetical world are assumed to be risk averse. This notion, which agrees for once with the world most of us know, implies that investors demand compensation for taking on risk. In financial markets dominated by risk-adverse investors, higher risk securities are priced to yield higher expected returns than lower risk securities.

A simple equation expresses the resulting positive relationship be-

EXHIBIT 2
Reduction of Unsystematic Risk through Diversification

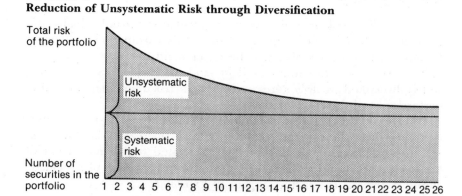

tween risk and return. The risk-free rate (the return on a riskless investment such as a T-bill) anchors the risk/expected return relationship.
The expected return on a risky security, R_s, can be thought of as the
risk-free rate, R_f, plus a premium for risk:

$$R_s = R_f + \text{risk premium}$$

The reward for tolerating CAPM's unrealistic assumptions is in having a measure of this risk premium and a method of estimating the
market's risk/expected return curve. These assumptions and the risk-
reducing efficacy of diversification lead to an idealized financial market
in which, to minimize risk, CAPM investors hold highly diversified portfolios that are sensitive only to market-related risk.

Since investors can eliminate company-specific risk simply by properly diversifying portfolios, they are not compensated for bearing unsystematic risk. And because well-diversified investors are exposed only
to systematic risk, with CAPM the relevant risk in the financial market's
risk/expected return trade-off is systematic risk rather than total risk.
Thus an investor is rewarded with higher expected returns for bearing
only market-related risk.

This important result may seem inconsistent with empirical evidence
that, despite low-cost diversification vehicles such as mutual funds, most
investors do not hold adequately diversified portfolios. Consistent with
CAPM, however, large investors such as the institutions that dominate
trading on the New York Stock Exchange do typically hold portfolios
with many securities. These actively trading investors determine securities prices and expected returns. If their portfolios are well diversified,
their actions may result in market pricing consistent with the CAPM
prediction that only systematic risk matters.

Beta is the standard CAPM measure of systematic risk. It gauges
the tendency of the return of a security to move in parallel with the
return of the stock market as a whole. One way to think of beta is as
a gauge of a security's volatility relative to the market's volatility. A
stock with a beta of 1.00—an average level of systematic risk—rises
and falls at the same percentage as a broad market index, such as Standard & Poor's 500 Stock Index.

Stocks with a beta greater than 1.00 tend to rise and fall by a greater
percentage than the market—that is, they have a high level of systematic
risk and are very sensitive to market changes. Conversely, a stock with
a beta less than 1.00 has a low level of systematic risk and is less sensitive
to market swings.

The Security Market Line

The culmination of the sequence of conceptual building blocks is
CAPM's risk/expected return relationship. This fundamental result fol-

lows from the proposition that only systematic risk, measured by beta (β), matters. Securities are priced such that:

$$R_s = R_f + \text{risk premium}$$
$$R_s = R_f + \beta_s \ (R_m - R_f)$$

where:

R_s = the stock's expected return
    (and the company's cost of equity capital).
R_f = the risk-free rate.
R_m = the expected return on the stock market as a whole.
β_s = the stock's beta.

This risk/expected return relationship is called the security market line (SML). I have illustrated it graphically in Exhibit 3. As I indicated before, the expected return on a security generally equals the risk-free rate plus a risk premium. In CAPM the risk premium is measured as beta times the expected return on the market minus the risk-free rate. The risk premium of a security is a function of the risk premium on the market, $R_m - R_f$, and varies directly with the level of beta. (No measure of unsystematic risk appears in the risk premium, of course, for in the world of CAPM diversification has eliminated it.)

In the freely competitive financial markets described by CAPM, no security can sell for long at prices low enough to yield more than its appropriate return on the SML. The security would then be very attrac-

EXHIBIT 3
The Security Market Line

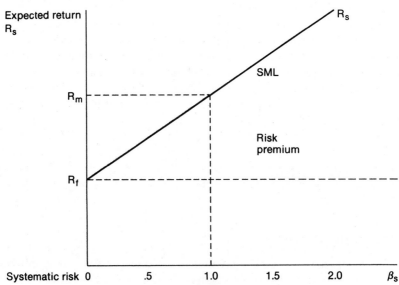

tive compared with other securities of similar risk, and investors would bid its price up until its expected return fell to the appropriate position on the SML. Conversely, investors would sell off any stock selling at a price high enough to put its expected return below its appropriate position. The resulting reduction in price would continue until the stock's expected return rose to the level justified by its systematic risk.

(An arbitrage pricing adjustment mechanism alone may be sufficient to justify the SML relationship with less restrictive assumptions than the traditional CAPM. The SML, therefore, can be derived from other models than CAPM.)

One perhaps counterintuitive aspect of CAPM involves a stock exhibiting great total risk but very little systematic risk. An example might be a company in the very chancy business of exploring for precious metals. Viewed in isolation the company would appear very risky, but most of its total risk is unsystematic and can be diversified away. The well-diversified CAPM investor would view the stock as a low-risk security. In the SML the stock's low beta would lead to a low risk premium. Despite the stock's high level of total risk, the market would price it to yield a low expected return.

In practice, such counterintuitive examples are rare; most companies with high total risk also have high betas and vice versa. Systematic risk as measured by beta usually coincides with intuitive judgments of risk for particular stocks. There is no total risk equivalent to the SML, however, for pricing securities and determining expected returns in financial markets where investors are free to diversify their holdings.

Let me summarize the conceptual components of CAPM. If the model correctly describes market behavior, the relevant measure of a security's risk is its market-related, or systematic, risk measured by beta. If a security's return bears a strong positive relationship with the return on the market and thus has a high beta, it will be priced to yield a high expected return; if it has a low beta, it will be priced to yield a low expected return.

Since unsystematic risk can be easily eliminated through diversification, it does not increase a security's expected return. According to the model, financial markets care only about systematic risk and price securities such that expected returns lie along the security market line.

HOW CAN IT BE USED?

With its insight into the financial markets' pricing of securities and the determination of expected returns, CAPM has clear applications in investment management. Its use in this field has advanced to a level of sophistication far beyond the scope of this introductory exposition.

CAPM has an important application in corporate finance as well. The finance literature defines the cost of equity as the expected return on a company's stock. The stock's expected return is the shareholders' opportunity cost of the equity funds employed by the company.

In theory, the company must earn this cost on the equity-financed portion of its investments or its stock price will fall. If the company does not expect to earn at least the cost of equity, it should return the funds to the shareholders, who can earn this expected return on other securities at the same risk level in the financial marketplace. Since the cost of equity involves market expectations, it is very difficult to measure; few techniques are available.

Cost of Equity

This difficulty is unfortunate in view of the role of equity costs in vital tasks such as capital budgeting evaluation and the valuation of possible acquisitions. The cost of equity is one component of the weighted average cost of capital, which corporate executives often use as a hurdle rate in evaluating investments. Financial managers can employ CAPM to obtain an estimate of the cost of equity capital.

If CAPM correctly describes market behavior, the security market line gives the expected return on a stock. Because this expected return, R_s, is by definition the company's cost of equity, k_e, the SML provides estimates of equity costs as well. Thus:

$$k_e = R_s = R_f + \beta_s(R_m - R_f)$$

Arriving at a cost of equity for evaluating cash flows in the future requires estimates of the future values of the risk-free rate, R_f, the expected return on the market, R_m, and beta, β_s.

Over the past 50 years, the T-bill rate (the risk-free rate) has approximately equaled the annual inflation rate. In recent years, buffeted by short-term inflationary expectations, the T-bill rate has fluctuated widely. Although sophisticated techniques could be employed to estimate the future inflation and T-bill rates, for the purposes of this exposition let us make a rough estimate of 10 percent.

Estimating the expected return on the market is more difficult. A common approach is to assume that investors anticipate about the same risk premium $(R_m - R_f)$ in the future as in the past. From 1926 to 1978, the risk premium on the Standard & Poor's 500 Stock Index averaged 8.9 percent. Benchmark estimates of 9 percent for the risk premium and 10 percent for the T-bill rate imply an estimated R_m of 19 percent.

This is substantially higher than the historical average of 11.2 percent. The difference reflects the long-term inflation rate of 10 percent incorporated in our estimated T-bill rate. The future inflation rate is assumed to be 7.5 percent higher than the 2.5 percent average rate over the 1926–78 period. Expected returns (in nominal terms) should rise to compensate investors for the anticipated loss in purchasing power.

As elsewhere, more sophisticated techniques exist, but an estimate of 19 percent for R_m is roughly consistent with historical spreads between stock returns and the returns on T-bills, long-term government bonds, and corporate bonds.

Statistical techniques that gauge the past variability of the stock relative to the market can estimate the stock's beta. Many brokerage firms and investment services also supply betas. If the company's past level of systematic risk seems likely to continue, beta calculations from historical data can be used to estimate the cost of equity.

Plugging the assumed values of the risk-free rate, the expected return on the market, and beta into the security market line generates estimates of the cost of equity capital. In Exhibit 4 I give the cost of equity estimates of three hypothetical companies.

EXHIBIT 4
Examples of Estimating the Cost of Equity Capital

Security market line:
$$k_e = R_s = R_f + \beta_s (R_m - R_f)$$
$$= 10\% + \beta_s (19\% - 10\%)$$
$$= 10\% + \beta_s (9\%)$$

Electric utility
$$\beta_U = .75$$
$$R_U = 10\% + \beta_U (9\%)$$
$$= 10\% + .75 (9\%)$$
$$= 16.75\%$$
$$k_e = 17\%$$

Chemical company
$$\beta_C = 1.10$$
$$R_C = 10\% + \beta_C (9\%)$$
$$= 10\% + 1.10 (9\%)$$
$$= 19.9\%$$
$$k_e = 20\%$$

Airline
$$\beta_A = 1.55$$
$$R_A = 10\% + \beta_A (9\%)$$
$$= 10\% + 1.55 (9\%)$$
$$= 23.95\%$$
$$k_e = 24\%$$

Assumptions:
$R_f = 10\%$, $R_m = 19\%$.

The betas in Exhibit 4 are consistent with those of companies in the three industries represented. Many electric utilities have low levels of systematic risk and low betas because of relatively modest swings in their earnings and stock returns. Airline revenues are closely tied to passenger miles flown, a yardstick very sensitive to changes in economic activity. Amplifying this systematic variability in revenues is high operating and financial leverage. The results are earnings and returns that vary widely and produce high betas in these stocks. Major chemical companies exhibit an intermediate degree of systematic risk.

I should stress that the methodology illustrated in Exhibit 4 yields

EXHIBIT 5. Risk/Expected Return Spectrum

Methodology and assumptions:

$$k_e = R_s = R_f + \beta_s(R_m - R_f) = 10\% + \beta_s(19\% - 10\%)$$

Estimated Cost of Equity (percent)	Beta	Industry		Beta	Industries (spectrum)
High-risk stocks 26.20%	1.80	Air transport		1.80	Air transport
				1.75	
				1.70	Real property
				1.65	Travel, outdoor recreation
24.40	1.60	Electronics		1.60	Miscellaneous finance; Electronics
				1.55	
				1.50	Nondurables, entertainment
23.05	1.45	Consumer durables		1.45	Business machines; Consumer durables
				1.40	Retail, general; Media
				1.35	Insurance; Trucking freight
21.70	1.30	Producer goods		1.30	Aerospace; Business services; Construction; Motor vehicles
				1.25	Photographic, optical; Chemicals; Energy, raw materials; Tires, rubber goods
20.80	1.20	Railroads, shipping		1.20	Forest products, paper
20.35	1.15	Miscellaneous, conglomerate		1.15	Drugs, medicine; Domestic oil

	Beta
Soaps, cosmetics	1.10
Steel Containers	1.05
Agriculture, food	1.00
	.95
Liquor	.90
Banks	.85
Tobacco	.80
Telephone	.75
	.70
	.65
Energy utilities	.60
	.55
	.50
	.45
	.40
Gold	.35

Medium-risk stocks	19.00	1.00 Nonferrous metals
	17.65	.85 International oil
	16.75	.75
Low-risk stocks	15.40	.60
	13.15	.35

Source of betas:
Barr Rosenberg and James Guy, "Prediction of Beta from Investment Fundamentals," *Financial Analysis Journal*, July–August 1976, p. 62.

only rough estimates of the cost of equity. Sophisticated refinements can help estimate each input. Sensitivity analyses employing various input values can produce a reasonably good range of estimates of the cost of equity. Nonetheless, the calculations in this exhibit demonstrate how the simple model can generate benchmark data.

Exhibit 5 shows the SML risk/expected return spectrum employing the average betas for companies in more than three dozen industries. The result is a pricing schedule for equity capital as a function of risk. The spectrum represents shareholders' risk/expected return opportunities in the financial markets and, therefore, shareholder opportunity costs to the particular company.

Employment of CAPM

Applications of these concepts are straightforward. For example, when a manager is calculating divisional costs of capital or hurdle rates, the cost of equity component should reflect the risk inherent in the division's operations rather than the parent company's risk. If the division is in one of the risky businesses listed in Exhibit 5, a cost of equity commensurate with this risk should be employed even though it may be much higher than the parent's cost of equity.

One approach to estimating a division cost of equity is to calculate CAPM estimates of the cost of equity for similar, independent companies operating in the same industry. The betas of these companies reflect the risk level of the industry. Of course, refinements may be necessary to adjust for differences in financial leverage and other factors.

A second example concerns acquisitions. In discounted cash flow evaluations of acquisitions, the appropriate cost of equity should reflect the risks inherent in the cash flows that are discounted. Again, ignoring refinements required by changes in capital structure and the like, the cost of equity should reflect the risk level of the target company, not the acquiror.

DOES CAPM WORK?

As an idealized theory of financial markets, the model's assumptions are clearly unrealistic. But the true test of CAPM, naturally, is how well it works.

There have been numerous empirical tests of CAPM. Most of these have examined the past to determine the extent to which stock returns and betas have corresponded in the manner predicted by the security market line. With few exceptions the major empirical studies in this field have concluded that:

> As a measure of risk, beta appears to be related to past returns. Because of the close relationship between total and systematic risk, it is difficult

to distinguish their effects empirically. Nonetheless, inclusion of a factor representing unsystematic risk appears to add little explanatory power to the risk/return relationship.

The relationship between past returns and beta is linear—that is, reality conforms to what the model predicts. The relationship is also positively sloped—that is, there is a positive trade-off between the two (high risk equals high return, low risk equals low return).

The empirical SML appears less steeply sloped than the theoretical SML. As illustrated in Exhibit 6, low-beta securities earn a return somewhat higher than CAPM would predict, and high-beta stocks earn less than predicted. A variety of deficiencies in CAPM and/or in the statistical methodologies employed have been advanced to explain this phenomenon.

Although these empirical tests do not unequivocally validate CAPM, they do support its main implications. The systematic risk measure, beta, does appear to be related to past returns; a positive risk/return trade-off does exist; and this risk/return relationship does appear to be linear. The contradictory finding concerning the slope of the SML is a subject of continuing research. Some researchers suggest using a more gradually sloped "empirical market line" based on these findings instead of the theoretical SML.

Recent work in the investment management field has challenged the proposition that only systematic risk matters. In a complex world it would be unlikely to find only one relevant type of risk—market risk.

Much progress has been made in the development of richer asset-

EXHIBIT 6
Theoretical and Estimated Security Market Lines

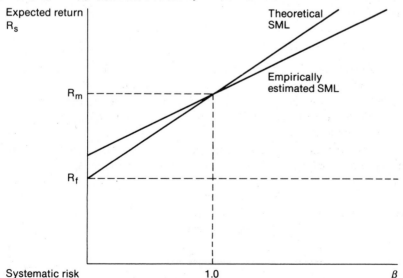

pricing models. As of yet, however, none of these more sophisticated models has proved clearly superior to CAPM. This continues to be a fertile area of research, focused primarily on investment management applications.

Application Problems

In corporate finance applications of CAPM, several potential sources of error exist. First, the simple model may be an inadequate description of the behavior of financial markets. (As I just noted, empirical work to date does not unequivocally support the validity of CAPM.) In attempts to improve its realism, researchers have developed a variety of extensions of the model.

A second problem is that betas are unstable through time. This fact creates difficulties when betas estimated from historical data are used to calculate costs of equity in evaluating future cash flows. Betas should change as both company fundamentals and capital structures change. In addition, betas estimated from past data are subject to statistical estimation error. Several techniques are available to help deal with these sources of instability.

The estimates of the future risk-free rate and the expected return on the market are also subject to error. Here too, research has focused on developing techniques to reduce the potential error associated with these inputs to the SML.

A final set of problems is unique to corporate finance applications of CAPM. There are practical and theoretical problems associated with employing CAPM, or any financial market model, in capital budgeting decisions involving real assets. These difficulties continue to be a fertile area of research.

Dividend Growth Model

The deficiencies of CAPM may seem severe. They must be judged, however, relative to other approaches for estimating the cost of equity capital. The most commonly used of these is a simple discounted cash flow (DCF) technique, which is known as the dividend growth model (or the Gordon-Shapiro model).

This approach is based on the proposition that the price of a company's stock equals the present value of future dividends per share discounted by the company's cost of equity capital. With the assumption that future dividends per share are expected to grow at a constant rate and that this growth rate will persist forever, the general present value formula collapses to a simple expression:

$$P = \frac{dps}{k_e - g}$$

where:

P = the current price of the stock.
dps = next year's dividends per share.
g = the perpetuity growth rate in dividends per share.
k_e = the company's cost of equity capital.

If the market is pricing the stock in this manner, we can infer the cost of equity impounded in the stock price. Solving for the cost of equity yields:

$$k_e = \frac{dps}{P} + g$$

The cost of equity implied by the current stock price and the assumptions of the model is simply the dividend yield plus the constant growth rate.

Like CAPM, two of the model's assumptions limit the dividend growth technique. One is the assumption of a constant, perpetual growth rate in dividends per share. Second, to permit the general present value formula to collapse to the simple stock price equation I gave, the perpetual constant growth rate must be less than the company's cost of equity. If this is not the case, the equation is not valid.

These two assumptions sharply limit the applicability of the dividend growth model. The model cannot be used in estimating costs of equity for companies with unstable dividend patterns or for rapidly growing companies where g is likely to be greater than k_e. (Obviously, the model also does not apply to companies paying no dividends.) Unlike CAPM, the model is limited mainly to companies enjoying slow, steady growth in dividends. More complex DCF techniques can, however, handle a wider range of companies.

Another problem with using the dividend growth model to estimate costs of equity is in gauging g. To derive a sound cost of equity figure, one must estimate the growth rate investors are using to value the stock. Thus it is the market's current estimate of g that matters, not the company's. This is a major source of error in the dividend growth model.

In contrast, the only company-specific input to the SML is the beta, which is derived by an objective statistical method. Even more sophisticated DCF techniques require as an input the market's estimate of the company's future dividends per share.

When compared with the dividend growth model and other DCF approaches, CAPM's deficiencies do not appear so severe. There is no reason, however, to consider CAPM and the dividend growth model as competitors. Very few techniques are available for the difficult task of measuring the cost of equity. Despite the shortcomings, investors should use both the DCF and CAPM models as well as sound judgment to estimate the cost of equity.

IMPERFECT, BUT USEFUL

Investment managers have widely applied the simple CAPM and its more sophisticated extensions. CAPM's application to corporate finance is a recent development. Although it has been employed in many utility rate-setting proceedings, it has yet to gain widespread use in corporate circles for estimating companies' costs of equity.

Because of its shortcomings, financial executives should not rely on CAPM as a precise algorithm for estimating the cost of equity capital. Nevertheless, tests of the model confirm that it has much to say about the way returns are determined in financial markets. In view of the inherent difficulty in measuring the cost of equity, CAPM's deficiencies appear no worse than those of other approaches. Its key advantage is that it quantifies risk and provides a widely applicable, relatively objective routine for translating risk measures into estimates of expected return.

CAPM represents a new and different approach to an important task. Financial decision makers can use the model in conjunction with traditional techniques and sound judgment to develop realistic, useful estimates of the costs of equity capital.

23.

The Cost of Capital and U.S. Capital Investment: A Test of Alternative Concepts*

J. WALTER ELLIOTT

I. INTRODUCTION

In the recent literature on corporation finance, the role of the cost of capital in financial structure decisions has come under debate. Charles W. Haley and Lawrence D. Schall argue that the concept can be misleading when applied to decisions on capital structure. Other difficulties with the concept applied to capital structure problems have been pointed out by Stewart Myers and clarified by D. J. Ashton and D. R. Atkins, while a defense of its use in this context is presented by Timothy Nantell and C. R. Carlson.

The more widespread use of the cost of capital as a hurdle rate for investment has also spurred recent debate by Fred Arditti, James Ang, as well as by Haley and Schall. Objections raised regarding the use of the cost of capital in this context are less severe than for capital structure decisions, and are at least partially matters of semantics. A defense of the cost of capital used in this context is contained in Nantell and Carlson as well as in a recent paper by William Beranek. Haley and Schall summarize the difficulties with the weighted average cost

---

* *Journal of Finance* 35, no. 4 (September 1980), pp. 981–94.

of capital as being concerned with two points, (a) there may be a different cost of capital for different risk levels and for different time periods and (b) internal and external financial investments can have differing rates of return under certain conditions.

Although technical problems such as those now cited remain with the concept of the cost of capital used as a hurdle rate, they appear to be of a refined and relatively minor nature when compared to the unresolved empirical questions associated with the cost of capital. The cost of equity alone accounts for much of the difficulty. It has been variously represented in the literature as a dividend yield, an earnings yield, an ex-post return on stock, and as the return on the general class of real assets. In addition, at least four substantively different groups of ideas have emerged over the past several decades as to how we may best represent fluctuations in the overall cost of capital through time. This produces a dilemma for those interested in empirical research into capital and investment theory. For, even if we agree upon the theoretical role of the cost of capital, which measure should be used to represent this role and why? Virtually no empirical results exist at present to support either the choice of one cost of capital measure over another or to support the decision that we may remain indifferent among the alternatives that have been presented.

Moreover, there has not been much of a consensus on the empirical significance of theory's role for the cost of capital in investment spending. Dale Jorgenson's work uses one specific representation of the cost of capital embedded in a rental price of capital term. This produces the result that capital investment is highly inelastic relative to the cost of capital. Other econometric investment models oriented toward prediction such as those of Michael Evans or Robert Resek add an interest rate representation of the cost of capital as a term in a linear regression model having investment as the dependent variable. These terms are found to be of statistical significance. However, translating this into a test of the significance of the theoretical role of the cost of capital in investment has not been done in the regression models.

This paper seeks to examine empirically and at the aggregate level the influence of the marginal cost of capital upon investment. It does this by formulating an investment model structure that reflects explicitly and uncompromisingly the theoretical role of the cost of capital in investment. This model is used to compare and evaluate the usefulness of alternative measures of the marginal cost of capital in explaining investment. Two types of results are produced. First, we produce findings about the influence of the cost of capital on investment that are largely independent of how we represent the cost of capital. These results are important in establishing the extent to which the evidence affirms the theoretical role of the cost of capital regardless of how we measure that variable. Second, our tests produce results on differences in the relative performance of various cost of capital measures, which help establish the extent to which one measure of the cost of capital is preferable to another.

We proceed by first defining four measures of the marginal cost of capital that reflect major concepts proposed to date. We use each of these measures in an investment model structure that is based on the conventional premise of maximizing net present value of the firm.

Our tests find a clearly significant cost of capital effect upon investment regardless of the measure we use. We also find that the restrictions upon model parameters implied by the underlying theory are met by all the cost of capital measures used.

We find some substantive differences in the relative performance of the cost of capital measures examined. However, the alternatives are in general more alike than different, and do not allow a clear choice of one cost of capital measure.

II. THE COST OF CAPITAL MEASURES

The cost of capital measures and the marginal return on investment are measured in nominal terms following the usual pattern in the literature. Taking explicit account of inflationary expectations could lead to their alternate formulation in real terms. While this is conceptually more pleasing, there is little reason to believe it would affect the comparisons among cost of capital measures that are our main concern.

The first cost of capital measure is a debt interest rate. It is common in the empirical literature on capital investment to represent the cost of capital by a rate of interest on corporate bonds. Macroeconomic theorists also almost uniformly follow this same pattern, employing a debt interest rate in aggregate demand functions to represent cost of capital effects in investment spending as well as interest rate effects on consumption spending. With a stable term structure, fluctuations in a debt rate of interest should presumably approximate fluctuations in the costs of all types of capital.

Thus, movements in a debt rate conceivably can be a simple and observable indicator of movements in broader and more complex cost of capital measures. Along these lines, Joseph Stiglitz has developed a model that shows that under conditions of certainty and under certain market efficiency restrictions, a pre-tax debt rate of interest is the theoretically correct representation of the marginal cost of capital. Without going this far, we make the less restrictive hypothesis that the marginal cost of capital, denoted as C_t is proportional to a bond rate of interest, i_t:

$$C_t = \gamma \cdot i_t \qquad \gamma > 0 \qquad (1)$$

The second and third measures of C_t we examine define the marginal cost of capital in the context of corporate business. This approach treats C_t as a weighted average of the marginal costs of debt, equity, and retained earnings, where the weights are the optimal proportions of each type of capital in the firm's financing mix. This way of measuring the cost of capital has been developed in the literature on corporation finance and capital budgeting. An earnings rate on new investment of equal risk to that of the firm's accumulated assets that yields a return equal to the weighted cost of capital is just sufficient to pay all suppliers of capital their required returns. Thus, the weighted cost of capital is the combined opportunity cost of funds available for new investment projects of homogeneous risk. Before tax adjustment, the weighted marginal cost of capital, $W_{b,t}$ is

$$W_{b,t} = \rho_{i,t} i_t + \rho_{e,t} \cdot e_t + \rho_{r,t} \cdot r_t \tag{2}$$

where ρ_i, ρ_e, and ρ_r are the optimal proportions of debt, equity, and retained earnings respectively, and e_t and r_t are the marginal costs of equity capital and retained earnings respectively. Disregarding taxes, $r_t = e_t$ since both new equity and retained earnings are funds belonging to residual owners. Taxes alter expression (2) in two ways. First, corporate income taxes reduce the effective cost of debt below its nominal cost. Second, dividend taxes must be taken into account. Specifically with marginal dividend tax rates equal to $t_{d,t}$, $r_t = e_t(1 - t_{d,t})$. The resulting tax-adjusted weighted cost of funds, $W_{a,t}$, is:

$$W_{a,t} = \rho_{i,t} \cdot i_t(1 - t_{p,t}) + \rho_{e,t} \cdot e_t + \rho_{r,t} \cdot (1 - t_{d,t}) \tag{3}$$

where $t_{p,t}$ is the marginal tax rate on corporate profits.

The two alternative weighted average measures of C_t we examine differ according to how each measures the cost of equity funds. The first alternative assumes the aggregate cost of equity to be equal to the earnings/price ratio for all corporations. Denoting the aggregate earnings/price ratio by $(E/P)_t$, this gives;

$$C_t = \rho_{i,t} i_t(1 - t_{p,t}) + \rho_{e,t} \cdot (E/P)_t + \rho_{r,t} \cdot (E/P)_t \cdot (1 - t_{d,t}) \tag{4}$$

The earnings/price ratio as a measure of the cost of equity is an idea suggested in the accounting literature and in parts of the literature on capital investment. In this view, new equity funds that cannot produce added profits in proportion to (E/P) will not meet investor expectations and will presumably lead to a lower share price. Proponents of the use of (E/P) recommend its use to measure the cost of equity because it is simple to calculate and is fully observable. Critics of the earnings/price ratio point out that (a) it is distorted by the use of after-tax earnings whereas most capital budgeting is designed to identify cash flow rates of return on new investment and (b) it uses actual rather than expected earnings which usually differ substantively.

The literature on capital investment theory stresses that the cost of equity is the expected return to shareholders on funds invested in the firm. However, there is little if any past work that formulates empirical measures of the cost of equity treated explicitly as a measure of expectations.

Fundamentally, the cost of equity is a long-run perception by investors of the dividend and capital gains income they expect on this component of financial wealth, expressed as a rate of return. Interestingly, there has now accumulated growing experience with measuring long-run expected income from total household stocks of financial and other wealth. This work is in connection with the permanent income theory of consumption, and has produced highly satisfactory empirical results. The techniques developed in the permanent income literature can be directly applied to measuring the long-run expected income from equity investment. Following this approach, permanent nonhuman or financial income is defined as the expected long-run return on financial wealth. The stock of equity capital is a component of the stock of total financial wealth. Accordingly, the income expected from equity wealth can be approximated in the same way that the income expected from total wealth is approximated in the permanent income literature. Michael Darby's version of this procedure involves isolating a "permanent" component of the observable income from wealth.

This measure of permanent income views the typical investor as forming an expectation of future long-run equity earnings partly on the basis of the past pattern of actual accrued earnings and partially on the basis of current earnings and prices. Statistically, permanent income is essentially a trend component of measured income modified by successive realizations of the actual income series. For equity, the observable income Y_e, is the flow of dividends plus changes in capital value. To quantify permanent equity income, we follow Darby's use of a difference equation that relates permanent income to observable income and past values of permanent income. This equation applied to income from equity is:

$$Y_{p,t} = \beta \cdot Y_{e,t} + (1 - \beta)(1 + g) \cdot Y_{p,t-1} \tag{5}$$

where β is the weight of current observable income upon permanent income and g is the long-run growth rate of permanent income. The value of $Y_{p,t}$ calculated from (5) measures the expected or permanent income from equity. It has the advantage of following from a fairly well-known procedure that has proved successful in estimates of aggregated permanent income from total wealth. The cost of equity that follows from its use is $Y_{p,t}/P_{t-1}$. This permanent income measure of the cost of equity gives a third measure of C_t:

$$C_t = \rho_{i,t} \cdot i_t(1 - l_{p,t}) + \rho_{e,t} \cdot Y_{p,t}/P_{t-1} + \rho_{r,t} \cdot Y_{p,t}/P_{t-1} \cdot (1 - l_{d,t}) \tag{6}$$

The fourth cost of capital measure we examine is that of Franco Modigliani and Merton Miller, in conjunction with their provocative analyses of the relationship between capital structure, the cost of capital, and the market value of the firm. Basically, the Modigliani-Miller work shows that for certain well specified capital market conditions the only impact of debt financing upon the cost of capital arises from the tax deductability of interest payments. Accordingly, the weighted cost of capital is not appropriate for the Modigliani-Miller formulation. The Modigliani-Miller cost of capital measure we examine is taken from their application of their theory to measuring cost of capital effects in the utility industry. At the aggregate level, the Modigliani-Miller measure is given as follows:

$$C_t = \frac{E_t + (1 - t_{p,t}) \cdot F_t}{V_t - t_{p,t} \cdot D_t - G_t} (1 - t_{p,t} \cdot \rho_{i,t}) \tag{7}$$

where E_t is after-tax corporate profits, F_t is total corporate interest payments, V_t is the market value of all corporations as reflected by the market value of outstanding stocks and bonds, D_t is the total stock of corporate debt, G_t is the market's valuation of expected growth in V_t, and as before $t_{p,t}$ and $\rho_{i,t}$ are the marginal profits tax rate and the optimal debt proportion respectively.

The Investment Model Structure

The investment model used to evaluate these cost of capital measures is based upon the capital investment theory that has emerged over the past two decades in the literature in capital budgeting and finance. This theory follows from a shareholder wealth-maximizing criterion. Each time period, the state of the world produces an array of new or revised investment opportunities. These opportunities include additions to, or replacement of, homogeneous capital, investment in new production technology, investment required to enter new product areas, or almost any other purchase of business assets. The net present value of each opportunity is based on each firm's expected future profit flow from the investment and upon its marginal cost of capital. Spending on new investment projects proceeds to the point where marginal projects earn zero net present value. This investment policy maximizes the present value of shareholder wealth for temporally independent sets of investment opportunities. At the aggregate level of our analysis, we may abstract from the types of conditions set forth by Varouj Awazian and Jeffrey Callen where investment may stop short of, or proceed beyond, the usual point of zero net present value.

To represent this theory, we begin with the following statement of the cumulative net present value, N, of any volume of investment, I:

$$N = E^* \left[\frac{1}{(1 + C)} + \frac{1}{(1 + C)^2} + \cdots + \frac{1}{(1 + C)^n} \right] + \frac{S}{(1 + C)^{n+1}} - I \tag{8}$$

where E^* is the annual earnings over an n-period planning horizon expected from new investment of I funds, S is the scrap value of I which we assume is realized during the period following the last income producing period of the asset, i.e., at $n + 1$, C is as before the cost of capital, and where t subscripts have been dropped from N, E^*, C, S, and I for convenience.

To formulate an investment model from (8), we first take the expected scrap value to be approximately equal to one year's expected earnings. We can then rewrite (8) as:

$$N = E^* \left[\frac{(1 + C)^{n+1} - 1}{C(1 + C)^{n+1}} \right] - I \tag{9}$$

or by letting $\dfrac{(1 + C)^{n+1} - 1}{C(1 + C)^{n+1}} = F(C)$

as

$$N = E^* \cdot F(C) - I \tag{9a}$$

We follow the approach in the finance literature of interpreting C as a hurdle date that has an exogenous influence upon investment. Accordingly, $F(C)$ is assumed to influence N and therefore I without feedback effects. This interpretation of C is somewhat questionable for at least some of our alternative representations of C. When the adjustment mechanism is defined below, the possibility of feedback effects is explicitly addressed. According to the theory, the value of E^* should rise with I at a falling rate. E^* should also reflect the impact that the state of the world has upon investment opportunities of firms. With little theoretical guidance as to how to structure these effects upon E^*, we take them to be related in a simple log linear fashion:

$$E^* = a \cdot I^b \cdot Z^d \qquad \begin{array}{l} 0 < b < 1 \\ d > 0 \end{array} \tag{10}$$

where a, b, and d are parameters and Z is a measure of profit expectations regarding I that reflects the way the state of the world impacts upon E^*. Combining (9a) and (10) gives:

$$N = aI^b Z^d F(C) - I \tag{11}$$

Maximum cumulative net present value from current investment occurs where $\dfrac{dN}{dI} = 0$ and $\dfrac{d^2N}{dI^2} < 0$, or where:

$$I^* = [abZ^d F(C)]^{\frac{1}{1-b}} \tag{12}$$

where I^* denotes the wealth maximizing or desired volume of investment.

Denoting $x^* = \log I^*$, $z = \log Z$, and $f(c) = \log F(C)$, and restoring the t subscripts, we can rewrite (12) as:

$$x_t^* = \gamma_0 + \gamma_1 z_t + \gamma_2 f(c)_t \tag{13}$$

where $\gamma_0 = \log(a \cdot b)/(1 - b)$, $\gamma_1 = d/(1 - b)$, and $\gamma_2 = 1/(1 - b)$. Expression (13) can be converted into a model of investment behavior by specifying the mechanism by which changes in the actual level of investment respond to changes in the desired level. Using the generalized Koyck adjustment process developed by Jorgenson, we can write:

$$x_t - x_{t-1} = \sum_{i=0}^{m} w_i [x_{t-1}^* - x_{t-i-1}^*] \tag{14}$$

where we constrain $\sum_{i=0}^{m}$ to unity. Combining (14 and (13) gives:

$$x_t - x_{t-1} = \gamma_1 \sum_{i=0}^{m} w_i \Delta z_{t-i} + \gamma_2 \sum_{i=0}^{m} w_i \Delta f(c)_{t-i} \tag{15}$$

To approximate the nonobserved profit expectations variable Z, it is appealing to follow Yehda Grunfeld in supposing that changes in security market values sensitively reflect perceived changes in the way the state of the work impacts upon investors' profit expectations. Given that securities markets are in equilibrium where expected returns are at required levels, the value of stocks and bonds, V_t, can be related to earnings expectations as:

$$V_t = \frac{A_t^*}{C_t} \tag{16}$$

where A^* is the market expectation of the annual flow of returns from amassed business assets and C_t is, as before, the cost of capital. We assume that state-of-the-world impacts on profit expectations regarding new investment are closely related to the same impacts on profit expectations regarding amassed business assets. Accordingly, we write:

$$Z_t = f \cdot (A_t^*) = f \cdot (C_t \cdot V_t) \quad f > 0 \tag{17}$$

where f is a constant value. Taking logs of (17) to obtain z_t gives $z_t = \log f + \log (C \cdot V)_t$. Differencing and inserting this into (15) completes the investment model

$$x_t - x_{t-1} = \gamma_1 \sum_{i=1}^{m} w_i \Delta \log(C \cdot V)_{t-i} + \gamma_2 \sum_{i=1}^{m} w_i' \Delta f(c)_{t-i} \tag{18}$$

where also the first term in each of the distributed lags has been constrained to zero to avoid problems of simultaneity in statistical estimation, especially due to $F(c)$. Constraining $w_0 = 0$ is consistent with a body of studies on the lags in the capital investment process. We also constrain the distributed lag weights w_i for both terms to lie along a polynomial of the same degree and length, but not necessarily the same curvature. We write the weights as w_i and w'_i in (18) to reflect this generalization.

Empirical Analysis

For our purposes, the most direct and meaningful empirical results are produced by successively estimating Equation (18) with each of the cost of capital measures. This gives information on both the common and unique features of each measure. To do this, quarterly data are taken for all variables sufficient to enable regressions to be run over the period 1955.1 to 1978.3.

Each of the cost of capital measures is inserted into expression (18). The length of the distributed lag is fit separately for each cost of capital measure by adding terms to the lag as long as the standard error is reduced. Both lags begin at $t - 1$ and multicollinearity is not a significant characteristic of the data. Accordingly, no special estimating procedures are required. The results below are obtained using OLS.

The dependent variable, investment spending, is defined in two ways. First, the GNP series, Fixed Nonresidential Investment, is used. Second, the narrower BEA New Plant and Equipment series is used. Table 1 presents the results for each cost of capital measure using the GNP investment expenditure series. The F-statistic for the cost of capital term in Table 1 tests the null hypothesis that the coefficients in the cost of capital lag distribution, $\sum_{w_i}$, are zero. We can reject this hypothesis in all four cases in favor of the alternative that a significantly nonzero cost of capital effect occurs. We may conclude that a cost of capital effect upon investment that is significant beyond the 1 percent level occurs regardless of which of the four cost of capital measures we use. This is positive empirical affirmation of the role expression (18) prescribes for the cost of capital in investment spending, regardless of how we measure the cost of capital.

Comparing the standard errors and R^2 values, we find a noticeable difference between the best fitting weighted average-permanent income equation (#3) and the worst fitting Modigliani-Miller equation (#4). The standard error is increased by almost 17 percent by using the Modigliani-Miller measure instead of the weighted average measure, while the R^2 falls from .567 to .413. The data thus tends to support the weighted average concept of the cost of capital distinctly more strongly than it supports the Modigliani-Miller concept.

The other two cost of capital measures show less pronounced differences. The results using the interest rate measure (#1) are quite close to those using the weighted average-permanent income measure. And,

TABLE 1
Statistics for GNP Investment Equations

$$x_t - x_{t-1} = \gamma_0 + \gamma_1 \sum_{i=1}^{m} w_i \Delta \log(C \cdot V)_{h-i} + \gamma_2 \sum_{i=1}^{m} w_i' \Delta f(C)_{h-i}$$

Cost of Capital Definition	γ_0	γ_1	γ_2	R^2 (Std. Error)	Regression F-Statistics*	F-Statistic for Cost of Capital Term†	D.W.	Calculated b: d	m
1. Interest rate	.0030 (0.80)	0.472 (4.50)	2.229 (7.41)	.544 (.0178)	12.85	14.95	1.69	.551	7
2. Weighted average: Earnings/price version	−.0035 (1.15)	0.658 (6.45)	1.671 (7.43)	.505 (.0185)	10.97	14.80	1.63	.212 .402 .393	5
3. Weighted average: Permanent income version	−.0073 (2.51)	0.924 (7.90)	4.216 (4.12)	.567 (.0173)	14.09	4.40	1.73	.763 .219	9
4. Modigliani-Miller	−.0005 (0.20)	0.424 (6.24)	2.842 (5.08)	.413 .0202	7.55	8.08	1.31	.648 .149	7

Note: Numbers in parentheses are absolute values of t-statistics.
† Significant beyond 1 percent level (4, 86) d.f.
* Significant beyond 1 percent level (8, 86) d.f.

while the weighted average earnings/price measure (#2) explains investment less sensitively than either the interest rate of permanent income measure, the difference is not large.

The estimated coefficient values show that both distributed lag sequences have significantly large t statistics in all four equations. Regression F-statistics show each of the equations provides a statistically significant explanation of fluctuations in investment. Indeed, both the F-statistics and the R^2 values in Table 1 support the model structure of Equation (18) solidly given that the dependent variable in our regressions is a percent change in investment.

The estimated coefficients enable calculations of the structural parameters b and d in expression (10). These are shown in the next to last column in Table 1. The coefficient b shows the net present value impact of changes in investment, and can be interpreted as the long-run elasticity of expected net present value relative to investment. The value of b is between zero and one for all four cost of capital measures, consistent with the expectation of a declining marginal net present value product of investment. The estimated b values thus uniformly support the theory regardless of our choice of cost of capital measures.

The coefficient d shows the net present value impact of shifts in expectations. The estimated d values are all greater than zero, also corresponding to the expectation of our theory in every case.

The values of b and d also show that cost of capital effects on expected net present value are quantitatively greater than profit-expectations effects for all four measures, with the difference being quite pronounced in all cases except the weighted average-earnings/price model (#2). For the best-fitting weighted average-permanent income model (#3), the cost of capital elasticity is about 3½ times as large as the profit expectations elasticity. These results suggest that cost of capital influences on investment are relatively important compared to profit expectations influences.

Table 2 gives results for the same estimations using the narrower BEA Plant and Equipment series rather than the GNP investment series. The statistics in Table 2 are largely the same as Table 1. The best-fitting model is again the weighted average-permanent income version (#3) while the worst fitting is the Modigliani-Miller model (#4), with the standard error in the latter case 16 percent higher than in the former case. Again, these data support the weighted average concept more strongly than the Modigliani-Miller concept.

F-statistics for the cost of capital term are significant beyond the 1 percent level for the first three cost-of-capital terms, and significant at about the 2 percent level for the Modigliani-Miller term. As earlier, the evidence suggests a statistically significant cost of capital effect upon investment regardless of how we define the cost of capital.

Furthermore, T-Statistics for the γ_2 coefficient are significant beyond

TABLE 2
Statistics for Plant and Equipment Equations

$$x_t - x_{t-1} + \gamma_0 + \gamma_1 \sum_{i=1}^{m} w_i \Delta \log(C \cdot V)_{t-i} + \gamma_2 \sum_{i=1}^{m} w_i' \Delta f(c)_{t-i}$$

Cost of Capital Definition	γ_0	γ_1	γ_2	R^2 (Std. Error)	Regression F-Statistics*	F-Statistics for Cost of Capital Term	D.W.	Calculated b		m
								b	d	
1. Interest rate	.0017 (0.32)	0.586 (3.78)	2.244 (5.29)	.430 (.0227)	8.11	8.80†	1.71	.554	.261	8
2. Weighted average: Earnings/price version	−.0076 (1.96)	0.781 (5.62)	1.831 (6.00)	.439 (.0225)	8.41	9.27†	1.70	.454	.426	6
3. Weighted average: Permanent income version	−.0102 (2.64)	1.060 (6.50)	6.179 (4.61)	.485 (.0216)	10.13	5.75†	1.88	.838	.172	11
4. Modigliani-Miller	−.0004 (0.11)	0.376 (4.42)	2.246 (3.24)	.301 (.0251)	4.64	3.53‡	1.52	.555	.167	7

Note: Numbers in parentheses are absolute values of t-statistics.
* Significant at the 5 percent level with (4, 86) d.f.
† Significant beyond 1 percent level with (8, 86) d.f.
‡ Significant beyond 1 percent level with (4, 86) d.f.

the 1 percent level for all four measures. Computed *b* values all lie between 0 and 1, thus conforming to the expectation of theory. Values of *d* are all greater than zero, also in conformance with theory. And, as before, cost of capital influences upon net present value are several times larger than profit expectations influences in all cases except the weighted average-earnings/price model (#2). In summary, Table 2 suggests that our conclusions on the influence of the cost of capital are largely independent of whether we define investment by the GNP series or by the Plant and Equipment series.

The Elasticity of Investment Relative to the Cost of Capital

As a result of the form of $F(c)$, the elasticity of investment relative to the cost of capital depends on the level of investment and the value of the cost of capital. In addition, the cost of capital influences investment in Equation (18) with a distributed lag. These attributes suggest a dynamic simulation is a useful way to measure the elasticity in this case. To do this, a nonturbulent time period, 1964–1967 was chosen, and baseline results obtained for all four models using the GNP definition of investment. Then, a 10 percent one-time increase in the cost of capital was made in 1964.1. Table 3 gives elasticities calculated from the resulting deviations of investment from the baseline. All four cost-of-capital measures show small initial elasticities, ranging from −.04 to −.14 one quarter after the change. By five quarters after the change, the elasticities range more widely, from −.35 to −.87. The long-run or steady state values show an even wider range, from −.35 to −1.47.

The weighted average-permanent income measure of the cost of capital produces a long-run elasticity that is more than twice as large as the next highest measure. This measure shows a relatively elastic

TABLE 3
Elasticity of Investment Relative to the Cost of Capital

Quarters after Change	Interest Rate	Weighted Average: Earnings/ Price	Weighted Average: Permanent Income	Modigliani- Miller
		Elasticities		
1	−.07	−.07	−.14	−.04
3	−.31	−.23	−.50	−.29
5	−.48	−.35	−.87	−.46
7	−.67	−.35	−1.17	−.56
9	−.67	−.35	−1.39	−.56
Long-run	−.67	−.35	−1.47	−.56

Note: Values shown are elasticities for the cumulative investment response to a 10 percent one-time change in the cost of capital introduced in 1964.1.

response of investment to changes in the cost of capital for a response period of seven quarters or longer. Since this weighted average-permanent income measure gave the lowest standard error in explaining investment, the reader may wish to place somewhat more emphasis on the elasticity calculated from it than upon elasticities calculated for the other alternatives. The weighted average measure in particular gives elasticities considerably higher than elasticities measured elsewhere.

Conclusions and Implications

We have found that none of the four alternative concepts of the cost of capital examined can be rejected as being inconsistent with data on U.S. investment. All make a statistically significant contribution to explaining fluctuations in investment, and all have structural coefficient values that conform to the restrictions implied by underlying theory. This result is of particular interest, since the explanatory role we have found for the cost of capital in investment spending is independent of how we define the cost of capital.

The largest difference in the goodness of fit due to the cost of capital measures is between the weighted average concept of the cost of capital and the Modigliani-Miller concept. The weighted average-permanent income measure lowers the standard error by 17 percent compared to the Modigliani-Miller measure. This difference is large enough to support the conclusion that the weighted average cost of capital measure leads to a better explanation of fluctuations in investment than the Modigliani-Miller measure. Similar comparisons among other alternative cost of capital measures are not as clear. Indeed, other important differences in explanatory significance are not present.

The elasticity of investment relative to the cost of capital varies more widely among the alternative cost of capital measures than do any other statistical results associated with these measures. Using the best-fitting weighted average (permanent income) concept of the cost of capital, we find a long-run elasticity of investment of nearly 1.5, indicating a much greater level of sensitivity of investment to cost of capital fluctuations than has heretofore been found in empirical investment studies. However, elasticities for the other cost of capital measures are smaller and more in line with prior results.

The weighted average cost of capital measure ranks highest among the alternatives examined using goodness of fit criteria. Accepting this as the most appropriate representation of the cost of capital has some interesting implications regarding the channel through which monetary policy may impact upon real markets. If we examine representative weights for debt versus equity costs over the period of our study, we find that roughly 75 percent of the fluctuation in the cost of capital is due to fluctuations in tax-adjusted equity costs while only 25 percent is due to fluctuations in debt costs. Costs of debt and of equity may not always move closely together. In cases where they do not, monetary policy efforts to influence investment by changing the cost of capital will have a much greater impact if they succeed in influencing equity costs than if they are primarily confined to debt markets influences. Indeed, in these times activist monetary policy may have a more important concern with stock market conditions than with bond market conditions.

24.

Residential Real Estate versus Financial Assets*

THOMAS J. COYNE
WALDEMAR M. GOULET
MARIO J. PICCONI

The conventional wisdom of the late 1960s to early 1970s was that common stocks provided the best hedge against inflation. Sophisticated investors believed stock price movement to be highly correlated with inflation. On the other hand, two of the authors of this article concluded that "from 1969 to 1975, a golden era of excess returns to real estate existed vis-a-vis returns to alternative investment opportunities." This study examines the validity of that statement when financial leverage is considered.

We use monthly data of returns to stocks, bonds, and real estate. The time period we studied was from January 1969 through December 1977. "Stock" returns are calculated by monthly changes in the value of a market index; "bonds" are monthly changes in a bond index. We calculated imputed returns for residential real estate from mean values of existing single-family homes sold in the United States. The data assume reinvestment of dividends and interest for stocks and bonds, respectively, while real estate returns result solely from monthly changes in market value, since no intermediate cash flow occurs. The formula for calculating returns in the earlier study was:

* *Journal of Portfolio Management* 7, no. 1 (Fall 1980), pp. 20–24.

$$r_t = \frac{V_t + A_t - V_{t-t}}{V_{t-1}}$$

where

> r_t = the rate of return to the investment at the end of period t,
> V_t = the market value of the investment at the end of period t,
> A_t = the net cash flow (interest or dividends) received at the end of period t, and
> V_{t-1} = the market value of the investment at the end of period $t-1$.

We have adjusted this formula slightly here to allow for consideration of financial leverage: We reduced the original gross returns by the carrying cost of the investment; i.e., by interest in the numerator. But we deducted the amount borrowed from the denominator in order to reflect the equity investment. Consequently, the formula for stocks and bonds is

$$r_t = \frac{V_t + A_t - V_{t-1} - (1 - m)(V_{t-1})(c)}{m \cdot V_{t-1}}$$

where

> m = margin rate (percent downpayment),
> c = call rate $\pm$ plus one percent; i.e., investor's borrowing rate,
> $(1 - m)$ = percent borrowed (because m = margin downpayment),
> $(1 - m)(V_{t-1})$ = dollars borrowed,
> $(1 - m)(V_{t-1})(c)$ = interest paid on dollars borrowed,
> V_{t-1} = gross original investment, and
> $(m)(V_{t-1})$ = dollar downpayment or equity investment.

The leverage formula for real estate is

$$h = \frac{H_t + R - H_{t-1} - (e)(H_{t-1}(f/12)}{(1 - e)H_{t-1}}$$

$$h = \frac{H_t - H_{t-1}(1 - e \cdot f/12)}{(1 - e)H_{t-1}}$$

where

> H_t = house price in t,
> H_{t-1} = house price in $t-1$,
> R = rental income (assumed zero),
> d = downpayment in percent, or $(1 - e)$,
> $D = d \cdot H_{t-1}$ = downpayment,
> e = percent borrowed, or $(1 - d)$,
> L = amount borrowed = loan = $e \cdot H_{t-1}$,

f = annual interest rate on mortgage,

$f/12$ = monthly mortgage interest rate,

h = rate of return on leveraged purchase.

SOURCE OF DATA

The NYSE returns from the CRSP computer file at the University of Chicago act as the market index for stock values. For purposes of this study, we needed a common stock index that is broad-based; the NYSE series appears to provide a representative sample of investors' actual experiences. The data assume reinvestment of dividends and interest for stocks and bonds, respectively.

The bond index data consistent with our purposes also came from a widely used source, namely, *Salomon Brothers High-Grade, Long-Term Corporate Bond Total Rate of Return Index.* In addition to its availability, its major advantage is that high-grade bonds represent a practical choice for an investor interested in stability of interest income.

Monthly residential real estate mean sales values for new and existing single family homes as presented in the *Journal of the Federal Home Loan Bank Board* form the raw data for purposes of generating monthly rates of return to investment in residential real estate. More precisely, the rate of return is the monthly change in mean sales price for consecutive months. The calculation is: mean sales price at the end of any current month, minus the mean sales price at the end of the previous month, divided by mean sales price at the beginning of the current month, adjusted for financial leverage.

Whether the investor is buying stocks, bonds, or residential real estate, we assume that he is free at the end of each month to buy, sell, or hold a position. Investors have the same problem of timing a buy-or-sell decision in residential real estate as they have for alternative assets; yet this assumption may be more realistic for stocks or bonds than it is for real estate.

Tables 1, 2, and 3 display the performance of stocks, bonds, new real estate, and existing housing for the overall period studied as well as for the recessionary periods, on both an unleveraged and leveraged basis.

The following discussion focuses on the impact of financial leverage on risk and return, traces the performance during the overall and recessionary periods, and concludes with the contrasts between new real estate and existing housing as investment portfolio strategy options.

LEVERAGE

Column 1 in Table 1 shows the unleveraged overall average monthly return for stocks, bonds, new real estate, and existing housing. These

TABLE 1
Leverage, Risk and Rates of Return: Overall Period. January 1969–December 1977
(Percent per Month)

	(1) Unleveraged	(2) Unleveraged	(3)	(4) Leveraged	(5)
	Return	Standard Deviation	Downpymt (margin)	Return	Standard Deviation
Bonds	.5831%	2.9885	51.402%	.5184%	5.9173
Stocks	.5320	4.9659	59.252	.6327	8.7926
New real estate	.5502	2.5443	24.781	.1345	1.0438
Existing real estate	.5853	3.1624	26.392	.2577	1.2200

returns are valid only when the investor purchases the asset for cash; otherwise, the financing charges must be subtracted to derive the net nominal return.

The investor without financing could earn about 0.5 percent per month on each of the assets. Then, to the extent that one uses the standard deviation of returns as a proxy for risk, column 2 shows more widely varied risk figures.

The risk-return trade-off is illustrated graphically in Figure 1. Bonds, existing real estate, and new real estate receive about the same return

FIGURE 1
Unleveraged: 1969–1977

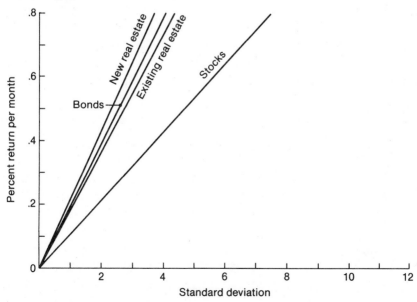

per unit of risk. On the other hand, stocks have a slightly lower positive return together with statistically significantly greater risk.

The leverage effects appear in columns 4 and 5 of Table 1. Price appreciation must exceed interest expense before one can enjoy a positive net nominal return. As we can see in column 4, this occurred in all four investment strategies, with stock and bonds enjoying the highest returns. Both new and existing real estate produced significantly lower average monthly returns. Even at the same rate of interest, the total interest expense will be higher for real estate because, as we show in column 3, the downpayment on either form of real estate is about half the margin requirements for stocks and bonds. Therefore, absolute price appreciation must be much higher on real estate than on the financial instruments if the investor is to avoid cash losses.

Risk for stocks and bonds about doubled when considering leverage. On the other hand, the standard deviations for new real estate and existing housing declined sharply. (column 5 vs. column 2 of Table 1).

From Figure 1 (unleveraged) to Figure 2 (leveraged), stocks and bonds lines became more horizontal as the relationship between returns and risk changed, meaning less return per unit in each case. Both strategies, however, appear to be viable investment alternatives, with stocks having greater return but also much greater risk.

The real estate lines in Figures 1 and 2 are almost unchanged as

FIGURE 2
Leveraged: 1969–1977

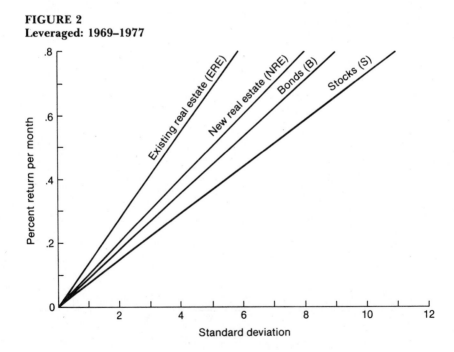

one moves from an unleveraged position to a leveraged one. Average returns for real estate are lower in the leveraged than the unleveraged model, but, in view of the much lower risk statistic associated with these returns, they may be the best buy. Before considering leverage, in other words, one would be more or less indifferent between bonds, new real estate, and existing housing; when the investor takes both risk and return into consideration, existing and new real estate after leverage clearly emerge as the most feasible investment alternative.

Figure 3 allows one to view the risk-to-return relationship between unleveraged bonds and stocks on the one hand and leveraged real estate, new and existing, on the other. This comparison is important, because people borrow money for acquisition of real estate both more frequently and in larger amounts than when they purchase other investment alternatives. Figure 3 demonstrates that existing real estate, leveraged, is the most attractive asset, followed in order by unleveraged bonds, leveraged new real estate, and, lastly, unleveraged stocks.

RECESSIONARY PERIODS

As we can see from Tables 2 and 3, the performance of real estate during recessions differed significantly from what it was during the overall period studied. During 1960–70, leveraged real estate incurred losses, whereas gains were realized during 1973–75. Yet, by examining Tables

FIGURE 3
Unleveraged (U) and Leveraged (L): 1969–1977

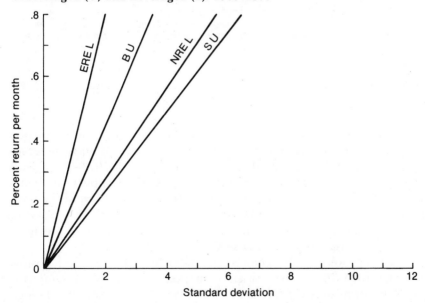

2 and 3, one can readily see that stocks performed worst of all during recessions. Margined stocks not only lost 0.65 percent per month in 1969–70 but also had the highest risk. Stocks lost 2.46 percent per month in the 1973–75 period and, again, the risk factor was the highest of any investment strategy considered.

TABLE 2
Leverage, Risk and Rates of Return: 1st Recession December 1969–November 1970
(Percent per Month)

	(1) Unleveraged	(2)	(3)	(4) Leveraged	(5)
	Return	Standard Deviation	Downpymt (margin)	Return	Standard Deviation
Bonds	1.0279%	2.6642	53.333%	1.2742%	5.1764
Stocks	−.2596	5.7200	70.000	−.6504	8.4325
New real estate	.0261	2.2840	28.283	−1.7648	8.0841
Existing real estate	.2116	1.9619	28.942	−.0952	6.8415

TABLE 3
Leverage, Risk and Rates of Return: 2nd Recession November 1973–March 1975
(Percent per Month)

	(1) Unleveraged	(2)	(3)	(4) Leveraged	(5)
	Return	Standard Deviation	Downpymt (margin)	Return	Standard Deviation
Bonds	.1337%	3.1629	50.000%	−.6763%	6.3516
Stocks	−.9295	7.4643	50.882	−2.4601	14.5599
New real estate	.8326	2.7796	24.300	1.1616	11.5123
Existing real estate	.9495	3.5912	27.518	1.6005	13.3235

Leveraged bonds were the least risky and also continued to show a positive net nominal return. The returns to these bonds increased during the 1969–70 recession but declined sharply in 1973–75. Indeed, consistency of returns to stocks and bonds does not appear any better than returns to real estate during recessions. The decrease in bond returns in 1973–75 and the drastic decline to stock returns occurred as many investors left these markets when the economy was depressed— but not so in real estate in 1973–75!

Existing housing, like new real estate, had an improved positive return in 1973–75; however, risk also jumped significantly. This improvement in returns to real estate in 1973–75 may reflect investor psychology.

Speculation in stocks and bonds is generally common during growth periods, but a conservative investment strategy frequently dominates during a recession. Investors see property as tangible, and if the recession continues, they still have a house; financial instruments, on the other hand, may become basically worthless if the company's fortunes decline.

EXISTING HOUSING VERSUS NEW REAL ESTATE

Figures 1 and 2 show only modest differences between existing and new housing. The returns are greater in the unleveraged model but, of course, so is the risk. Existing housing, under leveraged conditions, however, appears to be clearly superior in the 1973–75 recessionary period. The risk adjusted return is highest for used homes, because returns are higher than on any other investment, while the risk is similar to stocks and new real estate (Table 3, columns 4 and 5).

The positive returns to existing housing during this recessionary period stem from both the terms of mortgages and the demand for housing. Mortgages on existing homes are smaller in dollar amounts than on new homes because of lower prices and higher downpayments. With interest rates similar to new housing rates, a smaller amount of interest is paid, lowering the financing cost.

In recessionary periods, lay-offs of blue collar workers may reduce the demand for existing housing *purchases* (even though demand for housing *services* may not decrease); this affects potential new home purchasers in their ability to "trade up." Hence, new home prices tend to fall, or at least tend not to rise quickly, but upward pressure is put on existing home prices as the stock of housing may lag behind the need for housing services.

USING COMBINATIONS OF ASSETS

Modern portfolio theory suggests that the analyst must also examine the correlations between investment alternatives. Investments can be combined in such a way as to reduce the risk of losses without reducing the return as much.

Correlation coefficients reflect how returns move with one another. Values of r equal to $+1.0$ indicate perfect positive correlation. If we combine highly correlated returns, we will increase returns during sound economic conditions, but this procedure will magnify the losses during downturns because both will move down together.

An r value of -1.0 depicts negative correlation. When one asset's return is down, the other's is up. This diversification effect protects the investor from large losses during periods of adverse economic conditions.

As shown in Table 4, columns 2 and 3, the r value (correlation coefficient) of unleveraged bonds with stock returns increased during the first recession, but then it decreased slightly in the second. Approximately the same condition existed using leveraged data (Table 5). The investor who combined these holdings in a portfolio might result in increased return *and* risk during contractions, when portfolio managers are usually willing to sacrifice some return in order to reduce risk.

TABLE 4
Correlations between Investment Alternatives
(Unleveraged Data)

Investment Types	(1) Overall Period	(2) Recession I 12/1/69–11/31/70	(3) Recession II 11/1/73–3/31/75
Bond to stock returns	.1697	.7797	.6554
Bond to new real estate	.0055	−.2078	.0002
Bond to existing real estate	−.0932	−.1693	−.2377
Stock to new real estate	−.0224	.0442	.0083
Stock to existing real estate	−.0146	−.3304	.0709
New real estate to existing real estate	.3592	.3925	.0223

TABLE 5
Correlations between Investment Alternatives
(Leveraged Data)

Investment Types	(1) Overall Period	(2) Recession I 12/1/69–11/31/70	(3) Recession II 11/1/73–3/31/75
Bond to stock returns	.2069	.8046	.6867
Bond to new real estate	.0164	−.2333	.0255
Bond to existing real estate	−.0794	−.1798	−.2342
Stock to new real estate	−.0408	.1000	.0110
Stock to existing real estate	−.0264	−.3733	.0421
New real estate to existing real estate	.3518	.3871	−.0025

Coefficients of returns to bonds with existing housing are negatively correlated for both the overall period and recessionary periods. During the 1969–70 recessionary period, however, new real estate returns became negatively correlated with bonds and then shifted to positive correlations in 1973–75. Hence, existing housing appears to be the preferable alternative to be combined with bonds.

The relatively low correlations between corporate issues and real estate in expansion and contraction of the economy indicates that real estate included in a portfolio with financial assets reduces systematic risk. The investor can accomplish the greatest risk reduction by combining bonds with existing housing, as indicated by the negative correlation between these investments in Tables 4 and 5. Furthermore, this would alleviate the dramatically low portfolio returns during the 1973–75 recessionary period, since the low returns (−.6763% monthly) to the bond component of the portfolio would tend to be offset by the substantially higher returns (1.60% monthly) to the existing housing component.

LIMITATIONS AND ATTRACTIONS

The true returns to real estate may be greater than shown here, as no rental receipts are included in these calculations; in addition, tax considerations are conspicuous by their absence. These limitations notwithstanding, the inclusion of real estate in a portfolio of stocks and bonds results in a reduction of risk as indicated by the negative correlation coefficients between real estate and these financial assets. The most substantial benefits occurred during the most recent recessionary period under leveraged conditions for investments in existing housing.

The earlier the recognition of the changing economic environment, the sooner the portfolio manager can begin adjusting the proportions of various assets. The tentative substitution of existing real estate for common stock (and vice versa, depending upon the direction of the economy) by the portfolio manager could be one of the primary considerations in the continuous balancing of the risk-return relationship.

Admittedly, portfolio managers may have difficulty in diversifying into the residential real estate area. It is practicable to invest in residential mortgages via the secondary mortgage market and through AMMINET, which provides a direct communications network that lists for its subscribers specific terms on individual mortgages. Outright purchases of residential real estate by portfolio managers may not be feasible currently because of search and other costs; nonetheless, as the electronic and computer integration of boards of realtors are linked and as more real estate brokerage firms become franchised on a nationwide basis, regional or national home purchase markets are likely to emerge, to the benefit of the portfolio managers.

25.

Inventory Demand and Cost of Capital Effects*

CHARLES LIEBERMAN

1. INTRODUCTION

Theoretical models of inventory investment including Belsley, Holt et al., Whitin and others invariably suggest that the opportunity cost of inventories should be included as a key explanatory variable in any empirical study of inventory behavior. In the absence of an opportunity cost (or other holding costs), the theoretically optimal inventory holding is infinitely large. Even so, it is rather rare that any financial variable emerges as statistically significant in empirical studies of inventories. Michael Lovell, who has written extensively on inventory investment, goes so far as to comment "that the probability of obtaining an interest-rate coefficient with negative sign is 50 percent." Even the MIT-Pennsyl-vania-Social Science Research Council model, which represents an explicit attempt to specify in detail the channels of monetary policy, fails to include monetary variables in its inventory equation.

The absence of empirical evidence in support of a cost of capital effect on inventory investment renders uncertain what many economists regard as a major channel of monetary policy. It is often commented that roughly three quarters of the variance in GNP is accounted for by changes in inventory investment. Since monetary policy is commonly viewed as very powerful, it is truly remarkable that so little econometric

* *Review of Economics and Statistics* 62, no. 3 (August 1980), pp. 348–55.

evidence exists to indicate a cost of capital effect on the most variable component of GNP.

This study attempts to reexamine the size and significance of the theoretically important cost of capital effect on inventory investment by utilizing firm specific cost of capital measures, as suggested by the finance theory literature, in a pooled cross section econometric analysis of inventory behavior. The cost of capital measure is computed using the actual balance sheet capitalization particular to each firm in the sample for each point in time. Use of a firm specific cost of capital measure instead of a market interest rate avoids the measurement errors introduced into the analysis by the latter procedure. Risk differences among firms, such as between General Motors and Chrysler, imply substantial differences in capital costs. The errors in measurement problem introduced by a market interest rate will bias towards zero the cost of capital effect. Thus a firm specific cost of capital measure may serve as a more effective opportunity cost variable in an econometric analysis of inventory investment.

Perhaps even more critical than the use of firm specific cost of capital measures, the econometric analysis is conducted using two samples of firms with each sample disaggregated by stage of fabrication. The first sample, which includes heavy machinery producing companies, attempts to explain inventory investment behavior for companies that produce output in response to orders. The second sample consists of textile companies that produce output predominantly to stock in anticipation of orders. Aggregation of firms that produce to stock and that produce to order—and, in addition, aggregation of inventories across stages of fabrication—may obscure the underlying behavioral characteristics that operate, in fact, at the individual firm level. As suggested by theory, the findings of this study indicate that the cost of capital is a highly significant explanatory variable in inventory demand equations.

II. THE THEORETICAL MODEL

The traditional empirical formulation of Bosworth, Darling, Darling and Lovell, Klein, Kuznets, Lui, Lovett, and others employs a stock adjustment equation between desired and actual inventories (or planned investment) and between expected and actual sales (or unplanned investment).

$$I_t - I_{t-1} = \lambda(I_t^* - I_{t-1}) + \delta(S_t^e - S_t). \tag{1}$$

Feldstein and Auerbach have demonstrated that as little as three or four days worth of production or deliveries of materials are equivalent to an entire year's worth of change in inventory investment. Moreover, the empirical evidence suggest improbably that firms react very rapidly to unanticipated sales—reaching 95 percent adjustment within one *quar-*

ter—in contrast to the slow 25 percent adjustment per year with respect to desired inventory levels. In light of the argument of Feldstein and Auerbach and these dubious empirical findings, this paper assumes complete adjustment to discrepancies between desired and actual inventory stocks within one year.[1]

Desired inventories are commonly taken to be a function of sales, the opportunity cost of holding inventories, and in the case of goods produced to order, order backlogs. The theoretical justification for this model is presented in Belsley, Childs, Holt et al., Whitin, and Zarnowitz, and therefore requires no elaboration here. The functional form commonly employed in previous studies has generally been linear, although Whitin's and many other theoretical models suggest a nonlinear function. The simple square root rule or variations of it may be specified for estimation as a linear in logs equation, as indicated by Equation (2). In this equation, I_t is the firm's real inventory level in period t, S_t is the level of real sales, CK_t is the real cost of capital and OB_t is the real order backlog.

$$\ln I_t = \alpha_0 + \alpha_1 \ln S_t + \alpha_2 \ln CK_t + \alpha_3 \ln OB_t + v_t. \tag{2}$$

Four cost of capital measures, as suggested by the finance theory literature are employed in this analysis. The first measure provides a weighted average of each firm's after-tax cost of debt *(W_D)*, preferred stock (if any) *(W_{PS}) and common stock (W_{CS})*, as indicated by Equation (3).

$$CK = (1 - t)i_D W_D + i_{PS} W_{PS} + i_{CS} W_{CS}, \tag{3}$$

where

t = corporate tax rate of the firm,
i_j = cost of financing via source j,
W_j = weight for financing via source j.

The weights are the percentage of the firm's capitalization accounted for by each means of financing. The financing costs, i_j, are the actual after tax rates paid by each firm. Thus, the cost of debt is the actual average interest rate paid by the firm on its outstanding debt adjusted for taxes, while the preferred stock cost is taken as the preferred stock's average dividend yield.[2] A tax rate was computed for each firm for each

---

[1] Since the data employed in this paper are annual rather than the quarterly data more commonly used in inventory equations, the assumption of complete adjustment within the time unit of measurement is relatively innocuous.

[2] The measured cost of financing using debt or preferred stock may understate the actual cost to the extent that the firm employed convertible issues. Generally, convertible issues represent a small portion of the total capitalization of firms so the bias should be small. These problems are avoided, however, by the marginal cost measures which will be discussed shortly.

year using its reported tax payments. Theoretically, the cost of common stock is taken as the sum of the common stock dividend rate and an estimated growth rate of future dividends.[3] The average of the year's high and low prices of the firm's common stock was used to calculate the dividend yield, while the average annual growth rate of cash flow over five years was used as a proxy for the expected future growth rate of dividends.[4]

The procedures described above provide average historic cost of capital measures in the sense that each firm's cost of debt and preferred stock financing depends upon its own history of when it issued new securities and the rates which prevailed at that point in time. Although marginal and average cost of capital measures may have moved together so that the average cost of capital may serve as a crude proxy for the marginal cost of capital, a marginal cost of capital measure would clearly be preferred.

A marginal cost of capital is available, however, from a component of the average historic computation. The cost of a new equity issue depends upon current dividends, the current price of the firm's shares in the market and prospective growth rate of the firm. All of these measures are based upon or are derived from current market values. Since the risk adjusted costs of all sources of financing must be equal at the margin, the equity cost of capital can serve as a proxy for the total marginal cost of financing from all sources. Thus, another set of cost of capital measures employs only the estimated cost of equity capital as a proxy for the firm's total marginal cost of capital, using cash flow and sales growth rates, respectively, as alternative measures of expected future dividend growth rates.[5]

III. THE DATA

The data employed in this paper are from the annual industrial (expanded) Compustat tapes which are produced by the Standard and Poor's Corporation. The tapes included as many as 120 items of data per firm per year over a 20-year period from 1957 through 1976. The

---

[3] Firms with negative growth rates of sales or cash flow were deleted from the sample. Financial theory provides measures of a firm's cost of capital only for firms with nonnegative growth rates. The cost of common stock represents a marginal (current market) cost of capital as compared to the bond and preferred stock costs that are historic measures. This point will be discussed in detail.

[4] The average five-year growth rate of sales was also employed as an alternative proxy for expected dividend growth in the above calculation to produce a second measure of the equity cost of capital. The five-year period of 1971–76 was used for all of the firms in the sample.

[5] Since the equity cost of capital measure carries a substantial weight in the average cost of capital calculation, movements in the average are also heavily influenced by the marginal component.

completeness of the data set varies by firm, with a general overall tendency for more complete data for the more recent past. The data relevant for this study are available almost exclusively for the period 1970 to 1976 for a limited sample of firms. As a result, entire firms or individual observations for a particular firm were excluded from this study whenever the corporation failed to provide sufficient information for that year for the variables included in the model. The data for the remaining firms were adjusted for stock splits and were pooled with data from other firms for use in the regression analysis.

Firms were also deleted if a substantial portion of the firm's business was in areas other than heavy machinery or textiles, as is obviously the case for conglomerates. Some machinery firms were also deleted since they produce to stock, such as Black and Decker which produces hand tools. Outside sources such as Standard and Poor's and Value Line were employed to determine which companies to delete. Thus, the machinery firms included in the study produce primarily heavy machinery in response to orders (although not necessarily to the specifications of the purchaser).

Firm inventory data are reported on different accounting bases along with the inventory valuation method used each year. Most firms employ the first-in-first-out (FIFO) method, others employ last-in-first-out (LIFO) and the remaining firms employ some average or combination of methods. The reported empirical findings employed only firms that use the FIFO method since there were not enough observations for firms which employ other accounting techniques.[6]

Since the inventory and other measures included in the Compustat data set are in current dollars, an appropriate price index is necessary to obtain real magnitudes. The wholesale price index for machinery and equipment (not seasonally adjusted) was used to deflate nominal magnitudes associated with the machinery industry while the wholesale price index for textile products and apparel (not seasonally adjusted) was used for the textile industry.[7]

Since different firms report their data on the basis of different fiscal years, a calendar year price index is inappropriate. To overcome this problem, an annual price index was computed for each individual firm based upon its own fiscal year using the appropriate monthly wholesale price data. Thus, the unit of observation is the firm-year, and the data are ajusted so as to correspond with the fiscal year of each firm.

---

[6] Most firms employ the FIFO method although many firms have switched to LIFO accounting in the last five years. When a firm switches inventory valuation methods, data for that firm are used in the analysis only for those years during which the firm employed FIFO accounting.

[7] The price deflators employed by the Department of Commerce to obtain real magnitudes take into account inventory turnover. The price deflators employed in this study are not adjusted for inventory turnover.

IV. THE EMPIRICAL FINDINGS

Table 1 reports inventory demand equations for a pooled time-series sample of heavy machinery companies which produce output predominantly in response to orders.[8] By limiting the sample to firms within a single industry, technology is implicitly held constant, thereby avoiding potential bias in the estimated coefficients. Firm dummmies are employed for each firm whenever at least four observations are available.[9] The equations are arranged by stage of fabrication. The dependent variables are the log of real total inventories, raw materials, work in process, and finished goods inventories, respectively. Since machinery companies produce output predominantly in response to orders, order backlogs, in addition to 'sales and the cost of capital, ought to be an important explanatory variable in an inventory equation.

All of the equations employ the nominal cost of capital and the inflation rate separately although it is the real rate that belongs directly in the equations. This is because in several periods the inflation rate exceeded the nominal cost of capital. Since there is no theoretical basis for rejecting a negative real cost of capital, at least for limited periods, these observations were retained by including separately the nominal cost of capital and the rate of inflation.

The first four equations of Table 1, which employ the "marginal" measure of the cost of capital and use cash flow to estimate the growth rate of dividends, support the theoretical propositions presented above. The work in process and total inventory equations are quite strong and provide a cost of capital coefficient that is statistically significant with the theoretically correct sign. Previously, inventory opportunity cost measures tended to provide either positive or insignificant coefficients in studies of inventories. The coefficients of sales and order backlogs are also highly significant and indicate that higher sales and larger order backlogs increase work in process inventories. Moreover, the magnitudes of the estimated coefficients are generally consistent with the values suggested by theory. The sales elasticity of 0.436 suggests substantial economies of scale while the cost of capital elasticity, at -1.119, suggests that work in process inventories are quite sensitive to the cost of capital. Moreover, the cost of capital coefficient is sizeable, significant, and of the theoretically expected sign in all of the equations except raw materials where it fails to achieve significance but nevertheless remains of negative sign. These findings also suggest that delivery times lengthen with rising

---

[8] Complete data are available for eleven machinery firms. Except for the first such company, firm dummies were employed whenever at least four observations were available.

[9] Year dummies were also employed in addition to firm dummies but these rarely achieved statistical significance. As a result, no year dummies were employed in the equations reported here.

TABLE 1
Inventory Demand Equations for Heavy Machinery Firms
(Output Produced to Order)

Dependent Variable	Observations	Constant	In S	In CK	In Prate	In OB	R^2	S.E.
"Marginal" cost of capital equations								
Total inventory	40	-2.23 (-16.52)	0.623 (12.56)	-0.599 (-10.36)	0.018 (0.73)	0.155 (4.23)	.977	.12
Raw materials	40	-2.91 (-4.96)	0.767 (3.57)	-0.292 (-1.17)	0.081 (0.76)	0.155 (0.98)	.675	.52
Work in process	40	-4.21 (-7.54)	0.436 (2.13)	-1.119 (-4.69)	-0.002 (-0.02)	0.390 (2.59)	.812	.49
Finished goods	40	-4.34 (-11.07)	1.250 (8.70)	-0.681 (-4.07)	-0.107 (1.52)	0.001 (0.01)	.922	.35
"Average" cost of capital equations								
Total inventory	40	-2.50 (-19.91)	0.652 (16.31)	-0.632 (-13.13)	-0.016 (-0.77)	0.165 (5.47)	.984	.10
Raw materials	40	-3.02 (-4.58)	0.782 (3.73)	-0.300 (-1.19)	0.065 (0.61)	0.160 (1.01)	.676	.52
Work in process	40	-4.84 (-8.28)	0.477 (2.57)	-1.236 (-5.52)	-0.067 (-0.71)	0.407 (2.90)	.838	.46
Finished goods	40	-4.49 (-9.92)	1.299 (9.02)	-0.654 (-3.77)	-0.142 (-1.95)	0.015 (0.14)	.918	.35

Notes: The variables S, CK, Prate and OB are the log of real sales, the nominal cost of capital, the inflation rate and real order backlogs, respectively. The values in parentheses are t-ratios and S.E. is the standard error of the equation. These equations also included two firm dummies for those firms for which at least four observations were available.

opportunity costs as work in process inventories become more costly to carry.

With the exception of the finished goods equations, all of the sales coefficients demonstrate support for substantial economies of scale. Even the finished goods equations fit surprisingly well.[10] The sales and the cost of capital coefficients were significant and of the correct signs. And it is reasonable that order backlogs are insignificant in explaining finished goods inventories of firms producing to order. The order backlogs coefficients are nevertheless sizeable and significant in the total inventories and work in process equations. This coefficient is also, in every case, of the theoretically expected sign.

Only the inflation rate coefficient often turns up with a theoretically unexpected negative sign. Even so, it is always insignificant except for some finished goods equations where its meaningfulness may be questioned. This result will be discussed more carefully with regard to textile firms.

The second set of four equations employs a historical average cost of capital instead of the marginal measure employed in the first four equations. On the whole, the average cost of capital equations are little different from the marginal cost of capital findings since much of the variation in the average measure is produced by the marginal equity cost of capital. When the average and marginal cost-of-capital measures employed the growth rate of sales instead of the growth rate of cash flow, the results also were similar.

Thus, the equations of Table 1 provide strong evidence that total inventories and, in particular, work in process inventories are sensitive to the firm's cost of capital. The cost of capital coefficient is negative, significant, and well within the bounds suggested by theory. Moreover, the cost of capital effect emerges most clearly in work in process and total inventories over which firms producing to order might be expected to have greatest discretion. And as usual, sales and order backlogs also emerge as important explanatory variables in these inventory equations.

Table 2 reports a sample of estimated equations of inventory demand by stage of fabrication for textile companies, an industry which produces output to stock.[11] The first four equations employ the "marginal" cost of capital measure, which uses cash flow to estimate the expected growth rate of dividends. Unlike firms producing to order, firms producing to

---

[10] Inventories of finished goods are likely beyond the control of firms producing to order and may be more related to delivery and train schedules, customer preferences, weather, and cancellations than to the explanatory variables employed in such equations.

[11] Data are available for six firms with at least two observations per firm. Firm dummy variables were included in the estimated equations for three of the four firms for which at least three observations were available, excluding the first such firm. These results are reported in Table 2. A firm dummy variable was also added for firms with inventory holdings above the mean for the sample but these findings were similar to the results reported here.

TABLE 2
Inventory Demand Equations for Textile Firms
(Output Produced to Stock)

Dependent Variable	Observations	Constant	ln S	ln CK	ln Prate	R^2	S.E.
"Marginal" cost of capital equations							
Total inventory	19	-2.76	0.975	-0.454	-0.147	.994	.12
		(-10.37)	(15.77)	(-3.75)	(-3.12)		
Raw materials	19	-2.50	0.153	-0.074	0.202	.979	.15
		(7.10)	(1.87)	(-0.46)	(3.24)		
Work in process	19	-3.45	1.596	-0.022	-0.196	.986	.23
		(-6.51)	(12.97)	(-0.09)	(-2.08)		
Finished goods	19	-4.69	1.381	-0.662	-0.332	.995	.13
		(-15.83)	(20.09)	(-4.91)	(-6.32)		
"Average" cost of capital equations							
Total inventory	19	-2.85	1.000	-0.409	-0.148	.989	.16
		(-3.51)	(8.97)	(-1.20)	(-2.26)		
Raw materials	19	-1.59	0.070	0.330	0.204	.981	.15
		(-2.14)	(0.68)	(1.06)	(3.38)		
Work in process	19	-2.28	1.485	0.488	-0.193	.987	.22
		(-2.05)	(9.73)	(1.05)	(-2.15)		
Finished goods	19	-6.09	1.537	-1.143	-0.336	.992	.16
		(-7.57)	(13.92)	(-3.39)	(-5.16)		

Note: See Table 1 for an explanation of the variables and symbols. Firm dummies were included in these estimates, as discussed in footnote 11.

stock might be expected to have greatest discretion and control over finished goods inventories. The finished goods equation provides significant cost of capital coefficients of the theoretically expected sign. Surprisingly, the sales coefficients are somewhat on the high side. The sales coefficients exceed unity in several equations whereas theory suggests economies of scale. This result may be due to anticipation by firms of higher future orders which provides an incentive to increase finished goods and work in process inventories to satisfy the expected surge in demand. The sales coefficients may also suggest longer production runs to take advantage of economies of scale. Unfortunately, given the limited number of observations and data available, it is difficult to test these possibilities.

The cost of capital coefficient is especially noteworthy in the finished goods equation. It is highly significant and, at −0.662, indicates that inventories of finished goods are quite sensitive to the cost of capital. Once again, such a large response of finished goods inventories to the cost of capital is at sharp variance with the evidence presented previously in the literature.

Total inventories are also rather sensitive to the cost of capital variable with an estimated coefficient of −0.454. The work in process inventory category, which was expected to be more difficult to explain for firms which produce to stock, in some cases yields positive but insignificant cost of capital coefficients and unusually large sales elasticities. As expected, work in process inventories were difficult to explain, perhaps due to the lack of control firms have over the minimum efficient size of a production run.

Even so, the estimated inventory equations for textile firms confirm the behavior expected for firms that produce output to stock. Finished goods inventories and total inventories are quite sensitive to the cost of capital with the theoretically expected sign. The raw material equation provides a negative but insignificant cost of capital effect while, as expected, the work in process equation produces the most unreasonable results for firms that produce to stock.[12]

The role performed by the inflation rate in these equations is uncertain as its coefficient is often negative and significant, contrary to theory. If the real cost of capital is the difference between the nominal cost of capital and the expected rate of inflation (with the actual rate employed as a proxy for the expected rate), the inflation rate coefficient should be positive.

There are, however, at least two additional effects that may be included in the estimated coefficient. To the extent firms speculate to profit by increasing inventories in anticipation of an increased inflation

---

[12] When corporate sales were used instead of cash flow to estimate the dividend growth rate for the textile firms, the cost of capital variable was generally insignificant in these equations.

rate, the positive cost of capital effect would be reinforced by a positive speculative behavior effect. Even so, a spurious correlation may exist that could swamp these expected positive effects. Since all of the firms in the sample use FIFO accounting, accelerations (decelerations) in the rate of inflation will tend to depress (increase) the measured real value of inventories, which is the left-hand variable, thereby introducing a spurious negative effect between real inventories, as measured, and the rate of inflation. This result arises because nominal inventories are valued at prices that prevailed when they entered stocks but are deflated by higher current prices. Thus, a negative coefficient could be obtained strictly due to the spurious correlation.

The degree to which a spurious correlation is introduced between inflation rates and real inventories could be clarified if data were available for firms employing alternative accounting practices, in particular, the LIFO method. Unfortunately, very few additional observations are available for firms using any alternative accounting system. The 1971–75 period is one in which many firms switched partially toward LIFO accounting, so that the data commonly indicate the use of a mixture of accounting methods. It is therefore not feasible, at the present time, to reestimate these equations for alternative accounting methods.[13]

Although it is likely that the inflation rate coefficient is biased due to this spurious correlation, since the inflation rate variable picks up the positive price effect as well as the spurious inventory pricing bias there is little reason to believe that other coefficients are also biased as a result. The unraveling of these effects must await the arrival of additional data.

The equations of Tables 1 and 2 were also reestimated employing the 4–6 month commercial paper rate in place of the firm specific cost of capital. The commercial paper rate, which reflects current short-term market conditions, should serve as a good proxy for the cost of short-term financing to firms to carry inventories. Thus, it is possible to determine whether the statistically significant cost of capital effects are due to the firm specific measures employed in the analysis or due to disaggregating by production to stock and to order and by stage of fabrication.

None of the equations that included a commercial paper rate as a measure of opportunity cost of holding inventories yielded a statistically significant commercial paper coefficient. This result therefore suggests

---

[13] Since the sample is restricted to firms employing the FIFO accounting system and since FIFO accounting requires firms to pay unnecessarily high taxes during inflationary periods, it is conceivable that the firms in this sample substantially underestimated the rate of inflation. If this is the case, such firms would interpret higher nominal yields due to higher inflation expectations as representing higher real rates and would tend to decrease real inventories. Since the use of FIFO accounting is still very widespread, inertia and various institutional constraints, rather than expectations of declines in the rate of inflation, probably account for the only gradual replacement of FIFO accounting by the more beneficial LIFO procedure.

that the significant cost of capital effects obtained by this analysis is due to the use of a theoretically more appropriate cost of capital measure.

None of the equations of Table 2 contains an order backlog variable. Firms that produce to stock ought to be less sensitive to order backlogs than firms that produce output in response to orders. If the actual speed of adjustment between actual and desired inventories is slow, a case can be made that an order backlog variable might be expected to provide a negative effect on inventories of firms, especially on finished goods inventories. An increase in orders would deplete finished goods inventories of firms that produce to stock in contrast to the expected positive order backlog effect on firms that produce output in response to orders. If adjustment to desired inventory levels is sufficiently rapid, as assumed in this analysis, this effect will be zero. In fact, the order backlog variable was always statistically insignificant whenever it was added to any of the equations of Table 2, thereby providing support for the assumption of rapid speeds of adjustment.

A modest attempt was also made to test for capacity constraints that might affect inventory holdings. If production levels of firms producing to stock rise sufficiently close to capacity, inventories may be reduced as finished goods are reduced below normal levels in response to growing and unfilled orders. An analogous argument may be made for firms which produce to order to the extent that actual work in process inventories are too low due to capacity ceilings which prohibit a satisfactory response to high sales and orders.

The Federal Reserve's index of capacity utilization and the national unemployment rate were included in the equations presented in Tables 1 and 2 to test for inventory changes due to capacity constraints.[14] The variables employed, however, were aggregate measures for the economy and, thus, neither firm nor even industry specific. When included in the estimated equations, these variables were statistically insignificant.

V. SUMMARY AND CONCLUSIONS

This study has employed firm specific cost of capital measures in inventory demand equations and panel data to provide econometric support for theoretical models which indicate that inventories are influenced significantly by their opportunity costs. Evidence has been presented in this regard for firms that produce output in response to orders (for heavy machinery firms) as well as for firms that produce output to stock in anticipation of orders (textile firms). These findings are sup-

---

[14] Capacity utilization was available only on a quarterly basis, which may not have coincided with the fiscal year basis employed by some firms. In this case, the quarterly capacity utilization series was employed so that the annual average would lead or lag the fiscal year by no more than one month.

ported by equations estimated to explain total inventories as well as by equations that explain inventory components by stage of fabrication.

Finished goods inventories are quite sensitive to the cost of capital for firms that produce to stock while work in process inventories are most sensitive to the cost of capital for firms that produce to order. The elasticity of inventories to the cost of capital ranged as low as −1.2, suggesting that inventories may be considerably more sensitive to financial conditions than indicated by previous empirical research. Evidence is therefore provided for an inventory channel of monetary policy.

The analysis presented here provides results which are at sharp variance with the previously published econometric evidence on inventory investment, and these findings seem attributable to the use of a firm specific cost of capital measure and partly due to the breakdown of inventory holding by stage of fabrication. Aggregate analysis may lose much of the underlying response of the components of inventories due to the different responses depending upon whether the firm produces to order or to stock. Other firm specific cost of capital measures would be useful to confirm or question these findings. The results also suggest that considerable study of inventory behavior is warranted at the firm or industry rather than the aggregate level. If we are to employ countercyclical policy productively, more research and better data are clearly necessary to obtain more reliable information on the determinants of inventory investment.

PART SIX

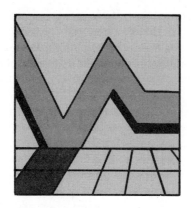

RISK, UNCERTAINTY, AND FACTORS TO CONSIDER WHEN MAKING BUSINESS DECISIONS

INTRODUCTION

For most managers, the easiest approach to risk adjustment is to increase or decrease the cost of capital to be used in discounting, depending on how risky the project looks. If the project appears to have higher risk than average, something can be added to cost of capital as a risk premium. On the other hand, if the project is thought to have lower risk than average, something can be subtracted from costs of capital.

Each projected cash flow is actually the mean of the expected values in a subjective probability distribution. If these subjective distributions take the normal form, variability of project results can be quantified by calculating coefficients of variation.

Amos Tversky and Daniel Kahneman explain in their article that the subjective assessment of probability resembles the subjective assessment of physical quantities such as distance or size. These judgments are based on data of limited validity. Their article describes three methods of helping to discover or learn more about how to make judgments under conditions of uncertainty. Tversky and Kahneman look for representativeness, which is usually employed when people are asked to judge the probability of an object or event; availability of instances, which is often employed when people are asked to assess the frequency of a class or the plausibility of a particular development; and adjustment from an anchor, which is usually employed in numerical prediction when a relevant value is available.

Risk and uncertainty exist in many business transactions. The article by Robert J. Eck argues that *the* primary function of the risk manager is to alleviate the uncertainty surrounding the risk of financial loss. To do this he/she often designs a program of insurance and self-insured retention. In other words, risk exists and must be accommodated to the greatest extent possible. Eck explains how the manager of scarce and costly resources should determine the most cost-effective combination of conventionally purchased insurance and self-insured retention.

In dealing with risk, uncertainty, and methods of measuring business decisions, the business economist at times leans heavily upon econometrics. Edward E. Leamer wants the *con* removed from *econometrics*. He suggests that many inferences drawn from econometric data are too fragile to be taken seriously.

Regardless of whether one uses a qualitative or quantitative method of analysis, David B. Hertz and Howard Thomas illustrate the linkage between risk analysis and strategy for the firm. They discuss the application of decision and risk analysis to a new product and facilities planning problem.

Concluding this Part Six on risk, uncertainty, and various theories related to the decision-making process is the research piece by Herbert Simon. Simon wants the managerial economist to look beyond the concepts found in economics. He argues for recognition of the numerous instances where applied price theory overlaps the areas of psychology and sociology. He wants one to realize the consumer as well as the entrepreneur is a compassionate person who hopes to gain and maintain a variety of objectives—only one of which might be profit.

How closely one chooses to weave other disciplines into economics depends primarily upon the range of questions being answered and the confidence placed by the economist in assumptions dealing with such things as static equilibrium.

Assumptions made by economists dealing with the behavior of consumers and entrepreneurs leans heavily upon psychology; assumptions regarding their lifestyle, number of persons in the family, education, and ethnic background are rooted in sociology. Surveys of consumer and managerial behavior often rely upon theories of statistical induction, stochastic learning, and concept formation. The manager of scarce and costly resources, namely, the managerial economist, should consider these variables; otherwise, he or she may be overlooking a significant and very helpful managerial tool.

26.

Judgment under Uncertainty: Heuristics and Biases*

AMOS TVERSKY
DANIEL KAHNEMAN

Many decisions are based on beliefs concerning the likelihood of uncertain events such as the outcome of an election, the guilt of a defendant, or the future value of the dollar. These beliefs are usually expressed in statements such as "I think that . . . ," "chances are . . . ," "it is unlikely that . . . ," and so forth. Occasionally, beliefs concerning uncertain events are expressed in numerical form as odds or subjective probabilities. What determines such beliefs? How do people assess the probability of an uncertain event or the value of an uncertain quantity? This article shows that people rely on a limited number of heuristic principles which reduce the complex tasks of assessing probabilities and predicting values to simpler judgmental operations. In general, these heuristics are quite useful, but sometimes they lead to severe and systematic errors.

The subjective assessment of probability resembles the subjective assessment of physical quantities such as distance or size. These judgments are all based on data of limited validity, which are processed according to heuristic rules. For example, the apparent distance of an object is determined in part by its clarity. The more sharply the object is seen, the closer it appears to be. This rule has some validity, because in any given scene the more distant objects are seen less sharply than

---

* *Science* 185 (September 27, 1974), pp. 1124–31. Copyright 1974 by the AAAS.

nearer objects. However, the reliance on this rule leads to systematic errors in the estimation of distance. Specifically, distances are often overestimated when visibility is poor because the contours of objects are blurred. On the other hand, distances are often underestimated when visibility is good because the objects are seen sharply. Thus, the reliance on clarity as an indication of distance leads to common biases. Such biases are also found in the intuitive judgment of probability. This article describes three heuristics that are employed to assess probabilities and to predict values. Biases to which these heuristics lead are enumerated, and the applied and theoretical implications of these observations are discussed.

REPRESENTATIVENESS

Many of the probabilistic questions with which people are concerned belong to one of the following types: What is the probability that object A belongs to class B? What is the probability that event A originates from process B? What is the probability that process B will generate event A? In answering such questions, people typically rely on the representativeness heuristic, in which probabilities are evaluated by the degree to which A is representative of B, that is, by the degree to which A resembles B. For example, when A is highly representative of B, the probability that A originates from B is judged to be high. On the other hand, if A is not similar to B, the probability that A originates from B is judged to be low.

For an illustration of judgment by representativeness, consider an individual who has been described by a former neighbor as follows: "Steve is very shy and withdrawn, invariably helpful, but with little interest in people, or in the world of reality. A meek and tidy soul, he has a need for order and structure, and a passion for detail." How do people assess the probability that Steve is engaged in a particular occupation from a list of possibilities (for example, farmer, salesman, airline pilot, librarian, or physician)? How do people order these occupations from most to least likely? In the representativeness heuristic, the probability that Steve is a librarian, for example, is assessed by the degree to which he is representative of, or similar to, the stereotype of a librarian. Indeed, research with problems of this type has shown that people order the occupations by probability and by similarity in exactly the same way. This approach to the judgment of probability leads to serious errors, because similarity, or representativeness, is not influenced by several factors that should affect judgments of probability.

Insensitivity to Prior Probability of Outcomes

One of the factors that have no effect on representativeness but should have a major effect on probability is the prior probability, or base-rate frequency, of the outcomes. In the case of Steve, for example, the fact that there are many more farmers than librarians in the population should enter into any reasonable estimate of the probability that Steve is a librarian rather than a farmer. Considerations of base-rate frequency, however, do not affect the similarity of Steve to the stereotypes of librarians and farmers. If people evaluate probability by representativeness, therefore, prior probabilities will be neglected. This hypothesis was tested in an experiment where prior probabilities were manipulated. Subjects were shown brief personality descriptions of several individuals, allegedly sampled at random from a group of 100 professionals—engineers and lawyers. The subjects were asked to assess, for each description, the probability that it belonged to an engineer rather than to a lawyer. In one experimental condition, subjects were told that the group from which the descriptions had been drawn consisted of 70 engineers and 30 lawyers. In another condition, subjects were told that the group consisted of 30 engineers and 70 lawyers. The odds that any particular description belongs to an engineer rather than to a lawyer should be higher in the first condition, where there is a majority of engineers, than in the second condition, where there is a majority of lawyers. Specifically, it can be shown by applying Bayes' rule that the ratio of these odds should be $(.7/.3)^2$, or 5.44, for each description. In a sharp violation of Bayes' rule, the subjects in the two conditions produced essentially the same probability judgments. Apparently, subjects evaluated the likelihood that a particular description belonged to an engineer rather than to a lawyer by the degree to which this description was representative of the two stereotypes, with little or no regard for the prior probabilities of the categories.

The subjects used prior probabilities correctly when they had no other information. In the absence of a personality sketch, they judged the probability that an unknown individual is an engineer to be .7 and .3, respectively, in the two base-rate conditions. However, prior probabilities were effectively ignored when a description was introduced, even when this description was totally uninformative. The responses to the following description illustrate this phenomenon:

> Dick is a 30-year-old man. He is married with no children. A man of high ability and high motivation, he promises to be quite successful in his field. He is well-liked by his colleagues.

This description was intended to convey no information relevant to the question of whether Dick is an engineer or a lawyer. Consequently, the probability that Dick is an engineer should equal the proportion of engineers in the group, as if no description had been given. The subjects, however, judged the probability of Dick being an engineer to be .5 regardless of whether the stated proportion of engineers in the group was .7 or .3. Evidently, people respond differently when given no evidence and when given worthless evidence. When no specific evidence is given, prior probabilities are properly utilized; when worthless evidence is given, prior probabilities are ignored.

Insensitivity to Sample Size

To evaluate the probability of obtaining a particular result in a sample drawn from a specified population, people typically apply the representativeness heuristic. That is, they assess the likelihood of a sample result, for example, that the average height in a random sample of 10 men will be six feet (180 centimeters), by the similarity of this result to the corresponding parameter (that is, to the average height in the population of men). The similarity of a sample statistic to a population parameter does not depend on the size of the sample. Consequently, if probabilities are assessed by representativeness, then the judged probability of a sample statistic will be essentially independent of sample size. Indeed, when subjects assessed the distributions of average height for samples of various sizes, they produced identical distributions. For example, the probability of obtaining an average height greater than six feet was assigned the same value for samples of 1,000, 100, and 10 men. Moreover, subjects failed to appreciate the role of sample size even when it was emphasized in the formulation of the problem. Consider the following question:

> A certain town is served by two hospitals. In the larger hospital about 45 babies are born each day, and in the smaller hospital about 15 babies are born each day. As you know, about 50 percent of all babies are boys. However, the exact percentage varies from day to day. Sometimes it may be higher than 50 percent, sometimes lower.
> For a period of one year, each hospital recorded the days on which more than 60 percent of the babies born were boys. Which hospital do you think recorded more such days?
>
> a. The larger hospital (21).
> b. The smaller hospital (21).
> c. About the same (that is, within 5 percent of each other) (53).

The values in parentheses are the number of undergraduate students who chose each answer.

Most subjects judged the probability of obtaining more than 60 percent boys to be the same in the small and in the large hospital, presumably because these events are described by the same statistic and are therefore equally representative of the general population. In contrast, sampling theory entails that the expected number of days on which more than 60 percent of the babies are boys is much greater in the small hospital than in the large one, because a large sample is less likely to stray from 50 percent. This fundamental notion of statistics is evidently not part of people's repertoire of intuitions.

A similar insensitivity to sample size has been reported in judgments of posterior probability, that is, of the probability that a sample has been drawn from one population rather than from another. Consider the following example:

> Imagine an urn filled with balls, of which ⅔ are of one color and ⅓ of another. One individual has drawn 5 balls from the urn, and found that 4 were red and 1 was white. Another individual has drawn 20 balls and found that 12 were red and 8 were white. Which of the two individuals should feel more confident that the urn contains ⅔ red balls and ⅓ white balls, rather than the opposite? What odds should each individual give?

In this problem, the correct posterior odds are 8 to 1 for the 4:1 sample and 16 to 1 for the 12:8 sample, assuming equal prior probabilities. However, most people feel that the first sample provides much stronger evidence for the hypothesis that the urn is predominantly red, because the proportion of red balls is larger in the first than in the second sample. Here again, intuitive judgments are dominated by the sample proportion and are essentially unaffected by the size of the sample, which plays a crucial role in the determination of the actual posterior odds. In addition, intuitive estimates of posterior odds are far less extreme than the correct values. The underestimation of the impact of evidence has been observed repeatedly in problems of this type. It has been labeled "conservatism."

Misconceptions of Chance

People expect that a sequence of events generated by a random process will represent the essential characteristics of that process even when the sequence is short. In considering tosses of a coin for heads or tails, for example, people regard the sequence H-T-H-T-T-H to be more likely than the sequence H-H-H-T-T-T, which does not appear random, and also more likely than the sequence H-H-H-H-T-H, which does not represent the fairness of the coin. Thus, people expect that the essential characteristics of the process will be represented, not only globally in the entire sequence, but also locally in each of its parts. A locally representative sequence, however, deviates systematically from chance expectation; it contains too many alternations and too few runs. Another consequence of the belief in local representativeness is the well-known gambler's fallacy. After observing a long run of red on the roulette wheel, for example, most people erroneously believe that black is now due, presumably because the occurrence of black will result in a more representative sequence than the occurrence of an additional red. Chance is commonly viewed as a self-correcting process in which a deviation in one direction induces a deviation in the opposite direction to restore the equilibrium. In fact, deviations are not "corrected" as a chance process unfolds, they are merely diluted.

Misconceptions of chance are not limited to naive subjects. A study of the statistical intuitions of experienced research psychologists revealed a lingering belief in what may be called the "law of small numbers," according to which even small samples are highly representative of the populations from which they are drawn. The responses of these investigators reflected the expectation that a valid hypothesis about a population will be represented by a statistically significant result in a sample—with little regard for its size. As a consequence, the researchers put too much faith in the results of small samples and grossly overestimated the replicability of such results. In the actual conduct of research, this bias leads to the selection of samples of inadequate size and to overinterpretation of findings.

Insensitivity to Predictability

People are sometimes called upon to make such numerical predictions as the future value of a stock, the demand for a commodity, or the outcome of a football game. Such predictions are often made by representativeness. For example, suppose one is given a description of a company and is asked to predict its future profit. If the description of the company is very favorable, a very high profit will appear most representative of that description; if the description is mediocre, a mediocre performance will appear most representative. The degree to which the description is favorable is unaffected by the reliability of that description or by the degree to which it permits accurate prediction. Hence, if people predict solely in terms of the favorableness of the description, their predictions will be insensitive to the reliability of the evidence and to the expected accuracy of the prediction.

This mode of judgment violates the normative statistical theory in which the extremeness and the range of predictions are controlled by considerations of predictability. When predictability is nil, the same prediction should be made in all cases. For example, if the descriptions of companies provide no information relevant to profit, then the same value (such as average profit) should be predicted for all companies. If predictability is perfect, of course, the values predicted will match the actual values and the range of predictions will equal the range of outcomes. In general, the higher the predictability, the wider the range of predicted values.

Several studies of numerical prediction have demonstrated that intuitive predictions violate this rule, and that subjects show little or no regard for considerations of predictability. In one of these studies, subjects were presented with several paragraphs, each describing the performance of a student teacher during a particular practice lesson. Some subjects were asked to *evaluate* the quality of the lesson described in the paragraph in percentile scores, relative to a specified population. Other subjects were asked to *predict*, also in percentile scores, the standing of each student teacher five years after the practice lesson. The judgments made under the two conditions were identical. That is, the prediction of a remote criterion (success of a teacher after 5 years) was identical to the evaluation of the information on which the prediction was based (the quality of the practice lesson). The students who made these predictions were undoubtedly aware of the limited predictability of teaching competence on the basis of a single trial lesson five years earlier; nevertheless, their predictions were as extreme as their evaluations.

The Illusion of Validity

As we have seen, people often predict by selecting the outcome (for example, an occupation) that is most representative of the input (for example, the description of a person). The confidence they have in their prediction depends primarily on the degree of representativeness (that is, on the quality of the match between the selected outcome and the input) with little or no regard for the factors that limit predictive accuracy. Thus, people express great confidence in the prediction that a person is a librarian when given a description of his personality which matches the stereotype of librarians, even if the description is scanty, unreliable, or out-dated. The unwarranted confidence which is produced by a good fit between the predicted outcome and the input information may be called the illusion of validity. This illusion persists even when the judge is aware of the factors that limit the accuracy of his predictions. It is a common observation that psychologists who conduct selection interviews often experience considerable confidence in their predictions, even when they know of the vast literature that shows selection interviews to be highly fallible. The continued reliance on the clinical interview for selection, despite repeated demonstrations of its inadequacy, amply attests to the strength of this effect.

The internal consistency of a pattern of inputs is a major determinant of one's confidence in predictions based on these inputs. For example, people express more confidence in predicting the final grade-point average of a student whose first-year record consists entirely of B's than in predicting the grade-point average of a student whose first-year record includes many A's and C's. Highly consistent patterns are most often observed when the input variables are highly redundant or correlated. Hence, people tend to have great confidence in predictions based on redundant input variables. However, an elementary result in the statistics of correlation asserts that, given input variables of stated validity, a prediction based on several such inputs can achieve higher accuracy when they are independent of each other than when they are redundant or correlated. Thus, redundancy among inputs decreases accuracy even as it increases confidence, and people are often confident in predictions that are quite likely to be off the mark.

Misconceptions of Regression

Suppose a large group of children has been examined on two equivalent versions of an aptitude test. If one selects 10 children from among those who did best on one of the two versions, he will usually find their performance on the second version to be somewhat disappointing. Conversely, if one selects 10 children from among those who did worst on one version, they will be found, on the average, to do somewhat better on the other version. More generally, consider two variables X and Y which have the same distribution. If one selects individuals whose average X score deviates from the mean of X by k units, then the average of their Y scores will usually deviate from the mean of Y by less than k units. These observations illustrate a general phenomenon known as regression toward the mean, which was first documented by Galton more than 100 years ago.

In the normal course of life, one encounters many instances of regression toward the mean, in the comparison of the height of fathers and sons, of the intelligence of husbands and wives, or of the performance of individuals on consecutive examinations. Nevertheless, people do not develop correct intuitions about this phenomenon, First, they do not expect regression in many contexts where it is bound to occur. Second, when they recognize the occurrence of regression, they often invent spurious causal explanations for it. We suggest that the phenomenon of regression remains elusive because it is incompatible with the belief that the predicted outcome should be maximally representative of the input, and, hence, that the value of the outcome variable should be as extreme as the value of the input variable.

The failure to recognize the import of regression can have pernicious consequences, as illustrated by the following observation. In a discussion of flight training, experienced instructors noted that praise for an exceptionally smooth landing is typically followed by a poorer landing on the next try, while harsh criticism after a rough landing is usually followed by an improvement on the next try. The instructors concluded that verbal rewards are detrimental to learning, while verbal punishments are beneficial, contrary to accepted psychological doctrine. This conclusion is unwarranted because of the presence of regression toward the mean. As in other cases of repeated examination, an improvement will usually follow a poor performance and a deterioration will usually follow an outstanding performance, even if the instructor does not respond to the trainee's achievement on the first attempt. Because the instructors had praised their trainees after good landings and admonished them after poor ones, they reached the erroneous and potentially harmful conclusion that punishment is more effective than reward.

Thus, the failure to understand the effect of regression leads one to overestimate the effectiveness of punishment and to underestimate the effectiveness of reward. In social interaction, as well as in training, rewards are typically administered when performance is good, and punishments are typically administered when performance is poor. By regression alone, therefore, behavior is most likely to improve after punishment and most likely to deteriorate after reward. Consequently, the human condition is such that, by chance alone, one is most often rewarded for punishing others and most often punished for rewarding them. People are generally not aware of this contingency. In fact, the elusive role of regression in determining the apparent consequences of reward and punishment seems to have escaped the notice of students of this area.

AVAILABILITY

There are situations in which people assess the frequency of a class or the probability of an event by the ease with which instances or occurrences can be brought to mind. For example, one may assess the risk of heart attack among middle-aged people by recalling such occurrences among one's acquaintances. Similarly, one may evaluate the probability that a given business venture will fail by imagining various difficulties it could encounter. This judgmental heuristic is called availability. Availability is a useful clue for assessing frequency or probability, because instances of large classes are usually recalled better and faster than instances of less frequent classes. However, availability is affected by factors other than frequency and probability. Consequently, the reliance on availability leads to predictable biases, some of which are illustrated below.

Biases Due to the Retrievability of Instances

When the size of a class is judged by the availability of its instances, a class whose instances are easily retrieved will appear more numerous than a class of equal frequency whose instances are less retrievable. In an elementary demonstration of this effect, subjects heard a list of well-known personalities of both sexes and were subsequently asked to judge whether the list contained more names of men than of women. Different lists were presented to different groups of subjects. In some of the lists the men were relatively more famous than the women, and in others the women were relatively more famous than the men. In each of the lists, the subjects erroneously judged that the class (sex) that had the more famous personalities was the more numerous.

In addition to familiarity, there are other factors, such as salience, which affect the retrievability of instances. For example, the impact of seeing a house burning on the subjective probability of such accidents is probably greater than the impact of reading about a fire in the local paper. Furthermore, recent occurrences are likely to be relatively more available than earlier occurrences. It is a common experience that the subjective probability of traffic accidents rises temporarily when one sees a car overturned by the side of the road.

Biases Due to the Effectiveness of a Search Set

Suppose one samples a word (of three letters or more) at random from an English text. Is it more likely that the word starts with r or that r is the third letter? People approach this problem by recalling words that begin with r (road) and words that have r in the third position (car) and passes the relative frequency by the ease with which words of the two types come to mind. Because it is much easier to search for words by their first letter than by their third letter, most people judge words that begin with a given consonant to be more numerous than words in which the same consonant appears in the third position. They do so even for consonants, such as r or k, that are more frequent in the third position than in the first.

Different tasks elicit different search sets. For example, suppose you are asked to rate the frequency with which abstract words (thought, love) and concrete words (door, water) appear in written English. A natural way to answer this question is to search for contexts in which the word could appear. It seems easier to think of contexts in which an abstract concept is mentioned (love in love stories) than to think of contexts in which a concrete word (such as door) is mentioned. If the frequency of words is judged by the availability of the contexts in which they appear, abstract words will be judged as relatively more numerous than concrete words. This bias has been observed in a recent study which showed that the judged frequency of occurrence of abstract words was much higher than that of concrete words, equated in objective frequency. Abstract words were also judged to appear in a much greater variety of contexts than concrete words.

Biases of Imaginability

Sometimes one has to assess the frequency of a class whose instances are not stored in memory but can be generated according to a given rule. In such situations, one typically generates several instances and evaluates frequency or probability by the ease with which the relevant instances can be constructed. However, the ease of constructing instances does not always reflect their actual frequency, and this mode of evaluation is prone to biases. To illustrate, consider a group of 10 people who form committees of k members, $2 \leqslant k \leqslant 8$. How many different committees of k members can be formed? The correct answer to this problem is given by the binomial coefficient $\binom{10}{k}$ which reaches a maximum of 252 for $k = 5$. Clearly, the number of committees of k members equals the number of committees of $(10 - k)$ members, because any committee of k members defines a unique group of $(10 - k)$ nonmembers.

One way to answer this question without computation is to mentally construct committees of k members and to evaluate their number by the ease with which they come to mind. Committees of few members, say 2, are more available than committees of many members, say 8. The simplest scheme for the construction of committees is a partition of the group into disjoint sets. One readily sees that it is easy to construct five disjoint committees of 2 members, while it is impossible to generate even two disjoint committees of 8 members. Consequently, if frequency is assessed by imaginability, or by availability for construction, the small committees will appear more numerous than larger committees, in contrast to the correct bell-shaped function. Indeed, when naive subjects were asked to estimate the number of distinct committees of various sizes, their estimates were a decreasing monotonic function of committee size. For example, the median estimate of the number of committees of 2 members was 70, while the estimate for committees of 8 members was 20 (the correct answer is 45 in both cases).

Imaginability plays an important role in the evaluation of probabilities in real-life situations. The risk involved in an adventurous expedition, for example, is evaluated by imagining contingencies with which the expedition is not equipped to cope. If many such difficulties are vividly portrayed, the expedition can be made to appear exceedingly dangerous, although the ease with which disasters are imagined need not reflect their actual likelihood. Conversely, the risk involved in an undertaking may be grossly underestimated if some possible dangers are either difficult to conceive of, or simply do not come to mind.

Illusory Correlation

Chapman and Chapman have described an interesting bias in the judgment of the frequency with which two events co-occur. They presented naive judges with information concerning several hypothetical mental patients. The data for each patient consisted of a clinical diagnosis and a drawing of a person made by the patient. Later the judges estimated the frequency with which each diagnosis (such as paranoia or suspiciousness) had been accompanied by various features of the drawing (such as peculiar eyes). The subjects markedly overestimated the frequency of co-occurrence of natural associates, such as suspiciousness and peculiar eyes. This effect was labeled illusory correlation. In their erroneous judgments of the data to which they had been exposed, naive subjects "rediscovered" much of the common, but unfounded, clinical lore concerning the interpretation of the draw-a-person test. The illusory correlation effect was extremely resistant to contradictory data. It persisted even when the correlation between symptom and diagnosis was actually negative, and it prevented the judges from detecting relationships that were in fact present.

Availability provides a natural account for the illusory-correlation effect. The judgment of how frequently two events co-occur could be based on the strength of the associative bond between them. When the association is strong, one is likely to conclude that the events have been frequently paired. Consequently, strong associates will be judged to have occurred together frequently. According to this view, the illusory correlation between suspiciousness and peculiar drawing of the eyes, for example, is due to the fact that suspiciousness is more readily associated with the eyes than with any other part of the body.

Lifelong experience has taught us that, in general, instances of large classes are recalled better and faster than instances of less frequent classes; that likely occurrences are easier to imagine than unlikely ones; and that the associative connections between events are strengthened when the events frequently co-occur. As a result, man has at his disposal a procedure (the availability heuristic) for estimating the numerosity of a class, the likelihood of an event, or the frequency of co-occurrences, by the ease with which the relevant mental operations of retrieval, construction, or association can be performed. However, as the preceding examples have demonstrated, this valuable estimation procedure results in systematic errors.

ADJUSTMENT AND ANCHORING

In many situations, people make estimates by starting from an initial value that is adjusted to yield the final answer. The initial value, or starting point, may be suggested by the formulation of the problem, or it may be the result of a partial computation. In either case, adjustments are typically insufficient. That is, different starting points yield different estimates, which are biased toward the initial values. We call this phenomenon anchoring.

Insufficient Adjustment

In a demonstration of the anchoring effect, subjects were asked to estimate various quantities, stated in percentages (for example, the percentage of African countries in the United Nations). For each quantity, a number between 0 and 100 was determined by spinning a wheel of fortune in the subjects' presence. The subjects were instructed to indicate first whether that number was higher or lower than the value of the quantity, and then to estimate the value of the quantity by moving upward or downward from the given number. Different groups were given different numbers for each quantity, and these arbitrary numbers had a marked effect on estimates. For example, the median estimates of the percentage of African countries in the United Nations were 25 and 45 for groups that received 10 and 65, respectively, as starting points. Payoffs for accuracy did not reduce the anchoring effect.

Anchoring occurs not only when the starting point is given to the subject, but also when the subject bases his estimate on the result of some incomplete computation. A study of intuitive numerical estimation illustrates this effect. Two groups of high school students estimated, within five seconds, a numerical expression that was written on the blackboard. One group estimated the product

$$8 \times 7 \times 6 \times 5 \times 4 \times 3 \times 2 \times 1$$

while another group estimated the product

$$1 \times 2 \times 3 \times 4 \times 5 \times 6 \times 7 \times 8$$

To rapidly answer such questions, people may perform a few steps of computation and estimate the product by extrapolation or adjustment. Because adjustments are typically insufficient, this procedure should lead to underestimation. Furthermore, because the result of the first few steps of multiplication (performed from left to right) is higher in the descending sequence than in the ascending sequence, the former expression should be judged larger than the latter. Both predictions were confirmed. The median estimate for the ascending sequence was 512, while the median estimate for the descending sequence was 2,250. The correct answer is 40,320.

Biases in the Evaluation of Conjunctive and Disjunctive Events

In a recent study by Bar-Hillel subjects were given the opportunity to bet on one of two events. Three types of events were used: (1) simple events, such as drawing a red marble from a bag containing 50 percent red marbles and 50 percent white marbles; (2) conjunctive events, such as drawing a red marble seven times in succession, with replacement, from a bag containing 90 percent red marbles and 10 percent white marbles; and (3) disjunctive events, such as drawing a red marble at least once in seven successive tries, with replacement, from a bag containing 10 percent red marbles and 90 percent white marbles. In this problem, a significant majority of subjects preferred to bet on the conjunctive event (the probability of which is .48) rather than on the simple event (the probability of which is .50). Subjects also preferred to bet on the simple event rather than on the disjunctive event, which has a probability of .52. Thus, most subjects bet on the less likely event in both comparisons. This pattern of choices illustrates a general finding. Studies of choice among gambles and of judgments of probability indicate that people tend to overestimate the probability of conjunctive events and to underestimate the probability of disjunctive events. These biases are readily explained as effects of anchoring. The stated probability of the elementary event (success at any one stage) provides a natural starting point for the estimation of the probabilities of both conjunctive and disjunctive events. Since adjustment from the starting point is typically insufficient, the final estimates remain too close to the probabilities of the elementary events in both cases. Note that the overall probability of a conjunctive event is lower than the probability of each elementary event, whereas the overall probability of a disjunctive event is higher than the probability of each elementary event. As a consequence of anchoring, the overall probability will be overestimated in conjunctive problems and underestimated in disjunctive problems.

Biases in the evaluation of compound events are particularly significant in the context of planning. The successful completion of an undertaking, such as the development of a new product, typically has a conjunctive character: for the undertaking to succeed, each of a series of events must occur. Even when each of these events is very likely, the overall probability of success can be quite low if the number of events is large. The general tendency to overestimate the probability of conjunctive events leads to unwarranted optimism in the evaluation of the likelihood that a plan will succeed or that a project will be completed on time. Conversely, disjunctive structures are typically encountered in the evaluation of risks. A complex system, such as a nuclear reactor or a human body, will malfunction if any of its essential components fails. Even when the likelihood of failure in each component is slight, the probability of an overall failure can be high if many components are involved. Because of anchoring, people will tend to underestimate the probabilities of failure in complex systems. Thus, the direction of the anchoring bias can sometimes be inferred from the structure of the event. The chainlike structure of conjunctions leads to overestimation, the funnel-like structure of disjunctions leads to underestimation.

Anchoring in the Assessment of Subjective Probability Distributions

In decision analysis, experts are often required to express their beliefs about a quantity, such as the value of the Dow-Jones average on a particular day, in the form of a probability distribution. Such a distribution is usually constructed by asking the person to select values of the quantity that correspond to specified percentiles of his subjective probability distribution. For example, the judge may be asked to select a number, X_{90}, such that his subjective probability that this number will be higher than the value of the Dow-Jones average is .90. That is, he should select the value X_{90} so that he is just willing to accept 9 to 1 odds that the Dow-Jones average will not exceed it. A subjective probability distribution for the value of the Dow-Jones average can be constructed from several such judgments corresponding to different percentiles.

By collecting subjective probability distributions for many different quantities, it is possible to test the judge for proper calibration. A judge is properly (or externally) calibrated in a set of problems if exactly II percent of the true values of the assessed quantities falls below his stated values of X_{II}. For example, the true values should fall below X_{01} for 1 percent of the quantities and above X_{99} for 1 percent of the quantities. Thus, the true values should fall in the confidence interval between X_{01} and X_{99} on 98 percent of the problems.

Several investigators have obtained probability distributions for many quantities from a large number of judges. These distributions indicated large and systematic departures from proper calibration. In most studies, the actual values of the assessed quantities are either smaller than X_{01} or greater than X_{99} for about 30 percent of the problems. That is, the subjects state overly narrow confidence intervals which reflect more certainty than is justified by their knowledge about the assessed quantities. This bias is common to naive and to sophisticated subjects, and it is not eliminated by introducing proper scoring rules, which provide incentives for external calibration. This effect is attributable, in part at least, to anchoring.

To select X_{90} for the value of the Dow-Jones average, for example, it is natural to begin by thinking about one's best estimate of the Dow-Jones and to adjust this value upward. If this adjustment—like most others—is insufficient, then X_{90} will not be sufficiently extreme. A similar anchoring effect will occur in the selection of X_{10}, which is presumably obtained by adjusting one's best estimate downward. Consequently, the confidence interval between X_{10} and X_{90} will be too narrow, and the assessed probability distribution will be too tight. In support of this interpretation it can be shown that subjective probabilities are systematically altered by a procedure in which one's best estimate does not serve as an anchor.

Subjective probability distributions for a given quantity (the Dow-Jones average) can be obtained in two different ways: (1) by asking the subject to select values of the Dow-Jones that correspond to specified percentiles of his probability distribution and (2) by asking the subject to assess the probabilities that the true value of the Dow-Jones will exceed some specified values. The two procedures are formally equivalent and should yield identical distributions. However, they suggest different modes of adjustment from different anchors. In procedure (1), the natural starting point is one's best estimate of the quantity. In procedure (2), on the other hand, the subject may be anchored on the value stated in the question. Alternatively, he may be anchored on even odds, or 50–50 chances, which is a natural starting point in the estimation of likelihood. In either case, procedure (2) should yield less extreme odds than procedure (1).

To contrast the two procedures, a set of 24 quantities (such as the air distance from New Delhi to Peking) was presented to a group of subjects who assessed either X_{10} or X_{90} for each problem. Another group of subjects received the median judgment of the first group for each of the 24 quantities. They were asked to assess the odds that each of the given values exceeded the true value of the relevant quantity. In the absence of any bias, the second group should retrieve the odds specified to the first group, that is, $9:1$. However, if even odds or the stated value serve as anchors, the odds of the second group should be less extreme, that is, closer to $1:1$. Indeed, the median odds stated by this group, across all problems, were $3:1$. When the judgments of the two groups were tested for external calibration, it was found that subjects in the first group were too extreme, in accord with earlier studies. The events that they defined as having a probability of .10 actually obtained in 24 percent of the cases. In contrast, subjects in the second group were too conservative. Events to which they assigned an average probability of .34 actually obtained in 26 percent of the cases. These results illustrate the manner in which the degree of calibration depends on the procedure of elicitation.

DISCUSSION

This article has been concerned with cognitive biases that stem from the reliance on judgmental heuristics. These biases are not attributable to motivational effects such as wishful thinking or the distortion of judgments by payoffs and penalties. Indeed, several of the severe errors of judgment reported earlier occurred despite the fact that subjects were encouraged to be accurate and were rewarded for the correct answers.

The reliance on heuristics and the prevalence of biases are not restricted to laymen. Experienced researchers are also prone to the same biases—when they think intuitively. For example, the tendency to predict the outcome that best represents the data, with insufficient regard for prior probability, has been observed in the intuitive judgments of individuals who have had extensive training in statistics. Although the statistically sophisticated avoid elementary errors, such as the gambler's fallacy, their intuitive judgments are liable to similar fallacies in more intricate and less transparent problems.

It is not surprising that useful heuristics such as representativeness and availability are retained, even though they occasionally lead to errors in prediction or estimation. What is perhaps surprising is the failure of people to infer from lifelong experience such fundamental statistical rules as regression toward the mean, or the effect of sample size on sampling variability. Although everyone is exposed, in the normal course of life, to numerous examples from which these rules could have been induced, very few people discover the principles of sampling and regression on their own. Statistical principles are not learned from everyday experience because the relevant instances are not coded appropriately. For example, people do not discover that successive lines in a text differ more in average word length than do successive pages, because they simply do not attend to the average word length of individual lines or pages. Thus, people do not learn the relation between sample size and sampling variability, although the data for such learning are abundant.

The lack of an appropriate code also explains why people usually do not detect the biases in their judgments of probability. A person could conceivably learn whether his judgments are externally calibrated by keeping a tally of the proportion of events that actually occur among those to which he assigns the same probability. However, it is not natural to group events by their judged probability. In the absence of such grouping it is impossible for an individual to discover, for example, that only 50 percent of the predictions to which he has assigned a probability of .9 or higher actually came true.

The empirical analysis of cognitive biases has implications for the theoretical and applied role of judged probabilities. Modern decision theory regards subjective probability as the quantified opinion of an idealized person. Specifically, the subjective probability of a given event is defined by the set of bets about this event that such a person is willing to accept. An internally consistent, or coherent, subjective probability measure can be derived for an individual if his choices among bets satisfy certain principles, that is, the axioms of the theory. The derived probability is subjective in the sense that different individuals are allowed to have different probabilities for the same event. The major contribution of this approach is that it provides a rigorous subjective interpretation of probability that is applicable to unique events and is embedded in a general theory of rational decision.

It should perhaps be noted that, while subjective probabilities can sometimes be inferred from preferences among bets, they are normally not formed in this fashion. A person bets on team A rather than on team B because he believes that team A is more likely to win; he does not infer this belief from his betting preferences. Thus, in reality, subjective probabilities determine preferences among bets and are not derived from them, as in the axiomatic theory of rational decision.

The inherently subjective nature of probability has led many students to the belief that coherence, or internal consistency, is the only valid criterion by which judged probabilities should be evaluated. From the standpoint of the formal theory of subjective probability, any set of internally consistent probability judgments is as good as any other. This criterion is not entirely satisfactory, because an internally consistent set of subjective probabilities can be incompatible with other beliefs held by the individual. Consider a person whose subjective probabilities for all possible outcomes of a coin-tossing game reflect the gambler's fallacy. That is, his estimate of the probability of tails on a particular toss increases with the number of consecutive heads that preceded that toss. The judgments of such a person could be internally consistent and therefore acceptable as adequate subjective probabilities according to the criterion of the formal theory. These probabilities, however, are incompatible with the generally held belief that a coin has no memory and is therefore incapable of generating sequential dependencies. For judged probabilities to be considered adequate, or rational, internal consistency is not enough. The judgments must be compatible with the entire web of beliefs held by the individual. Unfortunately, there can be no simple formal procedure for assessing the compatibility of a set of probability judgments with the judge's total system of beliefs. The rational judge will nevertheless strive for compatibility, even though internal consistency is more easily achieved and assessed. In particular, he will attempt to make his probability judgments compatible with his knowledge about the subject matter, the laws of probability, and his own judgmental heuristics and biases.

SUMMARY

This article described three heuristics that are employed in making judgments under uncertainty; (1) representativeness, which is usually employed when people are asked to judge the probability that an object or event A belongs to class or process B; (2) availability of instances or scenarios, which is often employed when people are asked to assess the frequency of a class or the plausibility of a particular development; and (3) adjustment from an anchor, which is usually employed in numerical prediction when a relevant value is available. These heuristics are highly economical and usually effective, but they lead to systematic and predictable errors. A better understanding of these heuristics and of the biases to which they lead could improve judgments and decisions in situations of uncertainty.

27.

An Economic Analysis of
Self-Insured Retention*

ROBERT J. ECK

The primary function of the risk manager is to alleviate the uncertainty
surrounding the risk of financial loss by designing a program of insurance
and self-insured retention. Through this program, risks can be assessed
in a more rational manner. It is the risk manager's job, then, to determine
the most cost-effective combination of conventionally purchased insurance and self-insured retention. In making this decision, three variables
are considered: the first is flexibility of the insurance market, the second
is predictability of the number of losses of a particular size that may
occur, and third is financial strength of the company assuming the risk—
how much loss it can absorb and continue to operate unimpaired.

This article analyzes the economic forces at work in shaping this
decision. I intend to show that risk aversion or preference is determined
by the interaction of the variables mentioned, and that risk preference,
in terms of relatively high retention levels, is the result of good financial
strength, relatively predictable loss frequency and a responsive insurance
market.

Before beginning the analysis, one major assumption I have made
must be addressed—that given the financial ability to absorb a loss,
the self-insurer can administer retained losses more efficiently than an
insurance company. There are three considerations behind this assumption. The first is that the insurance company cannot adjust claims more

---

* *Risk Management* 30, no. 5 (May 1983), pp. 20–28.

cost-effectively than a self-insurer. The reason, I feel, is that claims handling is a manual function in its very nature. The adjuster investigates the accident, sets reserves and authorizes payments on a claim-by-claim basis. I don't think this process can be automated because a variety of damage or medical reports must be studied so that conclusions may be drawn regarding the extent of liability for each loss. This same process is undertaken by the claims adjuster for the self-insurer.

With the advent of word processors and microcomputers, automated claims recordkeeping is accessible even to relatively small firms at low cost. This is particularly true when one considers that the microcomputer can be used for a variety of functions in addition to claims adjusting support. I believe the self-insured has ready access to talented and experienced claims personnel, and can afford to offer the salary needed to attract the claims professional because it has not borne the cost of training the adjuster. In a competitive labor market, these costs will trade off so that the cost of an adjuster to the insurance company will be equivalent to the cost of a self-insurer.

The second consideration in my assumption concerns the fact that the self-insurer does not incur marketing costs in retaining some part of a risk, whereas the marketing costs would be incurred by an insurance company, which then passes these marketing costs down to the insured in the premium charge. So, in terms of easily identifiable and measurable costs, it seems the self-insurer can operate more efficiently.

There is, however, one final consideration which is more difficult to quantify—that the insurance company may handle losses more aggressively than the insured desires. For example, consider the possible employee relations costs that may result if an insurance company aggressively denies or litigates workers' compensation cases. Or the customer bad will that could result from aggressively handled general or products liability claims. Thus, the following analysis will assume that the self-insurer can retain risk more cost-effectively than it can insure it, given the ability to absorb the loss and continue operating.

TAKING ADVANTAGE OF MARKET CONDITIONS

To begin, the insurance market can serve as either primary obstacle or boon to cost-effective risk management. Presently, the market is fairly flexible, giving the risk manager a variety of options. This responsiveness solves the first part of the decision-making process by allowing the risk manager to choose between full or low deductible insurance and high levels of self-insured retention for many risks. Captive insurance companies have also proliferated, some very closely held and others serving a broader market. And access to captive reinsurance has also enhanced the flexibility in the insurance market.

To better understand market variations, the insurance market can

FIGURE 1

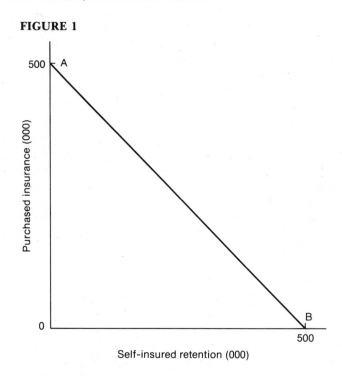

be depicted graphically. The graph represents the first part of the deci-sion concerning self-insured retention. The curve can be called the Risk Management Opportunities Curve because it depicts the options be-tween full insurance and full retention at a given loss size. Figure 1 represents the flexible insurance market. In this case, the risk manager is considering how to provide for a possible $500,000 loss.

Point A in Figure 1 represents full insurance and point B, full reten-tion. Depending on financial and probabilistic considerations, the risk manager will choose some point on this curve. To consider the situation presented by a restrictive market, examine Figure 2. In this case, no deductible smaller than $100,000 is available, due perhaps to the insur-ance market's belief that this type of loss is prone to a high frequency of occurrences. This restrictive market favors financially strong compa-nies that are capable of absorbing this deductible level with some fre-quency. Due to the restriction, the graph is vertical at $100,000 retention, until the $400,000 insurance level at point A. The reason is that no less than $100,000 can be retained. For the $500,000 loss being consid-ered, the maximum amount of insurance available is $400,000.

To complete this stage of the analysis, one must understand that the risk manager faces a different Risk Management Opportunities Curve for each type of loss. This is because the firm encounters a different

FIGURE 2

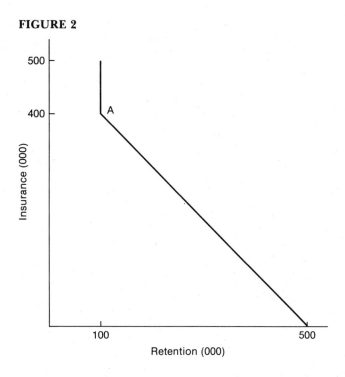

potential for loss, when all factors are considered, for each type of loss (e.g., auto liability versus ocean marine). Hence, the first stage in the decision process will be repeated when each line of coverage is considered.

CONSIDERING LOSS FREQUENCY AND SEVERITY

The second factor in the decision to insure or retain varying amounts of a potential loss is the probability of such a loss occurring. This includes not only the probability of the incident occurring, but also the probability that the magnitude of the loss will be the amount predicted. These frequency and severity considerations differ in nature for each coverage or type of loss. The point here is fairly simple: if there is a high probability that a loss or number of losses of x value will occur during one year, then the risk manager has good information on which to base the decision. If the probability is low, there is a high potential that the frequency of loss will deviate from the estimate. In this case, the risk manager might opt to buy more insurance, because he or she is trading off the uncertain total loss amount for the certain cost of insurance. If the probability regarding the size of each loss changes, this will not have much effect on retention. This is because retention is based on severity, finance, and the insurance market. If the size of loss changes, with the other factors static, the risk manager will respond by buying more insurance. A change in the loss size will present a change in total liability, but not in how much risk a firm can afford to retain.

FACTORING IN FINANCIAL CONSIDERATIONS

At this point, consideration turns to the financial factors in the retention decision. There are four major factors which must be understood and addressed by the risk manager when deciding how much risk to retain. The first is the most basic—the trade-off between deductibles and premiums. First dollars of insurance protection are more expensive than later dollars because smaller value losses are more likely to occur. The frequency associated with smaller value losses translates into a proportionally greater premium charge for the first dollars of coverage. The higher value losses are less frequent and less predictable. Insurance is a tool to spread these unpredictable losses among many policyholders.

However, at lower loss levels policyholders pay proportionally greater premiums to cover their own losses. So, based on the frequency of low-cost losses and relatively high premium levels, the risk manager begins to frame some idea of a cost-effective deductible level. At this point, the second factor is considered. This factor is concerned with how much loss the firm can absorb and continue to operate profitably. This is integrally associated with the above consideration because the cost-effectiveness of a high deductible is meaningless if a firm fails in the aftermath of a retained loss that it could not afford. In the past, this subject has been addressed at length, considering ratios of profits, sales, net assets, etc. The point here is that the risk manager must look to some valid measure to determine how much loss the firm can successfully retain. Further, he or she must realize that the firm may have to absorb this loss some number of times each year, and in consecutive years.

Two factors remain to be considered: tax costs or benefits, and cash flow considerations. The cash flow consideration has changed significantly in recent years. Currently, firms paying large premiums have access to cash flow payment plans, or "paid loss retro" plans, in which premium payments are based on actual losses and spread out over the time span that the losses will liquidate. This is much the same as the situation faced by the self-insurer. However, the noteworthy differences are twofold. First, the self-insurer does not pay the marketing costs incurred in selling the plan. Second, cash flow plans include a factor for the investment income lost by the insurance company in offering the plan. An additional benefit the self-insurer garners is the income from investing the reserves set against future liabilities from existing claims.

However, the cash flow plan, or paid loss retro plan, is usually only available for workers' compensation at full insurance. If the risk manager is considering some other line of insurance, or self-insuring workers' compensation, then more traditional payment plans apply. In this case, cash flow is sacrificed completely. Premiums must be paid yearly, regardless of loss liquidation. Further, the insurance company gains investment income from money held in reserve against future losses. From this point of view, insuring retainable loss levels is clearly a costly proposition. So, greater retention will result in better cash flow and investment income from loss reserves.

A CLOUDY ISSUE—TAXES

This leaves the final financial consideration—taxes. The courts and the IRS have left this issue somewhat cloudy in the United States. IRS regulations state that a self-insurer cannot deduct its loss reserves as an expense, but can only deduct loss payments as they are paid out. So, from a tax point of view, the paid loss retro option becomes attractive. The insured deducts the total premium the year it is incurred, but only pays it as the losses liquidate—usually about a 10-year period. But, the Ninth Federal District Court has ruled that a self-insurer can deduct loss reserves the year the loss occurs. Therefore, the tax issue is rather uncertain, but must be discussed with legal counsel to determine an appropriate retention level. (In the case of property losses, this decision is easier because the amount of the loss is known quickly and also paid relatively quickly.)

TRANSFERRING THE DECISION TO A DIAGRAM

Now the risk manager has amassed the information needed to decide how much of a given loss level to retain. The probability of the loss occurring, the financial factors and the options in the insurance market will be considered together to determine the retention level. This decision can be depicted diagrammatically, as in Figure 3. Point A represents the risk manager's choice of retention and insurance. In Figure 3, the risk manager is faced with a possible $500,000 loss. The isoquant P_A represents the decision-making process. The slope and position of P_A is determined by the factors considered above. (Remember that the Risk Management Opportunity Curve is determined by the insurance market.) Isoquant P_A can be referred to as the Risk Preference Curve. When one of the factors changes, the position of the curve will change. In Figure 4, the same loss is being assessed. However, Risk Preference Curve P_B represents a change in the probable frequency of occurrence. In this case, the frequency has doubled, so the risk manager has decided to retain $50,000 of each occurrence, as opposed to $100,000 in Figure

FIGURE 3

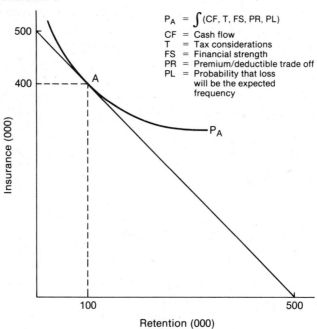

FIGURE 4

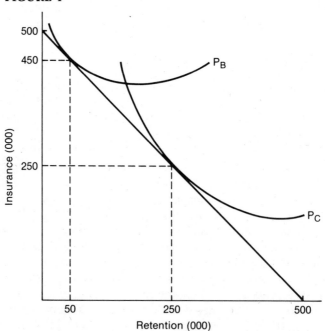

FIGURE 5

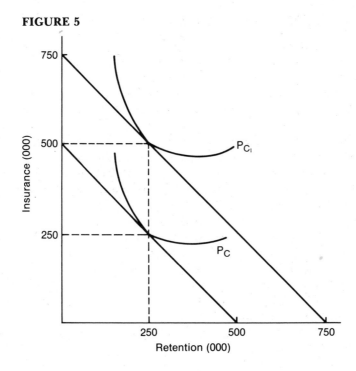

3. P_C, however, represents a change in probability toward a lower frequency, causing the risk manager to retain a greater portion of each loss—$250,000 in the example. The same movements can be caused by changes in the financial considerations. P_B would represent a weaker financial situation than P_C if severity were static.

Two further points regarding probability should be discussed. First, if the probable severity increases, the Risk Management Opportunities Curve will move to the right. The Risk Preference Curve will also move in response to this change. If, for example, all frequency and financial considerations comprising P_C remained static, then P_C will move straight upwards as in Figure 5 to P_{C_1}. Total loss retained remains the same because the retention was determined based on the number of occurrences expected in one year and the amount of that total liability the firm could absorb during the year and still operate profitably. Another probability consideration is the credibility of the data base used to determine frequency. If the data points are widely divergent within the sample, then potential total annual liability is more difficult to estimate. The result will be to retain less of each loss to reduce financial uncertainty.

ANOTHER OPTION—LAYERING RETENTION

At this point, another consideration can be introduced. This consideration is financial, and will encourage greater risk retention. The idea is that the risk manager can optimize risk retention and limit the insurance premium by layering various levels of retention and insurance. This tool is particularly useful in handling relatively frequent losses.

A good example would be auto liability for a fleet of automobiles used by salesmen, for which losses may occur fairly frequently and will tend to be lower in value. The risk manager could choose a conventional policy with a $1,000 deductible and a $250,000 limit of liability, and would then retain losses between $250,000 and $500,000, with losses over $500,000 covered by an excess policy. The excess limits would be set to cover the maximum probable loss.

The effect of such an arrangement is that premiums are minimized while the risk manager limits exposure to serious loss. This type of program is clearly most beneficial when a firm cannot risk the potential financial harm presented by retaining many losses between $1,000 and $250,000. The risk manager is assuming in this case that only rarely will a loss penetrate the $250,000 level. If, for example, a loss hits $350,000, and the firm is in a 45 percent tax bracket, the actual loss absorbed will be $45,450. This tax consideration is critical to understanding such a layering program. Therefore, by layering retention, a self-insurer can increase retention, reduce premiums, and reduce total annual loss liability.

As has been shown above, the insurance market can greatly limit or extend the options available to the risk manager, and a flexible market will allow for a variety of retention levels as determined by other factors. Second, the probability that a loss of a given size will occur, and how often that loss will repeat itself during a specified period of time must be considered. If the data base is credible, the risk manager will tend to retain a greater portion of each loss due to the certainty of financial loss over a period of time. This conclusion is tempered by the risk manager's third consideration—financial strength. As discussed, financial strength is composed of the following considerations: cost trade-offs between premiums and deductibles, taxes, cash flow, balance sheet conditions, and layering method.

A strong financial position will encourage higher retention because the risk manager can administer retained losses more cheaply than provide for them with insurance. The exception to this is catastrophic loss levels, which will be insured. Therefore, risk preference, in terms of higher risk retention, will occur when a risk manager encounters somewhat predictable loss frequency, strong financial position, and a responsive insurance market.

28.

Let's Take the Con out of Econometrics*

EDWARD E. LEAMER

Econometricians would like to project the image of agricultural experimenters who divide a farm into a set of smaller plots of land and who
select randomly the level of fertilizer to be used on each plot. If some
plots are assigned a certain amount of fertilizer while others are assigned
none, then the difference between the mean yield of the fertilized plots
and the mean yield of the unfertilized plots is a measure of the effect
of fertilizer on agricultural yields. The econometrician's humble job is
only to determine if that difference is large enough to suggest a real
effect of fertilizer, or is so small that it is more likely due to random
variation.

This image of the applied econometrician's art is grossly misleading.
I would like to suggest a more accurate one. The applied econometrician
is like a farmer who notices that the yield is somewhat higher under
trees where birds roost, and he uses this as evidence that bird droppings
increase yields. However, when he presents this finding at the annual
meeting of the American Ecological Association, another farmer in the
audience objects that he used the same data but came up with the conclusion that moderate amounts of shade increase yields. A bright chap in
the back of the room then observes that these two hypotheses are indis-
tinguishable, given the available data. He mentions the phrase *identification problem*, which, though no one knows quite what he means, is said

* *The American Economic Review* 73, no. 1 (March 1983), pp. 31–43.

with such authority that it is totally convincing. The meeting reconvenes in the halls and in the bars, with heated discussion whether this is the kind of work that merits promotion from Associate to Full Farmer; the Luminists strongly opposed to promotion and the Aviophiles equally strong in favor.

One should not jump to the conclusion that there is necessarily a substantive difference between drawing inferences from experimental as opposed to nonexperimental data. The images I have drawn are deliberately prejudicial. First, we had the experimental scientist with hair neatly combed, wide eyes peering out of horn-rimmed glasses, a white coat, and an electronic calculator for generating the random assignment of fertilizer treatment to plots of land. This seems to contrast sharply with the nonexperimental farmer with overalls, unkempt hair, and bird droppings on his boots. Another image, drawn by Orcutt, is even more damaging: "Doing econometrics is like trying to learn the laws of electricity by playing the radio." However, we need not now submit to the tyranny of images, as many of us have in the past.

I. IS RANDOMIZATION ESSENTIAL?

What is the real difference between these two settings? Randomization seems to be the answer. In the experimental setting, the fertilizer treatment is "randomly" assigned to plots of land, whereas in the other case nature did the assignment. Now it is the tyranny of words that we must resist. "Random" does not mean adequately mixed in *every* sample. It only means that on the average, the fertilizer treatments are adequately mixed. Randomization implies that the least squares estimator is "unbiased," but that definitely does not mean that for each sample the estimate is correct. Sometimes the estimate is too high, sometimes too low. I am reminded of the lawyer who remarked that "when I was a young man I lost many cases that I should have won, but when I grew older I won many that I should have lost, so on the average justice was done."

In particular, it is possible for the randomized assignment to lead to exactly the same allocation as the nonrandom assignment, namely, with treated plots of land all being under trees and with nontreated plots of land all being away from trees. I submit that, if this is the outcome of the randomization, then the randomized experiment and the nonrandomized experiment are exactly the same. Many econometricians would insist that there is a difference, because the randomized experiment generates "unbiased" estimates. But all this means is that, if this particular experiment yields a gross overestimate, some other experiment yields a gross underestimate.

Randomization thus does not assure that each and every experiment is "adequately mixed," but randomization does make "adequate mixing" probable. In order to make clear what I believe to be the true value of randomization, let me refer to the model

$$Y_i = \alpha + \beta F_i + \gamma L_i + U_i, \qquad (1)$$

where Y_i is the yield of plot i; F_i is the fertilizer assigned to plot i; L_i is the light falling on plot i; U_i is the unspecified influence on the yield of plot i, and where β, the fertilizer effect, is the object of the inferential exercise. We may suppose to begin the argument that the light level is expensive to measure and that it is decided to base an estimate of β initially only on measurement of Y_i and F_i. We may assume also that the natural experiment produces values for F_i, L_i, and U_i with expected values $E(U_i|F_i) = 0$ and $E(L_i|F_i) = r_0 + r_1 F_i$. In the more familiar parlance, it is assumed that the fertilizer level and the residual effects are uncorrelated, but the fertilizer level and the light level are possibly correlated. As every beginning econometrics student knows, if you omit from a model a variable which is correlated with included variables, bad things happen. These bad things are revealed to the econometrician by computing the conditional mean of Y given F but not L:

$$\begin{aligned} E(Y|F) &= \alpha + \beta F + \gamma E(L|F) \\ &= \alpha + \beta F + \gamma (r_0 + r_1 F) \\ &\equiv (\alpha + \alpha^*) + (\beta + \beta^*)F, \end{aligned} \qquad (2)$$

where $\alpha^* = \gamma r_0$ and $\beta^* = \gamma r_1$. The linear regression of Y on F provides estimates of the parameters of the conditional distribution of Y given F, and in this case the regression coefficients are estimates not of α and β, but rather of $\alpha + \alpha^*$ and $\beta + \beta^*$. The parameters α^* and β^* measure the bias in the least squares estimates. This bias could be due to left-out variables, or to measurement errors in F, or to simultaneity.

When observing a nonexperiment, the bias parameters α^* and β^* can be thought to be small, but they cannot sensibly be treated as exact zeroes. The notion that the bias parameters are small can be captured by the assumption that α^* and β^* are drawn from a normal distribution with zero means and covariance matrix M. The model can then be written as $Y = \alpha + \beta F + \epsilon$, where ϵ is the sum of three random variables: $U + \alpha^* + \beta^* F$. Because the error term ϵ is not spherical, the proper way to estimate α and β is generalized least squares. My 1974 article demonstrates that if (a,b) represent the least squares estimates of (α,β), then the generalized least squares estimates $(\hat{\alpha},\hat{\beta})$ are also equal to (a,b):

$$\begin{pmatrix} \hat{\alpha} \\ \hat{\beta} \end{pmatrix} = \begin{pmatrix} a \\ b \end{pmatrix}, \qquad (3)$$

and if S represents the sample covariance matrix for the least squares estimates, then the sample covariance matrix for $(\hat{\alpha},\hat{\beta})$ is

$$Var\ (\hat{\alpha},\hat{\beta}) = S + M, \tag{4}$$

where M is the covariance matrix of (α^*,β^*).

The meaning of Equation (3) is that unless one knows the direction of the bias, the possibility of bias does not call for any adjustment to the estimates. The possibility of bias does require an adjustment to the covariance matrix (4). The uncertainty is composed of two parts: the usual sampling uncertainty S plus the misspecification uncertainty M. As sample size grows, the sampling uncertainty S ever decreases, but the misspecification uncertainty M remains ever constant. The misspecification matrix M that we must add to the least squares variance matrix is just the (prior) variance of the bias coefficients (α^*,β^*). If this variance matrix is small, the least squares bias is likely to be small. If M is large, it is correspondingly probable that (α^*,β^*) is large.

It would be a remarkable bootstrap if we could determine the extent of the misspecification from the data. The data in fact contain no information about the size of the bias, a point which is revealed by studying the likelihood function. The misspecification matrix M is therefore a pure prior concept. One must decide independent of the data how good the nonexperiment is.

The formal difference between a randomized experiment and a natural experiment is measured by the matrix M. If the treatment is randomized, the bias parameters (α^*,β^*) are exactly zero, or, equivalently, the matrix M is a zero matrix. If M is zero, the least squares estimates are consistent. If M is not zero, as in the natural experiment, there remains a fixed amount of specification uncertainty, independent of sample size.

There is therefore a sharp difference between inference from randomized experiments and inference from natural experiments. This seems to draw a sharp distinction between economics where randomized experiments are rare and "science" where experiments are routinely done. But the fact of the matter is that no one has ever designed an experiment that is free of bias, and no one can. As it turns out, the technician who was assigning fertilizer levels to plots of land, took his calculator into the fields, and when he was out in the sun, the calculator got heated up and generated large "random" numbers, which the technician took to mean no fertilizer; and when he stood under the shade of the trees, his cool calculator produced small numbers, and these plots received fertilizer.

You may object that this story is rather fanciful, but I need only make you think it is possible, to force you to set $M \neq 0$. Or if you think a computer can really produce random numbers (calculated by a mathematical formula and therefore perfectly predictable!), I will bring up mismeasurement of the fertilizer level, or human error in carrying out the computer instructions. Thus, the attempt to randomize and the attempt to measure accurately ensures that M is small, but not zero, and the difference between scientific experiments and natural experiments is difference in degree, but not in kind. Admittedly however, the misspecification uncertainty in many experimental settings may be so small that it is well approximated by zero. This can very rarely be said in nonexperimental settings.

Examples may be ultimately convincing. There is a great deal of empirical knowledge in the science of astronomy, yet there are no experiments. Medical knowledge is another good example. I was struck by a headline in the January 5, 1982 *New York Times:* "Life Saving Benefits of Low-Cholesterol Diet Affirmed in *Rigorous* Study." The article describes a randomized experiment with a control group and a treated group. "Rigorous" is therefore interpreted as "randomized." As a matter of fact, there was a great deal of evidence suggesting a link between heart disease and diet before any experiments were performed on humans. There were cross-cultural comparisons and there were animal studies. Actually, the only reason for performing the randomized experiment was that someone believed there was pretty clear nonexperimental evidence to begin with. The nonexperimental evidence was, of course, inconclusive, which in my language means that the misspecification uncertainty M remained uncomfortably large. The fact that the Japanese have both less incidence of heart disease and also diets lower in cholesterol compared to Americans is not convincing evidence, because there are so many other factors that remain unaccounted for. The fact that pigs on a high cholesterol diet develop occluded arteries is also not convincing, because the similarity in physiology in pigs and humans can be questioned.

When the sampling uncertainty S gets small compared to the misspecification uncertainty M, it is time to look for other forms of evidence, experiments or nonexperiments. Suppose I am interested in measuring the width of a coin, and I provide rulers to a room of volunteers. After each volunteer has reported a measurement, I compute the mean and standard deviation, and I conclude that the coin has width 1.325 millimeters with a standard error of .013. Since this amount of uncertainty is not to my liking, I propose to find three other rooms full of volunteers, thereby multiplying the sample size by four, and dividing the standard error in half. That is a silly way to get a more accurate measurement, because I have already reached the point where the sampling uncertainty S is very small compared with the misspecification uncertainty M. If I want to increase the true accuracy of my estimate, it is time for me to consider using a micrometer. So too in the case of diet and heart disease. Medical researchers had more or less exhausted the vein of nonexperimental evidence, and it became time to switch to the more expensive but richer vein of experimental evidence.

In economics, too, we are switching to experimental evidence. There are the laboratory experiments of Charles Plott and Vernon Smith and Smith, and there are the field experiments such as the Seattle/Denver income maintenance experiment. Another way to limit the misspecification error M is to gather different kinds of nonexperiments. Formally speaking, we will say that experiment 1 is qualitatively different from experiment 2 if the bias parameters (α_1^*, β_1^*) are distributed independently of the bias parameters $(\alpha_2^*, (\beta_2^*)$. In that event, simple averaging of the data from the two experiments yields average bias parameters $(\alpha_1^* + \alpha_2^*, \beta_1^* + \beta_2^*)/2$ with misspecification variance matrix $M/2$, half as large as the (common) individual variances. Milton Friedman's study of the permanent income hypothesis is the best example of this that I know. Other examples are hard to come by. I believe we need to put much more effort into identifying qualitatively different and convincing kinds of evidence.

Parenthetically, I note that traditional econometric theory, which does not admit experimental bias, as a consequence also admits no "hard core" propositions. Demand curves can be shown to be positively sloped. Utility can be shown not to be maximized. Econometric evidence of a positively sloped demand curve would, as a matter of fact, be routinely explained in terms of simultaneity bias. If utility seems not to have been maximized, it is only that the econometrician has misspecified the utility function. The misspecification matrix M thus forms Imre Lakatos' "protective belt" which protects certain hard core propositions from falsification.

II. IS CONTROL ESSENTIAL?

The experimental scientist who notices that the fertilizer treatment is correlated with the light level can correct his experimental design. He can control the light level, or he can allocate the fertilizer treatment in such a way that the fertilizer level and the light level are not perfectly correlated.

The nonexperimental scientist by definition cannot control the levels of extraneous influences such as light. But he can control for the variable light level by including light in the estimating equation. Provided nature does not select values for light and values for fertilizer levels that are perfectly correlated, the effect of fertilizer on yields can be estimated with a multiple regression. The collinearity in naturally selected treatment variables may mean that the data evidence is weak, but it does not invalidate in any way the usual least squares estimates. Here, again, there is no essential difference between experimental and nonexperimental inference.

III. ARE THE DEGREES OF FREEDOM INADEQUATE WITH NONEXPERIMENTAL DATA?

As a substitute for experimental control, the nonexperimental researcher is obligated to include in the regression equation all variables that might have an important effect. The NBER data banks contain time-series data on 2,000 macroeconomic variables. A model explaining gross national product in terms of all these variables would face a severe degrees-of-freedom deficit since the number of annual observations is less than thirty. Though the number of observations of any phenomenon is clearly limited, the number of explanatory variables is logically unlimited. If a polynominal could have a degree as high as k, it would usually be admitted that the degree could be $k + 1$ as well. A theory that allows k lagged explanatory variables would ordinarily allow $k + 1$. If the level of money might affect *GNP*, then why not the number of presidential sneezes, or the size of the polar ice cap?

The number of explanatory variables is unlimited in a nonexperimental setting, but it is also unlimited in an experimental setting. Consider again the fertilizer example in which the farmer randomly decides either to apply F_1 pounds of fertilizer per acre or zero pounds, and obtains the data illustrated in Figure 1. These data admit the inference that fertilizer level F_1 produces higher yields than no fertilizer. But the farmer is interested in selecting the fertilizer level that maximizes profits. If it is hypothesized that yield is a linear function of the fertilizer intensity $Y = \alpha + \beta F + U$, then profits are

$$Profits = pA(\alpha + \beta F + U) - p_F A F,$$

where A is total acreage, p is the product price, and p_F is the price per pound of fertilizer. This profit function is linear in F with slope

FIGURE 1
Hypothetical Data and Three Estimated Quadratic Functions

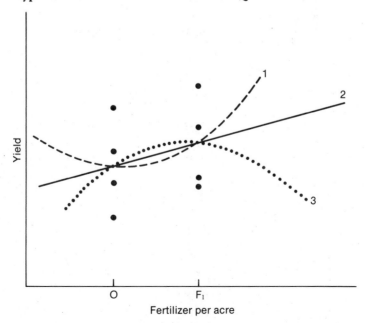

Fertilizer per acre

$A(\beta p - p_F)$. The farmer maximizes profits therefore by using no fertilizer if the price of fertilizer is high, $\beta p < p_F$, and using an unlimited amount of fertilizer if the price is low, $\beta p > p_F$. It is to be expected that you will find this answer unacceptable for one of several reasons:

1. When the farmer tries to buy an unlimited amount of fertilizer, he will drive up its price, and the problem should be reformulated to make p_F a function of F.
2. Uncertainty in the fertilizer effect β causes uncertainty in profits, $Variance\ (profits) = p^2 A^2 F^2 Var(\beta)$, and risk aversion will limit the level of fertilizer applied.
3. The yield function is nonlinear.

   Economic theorists doubtless find reasons 1 and 2 compelling, but I suspect that the real reason farmers don't use huge amounts of fertilizer is that the marginal increase in the yield eventually decreases. Plants don't grow in fertilizer alone.

   So let us suppose that yield is a quadratic function of fertilizer intensity, $Y = \alpha + \beta_1 F + \beta_2 F^2 + U$, and suppose we have only the data illustrated in Figure 1. Unfortunately, there are an infinite number of quadratic functions all of which fit the data equally well, three of which are drawn. If there were no other information available, we could conclude only that the yield is higher at F_1 than at zero. Formally speaking, there is an identification problem, which can be solved by altering the experimental design. The yield must be observed at a third point, as in Figure 2, where I have drawn the least squares estimated quadratic

FIGURE 2
Hypothetical Data and Estimated Quadratic Function

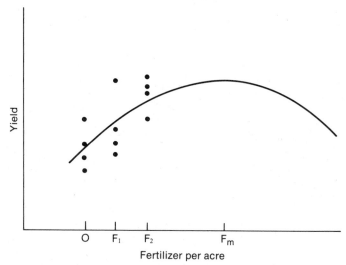

function and have indicated the fertilizer intensity F_m that maximizes the yield. I expect that most people would question whether these data admit the inference that the yield is maximized at F_m. Actually, after inspection of this figure, I don't think anything can be inferred except that the yield at F_2 is higher than at F_1, which in turn is higher than at zero. Thus I don't believe the function is quadratic. If it is allowed to be a cubic then again there is an identification problem.

This kind of logic can be extended indefinitely. One can always find a set of observations that will make the inferences implied by a polynomial of degree p seem silly. This is true regardless of the degree p. Thus no model with a finite number of parameters is actually believed, whether the data are experimental or nonexperimental.

IV. DO WE NEED PRIOR INFORMATION?

A model with an infinite number of parameters will allow inference from a finite data set only if there is some prior information that effectively constrains the ranges of the parameters. Figure 3 depicts another hypothetical sequence of observations and three estimated relationships between yield and fertilizer. I believe the solid line A is a better representation of the relationship than either of the other two. The piecewise linear form B fits the data better, but I think this peculiar meandering function is highly unlikely on an a priori basis. Though B and C fit the data equally well, I believe that B is much more likely than C. What

FIGURE 3
Hypothetical Data and Three Estimated Functions

Yield

Fertilizer per acre

I am revealing is the a priori opinion that the function is likely to be smooth and single peaked.

What should now be clear is that data alone cannot reveal the relationship between yield and fertilizer intensity. Data can reveal the yield at sampled values of fertilizer intensities, but in order to interpolate between these sampled values, we must resort to subjective prior information.

Economists have inherited from the physical sciences the myth that scientific inference is objective, and free of personal prejudice. This is utter nonsense. All knowledge is human belief; more accurately, human opinion. What often happens in the physical sciences is that there is a high degree of conformity of opinion. When this occurs, the opinion held by most is asserted to be an objective fact, and those who doubt it are labelled "nuts." But history is replete with examples of opinions losing majority status, with once-objective "truths" shrinking into the dark corners of social intercourse. To give a trivial example, coming now from California I am unsure whether fat ties or thin ties are aesthetically more pleasing.

The false idol of objectivity has done great damage to economic science. Theoretical econometricians have interpreted scientific objectivity to mean that an economist must identify exactly the variables in the model, the functional form, and the distribution of the errors. Given these assumptions, and given a data set, the econometric method produces an objective inference from a data set, unencumbered by the subjective opinions of the researcher.

This advice could be treated as ludicrous, except that it fills all the econometric textbooks. Fortunately, it is ignored by applied econometricians. The econometric art as it is practiced at the computer terminal involves fitting many, perhaps thousands, of statistical models. One or several that the researcher finds pleasing are selected for reporting purposes. This searching for a model is often well intentioned, but there can be no doubt that such a specification search invalidates the traditional theories of inference. The concepts of unbiasedness, consistency, efficiency, maximum-likelihood estimation, in fact, all the concepts of traditional theory, utterly lose their meaning by the time an applied researcher pulls from the bramble of computer output the one thorn of a model he likes best, the one he chooses to portray as a rose. The consuming public is hardly fooled by this chicanery. The econometrician's shabby art is humorously and disparagingly labelled "data mining," "fishing," "grubbing," "number crunching." A joke evokes the Inquisition: "If you torture the data long enough, Nature will confess" (Coase). Another suggests methodological fickleness: "Econometricians, like artists, tend to fall in love with their models" (wag unknown). Or how about: "There are two things you are better off not watching in the making: sausages and econometric estimates."

This is a sad and decidedly unscientific state of affairs we find ourselves in. Hardly anyone takes data analyses seriously. Or perhaps more accurately, hardly anyone takes anyone else's data analyses seriously. Like elaborately plumed birds who have long since lost the ability to procreate but not the desire, we preen and strut and display our *t*-values.

If we want to make progress, the first step we must take is to discard the counterproductive goal of objective inference. The dictionary defines an inference as a logical conclusion based on a set of facts. The "facts" used for statistical inference about θ are first the data, symbolized by *x*, second a conditional probability density, known as a sampling distribution, $f(x|\theta)$, and, third, explicitly for a Bayesian and implicitly for "all others," a marginal or prior probability density function $f(\theta)$. Because both the sampling distribution and the prior distribution are actually *opinions* and not *facts*, a statistical inference is and must forever remain an *opinion*.

What is a fact? A fact is merely an opinion held by all, or at least held by a set of people you regard to be a close approximation to all. For some that set includes only one person. I myself have the opinion that Andrew Jackson was the 16th president of the United States. If many of my friends agree, I may take it to be a fact. Actually, I am most likely to regard it to be a fact if the authors of one or more books say it is so.

The difference between a fact and an opinion for purposes of decision making and inference is that when I use opinions, I get uncomfortable. I am not too uncomfortable with the opinion that error terms are normally distributed because most econometricians make use of that assumption. This observation has deluded me into thinking that the opinion that error terms are normal may be a fact, when I know deep inside that normal distributions are actually used only for convenience. In contrast, I am *quite* uncomfortable using a prior distribution, mostly I suspect because hardly anyone uses them. If convenient prior distributions were used as often as convenient sampling distributions, I suspect that I could be as easily deluded into thinking that prior distributions are facts as I have been into thinking that sampling distributions are facts.

To emphasize this hierarchy of statements, I display them in order: truths; facts; opinions; conventions. Note that I have added to the top of the order, the category truths. This will appeal to those of you who feel compelled to believe in such things. At the bottom are conventions. In practice, it may be difficult to distinguish a fact from a convention, but when facts are clearly unavailable, we must strongly resist the deceit or delusion that conventions can represent.

What troubles me about using opinions is their whimsical nature. Some mornings when I arise, I have the opinion that Raisin Bran is

better than eggs. By the time I get to the kitchen, I may well decide
on eggs, or oatmeal. I usually do recall that the 16th president distinguished himself. Sometimes I think he was Jackson; often I think he
was Lincoln.

A data analysis is similar. Sometimes I take the error terms to be
correlated, sometimes uncorrelated; sometimes normal and sometimes
nonnormal; sometimes I include observations from the decade of the
50s, sometimes I exclude them; sometimes the equation is linear and
sometimes nonlinear; sometimes I control for variable z, sometimes I
don't. Does it depend on what I had for breakfast?

As I see it, the fundamental problem facing econometrics is how
adequately to control the whimsical character of inference, how sensibly
to base inferences on opinions when facts are unavailable. At least a
partial solution to this problem has already been formed by practicing
econometricians. A common reporting style is to record the inferences
implied by alternative sets of opinions. It is not unusual to find tables
that show how an inference changes as variables are added to, or deleted
from, the equation. This kind of sensitivity analysis reports special features of the mapping from the space of assumptions to the space of
inferences. The defect of this style is that the coverage of assumptions
is infinitesimal, in fact a zero volume set in the space of assumptions.
What is needed instead is a more complete, but still economical way
to report the mapping of assumptions into inferences. What I propose
to do is to develop a correspondence between regions in the assumption
space and regions in the inference space. I will report that all assumptions
in a certain set lead to essentially the same inference. Or I will report
that there are assumptions within the set under consideration that lead
to radically different inferences. In the latter case, I will suspend inference and decision, or I will work harder to narrow the set of assumptions.

Thus what I am asserting is that the choice of a particular sampling
distribution, or a particular prior distribution, is inherently whimsical.
But statements such as "The sampling distribution is symmetric and
unimodal" and "My prior is located at the origin" are not necessarily
whimsical, and in certain circumstances do not make me uncomfortable.

To put this somewhat differently, an inference is not believable if
it is fragile, if it can be reversed by minor changes in assumptions. As
consumers of research, we correctly reserve judgment on an inference
until it stands up to a study of fragility, usually by other researchers
advocating opposite opinions. It is, however, much more efficient for
individual researchers to perform their own sensitivity analyses, and
we ought to be demanding much more complete and more honest reporting of the fragility of claimed inferences.

The job of a researcher is then to report economically and informatively the mapping from assumptions into inferences. In a slogan, "The
mapping is the message." The mapping does not depend on opinions

(assumptions), but reporting the mapping economically and informatively does. A researcher has to decide which assumptions or which sets of alternative assumptions are worth reporting. A researcher is therefore forced either to anticipate the opinions of his consuming public, or to recommend his own opinions. It is actually a good idea to do both, and a serious defect of current practice is that it concentrates excessively on convincing one's self and, as a consequence, fails to convince the general professional audience.

The whimsical character of econometric inference has been partially controlled in the past by an incomplete sensitivity analysis. It has also been controlled by the use of conventions. The normal distribution is now so common that there is nothing at all whimsical in its use. In some areas of study, the list of variables is partially conventional, often based on whatever list the first researcher happened to select. Even conventional prior distributions have been proposed and are used with nonnegligible frequency. I am referring to Robert Shiller's smoothness prior for distributed lag analysis and to Arthur Hoerl and Robert Kennard's ridge regression prior. It used to aggravate me that these methods seem to find public favor whereas overt and complete Bayesian methods such as my own proposals for distributed lag priors are generally ignored. However, there is a very good reason for this: the attempt to form a prior distribution from scratch involves an untold number of partly arbitrary decisions. The public is rightfully resistant to the whimsical inferences which result, but at the same time is receptive to the use of priors in ways that control the whimsy. Though the use of conventions does control the whimsy, it can do so at the cost of relevance. Inferences based on Hoerl and Kennard's conventional "ridge regression" prior are usually irrelevant, because it is rarely sensible to take the prior to be spherical and located at the origin, and because a closer approximation to prior belief can be suspected to lead to substantially different inferences. In contrast, the conventional assumption of normality at least uses a distribution which usually cannot be ruled out altogether. Still, we may properly demand a demonstration that the inferences are insensitive to this distributional assumption.

A. The Horizon Problem: Sherlock Holmes Inference

Conventions are not to be ruled out altogether, however. One can go mad trying to report completely the mapping from assumptions into inferences since the space of assumptions is infinite dimensional. A formal statistical analysis therefore has to be done within the limits of a reasonable horizon. An informed convention can usefully limit this horizon. If it turned out that sensible neighborhoods of distributions around the normal distribution 99 times out of 100 produced the same inference, then we could all agree that there are other more important things to worry about, and we may properly adopt the convention of normality. The consistency of least squares estimates under wide sets of assumptions is used improperly as support for this convention, since the inferences from a given finite sample may nonetheless be quite sensitive to the normality assumption.

The truly sharp distinction between inference from experimental and inference from nonexperimental data is that experimental inference sensibly admits a conventional horizon in a critical dimension, namely the choice of explanatory variables. If fertilizer is randomly assigned to plots of land, it is conventional to restrict attention to the relationship between yield and fertilizer, and to proceed as if the model were perfectly specified, which in my notation means that the misspecification matrix M is the zero matrix. There is only a small risk that when you present your findings, someone will object that fertilizer and light level are correlated, and there is an even smaller risk that the conventional zero value for M will lead to inappropriate inferences. In contrast, it would be foolhardy to adopt such a limited horizon with nonexperimental data. But if you decide to include light level in your horizon, then why not rainfall; and if rainfall, then why not temperature; and if temperature, then why not soil depth, and if soil depth, then why not the soil grade; ad infinitum. Though this list is never ending, it can be made so long that a nonexperimental researcher can feel as comfortable as an experimental researcher that the risk of having his findings upset by an extension of the horizon is very low. The exact point where the list is terminated must be whimsical, but the inferences can be expected not to be sensitive to the termination point if the horizon is wide enough.

Still, the horizon within which we all do our statistical analyses has to be ultimately troublesome, since there is no formal way to know what inferential monsters lurk beyond our immediate field of vision. "Diagnostic" tests with explicit alternative hypotheses such as the Durbin-Watson test for first-order autocorrelation do not truly ask if the horizon should be extended, since first-order autocorrelation is explicitly identified and clearly in our field of vision. Diagnostic tests such as goodness-of-fit tests, without explicit alternative hypotheses, are useless since, if the sample size is large enough, any maintained hypothesis will be rejected (for example, no observed distribution is exactly normal). Such tests therefore degenerate into elaborate rituals for measuring the effective sample size.

The only way I know to ask the question whether the horizon is wide enough is to study the anomalies of the data. In the words of the physiologist, C. Bernard:

A great surgeon performs operations for stones by a single method; later he makes a statistical summary of deaths and recoveries, and he concludes from these statistics that the mortality law for this operation is two out of five. Well, I say that this ratio means literally nothing scientifically, and gives no certainty in performing the next operation. What really should be done, instead of gathering facts empirically, is to study them more accurately, each in its special determinism . . . by statistics, we get a conjecture of greater or less probability about a given case, but never any certainty, never any absolute determinism . . . only basing itself on experimental determinism can medicine become a true science.

A study of the anomalies of the data is what I have called "Sherlock Holmes" inference, since Holmes turns statistical inference on its head: "It is a capital mistake to theorize before you have all the evidence. It biases the judgments." Statistical theory counsels us to begin with an elicitation of opinions about the sampling process and its parameters; the theory, in other words. After that, data may be studied in a purely mechanical way. Holmes warns that this biases the judgments, meaning that a theory constructed before seeing the facts can be disastrously inappropriate and psychologically difficult to discard. But if theories are constructed after having studied the data, it is difficult to establish by how much, if at all, the data favor the data-instigated hypothesis. For example, suppose I think that a certain coefficient ought to be positive, and my reaction to the anomalous result of a negative estimate is to find another variable to include in the equation so that the estimate is positive. Have I found evidence that the coefficient is positive? It would seem that we should require evidence that is more convincing than the traditional standard. I have proposed a method for discounting such evidence. Initially, when you regress yield on fertilizer as in Equation (2), you are required to assess a prior distribution for the experimental bias parameter β^*; that is, you must select the misspecification matrix M. Then, when the least squares estimate of β turns out to be negative, and you decide to include in the equation the light level as well as the fertilizer level, you are obligated to form a prior for the light coefficient γ consistent with the prior for β^*, given that $\beta^* = \gamma r_1$, where r_1 is the regression coefficient of light on fertilizer.[1]

This method for discounting the output of exploratory data analysis requires a discipline that is lacking even in its author. It is consequently important that we reduce the risk of Holmesian discoveries by extending the horizon reasonably far. The degree of a polynomial or the order of a distributed lag need not be data instigated, since the horizon is easily extended to include high degrees and high orders. It is similarly wise to ask yourself before examining the data what you would do if the estimate of your favorite coefficient had the wrong sign. If that makes you think of a specific left-out variable, it is better to include it from the beginning.

---

[1] In a randomized experiment with $r_1 = 0$, the constraint $\beta^* = \gamma r_1$ is irrelevant, and you are free to play these exploratory games without penalty. This is a very critical difference between randomized experiments and nonrandomized nonexperiments.

Though it is wise to select a wide horizon to reduce the risk of Holmesian discoveries, it is mistaken then to analyze a data set as if the horizon were wide enough. Within the limits of a horizon, no revolutionary inference can be made, since all possible inferences are predicted in advance (admittedly, some with low probabilities). Within the horizon, inference and decision can be turned over completely to a computer. But the great human revolutionary discoveries are made when the horizon is extended for reasons that cannot be predicted in advance and cannot be computerized. If you wish to make such discoveries, you will have to poke at the horizon, and poke again.

V. AN EXAMPLE

This rhetoric is understandably tiring. Methodology, like sex, is better demonstrated than discussed, though often better anticipated than experienced. Accordingly, let me give you an example of what all this ranting and raving is about. I trust you will find it even better in the experience than in the anticipation. A problem of considerable policy importance is whether or not to have capital punishment. If capital punishment had no deterrent value, most of us would prefer not to impose such an irreversible punishment, though, for a significant minority, the pure joy of vengeance is reason enough. The deterrent value of capital punishment is, of course, an empirical issue. The unresolved debate over its effectiveness began when evolution was judging the survival value of the vengeance gene. Nature was unable to make a decisive judgment. Possibly econometricians can.

In Table 1 you will find a list of variables that are hypothesized to influence the murder rate. The data to be examined are state-by-state murder rates in 1950. The variables are divided into three sets. There are four deterrent variables that characterize the criminal justice system, or in economic parlance, the expected out-of-pocket cost of crime. There are four economic variables that measure the opportunity cost of crime. And there are four social/environmental variables that possibly condition the taste for crime. This leaves unmeasured only the expected rewards for criminal behavior, though these are possibly related to the economic and social variables and are otherwise assumed not to vary from state to state.

A simple regression of the murder rate on all these variables leads to the conclusion that each additional execution deters 13 murders, with a standard error of 7. That seems like such a healthy rate of return, we might want just to randomly draft executees from the population at large. This proposal would be unlikely to withstand the scrutiny of any macroeconomists who are skilled at finding rational expectations equilibria.

The issue I would like to address instead is whether this conclusion

TABLE 1
Variables Used in the Analysis

a. Dependent variable.
    M = Murder rate per 100,000, FBI estimate.
b. Independent deterrent variables.
    Pc = (Conditional) Probability of conviction for murder given commission. Defined
    by $PC = C/Q$, where C = convictions for murder, $Q = M \cdot NS$, NS = state popula-
    tion. This is to correct for the fact that M is an estimate based on a sample
    from each state.
    PX = (Conditional) Probability of execution given conviction (average number of exe-
    cutions 1946–50 divided by C).
    T = Median time served in months for murder by prisoners released in 1951.
    $XPOS$ = A dummy equal to 1 if $PX > 0$.
c. Independent economic variables.
    W = Median income of families in 1949.
    X = Percent of families in 1949 with less than one-half W.
    U = Unemployment rate.
    LF = Labor force participation rate.
d. Independent social and environmental variables.
    NW = Percent nonwhite.
    AGE = Percent 15–24 years old.
    URB = Percent urban.
    $MALE$ = Percent male.
    $FAMHO$ = Percent of families that are husband and wife both present families.
    $SOUTH$ = A deummy equal to 1 for southern states (Alabama, Arkansas, Delaware,
    Florida, Kentucky, Louisiana, Maryland, Mississippi, North Carolina, Okla-
    homa, South Carolina, Tennessee, Texas, Virginia, West Virginia).
e. Weighting variable.
    $SQRTNF$ = Square root of the population of the FBI-reporting region. Note that
    weighting is done by multiplying variables by $SQRTNF$.
f. Level of observation.
    Observations are for 44 states, 35 executing and 9 nonexecuting. The executing states
    are: Alabama, Arizona, Arkansas, California, Colorado, Connecticut, Delaware, Florida,
    Illinois, Indiana, Kansas, Kentucky, Louisiana, Maryland, Massachusetts, Mississippi,
    Missouri, Nebraska, Nevada, New Jersey, New Mexico, New York, North Carolina,
    Ohio, Oklahoma, Oregon, Pennsylvania, South Carolina, South Dakota, Tennessee,
    Texas, Virginia, Washington, West Virginia.
        The nonexecuting states are: Idaho, Maine, Minnesota, Montana, New Hamp-
    shire, Rhode Island, Utah, Wisconsin, Wyoming.

is fragile or not. Does it hold up if the list of variables in the model is
changed? Individuals with different experiences and different training
will find different subsets of the variables to be candidates for omission
from the equation. Five different lists of doubtful variables are reported
in Table 2. A right winger expects the punishment variables to have
an effect, but treats all other variables as doubtful. He wants to know
whether the data still favor the large deterrent effect, if he omits some
of these doubtful variables. The rational maximizer takes the variables
that measure the expected economic return of crime as important, but
treats the taste variables as doubtful. The eye-for-an-eye prior treats

TABLE 2
Alternative Prior Specifications

Prior	PC	PX	T	XPOS	W	X	U	LF	NW	AGE	URB	MALE	FAMHO	SOUTH
Right winger	1	1	1	*	D	D	D	D	D	D	D	D	D	D
Rational maximizer	1	1	1	*	1	1	1	1	D	D	D	D	D	D
Eye-for-an-eye	1	1	D	*	D	D	D	D	D	D	D	D	D	D
Bleeding heart	D	D	D	*	1	1	1	1	1	1	1	1	1	1
Crime of passion	D	D	D	*	1	1	1	1	1	1	1	1	1	1

Notes: 1. *I* indicates variables considered important by a researcher with the respective prior. Thus, every model considered by the researcher will include these variables. *D* indicates variables considered doubtful by the researcher. * indicates *XPOS*, the dummy equal to 1 for executing states. Each prior was pooled with the data two ways: one with *XPOS* treated as important, and one with it as doubtful.

2. With five basic priors and *XPOS* treated as doubtful or important by each, we get ten alternative prior specifications.

all variables as doubtful except the probability of execution. An individual with the bleeding heart prior sees murder as the result of economic impoverishment. Finally, if murder is thought to be a crime of passion then the punishment variables are doubtful.

In Table 3, I have listed the extreme estimates that could be found by each of these groups of researchers. The right-winger minimum of −22.56 means that a regression of the murder rate data on the three punishment variables and a suitably selected linear combination of the other variables yields an estimate of the deterrent effect equal to 22.56 lives per execution. It is possible also to find an estimate of −.86. Anything between these two extremes can be similarly obtained; but no estimate outside this interval can be generated no matter how the doubtful variables are manipulated (linearly). Thus the right winger can report that the inference from this data set that executions deter murders is not fragile. The rational maximizer similarly finds that conclusion insensitive to choice of model, but the other three priors allow execution actually to encourage murder, possibly by a brutalizing effect on society.

TABLE 3
Extreme Estimates of the Effect of
Executions on Murders

Prior	Minimum Estimate	Maximum Estimate
Right winger	−22.56	−.86
Rational maximizer	−15.91	−10.24
Eye-for-an-eye	−28.66	1.91
Bleeding heart	−25.59	12.37
Crime of passion	−17.32	4.10

Note: Least squares is −13.22 with a standard error of 7.2.

I come away from a study of Table 3 with the feeling that any inference from these data about the deterrent effect of capital punishment is too fragile to be believed. It is possible credibly to narrow the set of assumptions, but I do not think that a credibly large set of alternative assumptions will lead to a sharp set of estimates. In another paper, I found a narrower set of priors still leads to inconclusive inferences. And I have ignored the important simultaneity issue (the death penalty may have been imposed in crime ridden states to deter murder) which is often a source of great inferential fragility.

VI. CONCLUSIONS

After three decades of churning out estimates, the econometrics club finds itself under critical scrutiny and faces incredulity as never before. Fischer Black writes of "The Trouble with Econometric Models." David Hendry queries "Econometrics: Alchemy or Science?" John W. Pratt and Robert Schlaifer question our understanding of "The Nature and Discovery of Structure." And Christopher Sims suggests blending "Macroeconomics and Reality."

It is apparent that I too am troubled by the fumes which leak from our computing centers. I believe serious attention to two words would sweeten the atmosphere of econometric discourse. These are whimsy and fragility. In order to draw inferences from data as described by econometric texts, it is necessary to make whimsical assumptions. The professional audience consequently and properly withholds belief until an inference is shown to be adequately insensitive to the choice of assumptions. The haphazard way we individually and collectively study the fragility of inferences leaves most of us unconvinced that any inference is believable. If we are to make effective use of our scarce data resource, it is therefore important that we study fragility in a much more systematic way. If it turns out that almost all inferences from economic data are fragile, I suppose we shall have to revert to our old methods lest we lose our customers in government, business, and on the boardwalk at Atlantic City.

29.

Decision and Risk Analysis in a New Product and Facilities Planning Problem*

DAVID B. HERTZ
HOWARD THOMAS

Risk analysis was originally presented as a useful addition to the range of techniques used in financial evaluations. It was seen as a logical extension to sensitivity analysis and as a means of explicitly taking account of uncertainty in financial forecasts. The proposition that risk and uncertainty could be more accurately defined by a simulation of input variables became widely accepted. It was emphasized, however, that risk analysis was a strategic decision aid and that eventually managerial judgment would be required in both input estimation and decision.

Although some readers saw this as an argument about methodology in investment appraisal, that was not the main intention. Rather, the aim was to alert businesspeople about the need to examine carefully the data and assumptions surrounding decision problems, given the pervasive uncertainties in both business and other environments.

Broader uses of the techniques of risk analysis have been explored in recent literature. For example, risk analysis is increasingly seen as a necessary and useful adjunct to a strategic planning and thinking process. It is viewed as an approach for forecast/uncertainty based planning (Stage II/III of Gluck's four stages of strategic planning), in which an

* *Sloan Management Review* (Winter 1983), pp. 17–30.

understanding of project risk, cash flow projections, and future scenarios is developed.

Underlying this article is the suggestion that risk, analysis can also help *strategic thinking* by encouraging constructive dialogue and debate about policy options. In such a dialogue process, risk analysis is an input for the strategy development process, aiding strategy formulation, evaluation, choice, and implementation. No distinction is drawn between strategic risk analysis and strategy formulation. Instead, both are viewed as parts of an iterative, adaptive, and flexible policy dialogue process. This dialogue involves the consideration by management of problem and policy formulation through a continual reexamination of potential alternative strategies and problem assumptions.

The role of strategic risk analysis in policy formulation and choice should, therefore, be to encourage serious thinking about the problem under consideration. The analysis should highlight the alternatives to be considered, examine the changing secondary effects, and anticipate the nature and extent of the impact of uncertainty for contingency planning. Nevertheless, it must be recognized that an initial risk analysis is no more than a first attempt at problem understanding. Its role should be to encourage controversy and to allow members of the decision-making group to discover where basic differences exist in problem assumptions, values, and uncertainties. This controversy should enable critical comment and review to be obtained, and should force the reanalysis, reexamination, and sensitivity testing of the problem solution. It is hoped that, after considerable dialogue, the quality and level of debate should facilitate compromise and consensus around a reasonable problem solution.

This article discusses the role of risk analysis in relation to a potential investment opportunity in the plastic egg carton market. The problem is somewhat disguised in regard to project chronology and magnitudes of input data, but the problem structure and new product area are unaltered.

The risk analysis approach involved three groups: the management at ABC (disguised company name), the ABC project team (charged with the responsibility for project evaluation), and the consultants (providing technical expertise and guidance). Various decision alternatives were considered, ranging from abandonment to expansion strategies. Abandonment would involve the loss of the pilot plant; expansion strategies would involve both the larger plants (known as superplants) and a series of smaller plants.

This article illustrates the step-by-step nature of the application of risk analysis and describes the procedures adopted at each stage of the analysis. The problem structure is developed in flow diagram form, and the problem assumptions are stated. This is followed by an initial sensitivity analysis where investment alternatives are developed, subjective probabilities are assigned, and the results of the risk analysis are presented. Finally, the article outlines the process of policy dialogue about the strategy to be chosen and summarizes the conclusions.

THE EGG'N FOAM PROJECT

The Egg'N Foam project at ABC involved a number of issues. The project represented a large investment in a new market area and a new product for ABC. For several years ABC had been developing Egg'N Foam, a plastic package produced as a competitive substitute for paper egg cartons. The product design had been refined, and a pilot plant in Pennsylvania had been operational for some time. Still, the project involved substantial amounts of uncertainty.

The project team selected to work on the Egg'N Foam decision consisted of representatives from the Research and Development Division, the Plastics Division, and the Corporate Controller's Office. Those involved had been associated with the Egg'N Foam project for a considerable period of time, and were familiar with the development, production, and marketing aspects of this project. This team used the step-by-step approach described below to study the attractiveness of investing more funds in Egg'N Foam.

THE RISK ANALYSIS PROCESS

Developing the Flowchart and Problem Structure

The first step in applying risk analysis to the Egg'N Foam project was to construct a flowchart of the investment analysis. The process started with an assessment of the basic economics of the investment project; each element was entered in a simple chart. The initial Egg'N Foam flowchart shown in Figure 1 consisted of six elements: the total market size for egg cartons, ABC's foam market share, the selling price, the manufacturing cost, total overhead, and the investment base.

The initial flowchart was then expanded backward to encompass a large set of input factors. This involved establishing a value for each factor and analyzing the determinants of that value, questioning the validity of the determining factors, and, where possible, exploding the elements into further detail. The final product was a flow diagram of all the factors relevant to determining the profitability of Egg'N Foam.

The final flowchart for Egg'N Foam was considerably more detailed than the initial chart. The manufacturing costs, overhead costs, and investment base were all expanded into a substantial number of inputs. However, the unavailability of sufficient market data limited the amount of analysis which could be undertaken on the marketing elements (i.e., market size, market share, and price).

FIGURE 1
Initial Egg'N Foam Flowchart

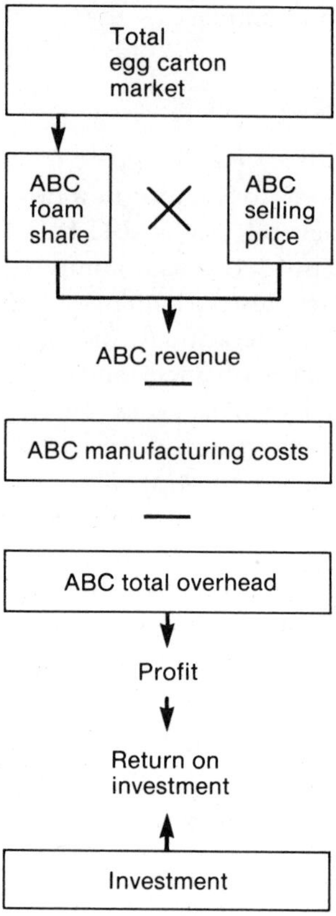

Stating the Assumptions

When the flowchart was completed, assumptions underlying each of the factors were stated explicitly and recorded. This step was particularly important, because it placed a limit on the amount of detail required to substantiate the data inputs. For example, if the project team assumed ABC would capture a 10 percent share of the carton market, little data would be needed to estimate ABC's sales volume.

Once assumptions have been stated, however, it is necessary to verify their reliability. Because invalid assumptions can result in misleading and inaccurate conclusions from analytic models, verification, and questioning of assumptions is an integral and important part of this phase of the analysis.

The Egg'N Foam project team was able to verify the validity of most of its data, including information about equipment rates supplied by Research and Development Division personnel, and forecasts of total egg production supplied by the U.S. Department of Agriculture. However, further study was considered necessary to determine the accuracy of some of the data and assumptions. In particular, more specific information was required about the percentage of eggs cartoned and future Egg'N Foam sales volume and price.

Analyzing Sensitivity

The next step in the analysis was to construct a nonprobabilistic computer model based on the flowchart. The model was built for a single plant, as each region represented a similar size market that would support a single plant operation. The model performed all the calculations indicated by the flowchart and provided answers in terms of the return on investment and cash flows.

The model was also used to determine the sensitivity of investment returns and cash flows to changes in input variables. The team could pose such questions as: "What would happen to the discounted rate of return if the price dropped by $0.50 per thousand cartons?" or "What would happen if, say, the thermoformer cycle time (in the production process) were improved to $4\frac{1}{2}$ seconds?" The results of the sensitivity analyses on Egg'N Foam are shown in Figure 2. Changes in two factors, caliper (or thickness) and demand, had a dramatic effect on the rate of return, whereas changes in the value of other factors had only a minor impact on profitability. The high sensitivity of the investment return to changes in caliper and demand indicated the extreme importance of the accuracy of the assumed sales volume of Egg'N Foam.

The sensitivity analysis was also valuable in identifying the optimal plant operation. It permitted the team to use the computer to experiment with different equipment combinations and plant sizes. When applied to Egg'N Foam, the sensitivity analysis suggested that one extruder could support two thermoformers instead of one thermoformer. The analysis also demonstrated the feasibility of building larger plants containing two extruders and four thermoformers.

Developing Investment Alternatives

After the sensitivity analysis was performed, the single plant model was used as a building block in constructing investment strategies for Egg'N Foam. The team developed four alternative strategies for ABC in the egg carton market; these strategies are shown in Figure 3 and are expressed in terms of the timing and sequence of equipment installation by plant location. Two strategies involved building superplants, each containing two extruders and four thermoformers; the other two

FIGURE 2
Sensitivity of Investment Return to Changes in Major Input Factors

Base Case:

One extruder
One thermoformer

Extruder rate = 525 lb./hr.
Thermoformer cycle time = 5.3 sec.
Caliper = .080 in.

Millions of cartons
	Year 1	Year 2	Year 3
Demand =	21	54	90

Physical capacity = 76 Million cartons
Discounted rate of return = 12.96%

Factor	Change	Change in rate of return	Adjusted rate of return[c]
Extruder rate	525 to 625 lb./hr.	+2.24%	15.20%
Thermoformer cycle time	5.3 to 4.2 sec.	+1.71%	14.67%
Raw material costs	15.0¢ to 13.5¢/lb. pellets	+1.40%	14.36%
Equipment costs	$790,000 to $999,000	−1.57%	11.39%
Caliper[a]	.080 to .100 in.	−10.25%	2.71%
Demand	Millions of cartons Year 1 / Year 2 / Year 3 From 21 / 54 / 90 To 21 / 54 / 66[b]	−4.17%	8.79%
Price	Decreased 50¢	−1.20%	11.76%
Direct labor	Extruder $11.00 to $13.29/hr. Thermoformer $26.94 to $32.34/hr.	−1.83%	11.13%

FIGURE 3
Egg'N Foam Investment Strategies

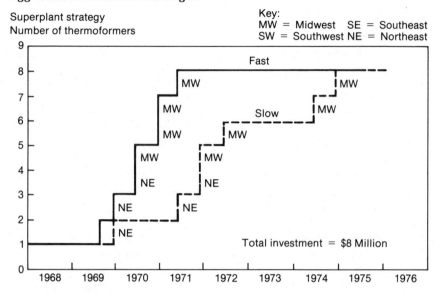

Superplant strategy
Number of thermoformers

Key:
MW = Midwest   SE = Southeast
SW = Southwest NE = Northeast

Total investment = $8 Million

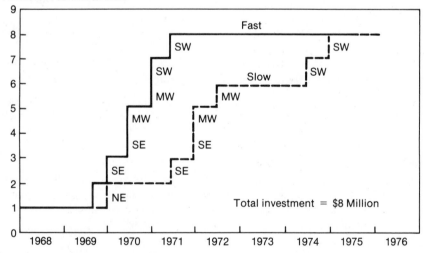

Small plant strategy
Number of thermoformers

Total investment = $8 Million

strategies called for small plants, each containing one extruder and two thermoformers.

The difference between the two superplant strategies and the two small plant strategies is speed of market entry. The slow, conservative investment pace suggested for both small and superplants required the addition of thermoformers only after the demand for the output of existing equipment was firmly established. The fast investment strategies assumed that ABC would act as quickly as possible to acquire equipment, to hire and train the necessary manpower, and to open the plants.

Assigning the Probabilities

The team next obtained probability information for values of input factors. Subjective probabilities were developed for the five inputs to the model that had either a significant impact on profitability or a considerable degree of uncertainty. Three of these inputs related to the production process (extruder rate, thermoformer cycle time, and caliper), and two were marketing variables (price and demand). The probability distributions were obtained using the fractile assessment method suggested by Raiffa, and represented the best judgment of ABC personnel who were most knowledgeable about the Egg'N Foam project.

The CDF Method.   Raiffa's fractile assessment procedure, sometimes called the CDF (cumulative distribution fractile) method, has found considerable acceptance as an approach for assessing subjective probability distributions. The horizontal axis of the cumulative distribution (CDF) shows possible values of the uncertain quantity, X (e.g., price of the new product), and the vertical axis gives the probability that the true value is X or less.

The following example demonstrates the implementation of this approach. It illustrates the actual assessment of the probability distribution for the price per thousand Egg'N Foam cartons for the first year of the new product launch. The series of questions might be as follows:

Analyst: Can you give me a value of the price (per thousand cartons) such that you feel there is only a very small chance, say 1 percent, that it will be exceeded during the first year of the Egg'N Foam launch? [Note that this establishes the value at which the CDF = 0.99.]

Manager: I guess I would say $27.

Analyst: Can you also give me a value of the price (per thousand cartons) such that you feel there is only a very small chance, say 1 percent, that it will be below that value during the first year of the launch? [Note that this establishes the value at which the CDF = 0.01.]

Manager: There is no way that it would go below $22.

Analyst: Can you give me a value for price that you feel has a 50 percent chance of being exceeded during the first year? [Note that this establishes the point at which the CDF = 0.50.]

Manager: Now, that's a hard thing to conceive. I suppose about $25.

Analyst: Are you sure about that? Would you find it extremely hard to choose between a bet on the interval above $25 ($25–$27) and on the interval below $25 ($22–$25)? [Note that this is a consistency check to ensure that $25 is the 0.50 fractile or the 50th percentile of the distribution.]

Manager: Yes.

Analyst: Now, suppose that the actual price during the first year will be below $25. Can you give me a value for price in the range of $22–$25 that you feel has a 50 percent chance of being exceeded?

Manager: Say $24. [Note that this establishes $24 as the 0.25 fractile, i.e., the value of price at which the CDF = 0.25.]

Analyst: Finally, given that the true value of the price during the year will exceed $25, can you give me a value for price that you feel has a 50 percent chance of being exceeded?

Manager: Well, I guess that I am beginning to understand what you are after now. My indifference point is about $26. (Note that this establishes $26 as the price at which the CDF = 0.75.)

From the set of five discrete points (namely, the 1 percent, 25 percent, 50 percent, 75 percent, and 99 percent fractiles) obtained from these questions, an approximate curve for the CDF can be drawn, as shown in Figure 4.

It is perhaps important to stress that, although the probability assessors felt confident about their short-term forecasting abilities (for, say, the next three years), they had some difficulty in thinking about future events (over a 3- to 10-year horizon) which would impact upon their longer-term assessments. Therefore, in order to structure their thought processes, certain assumptions were made that were the basis for their probability assessments over the 10-year period.

In the case of the three production variables, it was assumed that technological and design advances would improve the performance of extrusion and thermoformer equipment and would enable caliper thickness to be better and more uniformly controlled. It was anticipated

FIGURE 4
CDF Curve for Carton Price in First Year
(Per Thousand Cartons)

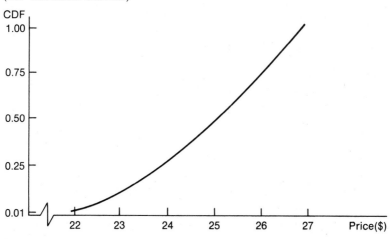

that such new equipment would be introduced approximately two to three years after product adoption.

In the case of the assessment of marketing variables, much stronger assumptions were made. Based on current evidence, it was felt that the price of a carton would decline linearly in real terms over the time horizon. Estimates of demand were based on the assumption that ABC would be able to capture a 10 percent market share in 6 years with the fast strategy or in 10 years with the slower strategy.

Risk Analysis, Capital Asset Pricing, and Project Appraisal

A weakness of the risk analysis approach is that it provides narrow, uncertainty-based information on the project's business risk and little or no information on the relationship between the project and the portfolio of risks faced by the company (or investor). It is, therefore, helpful to use the capital asset pricing model (CAPM) to assess the viability of the strategy alternatives associated with the project. The first step is to estimate the company's cost of equity capital that can then be used, assuming minimal debt, as the discount rate in capital budgeting calculations based upon NPV (net present value) criteria. The CAPM, which was developed in the context of financial securities markets, can be used to estimate this equity capital rate.

The CAPM divides a security's risk into two components: *unsystematic risk*, which is company specific, and *systematic risk*, which is related to the movement of the stock market and wider economic factors. It is further argued that investors can, through an efficient diversification process (say, by holding a portfolio of twenty stocks or more), largely eliminate the company-specific, or unsystematic, component of risk. The only relevant risk faced by investors is systematic risk.

The equilibrium CAPM can be stated as:

$$E(R) = R_f + \beta(E(R_m) - R_f),$$

where $E(R)$ is the required rate;

R_f is the risk-free rate;
β is the estimate of systematic risk;
$E(R_m)$ is the expected return on the market.

To derive the cost of equity capital, forecasts using historical market data must first be generated for the right-hand-side variables (R_f, β, $E(R_m)$) in the CAPM and then substituted into the equilibrium equation. The cost of equity capital is equivalent to the required rate, $E(R)$.

The CAPM's prescription for capital investment decision making can then be summarized in the following manner. It is assumed that the stated aim of management is to maximize the firm's value as measured by shareholder wealth. In addition, assets are assumed to be priced in financial markets by discounting cash flows at a risk-adjusted rate; this rate reflects both the market's risk premium and the volatility of the investment relative to the market. Therefore, for capital project appraisal, an individual project's expected cash flows should be discounted by the appropriate risk-adjusted rate derived from the CAPM and from consideration of the debt/equity ratio (which might modify the weighted average cost of capital). Any project that increases the value of the firm (i.e., that has a positive NPV) when discounted at the risk-adjusted rate should merit acceptance if it confirms other criteria concerning its competitive value for the firm.

Results of the "First Pass" Risk Analysis.   This section presents some results for the "first pass" risk analysis for the Egg'N Foam project. This single point estimate calculation is the NPV project appraisal using the risk-adjusted rate derived from the CAPM. The other calculations involve the direct use of risk simulation. The results for both the probabilistic risk analysis and the CAPM-based point estimate are summarized in Table 1. The cumulative density function (CDF) for the NPV for each of the strategies is presented in Figure 5.

According to the single point CAPM estimates in Table 1, Strategy 4 could be eliminated since it has a negative NPV. The last two columns in the table present two possible additional choice criteria for each strategy: the probability that the NPV is positive, and the value of NPV such that there is a 95 percent probability of exceeding that value. Using these criteria, it would again appear that Strategy 4 could be eliminated immediately.

In addition, using second-order principles of stochastic dominance, it would appear that Strategy 1 dominates all other strategies since its CDF lies *everywhere* to the right of the CDFs for the other three strategies (see Figure 5). Therefore, Strategy 1 appears to be the most viable alternative. However, as a contingency plan, Strategy 2 appears to be the next best alternative, if in the first four years, the market growth projections are revised downward considerably.

Policy Dialogue

Following the initial risk analysis, the dialogue about strategy choice between the project and management teams at ABC focused on two main concerns. Although it was agreed that the sensitivity and risk analyses had aided the process of strategy evaluation by indicating key uncertain variables and by forecasting uncertain cash flows, it was felt that further discussion and review were necessary before choosing a strategy. Much controversy centered on the inadequacy of the processes of problem identification (including key assumptions), and the lack of specificity

TABLE 1
Results in Terms of NPV

Strategy	Point Estimate ($ millions)	Risk-Analysis Simulation ($ millions)		Probability (NPV > 0)	NPV Such That 95% Probability of Exceeding That Value ($ millions)
		Mean	Standard Deviation		
1	4.12	3.53	0.84	0.99	2.0
2	0.85	0.74	0.45	0.94	0
3	2.90	0.94	1.37	0.88	−2.0
4	−1.38	−1.70	0.68	0	−3.0

Notes:
1. Discount rate in simulation calculation is assumed at 5 percent net-of-tax, i.e., the riskless rate.
2. Point estimate calculation is made using expected values for each input variable and appropriate net-of-tax risk-adjusted rate of return (using CAPM).
3. Strategy 1 = superplant/fast investment; strategy 2 = superplant/slow investment; strategy 3 = small plant/fast investment; strategy 4 = small plant/slow investment.

FIGURE 5
Graph of CDF for NPV for Each Strategy

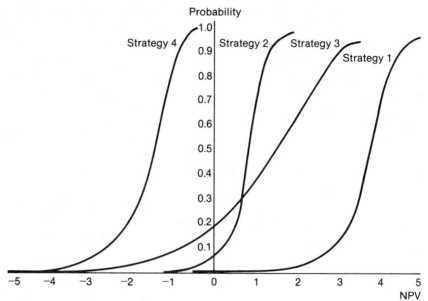

and clarity about ABC's objectives. The strategic issues raised are outlined below.

Problem Identification.   Typical critical comments from management included:

> The team seems to have considered heavily technologically oriented strategies, i.e., concentration on plant size and speed of introduction for the product. Little emphasis was placed on interpreting the demand picture, which seems to suggest that marketing-related strategies have either not been considered or assumed away.

or

> Why should the first step . . . be to construct a flowchart?

or

> The team's effectiveness might improve, if its composition were better balanced with the addition of some marketing personnel.

In general, it was felt that some problem assumptions and inputs should be examined and questioned more closely prior to a more effective "structuring" of the risk analysis model. It was agreed that both the initial listing of assumptions and the sensitivity analysis in Figure 2 provided a valuable starting point for examining problem structure and the influence of problem assumptions.

Some further observations were made about the assumptions. First, why did the ABC project team assume that ABC would produce its own sheets of foam when the option of purchasing from an outside source might be a worthwhile and cost-effective alternative? Second, what additional correlation effects (with their attendant measurement complications) should be included in the model in relation to price elasticity, demand, production rates, etc.? Third, why were market assumptions taken more or less as given, ignoring market-related strategies, thus reducing ABC's decision to an apparent choice of one of the four production strategies?

After considerable discussion, it was agreed that the greatest weakness concerned the marketing assumptions adopted in the model and the level of empirical or research effort available to support these assumptions. The following were some of the major areas in the treatment of marketing that were questioned:

> Market share will be 10 percent by 1978. (Should there be a spread of possible values?)
>
> No manufacturer other than Diamond National would enter the market before 1978.
>
> Paper carton manufacturers would not react violently to their share being cut from 50 percent to 5 percent in 10 years. (Why would they not start a price war? Could they afford to do so?)
>
> Market forecasts are assumed to be correct. (Has any attempt been made to check their methodology and forecast accuracy?)
>
> Selling would be undertaken by the plastics marketing department. (It seemed that the transfer price would become an increasingly important motivating factor; this might indicate the need to establish a separate department for marketing Egg'N Foam in the carton market.)
>
> Pricing must be at a predetermined level for foam cartons. (Why not, for example, consider the adoption of penetration pricing policies to gain share in an aggressive manner?)

This last point deserves further elaboration. Penetration pricing policies involve setting a price that maximizes a firm's market share penetration, probably at the expense of current profits. The goal is the maximization of long-run profitability through the rapid attainment of market share. In this instance, Egg'N Foam's strategy for market penetration would be to expand plant capacity as fast as possible (and certainly ahead of share) and to set the price lower than competitors in order to win share, achieve market growth, and discourage competition. In addition, ABC could take advantage of production and cost economies resulting from accumulated experience by continually lowering its price; such penetration pricing strategies are thus associated with exploitation of the experience curve strategy popularized by the Boston Consulting Group.

It was felt that two other financial management assumptions required further justification. First, working capital should not have been regarded as a single predetermined value. The amount required would depend upon the level of plant capacity, the accuracy of demand predictions (e.g., a stock pile-up might occur), the speed of payments by debtors, and many other (as yet unknown) factors. Second, the influence of inflation should not have been ignored. Inflation might, for example, affect foam more than pulp or vice versa, thus seriously changing the competitive balance within ABC. This could produce shortfalls in short-term cash flow, leading to an increase in short-term loans or in the time required to settle suppliers' accounts.

Specificity and Clarity of Objectives. Management felt that the project team was also uncertain about the criteria to be used in choosing among the available strategies. It was suggested, therefore, that attention be directed toward the criterion for strategy choice in relation to ABC's overall portfolio of investments, both current and projected. The main concerns were to relate single project risk to the firm's overall risk and to handle strategic issues. For example, it was necessary to consider whether the Egg'N Foam project would be too risky, not only in the sense of variability of returns, but also in terms of its effect on the firm's portfolio of projects, i.e., its long-term capital assets. Senior managers commented that the carton project might focus too great a proportion of the company's resources (financial, managerial, production, and marketing) on a single project to the detriment of other possible alternatives. This might weaken the firm's competitive edge in other strategic areas.

Conclusions of the Initial Policy Dialogue. It was agreed that certain tasks could be better performed by management than by the project team. It was also suggested that the project team, which was perhaps better balanced with marketing and financial expertise, should generate appropriate alternative strategies in line with management policy. Some form of strategic evaluation could be carried out later, using risk measures agreed upon jointly with management. Management's task should be to define guidelines for the range of strategies to be considered and to direct the project group in the decision-making task. A managerial dialogue process involving the consideration of other factors and attributes should ultimately determine the final strategy choice.

It should be emphasized that both groups stressed the importance of management's role in the problem finding and formulation process. It was felt that the current strategy placed too much emphasis on production and R&D. It was also agreed that the range of strategies for consideration should focus on a close scan of the internal and external environment, as well as on a screen of potential competitive market and technological uncertainties.

As a result, the following recommendations were made concerning further strategy formulation and evaluation through the analytic process. First, greater attention should be paid to the influence of competition, competitive reaction, and marketing forces on the Egg'N Foam decision. In other words, strategies that combine marketing and production considerations should be developed. Management felt that the most sensible approach would be to develop a number of marketing scenarios (using a Delphi-type approach) and, if appropriate, to carry out a simulation of each scenario. For example, the following types of scenarios should be developed in association with each production alternative:

Steady price.

Failure of the market to grow meaningfully.

Tough competitive reaction (e.g., price war initiated by Diamond National and others.

A price war started by ABC to discourage other potential market entrants (i.e., an attempt to build up share quickly as required by an experience-curve type of strategy.

Consumers preferring paper-based to plastic cartons.

Second, attention should be given in model development to working capital and cash flow management. For example, inflation effects and their impact on potential cash flow generation should be examined thoroughly. Third, output of the analytic process should be presented in terms of a series of performance measures (essentially policy indicator variables) over the project time horizon (15 years). This recommendation developed from the belief that the influence of contingencies on a series of measures (such as cash flow and sales projections and NPV measures) would give valuable input to the process of strategy choice and *perhaps* would lead to the generation of additional strategy alternatives for policy dialogue. The performance measures suggested were:

Total dollar sales.

Cash flow profile.

Gross profit as a percentage of sales.

Net profit after taxes.

Net profit as a return on investment.

Net present value.

Further sensitivity analysis of results to key changes in input factors.

Subsequent Policy Dialogue.   Management reviewed the subsequent output of the risk analysis, which showed the Strategy 1 (superplant/fast investment) was still dominant, except under adverse marketing and financial scenarios when Strategy 2 would be preferred. Interestingly, it was also determined (from the marketing scenarios) that ABC had a competitive strength with the plastic carton. As a result, if it adopted an even more aggressive capacity-building strategy, it might be able to obtain both the dominant market share position and the lowest relative cost position. This information provided a useful topic for discussion.

Management commented upon the value of the marketing and financial (e.g., cash flow) probabilistic forecasts provided by the "second pass" risk simulation. Quite apart from providing a better understanding of the influence of uncertain events on ABC's business activities, it was felt that these forecasts gave an insight into the relationship between this particular project and the firm's portfolio of activities.

Because the project's NPV (for Strategies 1 and 2) was positive when discounted at the required risk-adjusted rate (determined from capital asset pricing theories), the project merited acceptance in portfolio terms. This was reinforced by the strategic aspects of the risk simulation, which enabled management to judge the project's viability under a range of alternative future scenarios. Indeed, managers commented that the confirmatory positive indications of the set of performance measures under the range of scenarios enabled them to better understand the project and assess its competitive potential.

While management generally favored project acceptance, a closer examination of ABC's goals was desired. This was considered important to ensure that this project was compatible with the firm's long-term growth plans and objectives. In order to develop this strategic thinking process, the firm's portfolio was simulated, with the inclusion of either Strategy 1 or Strategy 2, over a 5- to 10-year horizon in terms of profitability and cash flow objectives. It was hoped that this would highlight other business areas with potential for decline or growth, and would provide an assessment of cash flow and financial implications for the Egg'N Foam project.

This subsequent portfolio analysis showed sound long-term viability, and strengthened management's view that some movement into the foam carton market would be a related business diversification providing the firm with a useful competitive edge. It was also felt that this project would be complementary in skills and growth potential to the firm's recent diversifications into the poultry processing and broiler chicken manufacturing areas.

RISK ANALYSIS AS A STRATEGIC INQUIRY SYSTEM

It is valuable to emphasize the link between risk analysis and strategic management. This can be conceptualized in terms of Churchman's development of inquiry systems. Churchman's inquiry systems are derived from interpretations of the writings of such philosophers as Leibnitz, Locke, Kant, Hegel, and Singer. Mitroff and Mason have also explained how these philosophical stances can be used to provide frameworks for understanding problem formulation and solving processes, particularly in the policy field.

Leibnitzian systems are characterized by the development of a single, near-optimal problem formulation, generally based upon some underlying theories and problem structures. This formulation of an analytic model of rational logical form is followed by data collection to support it and the generation of results, namely, deductive conclusions, which are consistent with the model. Lockean inquiry systems, however, have a much more empirical focus. Data are collected relevant to the decision problem, and the Lockean aim is to infer patterns from the data through inductive reasoning to support a single problem structure. Both Leibnitzian and Lockean systems are regarded as being suited to resolving well-structured problems.

Kantian and Hegelian systems are more appropriate for resolving ill-structured policy and planning problems (such as the Egg'N Foam diversification issue), which arise in business applications. Kantian inquiry systems are characterized by the existence of multiple frameworks for viewing problems and by the existence of differing conceptual viewpoints. These viewpoints are based upon the differing assumption bases of the members of the decision-making group. Efforts are made to combine these views and to achieve *consensus* by presenting each set of underlying assumptions. Hegelian inquiry systems also involve multiple frameworks and viewpoints, but they require the introduction of conflict—challenging and questioning of assumptions—to achieve a sound problem formulation process. Through conflict, structured debate, and dialectical inquiry, a synthesis emerges.

The initial risk analysis process shown in Figures 1 and 2 is a simple, somewhat naive form of a Leibnitzian inquiry system. In other words, a single "optimal" problem formulation is developed and data are collected to support this single "view of the world." After the first pass risk analysis, the ensuing policy dialogue indicated, *inter alia,* that increased effort should be directed toward focused questioning of assumptions, scenarios, and product market concepts. Indeed, managers took the "devil's advocate" position in their advocacy of extreme scenarios and alternative project assumptions. It should be noted that the use of risk analysis in the questioning and debate process indicates a significant change in the character of an inquiry system. The problem formulation system is now more complex and multidimensional, and is much closer to the inquiry systems described by Churchman, Kant, and Heggel. Several views about the problem are held, and it is believed that consensus and synthesis about problem formulation should be achieved through a process of group debate and dialogue. Further "passes" of risk analyses aid strategic dialogue by generating additional information for debate about the possible consequences of alternative assumptions, problem formulations, and future scenarios. This should lead to a continual review and updating of strategy options and to a resolution of conflicting viewpoints following structural debate.

CONCLUSIONS AND STRATEGIC IMPLICATIONS

The value of risk analysis in a facilities planning decision has been examined here in relation to a disguised planning situation called Egg'N Foam. Following Gluck's approach, risk analysis is presented as Stage II/III of a sensible strategic thinking process. That is, risk analysis is a vehicle for forecast/uncertainty based planning, in which an understanding of future scenarios, cash flow projections, and synergies between marketing and production activities is developed. This framework enables managers to search more creatively in order to identify the menu of strategic options.

The strategic risk analysis presented here differs from that presented by some other authors in the same area in terms of its treatment of risk preference and criteria for strategy choice. Risk preference involves the decision maker's attitude towards risk, and is commonly handled via utility function assessment and certainty equivalence concepts. In this case, however, management felt uncomfortable with the utility concept, even though they regarded risk preference as a policy question. They preferred to treat risk preference through a number of "lenses" by examining the risk simulation output in mean/variance terms using "risk of ruin" criteria (i.e., probability of NPV > 0), and by looking at future cash flow profiles. In addition, they accepted that a project with a positive NPV, when discounted at an appropriate "risk-adjusted" rate, would increase the value of the firm in portfolio terms (thus, accepting the relevance of a market-determined risk preference function).

Management also felt that, for strategy choice, both the project and the firm's portfolio should be examined in terms of a number of performance measures (cash flow, NPV, sales) specified over the 15-year project time horizon. This criterion, specified in terms of a time stream of indicator measures (cash flow, etc.) rather than in terms of a single value (such as expected utility), is consistent with the work on preferences over time.

In terms of strategic implementation, this risk analysis approach was successful. Its value lies in encouraging policy dialogue among the management group about future uncertainty impacts, rather than in imposing a deductive solution derived from an analytic model. The continued questioning of assumptions and problem formulation is essential for the effective formulation and evaluation of alternative strategy positions. In this case, by such continued questioning and dialogue a meaningful consensus about strategy choice emerged. This consensus process, which involved "three passes" of a risk analysis process, could not have been achieved without the adaptive mechanisms and flexibility built into the process during the course of dialogue and successive risk analysis passes. Interestingly, the outcome was to follow Strategy 2 (superplant/slow investment) with the proviso that should the market take off rapidly, a contingency plan for quickly adding further capacity would be immediately activated.

30.

Theories of Decision Making in Economics and Behavioral Science*

HERBERT A. SIMON

Recent years have seen important new explorations along the boundaries between economics and psychology. For the economist, the immediate question about these developments is whether they include new advances in psychology that can fruitfully be applied to economics. But the psychologist will also raise the converse question–whether there are developments in economic theory and observation that have implications for the central core of psychology. If economics is able to find verifiable and verified generalizations about human economic behavior, then these generalizations must have a place in the more general theories of human behavior to which psychology and sociology aspire. Influence will run both ways.

1. HOW MUCH PSYCHOLOGY DOES ECONOMICS NEED?

How have psychology and economics gotten along with little relation in the past? The explanation rests on an understanding of the goals toward which economics, viewed as a science and a discipline, has usually aimed.

* *American Economic Review* 49 no. 3 (June 1959), pp. 253–80.

Broadly speaking, economics can be defined as the science that de-scribes and predicts the behavior of several kinds of economic man—notably the consumer and the entrepreneur. While perhaps literally cor-rect, this definition does not reflect the principal focus in the literature of economics. We usually classify work in economics along two dimen-sions: (a) whether it is concerned with industries and the whole economy (macroeconomics) or with individual economic actors (microeconomics) and (b) whether it strives to describe and explain economic behavior (descriptive economics), or to guide decisions either at the level of public policy (normative macroeconomics) or at the level of the individual con-sumer or businessman (normative microeconomics).

The profession and literature of economics have been largely preoc-cupied with normative macroeconomics. Although descriptive macroeco-nomics provides the scientific base for policy prescription, research em-phases have been determined in large part by relevance to policy (e.g., business cycle theory). Normative microeconomics, carried forward un-der such labels as "management science," "engineering economics," and "operations research," is now a flourishing area of work having an uneasy and ill-defined relation with the profession of economics, traditionally defined. Much of the work is being done by mathematicians, statisticians, engineers, and physical scientists (although many mathe-matical economists have also been active in it).

This new area, like the old, is normative in orientation. Economists have been relatively uninterested in descriptive microeconomics—under-standing the behavior of individual economic agents—except as this is necessary to provide a foundation for macroeconomics. The normative microeconomist "obviously" doesn't need a theory of human behavior: he wants to know how people *ought* to behave, not how they *do* behave. On the other hand, the macroeconomist's lack of concern with individual behavior stems from different considerations. First, he assumes that the economic actor is rational, and hence he makes strong predictions about human behavior without performing the hard work of observing people. Second, he often assumes competition, which carries with it the implica-tion that only the rational survive. Thus, the classical economic theory of markets with perfect competition and rational agents is deductive theory that requires almost no contact with empirical data once its as-sumptions are accepted.

Undoubtedly there is an area of human behavior that fits these as-sumptions to a reasonable approximation, where the classical theory with its assumptions of rationality is a powerful and useful tool. Without denying the existence of this area, or its importance, I may observe that it fails to include some of the central problems of conflict and dynamics with which economics has become more and more concerned. A metaphor will help to show the reason for this failure.

Suppose we were pouring some viscous liquid—molasses—into a

bowl of very irregular shape. What would we need in order to make a theory of the form the molasses would take in the bowl? How much would we have to know about the properties of molasses to predict its behavior under the circumstances? If the bowl were held motionless, and if we wanted only to predict behavior in equilibrium, we would have to know little, indeed, about molasses. The single essential assumption would be that the molasses, under the force of gravity, would minimize the height of its center of gravity. With this assumption, which would apply as well to any other liquid, and a complete knowledge of the environment—in this case the shape of the bowl—the equilibrium is completely determined. Just so, the equilibrium behavior of a perfectly adapting organism depends only on its goal and its environment; it is otherwise completely independent of the internal properties of the organism.

If the bowl into which we were pouring the molasses were jiggled rapidly, or if we wanted to know about the behavior before equilibrium was reached, prediction would require much more information. It would require, in particular, more information about the properties of molasses: its viscosity, the rapidity with which it "adapted" itself to the containing vessel and moved towards its "goal" of lowering its center of gravity. Likewise, to predict the short-run behavior of an adaptive organism, or its behavior in a complex and rapidly changing environment, it is not enough to know its goals. We must know also a great deal about its internal structure and particularly its mechanisms of adaptation.

If, to carry the metaphor a step farther, new forces, in addition to gravitational force, were brought to bear on the liquid, we would have to know still more about it even to predict behavior in equilibrium. Now its tendency to lower its center of gravity might be countered by a force to minimize an electrical or magnetic potential operating in some lateral direction. We would have to know its relative susceptibility to gravitational and electrical or magnetic force to determine its equilibrium position. Similarly, in an organism having a multiplicity of goals, or afflicted with some kind of internal goal conflict, behavior could be predicted only from information about the relative strengths of the several goals and the ways in which the adaptive processes responded to them.

Economics has been moving steadily into new areas where the power of the classical equilibrium model has never been demonstrated, and where its adequacy must be considered anew. Labor economics is such an area, oligopoly or imperfect competition theory another, decision making under uncertainty a third, and the theory of economic development a fourth. In all of these areas the complexity and instability of his environment becomes a central feature of the choices that economic man faces. To explain his behavior in the face of this complexity, the theory must describe him as something more than a featureless, adaptive organism; it must incorporate at least some description of the processes and mechanisms through which the adaptation takes place. Let us list a little more concretely some specific problems of this kind:

(a) The classical theory postulates that the consumer maximizes utility. Recent advances in the theory of rational consumer choice have shown that the existence of a utility function, and its characteristics, if it exists, can be studied empirically.

(b) The growing separation between ownership and management has directed attention to the motivations of managers and the adequacy of the profit-maximization assumption for business firms. So-called human relations research has raised a variety of issues about the motivation of both executives and employees.

(c) When, in extending the classical theory, the assumptions of perfect competition were removed, even the definition of rationality became ambiguous. New definitions had to be constructed, by no means as "obvious" intuitively as simple maximization, to extend the theory of rational behavior to bilateral monopoly and to other bargaining and outguessing situations.

(d) When the assumptions of perfect foresight were removed, to handle uncertainty about the environment, the definition of rationality had to be extended in another direction to take into account prediction and the formation of expectations.

(e) Broadening the definition of rationality to encompass goal conflict and uncertainty made it hard to ignore the distinction between the objective environment in which the economic actor "really" lives and the subjective environment that he perceives and to which he responds. When this distinction is made, we can no longer predict his behavior—even if he behaves rationally—from the characteristics of the objective environment; we also need to know something about his perceptual and cognitive processes.

We shall use these five problem areas as a basis for sorting out some recent explorations in theory, model building, and empirical testing. In section II, we will examine developments in the theory of utility and consumer choice. In section III, we will consider somewhat parallel issues relating to the motivation of managers. In section IV, we will deal with conflict of goals and the phenomena of bargaining. In section V, we will survey some of the work that has been done on uncertainty and the formation of expectations. In section VI, we will explore recent developments in the theory of human problem solving and other higher mental processes, and see what implications these have for economic decision making.

II. THE UTILITY FUNCTION

The story of the reestablishment of cardinal utility, as a consequence of the introduction of uncertainty into the theory of choice, is well known.

When Pareto and Slutsky had shown that the theory of consumer demand could be derived from the properties of indifference curves, without postulating a cardinal utility function underlying these curves, it became fashionable to regard utility as an ordinal measure—a ranking of alternatives by preference. Indeed, it could be shown that only ordinal utility had operational status—that the experiments that had been proposed, and even tried in a couple of instances, to measure an individual's utilities by asking him to choose among alternatives could never distinguish between two cardinal utility functions that were ordinally equivalent— that differed only by stretchings and contractions of the unit of measurement.

It was shown by von Neumann and Morgenstern, as a by-product of their development of the theory of games, that if the choice situation were extended to include choices among uncertain prospects—among lottery tickets, say—cardinal utilities could be assigned to the outcomes in an unequivocal way. Under these conditions, if the subject's behavior was consistent, it was possible to measure cardinally the utilities that different outcomes had for him.

A person who behaved in a manner consistent with the axioms of choice of von Neumann and Morgenstern would act so as to maximize the expected value—the average, weighted by the probabilities of the alternative outcomes of a choice—of his utility. The theory could be tested empirically, however, only on the assumption that the probabilities assigned to the alternatives by the subject were identical with the "objective" probabilities of these events as known to the experimenter. For example, if a subject believed in the gamblers' fallacy, that after a run of heads an unbiased coin would be more likely to fall tails, his choices might appear inconsistent with his utility function, while the real difficulty would lie in his method of assigning probabilities. This difficulty of "subjective" versus "objective" probability soon came to light when attempts were made to test experimentally whether people behaved in accordance with the predictions of the new utility theory. At the same time, it was discovered that the problem had been raised and solved 30 years earlier by the English philosopher and mathematician Frank Ramsey. Ramsey had shown that, by an appropriate series of experiments, the utilities and subjective probabilities assigned by a subject to a set of uncertain alternatives could be measured simultaneously.

Empirical Studies

The new axiomatic foundations of the theory of utility, which show that it is possible, at least in principle, to determine empirically whether people "have" utility functions of the appropriate kind, have led to a rash of choice experiments. An experimenter who wants to measure utilities, not merely in principle but in fact, faces innumerable difficulties.

Because of these difficulties, most experiments have been limited to confronting the subjects with alternative lottery tickets, at various odds, for small amounts of money. The weight of evidence is that, under these conditions, most persons choose in a way that is reasonably consistent with the axioms of the theory—they behave as though they were maximizing the expected value of utility and as though the utilities of the several alternatives can be measured.

When these experiments are extended to more "realistic" choices—choices that are more obviously relevant to real-life situations—difficulties multiply. In the few extensions that have been made, it is not at all clear that the subjects behave in accordance with the utility axioms. There is some indication that when the situation is very simple and transparent, so that the subject can easily see and remember when he is being consistent, he behaves like a utility maximizer. But as the choices become a little more complicated—choices, for example, among phonograph records instead of sums of money—he becomes much less consistent.

We can interpret these results in either of two ways. We can say that consumers "want" to maximize utility, and that if we present them with clear and simple choices that they understand they will do so. Or we can say that the real world is so complicated that the theory of utility maximization has little relevance to real choices. The former interpretation has generally appeared more attractive to economists trained in classical utility theory and to management scientists seeking rules of behavior for normative microeconomics; the latter to behavioral scientists interested in the description of behavior.

Normative Applications

The new utility theory has provided the formal framework for much recent work in mathematical statistics—i.e., statistical decision theory. Similarly (it would be accurate to say "synonymously"), this framework provides the basis for most of the normative models of management science and operations research designed for actual application to the decision-making problems of the firm.[1] Except for some very recent developments, linear programming has been limited to decision making under certainty, but there have been far-reaching developments of dynamic programming dealing with the maximization of expected values of outcomes (usually monetary outcomes) in situations where future events can be predicted only in terms of probability distributions.

Again, there are at least two distinct interpretations that can be placed on these developments. On the one hand, it can be argued:

---

[1] This work relates, of course, to profit maximization and cost minimization rather than utility maximization, but it is convenient to mention it at this point.

"Firms would like to maximize profits if they could. They have been limited in doing so by the conceptual and computational difficulties of finding the optimal courses of action. By providing powerful new mathematical tools and computing machines, we now enable them to behave in the manner predicted by Alfred Marshall, even if they haven't been able to in the past." Nature will imitate art and economic man will become as real (and as artificial) as radios and atomic piles.

The alternative interpretation rests on the observation that, even with the powerful new tools and machines, most real-life choices still lie beyond the reach of maximizing techniques—unless the situations are heroically simplified by drastic approximations. If man, according to this interpretation, makes decisions and choices that have some appearance of rationality, rationality in real life must involve something simpler than maximization of utility or profit. In section VI, we will see where this alternative interpretation leads.

The Binary Choice Experiment

Much recent discussion about utility has centered around a particularly simple choice experiment. This experiment, in numerous variants, has been used by both economists and psychologists to test the most diverse kinds of hypotheses. We will describe it so that we can use it as a common standard of comparison for a whole range of theories and empirical studies.

We will call the situation we are about to describe the *binary choice* experiment. It is better known to most game theorists—particularly those located not far from Nevada—as a two-armed bandit; and to most psychologists as a partial reinforcement experiment. The subject is required, in each of a series of trials, to choose one or the other of two symbols— say, plus or minus. When he has chosen, he is told whether his choice was "right" or "wrong," and he may also receive a reward (in psychologist's language, a reinforcement) for "right" choices. The experimenter can arrange the schedule of correct responses in a variety of ways. There may be a definite pattern, or they may be randomized. It is not essential that one and only one response be correct on a given trial: the experimenter may determine that both or neither will be correct. In the latter case the subject may or may not be informed whether the response he did not choose would have been correct.

How would a utility-maximizing subject behave in the binary choice experiment? Suppose that the experimenter rewarded "plus" on one third of the trials, determined at random, and "minus" on the remaining two thirds. Then a subject, provided that he believed the sequence was random and observed that minus was rewarded twice as often as plus, should always, rationally, choose minus. He would find the correct answer two thirds of the time, and more often than with any other strategy.

Unfortunately for the classical theory of utility in its simplest form, few subjects behave in this way. The most commonly observed behavior is what is called *event matching*. The subject chooses the two alternatives (not necessarily at random) with relative frequencies roughly proportional to the relative frequencies with which they are rewarded. Thus, in the example given, two thirds of the time he would choose minus, and as a result would make a correct response, on the average, in five trials out of nine (on two thirds of the trials in which he chooses minus, and one third of those in which he chooses plus).[2]

All sorts of explanations have been offered for the event-matching behavior. The simplest is that the subject just doesn't understand what strategy would maximize his expected utility; but with adult subjects in a situation as transparent as this one, this explanation seems far-fetched. The alternative explanations imply either that the subject regards himself as being engaged in a competitive game with the experimenter (or with "nature" if he accepts the experimenter's explanation that the stimulus is random), or that his reponses are the outcome of certain kinds of learning processes. We will examine these two types of explanation further in sections IV and V respectively. The important conclusion at this point is that even in an extremely simple situation, subjects do not behave in the way predicted by a straightforward application of utility theory.

Probabilistic Preferences

Before we leave the subject of utility, we should mention one recent important development. In the formalizations mentioned up to this point, probabilities enter only into the estimation of the consequences that will follow one alternative or another. Given any two alternatives, the first is definitely preferable to the second (in terms of expected utility), or the second to the first, or they are strictly indifferent. If the same pair of alternatives is presented to the subject more than once, he should always prefer the same member of the pair.

One might think this requirement too strict—that, particularly if the utility attached to one alternative were only slightly greater or less than that attached to the other, the subject might vacillate in his choice. An empirical precedent for such vacillation comes not only from casual observation of indecision but from analogous phenomena in the psychophysical laboratory. When subjects are asked to decide which of two weights is heavier, the objectively heavier one is chosen more often

---

[2] Subjects tend to choose the more highly rewarded alternative slightly more frequently than is called for by event matching. Hence, the actual behavior tends to be some kind of average between event matching and the optimal behavior.

than the lighter one, but the relative frequency of choosing the heaviest approaches one half as the two weights approach equality. The probability that a subject will choose the objectively heavier weight depends, in general, on the ratio of the two weights.

Following several earlier attempts, a rigorous and complete axiom system for a utility theory incorporating probabilistic preferences has been constructed recently by Duncan Luce. Although the theory weakens the requirements of consistency in preference, it is empirically testable, at least in principle. Conceptually, it provides a more plausible interpretation of the notion of "indifference" than does the classical theory.

III. THE GOALS OF FIRMS

Just as the central assumption in the theory of consumption is that the consumer strives to maximize his utility, so the crucial assumption in the theory of the firm is that the entrepreneur strives to maximize his residual share—his profit. Attacks on this hypothesis have been frequent. We may classify the most important of these as follows:

(a) The theory leaves ambiguous whether it is short-run or long-run profit that is to be maximized.

(b) The entrepreneur may obtain all kinds of "psychic income" from the firm, quite apart from monetary rewards. If he is to maximize his utility, then he will sometimes balance a loss of profits against an increase in psychic income. But if we allow "psychic income," the criterion of profit maximization loses all of its definiteness.

(c) The entrepreneur may not care to maximize, but may simply want to earn a return that he regards as satisfactory. By sophistry and adept use of the concept of psychic income, the notion of seeking a satisfactory return can be translated into utility maximizing, but not in any operational way. We shall see in a moment that "satisfactory profits" is a concept more meaningfully related to the psychological notion of aspiration levels than to maximization.

(d) It is often observed that under modern conditions the equity owners and the active managers of an enterprise are separate and distinct groups of people, so that the latter may not be motivated to maximize profits.

(e) Where there is imperfect competition among firms, maximizing is an ambiguous goal, for what action is optimal for one firm depends on the actions of the other firms.

In the present section we shall deal only with the third of these five issues. The fifth will be treated in the following section; the first, second, and fourth are purely empirical questions that have been discussed at length in the literature; they will be considered here only for their bearing on the question of satisfactory profits.

Satisficing versus Maximizing

The notion of satiation plays no role in classical economic theory, while it enters rather prominently into the treatment of motivation in psychology. In most psychological theories the motive to act stems from *drives,* and action terminates when the drive is satisfied. Moreover, the conditions for satisfying a drive are not necessarily fixed, but may be specified by an aspiration level that itself adjusts upward or downward on the basis of experience.

If we seek to explain business behavior in the terms of this theory, we must expect the firm's goals to be not maximizing profit, but attaining a certain level or rate of profit, holding a certain share of the market or a certain level of sales. Firms would try to "satisfice" rather than to maximize.

It has sometimes been argued that the distinction between satisficing and maximizing is not important to economic theory. For in the first place, the psychological evidence on individual behavior shows that aspirations tend to adjust to the attainable. Hence in the long run, the argument runs, the level of aspiration and the attainable maximum will be very close together. Second, even if some firms satisficed, they would gradually lose out to the maximizing firms, which would make larger profits and grow more rapidly than the others.

These are, of course, precisely the arguments of our molasses metaphor, and we may answer them in the same way that we answered them earlier. The economic environment of the firm is complex, and it changes rapidly; there is no a priori reason to assume the attainment of long-run equilibrium. Indeed, the empirical evidence on the distribution of firms by size suggests that the observed regularities in size distribution stem from the statistical equilibrium of a population of adaptive systems rather than the static equilibrium of a population of maximizers.

Models of satisficing behavior are richer than models of maximizing behavior, because they treat not only of equilibrium but of the method of reaching it as well. Psychological studies of the formation and change of aspiration levels support propositions of the following kinds: *(a)* When performance falls short of the level of aspiration, search behavior (particularly search for new alternatives of action) is induced. *(b)* At the same time, the level of aspiration begins to adjust itself downward until goals reach levels that are practically attainable. *(c)* If the two mechanisms just listed operate too slowly to adapt aspirations to performance, emotional behavior—apathy or aggression, for example—will replace rational adaptive behavior.

The aspiration level defines a natural zero point in the scale of utility—whereas in most classical theories the zero point is arbitrary. When the firm has alternatives open to it that are at or above its aspiration level, the theory predicts that it will choose the best of those known to be available. When none of the available alternatives satisfies current aspirations, the theory predicts qualitatively different behavior: in the short run, search behavior and the revision of targets; in the longer run, what we have called above emotional behavior, and what the psychologist would be inclined to call neurosis.[3]

Studies of Business Behavior

There is some empirical evidence that business goals are, in fact, stated in satisficing terms. First, there is the series of studies stemming from the pioneering work of Hall and Hitch that indicates that businessmen often set prices by applying a standard markup to costs. Some economists have sought to refute this fact, others to reconcile it—if it is a fact—with marginalist principles. The study of Earley belongs to the former category, but its evidence is suspect because the questions asked of businessmen are leading ones—no one likes to admit that he would accept less profit if he could have more. Earley did not ask his respondents how they determined marginal cost and marginal revenue, how, for example, they estimated demand elasticities.

Another series of studies derived from the debate over the Keynesian doctrine that the amount of investment was insensitive to changes in the rate of interest. The general finding in these studies has been that the rate of interest is not an important factor in investment decisions.

More recently, my colleagues Cyert and March have attempted to test the satisficing model in a more direct way. They found in one industry some evidence that firms with a declining share of market strove more vigorously to increase their sales than firms whose shares of the market were steady or increasing.

Aspirations in the Binary Choice Experiment

Although to my knowledge this has not been done, it would be easy to look for aspiration-level phenomena in the binary choice experiment. By changing the probabilities of reward in different ways for different groups of subjects, we could measure the effects of these changes on search behavior—where amount of search would be measured by changes in the pattern of responses.

---

[3] Lest this last term appear fanciful, I should like to call attention to the phenomena of panic and broken morale, which are well known to observers of the stock market and of organizations but which have no reasonable interpretation in classical utility theory. I may also mention that psychologists use the theory described here in a straightforward way to produce experimental neurosis in animal and human subjects.

Economic Implications

It has sometimes been argued that, however realistic the classical theory of the firm as a profit maximizer, it is an adequate theory for purposes of normative macroeconomics. Mason, for example, in commenting on Papandreou's essay on "Problems in the Theory of the Firm" says, "The writer of this critique must confess a lack of confidence in the marked superiority, *for purposes of economic analysis,* of this newer concept of the firm over the older conception of the entrepreneur." The italics are Mason's.

The theory of the firm is important for welfare economics—e.g., for determining under what circumstances the behavior of the firm will lead to efficient allocation of resources. The satisficing model vitiates all the conclusions about resource allocation that are derivable from the maximizing model when perfect competition is assumed. Similarly, a dynamic theory of firm sizes, like that mentioned above, has quite different implications for public policies dealing with concentration than a theory that assumes firms to be in static equilibrium. Hence, welfare economists are justified in adhering to the classical theory only if: *(a)* the theory is empirically correct as a description of the decision-making process or *(b)* it is safe to assume that the system operates in the neighborhood of the static equilibrium. What evidence we have mostly contradicts both assumptions.

IV. CONFLICT OF INTEREST

Leaving aside the problem of the motivations of hired managers, conflict of interest among economic actors creates no difficulty for classical economic theory—indeed, it lies at the very core of the theory—so long as each actor treats the other actors as parts of his "given" environment, and doesn't try to predict their behavior and anticipate it. But when this restriction is removed, when it is assumed that a seller takes into account the reactions of buyers to his actions, or that each manufacturer predicts the behaviors of his competitors—all the familiar difficulties of imperfect competition and oligopoly arise.[4]

The very assumptions of omniscient rationality that provide the basis for deductive prediction in economics when competition is present lead to ambiguity when they are applied to competition among the few. The central difficulty is that rationality requires one to outguess one's opponents, but not to be outguessed by them, and this is clearly not a consistent requirement if applied to all the actors.

---

[4] There is by now a voluminous literature on the problem.

Game Theory

Modern game theory is a vigorous and extensive exploration of ways of extending the concept of rational behavior to situations involving struggle, outguessing, and bargaining. Since Luce and Raiffa have recently provided us with an excellent survey and evaluation of game theory, I shall not cover the same ground here. I concur in their general evaluation that, while game theory has greatly clarified the issues involved, it has not provided satisfactory solutions. Not only does it leave the definition of rational conduct ambiguous in all cases save the zero-sum two-person game, but it requires of economic man even more fantastic reasoning powers than does classical economic theory.

Power and Bargaining

A number of exploratory proposals have been put forth as alternatives to game theory—among them Galbraith's notion of countervailing power and Schelling's bargaining theory. These analyses draw at least as heavily upon theories of power and bargaining developed initially to explain political phenomena as upon economic theory. They do not lead to any more specific predictions of behavior than do game-theoretic approaches, but place a greater emphasis upon description and actual observation, and are modest in their attempt to derive predictions by deductive reasoning from a few "plausible" premises about human behavior.

At least four important areas of social science and social policy, two of them in economics and two more closely related to political science, have as their central concern the phenomena of power and the processes of bargaining: the theory of political parties, labor-management relations, international politics, and oligopoly theory. Any progress in the basic theory applicable to one of these is certain to be of almost equal importance to the others. A growing recognition of their common concern is evidenced by the initiation of a new cross-disciplinary journal, *Journal of Conflict Resolution.*

Games against Nature

While the binary choice experiment is basically a one-person game, it is possible to interpret it as a "game against nature," and hence to try to explain it in game-theoretic terms. According to game theory, the subject, if he believes in a malevolent nature that manipulates the dice against him, should "minimax" his expected utility instead of maximizing it. That is, he should adopt the course of action that will maximize his expected utility under the assumption that nature will do her worst to him.

Minimaxing expected utility would lead the subject to call plus or minus at random and with equal probability, regardless of what the history of rewards has been. This is something that subjects demonstrably do not do.

However, it has been suggested by Savage and others that people are not as interested in maximizing utility as they are in minimizing regret. "Regret" means the difference between the reward actually obtained and the reward that could have been obtained with perfect foresight (actually, with perfect hindsight!). It turns out that minimaxing regret in the binary choice experiment leads to event-matching behavior. Hence, the empirical evidence is at least crudely consistent with the hypothesis that people play against nature by minimaxing regret. We shall see, however, that event matching is also consistent with a number of other rules of behavior that seem more plausible on their face; hence we need not take the present explanation too seriously—at least I am not inclined to do so.

V. THE FORMATION OF EXPECTATIONS

While the future cannot enter into the determination of the present, expectations about the future can and do. In trying to gain an understanding of the saving, spending, and investment behavior of both consumers and firms, and to make short-term predictions of this behavior for purposes of policy making, economists have done substantial empirical work as well as theorizing on the formation of expectations.

Empirical Studies

A considerable body of data has been accumulated on consumers' plans and expectations from the Survey of Consumer Finances, conducted for the Board of Governors of the Federal Reserve System by the Survey Research Center of the University of Michigan. These data, and similar data obtained by others, begin to give us some information on the expectations of consumers about their own incomes, and the predictive value of their expenditure plans for their actual subsequent behavior. Some large-scale attempts have been made, notably by Modigliani and Brumberg and, a little later, by Friedman to relate these empirical findings to classical utility theory. The current empirical research on businessmen's expectations is of two main kinds:

1. Surveys of businessmen's own forecasts of business and business conditions in the economy and in their own industries. These are obtained by straightforward questionnaire methods that assume, implicitly, that businessmen can and do make such forecasts. In some uses to which the data are put, it is also assumed that the forecasts are used as one basis for businessmen's actions.

2. Studies of business decisions and the role of expectations in these decisions—particularly investment and pricing decisions. We have already referred to studies of business decisions in our discussion of the goals of the firm.

Expectations and Probability

The classical way to incorporate expectations into economic theory is to assume that the decision maker estimates the joint probability distribution of future events. He can then act so as to maximize the expected value of utility or profit, as the case may be. However satisfying this approach may be conceptually, it poses awkward problems when we ask how the decision maker actually estimates the parameters of the joint probability distribution. Common sense tells us that people don't make such estimates, nor can we find evidence that they do by examining actual business forecasting methods. The surveys of businessmen's expectations have never attempted to secure such estimates, but have contented themselves with asking for point predictions—which, at best, might be interpreted as predictions of the means of the distributions.

It has been shown that under certain special circumstances the mean of the probability distribution is the only parameter that is relevant for decision—that even if the variance and higher moments were known to the rational decision maker, he would have no use for them. In these cases, the arithmetic mean is actually a certainty equivalent, the optimal decision turns out to be the same as if the future were known with certainty. But the situations where the mean is a certainty equivalent are, as we have said, very special ones, and there is no indication that businessmen ever ask whether the necessary conditions for this equivalence are actually met in practice. They somehow make forecasts in the form of point predictions and act upon them in one way or another.

The "somehow" poses questions that are important for business cycle theory, and perhaps for other problems in economics. The way in which expectations are formed may affect the dynamic stability of the economy, and the extent to which cycles will be amplified or damped. Some light, both empirical and theoretical, has recently been cast on these questions. On the empirical side, attempts have been made: (a) to compare businessman's forecasts with various "naïve" models that assume the future will be some simple function of the recent past and (b) to use such naïve models themselves as forecasting devices.

The simplest naïve model is one that assumes the next period will be exactly like the present. Another assumes that the change from present to next period will equal the change from last period to present; a third, somewhat more general, assumes that the next period will be a weighted average of recent past periods. The term *naïve model* has been applied loosely to various forecasting formulas of these general kinds. There is some affirmative evidence that business forecasts fit such models. There is also evidence that elaboration of the models beyond the first few steps of refinement does not much improve prediction. Arrow and his colleagues have explored some of the conditions under which forecasting formulas will, and will not, introduce dynamic instability into an economic system that is otherwise stable. They have shown, for example, that if a system of multiple markets is stable under static expectations, it is stable when expectations are based on a moving average of past values.

The work on the formation of expectations represents a significant extension of classical theory. For, instead of taking the environment as a "given," known to the economic decision maker, it incorporates in the theory the processes of acquiring knowledge about that environment. In doing so, it forces us to include in our model of economic man some of his properties as a learning, estimating, searching, information-processing organism.

The Cost of Information

There is one way in which the formation of expectations might be reincorporated in the body of economic theory: by treating information gathering as one of the processes of production, so to speak, and applying to it the usual rules of marginal analysis. Information, says price theory, should be gathered up to the point where the incremental cost of additional information is equal to the incremental profit that can be earned by having it. Such an approach can lead to propositions about optimal amounts of information-gathering activity and about the relative merits of alternative information-gathering and estimating schemes.

This line of investigation has, in fact, been followed in statistical decision theory. In sampling theory we are concerned with the optimal size of sample (and in the special and ingenious case of sequential sampling theory, with knowing when to stop sampling), and we wish to evaluate the efficiencies of alternative sampling procedures. The latter problem is the simpler, since it is possible to compare the relative costs of alternative schemes that have the same sampling error, and hence to avoid estimating the value of the information. However, some progress has been made also toward estimating the value of improved forecast accuracy in situations where the forecasts are to be used in applying formal decision rules to choice situations.

The theory of teams developed by Marschak and Radner is concerned with the same problem. It considers situations involving decentralized and interdependent decision making by two or more persons who share a common goal and who, at a cost, can transmit information to each other about their own actions or about the parts of the environment with which they are in contact. The problem then is to discover the optimal communication strategy under specified assumptions about communication costs and payoffs.

The cost of communication in the theory of teams, like the cost of observations in sampling theory, is a parameter that characterizes the economic actor, or the relation of the actor to his environment. Hence, while these theories retain, in one sense, a classical picture of economic man as a maximizer, they clearly require considerable information about the characteristics of the actor, and not merely about his environment. They take a long stride toward bridging the gap between the traditional concerns of economics and the concern of psychology.

Expectations in the Binary Choice Experiment

I should like to return again to the binary choice experiment, to see what light it casts on the formation of expectations. If the subject is told by the experimenter that the rewards are assigned at random, if he is told what the odds are for each alternative, *and if he believes the experimenter,* the situation poses no forecasting problem. We have seen, however, that the behavior of most subjects is not consistent with these assumptions.

How would sequential sampling theory handle the problem? Each choice the subject makes now has two consequences: the immediate reward he obtains from it, and the increment of information it provides for predicting the future rewards. If he thinks only of the latter consequences, he is faced with the classical problem of induction: to estimate the probability that an event will occur in the future on the basis of its frequency of occurrence in the past. Almost any rule of induction would require a rational (maximizing) subject to behave in the following general manner: to sample the two alternatives in some proportion to estimate the probability of reward associated with each; after the error of estimate had been reduced below some bound, always to choose the alternative with the higher probability of reward. Unfortunately, this does not appear to be what most subjects do.

If we give up the idea of maximization, we can make the weaker assumption that the subject is adaptive—or learns—but not necessarily in any optimal fashion. What do we mean by adaptation or learning? We mean, gradually and on the basis of experience responding more frequently with the choice that, in the past, has been most frequently rewarded. There is a whole host of rules of behavior possessing this characteristic. Postulate, for example, that at each trial the subject has a certain probability of responding "plus," and the complementary probability of responding "minus." Postulate further that when he makes a particular response the probability of making the same response on the next trial is increased if the response is rewarded and decreased if the response is not rewarded. The amount of increment in the response probability is a parameter characterizing the learning rate of the particular subject. Almost all schemes of this kind produce asymptotic behaviors, as the number of trials increases, that are approximately event matching in character.

Stochastic learning models, as the processes just described are usually called, were introduced into psychology in the early 1950s by W. K. Estes and Bush and Mosteller and have been investigated extensively since that time. The models fit some of the gross features of the observed behaviors—most strikingly the asymptotic probabilities—but do not explain very satisfactorily the fine structure of the observations.

Observation of subjects in the binary choice experiment reveals that usually they not only refuse to believe that (or even to act as if) the reward series were random, but in fact persist over many trials in searching for systematic patterns in the series. To account for such behavior, we might again postulate a learning model, but in this case a model in which the subject does not react probabilistically to his environment, but forms and tests definite hypotheses about systematic patterns in it. Man, in this view, is not only a learning animal; he is a pattern-finding and concept-forming animal. Julian Feldman has constructed theories of this kind to explain the behavior of subjects in the binary choice experiment, and while the tests of the theories are not yet completed, his findings look exceedingly promising.

As we move from maximizing theories, through simple stochastic learning theories, to theories involving pattern recognition, our model of the expectation-forming processes and the organism that performs it increases in complexity. If we follow this route, we reach a point where a theory of behavior requires a rather elaborate and detailed picture of the rational actor's cognitive processes.

VI. HUMAN COGNITION AND ECONOMICS

All the developments we have examined in the preceding four sections have a common theme: they all involve important modifications in the concept of economic man and, for the reasons we have stated, modifications in the direction of providing a fuller description of his characteristics. The classical theory is a theory of a man choosing among fixed and known alternatives, to each of which is attached known consequences. But when perception and cognition intervene between the decision maker and his objective environment, this model no longer proves adequate. We need a description of the choice process that recognizes that alternatives are not given but must be sought; and a description that takes into account the arduous task of determining what consequences will follow on each alternative.

The decision maker's information about his environment is much less than an approximation to the real environment. The term "approximation" implies that the subjective world of the decision maker resembles the external environment closely, but lacks, perhaps, some fineness of detail. In actual fact the perceived world is fantastically different from the "real" world. The differences involve both omissions and distortions, and arise in both perception and inference. The sins of omission in perception are more important than the sins of commission. The decision maker's model of the world encompasses only a minute fraction of all the relevant characteristics of the real environment, and his inferences extract only a minute fraction of all the information that is present even in his model.

Perception is sometimes referred to as a *filter*. This term is as misleading as *approximation*, and for the same reason: it implies that what comes through into the central nervous system is really quite a bit like what is "out there." In fact, the filtering is not merely a passive selection of some part of a presented whole, but an active process involving attention to a very small part of the whole and exclusion, from the outset, of almost all that is not within the scope of attention.

Every human organism lives in an environment that generates millions of bits of new information each second, but the bottleneck of the perceptual apparatus certainly does not admit more than 1,000 bits per second, and probably much less. Equally significant omissions occur in the processing that takes place when information reaches the brain. As every mathematician knows, it is one thing to have a set of differential equations, and another thing to have their solutions. Yet the solutions are logically implied by the equations—they are "all there," if we only knew how to get to them! By the same token, there are hosts of inferences that *might* be drawn from the information stored in the brain that are not in fact drawn. The consequences implied by information in the memory become known only through active information processing, and hence through active selection of particular problem-solving paths from the myriad that might have been followed.

In this section we shall examine some theories of decision making that take the limitations of the decision maker and the complexity of the environment as central concerns. These theories incorporate some mechanisms we have already discussed—for example, aspiration levels and forecasting processes—but go beyond them in providing a detailed picture of the choice process.

A real-life decision involves some goals or values, some facts about the environment, and some inferences drawn from the values and facts. The goals and values may be simple or complex, consistent or contradictory; the facts may be real or supposed, based on observation or the reports of others; the inferences may be valid or spurious. The whole process may be viewed, metaphorically, as a process of "reasoning," where the values and facts serve as premises, and the decision that is finally reached is inferred from these premises. The resemblance of decision making to logical reasoning is only metaphorical, because there are quite different rules in the two cases to determine what constitute "valid" premises and admissible modes of inference. The metaphor is useful because it leads us to take the individual *decision premise* as the unit of description, hence to deal with the whole interwoven fabric of influences that bear on a single decision—but without being bound by the assumptions of rationality that limit the classical theory of choice.

Rational Behavior and Role Theory

We can find common ground to relate the economist's theory of decision making with that of the social psychologist. The latter is particularly interested, of course, in social influences on choice, which determine the *role* of the actor. In our present terms, a role is a social prescription of some, but not all, of the premises that enter into an individual's choices of behavior. Any particular concrete behavior is the resultant of a large number of premises, only some of which are prescribed by the role. In addition to role premises there will be premises about the state of the environment based directly on perception, premises representing beliefs and knowledge, and idiosyncratic premises that characterize the personality. Within this framework we can accommodate both the rational elements in choice, so much emphasized by economics, and the nonrational elements to which psychologists and sociologists often prefer to call attention.

Decision Premises and Computer Programs

The analysis of choice in terms of decision premises gives us a conceptual framework for describing and explaining the process of deciding. But so complex is the process that our explanations of it would have remained schematic and hypothetical for a long time to come had not the modern digital computer appeared on the scene. The notion of decision premise can be translated into computer terminology, and when this translation has been accomplished, the digital computer provides us with an instrument for stimulating human decision processes—even very complex ones—and hence for testing empirically our explanations of those processes.

A fanciful (but only slightly fanciful) example will illustrate how this might be done. Some actual examples will be cited presently. Suppose we were to construct a robot incorporating a modern digital computer, and to program (i.e., to instruct) the robot to take the role of a business executive in a specified company. What would the program look like? Since no one has yet done this, we cannot say with certainty, but several points are fairly clear. The program would not consist of a list of prescribed and proscribed behaviors, since what an executive does is highly contingent on information about a wide variety of circumstances. Instead, the program would consist of a large number of *criteria* to be applied to possible and proposed courses of action, of routines for *generating* possible courses of action, of computational procedures for *assessing* the state of the environment and its implications for action, and the like. Hence, the program—in fact, a role prescription—would interact with information to produce concrete behavior adapted to the situation. The elements of such a program take the form of what we have called decision premises, and what the computer specialists would call instructions.

The promise of constructing actual detailed descriptions of concrete roles and decision processes is no longer, with the computer, a mere prospectus to be realized at some undefined future date. We can already provide actual examples, some of them in the area of economics.

1. Management Science.   In the paragraphs on normative applications in section II, we have already referred to the use of such mathematical techniques as linear programming and dynamic programming to construct formal decision processes for actual situations. The relevance of these decision models to the present discussion is that they are not merely abstract "theories" of the firm, but actual decision-making devices. We can think of any such device as a simulation of the corresponding human decision maker, in which the equations and other assumptions that enter into the formal decision-making procedure correspond to the decision premises—including the role prescription—of the decision maker.

The actual application of such models to concrete business situations brings to light the information-processing tasks that are concealed in the assumptions of the more abstract classical models.

a. The models must be formulated so as to require for their application only data that are obtainable. If one of the penalties, for example, of holding too small inventories is the loss of sales, a decision model that proposes to determine optimal inventory levels must incorporate a procedure for putting a dollar value on this loss.

b. The models must call only for practicable computations. For example, several proposals for applying linear programming to certain factory scheduling problems have been shown to be impracticable because, even with computers, the computation time is too great. The task of decision theory (whether normative or descriptive) is to find alternative techniques—probably only approximate—that demand much less computation.

c. The models must not demand unobtainable forecast information. A procedure that would require a sales department to estimate the third moment of next month's sales distribution would not have wide application, as either description or prescription, to business decision making.

These models, then, provide us with concrete examples of roles for a decision maker described in terms of the premises he is expected to apply to the decision—the data and the rules of computation.

2. Engineering Design. Computers have been used for some years to carry out some of the analytic computations required in engineering design—computing the stresses, for example, in a proposed bridge design. Within the past two years, ways have been found to program computers to carry out synthesis as well as analysis—to evolve the design itself. A number of companies in the electrical industry now use computers to design electric motors, transformers, and generators, going from customer specifications to factory design without human intervention. The significance of this for our purpose here is that the synthesis programs appear to simulate rather closely the processes that had previously been used by college-trained engineers in the same design work. It has proved possible to write down the engineers' decision premises and inference processes in sufficient detail to produce workable computer programs.

3. Human Problem Solving. The management science and engineering design programs already provide examples of simulation of human decision making by computer. It may be thought that, since in both instances the processes are highly arithmetical, these examples are relevant to only a very narrow range of human problem-solving activity. We generally think of a digital computer as a device which, if instructed in painful detail by its operator, can be induced to perform rather complicated and tedious arithmetical operations. More recent developments require us to revise these conceptions of the computer, for they enable it to carry out tasks that, if performed by humans, we would certainly call "thinking" and "learning."

Discovering the proof of a theorem of Euclid—a task we all remember from our high school geometry course—requires thinking and usually insight and imagination. A computer is now being programmed to perform this task (in a manner closely simulating the human geometer), and another computer has been successfully performing a highly similar task in symbolic logic for the past two years. The latter computer is programmed to learn—that is to improve its performance on the basis of successful problem-solving experience—to use something akin to imagery or metaphor in planning its proofs, and to transfer some of its skills to other tasks—for example, solving trigonometric identities—involving completely distinct subject matter. These programs, it should be observed, do not involve the computer in rapid arithmetic—or any arithmetic for that matter. They are basically nonnumerical, involving the manipulation of all kinds of symbolic material, including words.

Still other computer programs have been written to enable a computer to play chess. Not all of these programs, or those previously mentioned, are close simulations of the processes humans use. However, in some direct attempts to investigate the human processes by thinking-aloud techniques and to reproduce in computer programs the processes observed in human subjects, several striking simulations have been achieved. These experiments have been described elsewhere and can't be reviewed here in detail.

4. Business Games. Business games, like those developed by the American Management Association, International Business Machines Corporation, and several universities, represent a parallel development. In the business game, the decisions of the business firms are still made by the human players, but the economic environment of these firms, including their markets, are represented by computer programs that calculate the environment's responses to the actions of the players. As the games develop in detail and realism, their programs will represent more and more concrete descriptions of the decision processes of various economic actors—for example, consumers.

The games that have been developed so far are restricted to numerical magnitudes like prices and quantities of goods, and hence resemble the management science and engineering design programs more closely than they do those we have described under the heading of human problem solving. There is no reason, however, to expect this restriction to remain very long.

Implications for Economics

Apart from normative applications (e.g., substituting computers for humans in certain decision-making tasks) we are not interested so much in the detailed descriptions of roles as in broader questions: (1) What general characteristics do the roles of economic actors have? (2) How do roles come to be structured in the particular ways they do? (3) What bearing does this version of role theory have for macroeconomics and other large-scale social phenomena?

Characterizing Role Structure. Here we are concerned with generalizations about thought processes, particularly those generalizations that are relatively independent of the substantive content of the role. A classical example is Dewey's description of stages in the problem-solving process. Another example, of particular interest to economics, is the hypothesis we have already discussed at length: that economic man is a *satisficing* animal whose problem solving is based on search activity to meet certain aspiration levels rather than a *maximizing* animal whose problem solving involves finding the best alternatives in terms of specified criteria. A third hypothesis is that operative goals (those associated with an observable criterion of success, and relatively definite means of attainment) play a much larger part in governing choice than nonoperative goals (those lacking a concrete measure of success or a program for attainment).

Understanding How Roles Emerge. Within almost any single business firm, certain characteristic types of roles will be represented: selling roles, production roles, accounting roles, and so on. Partly, this consistency may be explained in functional terms—that a model that views the firm as producing a product, selling it, and accounting for its assets and liabilities is an effective simplification of the real world, and provides the members of the organization with a workable frame of reference. Imitation within the culture provides an alternative explanation. It is exceedingly difficult to test hypotheses as to the origins and causal conditions for roles as universal in the society as these, but the underlying mechanisms could probably be explored effectively by the study of less common roles—safety director, quality control inspector, or the like—that are to be found in some firms, but not in all.

With our present definition of role, we can also speak meaningfully of the role of an entire business firm—of decision premises that underlie its basic policies. In a particular industry we find some firms that specialize in adapting the product to individual customers' specifications; others that specialize in product innovation. The common interest of economics and psychology includes not only the study of individual roles, but also the explanation of organizational roles of these sorts.

Tracing the Implications for Macroeconomics. If basic professional goals remain as they are, the interest of the psychologist and the economist in role theory will stem from somewhat different ultimate aims. The former will use various economic and organizational phenomena as data for the study of the structure and determinants of roles; the latter will be primarily interested in the implications of role theory for the model of economic man, and indirectly, for macroeconomics.

The first applications will be to those topics in economics where the assumption of static equilibrium is least tenable. Innovation, technological change, and economic development are examples of areas to which a good empirically tested theory of the processes of human adaptation and problem solving could make a major contribution. For instance, we know very little at present about how the rate of innovation depends on the amounts of resources allocated to various kinds of research and development activity. Nor do we understand very well the nature of "know-how," the costs of transferring technology from one firm or economy to another, or the effects of various kinds and amounts of education upon national product. These are difficult questions to answer from aggregative data and gross observation, with the result that out views have been formed more by armchair theorizing than by testing hypotheses with solid facts.

VII. CONCLUSION

In exploring the areas in which economics has common interests with the other behavioral sciences, we have been guided by the metaphor we elaborated in section I. In simple, slow-moving situations, where the actor has a single, operational goal, the assumption of maximization relieves us of any need to construct a detailed picture of economic man or his processes of adaptation. As the complexity of the environment increases, or its speed of change, we need to know more and more about the mechanisms and processes that economic man uses to relate himself to that environment and achieve his goals.

How closely we wish to interweave economics with psychology depends, then, both on the range of questions we wish to answer and on our assessment of how far we may trust the assumptions of static equilibrium as approximations. In considerable part, the demand for a fuller picture of economic man has been coming from the profession of economics itself, as new areas of theory and application have emerged in which complexity and change are central facts. The revived interest in the theory of utility, and its application to choice under uncertainty, and to consumer saving and spending is one such area. The needs of normative macroeconomics and management science for a fuller theory of the firm have led to a number of attempts to understand the actual processes of making business decisions. In both these areas, notions of adaptive and satisficing behavior, drawn largely from psychology, are challenging sharply the classical picture of the maximizing entrepreneur.

The area of imperfect competition and oligopoly has been equally active, although the activity has thus far perhaps raised more problems than it has solved. On the positive side, it has revealed a community of interest among a variety of social scientists concerned with bargaining as a part of political and economic processes. Prediction of the future is another element common to many decision processes, and particularly important to explaining business cycle phenomena. Psychologists and economists have been applying a wide variety of approaches, empirical and theoretical, to the study of the formation of expectations. Surveys of consumer and business behavior, theories of statistical induction, stochastic learning theories, and theories of concept formation have all been converging on this problem area.

The very complexity that has made a theory of the decision-making process essential has made its construction exceedingly difficult. Most approaches have been piecemeal—now focused on the criteria of choice, now on conflict of interest, now on the formation of expectations. It seemed almost utopian to suppose that we could put together a model of adaptive man that would compare in completeness with the simple model of classical economic man. The sketchiness and incompleteness of the newer proposals has been urged as a compelling reason for clinging to the older theories, however inadequate they are admitted to be.

The modern digital computer has changed the situation radically. It provides us with a tool of research—for formulating and testing theories—whose power is commensurate with the complexity of the phenomena we seek to understand. Although the use of computers to build theories of human behavior is very recent, it has already led to concrete results in the simulation of higher mental processes. As economics finds it more and more necessary to understand and explain disequilibrium as well as equilibrium, it will find an increasing use for this new tool and for communication with its sister sciences of psychology and sociology.

PART SEVEN

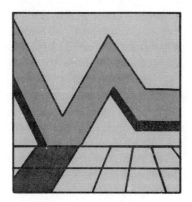

FORECASTING

INTRODUCTION

Some practicing business economists spend approximately 60 percent of their time forecasting. Agreement is not common among these forecasters about the relative merits of different methodological approaches to forecasting. However, there are two factors about which most economists agree: (1) economic forecasts are almost always wrong and (2) even when a forecast is reasonably accurate, more often than not, it is correct for reasons other than those related by the forecaster. This Part Seven explains some of the more common approaches to economic forecasts and provides an insight into a few of the various methods.

The general subject of forecasting may be divided according to the forecast period; in other words, whether short run or long run. It may also be classified according to forecasting method; is it subjective (judgmental) or objective (quantitative), based on economic relationships and statistical techniques? The article by John P. Lewis cuts across this classification and concerns itself with short-run forecasts. Lewis argues that many short-run methods are complementary, that a good combination of subjective and objective methods can achieve better forecasts than either method used alone.

Government spending at the federal, state, and local level appears to many forecasters to be increasing in quantity to such an extent and at such a rate that variables such as the federal government deficit may be very difficult to predict in the years immediately ahead. Associated with these government expenditures is the notion that a difference exists between nominal and real spending.

Nominal spending is converted to "real" terms by use of a price deflator. Peter S. Heller discusses the issues underlying the choice of an appropriate government price deflator and the various policy implications that arise in a situation where the growth of the government price deflator exceeds that of the gross domestic product deflator. Heller notes the divergence between the real burden of government expenditure, in terms of the taxpayer's opportunity cost, and the real value of publicly produced or purchased goods and services.

Objective, econometric methods of forecasting may be very useful if they predict short-range changes in, say, a dependent variable. But whether complex econometric methods provide more accurate forecasts than simpler ones is the subject of much debate. J. Scott Armstrong compares and contrasts the folklore and fact of forecasting with econometric methods.

Input-output analysis as a tool in economic forecasting is available to us primarily because of the pioneering effort of Nobel Prize-winning laureate, Wassily Leontief. His work relates the production of each industry to its consumption from every other industry. Input-output tables are provided for the entire economy by the United States government.

These tables differ in a statistical sense from those provided initially by Leontief; yet they are based on ideas initially revealed by him.

A research study in the late 1970s by Rodney L. Carlson investigated automobile demand for the 10-year period 1965 through 1975 using a disaggregate approach. The purpose of that study was to reveal the strength of model building as opposed to that of forecasting. The article here by Carlson and M. Michael Umble points out the forecasting accuracy of the market segmentation approach and estimates the effect of the energy crisis on automobile demand for the years 1979 through 1983. This article is of considerable interest in view of the importance of the auto industry to the nation's economy; in addition, it reveals again the merits of good econometric methodology when applied to short-range forecasting.

31.

Short-Term General Business Conditions Forecasting: Some Comments on Method*

JOHN P. LEWIS

The assignment that gave rise to this paper stipulated that I should first establish some kind of classification of general short-term forecasting techniques and then evaluate the several techniques on the basis of their showings during the past two or three years. What follows, however, does not really attempt the second of these tasks. One's impulse to construct batting averages is forestalled, for one thing, by the near impossibility of defining the universe from which a sample of representative forecasts might be drawn. Moreover, it is far harder to classify forecasters than forecasting techniques; few of us in practice are willing to stick exclusively to a particular technique, no matter how partisan to it we may be (and in this habit of mixed practice, I shall be saying, we are very wise.) Furthermore, insofar as one *can* associate particular forecasters or forecasting groups or exercises with particular techniques, the variance in recent performance is much greater between the best and worst records within particular categories than it is among the best per-

* "Short-Term General Business Conditions Forecasting: Some Comments on Methods," by John P. Lewis. Reprinted from *Journal of Business* 35, no. 4 (October 1962), pp. 343–56, by permission of The University of Chicago Press © Copyright 1962, The University of Chicago Press.

formances in the several categories. Finally, as one who must sometimes practice the art himself, I feel, in any event, that there is a certain basic indecency about displaying forecasters' comparative batting average publicly. To do so is too much like reading a paper to an open meeting of a county medical society in which one undertakes to spell out which local doctors lost the most patients last year.

Accordingly, my purpose here will be to dwell, rather than upon batting averages, upon the potentialities for complementarity among the several major forecasting approaches. In doing so, I hope largely to avoid contentiousness, of which we have already had altogether too much with respect to short-term forecasting methodology. The central, if pious, thesis of the paper is that all of us who find ourselves engaged in the forecasting enterprise rather urgently need every bit of quasi-respectable help we can get from one another.

I. SOME GROUND CLEARING

I propose to focus my discussion on five varieties of forecasting techniques that currently constitute the professional economic core of the activity—(1) leading indicators of the National Bureau of Economic Research (NBER) variety, (2) the leading monetary indicators that have been pioneered by Professor Milton Friedman and his associates, (3) use of those surveys of spenders' intentions and of other compilations of advance plans and commitments that, I believe, Martin Gainsbrugh was the first to label collectively as "foreshadowing indicators," (4) econometric model building, and (5) that looser, less elegant, but more comprehensive variety of model building that has been called many things, which I prefer to label "opportunistic."

These techniques have certain common characteristics. They share a certain professional respectability and orthodoxy; they are not, within the trade, regarded as crackpot approaches (although this, if one looks at the history of the art, is not necessarily a cause for reassurance). They all invite some use of the economists' trained skills; thereby they implicitly assume that a systematic marshalling of such skills can yield insights into the near-term economic future that an intelligent layman would be likely to miss. In this sense they are not diffident techniques. Finally, they all are genuinely professional techniques in that they are regimens for arriving by mainly dispassionate, quasi-objective procedures at technically honest answers to the question of what the unfolding condition of the economy is likely to be. They are not the best techniques, in other words, for telling bosses, presidents, congressmen, and other decision makers what they want to hear. All of these techniques, to be sure, can be twisted to yield preconceived answers, but at least they create tensions—they set up conflicts of loyalties—in any conscientious professional when he is called upon to abuse them in this fashion.

By concentrating on these five varieties of technique—the two kinds of leading-indicator analysis, the foreshadowing indicators, and the two kinds of model building—we shall be leaving out of account a fair part of the total methodological terrain. We shall pass over, for example, those analytical cults whose basic forecasting hypothesis is that inexorable, rhythmical cycles in activity are so deeply rooted in the laws of the economy that all the forecaster needs to do is, first, identify the relevant cycles by penetrating the cunning veil which nature seems to cast over them; second, locate the present position of the economy in the identified cycle or cycles; and then, third, proceed to read future business conditions right off the calendar. It would be presumptuous to say that the rhythmical cycle hypothesis has no place at all in sensible forecasting practice—it has certain, although limited, uses, for example, in the inventory field—but those who retain it as their principal general forecasting doctrine have, by now, been consigned to the crackpot category, and I think deservedly so.

We also shall be passing over a rather mixed bag of forecasting practices that I have labeled elsewhere as the "agnostic techniques"—meaning by that those more or less self-evidently weak methods for probing the future to which people resort when they doubt their capacity to do anything better. They may, for example, adopt a no-change hypothesis, projecting the latest period's level to the coming period, or, if they want to be a bit more sophisticated, they may extrapolate the recent trend to future periods. In the very best contemporary forecasting, of course, there are a number of points at which practitioners still fall back on precisely this procedure. However, if no-change extrapolations were the craft's universal methodology, it would be professionally bankrupt.

General expectations surveys also belong in the "agnostic" category. I am referring now to surveys, not of respondents' spending intentions or even of their own sales expectations, but of their anticipations of general business conditions. Such general expectations surveys may provide the forecaster with some useful data of a psychological sort, but if they are viewed as producing self-contained forecasts in their own right, their use rests on the hypothesis that the blind can lead the blind—if they do it collectively, that is. Then there is that variety of forecaster whom we might call "the parasitical agnostic"—the fellow who relies, via the Joe Livingston type of survey, upon the consensus of the experts. This, of course, is a fairly sensible, if unambitious, procedure, and, in fact, such surveys are of great utility to the experts themselves. For if there is any quality that ill suits a practicing forecaster it is arrogant indifference to what others in the trade are saying. All the same, the surveying of expert expectations obviously is a derivative forecasting methodology at best; it would cease to exist if the only experts were those who were expert in surveying experts' expectations.

Gerhard Colm has suggested to me one other methodological category that ought to be included in the list, but it too I shall largely pass over here. Colm's suggestion is the "cynical" forecast, and his example is the curious inability of the Council of Economic Advisers late in the Eisenhower Administration to detect the approach or even the start of the recession of 1960–61. I would prefer a slightly less harsh label—say, the "contrived" or "ulterior-motive" forecast—and, to balance things up politically, suggest as another example the present Administration's forecast of a $570 billion GNP for 1962. This last has not entailed any violent wrenching of professional standards, but Administration economists rather plainly have been looking on the bright side for a reason.

Having brought the matter up, I want to make a couple of quick comments on central-government forecasting, particularly that done within the executive office of the president. Two separable problems are involved. One is simply the feedback problem that besets any highly influential forecaster, public or private: Shall he allow himself to be deflected by the fact that his prognostications are likely, themselves, to have some impact upon business conditions in the forecast period? The accepted answer to this question, it seems to me, is "No." An agency like the Council of Economic Advisers should do the most accurate job it can of identifying the prospects likely to emerge under existing policies. But then when, by following this no-nonsense procedure, it finds itself about to release a pessimistic forecast, it also should do what it can to see that there comes, packaged with the forecast, a program of policies whose adoption would tend to make the disappointing forecast become untrue.

The other, and much stickier, problem under which official forecasters labor is that of occasional but stubborn direct political constraints. At least two economic-policy changes presently under discussion in Washington would relax the political inhibitions under which government forecasters lately have been working. One is the proposed delegation of increased standby stabilization powers to the president. This would weaken the presently inhibiting assumption that the tempo of adjustments in fiscal policy directed by business conditions necessarily should match the tempo of our congressional and electoral calendars. The second—and, in this context, the more important—reform may occur in the field of budgeting practice. Moves are under way to deflate further the traditional administrative budget concept and, in particular, to inject some sort of business-style distinction between capital and current outlays into federal accounting. Such a change, which would parallel the standard practice in most West European countries, could, as one of its by-products, greatly ease the constraint that the balanced-budget fetish has been imposing on responsible forecasters.

But I stray too far afield. For the ulterior-motive type, like the agnostic and rhythmical-cycle types, of forecasting lies beyond the boundaries to which I want to confine the burden of this discussion.

II. SOME LIMITATIONS OF THE TECHNIQUES USED SINGLY

As for the central core of professional short-term forecasting techniques, a commentator at this juncture, I think, must deliberately choose what the mood of his commentary is going to be. One could readily take a very bullish view of things, for the state of the art plainly is greatly improved from its condition a generation or even a decade ago. It would be equally legitimate, however, to adopt a thoroughly bearish stance and enlarge on the theme that, when you come right down to it, we are still practicing alchemy, not chemistry. So long as two intelligent persons or groups practicing the "same" techniques can come out with radically different forecasting answers, our scientific pretensions do not become us very well.

As indicated already, however, my own choice of a theme is neither gloom nor buoyancy but, rather, synthesis. I want to emphasize the complementarity of the several techniques we have under inspection, and this can best be done in two stages. First, I want to suggest some of the weaknesses that each of the five conventionally respectable techniques exhibits as a self-sufficient, go-it-alone device. But then, second, I want to underscore the contribution that each of these techniques can make to a properly comprehensive and synthesized forecasting exercise.

A. NBER Leading Indicators

The point has been rather widely made by now that the National Bureau of Economic Research type of leading indicator analysis constitutes a good bit less than a complete set of forecasting tools. This comes as no shock to the more responsible users and proponents of leads-and-lags analysis. However, a brief summary of the limitations of the method may still be in order. They seem to me to be these:

In the first place, the NBER leading indicators are inherently weak devices for detecting the *magnitude* of coming changes in business conditions. Their purpose is the detection of coming turning points, but, despite the improvements that Julius Shiskin lately has attempted in this regard, they have little capacity for disclosing how sharp the turn will be or how high or deep the upswing or downswing will go.

In the second place, the leading indicators as a group are quite short-range devices. Even if there were no problem of garbled signals, they would, as a group, give us no more than six months' advance notice of a coming downturn in the economy—and far less than that in the case of upturns.

In the third place, there *is* a problem of garbled signals. Looked at individually the leading indicators series run jagged courses. When any given wiggle occurs it usually takes two or three months to tell whether the leading indicator really has turned a significant corner or not, and by then, of course, much of its lead has been eaten up. Moreover, the leads of the particular indicators are not consistent from cycle to cycle, making it difficult to guess how soon a signaled change may occur. More important, the several leading indicators almost never all point in the same direction, especially in months just prior to general turns in business conditions. And while the "diffusion indexes" represent a natural and probably necessary attempt to cope with this last problem, they suppress most of the illuminating detail in the series that underlie them; typically they give no weight to the magnitudes of the expansions and contractions in the component series; they weight all of the components together as if they were of equal intrinsic importance; and, despite all of this, the diffusion indexes themselves are highly irregular in their movements.

Finally, as a self-sufficient technique, the leads-and-lags approach has this major limitation: it implicitly assumes a very high degree of structural rigidity in the economy. It has no adequate way of coping, for example, with major changes in the structure of demand. It is in such terms, I think, that one must explain the few past occasions—in 1951, 1956, and in 1959—on which the leading indicators have given concerted and prolonged false signals.

B. The Leading Monetary Indicators

The rest of us are much indebted to Friedman and his colleagues for emphasizing in recent years the degree to which the rate of change in the money supply tends to lead changes in general business activity, and changes in monetary reserves lead the money supply, and changes in central bank policy lead monetary reserves. The efforts to marshal the evidence underlying these assertions, to establish a format for the presentation of pertinent indicators, and to interest some of our reserve banks and other financial institutions in their publication have been all to the good.

Despite my reading of some of Friedman's writings on the subject and several lucid papers by Beryl Sprinkel, however, I confess to some confusion as to how far the proponents of the leading monetary indicators mean to go in claiming self-sufficiency for them as forecast devices. This confusion is rooted, in turn, in my confusion about the theoretical debate from which advocacy of the leading monetary indicators seems to emerge.

I am rather puzzled by the alleged contest between so-called modern quantity theory and the better contemporary versions of what is called income and expenditure theory. It seems to me just as evident that early Keynesian theory went much too far in underrating the role of money as a determinant of general economic activity even as the quantity theorists of the 20s went too far in overrating it. Surely it was a mistake to believe that the frail stem of the money rate of interest could bear the full burden of the impact of finance and financial institutions on investment activity, just as it was a mistake to talk as if monetary and credit conditions had a direct impact only on investment and not also upon such other sectors as consumer buying of durables and state and local government outlays. I should have supposed that today just about any journeyman analyst of the so-called income and expenditure persuasion, and certainly any sensible forecaster working in that tradition, is, therefore, vitally concerned with monetary prospects. That, indeed, is precisely why such analysts are very *much* interested in the current posture of the Federal Reserve and are sometimes critical of it. And that is why they prize the help Friedman et al. are giving us in identifying the time linkages that seem to relate changes in monetary policy to changes in the availability and cost of finance.

But to go beyond this to the opposite extreme and accept the leading monetary indicators as *sufficient* tools for predicting general business conditions would seem to me a most bizarre procedure. It would rest on the hypothesis that, for predictive purposes, the economy could be treated as if central bank decision making were the only significant independent variable in the system. For better or worse, things are more complicated than this. The capacity for influential autonomous decision making is far more widely dispersed. Considerable quantities of it lodge also, for example, in the Congress, in the White House, in the Finance Committee of the United States Steel Corporation, in Detroit, in all the great industrial houses and major labor organizations in the country and, even, in 50 million households. The responsible general forecaster must, somehow or other, directly concern himself with all of this pivotal decision making, not just with a particular slice of it. Academically, it is an interesting exercise to imagine that one had to settle for a single, go-it-alone set of predictive indicators and then debate the question of which would be the more reliable—the monetary set or some other? But this is a good deal like the question, with which good book would you most like to be cast on a desert isle? Neither question has much practical relevance. As a practical matter, there seems to be no reason for the general forecaster to confine himself to so spare and oversimplified a predictive hypothesis as sole reliance upon the leading monetary indicators would imply.

I do not mean to accuse Friedman and his associates of actually advocating exclusive reliance upon their wares, but some of their arguments have seemed to me susceptible to such a misinterpretation. The leading monetary indicators also have two more specific limitations.

First, the series on changes in monetary reserves and in the money supply, even after seasonal adjustment, are, like many of the NBER leading indicators, subject to rather violent gyrations. Thus it is much harder to detect, from the current data, a change of direction in the smoothed trends of these series than might first appear when one looks at the dramatic shifts in the ex post multimonth averages that the published charts of these series typically display.

Second, I would make the strange-sounding complaint that the average lead that the rate of change in the money supply is alleged to have over general cyclical downturns—namely, some 20 months since the mid-20s, is really too *long* to be very useful for forecasting purposes. Recent cyclical fluctuations in the American economy have appeared more or less to have followed a three-phase format. In a recession phase activity falls away from its long-term growth trend. In a second, recovery phase, it moves back up toward the long-term trend. But then, in a third, normal-growth or normal-prosperity phase, it moves *along* the trend. And this is the key point: Most of us would say that it is impossible to predict at the time it starts how long this third, along-the-trend phase of the cycle is likely to be. There are certain internal dynamics within the system that may tend roughly to govern the durations of most recession and recovery phases. But the duration of the prosperity phase probably is another matter; it appears to depend upon the particular sequence of demands—first, in autos, for example, then in plant and equipment or national defense, and then perhaps in state and local government—that happens to emerge as a result of the particular combination of decision making that occurs in a particular field.

Thus to tell me—as in effect the monetary change indicator does—that these periods of prosperity, along-the-trend phases of cycles since the 20s have *averaged* about 20 months really does not help very much. It gives me no confidence at all that such will be the case this particular time. Especially it gives me no such confidence if I believe, as I do, that there is nothing inevitable or immutable about cyclical rhythms and that deliberate discretionary changes in federal fiscal and monetary policies often decisively affect the duration of prosperity periods.

C. Foreshadowing Data

If it is jousting with a straw man to disprove the self-sufficiency of the leading indicators as forecast devices, it would be still worse to belabor the point that foreshadowing data—the spenders' intentions surveys, the federal budget, contract construction awards, new orders of durable goods manufacturers, and so on—do not in themselves constitute a full kit of forecasting tools. For I know of no serious developer or advocate of such data who has ever hinted that they can single-handedly generate a forecast. On the contrary, there has from the beginning been an alliance between the assemblers of foreshadowing data and model builders, especially of the less elegant, looser persuasion, with the former, of course, supplying much of the latter's inputs. For the sake of the present record, however, and because one still does occasionally encounter people who seem to think that if we could only finish the job of blanketing the GNP with intentions surveys, we would have the forecasting problem licked, let me venture just a few comments on the limitations of the foreshadowing series.

In the past the approach has been constrained by sheer problems of technique—for one thing, in the area of sampling and survey methods, and for another thing, with respect to the interpretation of the sequences of decreasingly tentative expectations and decreasingly conditional decisions into which the surveys from time to time dip. Franco Modigliani, however, has made sense of this latter matter, and certainly our better sampling and survey technology has become highly sophisticated. It is my layman's impression, therefore, that technical problems no longer are the real roadblocks in the area.

However, the coverage of the foreshadowing series is not yet all that it might be. There are some gaps—notably in the case of state and local government outlays—where spenders do indeed make advance plans, commitments, or conditional spending decisions (in the case of state and local governments they are a matter of public record) but where we simply have no agency yet that has assumed the task of systematically collecting or sampling and collating them.

But there are major segments of the GNP—notably in the area of consumer soft goods and services—that are destined, I should think, to remain effectively immune to intentions surveys, no matter how willing the surveyors may be, for the simple reason that buyers in these fields do not do enough coherent advance planning so that they themselves can recognize and report it.

Finally, there is the familiar but important point that the existence of plans, even strongly intentioned plans, offers no assurance that they will be carried out. The forecaster must convert the finding of an intentions survey into a forecast at his own peril. In particular when he makes such a conversion he must assume that the general economic developments that the expenditure planner does *not* foresee are not going to thwart his spending intentions. Modigliani has supplied us with a very intriguing refinement of this point—namely, that if the survey can canvass a respondent's sales or income expectations at the same time it canvasses his spending intentions and if it can be shown that past discrepancies between intended and actual outlays have been related to the discrepancies between expected and actual sales or incomes, it may be possible systematically to "correct" the intentions figure for forecasting purposes—*if* the forecaster is in a position to second-guess respondents' reported sales or income expectations. This approach seems to me to have considerable promise: perhaps even more in the fields of consumer intentions and of business inventory intentions, than in the plant and equipment sector where Modigliani first experimented with it. But as he emphasizes it must be used within the framework of a general model-building exercise. For only in such a context would the forecaster have any real basis for judging that spenders' expectations of future sales or incomes are unlikely to be realized. Modigliani's point, in other words, only underscores the conclusion that foreshadowing series are not go-it-alone devices.

D. Econometric Models

I shall focus my remarks about the limitations of general short-term econometric forecasting upon the single example of the present version of the original Klein-Goldberger model over which Daniel Suits now presides at the University of Michigan. This is one of the oldest econometric forecasting exercises with a continuous work record. It would appear to be fairly representative of its genus. And, for our purposes, it has the overwhelming advantage of just having been laid out for all of us to see in Suits's lucid article in the March 1962 *American Economic Review.*

Judging from this sample of one, we can draw the happy conclusion that econometric forecasting has been in process recently of getting constructively corrupted. In the course of drafting my book on *Business Conditions Analysis* about five years ago, I was casting about for a sharp distinction to be drawn between econometric model building and the less rigorous varieties that I call "opportunistic." I hit on these propositions. A true econometrician was a man, first, who insisted on cranking his forecast out of his explicit simultaneous-equation model without hedging or judgmental adjustment. He insisted, second, upon selecting all of the independent variables in his equations and deriving all of their parameters from an analysis of historical time series. By this definition, Suits no longer is an econometrician—which is to say, the definition is out of date.

There are two striking concessions that Suits's present methodology makes to the "practical" considerations espoused by opportunistic model builders. First, he now freely plugs in—instead of a rather lame investment function that makes business fixed-capital spending wholly dependent on last year's profits and last year's growth in plant-and-equipment stock—an intentions-survey result (in this case, the McGraw-Hill) as his business fixed-investment input. (Incidentally, he has not yet, so far as I can tell, adopted the Modigliani proposal for making a systematic correction in the intentions figure to compensate for the "error" in investors' sales expectations.) Second, the Michigan team now evidently feels free to tinker with the "*a*" constants in any or all of its linear equations to make allowance for judgmental considerations regarding the particular year at hand that it feels the formal model does not adequately encompass. In short, you might say that the Michigan group has become nothing but a bunch of elegant opportunists—and with good results. Its forecast record since it began corrupting its model in this considered fashion is a good bit better than it was in the early and middle 50s.

As it is represented by the present Michigan exercise, therefore, econometric model building already has gone a long way toward overcoming limitations with which I would have charged it a few years ago. But it is still far short of having surmounted its basic problem of excessive rigidity—that is, in effect, excessive simplification. To attempt to cram the myriad complexity of the economy into even a 32-equation model entails, as Suits is careful to emphasize, an heroic abstraction. This is evident if one considers the model's lack of nimbleness in adjusting to the sort of temporary and significant but unusual development that is forever cropping up and of which the looser model builder routinely takes account. For example, most opportunistic model builders, I should suppose, added a bit extra to their inventory investment estimates for the first quarter of 1962 to allow for some steel stockpiling and then shaved their second and/or third quarter estimates a compensating amount. The Suits model has no explicit, untinkered-with capacity for handling such refinements. Its limitations become most evident if one considers the stark simplicity of the theories of sector-demand determination that underlie some of its expenditure equations.

Indeed, I would urge sector-demand specialists who have not already done so to look carefully in Suits' March 1962 article in the *American Economic Review* at the demand functions for their own particular sectors—at the equations, for example, for automobiles, for other consumer durables, and for housing starts. They are apt to find themselves a bit amazed that a forecasting technique that indulges in such gross oversimplifications with respect to the particular sectors in which they are expert can produce such generally good GNP forecasts as the Michigan model has done in recent years. That it can, of course, is dramatic testimony to the importance in general forecasting of that quality which is econometric model building's particular strength—namely, the quality of internal consistency. Even when many of its sector legs rest on quite mushy foundations, a model of the economy whose income-distribution and receipts, expenditures, and savings relationships all are internally consistent, judged by past experience, has a pretty fair chance of hitting the aggregates. But this does not mean that mushy sector forecasting and an incapacity for encompassing the idiosyncrasies of a particular period are admirable qualities in their own right.

E. Opportunistic Model Building

It is almost a contradiction in terms to imagine the looser forms of model building as being self-sufficient with respect to the other techniques. For the very essence of this approach—the reason I call it "opportunistic"—is its scavenging quality. Opportunistic model building is a procedure for gathering data, information, and insights of just about any conceivably relevant kind and for assembling them, in some orderly manner, into a coherent and quantified statement of prospects. I already have mentioned this approach's particularly heavy dependence upon inputs of foreshadowing data; in addition, sensible practitioners have ravenous appetites for help of other kinds.

Nevertheless, as a kind of horrible example, one can conjure up an imaginary forecaster who might take some pleasure in thinking of himself as a model builder and would indeed express his outlook judgments in the form of a GNP breakdown. But his would be strictly a laundry-list style of forecasting. He would simply go down the sector list, making up forward estimates, one by one, by some intuitive process out of whatever mix of past data, current gossip, and recent comments in the business press he happened to have at hand. He would not even bother to avail himself of the foreshadowing data systematically. He would ignore the insights that the NBER leading indicators might give him into the timing of coming changes in general activity and the help that the leading monetary indicators could supply as to prospective money and credit conditions. He would simply put down his sector forecasts, tot them up, and call the sum his forecast. The entire theory of aggregate demand determination underlying his analysis would consist of the national-income accounting identity that the GNP equals the sum of its parts. His analysis would contemplate no intersectoral, no income-expenditure, and no asset-expenditure interactions. The only internal-consistency test to which it would submit would be one to make sure that the GNP components did, indeed, add up to the total. And his mathematical requirements would be limited, not just to arithmetic, but to addition and subtraction.

Although I have called the foregoing an imaginary horrible example, a good bit of the actual short-term forecasting being done today comes uncomfortably close to fitting this description. This serves only to prove that something fairly close to go-it-alone opportunistic model building is, indeed, possible. But it also, it seems to me, is almost self-evidently foolish.

III. THE OPPORTUNITY FOR SYNTHESIS

So much for my argument that none of our five major short-term forecasting techniques is an island—at least not a very successful island when a consolidation of the five is perfectly feasible. The case for consolidation already has been anticipated considerably in the case against separatism. Thus I propose to enlarge on it only briefly, and shall do so in a moment.

A. A Few Substantive Comments on Opportunistic Model Building

First, by way of an aside, I want to get in a few somewhat more explicit licks on the craft of opportunistic model building. These are intended mainly as discussion provokers; I shall put my points very sketchily and, in a couple of cases, vulnerably.

The Usefulness of a Capacity Concept. The most controversial of the points I want to make about model-building practice is that such analysis can be greatly assisted by the incorporation of an explicit capacity concept. One must grant, of course, that capacity is a fuzzy, ambiguous, imprecise, not directly measured variable. But it generalizes about characteristics of the economy that are objective, dated, and vitally important. In one guise or another it is an essential concept for the general forecaster if he is going to discharge his ultimate function, which is to predict the basic healthiness of economic activity in a coming period. For that healthiness will depend most pivotally not on the absolute level of output but on the relationship between output and normal productive capacity. Such is plainly the crucial consideration, for one thing, in the case of general price prospects. For it is quite impossible to formulate any working hypothesis about the price-output relationships that changes in demand will encounter during a forecast period without formulating, at least implicitly, some assumption about the level and growth rate of capacity during the period.

The prospective relationship of capacity to output, adjusted for cyclical variations in output per man-hour, in the labor force, and in average working hours, likewise is the pivotal consideration for unemployment forecasting. Thus, although a model-building group may keep its capacity estimates invisible to the naked eye, as, for example, Suits's group does at Michigan, implicitly they are present in one form or another if the group is attempting to do a comprehensive forecasting job. The best procedure, I think, is to bring the capacity estimates out into the open where they can be seen and be argued about.

The Need for Explicit Sector Income Estimates. A second practice that I would urge upon opportunistic model builders is the construction of a model that forces the analyst to make explicit the breakdown of the gross national income into net receipts of governments, net foreign transfers by government, gross retained earnings of business, and disposable personal income that he is setting over against his final-demand breakdown. For only by this means does one have a framework that facilitates allowance for the impacts of expenditures in one sector upon those in others and that permits very much of the internal-consistency testing that is model building's greatest potential advantage.

If I read him rightly, Friedman may raise an eyebrow at this suggestion on the ground that I am asking for models with built-in multipliers, and that it can be shown that in this economy during the past several decades "investment multipliers," or "autonomous sector" multipliers have in fact been highly unreliable phenomena. With Friedman's findings of fact I heartily agree; indeed, they are what I would expect since I believe that the stability characteristics of the economy have been considerably improved during the past generation, with most of that improvement taking the form of just such a weakening of the intersectoral cumulative mechanisms as Friedman's findings suggest. In particular, we beneficently have managed, partly thanks to the so-called built-in stabilizers, greatly to reduce the sensitivity of disposable personal income (DPI) to declines in the GNP.

However, the inference for forecasting practice that I draw from all this is not that multiplier effects therefore should be banned from outlook models but rather than they require considerably more elaborate treatment than our simplified textbook theories of a few years back seemed to suggest. In a little semiannual forecast exercise that we run at Indiana, for example, we do three things. First, we separate consumer durables from the rest of consumption and treat them as a quasi-autonomous sector of the same sort as housing or plant and equipment. This is on the thesis that the aggregate of consumer soft goods and services is a much more stable function of DPI than is total consumption. Second (and this is the newest wrinkle of the three in our practice) we nevertheless treat the relation between soft goods and services consumption as being cyclically variable within fairly narrow limits. Third, and most important, we explicitly forecast the ratios of DPI to personal income and of personal income to GNP, treating both of these also as being cyclically variable.

Thus, in effect, we systematically incorporate into the model a rather highly variable multiplier that, in particular, takes explicit account of the tax-less-transfers and retained-earnings leakages between GNP and DPI. Rightly or wrongly, we attribute most of the very good luck that we have had with the exercise the last two or three times around to the more careful efforts we have been making along these lines.

Inventories and Net Exports.   My other two substantive comments are far narrower in scope, and I shall no more than mention them. Both concern matters rather urgently in need of further investigation. First, it appears to me that our forecasting doctrines for inventory investment presently are in a state of some theoretical disarray. Having become rather thoroughly disenchanted with the practical usefulness of inventory-sales ratios as guides for inventory forecasting, many of us have become rather excited about the greater utility of new orders and order backlogs as indicators of prospective changes in manufacturers' inventories. In this we have followed the lead, for example, of the Duesenberry-Eckstein-Fromm model of a few years ago. The trouble, however, is that this new doctrine really makes sense only for those industries that produce to order, not to stock, and have little or no finished-goods inventory. Consequently, for improved inventory forecasting I suspect that we need a considerably more disaggregated approach than is now customary; we need to know a good bit more than published data presently reveal of the differing degrees to which different manufacturing sectors rely, on the one hand, upon order backlogs and, on the other, upon finished-goods inventories for cushioning the lags of their output behind their demand; knowing this, we need to forecast changes in manufacturing inventories by fabrication stages; and, I suspect, in the case of manufacturers' finished stocks as well as trade inventories we need to hark back to inventory-sales ratios but with renewed attention to inventory-cycle models.

The other point is simply that net-export forecasting is in a bad way because of the average forecaster's or forecasting group's inability to make any closely reasoned prediction of exports. With the passing of the dollar shortage it no longer is legitimate to assume that the volume of United States exports will be determined simply by the volume of dollars that the United States supplies to the rest of the world through its imports and its transfers abroad of public and private capital. But lacking this short cut, the general forecaster is left with an apparent but impossible need to predict demand developments the world over if he is to make a considered estimate of United States exports. Because of the comparatively narrow limits with which net exports move, the problem is not a particularly serious one for the aggregate domestic forecast. But if anyone can come up with a new legitimate short cut to export prediction, he certainly at least will ease the consciences of many of us.

B. Joining the Techniques Together

By way of conclusion, let me indicate how the five forecasting techniques upon which we have been focusing can sensibly complement one another. Perhaps this can be conveyed most succinctly by describing what I would regard as an ideal short-term forecasting exercise.

In the first place, this would be a group exercise. Outlook analysis is an activity, I think, in which the group has an inherent advantage over the lone wolf, partly because it benefits from a division of labor, partly because it must be considerably judgmental and gains from an effort to achieve a consensus. Second, it would be a continuing exercise. I frankly would become bored as a member of a staff that gave its uninterrupted attention to the business outlook, and there are comparatively few organizations that could afford a fairly elaborate staff that had this single function. However, we are conjuring up an ideal, and there is no denying the expertise that comes with daily immersion in the outlook problem. Third, it would be a rather highly structured exercise. The free-wheeling virtuosity of gifted seat-of-the-pants analysts always is impressive, but it also is commonly overrated, and it has very little transferability. One quality of an ideal forecasting organization would be a considerable ability to maintain continuity despite changes in personnel. Well-defined tasks, procedures, and analytical doctrines would all contribute to this end.

I would place at the head of such a staff a seasoned opportunistic model-builder with a good measure of forecasting experience, theoretical sophistication, and executive ability. I would associate with him three deputy directors, each of whom would have cognizance of the whole operation. One Friedman would be asked to nominate; one Geoffrey Moore or Arthur F. Burns would nominate; and the third would be a first-class econometrician whose professional sensibilities, however, did not bruise too easily. The balance of the staff would be composed mainly of specialists who were immersed in the lore and data of particular demand and/or industry sectors.

The format of my idealized exercise would be a simultaneous equation model—indeed, a far more elaborate model than that presently employed at Michigan—and all members of the staff would require the limited command of mathematics necessary for translating their views into the terminology of such a model and for comprehending its manipulation. The point here would be for the exercise to avail itself of the maximum internal-consistency insurance, and its feasibility would depend upon ready and continuing access to adequate electronic computer services.

The equations in the model, however, would be subject to constant tending. Variables (and, as necessary, equations) would be added or subtracted and parameters would be altered as fast as, and for whatever reason, the staff judged such changes appropriate. In fact, each equation would constitute a summary statement of the staff's presently operative forecasting doctrine for the particular demand sector or the particular income relationship involved. It would be the responsibility of each sector forecaster to keep his equation(s) in a continuing state of repair so that at any given moment the most accurate forecast of which the staff currently was collectively capable, with the help of a computer, could be cranked out of the model with minimum delay.

Foreshadowing data with built-in adjustments, where appropriate, along the lines that Modigliani suggests would figure very prominently as inputs into the model. Monetary and credit variables would be more explicitly knit into the model than has been customary with econometric models to date, with the leading monetary indicators being incorporated as lead devices for signaling later changes in the money supply and credit availability. Moreover, despite the realistic complexity that would be built into the model, the forecasting staff would not consider its findings to be inexorably bound to the model results. In particular, the NBER leading indicators would be used as an independent aid for timing prospective changes of course in the economy, a feat at which opportunistic model building is notoriously clumsy.

This, perhaps, is enough to convey the gist of what I have in mind. Few of us, probably, ever will work in circumstances that closely parallel the conditions just sketched. But at least we can strive for whatever intertechnique collaboration fits our particular scale of operations. We can recognize that not merely should the several respectable short-term forecasting techniques be able to coexist; they have far more to gain from outright alliance than they do from internecine bickering.

32.

Diverging Trends in the Shares of Nominal and Real Government Expenditure in GDP: Implications for Policy*

PETER S. HELLER

I. INTRODUCTION

A common trend throughout the world over the last 30 years has been the significant rise in the nominal share of public expenditure in total gross domestic product (GDP). This has often been viewed as verifying the theories propounded in the late 19th century by Adolph Wagner. Yet an analysis by Morris Beck of trends in real public expenditure in the industrial world reveals a considerably slower and less significant increase in the real share of public expenditure in total output. This has been particularly true for public consumption, as opposed to public transfers. In fact, Beck argues, in the period 1950–77 the real share of public consumption actually declined in a majority of developed countries.

The principal factor underlying this type of argument is that the observed statistical measure of the relative cost of providing government services and transfers, the government price deflator has been increasing

* *National Tax Journal* 34, no. 1 (March 1981), pp. 61–74.

more rapidly than the cost of other goods and services in the economy, such that the public sector has suffered a so-called adverse relative price effect (RPE) (i.e., the government price deflator has risen more rapidly than the GDP deflator). Yet the fact of an adverse RPE for the government sector raises far more serious conceptual, statistical, and policy questions than simply the validity of Wagner's law.

Specifically, what is the appropriate deflator for the activities of the public sector? How are such deflators actually calculated by different countries? Are Beck's results applicable to developing countries as well? What are the policy implications of differential movements in the share of real and nominal expenditure in total output? What do such movements imply about the demand for public services and the willingness of taxpayers to bear their costs? How should an adverse RPE be considered in budgetary planning?

This paper provides further analysis of some of these issues. Section II examines the role of a deflator for public sector activity and the problems that arise in calculating it. Section III provides additional comments on recent empirical analyses of real and nominal trends in public expenditure and examines recent trends among developing countries. Section IV explores the sources of an adverse RPE. Section V discusses the policy implications of these developments.

II. THE MEASUREMENT OF A DEFLATOR FOR PUBLIC EXPENDITURE

In discussing an adverse or favorable RPE, one must distinguish between past and future developments. The ex post RPE reflects the relative growth of the government price deflator and the GDP deflator over some past period. The ex ante RPE reflects the set of *anticipated* changes in the specific prices of the many goods and services that *could* be included in the government's budget relative to the changes projected for other goods and services in the economy. The ex post measure allows us to discern the difference between past real and nominal trends in expenditure and to compare the relative levels of public and private sector output. It ostensibly reflects the change in the cost of an unchanging basket of goods and services. The ex ante forecasting of the costs of public goods and transfers is an essential part of fiscal planning. It is directly analogous to a consumer taking account of relative price changes in determining his demand for different baskets of commodities. It allows the government decision maker to understand the financial and tax policy implications of alternative public programs and to guide choices among such programs and among technologies. Unlike the consumer, the government has some control over the RPE through its influence over the price it pays for certain goods and services. The possibility also exists for a change in the mix of goods and services purchased. It is important to make this distinction because one can too easily assume, from examination of past trends of a deflator, that an adverse RPE is an exogenous phenomenon over which the government has virtually no control. While much of the analysis of Beck's results focuses on the implications of trends in the ex post RPE, any discussion of the policy implications of an adverse RPE must focus on the ex ante concept.

The obvious starting point for determining past trends in real public expenditure and appraising the effect of any RPE is the calculation of an ex post deflator. In principle, this should measure the increase over time in the cost of providing a given basket of public sector output. The estimation of such a deflator involves many interesting issues, primarily because of the highly diverse character of public expenditure, ranging from the payment of salaries and the purchase of goods and services to different kinds of financial transfers. The last may include interest payments, consumption or production subsidies, income transfers to households, and subsidies to nonfinancial public enterprises or local governments. Most of the efforts of statisticians have been focused on developing a deflator to measure the cost to the government of purchasing the real goods and services traditionally labeled as public consumption or investment in a national income accounts sense. Only minimal attention has been paid to estimating a deflator for the totality of public expenditure, which requires a deflator for the non-GDP component of public expenditure. Equally important, the emphasis has been on estimating deflators to reflect the increase in the cost to government in its role as a *purchaser*. An equally valid point of view of the real cost of government purchases is the opportunity cost to the *taxpayer*. As we shall see, the policy implications of using a taxpayer-oriented deflator are very different from those obtained from the conventionally estimated deflator.

A short discussion on the methodology of computing the public consumption deflator provides some insight into the statistical and conceptual difficulties that arise. The UN guidelines for calculating public consumption in terms of the constant prices of a base period are an obvious starting point, since an aggregate public consumption deflator can then be derived. Public consumption includes principally wages and salaries paid to the civil service and the military and goods and services purchases from the private and external sectors. Such a measure should be based

> on the sum of estimates of real intermediate consumption and real primary inputs. . . . When compiling indicators of real primary inputs it would be desirable to take into account the consumption of fixed capital and changes in the mix of employees engaged in the various services. The adjustment of changes in the employee mix might be based on figures of average employ-

ment during the period of account or similar measures, coupled with base-period compensation per unit of work measurement, for various occupations and grades. *It is questionable whether reliable adjustments can be made for other factors contributing to labour productivity.* (Italics provided by author.)[1]

An analogous procedure could be used to estimate a deflator for public sector investement, as defined in the national income accounts.

In principle, the procedures used for calculating such a deflator, and the problems that arise, are similar to those involved in the calculation of a deflator for private consumption expenditure. The government, in its role as a purchaser, is buying both goods and services. As with the consumption deflator, the computation should presumably take account of changes in the quality of goods purchased and of changes in the productivity of purchased labor services. In practice, the latter is very difficult to do, especially for labor services. The difficulties of gauging changes in the efficiency and productivity of a teacher, bureaucrat, medical technician, or soldier should be obvious. Because of these difficulties, national accounts statisticians assume zero productivity growth for labor employed in the public sector. As a result, there is a clear bias toward an overestimation of the rate of growth of the government consumption and investment price deflators. Another problem that arises is that the use of a fixed basket of goods and services, and fixed weights for these, ignores the shifts in the mix of the consumption basket due to relative price changes. Choice of the base-year basket (a Laspeyres index) overestimates the effects of price changes on purchasing power, choice of the end year (a Paasche index) leads to an underestimation. This is a particularly serious problem when one considers the drastic changes that have occurred in the last 30 years in the types of programs for which the government is involved and in the types of goods and services it purchases. Beck's analysis relies on a Paasche index, and to this extent, there is a bias, in the index number procedure, toward underestimation of the deflator.

What is the appropriate deflator for government transfers, the other principal form of government expenditure? If one focuses on the recipient of the transfer, the deflator would measure the change in the price to the recipient of a given typical basket of goods and services. The estimated measure of real expenditure would indicate whether the transfer allows the recipient to purchase a different amount of real goods and services compared to an earlier period. This is, in effect, the approach described by Beck in his second article. He deflates government transfers by the price deflator for private consumption expenditure. Cor-

---

[1] Department of Economic and Social Affairs, Statistical Office of the United Nations, *A System of National Accounts, Studies in Methods,* Series F, No. 2, Rev. 3 (United Nations, New York, 1968), p. 144.

rectly applied, this approach would require that the many varied forms of financial transfers by the government be matched with deflators corresponding to the particular baskets of goods and services purchased by different categories of recipients. This is feasible as long as there is not too much variability in the composition of the particular recipient groups over time. Thus, for welfare or security payments, one could use a deflator such as the consumer price index (CPI), although separate deflators for the low-income or elderly groups of the population would be more appropriate.

To obtain a real measure of public loans, which are an important expenditure in developing countries, one could similarly examine the types of capital expenditure to which these loans give rise. One could distinguish loans to agriculturalists from those to industrialists. For transfers to state and local government, one would use separate state or local government consumption or investment deflators, reflecting the normal differences in the types of goods purchased at different governmental levels.

There remain, however, several classes of expenditure where the appropriate deflator is not obvious, such as interest payments, subsidies to nonfinancial public enterprises, etc. One could simply deflate such items according to an opportunity cost principle, namely, the increase in the price of the basket of other goods and services purchased by the public sector.

This approach, however, could easily be extended to develop an alternative deflator for public expenditure as a whole. For the opportunity cost of a particular type of public expenditure is not only defined in terms of other possible forms of public expenditure but also of other private expenditure by the taxpayer. While it is certainly of interest to know whether the real quantum of goods and services provided by the public sector has increased, the change in the real burden of the public sector to taxpayers is equally relevant.

In principle, one could construct a deflator according to the consumption basket of the "representative" taxpayer. The latter would represent the weighted consumption basket of taxpayers from different income groups, with the weights reflecting the share of the overall tax burden borne by each, a datum that could potentially be drawn from some tax incidence analyses. This would not necessarily be the same price index as the CPI or private consumption expenditure index in the National Accounts, depending on the regressivity or progressivity of the overall tax structure. Both of these consumption deflators are, however, obvious proxies in the absence of more refined data. What is compelling about this approach is that it is the mirror image of the earlier approach used for deflating financial transfers. If it is logical to deflate on the basis of the real value to the recipient of the transfers, it is equally reasonable to deflate on the basis of the real value to the taxpayer of the taxes paid to finance the expenditure.

Finally, we have noted that most statistical efforts have focused on the estimation of a deflator for government consumption. Since Beck's paper relies very heavily on the movement of this index for generating policy conclusions, it should be recognized that there are wide differences across countries in their procedures for deriving a deflator for government consumption. In practice, such procedures may be categorized according to whether the deflator is exogenously or endogenously estimated. In the endogenous cases, the deflator is derived from initial estimates of real public sector consumption, which are derived from specific quantity indices, such as the number of pupils in the school system, the number of patients in hospitals, indices of public employment, etc. In the most sophisticated exercise, one goes beyond raw quantity indicators and attempts to assess performance and real output within the public sector, thus obtaining indices of real output that may be inclusive of changes in productivity. Actual use of the latter procedure is quite unusual, having occurred only in the United Kingdom, and with unfortunate results.

The procedure whereby real output is itself derived by developing an exogenous price deflator series is far more common. The deflation procedure may occur at varying levels of detail. In some countries, total nominal government consumption expenditure is simply deflated by a particular proxy index or set of indices: namely, the retail price index, the wholesale price index (WPI) (or subcomponents of the latter), or an average of the urban and rural CPIs. In other countries, a distinction is made between purchases of goods and services and wages and salaries, with different procedures used for estimating the respective deflators for each class of expenditure.

In the latter countries, wages and salaries are generally deflated by some wage rate index, with little distinction being made between increases due to productivity change and increases to adjust for inflation or movements in productivity in the private labor market. Effectively, this imparts a downward bias to the observed measure of real salaries. Countries differ in the specificity with which the bundle of other purchased goods and services is decomposed for the purpose of estimating this component of the overall deflator. At one extreme, the CPI or WPI is used; at another, a detailed decomposition is made and the relevant commodity price series from the CPI or WPI used. Idiosyncratic procedures are common. What is important to emphasize is that there is sufficient heterogeneity in the procedures used to render cross-country comparisons of the trends in the share of government expenditure in GDP a questionable exercise. In fact, it is quite possible that the use of the same estimation procedure across countries would yield results quite different from those indicated in the Beck study.

III. OBSERVATIONS ON THE BECK RESULTS AND EMPIRICAL EXTENSIONS TO DEVELOPING COUNTRIES

The principal empirical focus of the Beck study was on the differential movement of the real and nominal shares of public expenditure in GDP. His results may be briefly summarized. For the 13 industrial countries under analysis for the period 1950–77, Beck notes a significant decline in the share of real public consumption in real GDP, in contrast to the increase in the nominal share of this type of expenditure. This reflected an adverse RPE for the public sector; for the median case, the total GDP deflator (P_y) rose by 369 percent over the period, in contrast to an increase of 681 percent for the government consumption deflator (P_g). On the other hand, the share in real GDP of total public expenditure, when deflated by a weighted government expenditure deflator, rose over the period, but wholly as a consequence of the sharp real growth in public transfers relative to GDP and of the fact that Beck's deflator for public sector transfers, the private consumption deflator (P_c), experienced a "favorable" RPE.[2]

A closer examination of Beck's statistical material suggests several other patterns in the development of public expenditure. First, Beck's own data suggests that the decline in the share of real public consumption in GDP for most of the countries in his sample appears to have ended in 1970 (Table 1); in 10 of the 13 countries the share of real public consumption increased between 1970 and 1977. Such increases occurred despite an adverse RPE of 1 to 3 percent per annum for public consumption and a significant increase in the real share of government transfers. Whether this represented the eventual reaction to the decline that took place over the previous 20 years or a more fundamental change in the responsibilities of the public sector cannot be readily determined from the aggregate data.

Second, the Beck results may be recast from the perspective of the taxpayer. As discussed above, one legitimate interpretation of the term "real" is in relation to what the resources applied to public expenditure could have purchased if devoted to private expenditure. If the private consumption expenditure deflator is used as a proxy for the deflator relevant to the "average" taxpayer, one observes a steadily increasing "real" share of both public consumption and total public expenditure in GDP over the period (Table 1). In fact, the increase in the real share of public expenditure in GDP in this sense has exceeded the growth of the nominal share in all of the countries in Beck's sample. While

---

[2] The deflator for total government expenditure is obtained by weighting the GDP deflators for private and public consumption by the shares of public transfers and consumption, respectively, in total public expenditure.

TABLE 1. Comparison of Nominal and Real Shares of Government Consumption and Total Government Expenditure in GDP, 1950–1977 (in percent)

	Nominal Shares				Real Share from Perspective of Government				Real Share from Perspective of Taxpayer			
	1950	1960	1970	1977	1950	1960	1970	1977	1950	1960	1970	1977
Government consumption												
Austria	11.3	12.7	14.6	17.4	11.3	8.7	7.5	7.5	11.3	14.4	17.0	20.2
Canada	10.3	13.9	19.2	20.3	10.3	11.4	12.7	11.6	10.3	14.9	21.6	25.1
Denmark	10.2	12.7	19.8	24.0	10.2	11.1	13.1	14.4	10.2	13.1	21.8	26.1
Finland	11.1	12.7	15.9	20.3	11.1	10.2	11.0	12.7	11.1	12.8	17.7	23.2
France	12.8	12.9	13.4	14.9	12.8	10.9	9.6	9.2	12.8	13.4	14.4	16.2
Germany, Federal Republic of	14.3	13.6	15.9	20.6	14.3	11.6	11.1	12.8	14.3	14.9	18.8	24.0
Greece	11.5	11.2	12.6	15.9	11.5	8.4	7.2	8.6	11.5	12.1	14.1	18.8
Ireland	13.7	12.4	14.8	18.6	13.7	12.3	13.2	15.5	13.7	12.7	16.7	21.3
Netherlands	12.2	13.4	16.3	18.3	12.2	11.7	9.3	9.0	12.2	14.5	19.0	21.1
Sweden	13.7	15.8	21.4	28.5	13.7	14.1	15.3	17.2	13.7	16.4	23.3	32.4
Switzerland	11.2	10.1	10.5	12.9	11.2	9.3	8.7	9.7	11.2	10.3	11.8	14.9
United Kingdom	16.3	16.5	17.7	20.3	16.3	14.2	13.3	14.4	16.3	17.5	19.1	22.2
United States of America	12.1	17.9	19.1	18.5	12.1	15.8	16.8	13.4	12.1	18.6	20.6	20.1
Total government expenditure												
Austria	21.2	25.6	33.1	39.8	21.2	23.3	28.7	33.7	21.2	28.9	38.2	46.5
Canada	19.0	25.7	32.2	36.9	19.0	23.8	27.3	32.3	19.0	27.4	36.2	45.9
Denmark	18.1	21.7	34.6	40.0	18.1	20.5	29.2	31.9*	18.1	22.5	36.7	45.7
Finland	20.4	22.2	27.6	35.6	20.4	20.5	24.0	30.4	20.4	22.7	30.9	40.9
France	26.7	30.2	34.7	41.8	26.7	28.9	32.3	38.5	26.7	31.4	37.2	45.5
Germany, Federal Republic of	28.3	28.2	31.6	41.3	28.3	27.6	29.6	38.3	28.3	31.0	37.2	49.6
Greece	19.6	17.8	22.4	29.0	19.6	14.2	18.3	24.6	19.6	17.9	25.2	34.2
Ireland	23.0	25.6	34.3	43.3	23.0	25.2	35.2	44.1*	23.0	25.6	38.8	49.8
Netherlands	23.9	27.8	39.6	52.3	23.9	26.6	36.4	48.3	23.9	30.0	46.0	60.4
Sweden	23.7	26.9	37.1	55.6	23.7	25.8	32.4	48.1	23.7	28.1	40.4	63.3
Switzerland	19.3	17.5	21.3	30.4	19.3	16.9	21.0	29.8	19.3	17.9	24.3	34.9
United Kingdom	30.2	29.0	33.3	40.8	30.2	27.8	29.8	35.8	30.2	30.8	35.5	43.6
United States of America	20.0	25.7	30.3	32.6	20.0	23.9	28.8	28.8	20.0	26.6	32.6	35.5

* Refers to 1976.

Source: The basic data for this table were drawn from Morris Beck, "Public Sector Growth: A Real Perspective," *Public Finance*, Vol. XXXVI, No. 3 (1979), pp. 313–56. The calculations in the last four columns were made by the author.

admittedly an imperfect measure of taxpayer's burden,[3] it suggests that the opportunity cost of the purchased public services has been steadily increasing.

In effect, this is no more than a restatement of the results obtained by comparing the government and private consumption deflators. There has been a steady decrease in the terms of trade between public and private consumption since 1950, a decrease even greater than that for GDP. In 1977, the price index for public consumption was 1.5 to 2.5 times higher than the price index for private consumption. As we shall discuss in Section IV, the reaction of the taxpayer as a consumer to the increasing relative cost of what are, admittedly, "essential" services is not surprising.

A third, and more puzzling aspect of Beck's results is the substantial amount of variability that exists across countries in the average adverse RPE that has characterized their public sector consumption over the period. Between 1950 and 1977, the average differential between the growth rates of the government consumption and GDP deflators ranged from 0.7 percent per annum in Ireland to 3.2 percent in Austria. In theory, there are two important factors that could explain this variability: differences across countries in the rate of growth of productivity and differences in the basket of goods and services purchased. Aggregate data do not allow an easy breakdown of such expenditure, but with the exception of the United States (due to its high military budget) one would not expect the latter factor to be a significant source of variability. An attempt was made, however, to relate the average annual RPE to the average annual productivity growth in these economies, but this also failed to explain the variability in the RPE.[4]

Equally puzzling is that there has been a decline in both the mean and variability of the RPE since 1970. During the period 1950–70, the adverse RPE averaged 1.9 percent per annum, with variance of 0.8 percent; between 1970 and 1977, the mean fell to 1.6 percent and standard deviation fell to 0.4 percent. This narrowing is also apparent from a tendency for countries to converge in their annual adverse RPEs.

There are two possible implications of these developments. It is possible that we are dealing with a statistical artifact, namely, that only

---

[3] There are obviously more sophisticated approaches to judging the increase in the real burden of taxation. At a minimum, one would want to relate total taxation to total personal income. At a more sophisticated level one would trace the increase in the net burden of taxes, net of transfer receipts, for different income groups over a period of time.

[4] A linear regression was estimated, both for Beck's sample and for a larger sample of developing countries, of the relationship between the average annual RPE (the differential in growth rate between the GDP deflator and the government consumption deflator) and the annual rate of real productivity growth. For Beck's sample of countries, the latter reflected output per man-hour; in the latter sample, it reflected output per member of the labor force. In both cases, the correlation coefficient was low (0.02 and 0.09, respectively) and insignificant.

TABLE 2
Percentage Growth of Deflators for GDP, Private Consumption, and Government Consumption in a Sample of Developing Countries, 1960–1975
(in percent)

Country	1960–1975			1965–1975			1970–1975		
	GDP Deflator	Government Consumption Deflator	Private Consumption Deflator	GDP Deflator	Government Consumption Deflator	Private Consumption Deflator	GDP Deflator	Government Consumption Deflator	Private Consumption Deflator
Argentina	7,043	12,400	6,567	2,400	2,930	2,281	1,076	1,199	987
Bolivia	324	290	282	236	208	232	171	165	190
Brazil	—	—	—	843	843	900	190	190	201
Colombia	590	687	533	282	331	256	136	139	135
Costa Rica	—	—	—	124*	166*	148*	92	114	111
Cyprus	75	206	52	62	130	51	40	52	46
Dominican Republic	93	101	78	66	92	49	54	47	48
Ecuador	—	—	—	149	230	135	95	99	89
Fiji	—	—	—	153	108	117	119	80	87
Ghana	274	225	282	159	162	120	81	73	78
Guatemala	56	67	61	58	47	63	46	40	52
Honduras	67	96	63	45	69	44	27	38	23
Hong Kong	102†	118†	76†	83	93	70	50	61	47
India	192	—	188	118	—	109	58	—	55

Indonesia	—	—	—	499	499	332	160	153	122
Iran	156	113	89	168	80	70	165	70	57
Kenya	—	—	—	69	49	118	54	29	105
Korea	1,063	1,105	1,090	383	525	367	136	154	146
Liberia	—	—	—	79	45	82	75	64	66
Malaysia	—	—	—	—	—	—	29‡	21‡	33‡
Mexico	153	177	143	113	140	103	79	89	72
Morocco	43	86	31	66	346	29	44	37	42
Nicaragua	85	143	102	78	85	99	56	39	68
Pakistan	191	231	191	162	191	162	113	136	116
Panama	70	97	63	59	82	58	46	35	55
Paraguay	156	116	150	106	66	103	87	55	86
Peru	344	449	315	203	232	188	83	82	90
Philippines	269	256	264	184	133	179	102	87	107
Singapore	60	65	59	54	50	53	46	43	42
Sri Lanka	—	—	—	57	78	65	30	35	39
Thailand	87	72	87	70	61	71	58	44	54
Tunisia	108	85	82	63	63	46	44	42	29
Uruguay	49,333	72,733	53,800	14,186	11,011	16,567	1,216	1,120	1,349
Zambia	67	104	98	68	80	85	7	51	44

* Calculated over the period 1966–1977.
† Calculated over the period 1961–75.
‡ Calculated over the period 1971–75.
Source: United Nations, *Yearbook of National Accounts Statistics*, Vol. I (1978).

in the last 10 years has there been a reasonable convergence in the degree of sophistication and comparability of methods to estimate this deflator. In the earlier period, the variability may have reflected differences in assumptions underlying the measure. The alternative implication is that there are genuine country-specific factors that lead to higher or lower adverse RPEs. The latter is certainly possible, but one would want to delve far more into the statistical bases for such differences before forming a judgment on this.

How does the Beck hypothesis fare when applied to countries in the developing world? In Table 2, the deflators for GDP, and private and government consumption, as derived from the National Accounts of 34 developing countries, are compared for the period 1960–75. Three points may be noted. First, over the entire period, Beck's observation that the government price deflator grew more rapidly than the GDP deflator is confirmed for 15 of the 24 countries examined. In 19 of these countries the terms of trade of government consumption vis-à-vis private consumption also declined. In terms of Beck's argument, it appears that the share of nominal public consumption in GDP rose (fell) more (less) rapidly than the share of real public consumption. However, unlike in the developed countries, there has been a marked shift since 1970 toward a "favorable" RPE. Between 1970 and 1975 $\dot{P}_g$ exceeded $\dot{P}_y$ in only 8 of these 23 countries, where $\dot{P}_g$ and $\dot{P}_y$ are the respective growth rates of the deflators for public consumption and GDP. $\dot{P}_g$ exceeds $\dot{P}_y$ in less than a third of the 32 countries for which data exist for the latter period. These countries were also different in that the private consumption deflator did not grow unambiguously at a slower rate than the public consumption deflator. Although this was true for three quarters of the countries between 1960 and 1970, the opposite was the case for 55 percent of the countries after 1970. This increase in the terms of trade between public and private consumption implies that from the taxpayer's perspective, any increase in the real share of public consumption in GNP is likely to be less onerous as a burden than is indicated by this measure of expenditure share.

Table 3 shows changes in the ratio of the nominal and real expenditure shares over different points of time. A value above 1 indicates an increase in the share. Any divergence between the change in nominal and real shares over a given period simply reflects the aforementioned change in the public consumption and GDP deflators. The trend in the share of real public consumption in GDP also does not support the Beck hypothesis, with at least two thirds of the countries displaying a constant or increasing share.

The reasons for the reversal in RPE cannot be readily determined but one obvious explanation is a lag in the adjustment to inflation by certain categories of government consumption expenditure, notably wages and salaries. Even if there is ultimately a full catch up of public

TABLE 3
Comparison of the Change in the Nominal and Real Shares of Government Consumption Expenditure in GDP, 1960–1975

Country	Ratio of Share in 1970 to Share in 1960		Ratio of Share in 1975 to Share in 1960		Ratio of Share in 1975 to Share in 1970	
	Nominal	Real	Nominal	Real	Nominal	Real
Argentina	1.04	0.71	1.11	0.68	1.07	0.98
Bolivia	1.21	—	1.29	—	1.07	1.23
Brazil	0.76	—	0.74	—	0.97	0.97
Colombia	1.23	1.09	1.19	1.04	0.97	0.95
Costa Rica	1.21	—	1.47	—	1.21	1.09
Cyprus	0.78	0.48	1.52	0.87	1.95	1.80
Dominican Republic	0.91	0.84	0.49	0.57	0.53	0.68
Ecuador	1.22	—	0.92	—	0.83	0.82
Fiji	1.18	—	1.00	—	0.86	1.04
Ghana	1.28	2.03	1.22	2.01	0.95*	0.99*
Guatemala	1.04	0.93	0.90	0.83	0.87	0.90
Honduras	1.07	0.99	1.21	1.03	1.13	1.05
Hong Kong	1.06†	0.98†	1.20	1.05	1.14	1.07
Indonesia	1.40†	—	1.59	—	1.13	1.16
Iran	1.72	—	2.30	—	1.34	2.07
Kenya	1.12‡	1.06‡	1.25	1.33	1.12	1.25
Korea	0.72	0.74	0.72	0.69	1.00	0.93
Liberia	0.90‡	1.04‡	0.98	1.12	1.09	1.08
Malaysia	1.33	—	1.42	—	1.07	1.09
Mexico	1.23	1.19	1.76	1.61	1.43	1.36
Morocco	0.94	0.93	1.21	1.27	1.29	1.36
Nicaragua	1.11	0.75	1.05	0.80	0.95	1.06
Pakistan	1.62	1.63	1.71	1.56	1.05	2.63
Panama	1.27	1.02	1.34	2.70	1.05	0.96
Paraguay	1.23	1.19	0.86	1.01	0.70	0.85
Peru	1.32	1.23	1.49	1.47	1.13	1.20
Philippines	1.06	1.03	1.23	1.27	1.15	1.24
Singapore	1.59	1.55	1.42	1.42	0.89	0.91
Sri Lanka	0.96†	0.89†	0.84	0.73	0.88	0.82
Thailand	1.16	1.15	1.06	1.13	0.91	0.98
Tunisia	1.03	—	0.86	—	0.83	0.88
Uruguay	2.11	1.33	1.87	1.27	0.89	0.95
Zambia	1.57	—	2.67	—	1.71	1.21

* End year used is 1974.
† Base year used is 1963.
‡ Base year used is 1965.
Source: United Nations, *Yearbook of National Accounts Statistics*, Vol. I (1978).

wage rates to inflation, the lags involved may statistically reveal a slower growth in the government consumption deflator than in the GDP deflator, relative to a given base period. Whether this will continue in a world where inflation is a deep-rooted, structural phenomenon is uncertain. The reversal was clearly not general, since it did not occur in the developed countries in Beck's sample. In any case, one would not expect the government deflator to get too far out of line with the GDP deflator because of such wage lags. There are limits to the size of the differential between public and private sector wages beyond which the impact on real productivity and morale in the public sector becomes particularly severe and the risk of corruption increases.

In his second paper, Beck constructed a deflator for *total* public expenditure as the weighted average of the deflators for public consumption and transfers. To extend such a methodology to developing countries requires the inclusion of capital expenditure, since such expenditure averages more than 30 percent of total public expenditure in these countries. Unfortunately, construction of such an index requires information on the economic composition of public expenditure, and there are no comparable cross-country disaggregated data bases available prior to 1970. However, the importance of using a weighted deflator rather than the simple public consumption deflator is apparent, even over the shorter period of four to five years.

Table 4, which is derived from data included in the IMF's *Government Finance Statistics,* shows the change in the share of total public expenditure in GDP, both in real and nominal terms, during the mid-1970s. Two deflators were used: a deflator for private consumption expenditure and a weighted index of the deflator for government consumption, total capital formation, and private consumption. For the latter, the weights are the shares in total public expenditure and net lending of (1) government expenditure on interest and on goods and services (including wages and salaries); (2) capital expenditure, capital transfers, and net lending; and (3) subsidies, respectively.

During the 1970s, there was some tendency among developing countries for the growth of the GDP deflator to exceed the growth of the deflator for government consumption. Given the composition of GDP it is obvious therefore that under such circumstances the private consumption deflator is likely to exceed that of the GDP deflator. As a result, there is also an inevitable bias for the weighted public expenditure deflator to at least fall between (if not exceed) that of the GDP deflator and government consumption deflators, since the weighted deflator draws on other deflators from the GDP accounts. In our sample of countries, the growth of the weighted deflator is so bounded in 17 of the 25 countries. In 5 of the remaining countries, the weighted deflator exceeds the GDP deflator. The obvious implication is that there will be an obvious tendency for the weighted public expenditure deflator to yield real shares that are closer to the nominal shares than would have been the case if the narrow government consumption deflator had been used.

This is also true for the countries in Beck's sample. For the period 1950–77, there was no more than a 25 percent differential between the total public expenditure deflator and the GDP deflator; this was in contrast to the differential between the public consumption and GDP

TABLE 4. Comparison of the Impact of Using Alternative Deflators on the Share of Total Government Expenditure in GDP (in percent)

Year	Country	Growth of:			Share of Total Government Expenditure in GDP		End Year	
		Government Consumption Deflator	Government Expenditure Deflator	GDP Deflator	Base Year	Nominal	Real Share A*	Real Share B†
1973–75	Brazil	74.5	68.6	74.5	16.1	18.2	18.0	18.2
1973–77	Costa Rica	117.0	95.8	110.9	20.5	20.1	20.8	19.3
1973–77	Cyprus	15.0	31.2	35.8	21.1	26.7	27.5	31.4
1973–77	Dominican Republic	–13.9	14.8	51.8	17.6	14.8	19.2	26.0
1973–77	Fiji	54.0	63.9	86.2	23.4	23.7	27.0	28.7
1973–77	Guatemala	54.8	68.1	72.5	9.5	10.6	10.9	11.8
1972–76	Honduras	26.4	31.8	31.3	15.2	18.5	18.5	19.3
1973–77	Indonesia	98.8	101.0	117.0	15.7	19.2	21.0	20.9
1973–76	Iran	65.1	66.4	102.4	27.1	41.2	50.1	50.5
1973–77	Kenya	40.7	56.3	77.7	20.7	20.0	21.8	24.9
1974–77	Korea	105.1	76.1	69.6	14.5	17.6	16.6	14.5
1974–77	Liberia	–12.6	18.2	32.9	20.2	26.1	29.4	39.7
1973–77	Malaysia	26.3	28.7	32.7	21.7	27.9	29.2	29.3
1972–76	Mexico	118.2	113.1	98.7	13.4	16.5	15.4	15.0
1973–77	Morocco	44.4	38.2	37.2	22.6	43.1	42.7	41.0
1973–77	Pakistan	65.3	72.6	64.9	12.9	14.6	13.9	14.6
1973–77	Paraguay	55.7	51.1	53.8	10.6	11.1	11.3	11.0
1974–77	Peru	118.0	126.7	121.5	16.0	16.1	15.7	16.3
1973–77	Philippines	93.0	86.9	66.7	14.0	13.4	12.0	11.6
1973–77	Singapore	30.2	30.2	21.8	15.6	20.6	19.3	19.3
1973–77	Sri Lanka	24.9	24.7	32.0	27.2	26.3	28.7	24.6
1974–77	Thailand	13.6	15.6	13.2	13.4	17.8	17.5	17.8
1973–77	Tunisia	30.5	40.2	34.9	25.8	35.0	33.6	36.1
1973–77	Uruguay	447.4	407.3	555.2	22.5	22.5	23.3	27.9
1973–77	Zambia	57.7	64.7	64.7	29.5	35.1	24.0	25.0

* Deflated using the weighted government expenditure deflator.
† Deflated using the government consumption expenditure deflator.

Sources: International Monetary Fund, *International Financial Statistics* and *Government Finance Statistics*; and United Nations, *Yearbook of National Accounts Statistics*, Vols. I and II (1978).

deflator, which averaged approximately 65 percent, and ranged from 18 percent to 133 percent.

IV. SOURCES OF AN ADVERSE RELATIVE PRICE EFFECT

The results of the previous section clearly imply that the RPE should be an important factor bearing on public policy decisions. There has been a steady erosion in the terms of trade of the public sector in virtually all the industrial countries over the last three decades. Although there has been a favorable shift in the RPE among developing countries in recent years, this is too recent a trend to be labeled as a clear structural change. What remains to be determined are the sources of the adverse RPE in the industrial countries and its significance for public policy.

Most attention in the literature has focused on the role of differential movements in labor productivity in the public and private sectors. In a seminal paper, Baumol predicted that the pressure on the public sector to maintain competitive wage rates, despite smaller productivity gains than in the private sector, would drive up unit labor costs in public sector programs, leading to precisely the type of adverse RPE effect witnessed above. Any attempt to maintain the real share of public output would then lead to an increase in the nominal share of the public sector in total output and an increasing differential between the real and nominal shares.

There is little doubt that the Baumol effect has some validity. Civil service rules and the particular characteristics of the production function for public sector output may limit the feasible range of alternative technologies and the possibility of productivity growth comparable to the private sector. Differences in the incentives and constraints facing public producers may also reduce their willingness or ability to respond to the adverse RPE for inputs through the use of alternative technologies. On the other hand, one might also note that the recent inflation has witnessed an erosion of real salaries in the civil service, in part as a form of incomes policy. Such lags in the growth of wages vis-à-vis the private sector suggest that a certain degree of wage disequilibrium in the labor market may exist, contrary to Baumol's assumption, and this would at least slow the deterioration of the RPE.

Furthermore, some of this RPE may be illusory, reflecting the recognized difficulties in measuring changes in public sector labor productivity and an understatement of the real output levels in the public sector. This would lead to an overstatement of the rate of growth of the price deflator for the public sector. This may be illustrated by a U.S. example. During the low inflation period of the 1950s and 1960s, U.S. budget planners prepared budget estimates based on the prices prevailing at the time the estimates were made, namely, one and a half years prior to the budget's execution. "It was argued that agencies should be able to offset price increases through increased productivity."[5] While there are no data to demonstrate that such productivity increases actually occurred, it is certainly plausible that certain technological developments (in word processing, photocopying, computers, etc.) facilitated their realization. If so, such productivity gains were not captured by the deflator.

How much of the adverse RPE is measurement error as opposed to a true productivity difference is not easily determined, but the answer is nevertheless critical for public policy. If government producers are able to innovate and respond as a normal private sector producer to changes in relative input prices, the whole controversy may be a statistical red herring. On the other hand, if an adverse RPE has actually occurred, then it indeed has significant implications for the character of the demand for public services and for future policies in public sector production.

The other obvious, but not very meaningful source of an adverse RPE is the higher proportion of purchases by the public sector of commodities and services produced by the private sector that are subject to relatively high rates of inflation. In the United States, for example, the increasing importance of public expenditure in the medical sector has contributed to an adverse RPE, since this sector has experienced one of the more rapid rates of inflation. There are two possible reasons why such goods and services are subject to higher rates of inflation: the first is simply that these are also the types of goods and services with lower potential rates of productivity growth and thus subject to the Baumol effect. Alternatively, it may be the character of their relationship with the public sector which fuels their relatively high inflation rates. If the effect of a substantial new involvement by the public sector is to increase demand sharply in a sector with limited capacity in the short run, this will drive up prices and produce rents to private sector producers.

Similarly, the rules under which the public sector purchases goods and services may not encourage efficiency in the private sector nor discourage demand in response to higher prices. Again, the U.S. experience in the medical care and defense sectors serve as ready examples. While there is nothing in principle that prevents the government from significantly altering its procurement procedures and its control over price movements in a sector (witness the National Health Insurance in the United Kingdom), such actions are, in fact, not common.

A final source of possible adverse RPE is the tendency toward indexation of some components of expenditure, particularly transfers. Such indexation occurs implicitly, in the choice of a deflator for such expenditure, since one usually assumes that an increase in the CPI or GDP deflator implies a reduction in the value of a given level of transfers.

---

[5] Office of Management and Budget, *Treatment of Inflation in the Budget,* (March 24–25, 1980) (mimeo.), p. 2.

This is the case whether or not such indexation is legislatively mandated. Thus, there is a built-in bias toward an adverse RPE, as the prices of some forms of expenditure are automatically growing at the level of one of the general price deflators. Whether there is, overall, an adverse RPE for total expenditure will therefore be determined by the degree of exogenous price changes in other purchased goods and services and of wages and salaries. If the latter is subject to the Baumol effect, and public sector wages do not lag, it is unlikely that one will observe a favorable RPE. What this suggests is the importance of an accurate estimator for the deflator for transfer programs, rather than the routine selection of a general price index. If one has reason to believe that the true price index for a transfer recipient rises at a slower rate than the CPI, this should be reflected in the formulation of the budget of the transfer program and in the statistical deflation procedure.

In summary, the adverse RPE derives primarily from (1) lower productivity growth in the public sector than in the private sector; (2) the tendency for the public sector to purchase goods and services from elements of the private sector experiencing relatively low productivity growth; (3) the increasing emphasis on the indexation of public transfers; (4) rigidities in the public sector production function that have limited the government's ability to respond to shifts in relative input prices; and (5) the inability of statisticians to measure correctly gains in productivity in the public sector.

V. POLICY IMPLICATIONS

What are some of the policy implications of an adverse RPE? Beck has taken the view that the public sector's real consumption has not grown appreciably as a share of total real output, and in fact has actually diminished in many industrial countries. The so-called Beck hypothesis is taken as a refutation of Wagner, at least as it applies to public consumption. Beck also argues that the growth in nominal shares has masked the decline in the provision of real essential services:

> The behavior of government consumption expenditures has important implications for the current controversy over the level of government spending. In real terms these outlays show a modest decline for the recent period, absolutely and as a proportion of GDP—on a nationwide basis. In many cities and states the decline has been substantial. State and local legislators' reacting to what is widely perceived as a taxpayer's revolt, may have in many cases jeopardized the public welfare in cuts in essential services."[6]

The implication is that the ire of the taxpayer is misplaced. Either there should be criticism of the rapid growth in transfer expenditure, one

---

[6] Beck, "Public Sector Growth: A Real Perspective," *Public Finance,* Vol. XXXVI, No. 3 (1979), pp. 313–56.

important source of the overall expenditure growth, or there should be greater "recognition" that there has not been a significant increase in the share of real services and that cuts in taxation would have to be matched by concomitant cuts in the level of real services that are provided.

Yet as we have argued above, the taxpayer's perception that the real burden of taxation has continued to rise is certainly valid. In many respects, what is most compelling about recent trends is that (1) the population is "willing" to buy such services at the higher effective real price; and (2) the adverse RPE creates difficult policy problems for the public sector decision maker.

Specifically, if the taxpayer as a consumer perceives that there has been a sharp increase in the relative price of public services, then some decline in the relative share of real goods and services purchased should be no surprise; of more interest is the fact that the nominal share rose as much as it did. This suggests that either (1) the perceived adverse RPE was less than measured or (2) the demand for public consumption was fairly price inelastic. In the former case, one is effectively arguing that the adverse RPE is a statistical artifact and is perceived as such. In other words, there has been a concomitant increase in the real share of public sector output corresponding to the increase in the nominal share. Productivity in the public sector has been actually higher than measured with significant increases in real output levels. The important policy question in this case is whether the increasing share reflects true public demand or a demand imposed by government decision makers. Subscribers to the various tax propositions in California would argue the latter.

For alternative (2) one also can raise the question of whether the inelasticity of demand is accepted or imposed on the population, but even where it is imposed, the policymaker is inevitably forced to confront the Baumol dilemma. There are clearly limits to the nominal share of the public sector in total GNP and these are effectively set by eventual increases in the price elasticity of demand for public sector services (for example, a "taxpayer revolt"), by a change in the mix of public sector output toward types of expenditure more in line with private sector output, or by technological changes in the production of public output. In this respect, one might view the increasing share of transfers as a rational approach by the public decision maker to the adverse terms of trade between public services and public transfers, although such transfers may not result in any more real services of the kind normally produced by the public sector.[7]

---

[7] Presumably, the cost to the private sector of producing goods comparable to the public sector is subject to the same types of wage-push pressure. As such, a transfer that maintains its value in terms of the GDP deflator, may still decline in real terms in terms of the basic services it can purchase.

Finally, there is little but "academic" consolation to the tax policy-maker in a shrinking size of the public sector in real terms while its nominal share in GDP continues to rise, for it imposes the need for a tax system equally elastic in nominal terms. This will prove a particularly serious problem for developing countries, where the share of progressive taxes, notably the income tax, is small and there is only limited potential in the foreseeable future, for expansion of such taxes.

If there are limits to the nominal share of taxes in GDP, there are only a limited number of options available to the public decision maker in response to true adverse trends in the RPE. Correct identification and analysis of such trends is absolutely essential for budget planning. In terms of substantive policy, short of allowing declines in the real share of output, one is forced to introduce innovations in the process of public sector production. Such innovations, which are not easy in any country, can include innovations in planning and budgeting, the introduction of more price-sensitive techniques in the evaluation of alternative project technologies, and reforms in procurement procedures. Once such innovations have been introduced, one must accept further adverse RPEs in the same way as one does other relative price changes, with associated shifts in relative demand.

33.

Forecasting with Econometric Methods: Folklore versus Fact*

J. SCOTT ARMSTRONG

INTRODUCTION

This paper is concerned with the use of econometric methods for forecasting in the social sciences. Although this is not the only use of econometric methods, it is one of the ways they are used; it is also the use that can most easily be validated. The paper examines only the predictive validity of econometric models. The importance of predictive validity has long been recognized by econometricians: "The ultimate test of an econometric model . . . comes with checking its predictions."

"Econometric methods" are defined in this paper as quantitative approaches that attempt to use causal relationships in forecasting. In particular, they refer to models based on regression analysis. This definition conforms to common usage of the term *econometric methods. Folklore* is used here to reflect what econometricians believe, as judged by what they do. *Fact* is based upon published empirical studies.

The first part of this paper draws upon evidence from social psychology to explain why folklore persists. Most of the evidence is based upon the behavior of people in general. However, there is evidence to suggest that scientists act as other people when testing their favored hypotheses.

Two examples of the discrepancy between folklore and fact are pro-

* *Journal of Business* 51, no. 4 (1978), pp. 549–63.

vided in the second part of the paper. These are only two of a number of possible examples, but they deal with two important questions. First, do econometric methods provide the most accurate way to obtain short-range forecasts? Second, do complex econometric methods provide more accurate forecasts than simple econometric methods?

The third part of the paper describes the method of multiple hypotheses. This method should help to overcome folklore.

THE PERSISTENCE OF FOLKLORE

Folklore persists because people who hold viewpoints on an issue tend to perceive the world so as to reinforce what they already believe; they look for "confirming" evidence and avoid "disconfirming" evidence. There is much literature on this phenomenon, commonly known as *selective perception*.

The tendency for intelligent adults to avoid disconfirming evidence was demonstrated by Wason. He provided three numbers (2, 4, 6) to subjects, and they were asked to determine what rule had been used to generate the three numbers. In order to gain additional information, the subjects were encouraged to generate other series of three numbers. The experimenter provided feedback on whether or not each new series was in agreement with the rule. What happened? The typical subject would think of a rule and then generate series that were consistent with that rule. It was unusual for a subject to try a series that was inconsistent with his own rule. Subjects who were told that their rules were incorrect were allowed to generate additional series. The majority of these subjects maintained the same rule that they had previously, but stated it in different terms. (It is like magic; it will work if one can pronounce it correctly!)

In cases where disconfirming evidence is thrust upon people, they tend to remember incorrectly. Fischhoff and Beyth, for example, found that subjects tended to remember their predictions differently if the outcome was in conflict with their prediction.

Wason's studies dealt with situations in which the person had no stake and no prior emotional attachment. When one has invested effort in supporting a particular viewpoint, the tendency to avoid disconfirming evidence would be expected to be stronger. The reward system in science encourages researchers to devote their energies to one viewpoint. The scientist gains recognition by being an advocate of a particular approach or theory. In such a case, the scientist can be expected to avoid disconfirming evidence.

Studies of scientists indicate that they are biased in favor of their own hypothesis. They interpret evidence so that it conforms to their beliefs. For example, in Rosenthal and Fode, experimenters were provided with two equivalent samples of rats, but they were told that one sample was gifted and the other was disadvantaged. In the subsequent "scientific tests," the gifted rats learned tasks more quickly than did the disadvantaged rats.

The above studies dealt with individuals rather than with groups. What happens when group pressures are involved—for example, when someone submits an article to be evaluated by his peers in the "marketplace of ideas"? What happens when learned societies, such as the Econometric Society, are formed to promote the advancement of the science? As the group pressures become stronger, one would expect stronger efforts to avoid evidence that disconfirms the group's opinions. Substantial literature shows how group judgment distorts reality. The study by Asch showed that most subjects would agree with the group that a given line B was longer than another line A, even though the reverse was obviously true.

In fact, the peer review process was studied in an experiment by Mahoney. A paper was sent to 75 reviewers. Some reviewers received the paper along with results that were supportive of the commonly accepted hypothesis in this group. Other reviewers received a copy of the identical study except that the results were reversed so that they disconfirmed the prevailing hypothesis. Reviewers with confirming results thought the study was relevant and methodologically sound. Reviewers with disconfirming results thought the study was not relevant and that the methodology was poor. The confirming paper was recommended for publication much more frequently.

The studies cited above provide only a portion of the evidence. Other relevant studies include Pruitt, Geller and Pitz, Chapman and Chapman, Rosenthal and Rosnow, and Greenwald. This evidence implies that scientists avoid disconfirming evidence. This tendency is stronger when the position is adopted by a group.

It is not surprising then, that great innovations in science have often met with resistance. There is little reason to expect that "modern science" is different. For illustration, one might examine the treatment of Immanuel Velikovsky, a case that is being followed closely by sociologists. This treatment was not the result of a lack of interest or a lack of time; rather it was an active attempt to suppress Velikovsky's theories and to discredit him.

Social scientists are expected to be more prone to group opinion than are physical scientists. Thus, they would experience serious difficulties in adopting new findings. Are econometricians also resistant to innovations? In a critique of what is being done by econometricians, Bassie implies that they are. He claims that econometricians display much conformity to their preconceptions.

Two examples from econometrics are examined below. These examples were selected because they represent an important part in the life of an econometrician—and also because there seem to be discrepancies between folklore and fact.

SHORT-RANGE FORECASTING

Most textbooks on econometrics discuss short-range forecasting. Although seldom stated, the implication is that econometric methods provide more accurate short-range forecasts than other methods. Brown asserted that econometric models were originally designed for short-range forecasting. Kosobud, in a paper on short-range forecasting, referred to ". . . the growing body of evidence on the predictive value of econometric models." In a review of a book on short-range economy-wide forecasting, Worswick said that "the value of econometric models in short-term forecasting is now fairly generally recognized." Various econometric services sell short-range forecasts, and one of their claims is improved accuracy. The press publishes short-range forecasts from well-known econometric models with the implication that these models will provide accurate forecasts.

Survey of Econometricians

In order to go beyond the indirect evidence cited in the preceding paragraph, a questionnaire was mailed to experts in econometrics in late 1975. The survey was based on a convenience sample. Of 56 questionnaires that were sent out, 21 were completed. An additional eight were returned incomplete by respondents who said they lacked the necessary expertise. Thus, replies were received from over 40 percent of the experts. The respondents were from some of the leading schools in econometrics—for example, MIT, Harvard, Wharton, Michigan State—and from well-known organizations that sell econometric forecasts. Many of the respondents are recognized as leading econometricians.

The questionnaire asked, "Do econometric methods generally provide more accurate or less accurate forecasts than can be obtained from competitive methods for short-term forecasting in the social sciences? Or is there no difference in accuracy?" A set of definitions was also provided.[1]

---

[1] These definitions were as follows: "(a) 'Econometric methods' include all methods which forecast by explicitly measuring relationships between the dependent variable and some causal variables. (b) 'Competitive methods' would include such things as judgment by one or more 'experts' or extrapolation of the variable of interest (e.g., by relating the variable to 'time' such as in autoregressive schemes). (c) By 'do,' we mean that comparisons should be made between methods which appear to follow the best practices which are available at the current time. In other words, the methods should each be applied in a competent manner. (d) 'Short-term' refers to time periods during which changes

The results of the survey, presented in Table 1, were that 95 percent of the experts agreed that predictions from econometric models are more accurate.

TABLE 1
Survey of Experts on Accuracy
of Short-Range
Econometric Predictions
($N = 21$)

Econometric Predictions Rated	Percentage
Significantly more accurate	33
Somewhat more accurate	62
No difference (or undecided)	0
Somewhat less accurate	0
Significantly less accurate	5

Respondents were asked how much confidence they had in their opinion on accuracy. Confidence was rated on a scale from 1 (no confidence) to 5 (extremely confident). (If the question was not clear to respondents, they were instructed to report a low level of confidence.) The average response was about 4. No one rated confidence lower than 3.0. Those who responded with "significantly more accurate" had the highest confidence level.

Another question asked how the respondent would rate himself ". . . as an expert on applied econometrics." Eight respondents rated themselves as "very much of an expert," six as "fairly expert," four as "somewhat of an expert," and two felt that they were "not much of an expert" (there was one nonresponsive on this question). Those who rated themselves as more expert felt that econometric methods were more accurate: Five of the eight who rated themselves as "very much of an expert" felt that econometric methods were significantly more accurate, a rating that was significantly higher than the ratings by the other respondents ($P < .05$ using the Fisher Exact Test).

In general, the survey supported the anecdotal evidence. Experts are confident that short-range econometric predictions are more accurate than predictions from other methods.

---

are relatively small. Thus, for forecasts of the economy, changes from year to year are rather small, almost always less than 10 percent. For some situations, however, one-year changes may be substantial. (e) 'Forecasts' refer to unconditional or *ex ante* forecasts only. That is, none of the methods shall use any data drawn from the situation which is being forecast. Thus, for time series, only data prior to time t could be used in making the forecasts. (f) The 'social sciences' would include economics, psychology, sociology, management, and so on. In short, any area where the behavior of people is involved."

Empirical Evidence

Turning to "fact," an examination was made of all published empirical studies that I could find in the social sciences. This survey was conducted primarily by examining references from key articles and by searching through journals. Respondents to the expert survey were asked to cite evidence, but this yielded few replies. Finally, early drafts of this paper were presented at conferences and were circulated for comments over a period of four years; this approach did lead to additional studies. The studies are summarized below.

Christ provided disconfirming evidence on the accuracy of econometric predictions. In the 1951 study, econometric forecasts were better than "no change" forecasts on six occasions and worse on four. These were conditional or *ex post* forecasts; nevertheless, the results were not encouraging. The reaction to these findings was similar to previously mentioned occasions when disconfirming evidence was thrust upon scientists. Two of the discussants for Christ's paper were Lawrence Klein and Milton Friedman. Klein, whose model had been examined by Christ, stated that ". . . a competent forecaster would have used an econometric model . . . far differently and more efficiently than Christ used his model." Friedman, however, was receptive. He said that additional evidence would tend to strengthen Christ's conclusion and that ". . . the construction of additional models along the same general lines [as Klein's model] will, in due time, be judged failures."

Additional evidence on the predictive validity of econometric methods since Christ's papers is described here. Most of these studies are recent. Some are only of a suggestive nature because they compare ex post predictions of econometric models with ex ante predictions from alternative methods. Comparisons between extrapolations and ex post econometric forecasts were made by Kosobud, Cooper, Nelson, Elliott, Granger and Newbold, Narasimham, Castellino, and Singpurwalla, Levenbach, Cleary, and Fryk, and Ibrahim and Otsuki. Extrapolations provided better forecasts than the econometric methods in all studies except Kosobud's and Levenbach's. In Levenbach's, there was a tie for the one-year forecast, and the econometric model was better for the two-year forecast. None of these eight studies claimed to find a statistically significant difference. A comparison between ex post econometric forecasts and judgmental forecasts was carried out by Kosobud, Fair, Haitovsky, Treyz, Su, and Rippe and Wilkinson. Although the econometric forecasts were superior in all but Rippe and Wilkinson, none of these studies reported on statistical significance. However, sufficient data were provided in the Rippe and Wilkinson study to allow for such a test; my analysis of their results indicated that the econometric forecasts were significantly poorer than the judgmental forecasts. Thus, the analyses of 13 ex post studies with 14 comparisons did not provide evidence that econometric methods were superior.

To obtain direct evidence on the short-range predictive validity of econometric methods, a review was made of studies involving *ex ante* or unconditional forecasts. To qualify for inclusion, a study must have compared econometric and alternative methods where each was carried out in a competent manner. The question of when a method was competently applied created some difficulty. The major effect of this restriction was to rule out studies where the alternative model was a "no-change" extrapolation. Some studies were retained, although the alternative models could have been improved.

In all, 12 studies involving 16 comparisons were found. These studies are summarized in Table 2. The criteria were taken from each study. In other words, they were the most appropriate criteria in the opinion of the researchers who did each study. Efforts were made to test for statistical significance where this had not been done in the published study. In general, serious difficulties were encountered; most of these studies did not provide sufficient data, others failed to use comparable time periods, and still others suffered small sample sizes. The most striking result was that *not one study was found where the econometric method was significantly more accurate.* Nor did the econometric method show any general superiority: Six comparisons showed the econometric method to be superior, three suggested no difference, and seven found that it was inferior.

To guard against biases that may have been held by the author and to ensure that this study could be replicated, two research assistants coded a sample of three studies. The coding was done independently (i.e., the coders did not meet each other) and it was done blindly (i.e., the coders were not aware of the hypotheses in this study). In each of the four comparisons from these studies, there was perfect agreement among the author and the two raters. In addition, five of the ex post prediction studies were coded. The only exception to perfect agreement occurred when one of the coders classified the econometric models as superior to extrapolation in Granger and Newbold. The agreement between the two raters and me (on eight out of nine comparisons) provides evidence that the ratings were reliable.

The 16 comparisons of predictive validity were in agreement with the 14 ex post comparisons. Econometric forecasts were not found to be more accurate.

SIMPLE VERSUS COMPLEX ECONOMETRIC METHODS

"Progress" in econometric methods appears to be reflected by an increase in complexity in the methods used to analyze data. Leser noted long-term tendencies toward the use of more variables, more equations, more complex functional forms, and more complex interactions among the variables in econometric models. This increase in complexity can be observed by examining various issues of *Econometrica* since 1933 or

TABLE 2
Accuracy of Econometric Methods for Short-Term Forecasting

Relative Accuracy of Econometric Methods	Source of Evidence	Forecast Situation	Alternative Forecasting Method	Criteria for Accuracy (RMSE = root mean square error; MAPE = mean absolute percentage error)	Test of Statistical Significance
	—	—	—	—	—
Significantly more accurate (P < .05)					
More accurate	Sims (1967)	Dutch economic indicators	Extrapolation	RMSE	None
	Ash and Smyth (1973)	U.K. economic indicators	Extrapolation	Theil's U	None
	McNees (1974)	U.S. economic indicators	Extrapolation	RMSE	None
	McNees (1974)	U.S. economic indicators	Judgmental	RMSE	None
	Haitovsky et al. (1974, table 7.3)	U.S. economic indicators	Judgmental	Average absolute error	None
No difference	Christ (1975)	U.S. economic indicators	Extrapolation	RMSE	None
	Sims (1967)	Norwegian economic indicators	Extrapolation	RMSE	None
	Ridker (1963)	Norwegian economic indicators	Extrapolation	(Five criteria used)	None
Less accurate	Christ (1975)	U.S. economic indicators	Judgmental	RMSE	None
	Vandome (1963)	U.K. economic indicators	Judgmental	Percentage changes	None
	Vandome (1963)	U.K. economic indicators	Extrapolation	MAPE	Armstrong
	Naylor et al. (1972)	U.S. economic indicators	Extrapolation	Average absolute error	None
	McNees (1975)	U.S. economic indicators	Judgmental	Theil's U	None
	Cooper and Nelson (1975)	U.S. economic indicators	Extrapolation	RMSE/Theil's U	Armstrong
	Liebling, Bidwell, and Hall (1976)	Nonresidential investment	Judgmental	MAPE	None
Significantly less accurate (P < .05)	Markland (1970)	Inventory control	Extrapolation	Coefficient of variation	Armstrong

by examining textbooks. The inference is that, because more complex procedures provide more realistic ways to represent the real world, they should yield more accurate forecasts.

Some researchers imply that complexity will lead to greater accuracy. For example, Suits states ". . . clearly the fewer the equations the greater must be the level of aggregation and the less accurate and useful the result." Of course, not all econometricians believe this. Bassie proposed a general rule, "the more a function is complicated by additional variables or by nonlinear relationships, the surer it is to make a good fit with past data and the surer it is to go wrong sometime in the future."

Survey of Econometricians

To gain further information on whether experts believe that increased complexity in econometric models leads to more accurate forecasts, my previously mentioned mail survey asked: "Do complex methods generally provide more accurate or less accurate forecasts than can be obtained from less complex econometric methods for forecasting in the social sciences?—or is there no difference in accuracy?" As shown in Table 3, there was substantial agreement on the value of complexity; 72 percent of the experts agreed and only 9 percent disagreed. The experts were confident in their ratings on the value of complexity. The average confidence level was 4.0 (where $5 =$ "Extremely confident").

TABLE 3
**Survey of Experts on Complexity
and Accuracy**
($N = 21$)

Complex Methods Rated	Percentage
Significantly more accurate	5
Somewhat more accurate	67
No difference (or undecided)	19
Somewhat less accurate	9
Significantly less accurate	0

Many factors could affect the relationship between complexity and accuracy. For example, Schmidt, working with psychological data, found simple unit weights to be superior to regression weights for small sample sizes where there were many predictors. Furthermore, the relationship may not be a linear one; that is, complexity up to a modest level might be desirable, and beyond that it could be undesirable.

A specific question asked the experts to make any qualifications they felt important in assessing the relationship. Most respondents did qualify their answers, but it was difficult to find factors that were mentioned by more than one person.

Empirical Evidence

To assess the value of complexity in econometric methods, an examination was made of all published empirical evidence that I could find in the social sciences. Some studies provided indirect evidence on the value of complexity. McLaughlin examined the accuracy of forecasts from 12 econometric services in the United States. These forecasts were made by models that differed substantially in complexity. There were no reliable differences in accuracy among these models: The rankings of accuracy for the models in 1971 were negatively correlated with those for 1972. If there are no reliable differences, then no differences would be found between accuracy and complexity. I reanalyzed data from the study by Jorgenson, Hunter, and Nadiri and found a perfect negative correlation between complexity of the four models (ranked by the number of variables in the model) and the stability of the regression coefficients from one period to the next; this lack of stability for more complex methods would suggest a loss in predictive validity. Friend and Taubman asserted their simple model was superior to more complex models. Fair found little difference between his simple model and the more complex Wharton model in a test of ex post predictive validity.

Direct evidence on the value of complexity was sought by using only studies with ex ante forecasts. Each of the models, whether simple or complex, was done in a competent manner. The results of this literature survey are summarized in Table 4.

To determine whether the coding of the studies in Table 4 was reliable, 8 of the 11 studies (all but Johnston and McNeal, Grant and Bray, and McNees) were independently coded by two research assistants. The coding was blind in that the assistants were unaware of the hypotheses. Discrepancies were noted on only 2 of these studies; one assistant coded Dawes and Corrigan to show that more complex methods were superior, and the other assistant reported complexity to be superior in Wesman and Bennett. The studies in Table 4 suggest that complexity and accuracy are not closely related. No study reported a significant positive relationship between complexity and accuracy. Overall, 7 comparisons favored less complexity and 4 favored more complexity.

The 11 studies that assessed provided validity directly were in agreement with the 5 studies that provided indirect evidence: Added complexity did not yield improvements in accuracy. The empirical evidence does not support the folklore in this area.

MULTIPLE HYPOTHESES: AN ALTERNATIVE RESEARCH STRATEGY

The first part of this paper suggested that econometricians often act as advocates; they attempt to find evidence to support their viewpoint. Furthermore, group opinion is often used to judge truth. Under such

TABLE 4
Accuracy of Simple versus Compex Methods

Relative Accuracy of Complex Methods / Source of Evidence	Forecast Situation	Criterion for Accuracy	Nature of Comparison	Test of Statistical Significance
Significantly more accurate (P < .05)				
More accurate	—	—	—	—
Stuckert (1958)	Academic performance	Percent correct	Unit weights versus regression	None
McNees (1974)	GNP	Theil coefficient; RMSE, mean absolute error	Small versus large models	None
Grant and Bray (1970)	Personnel	Correlation coefficient	Unit weights versus regression	Armstrong
Johnston and McNeal (1964)	Medicine	Correlation coefficient	Unit weights versus regression	Authors
No difference	—	—	—	—
Less accurate				
Dawes and Corrigan (1974)	Academic performance, simulated data, psychiatric ratings	Correlation coefficient	Unit weights versus regression	Armstrong
Lawshe and Shucker (1959)	Academic performance	Percent correct	Unit weights versus regression	None
Reiss (1951)	Criminology	Percent correct	Few versus many causal variables	None
Wesman and Bennett (1959)	Academic performance	Correlation coefficient	Unit weights versus regression	None
Scott and Johnson (1967)	Personnel selection	Percent correct, correlation coefficient	Unit weights versus regression	None
Significantly less accurate (P < .05)				
Claudy (1972)	Simulated data (typical of psychological data)	Correlation coefficient	Unit weights versus regression	Armstrong
Summers and Stewart (1968)	Political judgments	Correlation coefficient	Linear versus nonlinear models	Armstrong

conditions, it is likely the beliefs will persist even if unsupported by empirical evidence.

An alternative to the use of advocacy is to adopt the method of multiple hypotheses. Here, each scientist examines two or more reasonable hypotheses (or methods) at the same time. The role of the scientist is to determine which of the methods is most useful in the given situation. When two or more reasonable hypotheses are studied, it is less likely that the scientist will feel a bias in favor of "his" hypothesis—they are all "his" hypotheses. The orientation of the scientist is changed from one where he seeks to confirm a hypothesis to one where he seeks to disconfirm one or more hypotheses. Because the various hypotheses are tested within each study, there is less need to rely upon the opinions of other experts. The method of multiple hypotheses should help researchers to make more effective use of disconfirming evidence.

Although the method of multiple hypotheses would appear to be less prone to selective perception, and thus superior to the use of advocacy, surprisingly little evidence is available on this issue. This evidence, summarized in Armstrong, provides modest support for multiple hypotheses over advocacy. Most surprising again was the lack of evidence to support advocacy, the research strategy that appears to be most common among social scientists.

CONCLUSIONS

Certain hypotheses about econometric methods have been accepted for years despite the lack of evidence. Ninety-five percent of the experts agreed that econometric methods are superior for short-range forecasting. An examination of the empirical literature did not support this belief: Econometric forecasts were not shown to be significantly better in any of the 14 ex post and 16 ex ante tests. Furthermore, there was no tendency toward greater accuracy over these 30 tests. Similarly, 72 percent of the experts felt that complexity contributed to accuracy, but the examination of the literature did not support such a belief: Complex models were not significantly better in any of the 5 indirect and 11 direct tests.

Thrusting disconfirming evidence upon others provides an ineffective way of changing attitudes. Econometricians are more likely to be convinced by their own studies. The use of the method of multiple hypotheses provides a rational way for econometricians to test their beliefs.

In one sense the situation is encouraging. Twenty-three studies using the method of multiple hypotheses were found (see Tables 2 and 4). These studies are becoming more common; the oldest study was published in 1951 and almost half were published since 1970. This trend in research strategy should be useful in distinguishing folklore from fact.

34.

Input-Output Economics*

WASSILY W. LEONTIEF

If the great 19th-century physicist James Clerk Maxwell were to attend a current meeting of the American Physical Society, he might have serious difficulty in keeping track of what was going on. In the field of economics, on the other hand, his contemporary John Stuart Mill would easily pick up the thread of the most advanced arguments among his 20th-century successors. Physics, applying the method of inductive reasoning from quantitatively observed events, has moved on to entirely new premises. The science of economics, in contrast, remains largely a deductive system resting upon a static set of premises, most of which were familiar to Mill and some of which date back to Adam Smith's *The Wealth of Nations*.

Present-day economists are not universally content with this state of affairs. Some of the greatest recent names in economics—Léon Walras, Vilfredo Pareto, Irving Fisher—are associated with the effort to develop quantitative methods for grappling with the enormous volume of empirical data that is involved in every real economic situation. Yet such methods have so far failed to find favor with the majority of professional economists. It is not only the forbidding rigor of mathematics; the truth is that such methods have seldom produced results significantly superior to those achieved by the traditional procedure. In an empirical science, after all, nothing ultimately counts but results. Most economists therefore continue to rely upon their "professional intuition" and "sound judgment" to establish the connection between the facts and the theory of economics.

In recent years, however, the output of economic facts and figures by various public and private agencies has increased by leaps and bounds. Most of this information is published for reference purposes, and is unrelated to any particular method of analysis. As a result we have in economics today a high concentration of theory without fact on the one hand, and a mounting accumulation of fact without theory on the other. The task of filling the "empty boxes of economic theory" with relevant empirical content becomes every day more urgent and challenging.

This article is concerned with a new effort to combine economic facts and theory known as "interindustry" or "input-output" analysis. Essentially it is a method of analysis that takes advantage of the relatively stable pattern of the flow of goods and services among the elements of our economy to bring a much more detailed statistical picture of the system into the range of manipulation by economic theory. As such, the method has had to await the modern high-speed computing machine as well as the present propensity of government and private agencies to accumulate mountains of data. It is now advancing from the phase of academic investigation and experimental trial to a broadening sphere of application in grand-scale problems of national economic policy. The practical possibilities of the method are being carried forward as a cooperative venture of the Bureau of Labor Statistics, the Bureau of Mines, the Department of Commerce, the Bureau of the Budget, the Council of Economic Advisers and, with particular reference to procurement and logistics, the Air Force. Meanwhile the development of the technique of input-output analysis continues to interest academic investigators here and abroad. They are hopeful that this method of bringing the facts of economics into closer association with theory may induce some fruitful advances in both.

Economic theory seeks to explain the material aspects and operations of our society in terms of interactions among such variables as supply and demand or wages and prices. Economists have generally based their analyses on relatively simple data—such quantities as the gross national product, the interest rate, price and wage levels. But in the real world things are not so simple. Between a shift in wages and the ultimate working out of its impact upon prices there is a complex series of transactions in which actual goods and services are exchanged among real people. These intervening steps are scarcely suggested by the classical formulation of the relationship between the two variables. It is true, of course, that the individual transactions, like individual atoms and molecules, are far too numerous for observation and description in detail. But it is possible, as with physical particles, to reduce them to some kind of order by classifying and aggregating them into groups. This is the procedure employed by input-output analysis in improving the grasp of economic theory upon the facts with which it is concerned in every real situation.

The essential principles of the method may be most easily comprehended by consulting the input-output table in Figure 1. This table summarizes the transactions which characterized the U.S. economy during the year 1947. The transactions are grouped into 42 major departments of production, distribution, transportation, and consumption, set up on a matrix of horizontal rows and vertical columns. The horizontal rows of figures show how the output of each sector of the economy is distributed among the others. Conversely, the vertical columns show how each sector obtains from the others its needed inputs of goods and services. Since each figure in any horizontal row is also a figure in a vertical column, the output of each sector is shown to be an input in some other. The double-entry bookkeeping of the input-output table thus reveals the fabric of our economy, woven together by the flow of trade which ultimately links each branch and industry to all others. Such a table may of course be developed in as fine or as course detail as the available data permit and the purpose requires. The present table summarizes a much more detailed 500-sector master table which has just been completed after two years of intensive work by the Interindustry Economics Division of the Bureau of Labor Statistics.

For purposes of illustration let us look at the input-output structure of a single sector—the one labeled "primary metals" (sector 14). The vertical column states the inputs of each of the various goods and services that are required for the production of metals, and the sum of the figures in this column represents the total outlay of the economy for the year's production. Most of the entries in this column are self-explanatory. Thus it is no surprise to find a substantial figure entered against the item "products of petroleum and coal" (sector 10). The design of the table, however, gives a special meaning to some of the sectors. The outlay for "railroad transportation" (sector 23), for example, covers only the cost of hauling raw materials to the mills; the cost of delivering primary metal products to their markets is borne by the industries purchasing them. Another outlay requiring explanation is entered in the trade sector (sector 26). The figures in this sector represent the cost of distribution, stated in terms of the trade margin. The entries against trade in the primary metals column, therefore, cover the middleman's markup on the industry's purchases; trade margins on the sale of primary metal products are charged against the consuming industries. Taxes paid by the industry are entered in the row labeled "government" (sector 40), and all payments to individuals, including wages, salaries and dividends, are summed up in the row labeled "households" (sector 42). How the output of the metals industry is distributed among the other sectors is shown in row 14. The figures indicate that the industry's principal cus-

FIGURE 1
The Exchange of Goods and Services in the United States for the Year 1947

INDUSTRY (columns 1–23)

| 1 AGRICULTURE AND FISHERIES | 2 FOOD AND KINDRED PRODUCTS | 3 TEXTILE MILL PRODUCTS | 4 APPAREL | 5 LUMBER AND WOOD PRODUCTS | 6 FURNITURE AND FIXTURES | 7 PAPER AND ALLIED PRODUCTS | 8 PRINTING AND PUBLISHING | 9 CHEMICALS | 10 PRODUCTS OF PETROLEUM AND COAL | 11 RUBBER PRODUCTS | 12 LEATHER AND LEATHER PRODUCTS | 13 STONE, CLAY AND GLASS PRODUCTS | 14 PRIMARY METALS | 15 FABRICATED METAL PRODUCTS | 16 MACHINERY (EXCEPT ELECTRIC) | 17 ELECTRICAL MACHINERY | 18 MOTOR VEHICLES |

INDUSTRY PRODUCING

Row	1	2	3	4	5	6	7	8	9	10	11	12	13	14	15	16	17	18
1 AGRICULTURE AND FISHERIES	10.86	15.70	2.16	0.02	0.19	—	0.01	—	1.21	—		0.05	*	0.01	—	—	—	—
2 FOOD AND KINDRED PRODUCTS	2.38	5.75	0.06	0.01	*	*	0.03	*	0.79	—	¬	0.44	*	*	*	*	*	—
3 TEXTILE MILL PRODUCTS	0.06	*	1.30	3.88	*	0.29	0.04	0.03	0.01	*	0.44	0.09	0.03	—	0.01	0.02	0.05	0.15
4 APPAREL	0.04	0.20	—	1.96	—	0.01	0.02	—	0.03	—	—	*	*	—	*	*	*	0.10
5 LUMBER AND WOOD PRODUCTS	0.15	0.10	0.02	*	1.09	0.39	0.27	*	0.04	0.01	—	0.02	0.02	0.06	0.06	0.09	0.05	0.05
6 FURNITURE AND FIXTURES	—	—	0.01	—	—	0.01	0.01	—	—	—	—	—	—	—	—	*	0.01	0.10
7 PAPER AND ALLIED PRODUCTS	*	0.52	0.08	0.02	*	0.02	2.60	1.08	0.33	0.11	0.02	0.05	0.18	*	0.09	0.04	0.07	0.03
8 PRINTING AND PUBLISHING	—	0.04	*	—	—	—	—	0.77	0.02	—	—	—	—	—	—	0.01	0.01	0.01
9 CHEMICALS	0.83	1.48	0.80	0.14	0.03	0.06	0.18	0.10	2.58	0.21	0.60	0.13	0.12	0.18	0.13	0.08	0.20	0.11
10 PRODUCTS OF PETROLEUM AND COAL	0.46	0.06	0.03	*	0.07	*	0.06	*	0.32	4.83	0.01	*	0.05	0.90	0.02	0.04	0.02	0.03
11 RUBBER PRODUCTS	0.12	0.01	0.01	0.02	0.01	0.01	0.01	*	*	*	0.04	0.05	0.01	*	0.01	0.13	0.03	0.50
12 LEATHER AND LEATHER PRODUCTS	—	—	*	0.05	*	0.01	—	*	—	—	—	1.04	—	—	*	0.02	*	0.01
13 STONE, CLAY AND GLASS PRODUCTS	0.06	0.25	*	*	0.01	0.03	0.03	—	0.26	0.05	0.01	0.01	0.43	0.21	0.07	0.07	0.12	0.19
14 PRIMARY METALS	0.01	*	—	*	0.01	0.11	—	0.01	0.19	0.01	0.01	*	0.04	6.90	2.53	2.02	1.05	1.28
15 FABRICATED METAL PRODUCTS	0.08	0.61	*	0.01	0.04	0.14	0.02	*	0.13	0.08	0.01	0.02	*	0.05	0.43	0.62	0.34	0.97
16 MACHINERY (EXCEPT ELECTRIC)	0.06	0.01	0.04	0.02	0.01	0.01	0.01	0.04	*	0.01	—	0.01	0.07	0.28	1.15	0.17	0.63	
17 ELECTRICAL MACHINERY	—	—	—	—	—	—	—	—	*	—		0.01	0.05	0.24	0.58	0.86	0.62	
18 MOTOR VEHICLES	0.11	*	—	*	—	—	—	—	*	—	*	*	0.03	0.03	0.01	4.40		
19 OTHER TRANSPORTATION EQUIPMENT	0.01	—	—	—	—	—	—	*	*	*	—	*	*	—	*	0.01		
20 PROFESSIONAL AND SCIENTIFIC EQUIPMENT	—	—	—	—	—	*	0.01	0.03	0.01	—	—	*	*	0.04	0.04	0.01	0.07	
21 MISCELLANEOUS MANUFACTURING INDUSTRIES	*	0.01	*	0.26	*	0.02	0.01	—	0.03	—	*	0.02	0.01	*	0.02	0.05	0.11	0.02
22 COAL, GAS AND ELECTRIC POWER	0.06	0.20	0.11	0.04	0.02	0.02	0.12	0.03	0.19	0.56	0.04	0.02	0.20	0.35	0.08	0.10	0.05	0.06
23 RAILROAD TRANSPORTATION	0.44	0.57	0.09	0.06	0.14	0.05	0.22	0.07	0.29	0.27	0.04	0.04	0.15	0.52	0.13	0.16	0.07	0.23
24 OCEAN TRANSPORTATION	0.07	0.13	0.01	0.01	0.01	*	0.02	*	0.04	0.09	*	*	0.01	0.08	*	*	*	*
25 OTHER TRANSPORTATION	0.55	0.38	0.08	0.03	0.14	0.04	0.12	0.03	0.10	0.47	0.01	0.02	0.07	0.16	0.03	0.04	0.03	0.07
26 TRADE	1.36	0.46	0.23	0.37	0.06	0.06	0.18	0.03	0.17	0.02	0.05	0.06	0.05	0.36	0.20	0.26	0.14	0.06
27 COMMUNICATIONS	*	0.04	0.01	0.02	0.01	0.01	0.01	0.04	0.02	0.01	0.01	*	0.01	0.02	0.02	0.03	0.02	0.02
28 FINANCE AND INSURANCE	0.24	0.15	0.02	0.02	0.08	0.02	0.02	0.02	0.02	0.13	0.01	0.01	0.05	0.06	0.04	0.05	0.04	0.02
29 REAL ESTATE AND RENTALS	2.39	0.09	0.03	0.10	0.02	0.02	0.03	0.06	0.03	—	0.01	0.02	0.02	0.06	0.03	0.04	0.03	0.02
30 BUSINESS SERVICES	0.01	0.63	0.07	0.10	0.02	0.06	0.02	0.06	0.42	0.04	0.02	0.05	0.01	0.03	0.05	0.09	0.06	0.08
31 PERSONAL AND REPAIR SERVICES	0.37	0.12	*	*	0.04	*	*	0.02	0.01	0.01	*	*	0.03	0.01	0.01	0.01	*	*
32 NON-PROFIT ORGANIZATIONS	—	—	—	—	—	—	—	—	—	—	—	—	—	—	—	—	—	—
33 AMUSEMENTS	—	—	—	—	—	—	—	—	—	—	—	—	—	—	—	—	—	—
34 SCRAP AND MISCELLANEOUS INDUSTRIES	—	—	0.02	—	—	—	0.25	—	0.01	—	0.01	—	0.01	1.11	0.02	0.05	*	—
35 EATING AND DRINKING PLACES	—	—	—	—	—	—	—	*	—	—	—	—	—	—	—	—	—	—
36 NEW CONSTRUCTION AND MAINTENANCE	0.20	0.12	0.04	0.02	0.01	0.01	0.04	0.01	0.04	0.03	0.01	0.02	0.03	0.10	0.03	0.05	0.02	0.04
37 UNDISTRIBUTED	—	1.87	0.30	1.08	0.73	0.27	0.17	0.50	1.49	0.65	0.27	0.27	0.47	0.32	1.14	1.71	0.89	0.41
38 INVENTORY CHANGE (DEPLETIONS)	2.66	0.40	0.12	0.19	*	0.01	0.09	0.03	0.14	0.01	*	0.03	*	0.11	*	*	*	0.01
39 FOREIGN COUNTRIES (IMPORTS FROM)	0.69	2.11	0.21	0.28	0.18	0.01	0.62	0.01	0.59	0.26	*	0.04	0.14	0.62	0.01	0.05	*	0.02
40 GOVERNMENT	0.81	1.24	0.64	0.38	0.34	0.11	0.50	0.34	0.76	0.78	0.11	0.14	0.32	0.82	0.48	0.77	0.40	0.66
41 PRIVATE CAPITAL FORMATION (GROSS)	DEPRECIATION AND OTHER CAPITAL CONSUMPTION ALLOWANCES ARE INCLUDED IN HOUSEHOLD ROW																	
42 HOUSEHOLDS	19.17	7.05	3.34	4.24	2.72	1.12	2.20	3.14	3.75	5.04	1.08	1.20	2.35	5.53	4.14	6.80	3.41	3.39
TOTAL GROSS OUTLAYS	**44.26**	**40.30**	**9.84**	**13.32**	**6.00**	**2.89**	**7.90**	**6.45**	**14.05**	**13.67**	**2.82**	**3.81**	**4.84**	**18.69**	**10.40**	**15.22**	**8.38**	**14.27**

This interindustry table summarizes the transactions of the U.S. economy in 1947, for which preliminary data have just been compiled by the Bureau of Labor Statistics. Each number in the body of the table represents billions of 1947 dollars. In the vertical column at left the entire economy is broken down into sectors; in the horizontal row at the top the same breakdown is repeated.

PURCHASING   **FINAL DEMAND**

24	25	26	27	28	29	30	31	32	33	34	35	36	37	38	39	40	41	42	HOUSEHOLDS	TOTAL GROSS OUTPUT
RAILROAD TRANSPORTATION	OCEAN TRANSPORTATION	OTHER TRANSPORTATION	TRADE	COMMUNICATIONS	FINANCE AND INSURANCE	REAL ESTATE AND RENTALS	BUSINESS SERVICES	PERSONAL AND REPAIR SERVICES	NON-PROFIT ORGANIZATIONS	AMUSEMENTS	SCRAP AND MISCELLANEOUS INDUSTRIES	EATING AND DRINKING PLACES	NEW CONSTRUCTION AND MAINTENANCE	UNDISTRIBUTED	INVENTORY CHANGE (ADDITIONS)	FOREIGN COUNTRIES (EXPORTS TO)	GOVERNMENT	PRIVATE CAPITAL FORMATION (GROSS)		
—	*	*	—	*	*	0.01	—	*	—	—	—	—	0.12	—	0.87	0.09	0.17	1.01	1.28 0.57 0.02 9.92	44.26
—	0.01	0.02	*	0.08	0.01	0.03	0.07	0.01	—	—	—	*	0.25	*	0.02	3.47	*	0.42	0.88 1.80 0.73 —	40.30
0.01	0.05	0.08	0.07	—	0.01	0.01	0.03	*	—	—	*	0.03	*	—	0.01	—	0.05	0.52	0.06 0.92 0.10 0.02 1.47	9.84
0.01	*	*	*	*	*	*	0.02	*	—	—	—	0.02	0.02	*	0.01	0.02	*	0.15	0.21 0.30 0.28 * 9.90	13.32
0.03	*	0.06	0.06	—	0.01	*	0.03	*	—	0.14	*	*	*	—	0.11	0.01	2.33	0.35	0.17 0.17 0.01 0.04 0.07	6.00
0.02	*	—	*	—	—	*	—	*	0.04	0.08	—	*	—	—	—	0.20	0.20	0.08	0.03 0.05 0.57 1.46	2.89
0.02	0.08	0.07	*	*	—	*	0.57	*	*	—	*	0.06	0.03	—	0.68	0.06	0.17	0.31	0.04 0.15 0.06 — 0.34	7.90
—	*	—	*	0.04	*	0.02	0.10	0.03	0.21	—	2.45	0.03	0.17	0.01	0.01	0.03	—	0.68	* 0.07 0.16 0.09 1.49	6.45
0.02	0.05	0.17	0.06	0.03	0.01	0.02	0.07	*	*	—	0.01	0.20	0.22	*	0.03	0.04	0.64	1.25	0.30 0.81 0.19 — 1.96	14.05
0.01	*	0.01	0.47	0.27	0.09	0.45	0.20	*	0.01	0.78	*	0.06	0.06	*	0.01	0.01	0.62	0.36	0.06 0.68 0.18 * 2.44	13.67
0.01	*	0.04	*	*	—	0.13	0.06	*	0.01	*	—	0.07	*	—	*	*	0.06	0.47	0.09 0.17 0.02 0.01 0.71	2.82
*	0.01	0.01	*	—	—	*	*	—	—	—	—	0.03	0.01	—	0.01	—	*	0.29	0.11 0.08 0.03 0.02 2.83	3.81
0.01	0.03	0.06	0.02	0.01	*	*	0.04	—	—	*	—	0.02	0.01	—	*	0.06	1.74	8.36	0.10 0.21 0.02 0.01 0.34	4.84
0.43	0.07	0.20	0.05	0.20	—	0.01	—	*	—	—	—	—	*	—	0.15	*	1.19	1.24	0.16 0.77 0.02 — 0.02	18.69
0.10	0.07	0.04	*	0.03	*	0.01	0.06	*	—	—	*	0.03	0.01	—	0.06	0.02	3.09	1.44	0.21 0.39 0.05 0.28 0.95	10.40
0.22	0.03	*	0.03	0.06	—	0.01	0.01	—	0.02	—	—	0.15	*	—	0.07	—	0.51	2.24	0.37 1.76 0.18 5.82 1.22	15.22
0.12	0.03	0.02	0.02	0.04	—	0.01	0.01	0.05	—	0.01	0.09	*	—	0.04	—	0.77	1.27	0.25	0.44 0.17 1.75 0.93	8.38
*	—	—	0.01	*	—	0.13	0.02	*	—	*	—	1.05	*	—	0.07	*	0.04	0.67	0.40 1.02 0.15 2.98 3.13	14.27
0.30	—	—	*	0.04	0.08	0.13	—	—	—	—	—	*	—	—	0.01	—	*	0.46	0.02 0.32 1.25 1.20 0.17	4.00
0.02	0.18	0.02	*	—	—	*	—	*	—	—	0.01	0.05	0.18	—	0.01	—	0.02	0.24	0.03 0.18 0.08 0.26 0.62	2.12
*	0.03	0.16	*	*	*	*	0.01	*	—	—	0.15	0.16	0.05	0.05	0.11	0.02	0.03	0.68	0.04 0.19 0.08 0.51 1.89	4.76
0.03	0.01	0.03	1.27	0.44	*	0.09	0.49	0.01	0.06	3.15	*	0.31	0.16	0.05	—	0.22	0.03	0.02	0.03 0.35 0.20 — —	9.21
0.04	0.01	0.03	0.15	0.41	*	0.06	0.08	*	0.01	0.42	0.03	0.03	0.05	*	0.03	0.25	0.71	0.30	0.08 0.59 0.33 0.27 2.53	9.95
*	*	0.01	*	—	0.22	—	—	—	—	—	—	—	—	—	*	—	*	*	1.16 0.31 — 0.10	2.29
0.01	0.01	0.01	0.03	0.19	0.04	0.25	0.31	*	*	0.13	0.03	0.01	0.02	*	0.02	0.10	0.57	0.17	0.04 0.32 0.35 0.10 4.77	9.86
0.07	0.04	0.05	0.05	0.03	0.01	0.42	0.20	0.01	0.04	0.75	0.14	0.37	0.29	0.01	0.09	1.06	2.52	1.01	0.20 1.00 0.05 2.34 26.82	41.66
0.01	0.01	0.01	0.02	0.02	*	0.04	0.33	0.06	0.09	0.06	0.43	0.12	0.07	0.01	—	0.01	0.04	0.08	— 0.04 0.15 — 1.27	3.17
0.02	0.01	0.02	0.05	0.02	0.12	0.30	1.00	*	1.85	0.56	0.02	0.12	0.09	0.03	—	0.07	0.40	—	— 0.14 0.03 — 6.99	12.81
0.02	0.01	0.03	0.05	0.02	0.01	0.15	1.96	0.05	0.21	0.21	0.06	0.71	0.40	0.18	—	0.39	0.08	—	— — 0.22 0.80 20.29	28.86
0.01	0.05	0.06	0.01	0.02	*	0.03	1.71	0.09	0.14	0.04	0.06	0.12	0.02	0.10	—	0.06	0.13	0.42	— * 0.04 — 0.18	5.10
*	*	*	0.02	0.11	0.01	0.26	1.42	0.02	0.11	0.03	0.07	0.56	0.08	0.02	0.03	0.23	0.82	1.17	— — 0.08 0.27 8.35	14.30
—	—	—	—	—	*	*	—	*	—	0.02	—	—	0.09	—	—	—	—	0.16	— — 5.08 — 8.04	13.39
—	—	—	—	—	—	—	*	—	—	—	—	—	0.01	0.39	—	—	—	0.01	— 0.13 — — 2.40	2.94
—	*	—	—	—	—	0.04	0.39	0.01	0.11	0.03	0.02	*	*	0.01	—	—	*	0.01	— 0.03 * — —	2.13
—	—	—	—	—	—	0.01	—	—	—	—	—	—	0.15	—	—	—	—	—	— — 5.29 15.70 0.15	13.27
0.02	0.01	0.02	0.27	1.12	*	0.13	0.18	0.18	0.03	4.08	*	0.06	0.34	0.02	—	0.07	0.01	—	— — 5.29 15.70 0.15	28.49
0.34	0.19	0.87	0.25	0.10	0.04	0.03	2.59	0.01	0.71	0.36	0.31	1.13	0.91	0.22	—	0.59	0.43	—	— — — —	21.60
0.01	0.05	0.16	*	—	—	—	—	—	—	—	—	—	—	0.40	—	0.02	—	—	— — — —	4.43
0.01	0.05	0.14	0.01	0.04	0.50	0.08	—	0.03	0.10	—	—	—	*	0.07	—	—	0.01	—	1.31 — 1.32	9.52
0.12	0.13	0.19	1.14	0.91	0.26	0.77	3.30	0.44	1.11	4.00	0.21	0.50	0.17	0.32	0.07	1.41	0.47	2.19	0.34 0.83 3.46 0.22 31.55	63.69
1.95	0.90	2.17	5.11	5.70	0.90	6.20	26.42	2.15	7.93	14.06	1.08	8.20	9.41	1.50	—	4.20	10.73	2.27	— 0.85 30.06 — 2.12	223.58
4.00	2.12	4.76	9.21	9.95	2.29	9.86	41.66	3.17	12.81	28.86	5.10	14.30	13.39	2.94	2.13	13.27	28.49	21.60	5.28 11.21 51.29 33.29	194.12

When a sector is read horizontally, the numbers indicate what it ships to other sectors. When a sector is read vertically, the numbers show what it consumes from other sectors. The asterisks stand for sums less than $5 million. Totals may not check due to rounding.

tomers are other industries. "Households" and "government" turn up as direct customers for only a minor portion of the total output, although these two sectors are of course the principal consumers of metals after they have been converted into end products by other industries.

Coming out of the interior of the table to the outer row and columns, the reader may soon recognize many of the familiar total figures by which we are accustomed to visualize the condition of the economy. The total outputs at the end of each industry row, for example, are the figures we use to measure the size or the health of an industry. The gross national product which is designed to state the total of productive activity and is the most commonly cited index for the economy as a whole, may be derived as the grand total of the five columns grouped under the heading of final demand, but with some adjustments necessary to eliminate the duplication of transactions between the sectors represented by these columns. For example, the total payment to households, at the far right end of row 42, includes salaries paid by government, a figure which duplicates in part the payment of taxes by households included in the total payment to government.

With this brief introduction the lay economist is now qualified to turn around and trace his way back into the table via whatever chain of interindustry relationships engages his interest. He will not go far before he finds himself working intuitively with the central concept of input-output analysis. This is the idea that there is a fundamental relationship between the volume of the output of an industry and the size of the inputs going into it. It is obvious, for example, that the purchases of the auto industry (column 18) from the glass industry (row 13) in 1947 were strongly determined by the number of motor vehicles produced that year. Closer inspection will lead to the further realization that every single figure in the chart is dependent upon every other. To take an extreme example, the appropriate series of inputs and outputs will show that the auto industry's purchases of glass are dependent in part upon the demand for motor vehicles arising out of the glass industry's purchases from the fuel industries.

These relationships reflect the structure of our technology. They are expressed in input-output analysis as the ratios or coefficients of each input to the total output of which it becomes a part. A table of such ratios (Figure 2) computed from a table for the economy as of 1939, shows how much had to be purchased from the steel, glass, paint, rubber and other industries to produce $1,000 worth of automobile that year. Since such expenditures are determined by relatively inflexible engineering considerations or by equally inflexible customs and institutional arrangements, these ratios might be used to estimate the demand for materials induced by auto production in other years. With a table of ratios for the economy as a whole, it is possible in turn to calculate the secondary demand on the output of the industries which supply

FIGURE 2

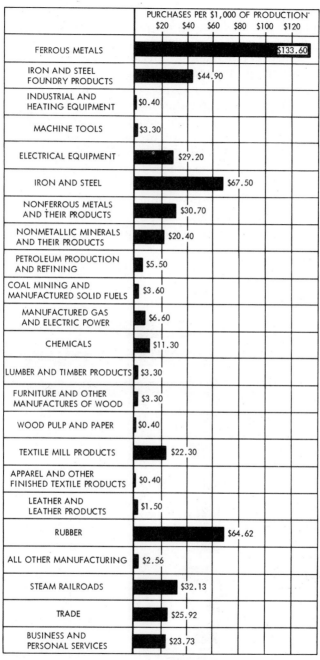

	PURCHASES PER $1,000 OF PRODUCTION					
	$20	$40	$60	$80	$100	$120
FERROUS METALS						$133.60
IRON AND STEEL FOUNDRY PRODUCTS		$44.90				
INDUSTRIAL AND HEATING EQUIPMENT	$0.40					
MACHINE TOOLS	$3.30					
ELECTRICAL EQUIPMENT	$29.20					
IRON AND STEEL			$67.50			
NONFERROUS METALS AND THEIR PRODUCTS	$30.70					
NONMETALLIC MINERALS AND THEIR PRODUCTS	$20.40					
PETROLEUM PRODUCTION AND REFINING	$5.50					
COAL MINING AND MANUFACTURED SOLID FUELS	$3.60					
MANUFACTURED GAS AND ELECTRIC POWER	$6.60					
CHEMICALS	$11.30					
LUMBER AND TIMBER PRODUCTS	$3.30					
FURNITURE AND OTHER MANUFACTURES OF WOOD	$3.30					
WOOD PULP AND PAPER	$0.40					
TEXTILE MILL PRODUCTS	$22.30					
APPAREL AND OTHER FINISHED TEXTILE PRODUCTS	$0.40					
LEATHER AND LEATHER PRODUCTS	$1.50					
RUBBER			$64.62			
ALL OTHER MANUFACTURING	$2.56					
STEAM RAILROADS	$32.13					
TRADE	$25.92					
BUSINESS AND PERSONAL SERVICES	$23.73					

Input to the auto industry from other industries per $1,000 of auto production was derived from the 1939 interindustry table. Comparing these figures with those for the auto industry in the 1947 table would show changes in the input structure of the industry due to changes in prices and technology.

the auto industry's suppliers and so on through successive outputs and inputs until the effect of the final demand for automobiles has been traced to its last reverberation in the farthest corner of the economy. In this fashion input-output analysis should prove useful to the auto industry as a means for dealing with cost and supply problems.

The table of steel consumption ratios (Figure 3) suggests, incidentally, how the input-output matrix might be used for the contrasting purpose of market analysis. Since the ultimate markets for steel are ordinarily buried in the cycle of secondary transactions among the metal-fabricating industries, it is useful to learn from this table how many tons of steel at the mill were needed in 1939 to satisfy each thousand dollars worth of demand for the products of industries which ultimately place steel products at the disposal of the consumer. This table shows the impressively high ratio of the demand for steel in the construction

FIGURE 3

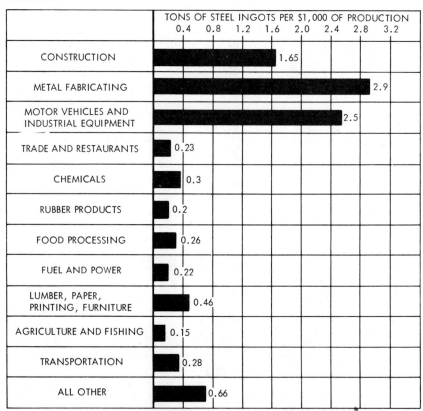

	TONS OF STEEL INGOTS PER $1,000 OF PRODUCTION
	0.4 0.8 1.2 1.6 2.0 2.4 2.8 3.2
CONSTRUCTION	1.65
METAL FABRICATING	2.9
MOTOR VEHICLES AND INDUSTRIAL EQUIPMENT	2.5
TRADE AND RESTAURANTS	0.23
CHEMICALS	0.3
RUBBER PRODUCTS	0.2
FOOD PROCESSING	0.26
FUEL AND POWER	0.22
LUMBER, PAPER, PRINTING, FURNITURE	0.46
AGRICULTURE AND FISHING	0.15
TRANSPORTATION	0.28
ALL OTHER	0.66

The output of the steel industry depends heavily on what kinds of goods are demanded in the ultimate market. This table shows the amount of steel required to meet each $1,000 of the demand for other goods in 1939. The current demand for the top three items is responsible for the steel shortage.

and consumer durable-goods industries which led the Bureau of Labor Statistics to declare in 1945 that a flourishing postwar economy would require even more steel than the peak of the war effort. Though some industry spokesmen took a contrary position at that time, steel production recently has been exceeding World War II peaks, and the major steel companies are now engaged in a 16-million-ton expansion program which was started even before the outbreak of the war in Korea and the current rearmament.

The ratios shown in these two tables are largely fixed by technology. Others in the complete matrix of the economy, especially in the trade and services and households sectors, are established by custom and other institutional factors. All, of course, are subject to modification by such forces as progress in technology and changes in public taste. But whether they vary more or less rapidly over the years, these relationships are subject to dependable measurement at any given time.

Here we have our bridge between theory and facts in economics. It is a bridge in a very literal sense. Action at a distance does not happen in economics any more than it does in physics. The effect of an event at any one point is transmitted to the rest of the economy step by step via the chain of transactions that ties the whole system together. A table of ratios for the entire economy gives us, in as much detail as we require, a quantitatively determined picture of the internal structure of the system. This makes it possible to calculate in detail the consequences that result from the introduction into the system of changes suggested by the theoretical or practical problem at hand.

In the case of a particular industry we can easily compute the complete table of its input requirements at any given level of output, provided we know its input ratios. By the same token, with somewhat more involved computation, we can construct synthetically a complete input-output table for the entire economy. We need only a known "bill of final demand" to convert the table of ratios into a table of magnitudes. The 1945 estimate of postwar steel requirements, for example, was incidental to a study of the complete economy based upon a bill of demand which assumed full employment in 1950. This bill of demand was inserted into the total columns of a table of ratios based on the year 1939. By arithmetical procedures the ratios were then translated into dollar figures, among which was the figure for steel, which showed a need for an absolute minimum of 98 million ingot tons. Actual production in 1950, at the limit of capacity, was 96.8 million tons.

Though its application is simple, the construction of an input-output table is a highly complex and laborious operation. The first step, and one that has little appeal to the theoretical imagination, is the gathering and ordering of an immense volume of quantitative information. Given the inevitable lag between the accumulation and collation of data for any given year, the input-output table will always be an historical document. The first input-output tables, prepared by the author and his associates at Harvard University in the early 1930s, were based upon 1919 and 1929 figures. The 1939 table was not completed until 1944. Looking to the future, a table for 1953 which is now under consideration could not be made available until 1957. For practical purposes the original figures in the table must be regarded as a base, subject to refinement and correction in accord with subsequent trends. For example, the 1945 projection of the 1950 economy on the basis of the 1939 table made suitable adjustments in the coal and oil input ratios of the transportation industries on the assumption that the trend from steam to diesel locomotives would continue throughout the period.

The basic information for the table and its continuing revision comes from the Bureau of the Census and other specialized statistical agencies. As the industrial breakdown becomes more detailed, however, engineering and technical information plays a more important part in determining the data. A perfectly good way to determine how much coke is needed to produce a ton of pig iron, in addition to dividing the output of the blast furnace industry into its input of coke, is to ask an ironmaster. In principle there is no reason why the input-output coefficients should not be entirely derived from "below," from engineering data on process design and operating practice. Thus in certain studies of the German economy made by the Bureau of Labor Statistics following World War II the input structures of key industries were set up on the basis of U.S. experience. The model of a disarmed but self-supporting Germany developed in these studies showed a steel requirement of 11 million ingot tons, toward which actual output is now moving. Completely hypothetical input structures, representing industries not now operating, have been introduced into tables of the existing U.S. economy in studies conducted by Air Force economists.

This brings us to the problem of computation. Since the production level required of each industry is ultimately dependent upon levels in all others, it is clear that we have a problem involving simultaneous equations. Though the solution of such equations may involve no very high order of mathematics, the sheer labor of computation can be immense. The number of equations to be solved is always equal to the number of sectors into which the system is divided. Depending upon whether a specific or a general solution of the system is desired, the volume of computation will vary as the square or the cube of the number of sectors involved. A typical general solution of a 42-sector table for 1939 required 56 hours on the Harvard Mark II computer. Thanks to this investment in computation, the conversion of any stipulated bill of demand into the various industrial production levels involves nothing more than simple arithmetic. The method cannot be used, however, in the solution of problems which call for changes in the input-output ratios, since each change requires a whole new solution of the matrix.

For the larger number of more interesting problems which require such changes, special solutions are the rule. However, even a special solution on a reasonably detailed 200-sector table might require some 200,000 multiplications and a greater number of additions. For this reason it is likely that the typical nongovernmental user will be limited to condensed general solutions periodically computed and published by special-purpose groups working in the field. With these the average industrial analyst will be able to enjoy many of the advantages of the large and flexible machinery required for government analyses relating to the entire economy.

A demonstration of input-output analysis applied to a typical economic problem is presented in Figure 4, which shows the price increases that would result from a general 10 percent increase in the wage scale of industry. Here the value of the matrix distinguishing between direct and indirect effects is of the utmost importance. If wages constituted the only ultimate cost in the economy, a general 10 percent rise in all money wages would obviously lead to an equal increase in all prices. Since wages are only one cost and since labor costs vary from industry to industry, it can be seen in the chart that a 10 percent increase in wages would have decidedly different effects upon various parts of the economy. The construction industry shows the greatest upward price change, as it actually did in recent decades. For each industry group the chart separates the direct effect of increases in its own wage bill from the indirect effects of the wage increases in other industries from which it purchases its inputs. Giving effect to both direct and indirect increases, the average increase in the cost of living is shown in the chart to be only 3.7 percent. The 10 percent money-wage increase thus yields a 6.3 percent increase in real wage rates. It should be noted, however, that the economic forces which bring increases in wages tend to bring increases in other costs as well. The advantage of the input-output analysis is that it permits the disentanglement and accurate measurement of the indirect effects. Analyses similar to this one for wages can be carried through for profits, taxes, and other ultimate components of prices.

In such examples changes in the economy over periods of time are measured by comparing before-and-after pictures. Each is a static model, a cross-section in time. The next step in input-output analysis is the development of dynamic models of the economy to bring the approximations of the method that much closer to the actual processes of economics. This requires accounting for stocks as well as flows of goods, for inventories of goods in process and in finished form, for capital equipment, buildings, and, last but not least, for dwellings and household stocks of durable consumer goods. The dynamic input-output analysis requires more advanced mathematical methods; instead of ordinary linear equations it leads to systems of linear differential equations.

FIGURE 4

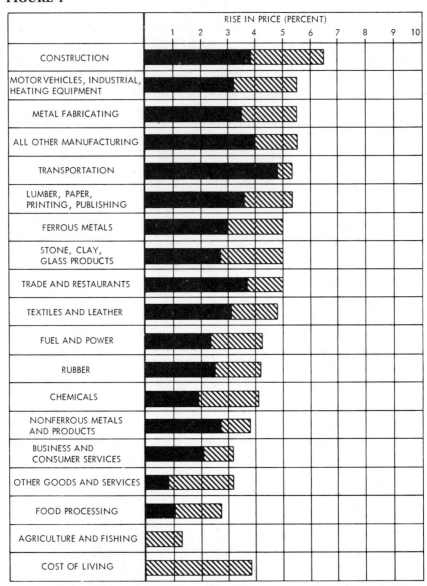

Price increases that would be caused by a 10 percent increase in wages were computed from the 1939 interindustry table. The increases include the direct effect of the rise in each industry's own wage bill (dark bars) and the indirect effect of price increases on purchase from others (striped bars).

Among the questions the dynamic system should make it possible to answer, one could mention the determination of the changing pattern of outputs and inventories or investments and capacities which would attend a given pattern of growth in final demand projected over a 5- or 10-year period. Within such broad projections, for example, we would be able to estimate approximately not only how much aluminum should be produced, but how much additional aluminum-producing capacity would be required, and the rate at which such capacity should be installed. The computational task becomes more formidable, but it does not seem to exceed the capacity of the latest electronic computers. Here, as in the case of the static system, the most laborious problem is the assembly of the necessary factual information. However, a complete set of stock or capital ratios, paralleling the flow ratios of all of the productive sectors of the U.S. economy for the year 1939, has now been completed.

This table of capital ratios shows that in addition to the flow of raw pig iron, scrap, coal, labor, and so on, the steel works and rolling mills industry—when operating to full capacity—required $1,800 of fixed investment for each $1,000 worth of output. This would include $336 worth of tools, $331 worth of iron and steel foundry production, and so on down to $26 worth of electrical equipment. This means that in order to expand its capacity so as to be able to increase its output by $1 million worth of finished products annually, the steel works and rolling mills industry would have to install $336,000 worth of tools and spend corresponding amounts on all other types of new fixed installations. This investment demand constitutes of course additional input requirements for the product of the corresponding capital goods industries, input requirements which are automatically taken into account in the solution of an appropriate system of dynamic input-output equations.

Active experimental work with the dynamic system is under way. Meanwhile the demonstrated power of input-output analysis has thoroughly convinced many workers in the field of its practical possibilities. Of wider consequence is the expectation of theoretical investigators that this new grasp on the facts of the subject will further liberate economics from the confines of its traditionally simplified postulates.

35.

Statistical Demand Functions for Automobiles and Their Use for Forecasting in an Energy Crisis*

RODNEY L. CARLSON
M. MICHAEL UMBLE

INTRODUCTION AND MODEL

A research study in 1976 by one of the authors investigated automobile demand over the period 1965–75 using a disaggregate approach. Previous studies by Chow, Nerlove, Suits, Smith, and others had explained auto purchase by aggregating all sizes and classes of automobile into one demand function. The 1976 study suggested that as little aggregation as possible is desirable in a model of the new car market and that automobile demand segmented into the five automobile classifications—subcompact, compact, intermediate, standard, and luxury—revealed much additional information.

While the purpose of this earlier study was model building (with emphasis on computing elasticities and demonstrating a practical application of "seemingly unrelated regression") and not forecasting, the implications for future demand were discussed, and the tentative fore-

---

* *Journal of Business* 53, no. 2 (April 1980), pp. 193–204.

casts made were quite accurate. The model forecast 1977 sales at 10.3 million, 1978 sales at 10.7 million, and 1979 sales at less than 11.0 million. Actual new car sales for 1977 and 1978 were 10.7 and 10.9 million cars, respectively, with 1979 sales projected around 11 million. One test for model validity is its ultimate forecasting ability, and the 1976 model has projected very accurately. This suggests that the model does reflect consumer purchase behavior in the automobile market and can be used to forecast the effects of a prolonged energy crisis on new car sales.

The automobile industry has already experienced temporary effects of the energy crisis on new car sales. These effects caused a change in consumer buying patterns in 1974 and 1975 and are described in detail in the earlier study. In 1976, however, consumer buying habits largely reverted to preembargo patterns because (1) the American public in general did not believe the energy crisis was real when gasoline prices stabilized and (2) the redistribution to smaller cars slowed because of the "American love affair with larger automobiles." Now, after 3 years of ominous silence, the energy crisis has again become a clear threat to economic stability. The price of gasoline is certain to continue to increase, especially if all government regulations are removed from the oil industry, and continued gasoline shortage is a definite possibility.

This paper is an addendum to the 1976 research and attempts to forecast automobile demand over the next five years. This research will (1) update the 1976 model using quarterly data from 1967 to 1978; (2) develop various forecasting scenarios requiring assumptions about the economy, automobile prices, gasoline price, and gasoline shortage; and (3) interpret these projections as to their implications for the automobile industry.

The theoretical model is basically the same as that used in the previous study. The only differences are in (1) the procedure used to account for population change and (2) the deleting of the variable "auto stock" from the model. The revised model uses an index of population change $(1967 = 100)$ to adjust auto sales and disposable income, while auto stock was not significant in preliminary research. The revised model can be written as

$$D_t^i = B_0 + B_1 Y_t^D + B_2 P_t^i + B_3 G_t + B_4 Z_t^E + B_5 Z_t + E_t \qquad (1)$$

where

$D_t^i =$ demand for car size i, $i = 1$ (subcompact), 2 (compact), 3 (intermediate), 4 (standard), and 5 (luxury), seasonally adjusted and adjusted for population size;

$Y_t^D =$ disposable income, seasonally adjusted and adjusted for population size and to constant dollars $(1967 = 100)$;

P_t^i = an average of car prices for size i, i = 1, 2, 3, 4, 5; adjusted to constant dollars (1967 = 100);

G_t = gasoline price in current dollars;

Z_t^E = 1, first and second quarter, 1974; gasoline shortage; and 0, otherwise;

Z_t = 1, fourth quarter, 1970; UAW strike; and 0, otherwise; and

E_t = the disturbance term.

Table 1 shows the results of estimating demand functions for each of the automobile classifications and suggests the following observations: (1) All variables seem to have correct signs, which is important since economic theory dictates certain relationships, *ceteris paribus*, in demand functions. (2) Disposable income is the variable of greatest impact in the model, which is to be expected, and is a result reported in all previous studies on automobile demand.[1] (3) Price is significant (at the .10 level) in all equations, which suggests it could be a significant factor in the depressed levels of auto sales. (4) Gasoline price is significant and positive in the subcompact and compact equations, significant and negative in the standard equation, not significant in the luxury equation (as expected), and absent from the intermediate equation. (5) The energy dummy indicates that in times of gasoline shortage the demand for subcompacts will increase, the demand for compacts will not significantly change, and that all other automobiles will decrease in sales. The implication is that consumers view subcompacts as the only true gasoline economy car and that shortage coupled with high gas prices will greatly increase the demand for this small car. Through 1978, however, these changes in demand had not occurred, as sales of intermediate sized cars led all others in 1977 and 1978 (see Figure 1 or 2). (6) The demand function for standard sized cars was modified because income (Y^D) had improper sign and was dropped from the equation. (Sales of standard sized cars have been decreasing since the late 1960s while income has been increasing.) A polynomial trend variable (T = 1, 1967) was added to the model in order that secular trend could be used as a proxy for income.

FORECASTING AUTOMOBILE DEMAND, 1979–1983

Two assumptions are made about each predictor variable in the next five years which can be labeled as optimistic and pessimistic. These different assumptions generate forecasts for each size of automobile which are aggregated into total automobile demand.

---

[1] If the regression coefficients are transformed into β-coefficients which reflect the relative importance of the variables, the income variable is of greatest magnitude.

TABLE 1
Demand Functions for the Different Sizes of Automobiles, 1967–1978

Dependent Variable	Constant	P_t^i	Y_t^D	G_t	Z_t^E	Z_t	T_t	T_t^2
Subcompact, D_t^1	−709,190	−275 (−3.37)	2570 (3.95) $R^2=.91$	3470* (1.67) D-W = 2.16	101000* (1.82)	—	—	—
Compact, D_t^2	209,010	−158 (−3.34)	760 (2.12) $R^2=.88$	2575 (2.48) D-W = 2.10	—	—	—	—
Intermediate, D_t^3	289,400	−161* (−1.68)	1136 (2.74) $R^2=.72$	— D-W = 2.24	−170100 (−4.84)	−82700 (−2.15)	—	—
Standard, D_t^4	3,565,600	−342* (−1.80)	— $R^2=.91$	−28030 (−5.01) D-W = 1.41	−171500 (−2.48)	−230100 (−4.62)	−42370 (−7.02)	636 (5.72)
Luxury, D_t^5	234,600	−53.1 (−4.13)	694 (6.16) $R^2=.83$	— D-W = 2.08	−56010 (−2.68)	−61900 (−3.54)	—	—

Note: Values in parenthesis are t-values; all coefficients are significant at .05 level except those with one asterisk, which are significant at .10; D-W is the Durbin-Watson statistic.

FIGURE 1
Automobile Sales, Classified by Size, Actual and Projected, Yearly Aggregates, 1967–1983
(Projections under No Gasoline Shortage Assumption)

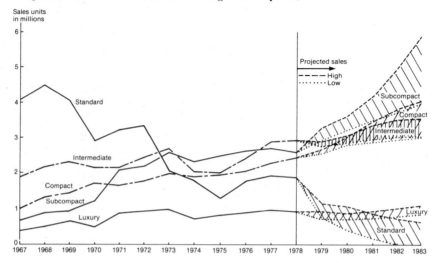

FIGURE 2
Automobile Sales, Classified by Size, Actual and Projected, Yearly Aggregates, 1967–1983
(Projections under Gasoline Shortage Assumption)

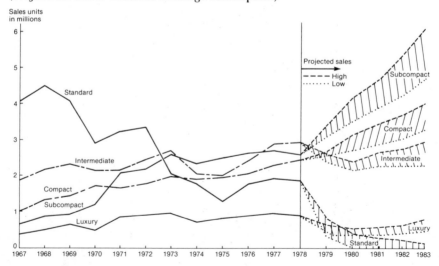

Disposable Income

From 1966 to 1978, 1974–76 excluded, disposable income in constant dollars, population adjusted, grew at an average rate of 2.7 percent. However, in the period 1974–76 average growth was around 1 percent, and forecasts the future growth vary considerably.

1. *Optimistic.*   Income growth to average 2.7 percent annually, which assumes minimal energy effects.

2. *Pessimistic.*   Income growth to average 1.0 percent annually, which assumes major energy effects.

Sales Price

While automobiles are certain to get smaller, they will probably become more expensive. In real terms, however, the automobile has usually been a bargain. The constant dollar price decreased from the early 1960s until 1974, when it increased dramatically through 1975. Since 1976 the constant dollar price of automobiles has decreased for some cars while increasing slightly for others.

1. *Optimistic.*   Price to remain constant (at 1978–79 new car levels) assuming that prices and inflation will stalemate, possibly due to government persuasion or outright control.

2. *Pessimistic.*   Price to remain constant during 1979 and then to increase at 2.0 percent annually plus another 10 percent for "gas guzzlers"—standard and luxury cars.

Gasoline Prices

The price of gasoline in the next five years will be a function of (1) pricing decisions of the Organizations of Petroleum Exporting Countries (OPEC) and (2) the degree of deregulation of the oil industry in the United States.

1. *Optimistic.*   Prices to climb to an average of $0.90 per gallon by late 1979 and then to increase at the rate of 5 percent per year. This should place the price of gasoline around $1.25 per gallon by 1983 and assumes partial stability in the Middle East and some government controls on price.[2]

2. *Pessimistic.*   Prices to climb to an average of $1 per gallon by late 1979 and then increase at the rate of 20 percent per year. (This assumes that gasoline could reach $2 levels before government controls are enacted. It is likely that the government would institute gasoline

---

[2] According to the *Oil and Gas Journal* the average price of gasoline was around $0.70 in early 1979. It was projected that prices could reach $0.90–$1.00 as an average around the United States by late 1979.

rationing at a price lower than \$2 and that gasoline price may not reach this level.)

Gasoline Shortage

A gasoline shortage is hard to define since industry analysts often disagree on (1) whether gasoline is in short supply or (2) whether the "quantity supplied" is being artificially restricted. This research defines shortage as any type of significant nationwide curtailment of gasoline supplies. Thus, significant weekend or weekday gasoline station closings, as happened in 1974 and in 1979, is assumed to have the same effect on automobile sales as actual rationing by allotment.

1. *Optimistic.* No shortage as defined will occur.
2. *Pessimistic.* Shortage to occur which would cause the annual demand for new automobiles (population adjusted) to change as estimated by the energy dummy in the five-equation model.

Subcompact	Compact	Intermediate	Standard	Luxury
+404,000	—	−680,000	−686,000	−224,000

While these figures reflect an increase in demand for subcompact cars in the advent of a shortage, they reveal a more definite tendency to refrain from purchasing larger cars during such a period.

The assumptions made in this section on income, sales price, and energy will generate 16 possible forecasts for automobile demand. These 16 scenarios are summarized in Table 2. Case 1a is strictly optimistic while case 8b is strictly pessimistic.

TABLE 2
A Catalog of Forecasting Scenarios Given Different Marketing Assumptions

Case	Income Change		Gas Price Change		Sales Price Change		Shortage	
	2.7%	*+1%*	*+5%*	*+20%*	*None*	*+2%*	*Yes*	*No*
1a	X		X		X			X
1b	X		X		X		X	
2a	X			X	X			X
2b	X			X	X		X	
3a		X	X		X			X
3b		X	X		X		X	
4a		X		X	X			X
4b		X		X	X		X	
5a	X		X			X		X
5b	X		X			X	X	
6a	X			X		X		X
6b	X			X		X	X	
7a		X	X			X		X
7b		X	X			X	X	
8a		X		X		X		X
8b		X		X		X	X	

FIGURE 3
Automobile Sales, Actual and Projected, Yearly Aggregates, 1967–1983
(Projections under No Gasoline Shortage Assumption)

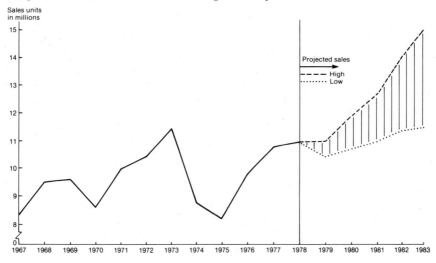

Forecasting Results and Conclusions

Figures 1–4 summarize graphically the different forecasts. All projections show high and low levels which are simply the high and low values for the 16 scenarios for that year. It should be noted that the high forecast levels are not all products of strictly optimistic assumptions.

FIGURE 4
Automobile Sales, Actual and Projected, Yearly Aggregates, 1967–1983
(Projections under Gasoline Shortage Assumption)

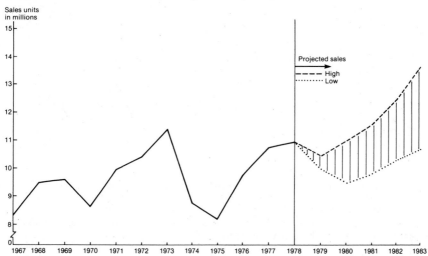

Subcompact demand is greatest, for example, when gasoline prices are the highest.

Comparing Forecasts for Each Car Size.   What is most apparent from these forecasts is the dominance of the subcompact automobile regardless of the assumptions used in the projections. If these estimates are correct, subcompact demand can be expected to average 35–45 percent of total demand by 1983. This is not surprising considering the energy crisis assumptions in this research; however, in 1978 subcompact sales totaled less than 25 percent of the market while the larger automobiles—intermediate, standard, and luxury—totaled 52.3 percent.

The forecasts for the other small car, the compact, are lower than expected. In general, compact demand shows projected increases of 5–7 percent by 1983. This supports the view that the compact automobile is in many cases a luxury subcompact, possessing significantly inferior fuel economy. Even though compact demand may not increase as much as subcompact demand, these projections do indicate that small car demand could make up 75 percent of the market in five years.[3]

In addition, these forecasts show that the demand for larger automobiles could be very unstable, particularly if gasoline prices rise dramatically and gasoline shortage is serious. The projected demand for intermediates shows a small increase (1%–2%) except in the case of gasoline shortage. In 1977 and 1978 intermediate automobiles led all others in sales because of (1) industry downsizing and (2) many new intermediates on the market designed to capture consumers "moving down" to small cars. If there is no gasoline shortage the intermediate could hold on to 25 percent of the market; however, if shortage does occur, their market share could drop to 18 percent or less.

The luxury automobile will, most probably, hold on to a 7.5–9 percent market share unless there is extreme gasoline shortage. Luxury sales have been very stable (except for 1974–75) since the late 50s. Projections show that this will continue, unless shortage occurs, which could cut luxury sales to under 6 percent.

As for the standard sized car, projections indicate little demand for this car by 1983. Only under strictly optimistic assumptions does the standard model retain any significant market share—5 percent. It is also possible that the automobile manufacturers will not retain this size classification through 1983, thus, little or no demand may not be unreasonable.[4]

---

[3] Small cars can be expected to remain defined as subcompacts and compacts until at least 1983. Intermediates may fall into this category in the near future; however, many cars in this size classification are already downsized standard models.

[4] Some assumptions under shortage conditions lead to negative demand for standard used cars by 1983. In these cases projected demand is assumed zero.

Comparing Forecasts of Total Sales. That the economy is the prime determinant of future automobile demand is certain. If gasoline shortage occurs, the two factors are certain to interact and produce a low level of consumer demand. The projections show that under these conditions automobile demand could drop as low as 9.4 million in 1980 before increasing to 10.9 million in 1983, the same level of sales as in 1978. However, if income growth is 2.7 percent or more (the optimistic assumption), then record levels of automobile sales are possible. Projections under the most favorable assumptions indicate that sales could increase to over 14 million. This is possible, as consumer demand for new cars has been depressed for some time. It is far more likely, however, that gasoline and automobile prices will continue to increase (at rates close to the pessimistic assumptions) and that total automobile demand will only reach 12–13 million by 1983.

This study suggests that unless disposable income increases at rates equal to pre-1974 levels the demand for automobiles could stagnate around 12.5 million even under favorable assumptions about energy and price levels. This is far short of the sales levels that auto makers anticipate by 1983. If the more realistic assumptions of high gasoline prices and gasoline shortages are made, total demand may not reach 11 million in a recessionary economy. This is not reassuring news for the auto industry.

Name Index

Subject Index

*This book has been set CAP, in 10 and 9 point Sabon, leaded
2 points. Part numbers and titles are 24 and 30 point Avant
Garde Demi-Bold. Reading numbers and titles are 60 point
and 18 point Avant Garde Demi-Bold. The size of the type
page is 27 by 47 picas.*